HOROS

Horos

Ancient Boundaries and the Ecology of Stone

Thea Potter

https://www.openbookpublishers.com

© 2022 Thea Potter

This work is licensed under a Attribution-NonCommercial 4.0 International (CC BY-NC 4.0). This license allows you to share, copy, distribute and transmit the text; to adapt the text for non-commercial purposes providing attribution is made to the authors (but not in any way that suggests that they endorse you or your use of the work). Attribution should include the following information:

Thea Potter, *Horos: Ancient Boundaries and the Ecology of Stone*. Cambridge, UK: Open Book Publishers, 2022, https://doi.org/10.11647/OBP.0266

Copyright and permissions for the reuse of many of the images included in this publication differ from the above. This information is provided in the captions and in the list of illustrations.

Every effort has been made to identify and contact copyright holders and any omission or error will be corrected if notification is made to the publisher.

In order to access detailed and updated information on the license, please visit https://doi.org/10.11647/OBP.0266#copyright. Further details about Creative Commons licenses are available at http://creativecommons.org/licenses/by-nc/4.0/

All external links were active at the time of publication unless otherwise stated and have been archived via the Internet Archive Wayback Machine at https://archive.org/web

Digital material and resources associated with this volume are available at https://doi.org/10.11647/OBP.0266#resources

ISBN Paperback: 9781800642669
ISBN Hardback: 9781800642676
ISBN Digital (PDF): 9781800642683
ISBN Digital ebook (epub): 9781800642690
ISBN Digital ebook (mobi): 9781800642706
ISBN XML: 9781800642713
DOI: 10.11647/OBP.0266

Cover image: ΗΟΡΟΣ ΕΙΜΙ ΤΕΣ ΑΓΟΡΑΣ, The Athenian Agora Museum [I 5510]. Reproduced with permission from the Hellenic Republic Ministry of Culture, Education and Religious Affairs, Directorate General of Antiquities and Cultural Heritage, Ephorate of Antiquities of Athens, Department of Prehistoric and Classical Sites, Monuments, Archaeological Research and Museums. Cover design by Anna Gatti.

Although there may be no outside that we can know, *there is a boundary.*

— Katherine Hayles

Να έχουμε μια πετρούλα. — PZ

Contents

Abbreviations	ix
List of Illustrations	xi
Acknowledgements	xiii
Prologue	xv
Introduction	xix
1. A New Ancient Petrography	2
2. Does the Letter Matter?	46
3. Breaking the Law	80
4. Terminological Horizons	118
5. The Presence of the Lithic	154
6. Geophilia Entombed or the Boundary of a Woman's Mind	196
7. Solon's Petromorphic Biopolitics	240
8. I Am the Boundary of the Market	278
Bibliography	286

Abbreviations

Ag.	*Agamemnon*
Alk.	*Alkestis*
And.	Andocides
Ant.	*Antigone*
Ap.	*Apology*
Ar.	Aristotle
Arist.	Aristophanes
Ath.	*Atheneion Politiea*
Cat.	Categoriae
de An.	de Anima
Cael.	de Caelo
Def.	Definitions
Int.	De Interpretatione
Deut.	Deuteronomy
Diog.	Diogenes Laertius
DK	Diels-Kranz
EN	*Ethica Nichomachea*
FDA	Federal Drug Authority
Gen.	*Genesis*
Grg.	*Gorgias*
Harp.	Harpocration
Hdt.	Herodotus
Hes.	Hesychius
Hom.	Homer
Hos.	*Hosiah*
Il.	*Iliad*
IG.	*Inscriptiones Graecae*
Job.	*Job*
KJ	*King James Bible*
LS	Liddell and Scott

Met.	*Metaphysics*
Meteor.	*Meteorologica*
Mor.	*Moralia*
MP	Member of Parliament
Myst.	*On the Mysteries*
Od.	*Odyssey*
OED	*The Shorter Oxford English Dictionary*
Phd.	*Phaedo*
Pl.	Plato
Plut.	Plutarch
Prov.	*Proverbs*
Pol.	*Politica*
NIV	*New International Version*
Rep.	*Republic*
Rev.	*Revelation*
Rhet.	*Rhetoric*
Sol.	Solon
Suid.	Suida
TGL	Thesaurus Graecae Linguae
Top.	*Topics*
Trach.	*Trachiniae*
Vit. Phil.	*Lives of the Philosophers*
WHO	World Health Organisation

List of Illustrations

Fig. 1. ΗΟΡΟΣ ΕΙΜΙ ΤΕΣ ΑΓΟΡΑΣ 'I am the *horos* of the *agora*', *IG* I³ 1087 [I 5510]. Photograph by M. Goutsourela, 2013. Rights belong to The Athenian Agora Museum © Hellenic Ministry of Culture and Sports/Hellenic Organization of Cultural Resources Development (H.O.C.R.E.D.) — 1

Fig. 2. ΑΧΡΙ ΤΕ[Σ] ΗΟΔΟ ΤΕΣΔΕ ΤΟ ΑΣΤΥ ΤΕΙΔΕ ΝΕΝΕΜΕΤΑΙ 'The city extends up until the edge of this road here,' *IG* I³ 1111. Photograph by T. Potter, 2021. Rights belong to the Epigraphic Museum, Athens © Hellenic Ministry of Culture and Sports/Hellenic Organization of Cultural Resources Development (H.O.C.R.E.D.). — 45

Fig. 3. ΗΟΡΟΣ ΤΕΣ ΟΔΟ ΤΕΣ ΕΛΕΥΣΙΝΑΔΕ '*horos* of the road to Eleusina' (end of the 5th c BC). Originally inscribed with HOROS TES ODO TES IERAS (520 BC). IG I³ 1096 [I 127] Photograph by M. Goutsourela, 2013. Discovered in the Eridanos river bed. Rights belong to the Kerameikos Museum, Athens. © Hellenic Ministry of Culture and Sports/Hellenic Organization of Cultural Resources Development (H.O.C.R.E.D.). — 79

Fig. 4. [Δ]ΕΥΡΕ ΠΕΔΙΕΟΝ ΤΡΙΤΤΥΣ ΤΕΛΕΥΤΑΙ ΘΡΙΑΣΙΟΝ ΔΕ ΑΡΧΕΤΑΙ ΤΡΙΤΤΥΣ 'Here ends the trittys Pedieis, while the trittys Thria begins' IG I³ 1128. Photograph by T. Potter, 2021. Rights belong to the Epigraphic Museum, Athens © Hellenic Ministry of Culture and Sports/Hellenic Organization of Cultural Resources Development (H.O.C.R.E.D.). — 117

Fig. 5. ΟΡΟΣ ΛΕΤΟΣ '[h]oros of Leto' Photograph courtesy of Paulos Karvonis, The Island of Delos, Ephorate of Antiquities of Cyclades, © Hellenic Ministry of Culture and Sports/Hellenic Organization of Cultural Resources Development (H.O.C.R.E.D.) — 153

Fig. 6.	Gravestones. Photograph by M. Goutsourela, 2013. Rights belong to the Kerameikos Museum, Athens. © Hellenic Ministry of Culture and Sports/Hellenic Organization of Cultural Resources Development (H.O.C.R.E.D.).	195
Fig. 6a.	ΗΟΡΟΣ ΜΝΗΜΑΤΟΣ, in Lalonde (1991) [I 7462]	195
Fig. 6b.	ΗΟΡΟΣ ΣΗΜΑΤΟΣ, in Lalonde (1991) [I 2528].	195
Fig. 7.	ΟΡΟΣ ΚΕΡΑΜΕΙΚΟΥ 'Oros of the Kerameikos' (4th c BC). Found outside the archaeological site in the area between Hippias Kolonos and Plato's Academy. [I 322] Photograph by M. Goutsourela, 2013. Rights belong to the Kerameikos Museum, Athens. © Hellenic Ministry of Culture and Sports/ Hellenic Organization of Cultural Resources Development (H.O.C.R.E.D.).	239
Fig. 8.	ΗΟΡΟΣ ΕΙΜΙ ΤΕΣ ΑΓΟΡΑΣ [retrograde] 'I am the *horos* of the agora.' *Horos* stone discovered in situ in the northeast corner of the Ancient Athenian Agora, by the Tholos. *IG* I^3 1088 [I 7039] Photgraph by M. Goutsourela, 2013. Rights belong to The Athenian Agora Museum © Hellenic Ministry of Culture and Sports/Hellenic Organization of Cultural Resources Development (H.O.C.R.E.D.)	277

Acknowledgements

Thanks to James K.O. Chong Gossard and John Rundell who supported the nomadic beginnings of this work during my doctoral studies at the University of Melbourne. Many thanks to Roger Scott and Penelope Buckley for their unwavering generosity in keeping me housed and fed at many crucial moments. Thanks also to Louis Ruprecht Jr. for feeding my enthusiasm and keeping it buoyant. A thousand thanks and more to Despoina Koi for looking after the boys and giving me the boon of uninterrupted time. Thanks too to the boys for interrupting me with such boisterous jollity. Maria Krystalidou and Elina Niarchou, ευχαριστώ πουλάκια μου, σας αγαπώ. The entire project would be inconceivable without my father's unswerving love and interest in things of the mind and things of the earth. I have never seen him refuse to engage in an argument no matter how unconventional, I have never seen him too tired to read another book or too busy to answer my questions about the composition of rocks or the identification of trees. I dedicate this book to him, because I know he will get more pleasure out of it than anyone, if only because it was his daughter who wrote it. Finally, many thanks to the whole team at Open Book Publishers!

The research for this book was conducted thanks to the Jessie Webb scholarship (University of Melbourne), during my stay at the British School at Athens, the Irish Institute of Hellenic Studies at Athens, and using the wonderful resources in the libraries of the American School of Classical Studies and French School at Athens. Photographic images from Archaeological sites in Athens are by myself and M. Goutzourela and are presented here by copyright permission from the Kerameikos Museum, Athenian Agora Museum and Epigraphic Museum © Hellenic Ministry of Culture and Sports/Hellenic Organization of Cultural Resources Development (H.O.C.R.E.D.).

All translations are by the author, unless otherwise indicated.

Prologue

When Edward Said visited Lebanon, he picked up and threw a stone across the border to Israel. For this act he was barred from attending certain institutions. During the French Revolution stones, frequently the humble cobble, were thrown against the troops and added to the piles of refuse forming the barricades. Again, in England, during the suffragette movement, women wrapped stones in paper, tied a string to and threw them at public offices, drawing the string to retrieve them and throw them again. During the Al-Aqsa Intifada in Palestine it was an iconic image of a young boy throwing stones, later killed by the Israeli army, that attracted the attention of the international media. In a simple protest in Athens against education cuts in 2008, a youth throwing stones was killed by police, causing a general revolt. In Egypt during the latest uprising, stones littered the streets even as the military was sending in tanks.

Must we be satisfied in agreeing with Blanqui that the stone is the principal article in urban battles because it is most ready to hand?[1] Or has the stone gathered this reputation for insurgency on account of history's momentum, resurfacing every time because of its presence in a former revolt? As Lacan said, perhaps the stone has become an *objet petit a* for the revolutionaries.[2]

But what if the symbolism of the stone is not limited to these recent acts of historical insurrection? What if the stone itself already marks our responsibility to struggle for what we know to be right? What if the stone actually stands as a testament to what we cannot see in the immediate world around us but presents a most substantial challenge to the status quo exactly because something has been missed, overlooked, or simply lost?

---

1   Blanqui (2003).
2   Roudinesco (1997) 336.

This work undertakes to bring before our gaze an intrinsic relation between stone and human, in a study that is inversely archaeological. It traces the earlier possibilities of the stone's task in archaic Greece and describes its subsequent modifications, losses, appropriations and occupations during the rise of the historical, political and *in utero* economic era of the classical world. Oddly enough, the resulting arc does not begin in corybantic times of cultic religious practice where the stone is presumed to be a fetish or animistic token, to find its epistemological culmination in materialism and utilitarianism. In fact, it would appear that, in relation to this base matter, we have been moving in the opposite direction. What began as simple (though not base) stone has gradually become fraught with all sorts of religious, political and economic investments in every aspect of life, that is, except insurrection. For although we employ stones, crushing them and piling them up in the construction of buildings, roads and walls, here the stone, in content and form, is in every way subordinated to the increasingly hostile environment we are building around us, blocking out strangers, ensuring swifter means of progress and limiting in every possible way the direct confrontation and interaction with others, human or otherwise.

We throw stones to bring us back to the matter at hand. As the marker of our graves the stone should be at once a material and metaphysical remainder of the fact that we are all strangers to life, regardless of nations, states and the self-interests of markets, corporations, security and defense. The stone stands as a marker of our ongoing and necessary relation with the more than human world. Although we dismiss stone as inanimate, it is the origin of animation, whether it disintegrates into its more readily available fertile components or erodes into the various formations upon which the diverse play of life is acted out.

It is in this light that the insurrectionary stone-throw should be understood. For it is an act directed against the hubristic violence of the border and the barrier, the wall and property. The stone-throw gestures towards what is common by putting such boundaries into question and by transgressing boundaries with the most solid (though not immutable) material that inevitably takes our place and even substitutes for us. For the stone-throw yet retains the possibility of the dissolution of the militarised border, or the armed aggressor. It is a symbol of friendship winning out over hostility. All who wish it are welcome to join the insurrection. The problem every insurrection faces is, however, how long the people are prepared to fight guns with stones before the injustices they have suffered compel them either to turn inward in despair and accept the terms of the victor or to embrace the same means of violence that are directed against them.

The rune-masters carved their runes in rock, wood or leather and then coloured them with magical ingredients, one of which was likely blood. In order to read the prophecies hidden within these objects the masters dispersed them upon the ground, and it was only those with the letter facing upward that provided the text for interpretation. This book could be said to follow a similar method. Since the text has (in the wake of deconstruction) proved itself exhausted, if not a mere ruin, this is an attempt to remain close to the material foundation of writing about writing. It is no coincidence, therefore, that the plinth upon which this text rests is literally a ruin. The earliest archaeological remains that will be considered here are mere traces of letters, found amongst the rubble, sometimes engraved in stone, other times in a text no less spoliated. They are literal remainders of an earlier, lapidary writing, whose name 'Horos' equally binds letter and stone: declarative letters whose stony annunciation would make a belligerent claim of precedence to any writing. *Horos* is the original material as well as the place-saver of Hermes' own statue in the Athenian market place. Though ancient, *Horos* remains throughout the hermetic period and into today when only interpretations and not positions are considered to be safe ground for thought.

There is a lot of talk of boundaries and bonds in the following pages. It is not my intention to wield bolt-cutters or claim to have found a key to dissolve these boundaries and free us of these bonds but rather to trace a path that should foreclose any arrival, such that the question remains. Questioning must begin somewhere. This book discusses the site or place of the question as both a matter of boundaries and definitions, where any question also allows the definition of words and things to remain open to the possibility of asking further questions. Here the boundary of the question is present in the stone as our trace or mark, with or without letters, of the potential distinctions and divisions in the material. In light of this return to the elemental material of stones and of letters it is necessary to ask what has been lost from our relations with the world and one another. Perhaps in what has been lost there is a chance of rediscovering a ground from which to resist and destroy the forces that occupy and with increasing aggression seek to manipulate the archaic frontiers of life.

Introduction

The market today resembles a Leviathan, a great beast growing in accordance with no law outside of the vain rapacity of its uncanny monstrosity, extending its boundaries beyond the nation-state, beyond government intervention, beyond ecologically safe limits and beyond our will to enter into it. It has become properly automatic, functioning for no purpose outside of itself, its masters simultaneously its slaves. And yet, this monstrous system originates with us. Have we lost control of this love child of unsatisfied desire and self-gratification? Are there no limits to its cancerous spread? Is there any way to assert our responsibility over and against the unlimited expansion of this voraciously consumptive automatism? Nobody can doubt the existence of material limits to economic developments, though there must be a huge discrepancy in the location, orientation, the matter and meaning attributed to such limits; otherwise there would not be such wide-ranging discussion concerning the mechanisms and alimentation required to keep the current system from collapse.

Here the basic argument will be that vital material limits both structure our relation in and with the world around us, comprising both humans and nonhumans, and call us back to an inclusive, inter-relational coexistence with all things in stark contrast to the reification of organic and inorganic natural resources required to maintain the unsustainable rate of technological advances in societies dominated by corporate, stakeholder capitalism (otherwise known as cartelism). To hold thus to the vitality of matter does not bracket out human subjectivity, its genesis and its boundaries; rather, it reinforces that the boundaries themselves separating the human being from everything else are not absolute, transcendental nor divinely given. But that does not mean that they are not substantial; they are, in fact, material. Because they are material, they are also subject to question. Therefore, as I will elaborate throughout this work, the project of Western human rationality is based upon a premise (that humans are 'rational animals' and distinct from other organic beings) that is epistemologically and ontologically secured by nothing but the very thing that the definition seeks to distinguish humans as separate from. This book is devoted to investigating this thing in the material origins of the philosophical and archaeological project of definition. The foundation that provides the definition distinguishing the human from the other inhabitants of the world, but also from the inorganic matter of the world is none other than 'insensate,' or 'inanimate,' matter itself.

Given that matter provides the substrate for all being, human or otherwise, why, it could be asked, the need to respond in like by advocating for the vitality of matter? The answer is that I agree wholeheartedly with Jane Bennett when she states that 'the image of dead or thoroughly instrumentalized matter feeds human hubris and our earth-destroying fantasies of conquest and consumption.'[1] In that light the project here is to trace a history of the vitality of matter and investigate how we have come to be psychologically, spiritually and linguistically disconnected from the world around us and the life inside us. This study reveals how the economically and politically dominant conceptualisations of matter, natural and otherwise, are contingent upon exclusions and exceptions that, reinvented within our language, could provide a deep kinship with the earth and open up the possibility of coming to terms with matter in a more involved, intra-active, symbiotic way.

How is matter vital? It is certainly vital to our survival, but it is vital in more ways than simply our dependence upon matter to provide us with warmth, food, and comfort. Matter is also vital to itself, and the relations of plants, fungi, animals, rocks, water, carbon dioxide, calcium, etc. all continue to interact regardless of human needs, intervention or even human existence, though no doubt these relations are increasingly modified and even hindered on account of human interventions (such as industrial farming depleting communities of biota in soil, the interactions between methane trapped under the ice with a heating atmosphere, or the affinity between asphalt and predatory birds). This then, might be the cause of the book, or what caused it to be written. The argument presented, however, requires these interrelations as an

---

1   Bennett (2010) ix.

assumed foundation upon which all human and nonhuman activity plays out. It is the ground upon which we stand. But it is also this ground that poses the dilemma I attempt to confront or abide by: do boundaries exist in nature? Conversely, is this problem inscribed in the human assumption of such boundaries in defining nature as separate to humans? Does 'nature' take everything into account except the human, and does 'matter' likewise exclude whatever is organic or has a soul? Are such boundaries even sensible given the predisposition of the human to say that nothing matters or is meaningful beyond human volition to make it so? The question must be raised as to what actually is the nature of the boundary that claims to distinguish humans from everything else; is it natural or is it in us? We have been taught that the boundary is located within the human. For example, the presence of reason within the human mind is what distinguishes the human as possessing subjectivity. Beyond or outside of this subjective position, there is no way to prove the nonexistence of other subjectivities. At least, any attempt to do so always recoils into the precedence of human subjectivity as the principal determination. It is this problem, then, that this book presents as intrinsic, not to the nature of what it means to be human, but within nature as the possibility to determine, define and divide.

It is the reflexive task of philosophy to unravel the meaning of words and things, to use language to define the use of language itself. Ancient Greek philosophy began as a play on words, a kind of game that illustrated philologically the relations between words and things, their meanings and non-meanings, and evolved into the Aristotelian project of definition and determination. Such a project may have become speculative but its origins are deeply embedded in the bedrock of the archaic psyche. We could also turn this around and say that the archaic psyche was embedded deeply in bedrock. The coincidence between thought, language and rocks might not seem likely. However, it is exactly this essential and most substantial coincidence that I reveal both in the material traces of archaeology as well as the no less material remains of Aristotelian philosophy and Solonic law. In fact, it becomes increasingly apparent that it is impossible to think about anything in the absence of some kind of lithic term cementing our path along the boundaries of human and nonhuman conceptual, that is to say non-concrete, experience.

This study has to do exclusively with this lithic term. I approach these limits without any attempt to transcend them, transgress them or erase them, taking in solidarity an archaic example of a stone: this stone I call *horos* because this is what it calls itself. A boundary-stone found during the excavations of the ancient Athenian market-place enunciates itself and with an inscription takes upon itself the responsibility for providing limits. Retaining even into the Classical period the archaic spelling (when the letter eta represented the aspirant rather than the long vowel sound), this stone reads ΗΟΡΟΣ ΕΙΜΙ ΤΕΣ ΑΓΟΡΑΣ, 'I am the boundary of the *agora*.' The Classical Athenian *agora*, the market-place, was demarcated by a number of these stones, which prohibited patricides and other criminals from entering the market-place. But they also prevented the activity of the market from leaving that sacred site. These stones thus demarcated the limits within which the work of the market was to take place, there where Athenians went about the unhindered task of exchanging, producing and reproducing verbal and more than verbal goods.

So, the *horos* stones demarcated the space of the *agora*, and it is believed that the *agora* took its name from the activities that were first conducted there, a space for the shared rituals of speaking (*agoreuein*) and the further tasks of more than linguistic exchange, of buying and selling (*agorazein*). As Socrates' presence there illustrates, the *agora* was a public space open to the redefinition of linguistic boundaries and questioning the value of words and other tangible and intangible goods. That questioning was based in and isolated within the same space as that committed to the exchange of goods, where measures and weights were brought into parallel with quantities of things, suggesting an (*unheimlich*) affinity between economics and philosophy. Both philosophy and exchange throw into question common values and, perhaps for that reason, were kept at a distance from domestic life, out of the household and its everyday activities, in a move that dissociated both tasks from their etymologically nested origins. There is a danger involved here, and the explanation of Marx might be well founded, although hypothetical, that exchange was first confined to the boundaries between tribes because of the risk of dissolving all communal bonds. The creation of a market-place within the confines of the ancient city may well be the first attack on the synergistic cohesion of the community.

Horos is a boundary-stone, a landmark, but it is also a term or definition, indicating a certain duration of time, a limit or boundary. It is also said to be a rule, a measure, an end or aim, the three terms of astrological measurement, notes of a musical scale, decree of a magistrate, and (apparently metaphorically) the boundary of a woman's mind. On top of, or rather underneath, this greater plurality of meanings, it is also the stone that marks a grave—gravestone. As this material monad embodying a plurality of linguistic configurations suggests, there is a vitality to this boundary that cannot be reduced to demarcating a separation between hostile territories. The *horos* defines and distinguishes, but that is precisely what the matter is with the word, and no matter how much we try to rub away the material connotations, its definition remains interminably solid, lithic, in fact. The *horos* cannot be read as choosing sides but does stand testament to our ability to distinguish between words and things, the human and the nonhuman. Nonetheless, when it comes to defining these things, us and itself, its own reflexivity confounds the attempt; the definition of *horos* cannot define the stone away out of presence, the stone is as vital to the *horos* as the word is to the definition of the boundary. It marks the differences that we read into the world, creating the distinction itself between the 'natural' and the human, while materialising the proof that this distinction is not in the least natural: or at least that what is natural in us, to read into stone something meaning more than base matter, creates the divide in nature and is exactly what determines us within and against the natural world while joining us to it inseparably.

The term 'nature' is conventionally proscriptive, describing all processes and beings other than the human and human creations. This book is structured around the distinction between the human and nature, between the human and nonhuman and describing the nonlinear history of this petrifyingly dualist construction. The irony is this: the presumption—that humanity alone raises the stone above its base materiality—is in fact the only basis for a theory of inanimate matter or a non-conscious cosmos. This division provides the framework for later economic developments based upon a non-synergistic or non-symbiotic relation with other beings, from bacteria, plants and animals to the gases that keep us alive and the geological formations that provide more than merely the substrate for life; today this is realised in the unbounded utilisation of the nonhuman world and the indubitably vain attempts of subjecting it to total human control. It is also the mystical origin of the project of Western scientific rationalism. This is the dilemma of human culture: it is based upon the reading of an unwritten division from (human) nature. The *horos* is a Greek concept, and its power is maintained within societies whose fundamental political and economic structures derive or in some significant way have been influenced by that specific heritage. That said, given that both the political form of democracy and the economic as a public structure of the unequal organisation of wealth are now exported worldwide, there is an expanding sense of importance in putting into question this unconscious rule of *horos*.

Foucault argued that there are rules—conceptual rules—common to different cultural practices and scientific disciplines, that work unconsciously to direct the many different fields toward their different goals as a 'positive unconscious of knowledge.'[2] I suggest that *horos* is one of these rules. However, unlike Foucault's rules that seem to be period-based, the *horos* is an economic rule, a rule fundamental to an entire form of economics grounded upon the unequal distribution of land and goods and unlimited natural recourse use. But it does not need to be this way. The *horos* could just as easily be an ecological rule resisting and rebutting the unbounded exploitation of the nonhuman as well as of the human.

This book is called an ecology both because its author would wish that our interactions with the lithic were less invasive, less aggressive, less consumptive and more involved and also because it has to do with the definitions that we use in order to build the possibly spectral house of human knowledge, culture and society. The presence of boundaries, from the material remains of ancient boundary-stones to the determinations in quantum physics, saturates the shared life of humans. Boundaries are placed, maintained and transgressed in order to facilitate the material practices and social theories through which we divide the world into a plethora of categories, not the least being that of the 'social' and the 'cultural, or 'human' and 'nature.' We require boundaries, in definitions or divisions, in order to make these categorical determinations. Ironically this also means that the boundaries must already exist as precedents to any subsequent determination. Does this mean they are

---

2 Foucault (2008) xi.

predetermined? And if they are predetermined, is meaning already inscribed within them? The main question that this book seeks to raise is whether boundaries exist in nature, but not in order to contrast natural with social boundaries or in any way privilege human ethics. Instead the intention is to draw attention to the human edifice of language and culture, the behemoth of our civilising project that has managed again and again to do away with any notion of boundaries (natural or human), including those that might limit industrial farming, land use and hyper-development, the biopolitical use of humans and animals, the corporate abuse of biopower, and the use of just about everything else as biofuel, not to mention all those rocks and minerals blasted into nonexistence in the search for precious rare earths required in electronics necessary to track, modify and manipulate further what it means to be human.

And yet a limit is out there, threateningly immanent though no less withdrawn than that vital distinction separating being and nonbeing or creation from extinction. Here our lives are lifted into the geological scale as if our inability to recognise boundaries in nature or limits in our own nature is obfuscated by a predetermined fate as inevitable as the wearing away of rocks by wind and water. No single actor can be held responsible for the market, for drawing up its limits, or opening them up. And yet a limit exists, and this limit names itself, declares a name for itself, and a place of belonging: 'I am the boundary of the market,' reads the stone. But it is read by us, and it is therefore us, the actors, who enter into the market place who read and are responsible for defending the limits and for expanding them, as much as we are the ones who inscribe the stone, read the stone and cross the boundary. The peculiarity of the ancient Athenian market-place as an exclusive site of exchange, of objects and money but also of words, culminates as the setting of Socratic dialogue. The danger the Athenians attributed to such activities is given as the cause for the erection of the stones upon its boundaries, while the activities themselves draw us to raise further questions about the notion of boundaries as such and the questionable subjectivity of this self-enunciating stone.

Horos means 'boundary,' but it is also a stone placed to mark a boundary. In a way, though, I'm not so interested in spatial boundaries that divide or demarcate two spaces opening them up to possession and the rights of the owner, nor even the piece of land they foreclose. What

I'm more interested in is the stone itself, both as matter and marker, and as obscuring the presence of a natural (human) marker. The intimacy of human culture with stone might be everywhere apparent, and yet studies into stone from a literary perspective are few. Two notable examples are the similarly titled John Sallis's *Stone* and Jeffery Cohen's *Stone: An Ecology of the Inhuman*. Both these works address the stone as something worth considering in its own right. Sallis takes up the stone in its sculpted form to investigate the sense of the sublime in stone, and in so doing he writes a philosophy of the cultural history and aesthetics of stone chiefly in art and architecture. Cohen is interested in the wide uses, practical but also literary, of stone during the Middle Ages in Europe. As the title suggests I would like to position my study in dialogue with Cohen's epic work. My topic might precede his chronologically, but it certainly follows his thematically. Luckily for me, neither Cohen nor Sallis take up the particular example of the stone *horos*. So, I hope that this work on the *horos* will be a useful addition to this as yet small lapidary field. If nothing else it should raise the problem of the *horos* and its relevance in the field of ancient economics and political philosophy.

In the tradition of apophatic theology, I begin by introducing this book in the negative, by what it is not. It is not a historical study, nor a philological or philosophical study. This book takes place on the boundary between literary criticism, social theory, classical studies and archaeology. Based on interpretations of Ancient Greek texts about terms and definitions and archaeological remains of boundaries, it remains within the margins of Ancient Greek society, though the only reason I am interested in these margins is because of the play of their absence/presence today. So, my perspective on these ancient phenomena is undisguisedly modern, though I hope for all that it is also a little untimely too. In addressing the problem of meaning and matter, or the matter of meaning, I have taken a cue from Karen Barad, who manages to reconfigure quantum entanglements and physical-semiotic relations in a way that I believe strongly resembles the problem raised (or founded) in the *horos*. Jane Bennett, Carolyn Merchant and Val Plumwood also significantly figure as theorists who provide me with alternative bases upon which to think through human relations with 'nature' and the material world. Finally, Jacques Derrida remains as always on the margins of the text, if only because he, with Levinas's assistance, framed a theory of hospitality that I believe to be essential when considering relations not only with humans in particular but also with the earth, mother of all hosts. If anywhere, the boundary is where friendship and the welcome given to the stranger (*philoxenia*) are at home. There might be something methodologically strange about this interweaving between modern and ancient conceptualisations of boundaries and matter and meaning. However, I would argue that a certain strangeness—even a lack of homeliness—is essential in order to remain with the boundary while simultaneously presenting this stone as the core that has remained with us, without remark and unnoticed since the introduction of philosophy into the central market of Athens.

The reader may, I fear, feel a certain disillusionment at the swinging timescale in the following pages. This, however, can be accounted for by the scarcity of early texts and the need to speculate upon changes that preceded the events described by later sources. On the other hand, no epoch exists in a vacuum, neither our own, nor that of the first few centuries of written history. Human activity is not only judged by reference to the present and the past alone but also by reference to the future. Therefore, it is as natural to look forward in order to look back as it is to look back in order to look forward. As Walter Benjamin stated, 'nothing that has ever happened should be regarded as lost to history.'[3] However, that does not mean that what is lost is overtly apparent in the present; rather, the task is to recognise what history, and its authors, have allowed and are in the process of allowing to slip away or leave concealed under thick layers of progressively more forceful interpretations. In my view, history is a significant factor in the composition of authority, and so for the authoritarian regime that we inhabit today to change, history itself must change, dominated as we are by market-based economics and a profitable version of the past as of the present sold to us in order to keep us from resisting.

To find a well-grounded site from which to rebel has always been a challenge, as the first thing dominant forces do when they assume power is to saturate the field, appropriate the land, and devitalise antagonistic elements. The battle is situated; it is over the earth itself and material gains as much as who has the power to enforce a translation of what that matter means. The catastrophic forces of the present can

---

3   Benjamin thesis III, in Löwy (2005) 34.

only be averted from a solid foundation, a grounded theory of the limit, fighting for the presence of boundaries in human economic and technological expansion, in antithesis to the prevailing powers that seek to manipulate the biological and geological foundations of life on earth (biometrics and terraforming). Present economies, no longer subject to the old state or ethnic borders, are all equally enslaved to the corporate interests of big tech and demand the highest price both of the human and the nonhuman, from the increasing presence of biotechnology in the facilitation and control of human activities to the exorbitant mineral demand these technologies make upon the surface of the earth. This means that to be a human embedded in the world and to take back our intra-active relation with other beings and things, we must take back our minds and bodies, free them from the technologies that seek to bind them within the limits of corporate and state control and demand the cessation of mining, deforestation, and the uses and abuses of organic beings.

To do this it may well be necessary to outsmart the very devices that control our slavish devotion to the system and discard the habitual and insidious technologies that have insinuated themselves into our lives. It might not be easy to realise these limits, but the alternative is unadulterated totalitarian dystopia. The trends in post-humanism and, of course, trans-humanism, to expand bodily boundaries into apparatuses fail to stress the negative impact such apparatuses might have on the environment and on human dignity.[4] The smartphone user might feel at one with her device and revel in the extension of her bodily boundaries to encapsulate this fantastic expansion of her senses, but she turns a blind eye to the mountainside exploded in search of metal or the bushland concreted over to provide a basis for the turbines necessary to charge it, not to mention the fact that every thought, every move she makes is subject to scrutiny. We are all implicated in the expansion of boundaries, and whether this is doing harm to us and the world we live in should be a subject not only of serious debate but should be reason enough to modify our thought, behaviour and limits of consumption. In any case our behaviour will be modified one way or the other, whether we like it or not. Biotechnological companies are keen to sell us products that expand the boundaries of consumption into

---

4   Barad (2007) 153ff.

previously untapped natural resources (including the modification of humanity itself), but ecological devastation (regardless of the colour of the flag flying over the military-industrial complex) will evidently enforce its own boundaries in any number of predictable and as yet unforeseen ways. Both alternatives will come to pass if we are too lazy to discover boundaries for ourselves, and the window of opportunity where we have the choice to change this future is becoming smaller day by day. The only alternative vision I can see that will in any way alleviate the decimation of humans, nature and human nature is by doing away with the belief in and exercise of false boundaries enforced by the power nexus of state, big tech and corporate wealth in order to include us as living beings within a world constituted by the vitality of interactions between all things.

The following chapters each riff upon different lexical meanings or translations of the word *horos* and provide a discussion centring around different examples of the word, whether in the archaeological record or in classical texts. Chapter One ('A New Ancient Petrography') provides an overview of the *horos* as it appears in the archaeological record and textual tradition. Given that the definition of its verbal cognate is 'to determine, divide, define,' it is suggested that this division is in the heart of language itself. Boundary markers must be read or interpreted as such, implying that the boundary is not a reductively material thing but is something dependent upon us, inside of us. Whatever it was that led us to create boundaries—to make distinctions—also bound us to our linguistic distinctions. This is what a materialist disposition would describe us as: the inscribers, the plinth-builders. The *horos*, at once stone and term, raises the problem of the boundary between nature and human, between worked stone and natural stone. This problem comes down to us in our distinctions of the physical world. In the absence of a demiurge, matter is supposed to be without meaning, and this is the basis for scientific rationalism. However, even the distinction between meaning and matter relies upon a conceptual acceptance that the boundary between the two is in some way naturally given. This chapter raises the problem of such distinctions and claims that any attempt to define humans as separate to everything else always ends up back at the coincidence of word and stone.

Chapter Two ('Does the Letter Matter?'), taking the definition 'boundary, landmark[...]pillar (whether inscribed or not)' as its starting point, returns to the earliest examples of the *horos* in the archaeological record. Here I confront the Derridean problem of writing as origin. Even if the stone was not marked with the word for boundary (*horos*), it does not cease to be a boundary because it was nonetheless read as a boundary. Therefore, I turn to the lexicons to discover how the Greeks themselves defined the *horos*. The result is twofold, like the boundary; a definition of the word must accept the *horos* as the boundary of writing and reading. It is always inferred in any act of reading because there must be something, whether the inscribed word or the natural rock, for us to read. *Horos* proliferates from the rock into our definitions of what words mean, and it always remains as the solid foundation of these works of 'definition.' It is the difference and bond that is co-terminal with language as such but does not for all that lose its base materiality as stone.

Chapter Three ('Breaking the Law') considers the legal implications of the *horos*, taking the meaning 'bounds, boundaries.' The regions that are thus separated are given definition by the boundary and exist as different spaces on account of the boundary but also share something in common: the boundary itself. I return to earlier examples of the boundary-stone in the Hebraic and Greek Biblical tradition, where variations of the *horos* appear repeatedly and ask the question as to why boundary-stones in the Old Testament required the double enforcement both as stone placed upon the land and as prohibition in the written text. The problem of legality is raised and followed into the work of Plato's *Laws*, where the first law is given as the prohibition against the removal of the boundary-stone. In these textual traditions, the prohibition that is to follow upon the *horos* implies that something has been lost from the base materiality, the bare presence of the stone, and this loss is exactly what supports the force of law. The final knife-twist in the letter of the law is described by a leap into the ephebic military service performed upon the boundaries of Attica, where failure to swear allegiance to the *horoi* meant exile from the Athenian city and its institutions.

The problem of determinate definition was assumed by Hegel and Heidegger but has been the problem for philosophy ever since Aristotle defined finding the 'essence' or being of something as the task of philosophy. The problem is always a terminological one, but we have inherited it also as a problem of translation. This problem belongs to the *horos*, the question of definition and the necessary overlap between words in both metonymy and metaphor. Chapter Four ('Terminological Horizons') focuses upon the translation of *horos* as 'term,' 'definition,' 'determination,' a sense of the word that is outlined by Aristotle in his *Topics* and *Categories* where he provides a definition of *horos* as the word that means 'what it is to be.' If *horos* (here 'definition') is a word that signifies the being of a thing, is it itself retained within the definition of a word even if in the form of a trace of this lithic term? Although the *horos* as 'definition' remains essential within the tradition of Western philosophy, its material presence has been confounded in the attempts at absolute conceptualisation and transcendental reasoning. That said, we do get a brief and telling glimpse of it in the preface to Hegel's *Phenomenology*. Its echo remains also in the work of Heidegger, inherited from Husserl, as that which frames our position in the world, as the 'horizon,' verbal cognate of the *horos*.

In Chapter Five ('The Presence of the Lithic') I illustrate the indebtedness of the conceptual structure and language of the geologic timescale to the Aristotelian formulation of time. I do not do this to assert that there is a debt modern thought owes to ancient thought but rather to raise the possibility of the divisive nature of the question of time itself. In the geologic timescale, as in Aristotelian time, linearity is important but not unproblematic. How the measurement of time is conceptualised both in geologic and in Aristotelian 'time' raises the problem of division in a continuum, or how to break time down into measurable units. For Aristotle the 'now' is the term distinguishing the past from the future, brought into alignment with the figure of the *horos*. Does this temporal boundary still retain a trace of stone? The stone is not only instrumental but also essential to the divisions of geologic time; it is simultaneously the tool and the unit of measure. Here, too, stone is read by us, and it is believed that it can tell us something determinate about the past, something at once concrete and abstract. That stone is given as a figure of the unit of time, interpreted as an indicator of time past, must alert us that the dynamics of existence are always read in material configurations which, as in the geological diagnostic of the Anthropocene, implicate a notion of human conjectural and material hegemony.

In Chapter Six ('Geophilia Entombed or the Boundaries of a Woman's Mind') I return once again to the archaeological record to discover the material remains of the *horos*. *Horos* was also inscribed upon the gravestone, a reminder for the living of this most basic of boundaries. Even here a limit remains, for it is only in our translation of the stone into a memorial that conjures up the ghost of the dead. With a study of ancient drama and the role burial rites play in the signification of death, I discover another aspect of the *horos*. Burial rites have long been associated exclusively with Sophocles' *Antigone* and the conflict between two different regimes of justice. *Horos* is what remains as the trace of our division from nature, and it also marks the futility of this division since we must all and without exception inevitably find a home for ourselves in the earth, inevitably engraving us all in a common fate. In this guise, the *horos* describes the boundary between the human and the organic world but is also dependent, in the archaic period in particular, on a reciprocal relationship between the living and the dead: I call this the economics of death.

The final chapter ('Solon's Petromorphic Biopolitics') resolves the former discussions on the *horos* by looking at one last meaning, 'decision of a magistrate.' The law-reformer Solon is famous for an act called the *seisachtheia*, where he was said to have relieved the earth from her burdens and freed men who were enslaved. The burdens he claims to have raised were none other than *horos*-stones. With the reforms of Solon, the web of meanings that the *horos* seems to have bound begins to unravel, and yet the word itself does not lose its multiplicity. Solon brings an end to a period of civil war and inaugurates an epoch that ensured the productivity of its citizens, limited their ease of movement, and opened the way to the eventual dominance of the market and its persuasive reasoning. He did so by claiming for himself the middle position: in his own words he stood as a *horos* in the midst of the people. I argue that this created a fracture in the traditions of Athens, disrupting the household and the place of women and their command over reproduction and production, generating, in contrast, a society based upon a centralised political economy. The novelty of this claim is in the idea of biological productivity as a regulative device within Athenian legal discourse. Therefore, I return to the first example of the *horos*, found in the Athenian *agora*, which marks this space for the exclusive valuation of words and things and where the work of exchange can go on because responsibility for the space that it encloses has been deferred. The argument draws to a close with the question of the reiteration of such boundaries and the need to reassert our communal life with things.

Fig. 1. ΗΟΡΟΣ ΕΙΜΙ ΤΕΣ ΑΓΟΡΑΣ 'I am the *horos* of the *agora*', *IG* I³ 1087 [I 5510]. Photograph by M. Goutsourela, 2013. Rights belong to The Athenian Agora Museum © Hellenic Ministry of Culture and Sports/Hellenic Organization of Cultural Resources Development (H.O.C.R.E.D.)

1. A New Ancient Petrography

ὁρίζω-divide or separate from, as a border or boundary, separate, delimit, 2. bound, 3. pass between or through, 4. part, divide.
    II. mark out by boundaries, limit one thing according to another. 2. trace out as boundary. III. ordain, determine, lay down. 2. define a thing.
    IV. Med., mark out for oneself, 2. determine for oneself, get or have a thing determined. 3. define a thing.[1]
    Define- 1. To bring to an end. 2. To determine the boundary or limits of. b. To make definite in outline or form. †3. To limit, confine. 4. To lay down definitely. †5. To state precisely. 6. To set forth the essential nature of. b. To set forth what (a word etc.) means. 7. transf. To make (a thing) what it is; to characterise. 8. To separate by definition.[2]

The ritual significance of the placement and shaping of stone is not uncommon in prehistoric cultures and ancient societies, some of these traditions even continuing into the present. From diverse countries with lithic arrangements ranging in scope and size, any number come to mind: for example, the enormous stone heads of Easter Island, the stone lines of the Aboriginal Australians, the megaliths of the Celts, the stone of Mecca, the obelisks of Egypt and the cute little Mesoamerican mushroom stones. In Greece there was the *omphalos* stone of Apollo at Delphi and of course all those stone altars and statues of gods. However, there were also the rather more discreet *horoi*, pretty much limited in range to Athens, Attica and its closest neighbours. Not unlike the stone arrangements found in many other countries and cultures, these were said to be boundary markers of one type or another.

The problem as to whether the site of the boundary can actually be said to be a place, natural or otherwise, is posed and deposed in the double gesture by which the stone assumes or vacates the position. Are these

---

1   LS: 1250.
2   OED: Onions (1962) 470.

boundaries permanent, do they describe natural boundaries or human boundaries, is their removal punishable, and is their transgression permitted? For example, the erection of the pyramids is attributed both to a mysterious, alien or divine intervention and to the weathered hands of an extensive human labour force, slave or skilled, and yet the stone, presumably, remains the same.³ And while the cobblestones lining the streets of Paris were torn up to aid the indomitable march of modernisation facilitating automobile speed and military access to the inner city, they were also raised in the name of the revolution, grasped at as material for the barricades or simply thrown in desperation against the armed forces. We should not dismiss as accident that this most solid and elementary material finds its place on the threshold between substantiality and insubstantiality, between life and death, comrade and enemy. Nor is it mere chance that the placement and displacement of the stone is characterised by a double gesture, of divinity and labour, construction and destruction.

I consider this a work of vital materialism, as phrased by Bennett, that nonetheless retains the problem of human subjectivity in the question of the boundary that would divide humans from other beings, other matter, and other objects with which we cohabit.⁴ I argue that any concept of the human is always already caught up in the aporetic structure of the meaning of stone or the matter of meaning. As Barad presented, matter is involved in a two-way creation of meaning, or even a plurality of involved meaning generating relations, where 'distinct agencies do not precede, but rather emerge through, their intra-action.'⁵ This entanglement of agencies, taking place for Barad upon the more epistemologically advanced plane of quantum physics, here can be seen to involve similar players and a similar vocabulary. Barad argues that 'the primary ontological unit is not independent objects with independently determinate boundaries and properties,' but rather 'phenomena' that are defined as 'the *ontological* inseparability of agentially intra-acting components.'⁶ It seems to me that from the *horos*, found as it is in its various contexts, material, textual and conceptual, it is possible to infer

---

3   Dio.Sic.64; Hdt.2.125; Fodor (1970) 335–363.
4   Bennett (2010) ix.
5   Barad (2007) 33.
6   Ibid. (original italics).

this intra-activity taking place both on the surface of the earth as well as in the minds of humans. This suggests to me that boundary-generating practices are inseparably material and conceptual so that ontology itself is caught up in this aporetic self-referentiality when it calls for the metaphysical independence of determinate boundaries. And no matter how much it tries it always defers to the definition, which in turn defers to the stone and back again to the boundary, in a cyclical dance between the constructs of meaning and materiality.

I elaborate this problem through the coincidence, the literal nexus of stone—boundary—writing. To say that matter is vital does not mean anthropomorphising the organisms and non-organisms, the stones, trees, and bacteria that share our world; rather, for me it means the necessary destabilising of the boundaries between the human and nonhuman and recognising dignity as something that inheres to all things; whether this is done via biology (reinhabiting the human with the microbiome etc), via ecopolitics (recognising the equal distribution of natural resources and the dignity of all beings) or, as is the case here through an intersection of the archaeological, via the ecological and, believe it or not, the classical. The stone that is the subject of this book is the very boundary that suggests the differences and commonalities between these different modes of being.

In this chapter I begin by providing an overview of the *horoi* in the archaeological record, the actual extant stones with a brief introduction to the translation of their inscriptions. Next, I present a brief excursion into the presence of *horoi* in the literary corpus, followed by a speculative discussion about their meaning and significance, both for the early archaic period as for today. Finally, this chapter presents an overview of how we comport ourselves ontologically in relation to the nonhuman and how two figures tend to surface (definition and stone) whenever the distinctions between our categories look precariously close to collapsing, breaking up or falling down.

Raising the Stakes

In the surrounds of the ancient Athenian polis, boundary-stones proliferated. Today, in the museums of Athens (and the gardens of the French School of Archaeology), examples of these stones can still be found if you look for them. One of these, found *in situ* east of the tholos and at the edge of the *agora*, legibly presents itself: ΗΟΡΟΣ ΕΙΜΙ ΤΕΣ ΑΓΟΡΑΣ, 'I am the boundary-stone of the agora.'[7] The inscription of this stone is conservatively dated to the beginning of the fifth century BC.[8] The unearthing of a number of other stones (and one with exactly the same inscription in retrograde) reinforced the notion that these were the remainders of an outline in stone, designating the boundaries of the *agora*, market-place, and marking off the area within as devoted to the activities of exchange and public speaking. Certain acts such as those that meant a person was deemed *atimos* (without honour) excluded people from the right to enter the *agora*, for example patricides and murderers were not permitted entry to the *agora*.[9] However, there were also activities that were not permitted within the *agora*. Diogenes Laertius tells a story about the controversial cynic Diogenes of Sinope eating within the bounds of the *agora*.[10] The implication is that it was not accepted to eat in the *agora*, though this may have been more a matter of custom rather than law. While it is known that the boundaries of the *agora* were for keeping certain actors and actions out, I think it is also worth looking at it the other way around, as boundaries meant for keeping certain activities in. If this is nothing more than a hunch on my part, it is nonetheless a hunch that Karl Marx also entertained as a significant factor in the rise of the capitalist economy and the dissolution of social bonds.

Marx was adamant that the original, or at least the earlier location of exchange was marginal. In *Capital* he states that 'the exchange of commodities begins where communities have their boundaries, at their points of contact with other communities, or with members of the latter. However, as soon as products have become commodities in the external relations of a community, they also by reaction, become commodities in

---

7   Epigraphic collections of horoi consulted beyond the field: Gerald Lalonde ed. et al. *Inscriptions: Horoi, Poleitai Records, Leases of Public Land* (1991); David Lewis and Lilian Jeffrey, 'Inscriptiones Atticae' in *IG* (1994); Lalonde, *Horos Dios* (2006); 'Horoi: Studies in Mortgage, Real Security and Land Tenure in Ancient Athens' Fine (1951).
8   Lalonde (1991) 5–7.
9   And.*Myst*.1.76.
10 Ὀνειδιζόμενός ποτε ὅτι ἐν ἀγορᾷ ἔφαγεν, "ἐν ἀγορᾷ γάρ," ἔφη, "καὶ ἐπείνησα." 'When he was upbraided for eating in the agora he replied "I was in the agora and I was hungry."' Diog. Laert. IV.58.

the internal life of a community.'[11] Again, in the *Grundrisse*, he says that 'money and the exchange which determines it play little or no role within the individual communities, but only on their boundaries, in traffic with others.'[12] And, in his *A Contribution to Political Philosophy*, he elaborates further and comes to the conclusion that exchange has a negative effect when it acts from within the community: 'in fact, the exchange of commodities evolves originally not within primitive communities, but on their margins, on their borders, the few points where they come into contact with other communities. This is where barter begins and moves thence into the interior of the community, exerting a disintegrating influence upon it.'[13]

The question that Marx would not entertain, however, is whether it is the interiorisation of the processes of exchange that spawns the community's dissolution or the preternatural force of the boundary itself. If the boundary and exchange are not in fact separate concepts, but two inseparable aspects of the one idea, then perhaps it is not only the presence of exchange that divides a community but the notion itself of division particularly as it is found in exchange, valuation and measurement, figured by the internalisation of the boundary. Perhaps this divisive presence in the heart of the city is what provokes a kind of consumptive sickness. Since the boundaries were, for the Greeks, always a site of mortal danger, of the transgression of the categories of mortal, immortal, wild and monstrous (where youths were sent out to perform their military service and return, having shaken off the savage instincts of childhood), perhaps exchange (transformation and instability of form) enters with the boundary, bringing with it a flux that the city must henceforth address and attempt to reform into a stable and solid representation. Perhaps the stone performed this sacred task, a kind of sacrificial host to the material, though not itself endowed with the sacred. The *horos* of the *agora* can be seen to provide the twofold work of restricting the dangerous and transgressive forces of the market, while simultaneously permitting and maintaining its presence. That this movement is double finds its complement in the duplicity of the limit itself. When it comes to surplus value, therefore, there is a unity

---

11   Marx (1990) 182.
12   Marx (1981) 103.
13   Marx (1904) 50.

of its production and of its realisation, as a process that requires an ever-increasing margin of circulation. Here too 'the limit is double, or rather the same regarded from both directions' and 'every limit appears as a barrier to be overcome.'[14] The overcoming of limits precedes the formal capitalist economy, being already present in the boundary as such, from its first representation within the city. It is this process that is twofold—the circulation and exchange of surplus value requires the continual enlargement of the 'periphery of circulation,' accompanied by 'the complementary tendency to create more points of exchange.'[15]

However, the result of this internalisation of the boundary and exchange into the city is not only economic, it is political but it also drives to the heart of social relations as well as relations with the nonhuman, reframing the world around the market as fat with objects, things and living beings for consumption, for use, to buy and to sell. Max Weber stated that 'not every stone can serve as a fetish, a source of magical power.'[16] He then suggested the employment of the word *charisma* to explain the phenomenon of a naturally endowed or artificially produced extraordinary power that inheres to an object or person.[17] The word *charisma* and its cognates (χάρισμα, χάρις, Χαρίτες) takes us back with a quantum leap to the archaic *polis*, where the reciprocity of the gift (*charis*) described an entire system of relations in which exchange was not measured according to a reciprocal valuation of abstract worth but was rather based upon the maintenance of a mutual relationship.[18] Does this mean that we can draw the conclusion that there is some kind of elusive link between relationships of mutuality and reciprocity and the vitality of objects, or the meaningfulness of matter? Is it possible that non-evaluative relations permit revelations of vibrant matter simply because their worth is not measured in terms of economic function but according to totally different, even disparate systems of belief? If this is the case, I find it intriguing to imagine that stone has within it an inherent power to divide and define the 'gift' of the boundary. To whom does this gift speak? Is it given to us or to the stone?

---

14   Grundrisse (1981) 408–415.
15   Ibid.
16   Weber (1978) 400.
17   McNeill (2021) 19–20.
18   Seaford (2003) 18.

Horos means 'boundary-stone,' but it also just means 'boundary.' This boundary prompts a great many questions that themselves seem to reflect upon the questionable nature of the boundary, asking what magic power is this that causes matter to move thought? What is this relation between matter and meaning given to us in flimsy conceptualisations but weighed down by stone? Can we separate the substance of the stone from the boundary or the inscription and the word from the stone? Without the inscription how can we tell a boundary-stone from any old stone? Without the stone marker, does the boundary remain nonetheless? And if so, if we read *horos* in the stone even without the inscription, where is the boundary inscribed, if not in us? Before writing, before difference there must be a mark. But must there not also be a marker? And yet the whole significance of this stone is that it assumes for itself the task of marking. It names itself, it is read, and takes on itself the responsibility of the writer by putting in question what was there before this mark and limit, before we could read the stone's self-declaration, before the stone assumed itself as the subject of the verb 'to be.' This is a lithic act of self identification, it is not a sign on the boundary or marking the boundary, but the stone itself declaring 'I am the boundary.'

And yet, despite this enunciative 'I am,' the *horos* does not cease to remain brute matter. In the archaeological record, this stone speaks from silence: it is *horos* before the inscription, before the adoption of script. It is not necessarily carved, let alone inscribed, and yet it can still be read. With or without letters the *horos* speaks to us and we read it. And yet, it could never have inscribed itself. If the boundary can be read even in the absence of an inscription is the boundary inscribed not only upon the land but also in us? We are implicated in this act of writing, even when we read what the stone already says. The stone therefore stands as the limit of our agency, between nature and human; mere thing and object for use; between our willingness to give definition to the land, the world and ourselves, and the project of definition that allows us to continue questioning these definitions. So, my task here is to return to the stone that is not under construction, not placed to support us, to be consumed or used, but is also no longer merely a thing or natural object. This example of a stone took upon itself the necessity of providing a limit and a definition by enunciating itself and allowing its marker to recede into the task of continual production, of speaking and re-producing without limits. As inscription and stone it could do this by marking our separation or division from nature and from our nature, providing the solid basis upon which the question of the origin of human culture could be deferred interminably.

Vital Matter

The earliest known example of a boundary-stone in Athens is an inscription upon a substrate rock dating to the seventh century BC. Usually hidden under grass, it can be easily missed. It bears the retrograde inscription ΗΟΡΟΣ ΔΙΟΣ (*horos* of Zeus) and marked the temple lands devoted to Zeus below the Athenian Pnyx.[19] The rock itself is in no way shaped or carved but retains its natural contours except for the surface, barely discernibly smoothed to support the inscription. There are many other examples of *horoi* marking the site of temple lands.[20] Later examples of *horoi* are those from the Athenian agora carved in the mid-sixth century BC. These are tall, upright rectangular plinths engraved with the phrase ΗΟΡΟΣ ΕΙΜΙ ΤΕΣ ΑΓΟΡΑΣ, 'I am the boundary of the market'.[21] Then there are *horoi* that are placed along roads to divide counties, which can be tall steles or smaller and set lower to the ground, for example the one that marked the ritually important road to Eleusis.[22] There are gravestone *horoi*, which stand tall and slim, inscribed ΗΟΡΟΣ ΣΗΜΑΤΟΣ or ΗΟΡΟΣ ΜΝΗΜΑΤΟΣ, with some variations thereof.[23] These are a little stranger to translate, and they prove that the multifaceted meaning of the word *horos*, as 'boundary of sign' and 'boundary of memory' does not cut it. Finally, there are *horoi* from the fourth century BC (on the later side of this study) that marked private lands encumbered with a mortgage and about which Moses Finley speculated.[24] These *horoi* were much smaller, about the size of a brick, and were inscribed, despite the changes that

---

19 *IG* I³ 1055A and B. Lalonde (2006).
20 See for example, ηόρος το τεμένος, *IG* I³ 1068; hόρος hιερο 1071, 1075; hόρος τεμένος Ἀθενάας 1082.
21 *IG* I³ 1087, 1088, 1089, 1090. Lewis and Jeffrey (1994) 711–712, 1087–1090; Lalonde (1991) H26 [1 7039].
22 *IG* I³ 1095, 1096.
23 *IG* I³ 1132,1134,1137.
24 Finley (1952).

had by that time occurred in the orthography of Greek, with the archaic word ΗΟΡΟΣ. These are all examples of *horoi* from the archaeological record.

However, it is worth noting that this is not even half the story, as the archaeological record would be seriously lacking in charm and intrigue if it were not accompanied by a fabulously rich textual tradition. So, throughout this study the apparently more definitive archaeological finds will be considered in the same breath as the rich gems of textual analysis. Here I simply list some of these references in order to give readers a sense of the *horos* in its various uses. I also apologise in advance to anyone without a knowledge of Greek not because I do not provide an adequate translation but because there will be times wordplay may be lost. I try to compensate by always flagging the use of the word *horos* in the English translation, placing the word in brackets beside the various translations of the term, which differ according to context.

The earliest references to the *horos* in the textual tradition are in the Homeric epic, the *Iliad*.

> ἣ δ'ἀναχασσαμένη λίθον εἵλετο χειρὶ παχείῃ
> κείμενον ἐν πεδίῳ μέλανα τρηχύν τε μέγαν τε,
> τόν ῥ' ἄνδρες πρότεροι θέσαν ἔμμεναι οὖρον ἀρούρης·
> τῷ βάλε θοῦρον Ἄρηα κατ' αὐχένα, λῦσε δὲ γυῖα.

> But she [Athena] gave ground, and seized with her stout hand a stone that lay upon the plain, black and jagged and great, that men of former days had set to be the boundary-mark [*ouron*] of a field. Therewith she smote furious Ares on the neck, and loosed his limbs.[25]

Again in the *Iliad* the boundary-stone is raised as a point of contention, in a simile for the walls of Troia.

> ἀλλ' ὥς τ' ἀμφ' οὔροισι δύ' ἀνέρε δηριάασθον
> μέτρ' ἐν χερσὶν ἔχοντες ἐπιξύνῳ ἐν ἀρούρῃ,
> ὥ τ' ὀλίγῳ ἐνὶ χώρῳ ἐρίζητον περὶ ἴσης,
> ὣς ἄρα τοὺς διέεργον ἐπάλξιες.[26]

> But as two men with measuring-rods in hand contend about the landmark stones [*houroisi*] in a common field, and in a narrow space contend each for his equal share, so did the battlements hold these foes apart.

---

25   Hom.*Il*.21.400–411. tr. Murray.
26   Hom.*Il*.12.417–426. tr. Murray.

In this example the *horoi* take a different form, given in the epic plural *ouroun/ouroisi* (οὖρον/οὖροισι). This form is unusual and will not be the form that appears throughout further discussion. Generally, I will use the transliteration *horos* or plural *horoi*. I will also not parse the English word according to its form within the original Greek text, unless it reveals something particular that I wish to draw attention to, though I will provide the verbal form if a verbal cognate of the word is being used. Otherwise, I will exclusively use the word *horos* to show that some form of this word appears in the original Greek text.

References to the *horoi* are also found in the Septuagint, for example, μη᾽μέταιρε ὅρια ἀώνια ἃ ἔθεντο οἱ πατέρες σου, 'remove not the ancient landmark, which thy *fathers* have set.'[27] This seemingly ancient command is repeated in Plato's *Laws*.

> Διὸς ὁρίου μὲν πρῶτος νόμος ὅδε εἰρήσθω· μὴ κινείτω γῆς ὅρια μηδεὶς μήτε οἰκείου πολίτου γείτονος μήτε ὁμοτέρμονος ἐπ᾽ ἐσχατιᾶς κεκτημένος ἄλλῳ ξένῳ γειτονῶν. [28]

> The first law, that of *Horos* Zeus shall be stated thus: do not move earth's *horoi*, whether they be those of a neighbour who is a native citizen or those of a foreigner with land on a frontier.

I have not found any particular reference to *Horos Zeus* outside this text of Plato, though that is not to say he does not exist. The *Horos Dios* from the Pnyx has the name of Zeus in the genitive, meaning that it was a *horos* 'of Zeus' rather than pointing to *Horos* as one of the epithets of Zeus. A reference to the word *horos* untainted by divinity can be found in the pseudo-Platonic work, aptly named, *Definitions*: ὅρος λόγος ἐκ διαφορᾶς καὶ γένους συγκείμενος, '*horos* is word composed of difference and genus.'[29] After Plato, Aristotle uses the verbal form of *horos* in his following explanation. He states that the 'essence,' the τί ἐστι (whatever that is) of things must be sought and defined, '*horizesthai*' (ζητεῖν καὶ ὁρίζεσθαι) in relation to matter, or at least not without matter (μὴ ἄνευ τῆς ὕλης).[30] In his physical, metaphysical and logical corpus *horos* is singly important for Aristotle in coming to terms with words. He uses the word in the same way we would use the word 'term' in logic,

---

27 Prov.22:28.
28 Pl.*Laws*.843A-B.
29 Pl.*Def*.414d10 in Plato (1972).
30 Ar.*Met*.1026a1–5.

or 'definition' when talking about what a word means. Significantly, the word *horos* appears in close proximity to Aristotle's definition for Being. In the *Metaphysics* he states that 'being is the only or main definition [*horos*] of beingness' (ἢ μόνον οὐσίας εἶναι ὅρον ἢ μάλιστα).³¹ In what should be one of his most well-known phrases, 'a definition [*horos*] is a phrase signifying what it is to be' (ἔστι δ ὅρος μὲν λόγος ὁ τὸ τί ἦν εἶναι σημαίνων), the *horos* plays a not insignificant role, though exactly what it signifies will be discussed later.³² In the *Physics* Aristotle uses the word *horos* as the point of difference in a temporal sense: 'coming to be and passing away are the terms (*horoi*) of being and not being' (γενέσει μὲν καὶ φθορᾷ τὸ ὂν καὶ τὸ μὴ ὂν ὅροι).³³ Again in a temporal sense he concludes that 'the now is the limit [*horos*] of the past and the future' (τὸ δὲ νῦν ὅρος τοῦ παρήκοντος καὶ τοῦ μέλλοντος).³⁴

It is worth noting one final reference in order to bring the *horos* into the political sphere. This is quoted in the work outlining the constitution of the city-state of Athens attributed to pseudo-Aristotle (hence called simply Aristotle for ease or perhaps laziness, though whenever we read ancient texts we should take authorship *cum grano salis*).³⁵ It is a piece of poetry, oddly enough, from one of the city's first statesmen. Solon was a political figure who rose to fame by dramatically altering the laws of Athens in order, as he claims, to bring an end to a state of civil war amongst the city's people. Using the opportunity of this state of exception (as do politicians today) he introduced many laws that apparently have nothing to do with the immediate problems, for example his laws forbidding women to travel with more than a certain number of garments or to carry more than a minimal amount of money on their person. He also limited the exuberant tendencies of the Athenians to mourn extended family members and maintain these rituals for long periods of time. But what he is most famous for doing is known as his *seisachtheia*. Though there are few exact details about this, it was supposedly an act he brought in that stopped Athenians from indebting their own persons into positions of slavery. So, what Solon claims to have done was to have lifted up the *horos* stones that were markers upon

---

31 Ar.*Met*.1039a21. See Chapter Four on terms and translating *ousia*.
32 Ar.*Top*.101b39. See Chapter Four.
33 Ar.*Phys*.261a34. See Chapter Five on *horos* and the 'now' in Aristotle's Physics.
34 Ar.*Phys*.222b1.
35 Ar.*Ath*. See Chapter Six.

the land that signified the presence of a debt, or of an Athenian who was so enslaved, and therefore represented that there was a certain burden of debt restricting the property's use. However, as Chapter Six discusses, this interpretation misses quite a lot in the significance of Solon's poetry.

> μήτηρ μεγίστη δαιμόνων Ὀλυμπίων
> ἄριστα, Γῆ μέλαινα, τῆς ἐγώ ποτε
> ὅρους ἀνεῖλον πολλαχῇ πεπηγότας,
> πρόσθεν δὲ δουλεύουσα, νῦν ἐλευθέρα.

> The mighty mother of the Olympian gods,/Black Earth, would best bear witness, for 'twas I/Removed her many boundary-posts [*horous*] implanted:/Ere then she was a slave, but now is free. [36]

These examples will be discussed separately in the following chapters. Here the point is that the word *horos* not only has many different meanings that complicate its direct translation into English but also that it was a significant word in its various contexts. As a word it always marked a point of difference, whether this is the turn in a battle scene, the distinction between words and things, between the past and the future, or between the free citizen and the slave. Some questions therefore must be asked about the nature of the *horos* itself, both as it appears in the archaeological and in the literary context. Can the literary use of the word be said to coincide in meaning with the material use of the stone as seen in the archaeological record? What do the different words have in common with the different stones? Is there a unifying idea and definition of the *horos*? What are its characteristics? Is lithic materiality as essential to the *horos* as the letters of the inscription? Is the boundary there even in the absence of the stone marker? Does the boundary not always slip away into either side in the absence of some kind of marker? And finally, what is this boundary, who is its original marker, and why and how does it and the space it demarcates come about? While this chapter attempts to resolve some of these questions, others flow into other chapters of the book and others still must remain as questions.

The use of *horoi* was not limited to one particular time period or any particular socio-political structure. They continued to be used from time immemorial, within the archaic period of the early *polis* (largely unknown, though we can speculate), through the classical period, and

---

36   Ar.*Ath*.12.4–5. tr. Rackham.

on into the Hellenistic. Over this time the city of Athens transitioned from an aristocratically organised system of government, through civil war, to a democracy, back again, through war, into imperialism and so forth. So, although the use of *horoi* might have changed throughout various political upheavals it nonetheless remained as a relatively stable presence both upon the land and within the language of the Athenians. It is interesting to note that despite Athenian imperialism, *horos* stones came into common usage only in the region of Attica and are only rarely apparent elsewhere, even in places where Athenians exercised political control. That said, if boundary-stones differ so widely and do not even necessarily have the word for boundary inscribed upon them, how they were to be known or recognised as such and how we would know if they were used elsewhere in the absence of the inscription remain silent problems.

In this chapter the main problem is the matter of the boundary. This also poses problems of definition. What is the boundary, and who decides its limits? How does *horos* arise as a mark upon the land that is read by us, and how did this single term come to encapsulate both the materiality of stone and the more conjectural ideas of boundary, term, limit and so forth? Does the boundary precede the stone and the stone stand testament to the boundary? Is the stone as marker secondary to the boundary? If so, where did the boundary come from? Was it a natural phenomenon or a human creation? Did human thought make the leap into abstraction, conceptualising boundaries and limits that are not otherwise present in nature and then erect the stone as the tangible marker of these abstractions? Is the boundary-stone an idolatrous manifestation of the primitive philosophy of early humans? The fact that the *horos* keeps sending us back into more questions is not a coincidence; rather, it is a coincidence in the absolute sense. But here in the archaic *polis* of Athens there is no such thing as 'chance,' because every time they questioned the origins and ends of their actions, the Athenians came face to face with stone and the original basis for all other *aporias* (problems) about what it meant to be human at that time.

It is difficult to imagine human culture without the assumption that there are boundaries, between you, me, the plants we eat, the air we breathe, the bacteria in our guts and everything else in physical proximity to this fluid, otherwise unbounded conception I have of what it means to be me. Such boundaries are obviously in constant contestation as well as reconfiguration. Perhaps this is why a figure—an actual form—is required to bring a conceptual halt to the indeterminate flow of thought. And yet, despite its lithic solidity, this mark does not cease to remain only metaphorically and figuratively static. The stone itself also is subject to natural processes. It keeps becoming, changing, devolving, subject to wearing away and entropy, while simultaneously representing the pause in this continual flux of change. As Barad explains, in the aptly named 'inscription model of constructivism, culture is figured as an external force acting on passive nature. There is an ambiguity in this model as to whether nature exists in any prediscursive form before its marking in culture.'[37] To this question I do not claim to have the answer. However, this exact problem is what I interpret the *horos* to embody. That it embodies it as a question without solution is significant because, as I argue, human culture requires the *horos* to materialise this question in order to progress into other questions. It is the material basis for the deferral, not the solution, of such a question. Only this intransigent material—the solidity of stone—could bear the burden of the weight of human culture.

So, marking boundaries is as much what the *horos* does as is. The proximity of the verbal cognate and frequency of its use to describe the activity of creating, making, and enacting boundaries remind us of the agency of the stone as a marker of boundaries even in the absence of that enunciative 'I am' of the *horos*. The *horos* is the literal configuration of the world through the differential enacting of boundaries, properties and meanings. And the epistemological and ontological practices that depend upon this configuration can make progress because ongoing, unfixed, indeterminate activity is deferred by binding questions of definition in a determinate, fixed, stable presence of stone. However, as Barad acknowledges, there is no fixity in matter, 'matter is substance in its intra-active becoming—not a thing but a doing, a congealing of agency. Matter is a stabilizing and destabilizing process of iterative intra-activity.'[38] Because there is no external position of knowledge outside the material world, the stone has meaning. Not that it does not anyway; but the meaning inherent to the stone itself is presumably unknowable to

---

37 Barad (2007) 176.
38 Ibid.

us (though psychedelics might help), whereas the meaning attributed to it as boundary-marker is essential to how we go about presuming to know anything and indeed separating ourselves from everything else as knowers of the un/knowable. Asking about the actual existence of boundaries at all is an interminable dilemma.

> The ecological project of thinking beyond anthropocentricity requires enlarged temporal and geographical scales. Yet expanded frames risk emphasizing separations at the expense of material intimacies.[39]

Horos is the materialisation of the problematic basis for any task of human thought, language or culture. Cohen states that the stone has a literally unequivocal power; it is a 'substantial force that exists outside of particular humans and often bluntly disregards their intentions, shaping and working and using and making with a startling autonomy, language responds to stone as matter to matter.'[40] What if, then, boundaries are not generated by human thought or language and are actually already present in nature, such that we read what was already written by nature, responding with script to a kind of cosmic writing, if I can put it like that? Can we accept the existence of places that are not endowed with the sacred by humans or human tradition but are rather intrinsically sacred? What if the stones that are present are placed by humans in recognition of a greater dividing force, a kind of reinscribing of a text that was always already written?

Aporias

As intimated by the self-declaration, the conjunction and disjunction of questions about relations between language and matter, words and stones, humans and nonhumans, these questions posed by, or on the boundary—that is, caught up in this aporetic structure in advance—are also indicative of the basic question of human subjectivity. So, this is the problem, our *aporia*, stuck on the meaning of matter, stopping us short even as it permits us to pass over and go on through it into other *aporias*, 'problems' literally 'without passage'. In his *Metaphysics*, Aristotle raises the problem thus:

---

39 Cohen (2015) 9.
40 Ibid. 8.

ἔστι δὲ τοῖς εὐπορῆσαι βουλομένοις προὔργου τὸ διαπορῆσαι καλῶς· ἡ γὰρ ὕστερον εὐπορία λύσις τῶν πρότερον ἀπορουμένων ἐστί, λύειν δ' οὐκ ἔστιν ἀγνοοῦντας τὸν δεσμόν, ἀλλ' ἡ τῆς διανοίας ἀπορία δηλοῖ τοῦτο περὶ τοῦ πράγματος· ᾗ γὰρ ἀπορεῖ, ταύτῃ παραπλήσιον πέπονθε τοῖς δεδεμένοις· ἀδύνατον γὰρ ἀμφοτέρως προελθεῖν εἰς τὸ πρόσθεν. διὸ δεῖ τὰς δυσχερείας τεθεωρηκέναι πάσας πρότερον, τούτων τε χάριν καὶ διὰ τὸ τοὺς ζητοῦντας ἄνευ τοῦ διαπορῆσαι πρῶτον ὁμοίους εἶναι τοῖς ποῖ δεῖ βαδίζειν ἀγνοοῦσι, καὶ πρὸς τούτοις οὐδ' εἴ ποτε τὸ ζητούμενον εὕρηκεν ἢ μὴ γιγνώσκειν·[41]

> Now for those who wish to find a way to answer problems [*euporēsai*] it is important to go into the problems thoroughly [*diaporēsai*]; for the subsequent answer [*euporia*] is a release from the previous problems [*aporoumenōn*], and release is impossible when we do not know the bond [*desmon*], but the problem [*aporia*] of thinking shows that this is what it is about; for when it is caught up in problems [*aporei*] it is much the same as those who are bound [*dedemenois*]: in both cases it is impossible to go on forward. Therefore we should first have studied all the difficulties, both for these reasons and also because those who begin their search without first going into the problems [*diaporēsai*] are like those who walk on without knowing where they are going, without even knowing whether what is looked for has been found or remains unknown.[42]

The *aporia* indicates difficulty in passing, a barrier or a dead end street where we lack the means or the wherewithal (*poros* also means 'wealth') to extricate ourselves from the dilemma. Aristotle tells us that the question, *aporia*, belongs to thinking (*dianoia*), that it points to a conceptual 'bond' (*desmos*) or as in Ross's translation 'knot in the subject' and that in so far as our thought is in difficulties so it is

---

41 Ar.*Met*.995a27–40.
42 This may not be the most serviceable translation, but my intention is to bring attention to the vocabulary used, in contrast with W. D. Ross's more fluent translation: 'Now for those who wish to get rid of perplexities it is a good plan to go into them thoroughly; for the subsequent certainty is a release from the previous perplexities, and release is impossible when we do not know the knot. The perplexity of the mind shows that there is a "knot" in the subject; for in its perplexity it is in much the same condition as men who are fettered: in both cases it is impossible to make any progress. Hence we should first have studied all the difficulties, both for the reasons given and also because those who start an inquiry without first considering the difficulties are like people who do not know where they are going; besides, one does not even know whether the thing required has been found or not.' Ar.*Met*.995a 27–40.

with those who are bound.⁴³ This knot or bond belongs as much to the subject matter of enquiry as it does to the subject engaged in raising the problems of the enquiry. And so, it is we who are all caught up in chains, caught up in these *aporias*, these non-passages of the problem raised between meaning and matter where it is impossible to go forward. Yet, if at the same time we only raise problems because we want to pass well over them (*euporēsai*) we must follow *aporias* in advance. Hence, to go forward, we must pass well across the *aporias* (*diaporēsai*). But while the *aporias* are literally things or thoughts about things that are without-passage, where it is impossible to go forward we must go forward, and the thing that marks the passage of human thought from being all entangled in the matter of meaning to passing easily on into divisions is the release from the bond or knot within human subjectivity. That said, the knot must be there first, a material bond made extraneous to the project of human thought in order to free human thought from being entangled in the processes of being.

The *aporia* is always already raised before any answer, solution or concept can be given (with declared or undeclared transcendental aspirations) because it lays down the boundaries that are to be 'passed over.' Derrida states that the *aporia* 'had to be a matter of [*il devait y aller du*] the nonpassage, or rather from the experience of the nonpassage, the experience of what happens [*se passe*] and is fascinating [*passionnel*] in this nonpassage, paralyzing us in this separation in a way that is not necessarily negative: before a door, a threshold, a border, a line, or simply the edge or the approach of the other as such.'⁴⁴ The 'way through' is presupposed in the question, whether or not this takes the form of an ineffectual demonstration (in spite of the lingering question) or of a forced passage to the other side (without asking further questions); 'it should be a matter of [*aller du*] what, in sum, appears to block our way or to separate us in the very place where it would no longer be possible to constitute a problem.'⁴⁵ Like *aporia*, the problem, also poses as a question of boundaries: *Problema* (πρόβλημα) means 'hindrance, barrier, bulwark,' but it also means 'task, or business'; in short it is

---

43   Examples of *aporias* in Aristotle: *Met*.993a25–30; *de An*.417a2; *Phys*.212b23. On *aporias*, see Derrida (1993), and Coope (2005) 17–30.
44   Derrida (1993) 12.
45   Ibid.

anything thrown forward (προβάλλω). Etymologically speaking it belongs to the same complex of difficulties that are posed and deposed on the boundary and around the *horos*. The situation resembles Antiphon's dilemma of the murder of a boy who placed himself exactly in the path between the arrow and the mark (τὸ ἀκόντιον ἔξω τῶν ὅρος τῆς αὐτοῦ πορείας. ἐξενεχθὲν ἔτρωσεν αὐτόν).[46] That is to say that it is not enough to substitute a letter as the end of your art; you also need to determine a just 'end' or 'aim' (*horos*).

The first task in Aristotelian philosophy is thus to raise problems (*diaporēsai*) in order to pass through or over them (*euporēsai*) into other problems. But this does not necessarily mean he arrives at a solution; in fact, this is an ongoing process where we only ever find ourselves confronted with further problems, problems that continue along with us, taking on new forms and shapes, shaping us along with them and our quest for further quests. And yet this task—of giving definition, of putting into language the *aporias*—had to begin somewhere. It is ours, our *desmos*, our 'bond' or 'knot' even though it cannot be said to belong to us, describe us or be inscribed fully by us. Since we are subjects divided by the matter of definition, it marks our passage into subjectivity. For, as Aristotle himself noted, while the later facility of resource is a solution of the former problems, yet to solve something is not to ignore the bond. Greek letters and matters are thus seen as structuring the initial example of the ancient *diaporēsai*, that interrogation into the meaning and matter of being that presses forward and raises questions, already forming antitheses in the midst of *logos* and finding equivocal slippages of an increasing exchange between stone and human.

There is an affirmation of an implicit reappropriation that provides the material departure for our position. But is there a static locale that can presuppose either an origin or a destination? Surely the supposition that there is no destination is all the confirmation required to assure us that this is just that—a position—which for all that does not foreclose the possibility that we find ourselves elsewhere, our thoughts shooting off into different directions, without answers, stuck and ridden by dissent, *stasis*; stuck to the spot and providing the material substrate (*hypostasis*) where the work of raising the question takes place. But

---

46 Antiphon, *The Second Tetralogy*, 2.4.

that does not mean that the matter or the position itself from which such questioning begins is not also subject to question. The problem is, however, how it is possible to put into question the matter of the stone without presupposing the word for this stone as the very point of division between language and matter.

For form's sake, one might ask: What does the name of the stone mean? And, after all, who is enunciating what? This stone seems to have contracted only with itself, without any chance that it might speak within the words, be present between the letters, and be itself, as the given presence of our *diaporēsai* already speaking in person. In such matters the Attic development of *diaporēsai* is not dependent upon any conceptual convention but solely on the nature of this monumental mediation of naming, or what is precisely called '*horos*.' And such a donation of naming must remain ontologically spontaneous, compacted and replete as stone. Thus, *diaporēsai*, delving into the depths of thoughtful problems usually follows the method of the *logos*, the logical *odos* 'road' (*via aporia*) that is given as linear, a *gramma*, and is also determined by a localised new ancient petrography. For the stone remains simply (ἁπλῶς) within itself, it is separate (χωριστόν) to such problems, inscribed as boundary that is not however inscribed within it.

The matter of matter is the boundary for further speculation about any definition of matter. There are two definitions that separate what the matter of matter is into different potentials for being present. 'But here' states Hegel 'also a want of connection of thought appears, even though all is subsequently united into an entirely speculative Notion.'[47] This notion is *hypostasis* (substance), that which takes up its position underneath, normally interpreted as rather more intrinsic than substantive, rarely thought of as conflictual. *Ousia* on the other hand, is a different type of being and not nearly as supportive despite its claim to femininity. Yet, as Hegel says, 'Aristotle distinguishes various elements in substance, insofar as the tendencies of activity and potentiality do not appear as a unity, but remain separate.'[48] These types of matter are not easily distinguished, and their interpretation is as riddled as their translation, which might alert us to the possibility that the boundaries between these two words are not as firm as they might seem.

---

47 Hegel (1894) 138.
48 Ibid. 141ff. [translation modified].

Horos comes into play as the figurative dilemma of this most substantial problem of the materiality of being. Because, in the words of Aristotle, a 'certain difficult question concerning definitions [*horous*] might be said to belong to it' (ἔχει τινὰ ἀπορίαν τὰ περὶ τοὺς ὁρισμούς), it might even be going too far to reduce everything down and discard the matter (ἀνάγειν οὕτω καὶ ἀφαιρεῖν τὴν ὕλην).[49] Which means that any reading of the word *horos* might just benefit from keeping in mind that the word is not all that matters.

Matter matters, but according to Aristotle at least the soul matters more.[50] Definition is intimately linked with motion or lack thereof. Matter is defined as inanimate while animals, us included, are called such because we are moved by the spirit; breath animates us. Traditionally only animals are privileged with the endowment of the *anima*, or soul (*psyche*). Must the movements of all other creatures, organisms and phenomena be explained away as mechanistic or automatic? Where are the terms of animation, the limits of the soul? How far can mind or consciousness be extended, and why has philosophy been so preoccupied with drawing up these limits so tightly around the human being? This chapter will revolve around these problems while suggesting that the definition of the relation between the stone and the human being is located exactly in this circling motion that necessarily opens up the possibility of an ensouled materiality in stone only to close it again with the advent of advanced metaphysics.

> αἰσθητὸν γάρ τι τὸ ζῷον, καὶ ἄνευ κινήσεως οὐκ ἔστιν ὁρίσασθαι, διὸ οὐδ' ἄνευ τῶν μερῶν ἐχόντων πώς. οὐ γὰρ πάντως τοῦ ἀνθρώπου μέρος ἡ χείρ, ἀλλ' ἢ δυναμένη τὸ ἔργον ἀποτελεῖν, ὥστε ἔμψυχος οὖσα: μὴ ἔμψυχος δὲ οὐ μέρος.[51]

> What is sensible about the living being is that is not defined [*horisasthai*] without motion nor without parts being in a definite condition, for it is not the hand in any condition at all that is a part of the human, but only when it can accomplish its function, and thus is an animate thing. If it is not animate it is not a part.

An ontologically significant metaphor retained since Aristotle (if not since Moses descended the mount, stone tablets in hand) is the hand

---
49 Ar.*Met*.1036b21.
50 Ar.*Met*.1036b23.
51 Ar.*Met*.1036b27–33.

of man grasping a tool, an image that dovetails with the deterministic, technologically-based concept of human progress.

But this is not to say that Aristotle arrives at a solution, rather this is an ongoing process, where he only ever finds himself confronted with further problems, problems that continue along with us, taking on new forms and shapes, shaping us along with them and our quest for further quests. And yet this task of giving definition, of putting into language the *aporias*, had to begin somewhere. This beginning could not have been an initial *aporia* or no through road. It is, on the contrary, a launching pad, something that sets us off and propels us forward into the proliferation of further questions: in the words of Hegel, 'such an order, such an absurdly rational product: a posited thing posing as being-in-itself. Its origin had to be placed into formal thought divorced from content; nothing else would let it control the material.'[52]

So, who placed this stone? Who drew up the boundaries of the market, and by doing so, who or what was excluded? When it comes to the *horos* drawing up the site of speaking and exchange in the archaic polis, the task of masculine activity must be assumed as prescribed. The earlier *horoi*, however, that mark other boundaries do not necessarily proscribe the feminine and the name itself should be proof enough that women were essential to the functioning economy despite whatever distinctions and regulations were ascribed to their behaviour and presence within the *polis*. But such divisions in the social body are problems that the *horos* precludes, exactly by enunciating itself and excising the necessity for someone in particular to take responsibility for such acts of division. A marker might be (out) here, as that which never sets within the stone, as the day of its giver (or the given cause of the inscription) did once and forever. And yet its possibility is already there, functioning not according to an old model that Aristotle would have preferred to be strictly natural, but rather automatically (τοῦ αὐτομάτου).[53] For that possible marker is not 'really a general implicit existence, which brings about the Aristotelian determinations, without producing one out of the other.'[54] It is always new, as is any purely productive activity now.

---

52 Adorno (2007) 21.
53 ὥστε φανερὸν ἐν τοῖς ἁπλῶς ἕνεκά του γιγνομένοις, ὅταν μὴ τοῦ συμβάντος ἕνεκα γένηται ὧν ἔξω τὸ αἴτιον, ἀπὸ τοῦ αὐτομάτου τότε λέγομεν. Ar.*Phys*.197b18.
54 Hegel (1894) 142.

And yet, it *could never have inscribed itself*, we are implicated in this act of naming, even there where we read what the stone already says. The stone therefore stands as the limit of our agency, between matter and human, human and nonhuman, between our willingness to give definitions and the precedent of definition that allows us to continue doing so.

The Greek name of fate (εἱμαρμένη), along with the words *meros* and *moira* ('share' and 'fate'), is derived from the verb μείρομαι (*meiromai*), 'divide out, allot, assign.' *Heimarmene* means the divine principle of *moirai*, that successive operation of something like a divine hand that allocates itself spatially within *topos* and spiritually within *logos*, regulating also the force that drives toward prediction and death. It, or rather 'she' opens a 'dialogue' between mythology and *logos*, between the past and the future, because, as Plutarch says,

ἡ εἱμαρμένη λόγος θεῖος ἀπαράβατος δι' αἰτίαν ἀναπόδραστον/ ἀνεμπόδιστον [...] ἡ εἱμαρμένη διχῶς καὶ λέγεται καὶ νοεῖται· ἡ μὲν γάρ ἐστιν ἐνέργεια, ἡ δ' οὐσία,

heimarmene (fate) is a divine word (*logos*) not to be transgressed due to a cause that is inescapable [...] *heimarmene* is said and thought of in two senses; since she is activity (*energeia*) and substance (*ousia*).[55]

The duplicity in speech and mind of the name of fate reveals her as the divided subject as such who directs the course of human lives. The trace of her hand is seen there in ours. As Hegel states, 'that the hand, however, must represent the in-itself of the individuality in respect of its fate is easy to see from the fact that, next to the organ of speech, it is the hand most of all by which a man manifests and actualises himself.'[56] Thus what we have to deal with in the first instance (the first division of chaos into cosmos) is something like a deity's hand that is extant (outside) and writes (is written also) upon stone.

Rational thought has always left out as what is left over from us, this divine principle of the divided subject of fate. The 'bondage to fate' was always construed not through a prediction of the course of the future

---

55 She is 'a law conforming to the nature of the universe, determining the course of everything that comes to pass' ... ' a divine law determining the linking of future events to events past and present.' 'On Fate' in Plut.*Mor*.568c-e.; also, Pl.*Phd*.115a.; *Grg*.512e.
56 Hegel (1977) 189.

but only through that which 'will' change upon their 'solid' encounter with the past, in 'a spirit that seeks its own security and the security of cognition in the extant.'[57] So that Adorno can say that 'what is irrational in the concept of the world spirit was borrowed from the irrationality of the world's course, and yet it remains a fetishistic spirit. To this day history lacks any total subject, however construable. Its substrate is the functional connection of real individual subjects.'[58] So, what I propose to do here is, like a palmist, to trace the lines of fate upon stone in an attempt to read what was never written, to remain with the stone upon the boundary, to draw out the outlines of its course into the historical era until we see ourselves writing and reading as if it were we who were subjects and divided. Until we face ourselves as limited beings unable to continue forward in indefinite expansion, nor able to remain still, in ignorance of the questions our (will to) productivity has raised.

Stressing that lapidary 'I am the boundary,' let this be said: agora is never a given; it is always a task. It is the 'dead substance' of an automatic procedure wherein the changes which matter passes through take place. Such an 'actuality' (in which I am now absorbed) articulates itself and sets people off like the *diaporēsai* set us off into further questions. In fact, this is just what the institution of *horos* enables us to avoid and what distinguishes *doxa*, 'everyday opinion' (seeking a variety of goods), from stony inscriptions with their obvious mystification. A simple stone that asserts itself from archaeology to philosophy, confounding any singular attempt to translate it or define it, the *horos* precedes us along the way (a necessary forerunner for any methodology) as the herald announcing this reflective task of definition and determination.

Monolithic Man

Here the human, standing on this side of life gazes, uncomprehending, over towards the idea of the afterlife, from the finite to the infinite, and erects a monument in honour of the awe of this incomprehension. From this vantage point it would seem that it is with the erection of the stone plinth that the idealist is born—the believer, the mythmaker, the toolmaker. And this plinth is the marker, at once vital metaphor

---

57   Adorno (2007) 305, 300.
58   Ibid. 304.

and primal tool, signifying the human being's turn away from other creatures and the conjectural point of departure from unity with nature, where the tool stands as the metaphor, at once material and ideal, of the self-alienating break with animality, that which literally allows us to carry ourselves across the divide into transcendent rationality.

Myth, made up of a multitude of powers, introduces the idea of functional differentiation. The separation of powers in a mythical worldview, says Blumenberg, is the substitution of the 'familiar for the unfamiliar, of explanations for the inexplicable, names for the unnameable,' a device that rationalises anxiety into fear and limits subjective value in phenomena.[59] It is the obelisk, or plinth, at once monumental, arcane and poetic, that appears out of nowhere causing the crisis of the anthropomorphic revolution and finds expression in the experience of existential *angst*, a sign of something greater from which the human being is horrified both to originate and break away from. It is the material metaphor whose function is 'to bridge over the sense of numinous indeterminacy into a sense of nominal determinateness,' transforming the threatening unity of nature into a multiplicity of powers and forces.[60] This plinth points away from worldly embeddedness and its outlines also bring into focus the force that potentially lies in sovereign man, a force manifested in the grasped tool and expressed in the will to power and the supremacy of man over humanity and humanity over and above all other creatures vindicated by the novelty of rational and technological advances. This is the sanctified, prosthetic monument (myth, figure, altar, temple) and apparatus (*logos*, science, state) representing an ontological distinction between humanity and the chaotic forces of nature, warding off the anxiety of living awash in chaos, an anxiety homogenous with the genesis of the human.

But what if this anthropology is grounded in nothing other than myth? It is likely that every anthropology is grounded in myth, even the great myth and metaphysics of observation and experimentation, Western scientific rationalism. Myth itself is, etymologically speaking, the beginnings of speech. And speech in turn is not much different when you think about it, from anthropology, which is basically the account (*logos*) humans give through language about humans (*anthropos*). What

---

59 Blumenberg (1990) 267.
60 Ibid. 32.

is significant about this myth of the genesis of monolithic man is how it obliquely casts humans as cause and effect, a persuasive endorsement of the sovereignty of human poetic reason. Today, even the laws of nature are supposed to have been formulated by men.

The myth of the exclusivity of human reason retains its power, even though we see daily proof as well as (ironically) scientifically discovered facts that human beings are not as unique as we thought we were.[61] There are ample examples of other creatures, birds, insects, animals and even plants and fungi who also employ tools. They, too, alter the environment in which they live in order to make it more congenial, making use of natural objects that they alter in order to render these changes. What is so special about the stone tool in the hand of man? Chimpanzees make spears to hunt with, crows craft their own feathers into tools with their beaks, bottlenose dolphins stir up the sea-floor with sponges while uncovering prey, sea otters use stones as hammers, gorillas use branches to test water-depth, octopuses use coconut shells as shields, the ophiocordyceps fungus uses carpenter ants to better distribute spores, and epiphytes use trees as supports in order to access sunlight. And yet, to some degree, humanity's use of the stone marks a meaningful point of definition, whether signifying the dominance of *Homo sapiens* against other human species or the leap into technological development and the supposed liberation of humanity from the whims of nature. Of course, it is entirely likely that a people employ tools yet continue to live in an embedded state with nature, and therefore the claim that we are separate from nature remains unfounded and much disputed. For example, even the quantum physicist Niels Bohr believed that 'we are a part of that nature that we seek to understand' and he therefore understood scientific practices as components of nature; this means that the tools we use to understand nature are also parts of nature.[62]

Despite our use of advanced technology, humanity is still entirely dependent upon the natural world, the moderation of its forces and the amiability of its climate. Meanwhile, the extended creation and use

---

61 Two exceptional books that span this divide are Merlin Sheldrake's *Entangled Life* (2020) and Monica Gagliano's *Thus Spoke the Plant* (2018). Both investigate how formerly exclusively human attributes, such as will, reason, memory and decision-making processes are evident in what have been thought to be relatively simple organisms, such as plants, fungi and slime moulds.

62 Barad (2007) 26.

of tools to the detriment of the natural landscape is only accelerating humanity further away from this ecologically comfortable niche. So, if the prosthetic device is considered to be the defining feature of humanity, it is also, unfortunately, a self-destructive tool in human hands. Just as I do not buy into constant technological advance, so too I do not buy into this definition of the tool. Although it might be historically factual, the interpretation alters significantly according to who you are and what kind of a device you're holding in your hand.

Carolyn Merchant presents the shift from an organic view to a mechanistic view of nature through the use of metaphor: 'Rational control over nature, society, and the self was achieved by redefining reality itself through the new machine metaphor.'[63] That the scientific revolution required the reformulation of the natural world, forces and individual organisms into machinic metaphors is reflective of the control that the men involved in these advances so obviously felt they both lacked and desired. That slime moulds (single-celled organisms) can make efficient logical choices and that plants have been proven to have memory and learning is enough to seriously shake the autocratically organised boat of human reason bobbing in the frothing sea of nonhuman cognition.[64] The pride of place of metaphor undergirding the bastion of rational deliberation and permitting torturous experimentation of other creatures should be construed as more than a literary trope. It implies the existence of a hierarchical system of cause and effect upon which man stands at the top with power devolving upon him from the architect of the machine. Meanwhile trees transfer information through the mycelial filaments running under the soil and engage in mutually beneficial signalling in tangible and intangible ways, not only putting into question but outright ridiculing the human being's exclusive claim to advanced conceptual processes and language.

Horatio's conventional philosophy might seem limited but it is the conclusion that can be drawn from the experience of the so-called preternatural or supernatural that makes contemporary scientific discoveries appear nothing more than natural or even instinctual. Such discoveries are manifestly timely. This is because for a while now we've been building our metaphorically weighted boats of human reason

---

63   Merchant (1990) 193.
64   Narby (2006) and Gagliano (2018).

upon the assumption that there was some kind of universally inherent right of humanity to make use of the trees, the plants, the animals, the rocks for a higher cause, for consumption and construction or boat-building in this case. But now that we find that most of our suppositions of human uniqueness are wrong, we must return to the drawing board in order to reconfigure our relations, our interactions and particularly our use of the nonhuman world. It seems obvious, at least to me, that such a reconfiguration might help us modify not only our actions and effects upon the nonhuman but also our needs and desires. Such needs are no doubt just as interwoven in the nonhuman, as are the sails made from hemp. Some of my needs are surely already deeply modified by the effect agrochemicals are having upon my gut flora and my libido or air and noise pollution upon my physical and mental health. It is well-known that a change in diet and some fresh country air can dramatically alter one's emotional well-being. Well, we need to change our emotional diet as a species so that we can think a little bit more in sync with the other creatures, organisms and non-organisms that make up the many worlds within our world.

What is really under discussion here is the stone as marker of definition, the human ability to make definitions and distinctions, and therefore also the definition or separation of humanity from the entirety of other worldly organisms and processes. The materialist worldview posits that there are no boundaries in nature. Lenin insisted upon 'the absence of absolute boundaries in nature, on the transformation of moving matter from one state into another, that from our point of view [may be] apparently irreconcilable with it, and so forth.'[65] Here, the idea of the boundary is as much a product as the stone that has been worked and shaped by labour. Once humans have created the stone, do they have the leisure to separate themselves from this construction, to stand back and view the distance the stone has demarcated between themselves and the non-productive coinhabitants of the world. The boundary between humankind and animals is distinguished *post factum*, and it is humankind who distinguishes it, not the animals, presumably. We have inherited this problem from Marx: How can we reconcile our animal nature, which drives us to produce, with the disclosure that our production separates us from our very nature? This boundary is

---

65 Lenin (1972) 258–266.

our Frankenstein; henceforth we are bound to the pursuit of resolving our two antipathetic natures (creator of a monster, father of science), of retracting the symptom of an unhinged humanity. There is a glitch though, for behind these two natures is the woman (Mary Shelley is the white goddess?) underlining the mistakes in our psychical developments, writing with the hand of fate and putting into question the outcome of tyrannical, omnipotent instrumental rationalism. The climax of our obsessive compulsion for control that humanity even now faces is yet another indication that progress in scientific and technological developments is not accompanied by progress in ethical consciousness.

Consequently, can we say that it is symptomatic of human nature to recognise boundaries, namely, to create boundaries that by nature are bound to be crossed? Here we will remain with the substance of the stone, on the literal side of *stasis*, where the negation of movement is a matter of will or decision to stay still so that thought can progress; or as Socrates explains, ἡ δὲ στάσις ἀπόφασις τοῦ ἰέναι βούλεται εἶναι which means something like '*stasis* is the negation of wanting-to-move.[66] Progress or the will to progress may be the very thing hindering our path to enlightenment or the expansion of human consciousness. The task, therefore, is to return to the material, the boundary-stone that by means of providing a static term allows revolutions in thought to circle and pass over it, though it is yet to be seen how far they get.

The vision of Herakleitos, where opposites morph and reform into one another is a world of constant motion, where movement between opposites resolves, ironically, into the law of *coincidentia oppositorum*, eternal movement, as a unifying principle. He expresses this unifying principle in the metaphorical figure of the river: 'representing beings in the flow of a river he says you cannot step twice into the same river' (ποταμοῦ ῥοῇ ἀπεικάζων τὰ ὄντα λέγει ὡς δὶς ἐς τὸν αὐτὸν ποταμὸν οὐκ ἂν ἐμβαίης).[67] Representation (*apeikazōn*, cognate with *eikon*- 'icon') takes place within speech, and it is how it is said that reveals the true nature of the world, hence the chiasmic play on form by Herakleitos. His words come and go as much as the content of his words signifies coming and going, coming-to-be and passing away.[68] *Logos* can be translated as

---

66 Pl.*Crat*.426d.
67 Pl.*Crat*.401D, 402A.
68 Many of his aphorisms engage in this wordplay between opposites, see DK, especially fragments 53,54,58 62, 63 p74–75 etc.

'word,' but it can also be 'language' and 'reason'; the most frequent use in philosophical texts might be in the sense of 'explanation,' 'account' (though I would not bet on it). That said, in the following aphorism, it is presumably being used as reason/language; nonetheless, in keeping with the spirit of the *horos*, I could not offer a definitive translation.

> Οὐκ ἐμοῦ, ἀλλὰ τοῦ λόγου ἀκούσαντας ὁμολογεῖν σοφόν ἐστιν ἓν πάντα εἶναί.
>
> Listening not to me but to the *logos* it is wise to agree [*omologein*] that all things are one.[69]

There is no room for dissent if all things are one; to argue would be futile. When Heidegger analyses this phrase, he does so by raising the problem of the origins of language. Reaching into 'the realm of the primordial, essential determination of language,' he states that speech or voice and signification 'are not capable of determining this realm in its primary characteristics.'[70] So what does he think determines this realm? According to Heidegger it is certain meanings of the word *legein*, cognate with *logos* and *omologein*, that take us back to the synthetic period before speech and thought came to be distinct. The synthetic meaning that he proposes for the verb *legein*, which in the classical period means 'to say, to mean, to read' (in much the same way as we can ask what a book 'says') allows him to trace the phrase back into a determinative position in the interpretation of the origin of speech. Speech, he says, develops from 'the unconcealment of what is present, and is determined according to the lying-before of what is present as the letting-lie-together-before.'[71]

This numinous revelation, where *logos* gathers meaning unto itself (regardless of etymological inconsistencies) might not be contestable, but this is not so significant here, because all I want to gesture towards is the primacy for Heidegger of some kind of 'essential determination' in the embryonic stages of pre-Socratic thinking. The determinative significance of the *logos* is not actually given as 'meaning' or 'reasoning,' but rather as dependent upon something that has precedence in its localised particular situation, it is lying there, 'picked up' (*legein*), laid

---

69 DK(22) 50: 73.
70 Heidegger (1984) 64.
71 Ibid.

down, fixed in place. This might be called the primal metaphor that permits language to start moving into the deferral of signification, where one word always points inherently on to others, as part of a larger structure. It might be poetic metaphor, but that does not mean it is not actually done or made, the literal and figurative carrying over of a determinative sign in speech.

In Herakleitos's fragment, reason or language stops the movement of opposites, breaking down the eternal motion of being into the monism of the arch-concept, the *logos*. In Hegel's words, the 'true and positive meaning of the antinomies is this: that every actual thing involves a coexistence of opposed elements. Consequently, to know, or, in other words, to comprehend an object, is equivalent to being conscious of it as a concrete unity of opposed determinations.'[72] In one way or another the presence of determination must be concretely represented but only in order to allow thought and the word to be definitive. According to the *Cratylus*, Herakleitos said that 'all beings move and nothing is still' or 'all passes and nothing stays' (τὰ ὄντα ἰέναι τε πάντα καὶ μένειν οὐδέν, or, πάντα χωρεῖ καὶ οὐδὲν μένει).[73] In a not-too-distant paraphrase this means that everything that is, is in the process of going, leaving no space (*chorei*) for a remainder. Obviously, this is a theory of everything (καὶ ἐκ πάντων ἕν καὶ ἐξ ἑνὸς πάντα), perhaps one of the earliest.[74] In a vexed way this is also the first step along the way toward reductionist science.

If, as Herakleitos suggested, motion is continuous, the definition of the instant or the cessation of movement within motion itself that provides the definable transition necessary for measuring time comes to revolve entirely around the boundaries it is ascribed. Aristotle addressed the problem of temporal boundaries by maintaining that neither motion nor rest is possible in the 'now.'[75] As he states, the 'now' is the *horos* between past and future.[76] This is the boundary between motion and rest that is also called the 'instant' and is treated in detail by Richard Sorabji along with other problems about defining the transition between moving and resting or stopping and starting.[77] Sorabji's language reflects

---

72   Hegel (1892) 100.
73   Pl. *Crat*.401D, 402A.
74   DK(23) 54: 68.
75   Ar. *Phys*.234a31–34. On a detailed discussion of time in Aristotle see Chapter Five.
76   Ar.*Phys*.222b1.
77   See Chapter Twenty-Six in Sorabji (1983).

the determining significance of the instant, though he never quotes Aristotle's use of the *horos*.

> For a start, I might suggest that an instant of motion falls *within* a period of motion, while an instant of rest will be one that falls within *or bounds* a period of rest.[78]

Fittingly, Herakleitos is himself difficult to position within particular temporal boundaries, as he never mentions any political events, people or even any easily dated natural phenomena. However, it is supposed that he was living around the late sixth century BC, the same time the *horoi* of the *agora* were being inscribed in the developing market-place. One thing is noteworthy though, for Herakleitos was as ethnocentric as the next man, and the *logos* according to him could only be understood in Greek. For Herakleitos, then, the *logos* does not only distinguish the logical supremacy of humans above all other creatures but of Greek speakers above the rest: 'Poor witnesses for men are their eyes and ears if they have barbarian souls' (βαρβάρας ψυχὰς ἐχόντων).[79] Since he is considered amongst the forerunners of Western philosophy and rationalism, it would appear that ethnic and linguistic bias was ingrained from the very beginning. Wittgenstein put the problem succinctly when he said *'the limits of my language* mean the limits of my world.'[80] Presumably this describes a reciprocal relation, in which the opposition between *logos* and *physis*, word and nature, became canonical in Greek philosophy on account of a simultaneous trend to claim power by assuming the side of the *logos* and dismissing any challenging systems of belief to the other category, be that no stranger than nature (*physis*). Suffice it to say that materiality was abandoned to the forces of nature, while meaning was written in to human language like a contract, ascribed as the exclusive property of rational man.

The Stone is Worldless

Plumwood argues that nature is a political rather than a descriptive category that developed as one half of Western dualism, in which the other 'protagonist super-hero of the western psyche' is reason.

---

78 Sorabji (1983) 415–416.
79 DK(22) 107: 81.
80 Wittgenstein (1922) 5.6. (original italics).

> The concept of reason provides the unifying and defining contrast for the concept of nature, much as the concept of husband does for that of wife, as master for slave. Reason in the western tradition has been constructed as the privileged domain of the master, who has conceived nature as a wife or subordinate other encompassing and representing the sphere of materiality, subsistence and the feminine which the master has split off and constructed as beneath him. The continual and cumulative overcoming of the domain of nature by reason engenders the western concept of progress and development.[81]

The *horos* marks this point of difference, retaining both the very materiality of stone and taking upon itself the distinction between *logos* and *physis*. The question is, do humans produce the stone, or does the stone produce humans? Is the stone a theological peak or *summa* of animal disputations, or a useful tool in the power politics of the *anima*? At first glance it would appear as if the stone issues in as the symbol that humans have sublated and sublimated nature, distanced by means of this from their animal origins. Perhaps that is the very nature of any dealings with a symbol, it is *thrown together* (*sym-ballein*), especially in the case of the stone whose brute materiality is not betrayed by the ideality of its impetus.[82] As Hegel states, in animistic religions, the divine itself was supposed to be visibly present in the animal, yet, 'the self-consciousness of spirit is what alone makes respect for the dark and dull inwardness of animal life disappear.'[83] This degradation itself, 'debasing the high dignity and position of the animal world,' is transformed into the content of thought. Aristotle remains the basis for the theory of the human soul even today.

> Νῦν δὲ περὶ ψυχῆς τὰ λεχθέντα συγκεφαλαιώσαντες, εἴπωμεν πάλιν ὅτι ἡ ψυχὴ τὰ ὄντα πώς ἐστιν· πάντα γὰρ ἢ αἰσθητὰ τὰ ὄντα ἢ νοητά, ἔστι δ'ἡ ἐπιστήμη μὲν τὰ ἐπιστητά πως, ἡ δ'αἴσθησις τὰ αἰσθητά.[84]

> And now let us sum up what has been said concerning the soul, let us say again that the soul is somehow all existent things. For they are all either objects of sensation or of thought; and knowledge is somehow what is known and sensation is what is sensed.

---

81 Plumwood (1994) 3.
82 Ar.*Pol*.1294a35
83 Hegel (1988) 445.
84 Ar.*Ath*.431b20ff.

Although things are here defined only by their existence as objects of thought or sensation, thought is also an object of thought. And from here it would be radically satisfying to reverse Aristotle's logic and force him into the quandary of the world soul or cosmic mind by stating that if the soul is all existent things, then all existent things are soul. The stone, being sensed and understood by the soul is simultaneously the subject of soul, creating sense and understanding. But Aristotle would not like this shifting of categories of one into another.

> ἀνάγκη δ' ἢ αὐτὰ ἢ τὰ εἴδη εἶναι. αὐτὰ μὲν δὴ οὔ· οὐ γὰρ ὁ λίθος ἐν τῇ ψυχῇ, ἀλλὰ τὸ εἶδος· ὥστε ἡ ψυχὴ ὥσπερ ἡ χείρ ἐστιν.[85]
>
> It is thus necessary that faculties are the same as the objects or their forms. But they are not the same, for the stone does not exist in the soul, but only its form. The soul, then, is like the hand.

The hand is the tool of division par excellence, and like the soul has the advantage of being a vital part of the human body, so that it is not even necessary to talk of prosthetics in order to discover the distinction between human and nonhuman. The distinction itself is immanently inherent. The facility to create shape as well as the ability to recognise form in nature is a characteristic of both the hand and the soul. According to Aristotle and perhaps Hegel as well *anima* or *psyche* is not so much descriptive as a figurative activity. Just as objects are taken in hand, so forms are taken into the soul. Aristotle arrives at a point of confusion in the question of the substance of division in bodies (*sōmata*)

> ὁμοίως ἔνεστιν ἐν τῷ στερεῷ ὁποιονοῦν σχῆμα: ὥστ' εἰ μηδ' ἐν τῷ λίθῳ Ἑρμῆς, οὐδὲ τὸ ἥμισυ τοῦ κύβου ἐν τῷ κύβῳ οὕτως ὡς ἀφωρισμένον.[86]
>
> for every shape is equally present in the solid, so that if 'Hermes is not in the stone,' nor is half of the cube in the cube as a determinate [*aphōrismenon*] shape.

The argument is that the stone subjected to the mason's tools already has its form within it as the potentiality of determinate (verbal cognate with *horos*) form. Agamben elaborated on Aristotle's notion of

---

85 Ar.Ath.431b30.
86 Arist.Met.1002a22,1017b7, Phys. 1.7 190b in wood: Met.1048a31, in painting: Met.1050a20.

potentiality, stressing, in a nice echo of Herakleitos, that a being that has potentiality is also capable of impotentiality, for example the potentiality of a child to learn but also not to learn to read. He explains that 'this is the origin (and the abyss) of human power, which is so violent and limitless with respect to other living beings.'[87] Agamben takes a more cynical position on the division of humans from the nonhuman. For him this division is located in the negation or *sterēsis* of potentiality, 'the potential for darkness:' 'other living beings are capable only of their specific potentiality. But human beings are the animals capable of their own impotentiality.'[88] Human freedom is therefore the potential to do both good and evil. Inertia or apathy is certainly a considerable cause of harm, though harm is just as often exerted through actions, whether devoid of thought or orchestrated and manipulated via the bad intentions of another. It is interesting that the negation of potentiality is here offered as a determinative ontological capacity of the construct of human subjectivity from an ethical perspective rather than a physical one. Here at least the tool is no longer the divisive force, but force itself or power, *dynamis*.

A less abstract way, and generally the more traditional way to distinguish animals from humans is to describe the human being as the animal with *logos*, the rational animal, the 'sick animal' as Hegel states, or as Castoriadis says 'the mad animal.'[89] Either way the intersection between human thought and language, whether rationalised or irrationalised, becomes the ontological lodestone for further developments in both aesthetics and epistemology, this is also known as the hermeneutic turn. Embeddedness within culture and the human sciences no longer justifies a distinct methodology, or set of rules to follow and apply, because humans are already situated within the discourse and dialogues that come under critique. As Gadamer states, a 'situation is not a case of something obeying a theoretical law and being determined by it; it is something that surrounds one and opens itself up only from a practical perspective.'[90] Both the authority of the speaker and the character of culture are found in

---

87 Agamben (1999) 182.
88 Ibid. 181–182.
89 Castoriadis (1997) 262.
90 Gadamer (1999) 74.

the same place (*ethos*), and it is within these practical constructs that determinations can be discovered, but not isolated. Nonetheless 'it is no objection that practical philosophy in Aristotle's sense presupposes a fixed, comprehensive ethical gestalt, the one that he himself found retrospectively in the ancient *polis*,' because as Gadamer states 'it is always the case that practical "philosophy" arises out of practically determined being and refers back to it.'[91]

But does modern hermeneutics really embed practical philosophy within the experience of the world? Being in the world is neither a property nor a relation that can be discarded and picked up at will. Heidegger describes Being-in-the-world as an essential characteristic of Dasein: 'Taking up relationships towards the world is possible only because Dasein, as Being-in-the-world, is as it is.'[92] However, that this is not a description of a mutual reciprocal relation between all things unequivocally is elaborated in his lecture course, *The Fundamental Concepts of Metaphysics* where he develops an unconventional method for distinguishing between humans and nonhumans.

Here the stone features as representing the opposite end of the spectrum to the human being. According to Heidegger the stone is emphatically 'worldless, it is without world it has no world,' while the animal is 'poor in world,' though not completely deprived, and the human being is 'world forming.'[93] He then attempts to answer the question as to how to characterise a living being, figuring the stone in a relation of non-reciprocity and (phallically) non-penetrative with the world it is within. He explains that the stone does not experience its embeddedness within the world, and that the 'stone cannot be dead because it is never alive.'[94]

> The stone is without world. The stone is lying on the path, for example. We can say that the stone is exerting a certain pressure upon the surface of the earth. It is 'touching' the earth. But what we call 'touching' here is not a form of touching at all in the stronger sense of the word. It is not at all like that relationship which the lizard has to the stone on which it lies basking in the sun. And the touching implied in both these cases is

---

91 Ibid. 75.
92 Heidegger (1962) 84.
93 Heidegger (1995) 176–177, 196.
94 Ibid. 179.

above all not the same as that touch which we experience when we rest our hand upon the head of another human being.[95]

Again, the human hand crops up as the tool of measurement. The human hand touches in a different way to the touch of the stone upon the earth. It is the stone in the hand that brings the stone to presence for us. The stone 'lying nearby is simply present at hand amongst other things.'[96] As an object the stone exists for us because we can and do take it in hand, that is, the stone becomes an object for us, while we do not become an object for the stone. Only we can wonder at 'what is plain and obvious, τὰ πρόχειρα,' that which 'lies right at hand.'[97] A similar significance of the hand also appeared in Aristotle. The hand's ability to grasp and touch was described as a metaphor for the grasping of thoughts in the soul (and vice versa).[98] Meanwhile the stone's existence is defined as nothing more than as something to be grasped, or something that touches but does not feel. The stone is worldless because it is defined as having no access to other beings. Perhaps another way of putting it would be to say that the stone cannot experience itself in relation to other beings in its immediate world, it is unable to penetrate the world (despite providing the ground and foundation of this world). This inability is what characterises the being of the stone:

> it lies upon the earth but does not touch it. The earth is not given for the stone as an underlying support which bears it, let alone given as earth. Nor of course can the stone ever sense this earth as such, even as it lies upon it. The stone lies on the path. If we throw it into the meadow then it will lie wherever it falls. We can cast it into a ditch filled with water. It sinks and ends up lying on the bottom. In each case according to circumstance the stone crops up here or there, amongst and amidst a host of other things, but always in such a way that everything present around it remains essentially inaccessible to the stone itself. Because in its being a stone it has no possible access to anything else around it, anything that it might attain or possess as such, it cannot possibly be said to be deprived of anything either.[99]

---

95 Ibid. 196.
96 Ibid. 198.
97 Heidegger (2003) 87.
98 Ar.*Phys*.1036b21–35.
99 Heidegger (1995) 197.

Sensation, motion and emotion are not new tropes in the exclusionary vocabulary of human beings, while possession and deprivation might be said to allude in a vague way to Aristotle's *dynamis*, albeit filtered through Agamben. Heidegger gives as the basis of the human being's presence in the world the ability to be attuned. '*Dasein as Dasein* is always already attuned in its very grounds. There is only ever a change of attunement.'[100] Attunement, though difficult to understand clearly, is comprised of an experience of profound boredom that leads to an indifference to existence. This indifference brings about the deprivation of world and this has to do with a change of temporality, in which the human being goes beyond the normal flow of existence, coming to a standstill.[101] As Kuperus puts it, the 'animal, in Heidegger's analysis, keeps going, without ever coming to a stop; the animal merely behaves and is not attuned. Human beings, instead, do not merely *move toward*, but can *keep a distance*; they are not absorbed in their worlds as the animal is. We humans *can* come to a stop in our otherwise driven existence.'[102] *Stasis* therefore appears for Heidegger to be essential to human consciousness.

How do we, therefore, access the stone? If we stop when everything around us keeps moving, surely it is we who become out of sync with the world. If the world is in flux and we are still, are we not left behind? How can we possibly hear, feel, understand the being of the stone if we do not experience it according to its own rhythm? Heidegger does not satisfactorily answer this question of how we access the stone.[103] Nonetheless, his response is interesting, for he finds himself caught in a 'circle' of thought which elucidates the problem, this globular problem: 'How are living beings as such—the animality of the animal and the plant-character of the plant—originally accessible? Or is there no possibility of any original access here at all?' and, 'what then of the stone—can we transpose ourselves into a stone?'[104] But why limit it to these basic categories? What about the bacterial-character of bacteria,

---

100 Ibid. 68.
101 Ibid. 146.
102 Kuperus, Gerard. 'Attunement, Deprivation, and Drive: Heidegger and Animality' in Painter and Lotz (2007) 23.
103 Krell (1992) 116.
104 Heidegger (1995) 179, 201.

the fungal-character of fungi, the watery-ness of water, the archaic nature of archaea? Heidegger's response is that

> these questions must be left open, but that also means that we must always have some answer ready, however provisional and tentative, in order to guide us as we pursue our comparative considerations. On the other hand, these comparative considerations can and must ultimately make some contribution toward the clarification and possible answering of these questions. Thus we constantly find ourselves moving in a circle. And this is an indication that we are moving within the realm of philosophy. Everywhere a kind of circling. This circling movement of philosophy of course is alien to ordinary understanding which only ever wants to get the job in hand over and done with as quickly as possible. But going round in circles gets us nowhere. Above all, it makes us feel dizzy, and dizziness is something uncanny.[105]

Should we not feel at home in considering all these other beings that constitute our world? These are our near neighbours, organic or no; often they are part of our very self. If we are not at home here, where else can we feel at home? Here we are at home, in the world, going around in circles.

It is worth stressing the duplicity of Heidegger's position here when he says that the questions must be left open and an answer must be at hand, no matter how tentative. Heidegger himself does not ground this duplicity, but it is clearly reminiscent of Aristotle's *diaporesai*, as well as the work of the *horos* standing in for definition so that further questioning of definitions can proceed. That Heidegger's progress comes to a standstill at this point, or rather keeps going in circles alerts us to the limits of the horizon, the frame in which he works. On the one hand, a cyclical motion would appear natural, after all many stones tend toward the spherical given enough time and space. On the other hand, Heidegger or rather his thought is trapped within the mouse hole of 'that dimension of truth pertaining to scientific and metaphysical knowledge.'[106] He states that we cannot transpose ourselves into stone, although he acknowledges that in myth and art it is in a way possible because this 'animates' them. This interesting investigation into transposition breaks off, because it comes up against 'quite different kinds of possible truth,' which do not fit into the project of western rationalism.

---

105 Ibid. 180.
106 Ibid. 204.

Since the mid-twentieth century there have been some concessions made within the tradition of human consciousness interacting with the nonhuman, through which different kinds of possible truths have filtered, especially when scientific explanations are not always ready to hand. Lately this has had noteworthy effects even within the edifice of science. As Alaimo states in her rereading of material nature,

> the pursuit of self-knowledge, which has been a personal philosophical, psychological, or discursive matter, now extends into a rather 'scientific' investigation into the constitution of our coextensive environments. Science, however, offers no steady ground, as the information may be biased, incomplete, or opaque and the ostensible object of scientific inquiry-the material world-is extremely complex, overwrought with agencies, and ever emergent.[107]

In terms of transposing ourselves into other beings, there are cases that cannot be dismissed as 'fantastical' or 'illusory.' For example, in Ecuador, humans have access to the minds of jaguars, monkeys, dogs and so forth.[108] Although even here our interpretation favours the activity of the human mind. It might not be as it seems, it might be the other way around: the jaguars may well have access to the human mind. Similarly, I might eat a psilocybin mushroom, but is it my mind that has access to the mushroom or the mushroom that accesses and makes use of my mind?[109] Many mental conditions have been found to respond well to an increase in gut flora, in which a patient ingests millions of microbiota, tiny little bacteria that live within the digestive tract and assist the functioning of the neurons therein. Such interactions are not limited to the living world. A lack of iron will cause me to feel foggy and lazy, while an increase in fulvic acid (the earth found in peat bogs) can cleanse my mind of the insanity of lead poisoning. Obviously, brittle bones are addressed by ingesting increased amounts of calcium and magnesium, both of which are rocks, while the mere proximity to other types of rock are said to alter human psychical states (from ruby crystals to uranium ore). These interactions should no longer be considered isolated events. All matter has an effect, whether negative or positive, on the mind or soul. Perhaps the real question should not be whether

---

107 Alaimo (2010) 20.
108 See Kuhn (2013).
109 See Sheldrake (2020).

the human mind is distinct from matter itself in which it is so deeply ensconced, but whether the existence of a soul common to all things can be excluded. 'If nature is to matter,' as Alaimo says, 'we need more potent, more complex understandings of materiality' but from where are we to extract these understandings?[110] We cannot all fall back upon indigenous knowledge as in many parts of the world such knowledge has been wiped out by the project of Western science and religion or remains only patchy. Can we change the limits of our world or at least recognise their historical development as inessential?

Graham Harman makes a smart move in relation to Heidegger's conception of the worldless stone; he inverts the experience of worldlessness to reflect us. It is then we who fail to experience the stone, it is we who cannot access its reality: 'the reality of things is always withdrawn or veiled rather than directly accessible, and therefore any attempt to grasp that reality by direct and literal language will inevitably misfire.'[111] What is interesting about object-oriented ontology is that it states a fact that is perhaps always implicitly understood but that nonetheless remains as an inherently faulty premise in human experience. Objects are not dismissed as devoid of relations unless they are subjected to human thought. Objects have relations and interactions amongst themselves and still bear little or no relevance for humankind.

From this perspective it could be said that the *horos*, that is, the coincidence of the boundary and the stone, is a relation that provided the precedent for what it means for the human to be human and not some other thing, though how the stone stands in relation to itself must remain a mystery. That this mystery has nothing to do with us might be factually true though it does not fail to play a role in how we experience the stone in itself. What I mean is that it might be the very fact that we interpret the stone as 'withdrawn' from us that means it can be invested with so much meaning. The stone matters to us exactly because its meaning always plays somewhere off in the distance, obscured and veiled by the bare materiality of stone. This might be a mystical way of saying what Harman phrases epistemologically: 'an object is whatever

---

110 Alaimo (2010) 2.
111 Harman (2018) 38.

cannot be reduced to either of the two basic kinds of knowledge: what something is made of, and what it does.'[112]

The material presence and proximity of stone is not enough for us to fully describe what it is in the world, nor what it does. This also holds for the stone in relation to itself. There is what Harman calls a fracture or 'gap *within* things, and we call it the object/qualities rift [...] The object precedes its qualities despite not being able to exist without them.'[113] Harman proposes that the gap between the object and our representation of it is internal to the presence of the object itself. This is very interesting if we consider *horos* as the object. Such an object seems to be the externalisation of this gap. Can we say that the boundary is the real object while the stone is the sensual object? The fracture of the *horos* would also be what provides the definition between the real and sensual, or between boundary and stone, and is in fact none other than the definition of the object as both real and sensual: that is *horos*. Perhaps this provides a basis for 'Aristotle's ancient claim in his *Metaphysics* that individual things cannot be defined since things are always concrete while definitions are made of universals.'[114] But if *horos* is the definition between real and sensual or concrete and universal it is also a figure that can be used to describe any object. This is why it cannot be reduced to anything but itself, because this reduction is its very being and purpose. It is always already fractured between its own materiality and its meaning, and this is what makes it mean something.

I am human so I cannot claim to observe the stone with anything but human sensibilities. Then again there's no way to know whether the boundary that the stone marks is of natural or human origin, prescribed by the hand of fate or inscribed in the nature of the stone. According to Heidegger, the being of the stone is taken entirely separately from any other worldly force. But do not the wind, the rain, the heat, and the motions of the earth turning interact with the stone, let alone lichen, plant life, animals and humans' use of it? What if these activities cannot be separated from the being of the stone because the stone's existence, shape, and place are entirely reliant upon them, just as we cannot

---

112 Ibid. 257.
113 Ibid. 259.
114 Ibid. 38

be separated from the air we breathe or the water, the food, and the microbes that constitute our bodies?

Heidegger's definition of the stone as worldless seems to be based largely upon the supposed fact that the stone is unable to locomote, to move or remove itself. The stone here is inert. This is the basic conceptual understanding for separating animate matter from inanimate. Absence of motion has long been used to justify the claim for absence of intelligence in plants, at least until it was proved that plants also move (as well as have the ability to change behaviour, remember and signal).[115] What about the long durée, where stone aggregates, dissolves, forms, reacts chemically, explodes, melts and so forth? The stone does not choose to be worn by water, they will say. But have not these kinds of interactions between stones or rocks flying through space created the world itself? Do planets form by choice or by accident? Is the world—the universe—devoid of consciousness except for smart little us? That matter is brute and devoid of soul asserted by reductionistscience does not even wash with reductionist science anymore.[116] The absence of world-creating spirit in stone is in no way something that can be taken for granted; it is well and truly beyond the realm of the human episteme and the opposite certainly seems more likely and better supported in the majority of the world's metaphysical belief systems.

---

115 Gagliano (2018) 65.
116 Barad (2007) 394.

Fig. 2. ΑΧΡΙ ΤΕ[Σ] ΗΟΔΟ ΤΕΣΔΕ ΤΟ ΑΣΤΥ ΤΕΙΔΕ ΝΕΝΕΜΕΤΑΙ 'The city extends up until the edge of this road here,' *IG* I³ 1111. Photograph by T. Potter, 2021. Rights belong to the Epigraphic Museum, Athens © Hellenic Ministry of Culture and Sports/Hellenic Organization of Cultural Resources Development (H.O.C.R.E.D.).

2. Does the Letter Matter?

Terminus, Limes, Fines: vt dicuntur regionis vel agri alicuius.¹

ὅρος, ὁ -*boundary, landmark* [...] *pillar* (whether inscribed or not) [...] in Logic, *term* of a proposition (whether subject or predicate) [...] *definition*.²

This chapter raises the problem of the materiality of the letter. The explicit problem confronted in the *horos* is the meaning of matter, where the inscription itself of the word upon stone can be read as the sign of a precedent natural script, of boundaries prescribed rather than inscribed. The stone itself raises this possibility, and this question: how do we read boundaries? Are boundaries written in 'nature' with the stone as marker and is the inscription of the word for boundary, then, a secondary script? In what capacity can the word *horos* be read simultaneously as script, stone and boundary? Is the stone itself the original proscription giving us pause, so that the separation of meaning from matter can be deployed into the dualism of the human and the nonhuman? In the hermeneutical course of writing on writing, and also of writing within writing, what is important in such an inscription is that regardless of its professed use the name remains the same: *Horos* is the name given by the Athenians to the words and letters upon the land.

Here I am working on the implicit hypothesis that words and things not only endure in a relation, but that the *horos*—given that it appears in philosophical texts, as in a philosophical 'term' or 'definition'— actually stands in for this relation as a boundary and limit, a point of division, simultaneously relating matter and language, the stone with the signifier for 'boundary,' and providing the very material basis for their distinctions. To pull this apart further, what can be seen is that *horos* stands equally within a scale of materiality beginning with

---

1 TGL: ὅρος. Estienne (1572) 1465.
2 LS: 1255–1256.

stone, moving then to the inscribed stone, and subsequently (though not chronologically later) the boundary invested in the stone, and the concept of boundary, as well as the word's other textual interpretations, such as definition, term, limit and so forth. Given its materiality the *horos* remains throughout the philosophical developments of Greece, despite claims to separate substance from word.

Horos is the matter that remains in any question of definition or what words mean. It does not just reinvest meaning with matter; it stands as a testament that matter means as much as meaning does. Wordplay is central, as psychoanalytic discourse shows, in revealing what is the matter, and should not be dismissed as *mere* words. Lacan states that 'metaphor is situated at the precise point at which meaning is produced in nonmeaning,' and it is not only the words we use, but also those we fail to use, employ idiosyncratically or poetically that reveal our psychical reality.[3] In human psychical disturbance, there is nothing immaterial about words nor more substantial than letters, though that does not make them any easier to understand. The point being that it does not matter all that much what we intended to say because the words themselves carry meaning independently of our will to use them, revealing what it was that we really wanted to say but did not or what we did not want to say at all.

Of course, that does not mean the existence of speech is absolute; it simply means that words reveal a psychical reality that is otherwise flooded within the babble of wanting to say something else or meaning to say nothing of any matter. If the accidental play of letters allows slips of consciousness to open up and reveal the crisis of symbolic meaning, perhaps there is more to letters than meets the eye. In hermetic traditions the letter has a meaning all of its own that is in no way distinct from its form and owes no debt to its appearance within otherwise meaningful words. The esoteric significance of letters is an earthly, lithic structure into which we must delve, 'excavate,' in order to even begin to understand the allusive and mysterious nature of the particular letters inscribing the word *horos*, and what they could possibly mean.

There is no intention here to reinscribe the *horos* into tradition, for what is significant about this stone is that although its history is unwritten, it

---

3   'The Instance of the Letter in the Unconscious or Reason Since Freud' in Lacan (2006) 423.

never ceased to be read. *Horos* (ΗΟΡΟΣ) appears inscribed upon stones small and large in the region of Attica, from the gardens of the French school of Archaeology to the cemetery in the Kerameikos. They are quite evident if you are looking, though their relation to the site of sight might be no more than formal (ὁράω, ὅρασις). These inscriptions were discovered in extraordinary numbers in the excavations of Athens.[4] This bounty found in such a limited area should alert us to the fact of their wider distribution throughout the city, suggesting a common use of these stones. But are they stones, or are they inscriptions? This is the heart of the problem.

To begin with, this chapter takes lexical definitions of the *horos* in an attempt to understand what the *horos* is, what is essential to the word *horos*. The readings of alternative manuscripts of Harpocration's lexicon entry for the term is taken for granted in the Liddell and Scott lexicon, in which the *horos* is described as 'boundary, landmark [...] pillar (whether inscribed or not, cf. Harp.)'[5] But this interpretation may well be based upon a misreading of the words for 'without letters' (χωρὶς γραμμάτων).[6] Given that Harpocration provides a definition almost word-for-word with that of the Suida, it seems likely that typographical error arose during the copying. Nonetheless this typographical slip, like a slip of the tongue, does not mean that it does not mean something or that it does not matter. The oversight of the copyist or transcriber, the lapse in concentration or proof of ignorance opens up the possibility of a deeper vision into the nature of stone. If the stone itself is the marker, what extraneous role does the inscription play? And if the stone already is read, whence come these lithic letters that draw up the boundaries of our relation with the land?

To begin again, however, it must be stated that *horos* is stone. And it does not cease to be stone once it is inscribed; its inscription is read and interpreted. The matter of the stone does not cease to matter once it is endowed and associated with script. But if it also does not require an inscription in order to be recognised or read as boundary, this poses a genuine challenge to the supposed precedence of speech over writing as well as human activity against nature's passivity or of meaning over

---

[4] Lalonde (1991); Lewis (1994); Finley (1952); Fine (1951).
[5] LS. ὅρος.
[6] Harp. (1833) 139; Harp. (1853) 226.

matter. The location of the boundary, assumed to be marked out by the human drive to determinism may well be read into what was already there: a kind of prehistoric script of stone. So, what of the stone? What does it tell us? What is its material, what does its materiality mean to us and what does it matter to the stone?

Aristotle says a synonym is where a single description corresponds to different nouns, 'so that there is no difference between the defined term (*horos*) and the name' (ὥστ' οὐδενὸς τῶν ὑπὸ τοὔνομα ὁ ἀποδοθεὶς ὅρος).[7] In translating the word *horos* can we do any better than simply offering a swathe of synonyms? Perhaps this plethora of proximate meanings is also essential to the *horos*. *Horos*, to paraphrase Aristotle wildly, is the very distinction between words, and the material basis for metonymy and the word itself is synonymous to some degree with its letters, insofar as it is a word inscribed upon stone at once giving and given meaning in terms of the material play of presence of letters.

Ever since Aristotle, if not before, matter has been denigrated in favour of abstract concepts such as the soul and reason. And since Plato, transcendence has been given as the aim of philosophical thought—transcendence beyond the quotidian things of experience. This is described in the figure of the cave, where humans begin locked up in the stone of their own ignorance, lacking the determination to come into the open. Within the cave, our shared, perceived reality is nothing more than a shadow play.[8] So long as we adhere within stone (the cave) we do not know the world for what it is, conscious reality elides us. But once we emerge and see that our previous habitation was nothing but stone, the symbolic (*sym-ballein*) play of meaning falls away and we are subject to a blast of the fresh air of reality.[9] Henceforth, being ensconced within stone, in the cave, becomes the symbol for an unexamined life. This allegory represents the Palaeolithic mind, literally old and stoned on the demands of bare existence, inseparable from nature, embedded within the earth. It could also be an allegory for the cosmic mind, or the world soul, that mythic reminder of meaningfully embedded cohabitation, though this would not make it any less derogatory in Plato's vainglorious eyes.

---

7   Ar.*Top*.148a25.
8   Pl.*Rep*.514–520.
9   Ar.*Pol*.1294a35

The material world is not just the basis or springboard for any more abstract thoughts, it is also the hole we fall into when, like Thales, our thought becomes too abstract and we stop looking where we step (βαδίζειν ἀγνοοῦσι).[10] Cohen points out the rocky substrate that underlies philosophical meanderings, from Petros (rock) as the foundation of the church to Latour's agency of the nonhuman: 'Stones are the partners with which we build the epistemological structures that may topple upon us. They are ancient allies in knowledge making.'[11] Philosophy has been based upon the speculation of the natural world from day one, whether that was wonder at the formation of the stars and the planetary bodies or the violent force of the rain and the sea as it wears away rock and crafts habitable zones. That sight (ὁράω 'to see') necessarily plays a part in this speculative world-view (*theoria*) and in the expansion of one's horizons reinforces the material intimacy of the term and stone, *horos*, with abstract human thought. As Chapter One argued, this term is the material representation of the constant motion of base materiality that needs to be passed over *diaporēsai* (διαπορῆσαι καλῶς) in order for thought to be freed from the material and go on into abstract thought, *euporēsai* (εὐπορῆσαι).[12] That there are determinations and certainties, static laws and rules in nature is entirely dependent upon being able to maintain a position within an otherwise constantly evolving world. And if this position is to have any meaning at all it has to exist in more than the symbolic realm of human thought and language, it has to obtain to 'reality.'

> Stone becomes history's bedrock as lithic agency impels human knowing. Neither dead matter nor pliant utensil, bluntly impedimental as well as collaborative force, stone brings story into being, a partner with language (just as inhuman), a material metaphor.[13]

The idea that stone undergirds flights of metaphor, of technological, artistic and philosophical creation seems a pretty radical cultural critique, especially as it must claim to be common to all cultures. It is in fact more than radical: roots are superficial in comparison to stone. In contrast, dominant cultural and economic practises today are reliant

---

10   Ar.*Met*.995a27–40.
11   Cohen (2015) 4.
12   Ar.*Met*.995a27–40.
13   Cohen (2015) 4.

upon stone being exactly nothing but dead matter and pliant utensil to be put to use according to human will. How does stone come to be thought 'dead matter' at all? It might be useful to consider this as a purposeful depletion of the meaning of matter, rather than a natural origin story in which matter begins as mute, base and void. If this is the case, then it is not matter itself that starts as lacking significance but human beings who strip matter of value or significance for or in itself. This stripping of meaning from matter is attributed to the project of scientific rationalism, the point at which the various disciplines of human knowledge abandoned notions of the existence of an immanent demiurge, animistic spiritual beliefs, or the *anima-mundi*, and restructured belief systems around the experimental understandings into mechanical processes of the organic world.[14]

That the world is the substrate or foundation for any more abstract thought rather than the other way around (where thought or *nous* brings the world into being) is also the basis for the supremacy of human meaning attribution. Even according to phenomenology (whose name derives from the things that appear) we experience objects only insofar as they mean something to us. This is the case both nominally or metaphorically and actually. For example, Aristotle's *physics* preceded his *metaphysics*, the stoics could be found in the marbled stoa earning a name for themselves, and even the peripatetics had to walk upon something in order for their name to get around.

Graphic Slips of the Tongue

Letters might not be as effective at persuading as stones are, but they can open up a correspondence between deeds and words in their indeterminable (a-orist) aspect of non-appropriation. The consubstantiality of letter and stone follows the path of writing crooked and straight (γραφέων ὁδὸς εὐθεῖα καὶ σκολιή), leading on the one hand to the play of absence and presence, but on the other to the interminable preoccupation with intercourse and copulation.[15]

The earliest extant *horoi* have been dated to the second half of the sixth century BC, and the archaic boundary-stones of the *agora* (which

---

14 Merchant (1990) 99f.
15 DK 59: 75. In keeping with the theme, there are variations in spellings here.

read 'I am the boundary of the *agora*') are believed to have been inscribed around 500 BC, while inscribed gravestones in Athens recede further back into the seventh century (though those inscribed with the ΗΟΡΟΣ are conservatively dated to the fifth century).[16] If we accept these rough dates we must also accept with a certain irony the fact that the *horos* of the agora, copulation and all, is among the earlier extant examples in the archaeological records of this stone (fifty years at the very most separates it from its predecessors). It is significant that attempts to date the earliest *horoi* upon archaeological evidence alone would suggest their coincidence with the foundation of the sixth-century archaic *polis*, with the period of the rise of the *agora* and the institutions that mark the beginnings of civic, political life in Athens. And yet, and this is unique, the literature suggests a considerably older heritage, intimated by references in the Homeric epics, as well as the important (if perplexing) role the *horos* plays in the poems and reforms of Solon, as we have received them from Aristotle (pseudo or not).

So, we face a curious problem. Our texts point to a prehistory of stone that the material evidence fails to support. It is more than a mere matter of precedence—the controversial relation between what is written and what is spoken—because here it would appear that the word, or the name of the stone, is older than the stone itself. But surely that is not possible. It is as if this early terminological identification between the stone and its various meanings (mark, limit, term and so forth) ridiculed the notions of precedence assumed in the school of archaeology, by inverting the *archē* and the *logos*. In order to excuse this lapse, of word before matter, the archaeologist may attribute these inconsistencies to the restrictions and limitations placed upon the epigraphist who is compelled to read script as a secondary writing upon stone.

The predisposition towards script can be observed in the self-evident distinction between the sculpted lumps of stone destined for museums and those inconsequent remainders dispersed among the weeds. How do archaeologists choose which stones are endowed with archaeological significance and which are discredited as meaningless matter? Obviously, the role the stones played in human society and culture provides the dividing line here for what is considered 'of archaeological interest' and what is not. But even here the lines are not so clear, since archaeologists

---

16   Lalonde (1991) 5–7.

are predominantly employed in the digging up of ancient rubbish heaps, the site dedicated to the remains of matter no longer invested with the significance of use. Matter itself and stones in particular are constantly enduring the recycling reconfigurations of social and cultural significance written upon their surface or implied in their disposal. From a paleontological perspective, of course, such differences break down and reconfigure into a different set of priorities attributed to the hierarchy of stone, but more on that in Chapter Five.

The pre-inscriptional *horoi* that are presumed to have sufficed in pre-literate times are necessarily speculative, as uninscribed stone cannot indubitably verify its name as *horos* to the epigraphist, even given the significance suggested by its position. The fact that ΗΟΡΟΣ was inscribed on waist-high pillars, wall blocks and even cut into natural rock façades would suggest that in pre-literate times more or less any rock surface could have sufficed as a *horos*. One such early rupestral *horos* of Zeus on the Hill of the Nymphs is easily missed and stepped over, carved as it is into the surface of a horizontal rock face.[17] If the words ΗΟΡΟΣ ΔΙΟΣ [retrograde] were not inscribed, it would be unrecognisable as a boundary of any kind. To our eyes this *horos* would be indistinguishable from stone: just another rock. But was this the case for its archaic observer? Does the word itself, '*horos*,' and therefore also the boundary it comprises, refer to its inscription, or did it inhere within the stone? Are boundaries found in language or presupposed in nature? What did the ancients themselves take the word *horos* to mean?

In order to address this problem, I will break the *horos* down into its respective parts: its multiple meanings and translations, its various archaeological remains, its textual examples and the letters themselves that constitute the inscription. The prehistory of the *horos* poses a particular difficulty to the epigraphist in identifying a stone *horos* in the absence of this inscription. As Lalonde suggests:

> The history of horoi in Athens, as in all of Greece, probably goes back before literate times, but the evidence for pre-inscriptional stones is slight and speculative; we might posit their use on the analogy of a variety of uninscribed natural and artificial boundary markers of the Classical and Hellenistic periods.[18]

---

17 Lalonde (2006).
18 Lalonde (1991).

And a note from Finley:

> The available evidence indicates that these *horoi* [meaning those later used as hypothecation markers], unlike the boundary-stones, were always inscribed; in fact, their very reason for existence would have been nullified by the absence of an inscription.[19]

Of course, both these statements indicate how the archaeological record cannot help but favour writing and the inscription over an implied act of reading. Both studies also intimate the probability that preclassical boundary-stones were not inscribed with the word *horos*. What is analogous about these arguments is an *argumentum ex silentio*, an archaeological proof of the symbolic invocation of reading—'I cannot say it because I cannot read it, but I say it anyway.' Speech from silence is the condition of speech as such; speech always issues out of silence. As Lacan notes in reference to St Augustine's *De locutionis significatione*, just as the words uttered by God in *Genesis* create *ex nihilo*, so speech is a 'symbolic invocation' that creates 'a new order of being in the relations between men.'[20]

Thus the stone speaks in the absence of script; the archaeologists hear the silence as proof for what they do not see before them, all those uninscribed *horoi*. The stone speaks to us *ex silentio*. In this, the *horos* is analogous with any other stone; it is *ana-logos*, *logos* drawn out of stone. Is this a kind of speech that is engraved upon the land and given to us aesthetically, not purely image but read nonetheless? One dictionary suggests the Indo-European root for *horos* is *ueru- 'draw,' *uoru-o-, with a further connection in Greek to ἐρύω, also 'to draw.'[21] But it also bears a close resemblance to seeing (ὁράω 'to look, see,' hence the Homeric form οὖρος, meaning 'watcher'), a theoretical origin which obviously should not be overlooked. In this case, the verbal action of the *horos* is drawn from speculation and said to precede any later attempts at definition (ὁρίζω). The *horos* is from the beginning a theoretical task that begins on the boundary and marks its path into the historical era as the term of the market.

There is also the possibility that the *horos* emerged along with its near neighbour 'mountain,' 'mountain range' (ὄρος) a natural boundary

---

19 Finley (1952) 197, n.13.
20 Lacan (1991) 239.
21 Beeks (2010) ὄρος.

par excellence, distinct from the *horos* on account of the oxytone on the first syllable rather than the last and lacking aspiration. It could also be distantly related to the more than verbal arousal, ὄρνυμι, 'to stir-up, excite, make to arise,' and would explain the habit of intervening within the texts at the most critical times. Nearby there is also the watery ὀρός, the 'whey' or because like engenders like, σπερματικὸς ὀρός, 'seminal fluid.' And yet my personal favourite is that *horos* is linked in some kind of devious way to the verb οὐρέω, 'to urinate,' drawing up the boundaries according to dogs, wild beasts and camping logic.[22] There is definitely a sort of libidinal coincidence of opposites inherent to these etymologies, whether originating from a protuberance or cleft the *horos* is indicative of a deeper penetration of stone than normally allowed in our frigid metaphysics. At least we can recognise that there is a bulging, autopoietic sense of boundary-creation, or something divisive, common to these etymologies. The *horos* need not proliferate or multiply since it is itself the same, amphibolous name given to division itself: 'one *horos*' suffices (εἷς ὅρος).[23]

The Liddell and Scott lexicon places the potential ambiguity of the word in parenthesis when it defines the *horos* as a *'pillar (whether inscribed or not...).'*[24] The parenthetical equivocation is presumably the result of a lexical comparison between the different manuscripts of Harpocration's lexicon. Harpocration's lexicon and the much later tenth-century AD lexical compilation, of the Suida, provide a similar definition for the word *horos*.

> Ὅρος· οὕτως ἐκάλουν οἱ Ἀττικοὶ τὰ ἐπόντα ταῖς ὑποκειμέναις οἰκίαις καὶ χωρίοις γράμματα, ἃ ἐδήλουν, ὅτι ὑπόκεινται δανειστῇ.[25]
>
> Horos: thus the Athenians called the letters set upon pledged households and lands, which showed that they were subject to a loan.

The text refers to the fourth-century BC usage of the *horoi* where they were placed upon properties to indicate fiscal encumbrance, a mortgage

---

22 Cf. ibid.
23 Thuc.4.92.4. I agree with Fine's objection to Wade-Gery's interpretation of this passage as providing an earlier reference to a mortgage stone, this is clearly the outer boundary-stone of a region. Fine (1951) 50–51. n.40.
24 LS: 1256 (II.b).
25 See entries for ὅρος in Suid. (1854) 786; Suid. (1705) Vol 2. 716 (with Latin translation). and Harp. (1833) 139; Harp. (1853) 266.

of sorts.²⁶ I've translated *grammata* as 'letters' to try to maintain the proximity to the written word, though the sense here is probably more like a 'deed,' as something that has been drawn up, or draws an outline, like a 'title deed.'²⁷ The alternate Harpocration manuscripts differ only slightly from the above definition but in an important way. For where this entry states that the Athenians drew letters 'upon the land,' the Harpocration manuscripts offer the alternative reading 'without letters.'²⁸ The χωρίοις γράμματα (letters upon the land) is replaced in the A manuscript with χωρὶς γράμμα, in the BC manuscript with χωρὶς γραμμάτων, and with χωρὶς γράμματος in the Aldine—all meaning 'without letters,' the 'letter' varying in case or number.²⁹ These readings have been rejected by the editor Dindorf, as by Bekker, as a corruption in favour of that of the χωρίοις γράμματα. And, judging by an earlier entry in the same work (ἄστικτον χωρίον, 'unmortgaged land') it would appear that the editor's addendum is accurate, for here we read ὅταν γὰρ ὑποκέηται, εἴθων ὁ δανείσας αὐτὸ τοῦτο δηλοῦν διὰ γραμμάτων ἐπόντων τῷ χωρίῳ, which is to say that the lender shows that a piece of land is pledged by means of letters set upon the land, with no mention of the *horos*.³⁰ Considering this coincidence of writing and speech, the *horos* is from the first a theoretical problem, the conjuncture of what is seen and heard as the initial margin of a similarity that is not primarily given to the senses, though it does not, for all that, cease to be represented aesthetically.

The difference is more than just a letter, though it is nothing less than a letter; it comes to provide a definition in which letters are themselves made absent or at least insignificant and even unnecessary, and the stone absorbs whatever remains in the absence of signification. As the Liddell and Scott lexicon states, the stone itself means *horos* 'with or without letters,' but does it mean this only because of a typographical error? Either way, there is a lack of letters, or a lapse of letters, whether in the text of Harpocration, in the Liddell and Scott, or on the stone itself

---

26 See Finley (1952).
27 The translation offered by Portus confirms this: *Attici vocabant libellos, vel titulos, cedibus & agris oppigneratis affixos, qui significabant, ea creditoribus obligata este*. Suid (1705) Vol 2. 716.
28 Harp. (1833) 139; Harp. (1853) 226.
29 Harp. (1853) 226.
30 Harp. (1853) 62. Also in Harp. (1833) 38 (with typographical variations/errors).

that does not need to be inscribed in order to say that it is *horos*. With or without letters, it reads *horos*.

Obviously, the interpretation of *horos* as being synonymous with 'letters' is also not without its difficulties. But, as Moses Finley notes in his study, it is 'more than probable that the two words [that is, *grammata* and *horos*] were here conceived as synonyms.'[31] What is common, then, is spelled out clearly in Aristotle's definition of the synonym:

συνώνυμα γὰρ ὧν εἷς ὁ κατὰ τοὔνομα λόγος· ὥστ᾽ οὐδενὸς τῶν ὑπὸ τοὔνομα ὁ ἀποδοθεὶς ὅρος, εἰ δὴ ὁμοίως ἐπὶ πᾶν τὸ ὁμώνυμον ἐφαρμόττει.[32]

Things are synonyms when there is a single description (*logos*) that corresponds to the name, so that the defined term (*horos*) is in no way different to these except in name, but is similarly joined to every homonym.

Aristotle introduces the notion of the 'homonym,' making it explicit that definition exists as overlapping boundaries between words. Definitions are paramount in conceptualising language as something more than merely conceptual; language begins to look like an interwoven structure rather than a list of discreet words. *Horos* is the definitory boundary or margin of definition that borders on every term. The *horos* is always there as the joint between the words' differences, and is what is likewise shared or similar, uniting them in a proximity despite nominal differences. *Horos* is there in the interstices as the name of this entire operation. In place of the name '*horos*,' then, one might also say letters, the common 'element' between words, on this at least the lexica are in agreement.[33]

'Drawing,' 'writing' or 'letters' are synonyms for the word *horos*. Unfortunately, the references to this 'drawing' upon the land deal exclusively with the later fourth-century *horoi* that undoubtedly have to do with actions taken by men to 'mark' encumbrance of a mortgage of some sort. It is pure speculation, but it is possible that the same language was used to talk about the earlier boundary-stones. If so, what did that earlier, earthly writing mean? Did it have to do with possession

---

31 Finley (1952) 199, n.22.
32 Ar.*Top*.148a25.
33 Except for Bekker (1814) 285.

and appropriation, with ownership or indebtedness as the later ones? Or were the boundary-stones implicated in 'natural' boundaries, in marking places given over to particular use, such as water holes, fertile land, easy passages between difficult terrain, or linguistic boundaries between tribes?

According to the precedence of speech over writing, it could be said that these stones are the supplement of the speech of the earth.[34] They are the sign of what the earth already signifies. But does the earth speak before it writes? Surely geo-forces take precedent here, and we read them and interpret them to mean something for us; that is what we call geology, geography, climatology and so forth. If, like the first pictograms, images replace sounds, what does the placement of stones upon the land reimagine or represent? Has there not been a prejudice towards literalism in always representing pictograms and ideograms as the first forms of writing, when, on the contrary the letter was never supposed to be taken literally? Writing is taken as a response from outside, a comment framed or outlined upon or against a natural surface, as if humans required a sense of their distinction and separation from the natural organic world, the self-consciousness of differentiation from the nonhuman, in order to 'represent' what they saw filtered through this consciousness. But it could just as easily be a trace that emerges from within. Is there anything more than an intellectual, even pedantic distinction between human script and the mark the dog leaves on the tree so that another dog can sniff it and thereby read into this scent the absent presence of the former dog? What if the traces of writing were read, sensible to begin with, though not necessarily intelligible?

There is a fracture within writing, according to Derrida, on account of the deferral of meaning within the sign that is always pointing somewhere else. There is therefore a spatial difference, but there is also a temporal difference, where writing defers to the meaning that it will be given when it is read in the future. This split within the text means that meaning is always absent, and no particular meaning can ever be definitively present. This slippage between difference and deferral gives rise to Derrida's coinage of the word *différance*, where sound remains one while meaning differs because of the mute phonetic play of a single letter. *Horos*, pronounced in modern Greek *oros* (and written without the

---

34 Derrida (2016) 305–306.

aspiration), might not be dissimilar. The letter itself, the archaic trace of an unknown phoneme, plays on the absence and presence of this sound (H) which might have ceased to be there by then, though exactly when 'then' is remains a question.

In any case the *horos* was written with an *H*. This letter remains as a trace of referral or deferral, both spatially and temporally, in the very least because we cannot say what it was originally supposed to mean or why it was kept even when its meaning had changed. That is to say that how the *horos* was supposed to be read as a spoken word remains a mystery, literally unspoken, locked up within stone. Perhaps it is along these lines that we can explain why Derrida disagrees with Lacan's articulation that 'the letter always arrives at its destination.'[35] For Derrida the destination is beside the point, as writing must function in the absence of the meaning-giving addressee of the text. For a letter to arrive it must have been sent. However, the origin of letters remains one of the great mysteries of human culture.

Lacan and Derrida both have innovative ways of escaping the limits of these atemporal boundaries. For Lacan it is to be found in the (literal) procedure or function of the unconscious, which, as Bruce Fink puts it, is 'composed of "letters" working, as they do, in an autonomous, automatic way, which preserves in the present what has affected it in the past.'[36] Or, as Lacan says himself, 'letters *make up* assemblages; not simply designating them, they *are* assemblages, they are to be taken as functioning as assemblages themselves,' and a little later, 'the unconscious is structured like the assemblages in question in set theory, which are like letters.'[37] These material elements have the capacity to break down and reform, where the act of reading meaning into them is never orchestrated fully by chance.

The letter's tendency toward dissolution and reformation marks it out as an element, or as Derrida will say a 'trace' of a structure that is not wholly described by the dichotomy of presence and absence. The letter returns from the past and interrupts, or erupts into, the present, even when its presence merely indicates absence. For Derrida the letter is the trace that always breaks into any predetermined project of

---

35 'Seminar on "The Purloined Letter"' in Lacan (2006) 30.
36 Bruce Fink, 'The Nature of Unconscious Thought or Why No One Ever Reads Lacan's Postface to the "Seminar on 'The Purloined Letter'"', in Feldstein (1996) 183.
37 Lacan (1988) 47–48.

archaeology which claims to escape the aporetic task of philosophy, and ascend to the heights of absolute presence: 'Such a *différance* would at once, again, give us to think a writing without presence and without absence, without history, without cause, without *archia*, without *telos*, a writing that absolutely upsets all dialectics, all theology, all teleology, all ontology.'[38]

Language is the structure into which every individual enters, but the role of writing is generally given in second place, just as in the case of the epigraphists, who read writing as a secondary script upon stone. Speech is obviously the main stage for psychoanalytic practice, its instrument, its material and framework. According to Lacan simile is paramount, so the unconscious is structured like a language; it is the place where signifiers loom large and generate the symbolic order. However, underneath, underpinning the symbolic order, sometimes undermining it, is the real. The real is the void of meaning and can never truly be known. It can only ever be mediated by the imaginary or the symbolic. The letter, for Lacan, is found here. The letter is part of the material substrate that buttresses the symbolic order. 'By "letter" I designate that material support that concrete discourse borrows from language.'[39] The letter therefore is always already there, in a peculiar way, found and brought up into the signifying chain. In Lacan's words the letter is 'the essentially localised structure of the signifier,' a component part or element that only gains meaning by being hauled out from the depths and forced into collusion with other letters.[40] Because the possibilities are endless the assemblages that are created are all the more indicative of the state of mind of the speaker, the author of (mis)meaning.

Derrida drew attention to the possibility that letters could be independent from speech in an entirely different way. For him writing does not function merely as a mnemonic device, it is not secondary to phonetic language. Rather, it belongs to the same world as that of objects. The letter is a thing without an inherent meaning attributed to it by the human imaginary. A scientific mind might say that it is therefore dead, an initiate into the mysteries might say that it is therefore full of the mystic depth of being, or something like that. For

---

38 'Ousia and Grammē: Note on a Note from Being and Time' in Derrida (1982) 67.
39 Lacan (2006) 413.
40 Ibid. 418.

a poet the letter is the raw material to be worked into song, just as stone is to the sculptor.

So, what is the difference between a stone and a letter? Both provide the basic structure of our world, and both support a living structure, into which we are born and grow. How different are they, then, if meaning and mattering are intra-active processes? Lacan asks whether 'the spirit could live without the letter. The spirit's pretensions would nevertheless remain indisputable if the letter hadn't proven that it produces all its truth effects in man without the spirit having to intervene at all.'[41]

Is it a coincidence, an accident, that the stone retains the outdated form of the letter? Or is this immaterial? Perhaps for the letter as such but for the term? Are not these terminal or temporal limits themselves the material boundary against which any system of definition comes? The letter's materiality is in the *horos*, the 'term, boundary, definition, stone, and landmark' etcetera. And yet surely the letter must precede all these definitions, not merely to give them form but even as the potential of reconstituting the similarity and difference of terms? The letters that compose the word, insofar as they draw up the boundaries, must also precede the determination of the stone as *horos*. This is the letter's bondage, not that it requires a master in order to convince the master that it is in fact the letter who reigns. The letter adheres to the term as closely as the gadfly to Socrates, and its protean pestering (or posturing) results in a different death each time. Pulling away from the term, it will reappear to reconstitute and be reconstituted in another term—the bondage of the letter is thus the *horos*.

That the *horos* is letters, with or without the inscription, suggests a regime where that which is already written in stone is more or less the material support of language, but where the difference between this more and less, the with or without, is the literal ground for the possibility of even the most miniscule differences in determination and terminology (hence the Socratic work takes place between these contraries). In order to express this difference is it necessary to coin a new term by changing an *e* to a little *a*? Perhaps it is dangerous and certainly acquisitive to thereby coin a new term (*différance*) and open a new market in the interstices of the text, at the risk of objectifying even fetishising something that has always been there. This name-giving also

---

41   'The Instance of the Letter in the Unconscious or Reason Since Freud' in Lacan (2006) 423–424.

gives the impression that one can claim a title to the trace that lingers throughout the history of philosophy, that one can give a name, inscribe one's mark on exactly that point at issue that always evades designation and determination. But this is exactly the mark of ownership that the *horos* proscribes by not even needing a letter to be read.

The stone cannot be left out since the base materiality of the *horos* acts as a dampening force amongst these spirited notions. For the stone is the *horos*, marked upon the land. The Athenians may well have called words and letters *horos*, but it is the stone that they read whether or not it could be said to boast inscription. The name *horos* belongs to the stone; its mark is inscribed upon it. It supports these marks and gives them (and) its identity thereby. The stone is recognisable because it tells us its name, it reads *horos*, and we may presume did so with or without the written word, the inscribed letters.

Fantasising the Letter

The origins of script are often given as a tool or a material support for human economic activity—that humans first wrote pictographs to begin with in order to represent material objects, to satisfy a need prompted by economic concerns.[42] The Indus-valley glyphs are supposed to be economic devices, the pictographs of Sumer designate quantities for exchange purposes, the logosyllabic script of the Maya primarily records events of the elite, the hieroglyphs are mnemonic devices for the rituals of the priestly caste. Other signs such as those on Greek pottery were supposed to have developed in order to represent ownership or authorship, while the incision of letters, *boustrophedon*, evolved from agriculture and from the most economic method of ploughing furrows.[43] Interestingly enough, these ideas about the origins of script tend to support the dominant economic and political systems, suggesting the development toward an elite-governed society structured around private ownership and an exchange-based economy.[44]

---

42 As Powell observed: 'The undoubted economic character of the protocuneiform tablets has coloured general histories of writing, suggesting that all writing has appeared in response to economic behaviour.' Powell (2009) 63. For the expanded economic theory, see Schmandt-Besserat (1992).
43 Derrida (2006) 313.
44 Gelb's language is itself an interesting case study. It is not coincidental that when describing the superiority of phonetic writing, many other assumed superiorities

The ancient cultures themselves had very different ideas about the origins of their scripts. For the most part they tell us clearly that writing came from the gods.[45] In Egypt, before Thoth, Seshat was the goddess who created writing, her name literally means 'scrivener,' so too does the name of the Northern African god 'Al Kutba.' The Sumerian goddess Nisaba was a goddess of writing and scribe of the gods, as was the ancient Mesopotamian Nuba and the Hindu god Chitragupta. In Celtic mythology the Ogham alphabet is attributed alternately to a Scythian king after the fall of Babel or to Ogma who used trees for letters and named the alphabet after himself. Perhaps the most impressive of all these is the story of Odin, who hung himself from the cosmic tree Yggdrasil for nine nights in order to obtain knowledge of the sacred runes. Meanwhile, in Japan, the deity Tenjin lost his former association with natural disasters (untimely) to become the god of calligraphy and scholarship. There are, no doubt, many more examples of scrivener gods amongst other less documented cultures. The monotheistic religions may have departed from the divine scrivener, putting writing into the hands of prophets. Nonetheless, Greek, Arabic and Biblical Hebrew all had mystical interpretations if not practices associated with their alphabets, much like the script of Easter Island and the runes. The actual act of writing as a practice seems to be the main point of interest here, rather than any oral tradition simply taken down in script.

Must we dismiss these origins as fantastic or fabulous and therefore inherently false? What kind of a phenomenon is writing? Did it develop as an economic tool in human hands, or was it created by some kind of transcendent deity? Or finally, was writing something that evolved 'naturally' to reflect our beliefs in our own 'naturally' evolved origins? That is to say, is writing the material proof of an autopoietic fantasy of deterministic evolution?

Given the presence of the origin of script in diverse cosmologies, what role does the letter play in the development of human cultures? If the earliest mythologies were based upon practices of prophecy or shamanism, the sole task of which was to read meaning into the

---

sneak in; from his use of the masculine article, his exclusive use of masculine examples, to his talk of primitives and primitive writing. This understanding of writing cannot be separated from its specific socio-cultural framework. Gelb (1952) see for example page 13.

45 Gelb (1952).

natural world around them, then surely the very basis of metaphysical belief is that earthly content or natural text that offered itself to such determinative practices. Perhaps these problems are only discoverable within an ontology of script, an ontogrammatology.

The privileged position that phonetic alphabets have held is not only culturally specific and outdated but, given the former belief in the divine origin of writing, presumably also something along the lines of heresy. The disjuncture between what linguists have called writing and what philologists called writing can be said to have been broken apart entirely by Derrida when he pointed out that the non-phonetic variability within writing should be proof that there is no purely phonetic writing.[46] Writing admits within itself and cannot function properly without the inclusion of non-phonetic signs, such as silent letters, archaic spellings, punctuation, spacings.[47]

The difference between graphemes is a silent play, neither always present to sight (they elude the reader in the dark) nor to hearing (like the *e* in granite), but the play is essential to the maintenance of the structure of language. 'Here, therefore, we must let ourselves refer to an order that resists the opposition, one of the founding oppositions of philosophy, between the sensible and the intelligible.'[48] Do human beings create deontological structures in order to wrestle life from the world around them, reforming it and denuding it within the pages of their control in order to put it to use, and appropriate it for their own ends without suffering pangs of conscious? If this is the case it is not only matter that has been subjected to this process of denuding but everything beyond the human.

Does the death of matter or the non-living of matter coincide with what Derrida calls the 'dead letter' or the death of writing?

> Writing in the common sense is the dead letter, it is the carrier of death. It exhausts life. On the other hand, on the other face of the same proposition, writing in the metaphoric sense, natural, divine, and living writing is venerated.'[49]

---

46 'Pictographs have no linguistic reference of any kind; they depict an event, or convey a message, by means of a series of drawings. Such a medium can hardly be called writing.' Hooker in Walker and Chadwick (1990) 6.
47 Derrida (1984) 5.
48 Ibid. 5.
49 Derrida (2006) 17.

Interpretations of the natural world as something to be read cast the earth as a book: the 'world is a manuscript' (Jaspers) and when we observe its phenomena we 'read in the great book of Nature' (Descartes).⁵⁰ The book of nature is the visible side of a deeper metaphor, 'which forces language to reside in the world, among the plants, the herbs, the stones, and the animals,' says Foucault.⁵¹ The idea of the book of nature has given a privileged place to the notion of an 'original' writing, while human writing is posed as secondary. And yet the two are indissolubly linked. These ideas of the book of nature were formed in the sixteenth century, just as scientific rationalism was gaining ground within the academies of Europe. What was important in generating new forms of knowledge was the non-distinction between 'what was seen and what was read, or between observation and relation,' an identification that provided the basis for the scientific method.⁵² This secondary writing served to implement the first as the basis for the laws of reason, of man and his dominance. First writing was associated immediately with the instigation of Law, whether as a product of a supreme demiurge, the hand of the Hebraic God or Scientific Man's laws of nature, the physical laws. These laws led to the unrestrained development of human technologies both of convenience and of death, which in turn led to the denuding of matter, the brutalising of matter, because behind matter were said to be laws, at once immutable and omniscient that governed whatever happened here below regardless of human actions, laws that could be understood only by human reason, and more specifically well-educated men inscribed in the institutions of power.

This first writing, the laws of the physical universe, was supposed to convey full-presence, fully legible in the world around us, indubitable and immutable, present to itself as subject. Of course modern physics, quantum physics, has proved that this was nothing more than a dream, a fantasy of clarity, control and unequivocality in a much more complex and involved universe. In fact the structure of the universe is much closer to what Derrida interpreted as the indefinite play of signs, where any sign is a representation of something else which is in its turn the representation of something else and so on ad infinitum: an assemblage

---

50 Ibid. 16.
51 Foucault (2008) 39.
52 Ibid. 43.

beyond imagining. Addressing the same problem from the other direction, Barad explains that

> Bohr's philosophy-physics (the two were inseparable for him) poses a radical challenge not only to Newtonian physics but also to Cartesian epistemology and its representationalist triadic structure of words, knowers, and things. Crucially, in a stunning reversal of his intellectual forefather's schema, Bohr rejects the atomistic metaphysics that takes "things" as ontologically basic entities. For Bohr, things do not have inherently determinate boundaries or properties, and words do not have inherently determinate meanings. Bohr also calls into question the related Cartesian belief in the inherent distinction between subject and object, and knower and known.[53]

The traditional (non-magic) definition of the sign is that it is a substitute for a thing, and that this substitution is secondary to the sign's substitution for the sound that the sign refers to. It is a threefold substitution in which the original material is lost earlier down the path on the way to advanced linguistics. But what if matter itself was already a sign for something, that is not fully present in the first place? According to Plato the material world was merely the shadow play of the realm of ideas. Nonetheless, for Plato language is quite sufficient at expressing both realms equally. In contrast, the reality of Brahman (also Tattva, Sat, Padārtha, Paramārtha) in Indian philosophy is not receptive to discursive intellect or speech, and nor is it sensible.

Writing need not be limited to a grapheme with a linguistic reference and a series of drawings representing an event or conveying a message can still be classified as writing. Writing therefore does not need to be a privileged, progressive medium limited to certain types of societies and cultures, and instead any pictorial depiction that conveys ideas in one way or another can be considered writing. Obviously drawing in caves or writing in the sand is writing, but what about a snail trail or the squiggles of a woodworm? Both of these can be read to mean something, that my lettuces have been nibbled on, and that the shelf is no longer strong enough for the weight of books. But how far can this go? If nature writes, it has then to be asked if nature also makes plans. Is our fate to be a punctuation mark in the book of nature, a very recent, brief, exotically musical and surprisingly destructive mark at that?

---
53   Barad (2003) 813.

Writing raises the question of the relation between human language and the environment in which this language is steeped. If there is no insensible realm of ideas from which human language devolves down to script, then the relationship must be the other way around, from the ground up. Observing a stone house Sallis reads into it the possibility of an inscribing that implicates the historical as well as the natural at play, evidence of the past marking its way into the present: 'If it is an old house, one will sense also in its worn stones the traces of an obscure lineage, a certain human history inscribed—without having been, in any active or intentional way, inscribed—on the stone. Nature and history—the opposition again violated, confounded.'[54] Is writing a kind of deep materialism, where letters themselves originate from an intimate connection to the objects that we share the world with? Is matter itself the origin of writing?

As Karen Barad states,

> matter is not little bits of nature, or a blank slate, surface, or site passively awaiting signification, nor is it an uncontested ground for scientific, feminist, or Marxist theories. Matter is not immutable or passive. Nor is it a fixed support, location, referent, or source of sustainability for discourse.[55]

Horos poses similar problems. The question, Does the stone mean *horos* in the absence of the inscription and in the absence of a reader? appears close to the breach intrinsic to writing. Again, if we take the *horos*, the typographical error of a letter is not even necessary because *horos* already is this non-identification between materiality and meaning, between sign and signifier. Is it identified as *horos* because it is inscribed with the letters, or is its identification found elsewhere, in the reader perhaps or some other earthly elsewhere? Despite itself, the *horos* does seem to be an unremitting example of arche-writing, in that it never is able to be identified with a single meaning or with itself as subject. The *horos* is never reducible down to its definition. There is always a slippage when it comes to definition, and yet the trace remains that cannot help but keep pointing to the gap within the definition. This gap is not however devoid of substance, it is stone and though its meaning is not present to it, it still matters.

---

54   Sallis (1994) 17.
55   Barad (2003) 821.

Is matter a blank page upon which human actions are written? In a sense Karen Barad returns to the book of nature when she comes up against the matter of meaning for Derrida. The dynamism of matter, she states, is noncontemporaneous with itself, it is 'regenerative un/doing.'[56] In the same sense as Derrida states that there is nothing outside of the text; for Barad the absence in the heart of presence is a concretely textual matter because matter and how matter performs, reconfigures, and differs from itself is a work of deconstruction. Paraphrasing Bohr's concept of complementarily, Barad explains that the intimate relationship between discourse and materiality paralleled with the discovery of quantum discontinuity undermines the notion of 'an inherent fixed (apparatus-independent, Cartesian subject-object) distinction.'[57] Entities cannot be said to be individual actors interacting with one another, rather 'boundaries and properties of objects become determinate by virtue of a cut between observed and agencies of observation which is enacted by the material-discursive apparatus.'

> Boundary-making practices, that is, discursive practices, are fully implicated in the dynamics of intra-activity through which phenomena come to matter. In other words, materiality is discursive (i.e., material phenomena are inseparable from the apparatuses of bodily production: matter emerges out of and includes as part of its being the ongoing reconfiguring of boundaries), just as discursive practices are always already material (i.e., they are ongoing material (re)configurings of the world). Discursive practices and material phenomena do not stand in a relationship of externality to one another; rather, the material and the discursive are mutually implicated in the dynamics of intra-activity. But nor are they reducible to one another. The relationship between the material and the discursive is one of mutual entailment. Neither is articulated/articulable in the absence of the other; matter and meaning are mutually articulated. Neither discursive practices nor material phenomena are ontologically or epistemologically prior. Neither can be explained in terms of the other. Neither has privileged status in determining the other.[58]

Barad calls into question the ground upon which are enacted the boundary-making practices that draw up the distinction between

---
56 Barad (2010) 268 n.11.
57 Barad (2003) 818.
58 Ibid. 816.

humans and nonhumans. For Barad discursivity is not a capacity that can be said to belong exclusively to humans, for the very reason that both the content and form of discourse is generated in conversation with the nonhuman and material world. 'Human' refers to a phenomenon, another part of matter that shifts, becomes and reconfigures, and if the boundaries and properties that humans attribute, interpret and observe in the world, like magma, rise, crust, melt and reform along with what it means to be human 'then the notion of discursivity cannot be founded on an inherent distinction between humans and nonhumans.' Discursivity is implicated in matter. She calls this a 'posthumanist account of discursive practices.'[59] Barad therefore uses the verbal neologism 'mattering' to explain how matter and meaning become-determinate as well as indeterminate.[60] In other words mattering is the process of coming-to-meaning that takes place across the division of the human/nonhuman and the organic/inorganic. As Barad concludes when she addresses the problem of what or how matter means, 'Nature is not mute, and culture the articulate one. Nature writes, scribbles, experiments, calculates, thinks, breathes, and laughs.'[61]

This reference to nature as subject of script is placed in a footnote, strange given the significance that such a concept of nature must have. Here it could be said that Barad's image of nature writing, breathing and laughing, resolves her new materialism in the same place where Derrida began his critique:

> The science of writing should therefore look for its object at the roots of scientificity. The history of writing should turn back toward the origin of historicity. A science of the possibility of science?[62]

It is interesting that contemporary theory in physics would take us back to the book of nature, as it were. However, this time the term 'nature' functions differently. It would seem to have become an all-inclusive term, crossing the boundaries generated by earlier versions of the 'book of nature,' bringing together the human and nonhuman, the organic/inorganic, but potentially also cosmos and chaos into the discursive processes of mattering. It is also a much more playful concept

---

59 Ibid. 818
60 Barad (2010) 254.
61 Ibid. 268 n.11.
62 Derrida (2016) 30.

of nature, one in which chance probably plays a more significant role than any all-powerful deterministic divinity, while the old physical laws resemble the gods of animism.

The belief that writing began as an economic aid or tool apparently serves to strip human artistic endeavours, such as poetry and literature of an originary, fantastic ingenuity. Basically what it effects is the banalisation of practical activities. However, there is nothing to say that the practical activities of finding food, of noting water-courses (for example in Aboriginal dot paintings) or describing the aim of the hunt (cave paintings in Sulawsi, Chauvet) cannot also be the subject of enlightened artistic and literary exploits, possibly accompanied by song, but also remaining in place to be read at later times. However, it could also be argued that writing does not begin and end with us. Despite the ubiquity of our signature upon the land, the earth is not inhabited exclusively by *Homo sapiens*, and we ought to be able to read the presence of other beings on the land with as much respect as we do our own. What is the justification for an economy of the nonhuman as a resource that can be used without natural limits and how does the history and philosophy of script intersect with the economic precedence of humankind? Economy in this sense is the management, organisation and redistribution, and extortion of the nonhuman beyond a philosophy of interspecial care or sense of ethical or ecological boundaries.

Where does the idea that the world and the nonhuman are ownable and disposable come from? It is certainly not an idea common to all peoples of the world; in fact, animism generally obfuscates the possibility of outright ownership.[63] The polytheism of Greece did include the powerful idea of *hubris* and of not challenging or offending the gods with human (overweening) pride, and yet nonalienability of property was introduced into the Athenian city with little resistance, as far as we know. Ownership of land tends to go hand in hand with its use and abuse, unfortunately, as does the ownership of anything. Obviously, slaves were owned and disposed of in whatever way the master saw fit, as were animals, according to his dictates and his economic interests.

---

63   See, for example in the Australian setting, Dark Emu by Yuin writer Bruce Pascoe, who argues that non-ownership does not necessarily foreclose the activity of land management. In contrast see also *Farmers or Hunter-Gatherers? The Dark Emu Debate* by Sutton and Walshe, arguing for an archaeology that reinfuses native practices of land-management with spiritual propagation, magic and the Dreamtime.

In Ancient Greece we see the requisite conditions for subjecting the nonhuman to human economic interests, but how possible would this be without the mark of ownership, authorship or authenticity? And, is it possible to reconfigure writing in order to obfuscate the demand or desire to own?

With or Without Letters

By the fourth century the term *horos* appears to be outdated and yet in continued use, this is what can be read into the appearance of the *eta* (H) that by this time had been dropped entirely. But on the fourth-century stones, is the inscription of the *horos* the remainder of a prehistorical letter? Here, the play of presence and absence, where the letter is read but not written and heard out of silence, has been capitalised upon (by Solon, the Athenians, epigraphists and archaeologists alike). The *horos* resembles, in time it comes to dissemble the capital 'H.' More or less than a letter, H is an aspiration.

A peculiar detail of the *horoi* is their retention, even into the Hellenistic era, of the archaic H (now known as the vowel-sound, lower-case η). The presence of the H where later literary texts substituted the sign for the *spiritus asper*—that is, the inverted apostrophe of a rough breath (') suspended over the subsequent vowel sound—is a trope misleading to epigraphists who tend to use such forms as indications of proximate dating. The spelling of HOPOΣ with the sign H for the *spiritus asper* is potentially misleadingly archaic and, as epigraphists maintain, continued to be used in conventional formulae until the period of the archonship of Euklides, fourth century AD.[64] Later, when the H was no longer used as a separate letter to indicate a rough breath, but the long vowel sound 'e,' the original H was cut in half vertically, where the first half was used to indicate a rough breath, the latter the soft breath. Finally, the trace of the eta was retained only as two right angles, facing in opposite directions. These then resolved into the diacritical marks marking the smooth breathing, ψιλὸν πνεῦμα or spīritus lenis; and the rough breathing, δασὺ πνεῦμα or spīritus asper, or simply *dasia*.[65]

---

64 Roberts (1905) xiii.
65 Christidis (2001) 990.

In contrast, with the *horoi* the continued usage of the H makes assigning a certain *terminus ad* or *ante quem* with which to date the *horoi* particularly difficult. And yet, a *terminus post quem* is easier to confer, as the H on the *horoi* is the open H, not the closed h of the earlier script, which was in use in inscriptions for the years around 600 BC. Toward the end of this period, there are remains of inscribed vases (which are considered to be the forerunners of change on account of the ease of adopting the cursive script on pottery and the reduced size of the inscription) by the painter Sophilos where the H is still closed, in which case the open H of the *horoi* can be assigned a later date, such as late sixth, early fifth century.

It can be viewed as more than mere coincidence that our information for the time of the *horos* in the archaeological record is dependent upon the letter. The *terminus* for the *horos* is the *letter*. Here synonyms abound, reduced though they are to a mere terminological difference where what remains is *horos*. Translating this in any way cannot evade the *horos'* resistance to further identification. So, when we try to date the *horos*, to assign it temporal boundaries by breaking it down into distinct and separate letters, we find ourselves confronted once again by a literal boundary, *horos*. As Jeffrey states, the letter H,

> hēt- seems to have been learnt originally by the Greeks as héta = hé, the whole, both aspirate and following vowel, being a more vigorous sound than that of hé. In dialects which used the aspirate, i.e. those of the Greek mainland (except Elis and Arkadia), the Doric Pentapolis, the central and southern Aegean islands (except Crete), and which needed therefore to express it in their script, the initial sound, the aspirate, naturally predominated over the following vowel.[66]

How exactly this initial sound was to be pronounced or heard remains a mystery. We do know, however, that in the absence of the *spiritus asper* (ʽ) that is amongst those peoples who dropped the rough breath and pronounced (-)oros, with a *spiritus lenis* (ʼ), the texts produce alternate spellings with an additional letter, such as the Ionic οὖρος, the Megarian ὅρρος, the lengthened Cretan ὦρος, not to mention the Corcyrean ὀρϝος /ὅρβος, where the much older *waw* intercedes. It might be a case of substitution, where the absence of one letter calls for

---

66 Jeffrey (1990) 28.

the presence of another. It is an ambiguous tendency to lament a silence, juxtaposing the dead nature of the letter's character with writing as a temporal gesture. As a rule the letter is capitalised upon, the *horoi* are never in lowercase. What can be remarked in any case is that given its presence or absence, this capital letter in particular, H, serves to mark the linguistic boundaries of the Greek-speaking world. And yet in the *horos* inscription dated from the period of the Athenian expansion, the letter ceased to convey such differences because it remained out of time. Perhaps it is itself nothing but the trace that remains when such differences disintegrate.

Letters have an esoteric interpretation, though in the Greek context this is not nearly as evident as in the Hebraic or Arabic traditions. In *Magical Alphabets*, Pennick describes the esoteric significance of the Greek letter, H:

> It is a character of balance, that quality of being in harmony with the world, being in the right place at the right time to achieve one's full potential. More specifically, as Eta this is manifested as the divine harmony of the seven planets and seven spheres of pre-Copernican cosmology. It can thus signify the music of the spheres. The Gnostic Marcus connected Eta with the third heaven: 'The first heaven sounds Alpha, and the one after that E (Epsilon), and the third Eta.'[67]

Meanwhile reinforcing the appropriateness of its place in the word *horos*, in the Hebraic tradition the earlier Hebraic form of the letter *cheth* means 'fence' or 'hurdle.'

> The fence is that which divides the inner from the outer. It is a barrier which serves an owner of something. It keeps those things in which the owner wants kept in, and keeps out those things which must be excluded. It is thus a letter of discrimination, the separation of things of worth from the worthless. Another related interpretation of Cheth is abundance and energy, the basic characteristics that separate the living from the dead. Esoterically, Cheth means 'distribution,' the primary function of energy. It has the number-equivalent of 8, Shemonah, fertility, and is connected astrologically with Libra.[68]

The advantage, as well as problem, with magic is that it is not easily subject to debate, but is a wily thing that slips beyond reason's grasp.

---
67   Pennick (1992) 51.
68   Ibid. 17.

Nonetheless, that writing is something in human history that was more than mere tool is a notion that should not be dismissed and should inform our subsequent conceptions of what writing does within culture. The important point being that there are traditions in which form cannot be wholly separated from content, or put otherwise, that the matter of the letter does matter, and the letter itself carries meaning distinct from its presence within words.

The earliest Greek form of the letter h (ḥēt) is the ancestor to the earlier Phoenician word for fence, wall or barrier (ḥēt). This would depend upon the assumption that a letter develops out of an image attributed with a meaning, that is to say Saussure's process of linking (the bar) signified and signifier. But what if in these early letters it was just this that was proscribed by the letter, that is to say the bar itself (unified materially as the hyphen)? After all, H is a letter, not an image and not a concept. All the same, fighting against meaningful resemblance even on the most literal level would appear to be a lost battle. As Aristotle was quoted saying, a noun, name [*onoma*] or a verb on its own 'resembles meaning (or concept) without combination and disjunction' (ἔοικε τῷ συνθέσεως καὶ διαιρέσεως νοήματι)[69]. If the name of the letter resembles the meaning of a word which it forms as in this particular case, admittedly in conjunction with other letters, it might be a case of, as Walter Benjamin puts it, 'non-sensuous similarity.'[70] And this is how we can read the history of this particular letter. Originally placed on its side by the Phoenicians, the precursor to the Greek letter H, outlines a stark physical resemblance to this hurdle of similitude. The letter is said to have taken form as an 'image' which means 'fence' or 'barrier' ⊫: Three posts, two on the extremes and a middle one separating unfilled space, while the horizontal lines protrude implying indefinite extension.

Put otherwise, and linking us back to the Suida, the letter is like a boundary (barrier/bar/hyphen) while the name of the letter is boundary (especially when it comes to distinguishing one letter from another). And in this sense perhaps every letter is a boundary imposed between meaning and non-meaning, marking out a word as something that can not only be read but also understood.[71] Since we are concerned

---

69   Ar.*Int*.16a14.
70   Benjamin (2005) 697.
71   Derrida (1995) 94; Derrida (1981) 16.

with letters, which Lacan defines as the 'material support' of language, the base elements for any chain of signifiers, any resemblance that they evoke must be purely circumstantial (we must therefore remain with the boundary, even if this means verging upon the position, not on it, but nearby or 'around' it). That is to say that any mimetic aspect of the letter ought not be wholly ascribed to the letter as our device for expressing meaning but could be equally ascribed to us who read it as the fence or barrier that draws us up short. Since the whole is already implied in the (Saussurian) 'bar' that would claim to perform the meaning-giving function, of jointure and division, it should go without saying that neither the *horos* nor the letter are defined (fully) by their aesthetic appearance.

But that is not to say that they are not material, that they cannot be seen or heard. Whether or not the Athenians were familiar with this particular semantic association between form and content, there does remain in the term (*horos*) that sense of 'joining' (ἐφαρμόττει), *hinging*, of coming in between *two*, whether this obtains to the letter or its time. But it is the *horos* that claims this task, not the letter. In fact, if anything, the letter made upright and deprived of two of its rungs, insists more on a relation between two poles rather than their disjunction. As if, to get the bar and the closed concept of linguistics we need to employ all forms of the letter, and bring them to their conclusion, their logical fulfilment in the spiritual caesura of the breath. But if we were to accept this schema we would have to resolve ourselves to recognising a distinction between the *horos* and the stone, the *horos* and the letter, the term, the limit and the end, that is by abstracting the name as a mere variation of speech, the modulated out-blowing of spirit.

The *horos* simultaneously divides letters (meaning they can be taken out of order, of a particular word) and joins them as what is common (meaning they can be reconfigured to produce a new word). This is the principal function of the *horos*, where the boundary is a material concept whose intent is both to create a barrier and offer trespass. It can never be a full concept and can never be wholly abstracted since it remains material whether any particular letter (for example the H) is marked as presence or absence.

This letter, then, might in its first impulse suggest some kind of barrier, but could more effectually be transferred into the metaphor of a linguistic portal. The letter defies the barrier; it always carries something over as what is left over from the past in the present. Is the problem raised by the letter seen better anywhere than in the institution more or less concurrent to the adoption and development of the Greek script, the *polis*? No doubt, the rapid proliferation of walls and fortifications and the corresponding need for doors, gates and passageways in the archaic *polis* (and their consequent protection in the form of property laws, immigration laws and so forth), coincide with the obsolescence in Ancient Greek of the closed form of the letter, and its lasting replacement with the open form (H). In the enclosed surrounds of the city and household walls, the blustery winds, along with the strange refuse carried upon the air, interrupting the clear categories of political allegiance (women, foreigners, gods and animals) could be momentarily shut out with the closure of a door and, with its opening, willingly admitted. Along the same lines, the aspiration came to lose its substance in the letter H, becoming a mere fixture or appendage that could be open (ʽ) or shut (ʼ). A door cannot afford a view or prospect, but it can give onto a hall or passageway, even an arcade. In the door the wall is brought to breaking point, where h or H is resolved into a moment of punctuation. A pause for breath. Everywhere, that is except in stone, ΗΟΡΟΣ.

And not even that any more. For even those stones have been subjected to classification techniques and a total subjection to the development and progress of letters, replaced *in situ*, installed in museums, set up in gardens, rubbed for squeezes elaborated upon in books. For in the aspirations of capitalist economies there is no time for what is lost to the past, or rather the glimmer of what is lost is relegated to dim corners in the floodlight of progress and punctuality. Henceforth, punctuations and dead spacing must bow in service to the hastening urge to press on, where simple breathing spaces are wasted breaths. So, the aspiration that marked the elision itself was elided, and in its most recent transformation, in the contemporary linguistic state, in place of the letter there is now as an unmarked elision, a term with no connection to its material past: όρος, what was in the past a marked elision, is remarked by nothing more than a lapse.

And yet, there is no call for resuscitating an unpronounceable phoneme in a new guise, nor to move ever forward with the 'storm of progress' excising any letter that no longer pays its due in speech.[72] But to have the time to recognise what is lost, even when this loss presents itself as a simple hiatus or caesura in the present, remains a marked possibility for thinking in an untimely way. A letter is more than just a sign, it is the briefest instant which stops our breath when we expire. The dead letter of the H, what we now cannot help but read as a capital or even as an entirely different letter from an entirely different language, succeeds 'cutting the breath short' as the 'principle of death and of difference,' where writing only presumes to interpolate itself from the beginning as the *aporia* that remains.[73] The point of the H is not to betray presence, to menace 'substantiality, that other metaphysical name of presence and of *ousia*.' The *horos* is not an inherently destructive force, not even a deconstructive one. On the other hand, what it is cannot be expounded by the dictates of identical reasoning.

Essentially, the *horos* is already drawn up in this outline of a letter. Any rhetorical exclamation (*apostrophē*) that would attempt to pronounce the letter would only come up against the apotropaic barrier of elision. Any claim to the possession of this letter has already been proscribed with the inverted possibility of an apostrophe (ὅρος). Always opening onto the other, exposed in quotation, the *horos* is the merest mark that distinguishes my word from yours, or brings into relief the bond of our communion, as Aristotle said 'the *horos* of life is breath' (τοῦ ζῆν ὅρον εἶναι τὴν ἀναπνοήν).[74] Is the *horos*, then, the door which can only be open or shut in its relations with other words or is it the switch in cybernetics that closes the circuit as it opens? When we read its inscription regardless of its form, the letter breaks open the barrier and maintains it, because the letter itself is exactly what is not represented in the image of a fence. Unlike the *horos* there is nothing aesthetic about the letter, certainly not, on principle, and yet that is not to say that it cannot be seen, heard or have its limits. You might not see the inscription in the dark, as 'the graphic difference itself vanishes into the night, cannot be sensed as a full term,' and the letter becomes illegible, indeed you might not even see the *horos*, but that does not mean you will not stub your toe against it.[75] So why have recourse to the other letter, to an alternate

---

72 Benjamin thesis IX in, Löwy (2005) 62.
73 Derrida (2016) 27–28.
74 Ar.*Ath*.404a9.
75 Derrida (1997) 27–28.

différance, which would itself reinscribe difference into the sensible text? Why? Perhaps because even here, a limit, that is to say a 'term' (even one that claims to defer its fullness) is required as a marker. Even Derrida at his most de(*con*)structive wants to mark the site between speech and writing, to fill it, albeit with something that it is not.[76]

The question is, however, whether these limits are imposed upon the letter from without, or within? Perhaps it is the interminability of this question that is posed in the *horos*. For what is fence-like or like a barrier in the letter is, of course, the boundary itself, the word that draws up the limits of identity and resemblance, without however becoming a bar for the very reason that it is simultaneously composed of letters, and the name of the letter. The *horos* provides the necessary scene onto which the letter steps, and knocks out a passageway through which every word must pass in order to become a word.

Just as you cannot abstract the letter from the *horos* (or vice versa), nor can you eliminate transgression from a barrier—such rules are made to be broken. And it is the letter that brings it to breaking point, by always going two ways. The letter is always implicated in the *horos*, which, however, brings it to its limit in the word by drawing up the limits, in definition, between one word and another. This is because there must be limits, even in the various combinations of letters—otherwise the fraternisation that is facilitated by an open door would erase any difference between inside and outside, would suppose that those who constructed the barrier are one with those who suffer to resist it. The *horos* literally limits the possibility of fraternising with the enemy, while it supposes the necessity of breaking the clear determinations between enemy and friend in the symbolic infringement of barriers. Hence all those thrown stones—projectiles of insurgency—against a regime that would follow the law to the letter, but of course, in this case the letter and the spirit of the law are indifferent.

---

76   'Différance,' in Derrida (1982) 5.

Fig. 3. ΗΟΡΟΣ ΤΕΣ ΟΔΟ ΤΕΣ ΕΛΕΥΣΙΝΑΔΕ *'horos* of the road to Eleusina' (end of the 5th c BC). Originally inscribed with HOROS TES ODO TES IERAS (520 BC). IG I³ 1096 [I 127] Photograph by M. Goutsourela, 2013. Discovered in the Eridanos river bed. Rights belong to the Kerameikos Museum, Athens. © Hellenic Ministry of Culture and Sports/Hellenic Organization of Cultural Resources Development (H.O.C.R.E.D.).

3. Breaking the Law

> ὁ ὅρος —*boundary, landmark*; the regions separated by the *boundary* usu. in gen. [...] also in pl., *bounds, boundaries* [...] *boundary-stone* marking the limits of temple-lands.[1]

Lithography works not only on the principle that oil and water repel one another but also on the principle that the stone itself has an affinity with both these antithetical substances. The stone, as the art's chance discoverer describes it, not only has

> an especial property of uniting with fats,—sucking them in and holding them,—but it has, also, the same propensity for taking all fluids that repel fats. Indeed, its surface unites so thoroughly with many of the latter that it forms a chemical union with them.[2]

Lithography therefore is founded upon the affinity of the stone to bring these antithetical substances together into a mutual relation of chemical repulsion.

> Lithography is founded on mutual and chemical affinities, which hitherto had never been applied to the art of engraving. The dislike which water has for all fat bodies, and the affinity which compact calcareous stones have both for water and greasy substances, are the bases on which rests this new and highly interesting discovery.[3]

However, the two substances, oil and water, have no need of the stone in manifesting their mutual repulsion for one another. In fact, it is only by means of their mutual affinity with stone that their reciprocal hostility is made coherent in the coagulation of script, the printed word. Although this affinity for bringing enmity into relief might not

---

1 LS: 1255–1256.
2 Senefelder (1911) 97.
3 Colonel (1821) 1.

be the essence of the philosopher's stone sought after in alchemy, it has, however, led to technologies that have proved their weight in gold.

> With lithography the technique of reproduction reached an essentially new stage. This much more direct process was distinguished by the tracing of the design on a stone rather than its incision on a block of wood or its etching on a copperplate and permitted graphic art for the first time to put its products on the market, not only in large numbers as hitherto, but also in daily changing forms. Lithography enabled graphic art to illustrate everyday life, and it began to keep pace with printing. But only a few decades after its invention, lithography was surpassed by photography.[4]

It is not without irony that when the art of printing aspired to mass production, it did so in so-called 'off-set lithography,' by substituting stone with more refined metal. While in the further 'advanced' science of cybernetics—for the production of circuit boards—another component was required—light: *photo*lithography. Do these technological advances shed a certain light on the stone? Even, or especially, given that the stone is absent or eclipsed the moment art manifests its potential to be reproduced, to be associated with a *logos* that transforms it into an ever-increasing demand to extend, proliferate, develop? Or do such material advances in human technologies *not* reflect the original affinities humans recognised (*read*) in the stone?

Horos is a word, but it does not, for all that, cease to be stone. The word itself refuses its abstraction from the material dilemma of the boundary, or, to be more precise, it raises the problem of the difference between word and material by always remaining between them and bringing them into distinction. Not only like, but exactly as the stone of lithography, the *horos* brings both sides into a relation, providing a contrast, if not an enmity. Here, we are confronted with the problem of the boundary. *Horos* is a fence-sitter, but this means that it presents us with a duplicitous problem, at once lexical and spatial. The *horos* is the stone which, according to Deuteronomy, 'men of old placed as a boundary upon the land.'[5] It is a boundary, marked

---

4 Benjamin (2002b) 102.
5 *Deut*. 19:14. This and all subsequent translations are from the *King James Bible* (KJ), unless referenced to the New International Version (NIV).

and marking. Can we distinguish that which marks the boundary from the boundary itself? Does either side of the boundary take its peculiarities from the boundary, or do their differences generate the boundary? What comes first, spatial opposition or the position in between? If the stone was 'placed,' then we could, along Hegelian lines, conceptualise this landmark as the point that negates space, and yet in the *horos* the point is confused with the line, as much as the word is with the stone.

For information about what archaeologists believe to be the 'primary'—the temporally first—use of the *horoi* as boundary-stones one is compelled to abandon the dubious connotations of lexicography and return to the obscure sphere of the sacred. Is this because first stones are always laid to the accompaniment of rites and rituals, the material remainder of cultic liturgy? Or because where further historical proofs are lacking, cultic worship, concerning which we now know so little, can be called upon to fill the void? Or are these past proceedings and present (lapse of) knowledge two sides of the same coin?

Upon approaching the *horos*, one is immediately confronted by the task of the translator. That one is destined to fail to pin down the word to any singular meaning reinvests this intransigent term with the peculiarity of an implicit prohibition: the prohibition against its removal, against a literal translation of the inscribed boundary. Even today, in the museums of Athens, the prohibition against the removal of the *horoi* holds, since we are unable to pick up this stone, to nurse it, and feel its grain upon our palms, to gauge its worth whether in the texts of Plato and Homer or in the archaeological museum ('hands off'). That is to say, with Walter Benjamin, any attempt at translating this term along with the inevitable failure to translate it fully, cannot help but reveal its essential nature: the proscription of translation itself, the prohibition of its removal.[6] Refusing movement, and in spite of the prescriptions of the boundary, like the Ka'aba, the *horos* offers itself to revolutions of thought which may circle near or far but never succeed in penetrating the profundity of stone.[7] Is this what makes a stone sacred?

---

6 Benjamin (2002a) 254.
7 Addas (1993) 213.

Sacred Boundaries

There is ample evidence for the significance of boundary-stones in the world's ancient religions. The removal of boundary-stones was prohibited and considered a serious crime according to Babylonian, Egyptian, Greek and Roman law.[8] Terminus was a Roman god (believed to be of Sabine origin) that could be said to deify the function of *horos*. A stone or altar of Terminus was located in the Temple of Jupiter Optimus Maximus on Rome's Capitoline Hill. Because of a belief that this stone had to be exposed to the sky, there was a small hole in the ceiling directly above it.[9] When the augurs took the auspices to discover whether the god or goddess of each altar was content for it to be moved, Terminus refused permission. The stone was therefore included within the Capitoline Temple, and its immovability was regarded as a good omen for the permanence of the city's boundaries.[10] Diocletian's decision in 303 AD to initiate his persecution of Christians on 23 February, a propitious day for the same god, has been seen as an attempt at enlisting Terminus 'to put a limit to the progress of Christianity.'[11]

In the Quaranic tradition, *Barzakh* is the limit between the realm of the living and that of the dead and is a phase of resurrection. It is 'the very thing that makes the activity of defining possible,' in which 'the separation between the things (defining) and the separating factor (that which defines) become manifest as one entity.'[12] The word *Barzakh* is used by Ibn al-'Arabî in his translations and interpretations of Aristotelian philosophy (see Chapter Four).[13] Meanwhile, the Hindu Bhaga is also worth looking at, if only because of his linguistic links with the Arabic word for boundary, *Barzakh*. In the *Rigveda*, Bhaga is the god who supervises the distribution of goods and destiny to each man corresponding to his merits. The word appears to be cognate with *Bhagavan* and *Bhagya*, terms used in several Indian languages to refer to God and destiny respectively. It is worth remembering that Pennick

---

8   Mills (1997) Boundary Stones: 122.
9   Dionysius of Halicarnassus, *Roman Antiquities* 2.74.2–5. 3.69.3–6.
10   Ovid, Fasti 2.639–684.
11   Liebeschuetz (1979) 247.
12   Bashier (2004) 87.
13   See Bashir (2004) for a thorough study on the concept of *Barzakh* in the works of the philosopher Ibn al-'Arabî.

also described the esoteric meaning of the Hebraic letter Cheth, 'barrier,' the earlier form of the Greek letter *eta* (H) as 'a letter of discrimination, the separation of things of worth from the worthless,' as well as having the esoteric meaning 'distribution, the primary function of energy.'[14] In these senses it seems that the concept of boundary has an ingrained relation to the economic, that is to the distribution and organisation of goods, as well as an economy of fate, that is the distribution of human destinies.

The earliest biblical reference to a boundary pillar in *Genesis*, 'and Jacob took a stone, and set it up for a pillar,' reflects a boundary covenant between Abraham and Laban at Mizpah, where neither party was to pass beyond the pillar (Heb. מצבה *matstsebah*) for purposes of doing harm to their neighbour.[15]

> And Laban said to Jacob, Behold this heap, and behold this pillar, which I have cast betwixt me and thee;
>
> this heap be witness, and this pillar be witness, that I will not pass over this heap to thee, and that thou shalt not pass over this heap and this pillar unto me, for harm.[16]

Many prohibitions against removing stones are found in the Old Testament.[17] Is this because the boundary-stone marks the site where the sacred coincides with law? Is it where awe and reverence unite in the form of a prohibition proscribing the former regime of power, and inscribing the deference due to the present regime, those who planted the pillar and enforced the law? Power is drawn not from a single actor but from an association including objects, specifically objects attributed with a steadfast authority. As Harman points out, the triumph of the Spaniards over the rituals of the Aztecs was 'not through the power of nature liberated from fetish,' but by an entire legion of authorities wearing the fetishistic garb of the Catholic Church and state.[18] Power requires the abstraction of certain objects from their original setting in order to invest them with a transcendent symbolism used to articulate

---

14 Pennick (1992) 17.
15 *Gen* 31:45–52.
16 Ibid.
17 *Deut*.19:14, 27:17, *Prov*.22:28, 23:10, *Job* 24:2, *Hos*.5:10.
18 Harman (2009) 21.

a very particular regime. In this sense Weber's statement that 'not every stone can serve as a fetish, a source of magical power' holds only within regimes that require bolstering in order to justify their reign and make use of only certain objects, a limited pick of earthly goods.[19] Other structures of belief, where goods are held in common, may well maintain that every stone is a source of magical power. Every object has the potentiality for resistance: 'a pebble can destroy an empire if the emperor chokes at dinner.'[20]

In Deuteronomy, the boundary-stone ensures the inheritance of land, marking ownership spanning over generations. However, it is also an appropriation of land from its earlier inhabitants.

> Thou shalt not remove thy neighbor's landmark, which they of old time have set in thine inheritance, which thou shalt inherit in the land that the Lord thy God giveth thee to possess it.[21]

This stone is erected within a chapter dedicated to dealing with the colonisation of territory and the destruction of its people:

> When the Lord your God has destroyed the nations whose land he is giving you, and when you have driven them out and settled in their towns and houses [...] Show no pity. You must purge from Israel the guilt of shedding innocent blood, so that it may go well with you.[22]

The boundary-stones are supposed to provide protection against the threat of those who were colonised, by acting as an objective proof of the new regime's authority over the land. Just as in the example with the Spaniards, here the previous chapter prohibited the engagement in the previous nation's occult practices, thereby establishing new systems of religious and secular power of the invaded territory.

> Let no one be found among you who sacrifices their son or daughter in the fire, who practices divination or sorcery, interprets omens, engages in witchcraft, or casts spells, or who is a medium or spiritist or who consults the dead. Anyone who does these things is detestable to the Lord; because of these same detestable practices the Lord your God will drive out those nations before you.[23]

---

19 Weber (1978) 400.
20 Harman (2009) 21.
21 *Deut* 19:14 KJ.
22 *Deut* 19:1 and 13 NIV.
23 *Deut.* 18:10–13 NIV.

Is this boundary-stone a type of signature marking the covenant protecting the colonisers from divine retribution? It could be said to act in the same way as the contemporary flag planted in the ground by the invading force. A symbol of the regime's power thrust into the earth and, like an injection, spreads the virus of colonisation down and through the filaments of the soil, causing contagion throughout the land. The invasion of territory requires these symbolic attributes in order to condone the violent acts conducted by otherwise innocent people, especially the gesture to a higher authority. The gesture to a heteronomous authority, in this case of both god and ancestors, reinforces the otherwise unjustifiable act of invasion and, potentially, genocide.

The Greek translation of *Deuteronomy* is more specific than the King James or New International version. Here it was the 'fathers' (*pateres*), not just those 'of old' or the 'predecessors' who set up the boundaries. The Septuagint reads:

οὐ μετακινήσεις ὅρια τοῦ πλησίον σου ἃ ἔστησαν οἱ πατέρες σου ἐν τῇ κληρονομίᾳ σου ᾗ κατεκληρονομήθης ἐν τῇ γῇ ᾗ κύριος ὁ θεός σου δίδωσίν σοι ἐν κλήρῳ.[24]

The new translation provides a translation closer to the original Hebrew, here the actors are 'men': 'You shall not remove your neighbor's landmark, which the men of old have set, in your inheritance which you will inherit in the land that the Lord your God is giving you to possess.' The Greek translation, commissioned during the Greco-Roman period of proprietorship and patriarchy, slips toward the name of the Father. The Hebrew text, however, has ראשׁון (*ri'shown*) which might be loosely translated as 'ancestors,' and the meaning tends more toward the temporal, 'men of former times,' 'earlier men.' These are men whose authority is not to be questioned. Again, in *Deuteronomy*, ἐπικατάρατος ὁ μετατιθεὶς ὅρια τοῦ πλησίον, 'Cursed be he that removeth his neighbour's landmark[s].'[25] Here, this prohibition follows upon another prohibition, that against graven images. The same synthesis appears again in *Proverbs*, μὴ μέταιρε ὅρια αἰώνια ἃ ἔθεντο οἱ πατέρες σου, 'remove not the ancient landmark[s], which thy fathers have set.'[26]

---

24 *Deut.* 19:14.
25 *Deut.* 27:17 KJ (the translation omitted the plural of *horia*).
26 *Prov.* 22:28 KJ (again the plural has been omitted).

The term used in *Deuteronomy* for the 'boundary-stone,' as it appears in later references, is different to that in *Genesis*. There it was a 'pillar' (מצבה *matstsebah*) and a 'heap' (גל *gal*). The term used in *Deuteronomy* is גבול *gĕbuwl*, translated by the Greek *horion*, while in the example from *Proverbs* it is in the plural form *horia*, the neuter noun of the masculine *horos*, and it continues to be translated thus throughout the Septuagint. The Hebrew (here given without diacritics) comprises a similar ambiguity to the Greek; the noun has multiple meanings ranging from 'boundary,' 'limit' and 'line' to 'land,' 'area' and 'territory.' The primitive root of the verb גבל means at once 'to bound' and 'to border.' And the added causative verbal stem, the Hiphil stem, where the effect caused is indirect or mediated, means 'to cause to set bounds,' generating the alternative translations of 'wall' and 'territory.'[27] Henceforth, the term encapsulates the coincidence between the boundary and the mark of the boundary, that is, the act of separating and the separator itself, much like the *Barzakh*, in the Arabic tradition and the *horos* in the Greek. The *horoi* enforce an atemporal (*aiōnia*), even eternal, regime (much like the phrase, 'the sun never sets on the British Empire.' The mark may have been placed by the forefathers, but the *horoi*, the stones that mark the invasion, themselves return to God himself, his eternity and his timelessness.

The text itself would suggest that it is not the boundary that is at risk of being transgressed as much as it is the mark that may go unheeded or be removed. But if it is a matter of recognising landmarks, why the need to stress the prohibition in a text? Is this not the task the boundary-stone itself performs? Presumably, the stone itself, the 'landmark,' is not prohibitive enough. If there is any prohibition here it adheres to the stone itself, the place of the stone as such, and the prohibition is directed not against crossing the boundary but against removing the stone. Or is the prohibition addressing itself to the people of the book, *as writing*, the mnemotechnique which assumes that there has or will have been a loss or lapse of memory? Perhaps the *horos* never uttered a prohibition at all but rather remained brute stone, the very material and boundary between the two realms of the sacred and the profane, between God and human laws and customs. Or, more essentially, the placement that is the one-time removal of the rock, is a symbol for the land itself

---

27 Waltke (1990) 433ff.

that has been appropriated. If this is what it is—a symbol of earthly domination—it can hardly be anything more than symbolic. In the era of the Anthropocene, such acts appear all too futile when we see daily how the devastation of the soil leads to the devastation of the people living upon it. What a futile attempt to appropriate the unappropriable. The people of the book, it would appear, are those who have forgotten to listen to the stone, to live with the land, to read in it the necessity to remain within earth's limits.

But this condemnation for a lack of memory is not a question of religion. It is a question of boundaries, not only of religio-ethical boundaries, nor even national boundaries, but more terrestrial boundaries. Today it is a political question, but it should be framed as an existential one. This is the question of how we live upon the land, not who owns it or has rights to it, but what are the relationships we should be forging and reforming with the earth, the plants and the variety of species (humans included) that the earth supports in order to refigure what it is the human being as a species does and gives to the land they are fed by.

No-Man's Land

The *horos* represented a rule of division and distinction which guided definitions within the space of knowledge in the ancient city and acted as an organising factor or principle common to a wide variety of cultural fields, from the rhetorical and martial arts to law, economics and philosophy. The *horos* and its various manifestations in other religions and languages, and found in foreign soils, is not wholly political. This is not because, in Athens at least, it precedes the institution of the *polis*, the city-state (and remember we have nothing outside of the city to confirm this) but because it generates a fundamental concept of division within the many different fields of knowledge. In economics it simultaneously draws up proprietal boundaries and calls the idea of possession into question, by the fact that a symbol (the stone itself) is required to enforce it. It would seem to suggest that there are limits to possession while implying that such possession is itself the limit between the human and the nonhuman (whatever can be taken possession of). The boundary comes in between, as much a rupture into our relationship with the land, which may have been assumed immanent or inherent before the stone separated us, and representing a covenant between humans and the things that can be disposed of because there is an unearthly principle (be this god, law or capital) that separates us from everything else.

Does this mean the boundary-stone is neutral ground, the intrepid security between borders? That is to say, is it inhuman in principle but also not natural? Is this the site of escalating tension, directed first and foremost at maintaining the line of division between those on either side of the barrier? Or is the stone a device deployed within this location to protect this spatial separation? Does it prompt the notion of the boundary that confronts us to choose sides? Did the *horos* function for the Athenians as an exclusionary principle, dividing their world into friends and enemies? The mere fact that the stone prompts these questions should already indicate that we are no longer on safe ground.

The ground is not secure both because we have found ourselves in no-man's land and because we are caught up in the aporetic structure of the letter of the law. The stone placed after the appropriation of the land raises the problem of any logical method in the law. The word *nomos*, 'law' or 'custom,' is related to the verb νέμομαι, which means 'to divide out,' 'distribute.' This aspect of division comes to signify possession—things that are divided up into different shares and titles, hence the later meaning 'to own,' 'manage.' The *horos* can be seen to have played an intrinsic role between the initial and more complex meanings, establishing the boundaries between what is divided. With a small shift of the oxytone the word *nomos* is a pasturage, the land apportioned for the use of livestock. The law is similar; it is that which is in habitual practice or subject to continual usage. In other words, in order for the law to hold it needs to be held habitually. In contrast to popular belief, laws are not made to be broken, for breaking laws habitually suspends their essential nature as laws. This is the *aporia* upon which the legal structure is built. For example, in Athens the ancient myths were renovated and deployed in order to establish differences between citizens and non-citizens.[28] But, naturally, these myths assumed the previous establishment of the city-state based as it was upon divine intervention—in this case the goddess Athena who

---

28   See Loraux (2006) 28.

engendered in an extraneous way, the first citizen who gave rise to the citizen population of Athens. The autonomy of the democracy and its citizens required the heteronomous establishment of the city and its laws in order for them to be maintained 'democratically.'

If law is supposed to be the basis for division, assumedly the fair distribution of goods and services, the fact that law in action promotes and underpins political inequality and the unequal redistribution of wealth, should alert us not only to the inefficiency of law but its termination. It is no longer 'law' as a process of equal distribution that is functioning; it is economic interests (aka wealth, capital) that exercise control.

In the archaic city and its surrounds the *horos* was found along roads, at the entrance to sacred sites and sanctuaries; generally it was to be found in public spaces. The *horos* described a boundary line not wholly representative of dimension. There is no certainty that the *horoi* were supposed to be linked between one another in order to describe a closed boundary or a fenced-off region.

> One should hardly imagine a continuous line drawn by means of numerous stones. More probably they stood at key points, at corners and where streets entered; here they would clearly say to any disqualified person, 'Thus far and no father.'[29]

The problem of the purpose of these *horoi*, how they demarcated boundaries, whether they demarcated space, becomes secondary when we ask why they were necessary in the first place. Who placed the *horos*, and whom did they mean to keep out? Further, who owned the right to describe boundaries? And, then consequently, by what law were others expelled or made the exception of the boundary?

In his study on the later fourth-century hypothecation *horoi*, Moses Finley suggests that the stones themselves, their particular use and the *terminology* that accompanied them was also particularly Athenian, tracing their appearance outside of Athens to the imperialist expansion of the mother city.

> From Athens they spread only to some of the Aegean islands, over all but one of which Athens held direct administrative control at certain

---

29 Thompson (1972) 118.

periods. How systematically this use of *horoi* was extended within the Athenian sphere and whether it was imposed more or less forcibly by the Athenians are interesting problems for the history of Greek law and interstate relations.[30]

The *horos* referred to here is its fourth-century use as a marker laid upon the land to signify that the owner has hypothecated their land, placing their land as insurance for a loan.[31] It can be assumed that the Athenians attempted to export the *horos* system during this period of imperial expansion in order to vouchsafe their imperial right to properties and taxes. No doubt this was not looked upon favourably by the local populations. It is significant for the present study that this question of the enforced *horos* remains unanswered by Finley, despite his suspicions of resistance against systematic Athenian imperialism.

> There was presumably strong resistance to the *horoi*, for not all the communities influenced by Athens, not even all those which had received cleruchies, seem to have adopted the institution [...] Hypothecation of land and houses was of course universal in Greece: only the *horos*-technique of public notice remained strictly localized. Why that should have happened is, I think, not answerable today. Nor is it too important; legal security is basic, the *horoi* merely a device.[32]

Nonetheless, it does pose the question of whether it was in fact the use to which the Athenians put the *horos* that led to such resistance. It might have been the imposition of taxes, but it also might have been the notion itself of division and possession that non-Athenians found offensive. Not all societies have the same ideas about land ownership, and presumably the notion of boundaries is very culturally specific. If the *horos* was merely a 'device' presumably it would be a simple task to discover to what end it was put to use. And indeed, there are references to these boundary-stones in Greek literature and enough have been found throughout the Greek world dating to the period of the Athenian expansion which can clearly be said to perform an economic function.[33] However, that it was 'put to use' at a later stage

---

30 Finley (1952) 6.
31 Finley (1952), Lalonde (1991); (2006), Harris (2006) 163–241.
32 Finley (1952) 6.
33 IG. II2, 2617–2619, 2581; and Merritt (1939) 50–55 and (1940) 53–56, Shear (1939) 205–206 and (1940) 266–267.

of Athenian history does not foreclose the possibility that it meant something else beforehand.

The boundary-stones of the *agora* signified a region into which the *atimoi*, those who had committed parricide and were therefore considered 'unclean,' were not permitted to enter, and one would assume the *horoi* that marked temple lands would have performed much the same function, while the fourth century mortgage *horoi* certainly demarcated a measured plot as being subject to certain interdictions. But how sure can we be that this stone presented a prohibition? The *horos* itself has no imperative attributed to it. And yet the *horos* that marks a grave, the *horos* that marks the boundary between one county and another, not to mention the *horos* in the philosophical text that means 'definition' or 'determination,' none of these particularly suggest prohibition. The problem that adheres to the *horos* is not that of prohibiting transgression so much as it is that of marking a boundary which otherwise would not be recognised.

If it is a matter of recognising boundaries, is this not rather a problem of reading? That is, is not this boundary found *in us* because we read it as such? Rather than any friend/enemy distinction, these questions remain with the boundary as generating a point of difference between he who reads the boundary and he who fails to do so. The question that is raised and remains with the boundary, as what belongs to the *horos* is not the generation of space on either side, but the question of difference, the question of similarity. On the one hand, we have different space to either side, on the other, different people. So long as it is recognised as mutual by those who inhabit either side, the boundary-stone raises the question of space by putting place into contention and materialising what is common to either side, i.e. the boundary. The *horos* raises a topography of contraries while simultaneously bringing these contraries together and uniting them in its own material. It is the matter that puts difference into question. It is therefore not only a spatial problem that is thus raised but also a problem of authority. For we must ask to whom the boundary belongs, and, thus also, who stands to either side, divided and opposed. Is this relation necessarily antagonistic? And then, consequently, who, if anyone, is expelled or made the exception of the boundary?

Let us proceed (for caution's sake) to one of the earliest literary references to the *horos*. The scene is no-man's land, on the battlefield. And this setting should come as no surprise given that the entire epic of the *Iliad* is set on the plain outside the walls of Troy, where the Danaans (Achaeans or Greeks) have pitched their camp and are engaged in the ten-year war with the Trojans (the armies themselves are composed of a multitude of different peoples with no common name to determine them). Here we see the Lycian contingent:

> οὔτε γὰρ ἴφθιμοι Λύκιοι Δαναῶν ἐδύναντο
> τεῖχος ῥηξάμενοι θέσθαι παρὰ νηυσὶ κέλευθον,
> οὔτέ ποτ' αἰχμηταὶ Δαναοὶ Λυκίους ἐδύναντο
> τείχεος ἂψ ὤσασθαι, ἐπεὶ τὰ πρῶτα πέλασθεν.
> ἀλλ' ὥς τ' ἀμφ' οὔροισι δύ' ἀνέρε δηριάασθον
> μέτρ' ἐν χερσὶν ἔχοντες ἐπιξύνῳ ἐν ἀρούρῃ,
> ὥ τ' ὀλίγῳ ἐνὶ χώρῳ ἐρίζητον περὶ ἴσης,
> ὣς ἄρα τοὺς διέεργον ἐπάλξιες·

> For neither could the mighty Lycians break the wall of the Danaans, and make a path to the ships, nor ever could the Danaan spearmen thrust back the Lycians from the wall, when once they had drawn near it. But as two men with measuring-rods in hand contend about the landmarks [*horoi*] in a common field, and in a narrow space contend each for his equal share, so did the battlements hold these foes apart.[34]

The *horoi* (here in the plural epic form- οὔροισι) present us with a simile for the wall of Troy. Just as the latter stands as the point of division and struggle (the Greeks want it to fall; the Trojans need it to stand firm), so the former is a point of contention. And yet, these *horoi* stand in a common field, and the arms at the men's disposal are measuring-rods, and their quarrel concerns equality in division. In the classical *polis* there was still something of a common-field system, even if these fields had come into the possession and disposal of the state. There were also lands that were attached to certain sanctuaries that may have been at the disposal of citizens (one would hope the less fortunate as well). One would presume that the small space in contention is the proposed site of each man's common agricultural efforts, a limited area of soil that he could work, sow and reap the benefits of for private use.

Other references to the *horos* in the Homeric epics also introduce this theme of measure and contention, whether it is an athlete's sprint surpassing another's that is the same as the length of furrows

---

34 Hom.*Il.*12.417–426. tr. A.T. Murray.

ploughed by a pair of mules (ἀλλ' ὅτε δή ῥ' ἀπέην ὅσσόν τ' ἐπὶ οὖρα πέλονται/ἡμιόνων) or the distance of a discus-throw exceeding another (ὅσσα δὲ δίσκου οὖρα κατωμαδίοιο πέλονται). What is consistent is, on the one hand the sense of proportion (ὅσσόν) which is generated, and on the other the *horos* as a simile for the comparative and combative deeds of men.[35] Although they refer to a struggle, all these similes intervene to describe a distance that is traced in shared, communal activities. Is this a mere literary device? Granted that the *horos* takes place in the text, despite its epic proportions, it appears as a reference to what is common beyond the text, the familiar and daily activities of life, with the implication that the measure of men in war is peace. And yet there is more to this than platitude since what the simile of the *horos* describes is a state of (peace-time) contention that is not one of aversion or hostility. There may be dissent or difference between the two athletes, but this is within measure. Not that they compromise, for the whole point of the simile is that of contention, but in the common field and in contrast to the battlefield they retain a (friendly) relation. The *horos* remains without place, the position of contention without, however, becoming a place. The measure that is described is in the midst of an opposition, describing a relation, and yet it does not facilitate mediation.

As it stands (the *horos*), the men remain united in their difference and, what is most important, regardless of their respective measurements, since it was not only the distance, shares of land between or claimed by each man that was the subject of the proportion, but the comparison between war and peace-time collaboration. Given that this simile occurs in epic poetry that was itself an intrinsic component of a youth's education, sung at feasts and in the competitive setting of rhapsodic festivals, it could be said that the measure of men was metric, that is, subject to a standard of measurement and division. And a standard and system of measurement and division is essential both for poetic metre and for the distribution of land and goods. Whether goods are subject to equal division or belligerent measures of seizure and rape, the yardstick stands witness to any disproportion. The *horos* reveals itself as a medial point but not necessarily a point of mediation. In these examples at least, it is a point of argumentative dissent.

---

35 Hom. *Il*.10, 351; 23.431, *Od*. 8.25.

This reflects upon the Athenian disposition toward the middle, towards being the middle of things, *in medias res*, and being 'the measure of all things.' The rise of the *agora* also meant the institution of a system of weights and measures, creating a system of values for the purpose of measuring disparate things in an equal way and determining a comparative value of equivalence. When Protagoras arrived in Athens in the fifth century BC, the *agora* was already a place of economic exchange and was probably already the place of disputation frequented by the Socrates. Protagoras's philosophy of the divisive fit right in. His treatise *The Art of Eristics* used wrestling as a rhetorical metaphor for the conflict between two arguments and expounded upon different argumentative techniques.[36] His philosophy has the human being acting and speaking about the value of things.

> Πάντων χρημάτων μέτρον ἄνθρωπον εἶναι, τῶν μὲν ὄντων, ὡς ἔστι, τῶν δὲ μὴ ὄντων, ὡς οὐκ ἔστιν.[37]
>
> Of all things the measure is the human: of things that are, that they are, and of things that are not, that they are not.

While it may have been something like an advertisement for his teaching, this phrase has a word that would subsequently become one of the most powerful words in the Greek language, *chrēmata*, 'money.' Although the 'things' of which the human is the measure may be of significance or not, the 'things' themselves are judged according to their use-value. This is what *chrēmata* means, 'property,' 'substance,' 'matter' or 'money.' The word signifies a relation with things that are already in existence in the economic life of the city. According to Plato one of Protagoras's aims in teaching was good economy.

> τὸ δὲ μάθημά ἐστιν εὐβουλία περὶ τῶν οἰκείων, ὅπως ἂν ἄριστα τὴν αὑτοῦ οἰκίαν διοικοῖ, καὶ περὶ τῶν τῆς πόλεως, ὅπως τὰ τῆς πόλεως δυνατώτατος ἂν εἴη καὶ πράττειν καὶ λέγειν.[38]
>
> This lesson is about good judgement in household matters, such as how to best manage one's household, and about matters of the city, such as to be most capable of acting and speaking about the matters of the city.

---

36 DK 520.1.
37 DK 518.27.
38 Pl.*Prot*. 318e–319a.

What we can see is that these ideas of division, argumentation and of taking sides may have been framed as comprising political thought; however, they form a network of analogies within different fields of study. These codes, influencing the gymnastic, martial and rhetorical arts as well as political, legal and economic thought and philosophical language, originated in ideas of separation and division. The space of knowledge in the ancient city was organised around the separating factor as a principle common to all fields. This principle (*horos*) existed in what Foucault phrased the 'positive unconscious' of the Athenians as a material guide or rule used to define the various objects of action and speech in the *polis*.[39]

In his *History of the Peloponnesian Wars*, Thucydides quotes a speech rallying for war,

> καὶ γνῶναι ὅτι τοῖς μὲν ἄλλοις οἱ πλησιόχωροι περὶ γῆς ὅρων τὰς μάχας ποιοῦνται, ἡμῖν δὲ ἐς πᾶσαν, ἢν νικηθῶμεν, εἷς ὅρος οὐκ ἀντίλεκτος παγήσεται.[40]
>
> know also that other tribes are constantly at war with their nearest neighbours over the boundaries of the land (*gēs horōn*), while if we win one battle, a single horos (*eis horos*) will be fixed once and for all.

Now it goes without saying that when two armies stand face to face there is a presupposed boundary of contention between them, a boundary which has been brought into question by the fact of war. So long as the war rages, a boundary remains. But the problem here is exactly where this boundary is located about which both sides are in disagreement. The location itself is at once the site of conflict and *in conflict*. In every sense it is over this very boundary that war is waged. But here we can understand the point of contention also as a unifier, where, in the words of Heidegger,

> strife is not a rift, as a mere cleft is ripped open; rather, it is the intimacy with which opponents belong to each other.[41]

However, there is a significant difference between peacetime contention on the one hand and war (*polemos*) and civil war (*stasis*) on the other.

---

39 Foucault (2008) xi.
40 Thuc.4.92.4.
41 Heidegger (2000) 188.

With war even though the boundary is in contention, it does not cease to be present as that which divides the hosts and unites them in hostility.[42] In *stasis*, however, there is not necessarily a distinct boundary that has been transgressed; there is no physical boundary (*horos*) within a singular community that divides it in two.

Stasis derives its meaning from the word 'to stand,' and we should understand this word in the same way as the Greeks, as the point when a community ceases its usual motion, comes to a standstill, comes up against a wall.[43] *Stasis* itself fulfils the function of division wherever it arises; however, this division is not linked to a particular place. It could be said to be the ethical experience of division. Vardoulakis states that 'the temporality of stasis in relation to the theologico-political is intimately linked to the impossibility of fixing stasis to a particular locus.'[44] *Stasis* is a creation of the community, within the community, that simultaneously calls into question the very character and unity of the community as such, so that, given its multivalence, 'stasis has the capacity to disturb the mutual support of presence and absence.'[45] Unlike the *horos*, the division in *stasis* has no immediate relation to a position, or the sacred; it is a political event even when it breaks in as an exception of political authority.

> If the law employs the exception—that is the suspension of law itself—as its original means of referring to and encompassing life, then a theory of the state of exception is the preliminary condition for any definition of the relation that binds and, at the same time, abandons the living being to law.[46]

The law that citizens had to choose sides in *stasis* meant that no fence-sitting was permitted in the democracy. The ideological formation that there are only and essentially two sides can be said to originate here, the basis of the idea that democracy means two-party politics. The contemporary enforcement of this law, for example, in Australia where fines are issued to those who refuse to vote, where the outcome

---

42 Plato, *Rep*.470b.
43 On stasis and Solon see Chapter Seven. For a full study of the concept of stasis in ancient Athens, see Loraux (2006).
44 Vardoulakis (2009)142.
45 Ibid. 127.
46 Agamben (2005) 1.

is foreclosed to be in favour of one of only two parties, maintains the idea that law is the mediator between citizens and state, having the right to intervene and enforce political engagement in one or the other way. Here the law is presented as the mythical, neutral ground, mediator and redistributor of goods, money and justice. But there's no such thing as a true middle in political economics or a neutral capitalist state (even neutral Switzerland engages in exporting banking systems to war-ravaged countries). Neutrality, or the disengaged middle, is nothing but a front for the establishment of economic interests that is none other than a coup d'état, a usurpation of control by a single faction. It can be argued that any representative democratic party in power, with less than fifty percent of the vote, is a usurpation of power under the auspices of the law.

Nonetheless, Vardoulakis reminds us that what appears to be an exception to politics is simultaneously the ground for a new political relation, but a ground that provides neither a foundation nor a sovereign. The non-state of civil war issues in the possibility for an ethical and political relation, thus a 'responsible politics is above all a politics that eschews the violent act of separation instituting the sovereign. Stasis solicits a politics of friendship.'[47] Here we can understand the point of contention also as a unifier. In the words of Heidegger, 'strife is not a rift,' rather it 'carries the opponents into the provenance of their unity by virtue of their common ground.'[48]

The German word for 'rift,' *Riß*, does not merely describe a crack or laceration; etymologically it is connected to the verb *reissen*, cognate with the English 'writing'; 'it is a basic design (*Grundriß*), an outline sketch (*Auf-riß*), that draws the basic features of the upsurgence into the clearing of beings.'[49] What is here *written* is the 'work,' something that is differentiated from its surrounding environment as 'figure' (*Gestalt*). And it is such because we allow it to become, or even, be *read* as something that has been sectioned off and fixed in place. Hence, 'this rift does not let the opponents break apart; it brings what opposes measure (*Maß*) and boundary (*Grenze*) into its common outline (*den einigen Umriß*).'[50] It

---

47 Vardoulakis (2010) 155.
48 Heidegger (2000) 188.
49 Ibid.
50 Ibid.

is in this sense that Heidegger uses the word strife to produce the work; it is a point of difference that marks out the boundaries between earth and world, in other words something like 'nature' and 'human activity.'

> Yet as a world opens itself the earth comes to tower. It stands forth as that which bears all, as that which is sheltered in its own law and always wrapped in itself. World demands its decisiveness and its measure and lets beings attain to the open region of their paths. Earth, bearing and jutting, endeavours to keep itself closed and to entrust everything to its law.[51]

World is experienced as something more than the material basis of the earth; it is where activity, work, significance and values, measures and divisions create an interpretation of living in the midst of 'nature,' here foreign in the sense of a foreign language, not understandable, despite our embedded origins. From this point on the earth exists as a value in the world of the human being. For Heidegger this seems to be the beginning of the cultural project and the wonder of the artwork.

And yet there is an uncanny resemblance with the *horos*, at least in terminology. The work does not cease to be composed of earth, in exactly the same way that the *horos*, whether engraved or not, does not cease to be stone: 'The rift must set itself back into the gravity of stone, the hardness of wood, the dark glow of colours.'[52] Although it resembles it, the *horos* is not quite akin to Heidegger's figure because it is not necessarily dependent upon a single authority, or author. It is not wholly placed or framed by us. Its position is already there, in its stoniness, and is only read by us as meaning bearing. Nor is it supposed to provide a definition to a question or a riddle. The *horos* never takes form beyond the possible coincidence between stone, letter and all those other meanings and matters. It is not a work as such, though that does not mean it is not read as something that works. It is exactly there where the artifice of script begins, but is itself not artificial. The word and boundary are never abstracted from stone, and it also never ceases to be mere stone. The divisive power of the *horos* is distinctly present as matter: the writing of division, the letter of the law. The *horos* does not cease to belong to the earth, standing as a rule that the human also

---

51 Ibid.
52 Ibid.

belongs in the nonhuman but also that there is a self-authorised break. Otherwise, there would be no distinction between whoever reads the *horos* as boundary and the rest of the world that does not.

How can the law be followed to the letter when the stone marks the impossibility of ever following the path without bringing the letter along with us? The stone is this *diaporia*; it marks the *aporia* and allows law and *logos* to transgress it but only in the form of the letter. Thus, the law, which would prohibit in order to foil transgression, is from the first naming of the stone always put into question by occupation of the letter, simultaneously composed of letters and destroyed by them. Because the *horos* is the base material upon which the letter is formed and the base material that gives form to letters, this convergence of form and matter provides the foundation and schema for the law, even as it undermines it. The *horos*, the boundary-stone, is the link, bond or knot in this aporetic structure, without which the law is illiterate and illegible. The stone, whether inscribed or not, marks a departure from the time before when the inscription was not subject to law, when what was engraved was without form and pointed nowhere. The *horos* might not precede the sacred, and yet it remains as the thin line that gives definition to either side, and describes an opposition between these spaces, which are not to be confused with *topoi*, topical places or places with a particular character localised in speech if not geographically (for example Aristotle's treatise *Topika* is the method of drawing conclusions from opinions).[53] But that does not stop the *horos* from remaining the position of unity, leaking opposition into division, before the *logos* intervened to show the way and to bar it.

Horos Zeus

Against a politics of walls and barriers, we can redefine the terms, raising the question once again to ask in what relation the *horos* stands with law, its transgression and its exception. In the *Laws*, Plato states that the prohibition against removing boundary-stones is the first law of Zeus, punishable twice over, first according to the justice of the gods, then by the laws of man.

---

53 Ar. *Top.* 100b21.

Διὸς ὁρίου μὲν πρῶτος νόμος ὅδε εἰρήσθω· μὴ κινείτω γῆς ὅρια μηδεὶς μήτε οἰκείου πολίτου γείτονος, μήτε ὁμοτέρμονος ἐπ' ἐσχατιᾶς κεκτημένος ἄλλῳ ξένῳ γειτονῶν, νομίσας τὸ τἀκίνητα κινεῖν ἀληθῶς τοῦτο εἶναι· βουλέσθω δὲ πᾶς πέτρον ἐπιχειρῆσαι κινεῖν τὸν μέγιστον ἄλλον πλὴν ὅρον μᾶλλον ἢ σμικρὸν λίθον ὁρίζοντα φιλίαν τε καὶ ἔχθραν ἔνορκον παρὰ θεῶν. τοῦ μὲν γὰρ ὁμόφυλος Ζεὺς μάρτυς, τοῦ δὲ ξένιος, οἳ μετὰ πολέμων τῶν ἐχθίστων ἐγείρονται. καὶ ὁ μὲν πεισθεὶς τῷ νόμῳ ἀναίσθητος τῶν ἀπ' αὐτοῦ κακῶν γίγνοιτ' ἄν, καταφρονήσας δὲ διτταῖς δίκαις ἔνοχος ἔστω, μιᾷ μὲν παρὰ θεῶν καὶ πρώτῃ, δευτέρᾳ δὲ ὑπὸ νόμου.[54]

> The first law, that of *Horos* Zeus shall be stated thus: Do not move earth's *horoi*, whether they be those of a neighbour who is a native citizen or those of a stranger (with adjoining land on a frontier), recognising that this is truly to move the immoveable; better to let someone try to move the largest rock which is not a *horos* than a small stone which marks the boundary between friendly and hostile ground under the oath of the gods. For of the one Kinship Zeus is witness, of the other Stranger Zeus; who, when aroused, brings wars most hostile. He that obeys the law shall not suffer the evils that it inflicts; but he who despises it shall be liable to a twofold justice, first and foremost from the gods, and second from the law.

Could it be assumed that every *horos* is the mark of the omnipresence of this Zeus of the *horos*? On the outskirts of Athens, there was a temple to an unknown Zeus marked by a *horos* of this name, dated amongst the oldest of the Athenian *horoi*, bearing the rupestral inscription ΗΟΡΟΣ: ΔΙΟΣ [retrograde] (*horos of Zeus*). As one epigraphical study suggests,

> this 'Horos of Zeus' is a type of abbreviated marker of shrines, in which the word ἱεροῦ or τεμένους [shrine or sanctuary] is either understood as part of the meaning of ὅρος, and a byname of the god was perhaps assumed as known.[55]

The implication is that the *horos*, by marking the site, consecrates it and is coterminous with the sacred quality of the place it identifies. If we take this to apply to all *horoi*, we could assume that for any boundary-stone to be recognised the reading of boundaries as such must be the guiding thread at once joining and distinguishing the sacred from the profane; it need not be accompanied by a prohibition as it already stands in order that the sacred remain inviolate. Therefore, as Plato informs us, the

---

54 Pl. *Laws*. 843A-B.
55 Lalonde, (2006) 6.

first law must be the prohibition against the removal of the boundary-stone, and he who is guilty of moving *horoi* is guilty of attempting to remove the very stones that draw up the outlines of power, that define the boundaries (and here we see the verbal form of the *horos* in action, ὁρίζοντα) sanctioned 'in oath by the gods' (ἔνορκον παρὰ θεῶν). And not only this, for the removal of the stone is also a trespass on logic, 'to move the immoveable' (τὸ τἀκίνητα κινεῖν).

The single stone protected by *Horos Zeus* comprises the internal confrontation or conjunction between two other epithets of Zeus named by Plato: Zeus of kinship, ὁμόφυλος Ζεὺς, and Zeus of strangers, ξένιος. The relational distinction between kin and stranger is 'hospitality,' *philoxenia*, the concrete relation barring friend from enemy (φιλίαν τε καὶ ἔχθραν). The relation of enmity is proscribed by the transgression of the boundary in friendship. It is essential to note that neither the stone nor this first law prohibits the transgression of the boundary. The intention is not the prohibition of people passing from one side to the other, but rather it has to do exclusively with the material of the boundary itself, with the boundary as marker. It is a law that does not deal with people's movements as such but with the matter of the boundary, the solidity and immovability of stone. It is not we who are prohibited from crossing the boundary, it is the boundary itself that must remain without motion, and, being put out of motion it is (according to Aristotelian physics) thus beyond nature, whether it is sacred or corroborated by law. It would be wrong to assume that this law, given its divine sanction, is therefore not a human law. It may not be inscribed on the tablets of the city, but this does not mean that it is not inscribed into human relations by human acts. The law of *horos* Zeus is, properly, topographical, but without actually being topical. It is written into the land as the first law of the land, the first law that protects the laws of logic. It draws up the boundaries between the possible and the impossible in language, for to remove the *horos* is to move the immoveable. This law thus finds its true *topothesia* in language, in *logos*, though that does not mean the stone is invested with reason.

Of course, this interpretation coincides perfectly with the archaeological history of the *horos*, which states that a *horos* is differentiated from other stones only insofar as it is read as such. The *horos* is the stone that is distinguished from the 'natural' stone according to archaeology because, to begin, with it is inscribed with the word.

The question, therefore, of the law is not here a question of authority or authenticity—of who wrote the law, in whose power the law resides. The question that must precede any question of writing is deflected by the question that the stone itself raises, which is: Who reads the *horos*? Who recognises the boundary? The difference that is thus generated by the *horos* is between those who read the *horos* as *horos* and those who fail to do so. This division takes place as the basis for the laws of the land, which subsequently belong to whoever has the capacity to distinguish them.

The difference the *horos* is said to mark is that between kin and stranger. This difference is that of hospitality itself, *xenia*, which should describe the relation one has with strangers. The word for the 'stranger,' *xenos*, is threefold; it also means 'guest' and includes the obligatory meaning to play 'host,' also *xenos*. Kinship Zeus must be presumed to protect relations within the clan, community, family, tribal group; that is always on this side of the boundary. *Xenios* Zeus stands guard over the relations between here and there, that is, between strangers; there, where, at least linguistically, we cannot be told apart except as what defines us in common. We are, both of us strangers to one another. Our identity is the reduplication of the signifier 'stranger' (*xenos/xenos*) with a boundary in between that transforms this relation into one of friendship, causing the double modification to alter to 'friend' (*philos/philos*). This transformative relation is called *'philoxenia,'* imperfectly translated as 'hospitality' (because *hospis* in your house still remains a hosted enemy, lacking the final metamorphosis into friend). But there is a boundary that nonetheless separates us and offers us the possibility of transgressing over into difference, of welcoming one another and introducing ourselves as something more than strangers, of learning the other's name, and also giving ourselves a name and family relation that extends beyond us. This boundary is the possibility of *xenia*, of the hospitable relation. The stone demands what the text prohibits, at least in regards to *crossing over*, or the maintenance of friendly relations. But, then, this can occur only if we both recognise the presence of a boundary that makes us both strangers, one to the other.

Therefore, the *horos* gives onto, and gives only, onto hospitality, to the possibility of two different people, two different spaces sharing something in common, even if this is none other than the boundary itself that divides them. It suggests a bond to those who transgress it in friendship, whether they belong to the same tribe or are bound in a relation of hospitality with that tribe. But it exactly ceases to be (read as) a boundary the minute that it is crossed in enmity because in that case the aggressor simply does not, or refuses to, recognise it as such by not making the appropriate transformation into 'friend.' Thus, the *horos* raises the possibility of hospitality and puts hostility out of the question. But this is because the hospitality itself already raises the possibility of hostility. In the words of Plato, the *horos* draws up the boundary (and he uses the participle of the verb, *horizon*) between friendship and enmity. This is no archaic Schmittian parallel maintaining a distinction of estrangement between friend and enemy.[56] On the contrary, since the *horos* binds these two epithets, it singularly permits, or rather demands, a relation that as such both makes possible and proscribes enmity. Hostility is only possible under the protectorate of *xenios Zeus*, as the potentiality of hospitality failed or perverted. Hospitality and hostility are not contrary; the latter is, rather, dependent upon the former as an inherent possibility. If hostility was not experienced as a possibility, hospitality ceases to be something freely given. This is the definition (*horos*) or horizon of hospitality.

Is this horizon experienced as a limitation? It is certainly a limit, just as the *horos* itself can be translated as 'limit,' but perhaps a limit that does not act as a restriction as such. And we must not fail to note the etymological link between the *horizon* and the *horos*, as if the nominal *horos* was put into action in the spectral limits of our world. Without this limit (*horos*), a term that must be read even though it provides no terms as such, hospitality retains the possibility of offering itself as hostility. But the *horos* is also the limit that asserts that hospitality must remain hospitality. Without such a limit, in the absence of some kind of term or boundary, hospitality is groundless. Here we could say, then, that the *horos* is necessary for hospitality, opening up the possibility of transgressing boundaries, of coming to terms with confrontation, whether in friendship or enmity, before any conditions are placed upon guest or host as to whom is accepted or with what intentions the boundary is crossed. Hospitality proceeds from this limit, opening up

---

56   Cf. Schmitt (2007).

the horizon to further transgression and abuse. Thus, Derrida suggested that 'pure' or 'unconditional' hospitality is an *aporia*; it always contains the possibility of flipping over into its opposite, or of failing to be given.[57] And consequently a 'pure' hospitality is, as Derrida states (unconsciously calling the *horos* into presence), 'without horizon.'[58] We could say it remains always on the boundary, that thin line, because it is the limit point as such (*horos*) that is itself unlimited.

> If, however, there is pure hospitality, or a pure gift, it should consist in this opening without horizon, without horizon of expectation, an opening to the newcomer whoever that may be. It may be terrible because the newcomer may be a good person, or may be the devil: but if you exclude the possibility that the newcomer is coming to destroy your house—if you want to control this and exclude in advance this possibility—there is no hospitality. In this case, you control the borders, you have customs officers, and you have a door, a gate, a key and so on. For unconditional hospitality to take place you have to accept the risk of the other coming and destroying the place, initiating a revolution, stealing everything, or killing everyone. That is the risk of pure hospitality and pure gift, because a pure gift might be terrible too.[59]

If we read this horizon as what remains of the *horos* in the present day then we can accept Derrida's conclusion, that hospitality appears as an *aporia*, a problem that does not permit passage, literally *a*- 'without,' -*poros* 'passage..' It is a problem that must remain irresolvable because what marks the boundary is exactly the task of reading, of the mutual recognition of the boundary. Moreover, the boundary is therefore either maintained because it is held in common, or transgressed because it is disputed. But that is not the real issue, for it is easy enough for those who are linguistically affiliated to the boundary, for those who are able to read the stone, to choose in what manner they cross the boundary. But how does the boundary stand for the real stranger, the foreigner who does not, cannot, read the stone as boundary, the foreigner who is unfamiliar with the laws of the land and therefore transgresses the boundary unwillingly or without the wherewithal to act in accordance with the laws of the land, and always at risk of defying this first law?

---

57 Derrida (1993) 11.
58 Derrida, 'Hospitality, Justice and Responsibility: A dialogue with Jacques Derrida' in Kearney (1999) 70.
59 Ibid.

This is where 'pure' hospitality is found, exactly where the boundary comes into question, not because it is revoked or removed, but simply because it is not read as such. Hence, the *horos*, in being unperceived by the stranger, signifies something beyond its own definition, term and limit. The *horos* itself always comes in between friendship and enmity, it is itself an open definition, but nonetheless material. The *horos* always remains with the boundary as the only position to which no determinate position belongs, and it is in this absolute relation with the boundary as such that we are all of us bound as strangers. In the words of Levinas,

> When in the *Iliad* the resistance to an attack by an enemy phalanx is compared to the resistance of a rock to the waves that assail it, it is not necessarily a matter of extending to the rock, through anthropomorphism, a human behaviour, but of interpreting human resistance petromorphically.[60]

The *horos* stands as and marks out the aporetic structure of hospitality, or, better, it provides a horizon in contention, a boundary of confrontation, where the *aporia* of *philoxenia*, the problem itself is always raised and given form in pure uncontested matter. Thus *philoxenia's* 'purity' is based upon a certain materiality always on the cusp of language, and that presents itself as a risk. So long as the *horos* remains and is unmoved, this problem refuses solution, because so long as the boundary is observed there will always be those on one side, and those on the other. Then, hospitality always remains as a possibility, whether offering it or receiving it, and so does hostility. If we put hospitality into question—as something that we might not give, if we conceptualise it not as a gift but as a right that must be permitted or held back, if we refuse it to some or place conditions on how it is to be received— then we put the boundary out of question. The boundary that does not remain open ceases to be mutual; it becomes proper to one side or the other, and ceases to be a boundary as such, it becomes a barrier and the boundary as such is deferred, and by being deferred, it is subject to question. Ironically enough, then, the state that privileges entry to some and refuses it to others can be seen to undermine the very existence of its own borders.

---

60   Levinas (1987) 78.

We can thus offer an alternate reading of Plato's first law against the removal of the boundary-stones by suggesting that it is not the transgression of the boundaries as such, but the transgression of the hospitable relation that rouses Zeus *Xenios* to inflict wars. Hostile is he who estranges himself from the obligation to play guest-host, not only to be the generous, bountiful host, but—and this is the harder— to be a stranger, to let oneself be defined as the other of the other.[61] This indebtedness (of self) to other is inscribed upon the land, both boundary and bond that cannot be proscribed or prohibited. Rather, as the question that would put the law of the 'same' out of play, it demands transgression by virtue of a certain similarity between guest and host that nonetheless remain bound together in a common estrangement. Any relation with the stranger automatically puts one in the parallel position of stranger, and it is this universal notion of estrangement before the other that binds us all to the breaking point of the boundary of the other. For Levinas this is where what is material breaks down into the presence of the face.

> Here the sensible presence desensibilizes to let the one who only refers to himself, the identical, break through directly. As an interlocutor he posits himself in front of me, and an interlocutor alone can properly speaking posit himself in a position facing me, without this 'facing' signifying hostility or friendship.[62]

Hospitality always has the possibility of giving onto friendship and enmity, hence Derrida's neologism 'hostipitalité,' adding the host into the otherwise exclusive reception of the enemy.[63] The point is that when it comes to reading the boundary-stone, one is not at liberty to choose sides. One contingently finds oneself on one side or the other, or else one might be so strange as to not even recognise the *horos* as such. The *horos*, however, gives only onto hospitality. In this case, however, the *horos* is not itself an *aporia*. It is not a problem to be solved, or a question as such, even though it gives onto or raises problems. If it is read as boundary then it is a boundary, if it is not read as such it retreats into its identity as stone. As Plato says, to move the largest stone that is not a *horos* is just fine ('sooner let someone move the largest rock which

---

61 Derrida (1999) 23.
62 Levinas (1987) 42.
63 See 'Hostipitality' in, Derrida (2002) 401–402.

is not a *horos* than a small stone which marks the boundary between friendly and hostile ground').⁶⁴ The assumption is that we already know which is which.

Swearing by the Horos

Looking at the *horos* from a distance, it becomes evident how central it was to the constitution of the Athenian citizen body and to the maintenance, even reverence, of the laws of the city. After performing their military service on the boundaries of the Athenian *polis* and before returning to the city, the ephebes swore an oath (Ὅρκος ἐφήβων). In order to be assumed into the body politic, the young men took an oath to obey the laws and protect the institutions of the city. The ephebes swore the oath upon returning from a two-year period spent serving upon the margins of the city's territory, supposedly doing the double duty of defense and of learning the art of an arms-bearing citizen. As Vidal-Naquet notes, this boundary area is both an actual geographical and symbolic space, where the boys are to make the transition into civilised young men.⁶⁵ The oath is their affirmation of this transition and their acceptance of the contractual bonds of civic life. At the end of this oath, they call as witnesses an intriguing variety of gods, plants, and, of interest to us here, the *horoi*.

> Ἵστορες θεοὶ Ἄγλαυρος, Ἑστία, Ἐνυάλιος, Ἄρης καὶ Ἀθηνᾶ Ἀρεία, Ζεύς, Θαλλώ, Αὐξώ, Ἡγεμόνη, Ἡρακλῆς, ὅροι τῆς πατρίδος, πυροί, κριθαί, ἄμπελοι, ἐλᾶαι, συκαῖ.

> Witnesses are the gods Aglauros, Hestia, Enyo, Enyalios, Ares and Athena Areia, Zeus, Thallo, Auxo, Hegemone, Herakles, *horoi* of the fatherland, wheat, barley, vines, olive-trees, fig-trees.⁶⁶

One might have expected that the *horoi* appear within the oath as something that needs protecting, along with the laws, authorities, institutions and affiliations of the city that are mentioned. But here they are included in a list of gods (with more or less obvious significance for the city) and certain fruit-bearing plants (that obviously provide basic

---

64 Pl. *Laws*. 843A-B.
65 Vidal-Naquet (1986) 107.
66 Siewert (1977) 103.

sustenance), called upon as *Histores*, 'witnesses.' An *histor* (cognate verb ἱστορέω, 'to inquire, examine, read,' as in history) is someone who knows the law, right and justice, thus it also means 'judge.' It is interesting to consider that the *horoi* might be considered plausible witnesses in the same sense as the gods. It seems reasonable to state that the *horoi* are called upon because of their role in maintaining friendly relations, or that failing, in defending against hostile forces. But, as was seen in both the Septuagint and Plato's Laws, the *horoi* also bear a significant relation with the past, and the 'ancestors' or 'men of old' who laid the stones or the gods and law that sanctified them. They are read and may even be said to provide, if not be, a kind of earthly narrative. These stones inscribe the history of the land. The narrative line read in the *horoi* might be that of hospitality, of the relation with friends and strangers. It is important that in this context the *horoi* are not in need of protection or maintenance by law, they are as autarchic as gods and trees (this does not mean self-sufficient). What does it mean that the *horoi* be called upon as witnesses to the oath and feature among a list of other nonhuman, some divine some organic, witnesses?

Oath, *horkos*, (ὅρκος) cognate with *herkos* (ἕρκος) meaning 'fence, enclosure,' has quite a lot in common semantically (if not syntactically, again the play of a letter) with the *horos*, except that the boundary of the oath closes the circle into a defensive barrier, while the *horos* leaves this possibility open, simply dividing. The oath presents us with a linguistic boundary, where, by swearing an oath one fences oneself in and is bound to one's words. The gods were said to swear their oaths upon the Styx, the river that encircles the universe and binds the gods to their words.[67] In this case, however, one's oath is the very paradigm of the truth (and divinity) of language itself, the power of the *logos* to be made flesh, to be actualised.[68] Therefore, as Agamben argues, in oath one takes responsibility not only for one's words but also constitutes oneself as 'the living being who has language.'[69] The oath expresses

> the demand, decisive in every sense for the speaking animal, to put its nature at stake in language and to bind together in an ethical and political connection words, things, and actions. Only by this means

---

67 Fletcher (2012) 74ff.
68 Agamben (2011) 21.
69 Ibid. 69.

was it possible for something like history, distinct from nature, and nevertheless, inseparably intertwined with it, to be produced.[70]

However, if these words, things, and actions had to be bound together, must they not first have been split? If the oath constitutes and ensures human nature as a speaking being and a being capable of living historically, the *horos* affirms the former split in which the human is divided from nature—and here there is no discernible difference between what would be human nature and nature absolutely. So, what we can *read* into the *horos* is exactly that split that divided human beings from (their) nature. Before this split, humans did not live historically, but fatefully. In the ancient world of Athens, this split was ascribed to the divine name of Fate, *Heimarmenē*— neither entirely god, nor entirely nature, this 'divine word' (λόγος θεῖος) as Plutarch refers to it, takes its root from the verb μείρομαι, 'to divide out, allot, assign' and is the principle of division:

> ἡ εἱμαρμένη δῖχως καὶ λέγεται καὶ νοεῖται· ἡ μὲν γάρ ἐστιν ἐνέργεια, ἡ δ'οὐσία.[71]
>
> Heimarmenē is said and thought in two ways: on the one hand as activity, on the other as substance.

She is divided (*dichōs*) between speech and thought but is also the singularity of fate; she is 'a law conforming to the nature of the universe, determining the course of everything that comes to pass' and 'the linking of future events to events past and present.'[72] Human fate is thus split between speech and thought, between what is said and what is done, between what is undertaken and what is. Does oath step into this division as an attempt to resolve it into a pure identity between speech, thought, act and being? It is this will to assert a unity that cannot help but point back to division. The oath is less about the risk of perjury than it is a declaration that this split belongs to the human, as if we are the subjects of this division and can in a single 'act' overcome our own nature. But the oath also gestures towards the possibility of lying. By asserting a correlation between language and truth it generates the very distinction between human and nature.

---

70 Ibid.
71 *On Fate*, Plut. *Mor*.568c-e.
72 Ibid. Also, Pl.*Phd*.115a, *Grg*.512e.

Can nature lie? For perhaps the majority of plants and animals, pretence would appear to be second nature, predisposed as they are to mimic the world around them or to mislead, trick or deceive their predator by pretending to be something they are not. Pretty much the entire insect world engages in some form of pretence, confusing their physiognomy or disguising themselves as leaves, bark, rocks even a different species of insect. Human beings, however, are not content with dissembling nature; they also claim to have exclusive mastery of truth. Perhaps lying can only exist in such a framework as this. Lying is not dissembling or deceiving for the purpose of self-defense or the defense of one's young. Lying occurs when someone speaks in opposition to a known truth. That said, that this is exclusively human is dubious. There are monkeys (for example, spider monkeys, brown capuchins and long-tailed macaques) who, upon finding a food source make the call that warns other monkeys in the area about the presence of a large predator, but they do this in the absence of said predator and purely for the purpose of hoarding the food themselves. A human being who lies rarely, if ever, does so for more noble causes.

If anything, lying resembles the oath in that they both have the potentiality to be entirely performative. Agamben suggests that the oath reveals a remnant stage in language when the connection between words and things was performative rather than denotative. This is not

> a magico-religious stage but a structure antecedent to (or contemporaneous with) the distinction between sense and denotation, which is perhaps not, as we have been accustomed to believe, an original and eternal characteristic of human language but a historical product (which, as such, has not always existed and could one day cease to exist).[73]

Foucault called this performative aspect of speech 'I swear,' 'I promise' etc, a 'veridiction,' where the subject constitutes itself as a performative speaker of the truth of their own affirmation and whose verbal act brings their own being into truth.[74]

> If one pretends to formulate a veridiction as an assertion, an oath as a denotative expression, and (as the Church began to do from the fourth century on by means of conciliar creeds) a profession of faith as dogma,

---

73 Agamben (2011) 55.
74 Ibid. 57.

then the experience of speech splits, and perjury and lie irreducibly spring up. And it is in the attempt to check this split in the experience of language that law and religion are born, both of which seek to tie speech to things and to bind, by means of curses and anathemas, speaking subjects to the veritative power of their speech, to their 'oath' and to their declaration of faith[75]

The oath sworn by the ephebes before returning and immersing themselves in the city, in obeisance of the city's laws and customs, trapped them into having to make a choice: that is, they are true to their oaths and return to the city, or they are true to themselves, refuse to make the oath and are deprived of the city's protection and benefits; or they commit perjury, performing the oath while knowing full well that they will not wholly abide by the city's laws. Considering the extremely litigious character of the ancient Athenian city, the last option, perjury, was obviously frequently the easiest choice.

This 'split' in the experience of language, which gives law and religion cause to intervene into the language of its subjects, would have no more power than the subjects' power to lie if it was not bound in some way to something more tangible than the spoken word. This explains the call within the oath to the trees and vines, the gods and *horoi* to witness the speech act and to act as representation of the boons that will be withdrawn from whomsoever enacts perjury. For this reason, the deities and things called to witness are singularly Athenian; they are the things that the city and the agricultural life around the city offer to its citizen. To go through them all would be tiresome, so, briefly we have the gods that protect the city in case of war (Athena and Ares), goddess of the economy (Hestia), of fertility (Thallo), and then the cultivated seeds of wheat and barley, grapes, olives, and of course the *horoi*.[76] These could all be contrasted, and no doubt they were in the minds of the ephebes, to the fruits of the wilderness, to the chase of the hunt, the self-sufficiency required while living outside the city walls.[77] The ephebes, having spent their last two years on the border zones of the land, had experienced this life in the wild and so knew what they were about when making their final decision (presumably life in the wild was also subject to the

---

75 Ibid. 58.
76 Siewert (1977) 103.
77 Vidal-Naquet (1986) 117ff.

threat of being killed by these adrenaline-charged young men roaming around the countryside like wild beasts). In the oath the ephebes were presented with nothing short of an ultimatum: society, law, religion, marriage, stable gender roles, cultivated crops and animals and wine or nothing.[78]

The split is in the core of what it means to be human, our own division (from 'organic' nature) that reduplicates itself in the world around us. It is the division falling to the hand of fate that constitutes who we are. As Hegel states, this 'formative education, regarded from the side of the individual, consists in his acquiring what thus lies at hand, devouring his inorganic nature, and taking possession of it for himself.'[79] The question (*horos*) that is devoured in the beginning is thus the human separation from (organic) nature, the necessary division before we take the letter as our own and begin to read and write the law. The ephebes accept their institutionalisation whether or not their oath is spoken in truth or lie, and re-enter the city as men willing to uphold the law, regardless, again of whether they are themselves lawful. In this way the myth of the identification between the actual bounded city, its citizens and its law is maintained in form if not in fact.

The *horos* is as solid as stone, and yet the oath that gives it substance in the creed of the city relies upon an unsubstantiated belief in civic law and myth. Was it a legal bond or religious bond, written (*legere*) on the land and then rewritten (*relegere*) in the human willing to abide by the mythically condoned and supported laws of the city? Does the mythic constitution and maintenance of law require something like a plinth, something solid to mark its advent into the human imaginary? Can such a simple structure bear the burden of belief? What happens when these imaginary systems collapse and the stone ceases to need to hold them up? This is what the *horos* is today, for us. It is just a stone, though it might be placed in museums and therefore be invested at least with a little historical significance. The structures of power, from democracy and law to philosophy and economics have been re-erected and now the burden, with increasing ecological destruction and the inequality of wealth of legal rights, is all the greater. But where or what are the boundary-stones that these structures require to maintain belief in these

---

78 On sexual inversion and the ephebes, see Vidal-Naquet (1986) 115–117.
79 Hegel (1977) 16.

systems and keep us to our words? Perhaps the material has given us up for dead and has abstracted itself from our metaphysical debates and our supernatural presumptions.

The *horos* does not stand as a warning against transgressing our bonds, boundaries or limits; that is up to our interpretation, our ability to read the bare facts of the matter. But that does not mean that the stone does not mean something to us, or that it cannot or should not. Just as an area the size of a football field ploughed flat in the once luscious Amazon does not need to mean hubris or the insane, ecocidal drive toward destruction. Of course, it can mean that, and perhaps as the earth burns and laws are continually refined to protect the pyromaniacs who fuel the fires, brute matter will sing out all the louder, making itself heard to those willing or forced to listen.

In the biblical text we saw the necessity of an additional prohibition (writing about writing) not to pass over the boundary for harm. It is no mark of hostility that would hinder correspondence with the other side. On the contrary, it is the *horos* that proscribes the steadfastness of such distinctions as self and other by always posing (as) problems of definition or difference. Law, on the other hand draws up the outlines of possession, putting the boundary out of question (*aporia*), in antithesis to the imposition of the *horos*. Law proposes a material barrier, enforcing the signature or title deed of proprietorship by means of which 'our fathers' asserted their right to the land, cutting themselves off from relations with the other side. Law prescribes relations before the problem of relations has been posed, limiting the possibility of confronting the boundary as the very site that would raise the problem of such relations. The letter of the law capitalises upon the *horos* and continues to do so.

And while the occupying force is bound to extend its boundaries, the displaced population is likewise bound to resist, and the first objects that come to hand will be none other than stones. The throwing of stones is the best means, as Blanqui noted, at the disposal of the insurgency, not because they are effective weapons (against armed forces this is obviously not the case), but because by throwing stones the resistance throws the symbol of what has been perjured, the bond to the oath permitting the sacrament of possession and the appropriation of land, in the face of the occupier. These stones mark the very bond that has been transgressed by the occupier every time they expand their boundaries into other territories. The bond itself is the subject of these catapults, a letter of dissent or a reminder of the necessary 'other' in every community, everywhere a technical, an actual barrier has been claimed to stand in place of a relation, whether as law, right or simple force. It is significant that it is the stone that falls into the hands of the dispossessed, right at the point when possession is at issue and a relation, of enmity or friendship, is displaced by an inequality in material force. War is only achieved when the sides have equal arms at their disposal. The stone-throw however, is directed against the unequal distribution of force. The stone only appears during people's uprisings, local insurgency and revolt while the possibility of unification is retained, the lines of battle are not yet drawn up. The point of difference in war is, unfortunately, usually an economic one; whoever has access to more advanced artillery is most likely to win.

The first law, the prohibition to move the stone that is *horos*, is swiftly followed by permission to the free use of the rest. This provides the possibility to engage in production and expansion, mining and building and limitless destruction in order to facilitate these processes. This is the condition without which colonialism and imperialism could not resolve into capital, globalisation and the indomitable march of technological expansion and development. The basis of today's institutions, both physical and nonphysical, is the matter, the bare matter upon, or with which they are built, from basalt and steel to rare earths.

But that is not to say that there are no limits. There are. The laws of nature, and the Law as such are dependent upon the notion that there is a limit (autonomous or heteronomous) out there. But what if the only limit is none other than the *horos*, that verbal and material term that raises the question of the law, that works alongside us as we talk about such limits and determinations? That is, it is a limit as much out there as in us. And the transgression of this limit is as dangerous in here as it is out there. Is the core, the very being of the human suffering because of the transgression of limits in the world, of ecological and environmental boundaries upon which human life is dependent?

In lithography the stone brings two antithetical substances into a kind of relation. It is important to note that it does not do so as a mediator, despite its apparent position in the middle. It does not effect a compromise or a change in relations between the antagonistic water and oil. In fact, it does not do anything at all. Perhaps it is simply empathetic. And yet because of a certain affinity (not an elective affinity) when oil and water in their mutual reactions are absorbed by stone and repelled by one another, from this alchemical dance of love and hate, the outline of shape is brought into distinction. And the letter is formed. The letter in this case is simultaneously the material proof of repulsion and affinity, alienation and friendship, distance and proximity. If it resembles any word upon the printed page, taking its place within the spaces left blank between letters and punctuations, the letter is brought to its limit in *horos*.

Fig. 4. [Δ]ΕΥΡΕ ΠΕΔΙΕΟΝ ΤΡΙΤΤΥΣ ΤΕΛΕΥΤΑΙ ΘΡΙΑΣΙΟΝ ΔΕ ΑΡΧΕΤΑΙ ΤΡΙΤΤΥΣ 'Here ends the trittys Pedieis, while the trittys Thria begins' IG I³ 1128. Photograph by T. Potter, 2021. Rights belong to the Epigraphic Museum, Athens © Hellenic Ministry of Culture and Sports/Hellenic Organization of Cultural Resources Development (H.O.C.R.E.D.).

4. Terminological Horizons

ὁ ὅρος —in Logic, *term* of a proposition (whether subject or predicate) [...] *definition*; defined as ἡ τοῦ ἰδίου ἀπόδοσις [...] in pl., title of pseudo-Platonic work [...] *premiss* of a syllogism [...] Math., *term* of a ratio or proportion [...] pl., *terms, conditions*.[1]

Neologisms are the bread and butter of lexicographers, providing novelty in an otherwise backward-looking field of study. One of the main differences between a lexicographer and a philosopher, who are both engaged in etymological studies about the relations between words and things and words and other words, is that the philosopher is in the habit of coming up with new terms. These may be new terms for new concepts or new terms for old concepts or new terms for concepts yet to be conceptualised or concepts resisting conceptualisation. The lexicographer, on the other hand, wields the axe over these terms, choosing which ones will be admitted into the annals of eternity by attributing them with an entry and deciding which ones will fade out of usage and be forgotten until another philosopher attempts a resuscitation of old terms.

Is the difference between a 'term' and a 'word' how deeply it is embedded in a language? A term still has the packaging, the slick of newness from the shop, while a word is ingrained within the language that it shapes and is shaped by. According to current dictionary entries, the difference between a term and a word is that the former is supposed to represent a concept in a particular field of study while a word is an element of language marked by a space to either side. In Ancient Greek philosophy the term *horos* stood in for both of these words, as well as the word for 'concept,' and in the ancient texts there are no spaces between words.

---

1 LS: 1255–1256.

Aristotle states that whoever is engaged in defining things must not coin new terms (οὐ ποιήσει ὁ ὁριζόμενος) because it would lead to a failure to be understood, for words are common, and it is necessary that they apply to something else as well.[2] To coin new terms on the one hand, and to embrace undiscovered forms on the other, oddly enough, presents the same picture. In bringing up the word '*horos*' from its hiding place within the texts of ancient philosophy or buried in archaeological remains, I am not coining a new term nor suggesting a new philosophical concept to add to an already prohibitively enormous repertoire. And yet if this is, as I suggest, a rule common to the positive unconscious of ancient thought and remaining with us as the material basis for our institutions today, there is no doubt that this word is here being transformed into a conceptual term, burdened with a plethora of meanings, both historical and cultural. In its original setting, however, the *horos* was certainly not a concept, nor a conceptual tool, though it was a term that could assist conceptualisation if that was necessary.

Terminology, unlike other *-logies* (biology, archaeology, philology, for example) is not a full science; it is not even in the humanities, not properly anyway, at least not yet. It is the use of technical terms within specific fields of study, such that every field has its own special system of nomenclature, and this is called its terminology. Every university course on the different fields of study ought to begin with the distribution of a dictionary of such terms; it would save students a lot of time. Of course, the different fields of study did not always have different terminologies. Ancient Greek philosophy is an excellent example of a common terminology used to address many fields of knowledge, though the fields were not distinct then, at least not before Aristotle's commentators came along and classified knowledge into separate books: *The Physics, The Metaphysics, The Ethics, Economics, Poetics, Politics,* and so forth.

As a science, the study of 'terminology' is considered to be a subsection or subcategory of linguistics where it finds its purpose in conformism, the attempt to get people to mean the same thing when they use the same term. 'Terminography,' on the other hand, finds its job description as the specialised field looking at the terms of specialised fields and then telling the lexicographer about it, who may or may not include it in the lexicon. A condemnation of an entire science out of

---

2   Ar.*Met*.1040a6–15.

hand is definitely imprudent; however, the one thing terminology fails to examine is the term itself. Terminology as a science is chiefly seen where it fails to express a common meaning: in biology seminars, in the stock exchange and in those illiterate manuals for electronic devices. But the truth is that the present use of terminology obscures its distinguished and notorious history.

Terminus was the Roman god of boundaries, and his worship was enshrined within the temple of Jupiter Optimus Maximus on the Capitoline Hill, the centre of ancient Roman religion, and an entire festival took its name from the god, the 'Terminalia.' If this is not glorification enough, turn to Aristotle, whose investigations, from the *Physics* through the *Metaphysics* (investigations into pretty much everything that is and is not), invariably feature as a guiding thread not only the question of the 'term,' *horos*, but an entire examination into the activity of the term, or, as he terms it *horismos*, the project of definition.

The *horos* is situated where definitions or determinations overlap, where words that are always composite (whether we place them in signifying chains or in dictionaries) cannot help but encroach upon another word's territory. Aristotle calls this particular force that unites word and being the '*chōriston*,' the 'divider.' However, if he listened to his own advice—not to coin new terms—he would perhaps have admitted that the same activity takes place in the *horos*. The *horos* simultaneously divides and unites, providing the (common) term and essential being of synonymity, where the crossover or overlap occurs between a word's description (*logos*) as well as marking out its (substantial) difference from other words.

The translation of the Greek terms in Aristotle is something that I am never quite satisfied by, and therefore the translations used in the subsequent chapter unfortunately require something of a preface. The translation of Aristotle has become something of a terminological debate, in both senses. To begin with, many terms were mistranslated long ago, chiefly in being filtered through mediaeval Christianity and the dominance of the Latin language.[3] Latin and Christian interpretations are largely responsible for slightly warped translations, such as 'substance' for *ousia*, which purposefully remove agency from anything other than

---

3   See Christophe Erismann, 'Aristotele Latinus: The Reception of Aristotle in the Latin World' in Falcon (2016) 439ff.

a single divine creator. The problem is, however, that these translations have for the most part been canonised, and to alter them risks alienating, or at least confusing, readers. That said, I cannot help but agree with Owens's explication of the absurdity of translating *ousia* as 'substance.'[4] However, his assumption that 'words and concepts merely signify as best they can the truth contained in things,' should not go unchallenged, specifically given the significance that this study places upon the precedence of the sign or writing.[5] Also, his argument that Aristotle's phrase *to ti en einai* is not to be understood as the articular infinitive but a novel coinage in which the *einai* is an infinitive of purpose ('in order to be') seems to me an unnecessary complication.

The frustrating fact is that it is not complicated in the original. The past tense of the third singular verb 'to be' is, according to Owens, supposed to ascribe timelessness to the verb. This would mean that the 'is' is not essentially present, but was and presumably, from the so-called infinitive of purpose, will continue to be. Owens translates *to ti en* as 'what-IS-being,' in his translation of Aristotle's *Metaphysics*, Sachs modifies this to 'what it is for it to be.' Basically, I am convinced by Sachs's argument for the translation of *ousia* as 'thinghood,' regardless of whether the word is derived from the feminine participle or the admittedly peculiar formation of an abstract noun from the neuter noun *on*, as he suggests in his introduction.[6] However, I have used neither of these translations, instead using a phrase as immediately close to the original as possible and then always including the Greek or a transliteration of the Greek in parentheses. I do not see any other way around these problems, other than to keep close contact with the original language.

In the following I therefore depart from the English tradition of translating *ousia* as 'substance.' In an effort to remain as close to the Greek language as possible, and in order to hold onto the material of language, that is not just the 'sense' or the feeling of a word but its essential nature, the translation used will always be accompanied by a transliteration of the Greek, especially where the wordplay is significant. So, because this chapter is devoted to the concept of definition, the following translations will be observed: *ousia* is translated as 'essence' or 'being,' given that it is

---

4   Owens (1978) 138–152; 180.
5   Ibid. 138.
6   Sachs (1999) xxxvii.

the feminine abstract participle of the verb 'to be'; essence is also derived from the Latin participle for the verb to be *'esse.'* *Hypostasis* is translated as 'substance,' for the simple reason that both words are composed of the same elements in their respective languages: In Greek, the prefix *hypo-* 'under' and *stasis* from the verb 'to stand, support'; in Latin, the prefix *sub-* 'under' and *stance* from the verb 'to stand, support.' I believe the similarity is sufficient to support the translation. I recognise that these translations are contrary to traditional usage. But the fact that a convention is established, does not mean that we have to keep doing it. And it has to be said that traditional translations of Aristotle do not make it any easier for someone without a knowledge of Greek to understand what on earth is being said, so I do not believe there is too much to lose. As the following will make clear, definition and determination, that is, what words mean, and how they are explained, are not only sidelines to understanding philosophy; they are, or at least they were for Aristotle, the core of any philosophical investigation.

As to the word 'substance,' given this study's focus upon mattering and meaning it would appear careless not to use the word with an appropriate sense of gravity. According to Owens, 'substance' fails to express the direct relation with Being denoted by *ousia* (οὐσία).[7] The translation 'substance' has filtered down through a history of philosophy that rendered ideas quite foreign to Aristotle's original setting. Substance denotes changeable things, the things that 'stand under' where solidity and extension seem to adhere to the definition; for example, Augustine struggles to attribute *substantia* to God. In this sense, substance is not being used as what is essential to all beings. But *ousia* describes the primary instance of being; for Aristotle that essentially means what something is before it is denoted by a word. Does this mean that *ousia* is a thought experiment? The word 'essence' does seem to go in the opposite direction to 'substance,' the one denoting the body of a thing, the other the soul, or at least something nonexistent. *Ousia* is not responsible for such binaries and they are not represented at all in the Greek.

In a sense the closest rendering of the word *ousia* might be 'object,' but only as the word is used by Harman to mean the being of anything, from a crystal to a war. At least here we can see how something's *ousia* does not need to relate to either a tangible or a conceptual being,

---

7   Owens (1978) 144.

though that does not mean that it does not denote the matter of a thing. Harman suggests that we cannot 'paraphrase an object, as if it were truly equivalent to a sum total of qualities or effects and nothing more.'[8] It cannot be reduced to our knowledge of it, as either a material object or an active one. According to Aristotle, all things depend upon *ousia*, but *ousia* is not universal to all things or the same in all things; something's *ousia* is peculiar to the thing itself and belongs to nothing else.[9] Its 'beingness' or its 'thinghood' is always primary.

A Question of Definition

To study the terms a science employs is not just to question the given definitions but to question the way a science expresses itself, its language, and hence, the science as such, its ends or aims. The actual practice of terminology is therefore where ethics meets logic, at the intersection between purpose and form in which words are used. Aristotle states that the 'essence' of a thing must be sought and defined (ζητεῖν καὶ ὁρίζεσθαι) 'not without matter' (μὴ ἄνευ τῆς ὕλης).[10] Are words twofold? Can a word be broken down to the matter of the word (sign), and the matter of what the word means (signifier and signified)? Is this what Aristotle means? Definition is one of the main tasks of Aristotelian philosophy because it is the first question asked, the question of a thing's essence (ἔστι δ' ὅρος μὲν λόγος ὁ τὸ τί ἦν εἶναι σημαίνων), 'horos is a word that means what a thing is.'[11] But this does not mean that philosophy has exclusively to do with matter, because the definition of a thing is also a word (ἐπειδὴ πᾶς ὁρισμὸς λόγος τίς ἐστιν).

Therefore, Aristotle finds his project located exactly in the margins between words and things, where 'definitions pose questions of similarity and difference' (καὶ γὰρ περὶ τοὺς ὁρισμούς, πότερον ταὐτὸν ἢ ἕτερον). 'So' Aristotle concludes, 'let us simply call everything definitory (*horika*) that follows this method of defining (*horismous*) things' (τὰ ὑπὸ τὴν αὐτὴν ὄντα μέθοδον τοῖς ὁρισμοῖς).[12] In this section from the *Topics*, the *horos* appears in various guises (adjectival, nominal, verbal),

---

8   Harman (2018) 257.
9   Ar. *Met*.1038b10.
10 Ar.*Met*.1026a1–5.
11 Ar.*Top*.101b39.
12 Ibid.

and it is singly important for coming to an understanding of how to deal with words and the problem of meaning. Take, for example, the following statement from the *Metaphysics*.

ἀλλὰ μὴν δοκεῖ γε πᾶσι καὶ ἐλέχθη πάλαι ἢ μόνον οὐσίας εἶναι ὅρον ἢ μάλιστα· νῦν δ' οὐδὲ ταύτης. οὐδενὸς ἄρ' ἔσται ὁρισμός· ἢ τρόπον μέν τινα ἔσται τρόπον δέ τινα οὔ.[13]

> But it seems to all, and was said a while ago, that being [*ousia*] is the only or main definition [*horos*]; but now it seems not even this is the so. Then there can be no definition of anything; or in a sense there can, and in a sense cannot.

It could also be said that Socrates was as focused upon definition as Aristotle, as he was frequently posed by Plato asking questions about the meaning of words, or abstract concepts (the good, beautiful, justice and so forth). Perhaps where Aristotle's project of definition differs from Socratic inquiry is the focus Aristotle places upon the matter of a thing, or rather, the coincidence between matter and word. It is not surprising then, to note the different usage of the word *horos* between Plato and Aristotle. Where in Plato the *horos* is firmly localised as the boundary-stone founded to maintain the law of a place (*topos*), for Aristotle the *horos* is the term that assists in his treatises on predication (*topika*) to talk about words as distinct from nouns or names (*onoma*) or logical phrases or arguments (*logos*). In Plato, it is the verbal form (*horizein*) that is pretty much exclusively used, while the noun *horos* is not identified with anything but the material (at least after avid searching I have not been able to find it to refer to anything other than actual boundary-stones in the land as in the *Laws*). In contrast, in Aristotle, *horos* is used frequently and in different contexts, and clearly means a 'term' or a 'definition.'

Here we must make ourselves aware of a difference in terms that is not apparent in translation between *horos* (ὅρος) and *horismos* (ὁρισμός). *Horismos* is the noun formed from the aorist stem of the verb *horizō*, 'to bound, mark out, define or determine, lay boundary-stones,' etcetera. To raise the spectre of Heidegger we might say that the latter refers to the project of determination. We can see the difference between these two terms in a significant introductory definition of the definition (*horos*) in Aristotle's *Topics*.

---

13   Ar.*Met*.1039a20.

ἔστι δ' ὅρος μὲν λόγος ὁ τὸ τί ἦν εἶναι σημαίνων. ἀποδίδοται δὲ ἢ λόγος ἀντ' ὀνόματος ἢ λόγος ἀντὶ λόγου· δυνατὸν γὰρ καὶ τῶν ὑπὸ λόγου τινὰ σημαινομένων ὁρίσασθαι. ὅσοι δ' ὁπωσοῦν ὀνόματι τὴν ἀπόδοσιν ποιοῦνται, δῆλον ὡς οὐκ ἀποδιδόασιν οὗτοι τὸν τοῦ πράγματος ὁρισμόν, ἐπειδὴ πᾶς ὁρισμὸς λόγος τίς ἐστιν. ὁρικὸν μέντοι καὶ τὸ τοιοῦτον θετέον, οἷον ὅτι καλόν ἐστι τὸ πρέπον. ὁμοίως δὲ καὶ τὸ πότερον ταὐτὸν αἴσθησις καὶ ἐπιστήμη ἢ ἕτερον· καὶ γὰρ περὶ τοὺς ὁρισμούς, πότερον ταὐτὸν ἢ ἕτερον, ἡ πλείστη γίνεται διατριβή. ἁπλῶς δὲ ὁρικὰ πάντα λεγέσθω τὰ ὑπὸ τὴν αὐτὴν ὄντα μέθοδον τοῖς ὁρισμοῖς. ὅτι δὲ πάντα τὰ νῦν ῥηθέντα τοιαῦτ' ἀστί, δῆλον ἐξ αὐτῶν.[14]

A 'definition' [*horos*] is a phrase signifying a thing's essence. It is rendered in the form either of a phrase [*logos*] in lieu of a word [*onoma*], or of a phrase in lieu of another phrase; for it is sometimes possible to define the meaning of a phrase as well. People whose rendering consists of a word only, try as they may, clearly do not render the definition [*horismos*] of the thing in question, because a definition is always a phrase of a certain kind [*logos tis*]. One may, however, use the word 'definitory' [*horiko*] also of a remark such as 'the 'becoming' is 'beautiful,' and likewise also of the question, 'are sensation and knowledge the same or different?,' for argument about definitions is mostly concerned with questions of sameness and difference. We may simply call 'definitory' everything that follows the same method as definitions; and that all the above-mentioned examples are such is clear by example.

What Aristotle is undertaking here is to provide the definition of definition, the boundary of the boundary, the limit of the limit. Is there any way to evade the inevitability of infinite regress?

Let us look closely at this definition. The first thing to note is that the word *horos* is placed in the foremost position and fails to reappear again. Henceforth, what Aristotle has to do with is not the noun *horos* but *horismos*, or the adjective (*horiko*) or different forms of the verb *horizō*. After positing *horos* as the signifying or indicative *logos* (to which we will return), Aristotle states that it pays its dues or is handed over and given away (*apodidotai*) as *either* a *logos* in place or instead of a name (noun or term) *or* a *logos* instead of a *logos*. Does this mean that the term of definition is given as a case of substitution, standing in for other descriptions where the determined place (*horikon theteon*) is only given in terms of a suspension of immediate meaning?

---

14 Ar.*Top.*101b39.

According to Agamben, in mediaeval philosophy a 'term' was 'a word that did not signify itself (*suppositio materialis*) but instead stood for the thing it signified, referring to something (*terminus supponit pro re, supposito personalis*).'[15] Is this what the *horos* is doing here? Does that mean that definition (*horos*) mediates signification, while it is itself an insignificant mediation of thought put into language? In a sense it is only qua *logos* as significant (*sēmainōn*) that *horos* can be defined. In defining a term an entire construct of language is required because otherwise, to simply place another word to explain the first word would not be a definition but mere metonymy. And within this construct, definition depends upon a relation between words that is based upon similarity and difference.

> δυνάμενοι γὰρ ὅτι ταὐτὸν καὶ ὅτι ἕτερον διαλέγεσθαι, τῷ αὐτῷ τρόπῳ καὶ πρὸς τοὺς ὁρισμοὺς ἐπιχειρεῖν εὐπορήσομεν· δείξαντες γὰρ ὅτι οὐ ταὐτὸν ἐστιν ἀνῃρηκότες ἐσόμεθα τὸν ὁρισμόν. οὐ μὴν ἀντιστρέφει γε τὸ νῦν ῥηθέν· οὐ γὰρ ἱκανὸν πρὸς τὸ κατασκευάσαι τὸν ὁρισμὸν τὸ δεῖξαι ταὐτὸν ὄν.[16]
>
> For if we are able to argue that two things are the same or are different, in the same way we shall be able [*euporēsamen*] to undertake an argument about the definitions [*orismous*]: for when we have shown that they are not the same thing we shall have demolished the definition.

The definition is a complex of words embedded within and dependent upon the already fully structured existence of a language. What then can be said to be 'logical' about the *horismos* is the fact that it follows a method that is in essence the same as its name, coming about in terms of same or other (*tauton/heteron*), of what it is and what it is not but always in the same way. Definitions that do not depend on metonymy alone require the proximity of other words whose significations are similar and different. So, what is in fact going on here is that definition (*horismos*) is being defined as a grammatical complex within a language, and a definition of this type is ascribed to *horos*. What is essential to philosophy in this case would be the *horismos*, which is in a way a *logos* (*logos tis*), that helps us to understand the meaning of words and their relations with other words within a language that generates meaning, while the meaning of *horos* is deferred in the essence of the thing.

---

15 Agamben (1999) 207.
16 Ar.*Top*.101b39;139a24.

ὥστε τὸ τί ἦν εἶναί ἐστιν ὅσων ὁ λόγος ἐστὶν ὁρισμός. ὁρισμὸς δ᾽ ἐστὶν οὐκ ἂν ὄνομα λόγῳ ταὐτὸ σημαίνῃ (πάντες γὰρ ἂν εἶεν οἱ λόγοι ὅροι: ἔσται γὰρ ὄνομα ὁτῳοῦν λόγῳ, ὥστε καὶ ἡ Ἰλιὰς ὁρισμὸς ἔσται) ἀλλ᾽ ἐὰν πρώτου τινὸς ᾖ: τοιαῦτα δ᾽ ἐστὶν ὅσα λέγεται μὴ τῷ ἄλλο κατ᾽ ἄλλου λέγεσθαι.[17]

> So what it is to be is such that the explanation [*logos*] is a definition [*horismos*]. It is not definition if the name [*onoma*] for the explanation signifies the same thing (for then all explanations [*logoi*] would be definitions [*horoi*]; for a name could be attributed to an explanation, so that even 'the Iliad' could be a definition), but only if it is something primary. These should not be said the one in place of the other.

The definition is not the name but something essential about the being of what is said. Therefore, substituting another name that has a similar meaning or explanation (*logos*) is not sufficient to provide a definition. According to Aristotle, these words should not be used interchangeably: explanation and homonymy are not the same thing.

Does that mean that *horos* is the boundary between every word, not as its definition but as the essential difference between words? Is it the meaningful boundary between same and other upon which the subsequent project of definition (*horismos*) works to bring difference and similarity together?

In the *Topics*, the 'signifying word,' *logos sēmainōn*, does not merely point to a *sign* but a *method*, reverting immediately from the simple *horos* to the *horismos*; as if the *horos* receded into its Aristotelian 'definition' as a *project* of definition, of the signifying word, or the alterity of creating meaning in process. Reading Hegel, Derrida suggests that it is semiopoetics that draws opposites together in more than a point of confrontation, in a resolution. This is something like, in Derrida's words, 'the resolution of the sign in the horizon of the non-sign.' For semiopoetics

> is a *Mittelpunkt*: both a central point on which all the rays of opposites converge, a middle point, a middle in the sense of element, of *milieu*, and also the medium point, the site where opposites pass one into the other.[18]

For Hegel this *Mittelpunkt* of sign-making is the 'productive imagination,' where what is one's own (das *Eigene*) and what is found along the way

---

17   Ar.*Met*.1030a5.
18   Derrida (1982) 80.

(*Gefundensein*), the universal and Being, become one.[19] But we must not forget through all this that the *horos* is still localised and material and is not merely a sign. So, what if this site (*topos*) of definition can only maintain its path (*meth-odos*) and keep producing more definitions by virtue of already proposing a limit that is also a question of productivity as such?

Aristotle gives us a definition where signifying or meaning cannot emerge from anything but the problem, or more precisely the raising of the question of what was there before, what being was. He said that *horos* is a phrase that means 'what it is to be' *to ti ēn einai* (ἔστι δ' ὅρος μὲν λόγος ὁ τὸ τί εἶναι σημαίνων). It is not quite what 'it is', but rather what 'it was' (ἦν), third-person singular imperfect. Though it could also be from the verb 'to say' (φημί), and in this case maybe it was 'what it said it was,' though this is unlikely. The point is that it is not that clear that it is what we thought it was, and in fact it might have been something else altogether. As Aristotle said before, when it comes to definitions, mostly we rub up against the different and the same (διατριβή).

The *horos* thus becomes a limit, a *terminus ad quem*, which proposes the question of what essence meant before it was localised in the *horos*. And indeed, what *was* being before it could be defined in language, before it could be put into question by the *logos*? Any search for essential beginnings, for principles (*archai*) and for a sure foundation, presumes exactly that something was (τι ἦν) before language and before the question of being. In the tradition of Heidegger, we could say that something began as revealed, only to be concealed and come into question later. However, what is significant about the *horos* is that, beginning only in division, it never fully began, not as a whole *archē*. Its principal meaning is always divided. It was nothing but the problem, as such and in itself, of the definition of essence (*einai*, 'to be'; *ousia*, 'being') at the same time as indicating the essence of the question itself. It draws up that first line of division that is necessary for us to ask the question of definition, to distinguish between word and essence (the 'being' of a thing, *esse* is the Latin form of the verb to be, *einai*). But in doing so, *horos* also resists its own definition because its essence is that point of difference between words, and the similarity to the material, both word and stone.

---

19   Ibid.

Before the *logos* came along and started meaning something, did the *horos* mean nothing? That is to say, was the *horos* nothing but the matter of the sign, signifying nothing, meaningless? And is this what matter or substance is, that is, definition without further meaning—brute stone?

For this reason, nothing is discovered by asking, 'what does *horos* signify?,' 'what does *horos* mean?' because, as Derrida explains about the question of the signification of signification, 'the very question would have brought us to the external border of its closure.'[20] And then there we are back on the boundary, immersed in rock assuming it does not matter at all. But of course the border cannot help but matter, even if that is all it does. The question itself, the 'what means,' 'what is' or even the why of metaphysics is already taking place within the confines, on the basis, that is, on account of a limit that proposes the meaningfulness of definition: *horos*. *Horos* refuses the definitive presence of any *archē*, any original, full presence since it gives definition only to the boundary as taking place as the split, between *ousia* and *logos*, that is however based upon the substance (*hypostasis*, that is in this case also very much stone), the matter that supports meaning, that must already be there in the raising of the question of definition.

In the Pseudo-Platonic work titled *Definitions* (Ὅροι) the *horos*, the definition, is thus defined:

Ὅρος λόγος ἐκ διαφορᾶς καὶ γένους συγκείμενος.

Horos is a *logos* comprised of difference and genus.[21]

It is both composed of difference and the matter itself that signifies how words differ from one another. The meaning of the word *horos*, then, is the question of definition as such. It questions its own signification, thus throwing into question its very identification with itself. And, of course, this was the problem from the very beginning, when we realised that we cannot tell the difference between a stone and a *horos* unless we have already identified it as such, and then the difference exists in *us* first and foremost, in *our division* between organic and inorganic nature. And it was also the problem raised by the untranslatability of the *horos*, not because it does not mean 'boundary, limit, letters, stone, landmark,

---

20 Derrida (1982) 81.
21 Pl.*Def*.414d10 in Plato (1972).

term, definition' and so forth, but because it means the contiguity, and existential contingence, of the different and similar. Its meaning, or signifying (something else, itself) remains on the boundary as what is common to all these terms, and they are definable in reference to what they are not, as much as to what they are. As definition it is the very difference that they have in common, binding them and making them distinct. The point is that it does not cease to be one while it is the other. As Hegel states, 'What is true of substances is also true of differences; for as synonyms they have both name and definition in common.'[22]

Aristotle's *Topics* raises the problem of the definition of particulars, while in the *Metaphysics* it is a question of essence (*ousia*) in *logos*, it is also a problem of substance; as anyone would realise should an example of the *horos* come hurtling through the air to land with a thud upon his head.

According to the Aristotelian definition, *horos* is a word whose meaning can be explicated by using a combination of other words, thus providing a similar meaning through difference. All words, when it comes to defining them, require us to indicate or point towards other words, and it is important to note that in this respect *horos* is just like any other word. It is just that what becomes apparent in the definition of *horos* is how the structure of language itself is determined by and dependent on this idea of *horos* as always indicating separation as well as contiguity, as if there is something alien within itself, as if it houses the collusion between the same and the different within its own definition. Is this because *horos* signifies the origin of writing, whether it is the stone that is read as the boundary-stone or the inscription or the definition that provides us with the essence of a thing? 'The sign,' states Hegel, 'is some immediate intuition, representing a totally different import from what naturally belongs to it; it is the *pyramid* into which a foreign soul has been conveyed, and where it is conserved.'[23] The sign, and this is its traditional position, comes in between the *logos* and the word, between the word and its definition. And yet, in the case of the *horos* the other words are only other words, that is, they can be defined as such because they must always be preceded by the split inherent to *horos*, hence the regressive definition of definition.

---

22 Hegel (1894) 217
23 Hegel (1971) 213. Cf. Derrida (1982) 83.

The *horos* as sign (inscription or raw stone) is the indication of the divisive force, the material intervention between *horos* and its definition, i.e. *horos*. It is not what *horos* signifies that is different or other; what it signifies is *horos*. *Horos* signifies what is other than *horos*, or to put it otherwise, a determined sign, a determinate or definite meaning is other than *horos*. *Horos*, 'definition,' is identical to itself only by signifying what it is not, that is the indefinite and the indeterminate which always falls to either side, of which it, *horos*, is the boundary.

The definition never seems to go anywhere without regress, without doubling back on our words. The *horos* interminably raises questions about meaning and essence, word and substance, by placing itself in an identical/non-identical relation with meaning, the sign, the letter and inscription, the stone as such. It is the materialisation of the problem, marking the *aporia* at the heart of the structure of language, or the passage without passage to anywhere, only to continue through and on towards further problems. *Horos*, as Aristotle states, is a matter of substitution, of giving a word in place of a name (*logos ant' onomatos*), or another word (or phrase) in place of a word (*logos anti logon*). That is, definition is necessarily a matter of substitution, as if nothing less than matter itself can step in to mediate the relation between words and their latent substitutability. *Horos* is peculiar as a name for the operation of replacing or substituting the name or word with something that has the potential of being both same and different. As such, it is the title that puts the authority of *logos*, the authenticity of the name into question every time and in this case the problem is that of all those indeterminate 'places' of logic (*ta topika*).

The *horos* demands that whatever is on either side of the sign, meets and joins in a relation of both same and other with the other side. Here the sign could be conceived as something like the Sausurrian bar, separating and joining at once and bringing into distinction what is meant and what is said, like a primeval curse that condemned our thoughts and our speech to be forever out of joint and our words always replacable. This juncture may seem accidental to language, as if the potential exists of actually saying what we meant if only we could find the right words, while in the meantime thought overflows into a mere trickle of language. Consequently we have a sense of alienation from our speech and what we mean or want to say, as if there is a disjuncture between language and meaning, writing and reading. This (dis)juncture is *horos*, bringing into definition the matter with and of language. Needless to say, language contained the seed of its discontent long before any more arboreal structures were attributed it. *Horos* was there from the beginning, a stone that was read by us, whether or not it was written, the line of definition between the human and the 'natural,' as such its meaning was already assured. But where did this faculty for meaning already invested in the stone come from? In terms of any significant meaning attributed to the stone, the distinction rests with us.

The Parenthetical *Horos*

To what degree does the *horos* in Aristotle's work retain the substantial meaning of being 'stone' even while it performs the function of meaning 'definition' or 'determination'? Finley believed that the context of the stone, the actual archaeological finding, changed the word's meaning so that every use of the *horos* became locally semantically specific. For example, the *horos* as boundary of temple lands was distinct from the *horos* that showed fiscal encumbrance, despite both being stones inscribed with the same word and with potentially no other noticeable differences.

> Whenever a Greek referred to a stone of either type, he said simply *horos*, without any qualifying adjective (or he used the related word *horizō*), because there could be no confusion between the two in context, just as there was no confusion between the *horos* as "boundary" and *horos* as "boundary stone."[24]

The *horos* might have had different meanings, but these were not homonyms. All the different meanings coalesce within the same semantic field, or perhaps more appropriately, on the boundary of the same semantic field. Its reticence to be pinned down or determined by a single meaning derives from the 'essence,' the *ti esti*, of the word itself. This could be why its matter is important, why the materiality of the *horos* always remains with it: the stone has to be there, keeping things, and us, grounded during the attempts at definition and determination

---

24 Finley (1952) 5.

of words and things. If *horos* is the convergence of sign, signifier and signified, word and meaning of 'term' or 'definition' as well as the letters inscribed, and without excepting the stone (whether inscribed or not), it cannot help but keep referring to itself as both identification and difference between word and thing, and between definition and essence. When we try to define it, we keep coming upon the same problem: we cannot help but put the term to use before we actually resolve upon its meaning or meanings.

Finley bewails the reduction of the diverse functions of the *horos* in translation, though acknowledging the difficulty of finding adequate substitutes. He assumes that lurking somewhere behind the *horos* there is a multiplicity of meanings that not only can but must be separated out in order to be both understood and used. And yet, this failure to adequately distinguish in translation the differences of meaning and use that adhere to the *horos* does of course reinforce the fact that in Greek these are different non-divisible aspects of the one term. That it remains one word means that if it engenders any effect upon us, it should certainly be that of pure perplexity, arriving as we do at the limit of meaningful definition or determination. And what does the *horos* signify if not the problem of arriving at the limit of determination or definition?

Perhaps the very difference that is underscored by its Latinate translations (definition, determination) is inherent to the *horos*—not yet arrived at philosophy's finale, nor quite deified, as if it represents the tendency to abstract (*de-*) from ontology to find its resolution in the question of either being or *logos*, but struggles to bring them together. The Romans resolved the problem by deifying the boundary (between being and language) as the god Terminus. Not only has Terminus lost his divinity in our eyes, but he has been reformed into the central station of our comings and goings, the electric opening to the possibility to further circuits, or the end point, pure and simple.

Assuming, then, that there's more than mere difference of spelling between these Latinate variations of the *horos*, could these undertakings lead us somewhere other than back to the *horos*? To somewhere else, an alibi of sorts, where the intention would presumably be to breach the *horos* or to define it, to understand the limit or to transcend it? The work of *horos* is definition. But why 'work'? Is the desire to define words what motivates philosophy, its determinative ontological impetus? Or is it, more accurately, its ontological impotence? As Hegel states in his preface,

> to judge a thing that has substance and solid worth is quite easy, to comprehend it is much harder, and to blend judgement and comprehension in a definitive description is the hardest thing of all.²⁵

How does whosoever it is go about defining this hardest thing? Is the 'hardest thing,' *das schwerste*, the matter with philosophy, the probably phallic preoccupation, and the *idée fixe* of determining philosophy itself? According to Hegel it is to be found only in philosophy's actualisation as science. The definition of the 'hardest thing of all' (already achieved by Hegel in his preface) is brought to fulfilment and actualised when the *philia* of philosophy is revoked by philosophy as a science. That is, when the coming night requires that we light the hard lamps of reason and no longer do it for the love of it, but because we know what it is. Is this a problem of desire or volition, as Hegel implies, 'freed from the material'?²⁶ Does philosophy find satisfaction in wisdom in the absence of love, and its *praxis* and *poiēsis*? And yet the determination to follow these desires or the desire to determine is aroused though never satisfied in philosophy, which takes place in the hours of leisure, in the space *between* production and reproduction. But must that mean that this space is infertile, insubstantial, and the work it engenders is abstract and lacks materiality? What is the difference between, on the one hand, occupation and love, and on the other their products, object and subject? What difference, in effect, is there between substance and *logos* other than their determinations, that is to say, definition itself?

Here in the earlier pages of Hegel's preface to the *Phenomenology of Spirit*, and nowhere else in the work, there is a brief encounter with the *horos*. Placed in the original text in the Roman alphabet, it is even capitalised in good Germanic form, as if Hegel could not help but retain the letter's material trace in the inscribed stone even when engaging with the most abstract or conceptual determination. The *horos*, shielded by parentheses from any reference to its lithic counterpart, is introduced as the object upon which the Romantics concentrate their contemptuous gaze.

---

25 Hegel (1977) 3. Cf. Hegel (2006) 5.
26 Hegel (1969) 13–14.

Dieses prophetische Reden meint gerade so recht im Mittelpunkt und der Tiefe zu bleiben, blickt verächtlich auf die Bestimmtheit (den Horos) und hält sich absichtlich von dem Begriffe und der Notwendigkeit entfernt, als von der Reflexion, die nur in der Endlichkeit hause.

Still less must this complacency which abjures Science claim that such rapturous haziness is superior to Science. This prophetic talk supposes that it is staying right in the centre and in the depths, looks disdainfully at determinateness (*Horos*), and deliberately holds aloof from Notion and Necessity as products of that reflection which is at home only in the finite.[27]

Ironically, if the romantics had gazed upon the *horos*, lying on its side, overgrown with chicory and chamomile in the shadow of the ravaged Parthenon I am sure they would have been thrilled. A textual confusion in regards to what remains of this ruin infiltrating the text of Hegel is worth noting. In the German text, the *horos* is parenthetical (*den Horos*). In the translation by Miller, the Greek word occurs capitalised in Latin script (*Horos*), while in the translation by Baille it is, oddly enough, transcribed back into the Greek (ὄρος).[28] In the German text of the Felix Meiner Verlag edition, it is given in Latin script with the German article. It would appear that the *horos* is already influencing the translation not of meaning but of the letters themselves, with the ambiguity of transliteration. What is the original: those Greek letters read by Hegel in the text of Aristotle and adopted by Baille but which leave out the capitalised 'H' that was read upon the stone? Or is it the term reinscribed in the Hegelian German having passed through a Roman heritage, inadvertently reinventing the archaic 'H'? Obviously the *horos* itself problematises this notion of an authentic writing. If this small extract is supposed to direct us toward finitude through determination, the translation once again obscures the clarity of such a path. Taken all together, the texts themselves betray the claim to a determined science through language, providing us with the textual proof of the problem of 'naming' (and after all is this said in the name of 'Spirit' or 'Mind,' *nous* or *anima*, or is *Geist* something else entirely?).

But it does seem like an odd place to reference the *horos*, especially given its significance within Aristotelian logic. For Hegel, parenthetical

---
27 Hegel (2006) 9; Hegel (1977) 6.
28 Hegel (2003) 6; Hegel (1977) 6.

'determinateness' (*Horos*) intervenes in the German text, has an end and aim, and is consistent with philosophy as a science tracing its history from Aristotle. It is the task of logic to provide determinations with their concept, to translate them into concepts, one might almost say, to relocate or *remove* (abstract) them to the middle point. The *horos* comes into the text this once and then never resurfaces, and yet what Hegel calls a *mittelpunkt* remains as something like a place-saver for the *horos*. As Hegel states in his *Science of Logic*,

> since the *real difference* belongs to the extremes, this *middle term is only the abstract neutrality*, the real possibility of those extremes; it is as it were, the theoretical element of the concrete existence of chemical objects, of their process and its result. In the material world water fulfils the function of this medium; in the spiritual world, so far as the *analogue of such a relation has a place there, the sign in general*, and more precisely language is to be regarded as fulfilling that function. [my emphasis] [29]

For Hegel 'only what is completely determined is at once exoteric, comprehensible, and capable of being learned and appropriated by all.'[30] Determination is really what is at issue in the *Logic*, even though the *horos* does not appear as such. Determination is in fact the 'real issue,' the search for that middle position that remains ever the same that would provide both method and content for the work of logic (or a philosophy that has exhausted the love of wisdom).

> [T]he real issue [*die Sache selbst*] is not exhausted by stating it as an aim, but by carrying it out, nor is the result the actual whole, but rather the result together with the process through which it came about.[31]

Once we've achieved a state of satisfaction, we want to remember how we got there. The question that Hegel entertains and that the Romantics spurn is then how one can arrive at what is definite (*horos*) from the same place, beginning here at home in the finite? Or must we concede the logic of the Irish joke, that if it is there that we want to be going to, we ought not to be starting from here? Such determinations must, according to Hegel, be freed for use. The bonds that hold them might be a not purely conceptual presence in material life.

---

29 Hegel (1969) 729.
30 Derrida (1982) 80.
31 Hegel (1977) 2.

> In real life, it is then a matter of making use of the thought determinations. From the honor of being contemplated for their own sake, such determinations are debased to the position of serving in the creation and exchange of ideas required for the hustle and bustle of social life. They are in part used as abbreviations, because of their universality. Indeed, what an infinite host of particulars relating to external existence and to action are summed up in a representation, for instance, of battle, war, nation, or of sea and animal, etc.![32]

If we return to Aristotle (who is both here at home with us and somewhere else entirely), we see that for him the real issue is the question of defining being, or substance; it is the problem of definition itself. It 'led those who questioned along the way and compelled them to the search' (αὐτὸ τὸ πρᾶγμα ὡδοποίησεν αὐτοῖς καὶ συνηνάγκασε ζητεῖν). For Aristotle as for Hegel this is neither 'real' nor an 'issue.'[33] If it must be considered in translation, that is as a matter of translation, the only 'thing' that *Sache* has in common with *pragma* is the 'same.' The thing itself (*die Sache selbst*/αὐτὸ τὸ πρᾶγμα) raises the same problem (*aporia*) or the problem of the same—τὴν ἐν ὕλης εἴδει λεγομένην, that is what the matter is. Kind of.

Giving one of his favourite examples, of the concave shaped versus the snub nose, Aristotle states that the 'essence' (whatever that is), the τί ἐστι of things must be sought and defined (ζητεῖν καὶ ὁρίζεσθαι) in relation to matter, not without matter (μὴ ἄνευ τῆς ὕλης).[34] Or, to return to Hegel, it is the limit or difference between the lifeless thing, bare matter or a 'corpse,' and the perfect living form. Aristotle and Hegel, then, have something in common. They have a common term, and the same thing propels the hunt and remains as the hunter's companion. This 'thing,' then, must be the same as its definition—it is given and what is given is what continues to need determination (*horizesthai*). Although this thing seems to come out of nowhere, and then 'walk alongside' (*sym-bainō*), Aristotle (and here he is at one with Hegel) would argue that this is no accident (*symbebēkos*). The organic unity 'in which truth exists can only be the scientific system of such truth,' which for Hegel is determined by the word *Gestalt*, for Aristotle the symbiosis between *morphē* and *physis*.[35]

---

32 Hegel (1969) 14–15.
33 Ar.*Met*.984a19.
34 Ar.*Met*.1026a1–5.
35 Hegel (1977) 5.

Once the determination is formulated and the term emptied of meaning, the search propels the philosopher onto further determinations.

And yet there is still something missing that would provide the substance for this work of bringing to definition, a tool of sorts, but a tool that must do a double duty, just as the arrow is provident of nutrition and harbinger of death, as in Herakleitos's aphorism 'the name of the bow is life, its work is death' (τῶι οὖν τόξωι ὄνομα βίος, ἔργον δὲ θάνατος).[36] That is, something whose name concurs with its work or activity. We are looking for something that is properly *aphoristic*, something that defines itself and is divided off from everything else (*apo-horizō*) but is not therefore discrete (*diōrismenon*). We might say the search is for 'perfect definition.' Is this why Nietzsche turned to the aphorism as the short, sweet answer to the question of form and method in philosophy?

The task of philosophy is to work upon each term so closely in order to find a definition that corresponds exactly with its substance that in the end the word itself is worn away, leaving nothing but what is left over, an abstraction that necessarily must also be subjected in turn. This is what Derrida calls the general economy of the philosophical text, the re-examination over and again of the same terms that are thereby simultaneously worn away and, in the history of philosophy, acquire too much interest.[37] Definitions abound and tend to circle about in the same place. Already we can feel the pull of the *agora* where certain stones are turned to profit and provide the outlines for denominative evaluations. Given that the *Categories* is the principal work of determination, we should have a glimpse of the intrinsic part played by the *horos* in the name itself which is situated quite unexpectedly in the *agora* (κατηγορίαι, *kata- agora*) as the theoretical task of drawing up accounts (*au logisamenos*) of speaking and intercourse (*agoreuō*).[38] In Adorno's words, 'nothing escapes the market-place,' and this holds emphatically in the philosophical work of definition.[39]

Ὅρος δὲ τοῦ μὲν ἀπὸ διανοίας ἐντελεχείᾳ γιγνομένου ἐκ τοῦ δυνάμει ὄντος, ὅταν βουληθέντος γίγνηται μηθενὸς κωλύοντος τῶν ἐκτός,[40]

---

36 Herakleitos, fr. 48 (DK 73).
37 'White Mythology' in Derrida (1982) 207ff.
38 Hegel (1894) 212.
39 Adorno (2007) 4.
40 Ar.*Met*.1049a5.

> The horos of that which comes to be in actuality by intention out of being in potentiality, comes to be if, when the thing is willed, nothing outside of it prevents this.

For Aristotle, definition in conjunction with the stone, a by-product of a willed becoming, is not actually found in nature. Why? Aside from the fact that the Greeks had no concept of nature, as we do today, it was because matter (*hylē*) is *aoristē*, like suffering it rejects such terms of definition. Aristotle says that both matter and suffering (*pathē*) are indeterminate (*aorista*).[41] And yet do *we* not give form to matter (form does not reproduce itself: 'men produce men, bedsteads do not produce bedsteads')?[42] We give expression to suffering because we are all bound up in determination so that our determination to draw up boundaries comes to be read (by us) in the world around us, as our point of resistance against a world where all is in flux.

> τὸ δ' ἄπειρον ἢ τὸ ἀδύνατον διελθεῖν τῷ μὴ πεφυκέναι διιέναι, καθάπερ ἡ φωνὴ ἀόρατος, ἢ τὸ διέξοδον ἔχον ἀτελεύτητον, ἢ ὃ μόλις, ἢ ὃ πεφυκὸς ἔχειν μὴ ἔχει διέξοδον ἢ πέρας· ἔτι προσθέσει ἢ ἀφαιρέσει ἢ ἄμφω.[43]

> The infinite [*apeiron*] is either that which cannot be traversed (just as sound is by nature invisible); or that which admits endless traverse; or scarcely admits of traverse; or, though it would naturally admit of traverse [*diexodon*] or limit [*peras*], does not do so. Whether in addition, subtraction or both.

So the *horos* permits the traversal between what is indeterminable and what is determined by drawing up the boundaries of definition (in us) without establishing an adamant barrier. It marks the place where we get stuck (*aporia*) and must go on asking (*diaporēsai*); even infinity comes to its *diexodos* in a determined refusal to suffer limit and definition and this is where we assume ourselves as subjects of our own experience. As Adorno puts it,

> where the thought transcends the bonds it tied in resistance—there is its freedom. Freedom follows the subject's urge to express itself. The need to lend a voice to suffering is a condition of all truth. For suffering is

---

41 Ar.*Met*.1049b1
42 Ar.*Phys*.193a-c.
43 Ar.*Met*.1066a35.

objectivity that weighs upon the subject; its most subjective experience, its expression, is objectively conveyed.[44]

The human being experiences movement passively, subjected to its motion, subjected to the necessities of (human) nature, the becoming and corruption of the environment, the rotation of the heavenly bodies and so forth. And yet human beings also experience themselves as separate, beyond this eternal flux but only because we have the potential to draw such distinctions, to infer that the boundaries and limits we experience are natural, already within us as our 'nature.' And so, they are written in us as much as they are written in the world around us.

Therefore, that distinction, which is found in the *horismos* between same and other, suddenly takes place on an entirely different site and scale. It is no longer the assimilation of the other into the same that Levinas diagnosed as the violence of ontology, the autarchy of the I and the betrayal of the ethical relation.[45] Definition is, rather, the obligation or the responsibility of recognising a still greater limit before a greater other, an absolute other that is ontologically irreducible to the same, what could be said to be the real limit or *horos*.[46] We could say, then, that here the chief definition of the *horos* is inescapable, it is the limit that human life is confronted by in the face of the desire for the divinity of the other.

On the Horizon of Temporality

The horizon as a notion and problem for philosophy could have originated in the determinative *horos* as it appears in Aristotle. Before modern philosophy, *horos* was already structuring the experience both of language and the actual world for the Ancient Greeks, especially in the setting of the Athenian market and Athenian imperialist expansion, where the problem of boundaries (or their transgression) became at once politically and philosophically charged. It is at the very least interesting to consider that for ancient philosophy it was the *horos*, boundary and stone, that was in some sense the determining element for the linguistic experience of

---

44 Adorno (2007) 17–18.
45 Levinas (2000) 180f.
46 Bashier (2004) 87.

the world, while in modern philosophy a derivative of the same word, expanded to the edge of our vision, plays 'the all-determining role' in the theory of horizon-intentionality.⁴⁷ To put it simply, you cannot take the *on* (the essence or 'being') out of the horizon, even when defining it (*horos*).

In Hegel's *History of Philosophy*, 'determinations' abound and are clearly associated with the principal task of defining everything from Aristotle's *Organon* to his *Metaphysics*.

> The Categories (κατηγορίαι), of which the first work treats, are the universal determinations, that which is predicated of existent things (κατηγορεῖται): as well that which we call conceptions of the understanding, as the simple realities of things. This may be called an ontology, as pertaining to metaphysics; hence these determinations also appear in Aristotle's Metaphysics.⁴⁸

But which 'determination' proliferates into ontology? Do the *horos* and the *horismos* perform differently in the *dénouement* from categorical determination to the ontological undertaking? And what does it signify that we cannot translate the *horos* or the *horismos* in their pure Latinate form (*fines, terminus*), but always as *de*finite, *de*termined? That is, without the *de-* of the absolute or the divinity (*deus*), that awe prefixed to the terror (δέος) that resounds in destruction? Certainly, these translations keep us at a distance from the boundary, but they also seem to push us off (*de-*) the path of pure ontology, as if the Roman god Terminus had taken upon himself the responsibility for maintaining a certain awed distance before the *horos*, binding our definitions and determinations with an interminable slip toward a deontological stance, especially when it comes to approaching linguistic boundaries. And yet there is something evocative about the *horismos*. Like an echo of a call to action (socialism, communism, nationalism, fascism) the *horismos* prompts movement, a kind of impetus found in saying regardless of form and content. Heidegger picks up on the project of definition.

> The question asks about being. What does being mean? Formally, the answer is: Being means this and that. The question seeks an answer which determines something which is somehow already given in the very questioning. The question is what is called a *question of definition*.⁴⁹

---
47 Geniusas (2012) 11.
48 Hegel (1894) 212.
49 Heidegger (1985) 143.

According to Heidegger the 'being-in-the-world of the human being is determined in its ground through its speaking.'[50] In his seminar on the *Basic Concepts of Aristotelian Philosophy*, Heidegger cannot resist the temptation to define this ground as his terminologically inherited square metre of Greek soil.

> We want to understand what definition means by questioning back to what it meant for the Greeks, for Aristotle. Ὁρισμός: "circumscription," "delimitation." Ὁρισμός: λόγος οὐσίας. What is meant by λόγος, by οὐσία, by λόγος οὐσίας?[51]

Are these questions bound to birth some kind of substantial resolution? The solution that is found in Heidegger is the return to the Greek, the return to the Aristotelian problem of determination: 'what is this λόγος? It is the fundamental determination of the being of the human being as such.'[52] Thus Heidegger also comes to the conclusion that each word relates interminably to the other. For Heidegger it is the word *logos* that bears the brunt of human determinism, rather than the *horos* or the *horismos*. And yet, he can project a limit, his project of determination. The *horismos* is then different from the *logos* insofar as it is also 'the title for Aristotelian fundamental research—or, more precisely, for Greek fundamental research as such—the basic concept per se, the term.'[53]

So here we are back at the beginning, to what should be a clear determination of the *horos*, both title and work. As it was for Aristotle, so for Heidegger, the (re)search presents itself as a knot or bond that we must follow; 'What is pre-given is a *bond* that is indeterminate as to content but determinate as to the way of actualization.'[54] And yet, this term is not as it appears. Heidegger is not talking about the *horos*; he is talking about the *project* of definition giving ground to philosophy itself: 'If it is genuine, a concretely determined problematic of philosophical research will run in its own directedness to the end, an end philosophy as such must have made fast for itself.'[55] The way is, of course, the *diaporēsai* made concrete in the posing of the question of definition (as the question of *being*). Ὁρισμός is a λόγος, a "speaking" about something,

---

50 Heidegger (2009) 13–15.
51 Ibid. 15.
52 Ibid. 14.
53 Heidegger (2009) 231.
54 Heidegger (2001) 17.
55 Ibid. 12.

an addressing of the matter "itself in that which it is," καθ' αὐτό.'[56] For Heidegger, this project of definition becomes the basic *horizon* of metaphysics. Belittling its nominative ancestor, *horos*, the horizon takes shape from the present participle of the verb *horizo* (ὁρίζω) and henceforth takes prominence as that which provides the outline of our world, our horizon. And with the horizon, the Greek *horismos* ceases to feature for Heidegger.

Heidegger never wrote a chapter on the horizon as such, almost as if he took it and its connection to the Aristotelian notion of 'determining' (*horismos*) for granted (it might be the original 'gift' -*es gibt*- upon which all determinations were thereafter based). It is important to remember that the Greeks needed to clarify the horizon by articulating the circle in addition to the determining participle, ὁ τοῦ ὁρίζοντος κύκλος, ὁ ὁρίζων κύκλος.[57] In a way the addition of the circle serves to expand the *horos* exponentially, but also to limit it, insofar as it forecloses its claim to the substantial, the lithic *horos*. Unlike so many of his concepts, Heidegger's horizon is not an immediate adoption of the Greek term; in using the word he is making explicit reference to a more widely used notion of the horizon.

Mediaeval European thought used the idea of the horizon as indicative of the boundary between the spiritual and human spheres, and although the horizon was a notion used in modern interpretations as an epistemological boundary opening onto human knowledge, as an idea it nonetheless remained largely a metaphor.[58] It is significant that Husserl, while retaining the idea of the horizon in its broadest sense as 'what consciousness co-intends in such a way that what is co-intended determines the sense of appearing objectivities,' ceased to use it as a metaphor for human experience.[59] For Husserl, the horizon is a perceptual notion of an object's twofold horizon, inner and outer. The inner horizon is constituted of the potential perception of an object from all angles; an object's outer horizon is extendible indefinitely through the object's relation to other objects, and these others' relation to others and so on. Here the indefinite extendability of the horizon is

---

56 Heidegger (2009) 14.
57 Ar.*Meteor*.363a27; *Cael*.297b34.
58 Geniusas (2012) 3–5.
59 Ibid. 7.

glimpsed in the object itself—as phenomenon—hence the horizon is defined as the outer extreme of our relation with the phenomenal world and simultaneously defines our co-existence with objects; 'horizon is a structure of determination that predelineates the purview within which each and every phenomenon appears.'[60] The horizon is 'intuitive emptiness' given and inseparable from intuitive fullness; it structures and is the structure of our experience in the world.

Where the horizon is normally experienced as a line, demarcated according to the objects which are within it—that within the perceptual field from here to there, or more generally still, an extendable limit, something to transcend— for the later Heidegger the horizon remains a limit, but a limit whose significance lies on the other side. The 'horizon, the sphere of the constant that surrounds man, is not a wall shutting man off; the horizon is *transparent*; it points beyond to what is not made fast, to what becomes and can become, to the possible.'[61] Upon the appearance of objects, and according to representational, calculative thinking, the being of the horizon is experienced only as a plane, this side that faces us of the surrounding 'openness.' *Gegnet*, a term awkwardly but perhaps necessarily translated as 'that-which-regions,' is 'an abiding expanse which, gathering all, opens itself, so that in it openness is halted and held, letting everything merge in its own resting.'[62] Heidegger seeks to shift this experience of the horizon into a relation, a suspension of 'calculative thinking,' through 'meditative thinking' (less thinking more thanking). This suspension is also a matter of space, or temporality, because meditative thinking maintains the 'openness' that lets the horizon be 'releasement to that-which-regions' (*Gelassenheit zur Gegnet*).[63] By having recourse to Heidegger's earlier texts, a different concept of the horizon can be found—one that is not subordinated, as it is in the *Conversation*, to the more fundamental concept of *Gegnet*.

Horizons proliferate in *Being and Time*. On the first page, we are presented with the schema of the horizon as the possibility of ontological interpretation, in the form of a simile. 'Our provisional aim is the Interpretation of *Time* as the possible *horizon* for any understanding

---

60 Ibid.
61 Inwood (1999) 99–100.
62 Heidegger (1966) 66.
63 Ibid. 74.

whatsoever of Being.'⁶⁴ In the final sentence on the last page we are again presented with the question of the horizon as something like a metaphor for time, 'Does *time* manifest itself as the horizon of *Being*?' What links temporality with the horizon, 'has *something like* a horizon'?⁶⁵ The answer can be addressed by his deference to the Greek 'determination' witnessed in his peculiar attempts to translate early Greek philosophy in its most material aspect, which is not to say a 'literal translation.' Heidegger's project of determination was undertaken under the aegis of an attempt to get to the 'root' of matters, the question of determination as such.

Hence, the similitude between temporality and horizon is represented in the grammatical form, so appropriately named, of the infinitive ὁρίζειν, 'that radical "determining" that occurs at the interface between language and being.'⁶⁶ The possibility, or more precisely, the potentiality, of determining provides the whereupon (*woraufhin*), out of where (*von wo aus*), the whence, dependent upon which the question of being is to be posed.⁶⁷ 'The prefiguration of horizons is but an alternative way of describing a foreshadowed structure of the hermeneutic situation.'⁶⁸ This location is the horizon; a horizonal-schema delineated in Heidegger's ecstatic translation of German into three basic Latinate tenses, a final task which remained incomplete. Hence the *whence* of temporality, the *vor von*, originates not only in the horizon as limit but in the determination (*horismos*) as such, where *logos* is the first horizon of being.

By means of *horismos* translated as 'circumscription,' 'delimitation,' Heidegger determined to seek in Aristotle the 'indigenous character' of the concept: 'We will have to seek out the *indigenous character* of conceptuality [...] We will have to consult the way the *Greek* conceptuality and its indigenous character look.'⁶⁹ Determination provides the ground of ontology, appropriating the Aristotelian task of definition as the first step—and the onward march—of the *diaporêsai*. However, there is a significant slip here toward *horismos*, which in Aristotle is the pre-determined project of definition. It is here that Heidegger finds his *worauf*,

---

64 Heidegger (1962) 364.
65 Ibid. 365.
66 Kisiel (1995) 446.
67 Heidegger (1962) 365, Kisiel (1995) 449–450.
68 Kisiel (1995) 447.
69 Heidegger (2009) 13–15.

his scene between the rising and setting (concealment-unconcealment) sun (of being). Within this horiz-*on* (the defined being) he discovers a land of ontological neutrality, rooting his philosophy to the ground, giving his inquiry a foundation.

The coming to be of terms is expressed in an economic formula and relates to what Heidegger calls the 'customary meaning' of *ousia*, 'property, possession and goods, household, estate.'[70]

> A determinate concrete context is discovered, seen anew for the first time—the word is missing, the word is *coined together with the matter*. An expression that was not at hand may immediately become a term, which later dissipates by entering into the general currency and ordinariness of speaking.[71]

This is the basis of Heidegger's economy where the ground for other concepts is prefigured in determination as the *logos* of *ousia*.

> The multifariousness of meaning of οὐσία is therefore not treated here for its own sake, but rather always only in the direction of the proper appropriation of matter, i.e., the understanding of what is addressed in ὁρισμός as λόγος.[72]

That determination is autochthonous, and that it can be discovered by returning to the place of its 'conception' betrays an appropriative desire. That said, the *horos* does have an intimate relation with the Greek soil, and in itself it is never far away from the economic and the legal bounds of possession. The law of the letter can be said to be exactly this estrangement or alienation written into the experience of time, denoting an elsewhere, an other origin, the fact of natality as the first disconnection with place, that is the prohibition against the 'return to the ground of definition.'[73] But when it comes to *horos*, the ground is always obfuscated by the stone. We have already seen that whatever was described in the *horos* was already inscribed in the lost figuration of the letter's migration, describing the *horos* just as the rising and setting sun outlines the horizon.

On the one hand, then, with Hegel, we have the preference for the Notion or Concept as determination taking shape; on the other, with

---

70 Ibid. 233.
71 Ibid. 18.
72 Ibid. 232.
73 Ibid. 13.

Heidegger we have definition as return to the 'soil' of determination. In both cases, *horismos* is appropriated into the work of thinking about being projected (into past and future). Can we overlook the appropriation of determination as the common ground of the human being?

Material Interventions

It is the task of theoretical first philosophy to determine such limits, to find the definition of being as such (*ousia*). It is a project of differentiation between the immediate identification of being with its name. The conjunction as in the statement of the subject 'Being as in being,' ὄντος ᾗ ὄν, or ὄν ᾗ ὄν (absurdly translated into Latin as 'being *qua* being') best describes this project since it is being that is presumed in the question (what is being?), but the method is speculative or theoretical, περὶ χωριστὰ καὶ ἀκίνητα, 'concerning whatever is separate and immobile.'[74] Metaphysics first names 'being' and then identifies it with itself through what it is not but resembles, in this case, a letter (eta, ᾗ)—a letter that breaks into identification (between being to either side) and interrupts this otherwise pure reduplication with similarity and difference.

This is none other than the name and work begun in the *Categories* as the project of definition and completed in the *Metaphysics*, in the 'determination' of substance as 'separate' (χωριστόν). Aristotle frequently uses the word *onoma* where we would expect *horos*, 'term'— the name of being and not being.[75] If anything can both be and not be— and this is the problem posed by potentiality—what causes them to be the one and not the other? Or, what is the difference, actually, between being and not being, εἶναι καὶ μὴ εἶναι? Aesthetically speaking, one could say it is the μή, the 'not.' Is it not a peculiarity that negation or deprivation expressed in the *logos* does not take something away from a positive but on the contrary requires a supplement, α-, μὴ, not, etc.? Privation, being a privation of substance is dependent upon a precedent definition that it can modify (this should put us in mind of the impotentiality inherent in potentiality): 'privation is negation from a determined (or defined) genus,' the absence of *horos*.[76] But there is also

---

74 Ar.*Met*.1026a15; 1026a30.
75 Ar.*Met*.1006a30, Ar.*Met*.1050b.
76 Ar.*Met*.1011a20.

the conjunction 'and,' in which case the question always takes a twofold form, 'both and not.' The name for being presents an *aporia*, while the conjunctions and disjunctions of language move across the plurality of *aporiai*.

That Aristotle presents metaphysics as the problem of the categories between language and thought is the subject of Derrida's critical article on Benveniste's thesis that the categories 'present different aspects, depending on whether they are categories of thought or language.'[77] This is an alleged opposition, which is, of course, the very subject of Aristotle's metaphysics since the question of being, τὸ τί ἦν εἶναι, is discussed in correspondence with the statement that 'being is said many ways,' πολλαχῶς λέγεται τὸ ὄν. But is the *chōriston*, the 'separate,' not a (product of) *logos*? Is it a name given to substance (*ousia*) that distinguishes it from everything else? So that οὐθὲν γὰρ τῶν ἄλλων χωριστόν ἐστι παρὰ τὴν οὐσίαν, 'none of the other [categories] are separate except substance,' yet everything must be said to have substance to be a subject.[78] To find the substance of a thing is supposed to complete the task Derrida calls 'usury,' of wearing away and abstracting terms.[79] In this case the 'separate' (*chōriston*) is at once the 'substance of substance' and the activity of philosophy. Put otherwise, it is natural (κατὰ φύσιν) that things have substance, but it is only the form that is 'by nature' (φύσει). Nature is form (μορφή), while its kind of form (εἶδος) is not separate from it except in language (οὐ χωριστὸν ὂν ἀλλ' ἢ κατὰ τὸν λόγον).[80] Substance as such comprises an *aporia* (ἔχει δὲ τὸ συμβαῖνον ἀπορίαν) that has to do entirely with 'definition.' The taking shape of nature as substance thus brings into definition the *aporia* of their separation and drives first philosophy as/to its determination. It is therefore the task of philosophy to explain the apparent accident of this *aporia*.

If there is only one 'definition' of substance (*ousia*), substance could not be said to be the determination of anything but itself (ἢ μόνον οὐσίας εἶναι ὅρον ἢ μάλιστα).[81] Hence the definition, *horos*, marks the

---
77 'The Supplement of Copula: Philosophy before Linguistics' in Derrida (1982) 175–205.
78 Ar.*Phys*.185a31; *Met*.1025b28.
79 Derrida (1982) 209.
80 Ar.*Phys*.193b5.
81 Ar.*Met*.1039a14;21.

twofold task, the 'problem' (*aporia*) of definition and its formulation or expression in *logos* which leads to further problems (*diaporiai*): definition as such both can and cannot be, yes and no. The reason for this ambiguity is that substance is said to be of two kinds, the *synolon* (the composition of word or description and matter) and the *logos*. But if there is a *logos* of a substance, it would be separate to the substance, that is, it would be separate only *as logos*. While if the description, *logos, and the form* (*eidos*) were separate from the substance, this would be an idea (the so-called 'third man' theory).

> διὸ δεῖ, τῶν πρὸς ὅρον ὅταν τις ὁρίζηταί τι τῶν καθ' ἕκαστον, μὴ ἀγνοεῖν ὅτι ἀεὶ ἀναιρεῖν ἔστιν· οὐ γὰρ ἐνδέχεται ὁρίσασθαι. οὐδὲ δὴ ἰδέαν οὐδεμίαν ἔστιν ὁρίσασθαι. τῶν γὰρ καθ' ἕκαστον ἡ ἰδέα, ὥς φασί, καὶ χωριστή· ἀναγκαῖον δὲ ἐξ ὀνομάτων εἶναι τὸν λόγον, ὄνομα δ' οὐ ποιήσει ὁ ὁριζόμενος (ἄγνωστον γὰρ ἔσται, τὰ δὲ κείμενα κοινὰ πᾶσιν· ἀνάγκη ἄρα ὑπάρχειν καὶ ἄλλῳ ταῦτα· οἷον εἴ τις σὲ ὁρίσαιτο, ζῷον ἐρεῖ ἰσχνὸν ἢ λευκὸν ἢ ἕτερόν τι ὃ καὶ ἄλλῳ ὑπάρξει.

> Therefore in cases relating to definition [*horizētai*], when we are trying to define any individual, we must not fail to realise that our definition may always be upset; because it is impossible to define (*horizesthai*) these things. Nor, indeed, can any Idea be defined; for the Idea is an individual, as they say, and separable; and the formula must consist of words, and the man who is defining must not coin a word, because it would not be comprehensible. But the words which are in use are common to all the things which they denote; and so they must necessarily apply to something else as well. E.g., if a man were to define you, he would say that you are an animal which is lean or white or has some other attribute, which will apply to something else as well.[82]

The problem with determining any definition is that one is compelled to use other words, and therefore, on the one hand, the definition always crosses over into other definitions as being reliant on these other words, along with all the baggage that comes with them. And on the other hand, the problem of determination simply allows one to continue into other problems of determination (and this is what is expressed by the verb *diapōresai*). Aristotle, who cannot accept the Platonic Ideas, solves this *aporia* by referring to incomposite substance

---

82 Ar.*Met*.1040a6–15.

as being 'in potentiality,' while it is only substance composite with *logos* that is separate absolutely.

> ἔστι δ' οὐσία τὸ ὑποκείμενον, ἄλλως μὲν ἡ ὕλη (ὕλην δὲ λέγω ἣ μὴ τόδε τι οὖσα ἐνεργείᾳ δυνάμει ἐστὶ τόδε τι), ἄλλως δ' ὁ λόγος καὶ ἡ μορφή, ὃ τόδε τι ὂν τῷ λόγῳ χωριστόν ἐστιν: τρίτον δὲ τὸ ἐκ τούτων, οὗ γένεσις μόνου καὶ φθορά ἐστι, καὶ χωριστὸν ἁπλῶς: τῶν γὰρ κατὰ τὸν λόγον οὐσιῶν αἱ μὲν αἱ δ' οὔ. [83]
>
> And the substrate is substance; in one sense matter (by matter I mean that which is not in actuality, but is potentially, an individual thing); and in another the word and shape (which is an individual thing and is separate in speech); and thirdly there is the combination of the two, which alone admits of generation and decay, and is separate absolutely— for of substances according to their word some are separate and some are not.

This definition for substance as *chōriston*, 'separate,' can be understood first and foremost in relation to contraries. As he says, substance has no contrary (ὑπάρχει δὲ ταῖς οὐσίαις καὶ τὸ μηδὲν αὐταῖς ἐναντίον εἶναι) that would provide it with something from which to differ.[84] But this is not what is particular (ἴδιον τῆς οὐσίας) to substance (quantity also has no contrary). What is particular to substance is that 'while remaining numerically one and the same, it is capable of admitting contrary qualities,' (ἡ δέ γε οὐσία ἓν καὶ ταὐτὸν ἀριθμῷ ὂν δεκτικὸν τῶν ἐναντίων ἐστίν).[85] It is its sameness that distinguishes and separates it, such that by changing itself, it can receive contraries, assimilating what is other to the same. But does this similarity, or identification with itself, mean that substance is one and the same (ἓν καὶ ταὐτὸν)?

It cannot be, and this is exactly why Aristotle calls or names substance the *chōriston*. Because the work of defining it is without substance, 'always away beyond it' (*chōris*, 'without' -*on*, 'being'). Or is it because substance is indeterminable? By making division (*chōrizein*) possible, is it the prospect of definition itself? Does the *chōriston* give substance to the potential conjunction of *logos* and substance?

According to Levinas, *chōriston* 'is the definition of freedom: to maintain oneself against the other, despite every relation with the other to

---

83 Ar.*Met*.1042a30.
84 Ar.*Cat*.3b25.
85 Ar.*Cat*.4a10-b20.

ensure the autarchy of the I.'[86] In the *name 'chōriston'* the relation between the contraries is resolved into a singular and separate reduction to the same. Perhaps the *chōriston* was a terminological 'solution' or release (*euporia* or *lysis*) to the interminable confrontation between Socratic contraries. That is, it is the essential step that would allow us, not in spite of our dialectic, but by means of it, to arrive at a logical conclusion that could resemble the thing itself (truth). This is the real issue, the reduction of the thing itself not to a common factor, but to the same thing from Aristotle to Hegel. Regardless of how each individual manipulates it, the thing itself remains the same, separate, the immaterial pledge of freedom, a 'place' (*topos*) of definition that prefigures the answer to the question posed in the absolute identification of Cartesian doubt between the question and the questioner. As Levinas states, 'Western philosophy has most often been an ontology: a reduction of the other to the same by interposition of a middle and neutral term that ensures the comprehension of being.'[87] Here philosophy might just succeed as a science but only because the erotic play of two has been replaced by the autonomous hegemony of the one.

And the truth of this self-identification is achieved in mathematics, where the indiscretion of *auto-philo-sophy* (love of one's own wisdom, or the knowledge of the same) is isolated *in situ*, freed from the bonds of pre-determined heteronomy. Pure mathematics, says Aristotle, deals with all things alike (ἡ δὲ καθόλου πασῶν κοινή). This might be because mathematics as a field of thought is extracted from the material. According to Aristotle it is because the objects of its study, numbers, have no common term or boundary (*horos*).

> τῶν μὲν γὰρ οὗ ἀριθμοῦ μορίων οὐδείς ἐστι κοινὸς ὅρος, πρὸς ὃν συνάπτει τὰ μόρια αὐτοῦ, οἷον τὰ πέντε εἰ ἔστι τῶν δέκα μόριον, πρὸς οὐδένα κοινὸν ὅρον συνάπτει τὰ πέντε καὶ τὰ πέντε, ἀλλὰ διώρισται.[88]

> In the case of the parts of a number, there is no common boundary [*koinos horos*] at which they join. For example: two fives make ten, but the two fives have no common boundary, but are separate; the parts three and seven also do not join at any boundary.

---

86 Levinas (1969) 47.
87 Ibid. 43.
88 Ar.*Cat*.4b20.

It is no coincidence that the proponents of mathematics are modern-day Platonists; something has to be out there *as the other* but that comes to *us*, touches *us*, it might even dawn upon us as a 'movement' or e-vent, coming from somewhere else. In mathematics the joint is there, but its community is lacking. Numbers can get it on with one another, break up, get back together, get others involved, but throughout all this, they remain distinct and unchanged. There is a promiscuity here that is, however, not social; numbers are not communal but atavistic. The truth of mathematics then can be 'defined' as freedom exactly because it shares no 'common boundary' (*koinos horos*), is without limit and substance, and is not nor has any necessary relation except to itself. There is indeed a violence here, as Levinas was aware, but it is the violence that masquerades as truth flying its banner of freedom for the same as it intervenes in the relations between others.

It is exactly because there is the 'common term' (*koinos horos*) in language that our attempts at definition are always 'upset' (*anairein*).[89] The task of definition has the potential of always going beyond its object, hence the verb *anairein*, which literally means 'to raise, lift,' a word that we could translate into the Hegelian *aufheben*. Every definition consists of something that is also applicable to something else, a certain common boundary or shared term, and can always be used in formulating its opposite; most evidently, we can always define something by what it is not or by giving its contrary.

---

[89] Ar.*Met*.1040a6.

Fig. 5. ΟΡΟΣ ΛΕΤΟΣ '[h]oros of Leto'. Photograph courtesy of Paulos Karvonis, The Island of Delos, Ephorate of Antiquities of Cyclades, © Hellenic Ministry of Culture and Sports/Hellenic Organization of Cultural Resources Development (H.O.C.R.E.D.)

5. The Presence of the Lithic

> ὁ ὅρος—*the time within which* one may marry [...]*the notes which limit* the intervals in the musical scale[...] I set the *limit* of human life at seventy years [...] Astrol, οἱ τρεῖς ὅ. the three *terms*, used in various calculations.[1]

The diagnostic of the Anthropocene as a new age in the geologic timescale introduces the human as an equivalent, nonhuman force of intemperate geological interference. Not only is the human being rendered as a subject of geomorphic and geological change but also as an intrinsic agent interacting within the geological materiality of the earth in such a way that the lithic record of time is both altered by human activity and is inherent to human agency. The rocks are changing, and the surface strata are being read differently by us, in a way that for the first time raises human beings to the position that human culture has long claimed us to be—as a dominant force, rewriting the fate of the world.

There is a complex of problems in this assertion of the new age of the *anthropos*. First, there are the problems that have to do with the human presence in the lithic: there is an underlying assumption that rocks present to us as a script that can be deciphered, interpreted and understood; stratigraphy requires humans to read into stone as if the earth's crust is a book. The other side of this problem is the authenticity of our rock-reading and the supposed equivalence between the human reader and the human content assumed within the Anthropocene. Since it was humans doing the reading, they were already superimposed upon or within the geological strata as those who read, interpret and make sense of a natural phenomenon. The Anthropocene reiterates the already intentional human presence in the lithic. Second, there are the problems that have to do with the measurement or definition of

---

1   Taken from LS: ὅρος.

geologic time and the question of whether this can ever be more than relative to the human act of reading. Is there such a thing as absolute time and if there is, is it possible for humans to experience it as such and transform it into a comprehensible measurement? Time itself has a habit of reconfiguring itself every time into space or spatial metaphors. Perhaps this is more essential to time than we allow. With this in mind this chapter will investigate the relation between rocks and time. In which case I will begin with the *horos* in the works of Aristotle, and its task of defining the present moment, or 'now.' Given the slippery nature of time, it should not come as a surprise if that is where I end up as well.

There can be no doubt that human beings are changing the surface of the earth through chemical use, industrial farming methods, fossil fuel extraction, and deforestation. That is not the issue. The issue is this: what lesson do we take from the introduction of a new name for a new age, and will it assist us in some way to make the necessary changes in our relations with the geomorphology of the earth? My suspicion is that this reiteration of the human as an age-inducing agent only reinforces the dangerous and destructive structures of belief endemic to the majority of human institutions (science, religion, architecture, politics) that actively segregate the human from the nonhuman. What would be more beneficial would be a reworking of a non-horizontal, non-vertical, non-linear history of human/nonhuman interrelations and interactions that is not just between humans and nonhumans but also between animals and rocks, plants and fungi, bacteria and viruses and so on—an entirely new multi-dimensional project that calls for the embeddedness of life and matter.

Perhaps the main problem with the designation of the Anthropocene is that it forebodes (nominally) an era in which humans presume to hold centre stage, when what it should really be suggesting is how we can reinvest ourselves within the subtle chain of life. The way climate change is being presented seems to suggest two possibilities only, on the one hand there is the technocratic, corporate world geo-engineered to suit humanity alone, on the other there is the imminent climatic chaos spawned by the rise of earthly, chthonic forces that do not give a damn about human lives or humanity as a whole. Climate change might be the scientific term for an aggregate of shifting climatic forces, but what we experience is a series of threateningly powerful interventions in the natural world: the disappearance of pollinators, barren oceans, genetically modified plant species spreading seeds across neighbouring fields, poisoned rivers, rising flood waters, out-of-season snow, firestorms of hellish proportions, chemicals that saturate the land, enter water sources and modify the reproductive health of our children and standing over it all devils with little resemblance to humanity, buying up land and expanding their dominion to the ends of the earth. The ancient monsters and old chthonic gods are awakening to fight a battle that will ravage our days and haunt our nights. All we need to do is keep our feet on the ground and stand firm to protect what is wild around and within us. 'The chthonic ones are precisely not sky gods, not a foundation for the Olympiad, not friends to the Anthropocene or Capitalocene, are definitely not finished. The Earthbound can take heart—as well as action.'[2] Donna Haraway proposes a new term, therefore, for the underside of the Anthropocene, a term that covers these chthonic forces and powers, the Chthulucene. As far as I understand, however, if we are diagnosing a problem rather than simply attributing a novel name to a time period then a name can be given but only to a small proportion of humanity whose cartel we could call the capitalocene. The conceptualisation of time since Aristotle and culminating in the designation of the Anthropocene reflects a human desire to flatten our experience of the world into a linear process of narcissistic complacency devoid of respect or mindfulness of the other beings and nonbeings that contribute to, or indeed form the very substrate of, our existence.

Here I will briefly outline the origins of the relation between stone and time in an attempt to rehabilitate the relation of present, dominant conceptualisations with the primordial intellectual and chemical swampland of geomorphous thought. In the geosciences, stratigraphy is the most important tool for measuring time, in which information contained within layers (strata) of rock is used to reconstruct the history of the earth. Similarly, biostratigraphy is the use of the palaeontological or fossil content of the stratigraphic record for the purpose of correlating a relative age of the stratigraphic unit (a body of rock characterised as a distinct entity, of identifiable origin and relative age). An abundance of fossils is designated a biozone, and the biohorizons are delimited by the first and last appearance of a particular fossil taxon. These biohorizons

---

2   Haraway (2016) 53.

are defined both spatially and temporally, and this duality generates the overarching concept of time as a linear, horizontal process. That said, evolution, as read in the geosciences, is anything but a linear process; on the contrary it is punctuated by flourishings, extinctions, dead-end evolutionary developments, about-faces, singular instances and interruptions. Nonetheless, how time is measured in the geosciences sets the stage for the representation of all biological, botanical and climatic events in earth's history.

The theory of time in the geosciences tends to begin and end here. However, cross-fertilisation between mineral and organic life goes in both directions, all the more so now that our technologies insinuate themselves within our own bodies. Human interraction with geology goes much deeper than merely extracting the earth's mineralogical deposits, exhuming them and exhausting them into the air we breathe and fail to sufficiently filter out. Is there something more than this infiltration between solid deposits of the past and the gaseous future of climatic destabilisation that changes the way time is inscribed in the rocks? The axiom of the Anthropocene is that human-geologic change is superficial or at least can be read superficially. But that is possibly because psychic disturbances on a planetary scale are not legible, at least not for any formally recognised science. Perhaps deeply embedded interaction between human activity and lithic life is always already present in the conceptualisation of time itself, at least since Aristotle defined it, if not from the beginning. Getting the moral in before the story is told: unbalanced interactions between creatures and rocky deposits on a cosmic scale cannot be solved by technological advances that require further destabilisation of natural beings and mineral entities.

In the history of philosophy spatial metaphors are deeply embedded within conceptualisations of time presumably because the extraction of matter from time is fundamentally problematic, if not inconceivable.

Heidegger criticises Aristotle's conception of time as 'vulgar,' by which he means cyclical. Nonetheless, as Derrida reveals, Heidegger's attempts to free time from its vulgar conception become themselves tangled once again because he wants to discover an originary but non-spatial time. He wants to, but cannot, divorce time from an economy of exteriority. I argue that at the crux of this dilemma (*aporia*) is the *horos*, which joins the terminology interminably, and the attempted determinations of time to the economy of exteriority in the base materiality of the *horos*, stone and boundary.

Predetermined by the Now

According to Aristotle, time is akin to a universal order, insofar as it consists of changes, and changes are all related to one another. All change exists within time, says Aristotle, but time is 'something of change.'[3] Ursula Coope also points out another sense in which time is a universal order, as all rational humans are able to count time by counting an order of defined 'nows.'[4] The 'now,' '*nun*' in Greek, something like an instant, is able to be distinguished temporally from other 'nows,' while the definition of all 'nows' remains the same. Put otherwise, all 'nows' are the same except insofar as they differ temporally, and this ordered series of similitude between 'nows' creates the temporal continuum. Because the 'nows' are all the same, there cannot be said to be any discrete parts of time, and so while the continuum can be divided into instants and between these instants further instants can be divided and therefore counted, time itself cannot be separated or interrupted. Ursula Coope explains this difference.

> What, then, is involved in dividing something continuous into parts? On Aristotle's view, we can only divide something into two by creating in it two boundaries: one boundary for each of the two parts. There are two different ways to create a double division of this sort in a line. One way is physically to cut the line in two, so that the two parts are separate from each other and each of them has its own boundaries. The other way is to move over the line, stopping when we are part way through the movement. By stopping at a certain point on a line and then starting out from that point, we create a double boundary. When we stop and then start at a point, we treat the point as two, allowing it to serve both as a boundary of the part to one side of it and as a boundary of the part to the other side.[5]

The original text that suggests this is in Aristotle's *Physics* Book IV, where he states that time is continuous 'in the now' (συνεχής τε δὴ ὁ χρόνος τῷ νῦν) and is divided according to the now (διῄρηται κατὰ τὸ

---

3 Coope (2005) 31.
4 Ibid. 172.
5 Ibid. 11.

νῦν).⁶ But beyond explaining how 'division' operates in the continuous line, Coope adds the idea of creating 'boundaries' on each side of the division. The word 'boundaries' here relates to the verb *horizo*, as it is used by Aristotle to describe the movement of an object. If a single object is being moved, its movement will be continuous not because the object remains the same but because it remains the same while it is moved, and this is what defines— *horizei*—the movement before and the movement after (ὁρίζει δὴ τὴν πρότερον καὶ ὕστερον κίνησιν τοῦτο).⁷ In much the same way, a moment, or point, both constitutes and defines linearity (ἡ στιγμὴ καὶ συνέχει τὸ μῆκος καὶ ὁρίζει) by tracing a path from beginning to end. This is where the concept of time as a continuous line with the now as an indivisible point on that line would seem to originate. On this line, each point is distinct (though not separate) from all others by a period of time, and hence, no two points can coexist temporally nor succeed one another immediately. What must distinguish each now from the others is the boundary that defines them temporally in relation to the line. Hence,

τὸ δὲ νῦν ὅρος τοῦ παρήκοντος καὶ τοῦ μέλλοντος.⁸

the now is the boundary [*horos*] of the past and future.

In this formulation, it appears that the 'now' and the 'boundary,' *horos*, are in an identical relation. Rather than there being an independent boundary on either side of the now giving definition to the now in contrast with whatever falls to either side, it is the now itself that marks the division between the past and the future, and it does so as boundary. Coope suggests that time can be attributed parts without actual divisions because it is impossible to actually interrupt time. Instead time can be understood by marking a 'potential division,' or as Aristotle puts it 'the "now" of time is on the one hand a divider according to potentiality, and on the other hand a limit (*peras*) and unifier of both future and past' (οὕτω καὶ τὸ νῦν τὸ μὲν τοῦ χρόνου διαίρεσις κατὰ δύναμιν, τὸ δὲ πέρας ἀμφοῖν καὶ ἑνότης).⁹ In itself the 'now' is at once a unifier and a divider (κατὰ ταὐτὸ ἡ διαίρεσις καὶ ἡ ἕνωσις), but it is not identical to itself.

---

6   Ar.*Phys*.220a5.
7   Ar.*Phys*.220a10.
8   Ar.*Phys*.223a7.
9   Ar.*Phys*.222a20.

> First, for Aristotle, indivisible things like points and instants exist only in so far as they are boundaries, divisions, or potential divisions, of a continuum. They are, thus, essentially dependent entities. A boundary must always be a boundary of something or other. Second, for a boundary to be (and hence for the part it bounds to be), it must be marked out in some way from its surroundings. A continuous thing that contains no such boundaries will not contain any parts (although it will, of course, be divisible). Third, when I mark a now I create a potential division, both in time and in whatever changes are then going on. It is thus by marking nows that we create parts in time and in changes.[10]

From the very moment when Aristotle gives form to the problem, he takes it as a problem of determination, of formulating a 'definition' of time. And, just as in English, so in Greek, this form is presupposed as one of boundaries, terms and limits. In short, he is putting the *horos* to work, both verbally and nominally, in order to draw up the boundaries of time. But can time itself not merely *have* but *be* a 'definition'? Can time itself be said to have boundaries? Not exactly. What Aristotle says is that we sense boundaries or limits of motion, and only from distinguishing these boundaries do we get a 'sense' of time.

> ἀλλὰ μὴν καὶ τὸ χρόνον γε γνωρίζομεν, ὅταν ὁρίσωμεν τὴν κίνησιν τὸ πρότερον καὶ ὕστερον ὁρίζοντες· καὶ τότε φαμὲν γεγονέναι χρόνον, ὅταν τοῦ προτέρου καὶ ὑστέρου ἐν τῇ κινήσει αἴσθησιν λάβωμεν. ὁρίζομεν δὲ τῷ ἄλλο καὶ ἄλλο ὑπολαβεῖν αὐτὰ καὶ μεταξύ τι αὐτῶν ἕτερον· ὅταν γὰρ ἕτερα τὰ ἄκρα τοῦ μέσου νοήσωμεν καὶ δύο εἴπῃ ἡ ψυχὴ τὰ νῦν—τὸ μὲν πρότερον τὸ δ' ὕστερον—τότε καὶ τοῦτό φαμεν εἶναι χρόνον· τὸ γὰρ ὁριζόμενον τῷ νῦν χρόνος εἶναι δοκεῖ.[11]

> We recognise a lapse of time when we determine [*horisōmen*] a movement by defining [*horizontes*] its first and last limit; and then we say that time has passed when we have a sense of a prior and posterior limit. And we distinguish between the initial limit and the final one, interpreting that what lies between them is distinct from both; for when we comprehend the difference between the extremes and what is between them, and the soul states that the "nows" are two—an initial and a final one—it is then that we say that there is time; for that which is determined [*horizomenon*] by a "now" seems to be time.

---

10 Coope (2005) 13.
11 Ar.*Phys*.219a25–30.

Not only the sense of time, but the sense of 'now' is thus subsequent to the determination of boundaries, and time is itself none other than this determining (*horizomenon*). The Greek text here is full of different forms of the *horos*. It is all about distinguishing and determining limits. There is a further question that would seem to present itself in the *Physics*; that is, to what do we owe this ability to determine limits? And what exactly *are* these limits (of past and future) that appear to present themselves to us without them actually being present as anything beyond the 'now'? For Aristotle, it is key to recognise that our experience of time is absolutely dependent upon our experience of change or our lapse in perception between one state and another. This lapse, or gap, is what provides us with the possibility to determine a change.

> συνάπτουσι γὰρ τὸ πρότερον νῦν τῷ ὕστερον νῦν καὶ ἓν ποιοῦσιν, ἐξαιροῦντες διὰ τὴν ἀναισθησίαν τὸ μεταξύ. ὥσπερ οὖν εἰ μὴ ἦν ἕτερον τὸ νῦν ἐπεὶ λανθάνει ἕτερον ὄν, οὐ δοκεῖ εἶναι τὸ μεταξὺ χρόνος. εἰ δὴ τὸ μὴ οἴεσθαι εἶναι χρόνον τότε συμβαίνει ἡμῖν ὅταν μὴ ὁρίζωμεν μηδεμίαν μεταβολὴν ἀλλ' ἐν ἑνὶ καὶ ἀδιαιρέτῳ φαίνηται ἡ ψυχὴ μένειν, ὅταν δ' αἰσθώμεθα καὶ ὁρίσωμεν, τότε φαμὲν γεγονέναι χρόνον, φανερὸν ὅτι οὐκ ἔστιν ἄνευ κινήσεως καὶ μεταβολῆς χρόνος.[12]

> So we join the former "now" to the latter "now" and make them one, making an exception of what comes between them since it is unperceived [*anaisthēsia*]. So, just as there would be no time if there were nothing other between this now and that now; since the other escapes our notice, there would appear to be no time in between. Since we do not suppose that time happens to us when we do not determine [*horisōmen*] any change, but the soul appears to remain in unity and undifferentiation, but when we sense and determine, then we say time has become, it is thus clear that time is not without movement and change.

Time appears before all else as the question of determining or defining the present 'now.' And yet, determination is first (and simultaneously) a sense or feeling of something other than the 'now,' which would provide a sense of definition between one 'now' and another. This is why Coope rests her interpretation of the continuity of time in Aristotle upon the idea that it is we who count time.

This sense would seem to work both ways, as a feeling of lapse, it would appear as a caesura, or a broken cog in the machine, interrupting

---

12 Ar.*Phys*.218b25–220a.

the continuous series of (undifferentiated) 'nows,' forward and back. It is therefore a feeling (of absence as well as of movement) that interrupts time, and brings time into distinction. And yet it is a feeling, a sense, and can be said to give time to us, by separating our sense that there is something other than immediacy but also something outside of perpetual motion. That time and movement are sensed, in a sense a matter of aesthetics (even if the matter itself is unperceived or unfelt), means that the exteriority of time is no longer an issue, it exists in us. Though this cannot be the end of the matter. As Derrida states, 'the transcendental exposition of time places this concept in an essential relation with movement and change, even while rigorously distinguishing it from them.'[13] The nature of time in Aristotle raises the problem of the matter of time, or time's exteriority as a problem of 'definition.'

According to Book IV of the *Physics* the present 'now' is not actually a part of time, although it pertains to time by bringing time into definition.

τὸ δὲ νῦν οὐ μέρος· μετρεῖ τε γὰρ τὸ μέρος, καὶ συγκεῖσθαι δεῖ τὸ ὅλον ἐκ τῶν μερῶν· ὁ δὲ χρόνος οὐ δοκεῖ συγκεῖσθαι ἐκ τῶν νῦν.[14]

[T]he now is not part [of time], for a part measures the whole, and the whole must be made up of the parts, but we cannot say that time is made up of nows.

And yet with its presence, the 'now' gives definition to time by joining past with future, which are themselves nonexistent, insofar as they only have been or will be a present 'now.' That is, they exist only by virtue of having crossed or potentially crossing over the boundary of the 'now.' Aristotle concedes that the future and the past have a common boundary (*koinos horos*) and that this boundary is identified as the present 'now.' What divides past from future is therefore also taken to be what gives definition to time as a whole. Still, this does not provide a continuous sense of time. For it is not enough to distinguish the boundary between past 'now' and future 'now'; one must also join them.

This is where the use of the word *horos* becomes pertinent because if the now were a limit as in the sense *peras*, which is a more finite type of limit, then there would be nothing to bind the past with the

---

13   Derrida (1984) 49.
14   Ar.*Phys*.218a5.

future; they would not have a common boundary. But since Aristotle identifies the 'now' with *horos*, he is able to create a definition of time that simultaneously divides and joins, that distinguishes and unites. Nonetheless, the leap in the definition is the synonymity between the present as a point or line of demarcation that distinguishes past from future, the definition itself (i.e. *horos*) and the 'now.'

> Φανερὸν δὲ καὶ ὅτι εἴτε χρόνος μὴ εἴη, τὸ νῦν οὐκ ἂν εἴη, εἴτε τὸ νῦν μὴ εἴη, χρόνος οὐκ ἂν εἴη·[...] καὶ συνεχής τε δὴ ὁ χρόνος τῷ νῦν, καὶ διῄρηται κατὰ τὸ νῦν.[15]
>
> It is clear that there would be no time if there were no "now," nor would "now" be if there were no time [...] and time owes its continuity to the "now," and yet is divided by reference to it.

In this sense the 'now' appears to give definition to time but problematically. By joining past and future, it ensures the continuity of time, and yet it is not itself part of time. And then also, the 'now' gives definition to time by dividing it up into past 'nows' and future 'nows,' but is not itself the definition of time. The 'now' is supposed to do the double task of both dividing and connecting past and future into a continuous sequence of 'nows.' This lapse of consciousness, however, gives Aristotle the grounds to separate the 'determination' of time into two limits, the double point or 'dyad' (τῇ γὰρ μέσῃ στιγμῇ ὡς δυσὶ χρήσεται).[16] At this point the now diverges as *peras*, the twofold limit, the beginning of time-to-come, and the end of time-past. Here the now is framed by similitude, 'the now is like a limit (*peras*), which is not time but only accidental to it' (ᾗ μὲν οὖν πέρας τὸ νῦν, οὐ χρόνος ἀλλὰ συμβέβηκεν).[17] But it is only temporarily like a limit for, as he stated from the very beginning, consciousness or its lapse joins the former now to the latter and makes them one excepting the non-sensation in between.

One 'now' differs from another, but in its actual holding of time continuously together it always remains the same; the 'now' is thus the contradiction of similars affirmed, it simultaneously divides and unites until we must accept that the 'now' is and is not the same. Therefore, as Derrida recognises, 'the very signification of coexistence or of presence

---

15 Ar.*Phys*.220a1–5.
16 Ar.*Phys*.219a20, 220a15, 30.
17 Ibid.220a20.

is constituted by this limit. Not to be able to coexist with an other [sic] (the same as itself), with an other [sic] now, is not a predicate of the now, but its essence as presence.'[18] However, as Aristotle himself notes, it is not at all clear whether the 'now' that divides (*diorizein*- from *diahorizein*) past and future remains always one and the same 'now' or is somehow subject itself to change.[19] According to Derrida, the question is whether 'in overturning the hypothesis, in demonstrating that the now is not part of time, does Aristotle extract the problematic of time from the "spatial" concepts of part and whole, from the predetermination of the *nun* as *meros* or even as *stigmé*?'[20] The problem does not lie with time as much as it does with the task of the definition (and its associated words) of time.

The line, as the solution of the problem of the nows, is the dialectical affirmation of the aporetic structure of time. The line resolves opposites: the now that is and is not the same, time is continuous and divided by the now, the now is only the point in terms of nonspatial spatiality.[21] Time is the name for the impossibility of the continuation of all these nows that are and are not the same, always flowing on from being into nonbeing, from presence into nonpresence. This is the *aporia* of time, that there are all these 'nows' that cannot be at the same time because then what happened a thousand years ago would be co-present with this 'now,' which it is not. And yet for time to be, rather than not be, it has to be possible to determine in the limit of the present 'now' and in the absence of a relation between the infinite number of 'nows' a continuously extended series of 'nows.' But it also needs to pass over this limit. Aristotle's conception of time is transitivity, transgression of a limit, passing over to ever more limits. The line cannot be a series of points, but only sensed as a series of potential 'nows,' a line 'thought on the basis of its extremities (*ta eskhata*) and not of its parts.'[22]

Heidegger explains, in a note to *Being and Time*, that the priority that is given to the 'now' contributes to the 'manner in which time is *ordinarily* understood.'[23]

---

18   Derrida (1982) 55
19   Ar.*Phys*.218a10.
20   Derrida (1984) 46.
21   Derrida (1984) 54.
22   Ibid. 60.
23   'Ousia and Grammé: Note on a Note from Being and Time' in Derrida (1984) 36.

> Aristotle sees the essence of time in the νῦν, Hegel in the "now". Aristotle takes the νῦν as ὅρος; Hegel takes the "now" as a boundary [*Grenze*]. Aristotle understands the νῦν as στιγμή; Hegel interprets the "now" as a point. Aristotle describes the νῦν as τόδε τι; Hegel calls the "now" the "absolute this". Aristotle follows tradition in connecting χρόνος with the σφαῖρα; Hegel stresses the "circular course" of time.[24]

The problem of the 'now,' as well as its importance in contributing to the 'traditional' definition of time, has normally overlooked the significance of its definition, that is the materiality of its definition, as *horos*. Heidegger does not reference the *horos* beyond the exclusionary, as well as foundational zone of the footnote. And yet the definition of the 'now' as the boundary, given its quiddity, its matter and its meaning (*to ti en einai*) remains within any subsequent determinations of time, haunting metaphysical determinations with base materiality. The problem of materiality, or, as Protevi puts it 'exteriority,' remains as an intimate exclusion within the definition of time, as much for Aristotle as for Hegel and Heidegger. This intimacy, a ghost in the room of Being, haunts Heidegger's hopes to remain terminologically vigilant, keeping vulgarity and originality, the line and the vector separate and at a distance.[25]

> This acceptation [of the mark "temporality"] must be kept clear from the vulgar time-concept by a rigorous policing of the terminological use of certain expressions that find their way into temporal discourse: "The conceptions of 'future,' 'past,' and 'present' have first arisen in terms of the authentic way of understanding time. In terminologically delimiting the primordial and authentic phenomena which correspond to these, we have to struggle against the same difficulty which keeps all ontological terminology in its grip". In such a policing of terminology, "violences [*Gewaltsamkeiten*]" are unavoidable here, Heidegger concedes.[26]

Such vigilance, however, requires the dematerialising of the terminology itself, but this is impossible. The words 'before' and 'after' create Aristotle's paradigm of the continuous flow of 'nows.' However, if, as Derrida notes in the word *hama* 'at the same time' 'together,' these words already have a spatial sense as well as a temporal sense, any definition of time that is generated on the basis of such words will necessarily bind a

---

24 Heidegger (1962) 500 note xxx.
25 Protevi (1984) 137.
26 Ibid.

spatial understanding of time with a temporal one. 'Time is that which is thought on the basis of being as presence, and if something—which bears a relation to time but is not time—is to be thought beyond the determination of being as presence, it cannot be a question of something that could still be called time.'[27] Since Aristotle already defined time as sensible, not in the sense of touch (though this is not absent from the word) but as a question of being determined by us, whether this is by counting or measuring, or 'sensing' movement in the soul, it seems vain to try to extract the question of 'sense' from the system of understanding being. Sense is irreducibly bound to the system of presence.

This is what Barad suggests when she says that there is a haunting within quantum physics. Haunting is the disruption of discontinuity; however, it is a destabilising that, like the 'now,' 'makes for the stability of existence itself.'

> Or rather, to put it a bit more precisely, if the indeterminate nature of existence by its nature teeters on the cusp of stability and instability, of possibility and impossibility, then the dynamic relationality between continuity and discontinuity is crucial to the open ended becoming of the world which resists acausality as much as determinism.[28]

According to Aristotle, there is only one way to get between two points, and that is by starting out at your home point and then moving across all the points in between until you arrive at your destination. The problem is that it is not the only way. On the one hand, because you were never at home, and on the other hand, because that was not actually your destination, the destination is always over there, deferred. But there is also a third way: because motion need not be continuous, and the 'now' need not be the divisive force it was cut out to be.

> In particular, the electron is initially at one energy level and then it is at another *without having been anywhere in between*. Talk about ghostly matters! A quantum leap is a dis/continuous movement, and not just any discontinuous movement, but a particularly queer kind that troubles the very dichotomy between discontinuity and continuity. Indeed, *quantum dis/continuity* troubles the very notion of *dicho-tomy*–the cutting into two– itself (including the notion of 'itself'!).[29]

---

27 Derrida in Protevi (1984) 150.
28 Barad (2010) 248.
29 Ibid. 246.

The quantum leap is a sure way to overcome an *aporia*, accept/except the problem and pass on.

Aristotle began his *Physics* with a series of *aporias*. Aristotle's basic *aporia* was that time is not among things or beings. The definition of time is that it is nothing because it is past or to come. In the words of Derrida, 'Being has been determined temporally as being-present in order to determine time as nonpresent and nonbeing.'[30] So far I concentrated on the *aporia* of the 'now,' and how the now can be simultaneously identical and nonidentical. However, there were other *aporias* in Aristotle's text, the main one revolving around the non-existence of time: 'one part of it has been and is not, another part of it will be and is not yet [...] But what is composed of non-beings might seem to be incapable of participating in being.'[31] Since, as he said in the beginning, 'we must advance from the concrete and particular,' because 'elements and principles are only accessible to us afterwards, as derived from the concrete' there can be only one place to start any attempt at solving or unravelling such *aporias*.[32] That is 'determination,' concrete, solid definition, *horos*. The point is that this was already there, in the text of Aristotle as the point of difference, the interruption of matter into the discourse on definition: that is what *horos* is. Any attempt to circumvent it only ends up in the sludge of the absolute, the muddy ground of transcendence, a slip or misstep that has us falling short of the path and the well-defined boundaries of the stepping-stone.

> In other words, the discourse that seeks to define and describe time uses terms haunted by the possibility of their iteration in bare spatial contexts. These defining and describing terms are inscribed in economies of exteriority with irreducible bare spatial moments—irreducible precisely because the possibility of iteration in bare spatial contexts cannot, *de jure*, be completely controlled.[33]

Aristotle describes that there is a sequence of dependence of movement upon magnitude (vector) and of time upon movement. The moving object is what brings our awareness to the point, the now and its passing between before and afterwards. This moving object that directs our

---

30   Derrida (1982) 50.
31   Ar.*Phys*.217b33. See Coope on the other *aporias* (2005) 18ff.
32   Ar.*Phys*.184a24.
33   Protevi (1984) 167.

attention, that shifts our gaze towards the timely is whatever intervenes into conscious thought, whether we call this a "point or a stone" (ἢ στιγμὴ γὰρ ἢ λίθος), it allows us to become aware of movement even while it retains its singular identity in speech (τῷ λόγῳ)[34].

Stone or the matter itself insistently, instantaneously intervenes within the text of Aristotle, interrupting time itself. But if this is so, and stone is also the very term of definition and boundary of the 'now' itself, it also is the foundation for any determination of time as a sequence of continuous nows. It is not a foregone conclusion how time can be said in the same breath as a rock. The lexicon puts the problem otherwise, stating that *horos* also means time as a period or duration of time, for example *'the time within which'* or the 'notes *which limit* the intervals of a musical scale', 'I set the *limit* of human life at seventy years.'[35] Apparently the word can be used to relate to time more broadly than in reference to the 'now' as an indivisible part of time. When considering these temporal translations, we must not forget the other meanings of the word and that the *horos* must always have raised this problem of the limits and of the limits of time even when all we saw was stone, landmark or boundary. This might suggest that the *horos* provides space and context for time, regardless of its content (though never without its form), the material substrate that can cut in on the continuum especially when we are not paying attention, which is most of the time.

In the *Physics*, Aristotle provides another example of the use of the word in relation to time, stating that 'coming to be and passing away are the terms (*horoi*) of being and not being,' γενέσει μὲν καὶ φθορᾷ τὸ ὂν καὶ τὸ μὴ ὂν ὅροι.[36] Meanwhile, in *The Laws*, Plato recommends the age within which marriage is to be permitted, the *horos* of marriage, between a boy and a girl (no doubt an uncomfortable discrepancy for the girl).

> γάμου δὲ ὅρον εἶναι κόρῃ μὲν ἀπὸ ἑκκαίδεκα ἐτῶν εἰς εἴκοσι, τὸν μακρότατον χρόνον ἀφωρισμένον, κόρῳ δὲ ἀπὸ τριάκοντα μέχρι τῶν πέντε καὶ τριάκοντα.
>
> the time [*horos*] of marriage for a girl is from sixteen until twenty years of age, the longest determined [*aphōrismenon*] time, and for a boy from thirty until thirty-five.[37]

---

34 Ar.*Phys*.219b20.
35 LS: 1255.
36 Ibid.261a34.
37 Pl.*Laws*.785b.

Herodotus also uses the same word (in dialect) when he has Solon give the limit (*horos*) of human life as seventy years (εἰς γὰρ ἑβδομήκοντα ἔτεα οὖρον τῆς ζόης ἀνθρώπῳ προτίθημι).[38] In English, we are able to pose this temporal aspect in similar terms, such as in the phrase, 'for the term of his natural life.' This term would seem to open up a determined space, describing as it does both the limits to either side as well as the monotonous time within. In all these examples, the time within is marked as common, characterised as identical or of a standard nature, comprehensively delimited for procreation, life or incarceration.

All these examples, nonetheless, reveal that the *horos* does not itself define time. On the contrary, it would appear to open up the possibility of bounded time, more often than not to be followed by determinative limits, such as 'from sixteen years of age until twenty' (ἀπὸ ἐκκαίδεκα ἐτῶν εἰς εἴκοσι). If the number of years or determinate boundaries of one type or another are required to give the limits on top of the temporal boundary itself, what kind of definition would the *horos* give to time beyond its arithmetical calculation? Is the horos the material form that opens up the potentiality of measuring time, that which we actually sense when we feel time passing, or a material, lithic substitute for the absence of an actual, tangible sense? Perhaps the *horos* is the equivalent on the level of the singular life, to the general conception of the horizon as the determination of a shared existence, as *that within whose limits we live*? Does the simple noun correspond to the particular, while its verbal form corresponds to all being under the vault of the heavens?

The question that should be posed, then, is how the *horos* was supposed to maintain or enforce itself as boundary, as place or (im)position between? This question of the maintenance or force of place presents us with the problem as to whether the past inscription of the *horos* is recognised in the present. There can be no doubt that the *horos*, even now as we read it in classical texts and see it in the museums, raises the question of time and perhaps all the more so now that the materiality of the terminus is increasingly indecipherable for us on account of the wear and tear, the scars of time passed. How is time supposed to fill out the space between two limits, when the *horos* leaves neither room nor space but on the contrary is itself already filled with brute matter? How can a concrete, spatial relation be forged between stone and time, if not in a relation of substitution?

---

38   Hdt.1.32.2.

The form of the letter provides epigraphists with a *terminus post quem* or a *terminus ad quem*. But in the *horos*, it is exactly the letter (H) that perplexes the indisputable determination of such *termini*. These *termini* are supposed to constrict the possibility of the archaeological object's extension in time to a space between an *ad* (or an *ante*) and a *post*; between a *before* and an *after*. The question of dating, which lingers with the *horos* in the absence of the inscription or in the presence of an archaic letter, is not merely accidental to the *horos*. The marking of the boundary and the materiality of definition cannot be sufficiently comprehended as a spatial metaphor of drawing up limits or of limiting extension. And yet we have seen enough examples that should make it evident that the *horos* was *placed*, that it was 'given' a determined site, that first of all it takes place substituting stone for the boundary and then substituting the letters of the inscription for the stone. The substitution of one thing for another or deferring of the original meaning in matter seems to be a movement that is natural to horos, whether the originary meaning is coincident with matter, inscribed upon the land, read on stone or written in the soul. We might say that the *horos* takes place as stone, but remains by raising the problem of the substitutability of temporal limits and spatial boundaries.

Geologic Time

Contemporary concepts of time might be helplessly indebted to Aristotle. However, it is Aristotle interpreted by Ibn Sina that has most significantly changed our conception of universal time experienced on earth, that is the longer, geologic timescale. In geology, time is immediately associated with rocks, rock strata and the contents of rocks. It does not seem too much of a stretch to state that here time is identified with and by rocks, and an assemblage of rocks is what allows geologists and archaeologists to presuppose the existence of temporal continuity, whether this allows for catastrophism or not. It is rocks as writing, 'stratigraphy,' that provides not just a tool but the content of measurement with which a definition of time can be isolated and temporal definition construed.

In al-Kindi's book *On the Definitions* (*Fi hudud al-ashya'*), as well as in Ibn Sina's larger *Book of Definitions* (*Kitab al-hudud*), the word employed to translate the Greek, or more particularly Aristotelian term *horos* is the

Arabic *hadd*. As Kennedy-Day puts it, Ibn Sina 'explicitly indicates his debt to Aristotle in the *Topics* in his technical definition of *hadd*.'

> The definition of definition [*hadd*] is what the wise man (Aristotle) mentions in the book, *Topics*: it is a *statement indicating (pointing to) the quiddity (mahiyya) of a thing*, that is, regarding the perfection of its essential existence. It (definition) is what is obtained from its proximate definition and its differentia (*fasl*).[39]

The word *hadd* is an astonishingly apposite translation for the *horos*. The lexicon entry gives its principal meanings in limiting terms: 'hindrance, impediment, boundary, frontier,' and so forth, but it also comes to mean the restrictive ordinances or statutes of Allah.

> Before assuming its philosophical meanings, the word *hadd* follows a semantic evolution comparable to that of the Greek words that it translates, ὁρισμός and ὅρος. From its meaning of "limit" it passes to that of "delimitation" or "definition", and from that of "furthest limit" or "extremity" to that of "extreme" or "term" in logic. In order to avoid any ambiguity between the two meanings, modern Arab authors who study mediaeval philosophy often follow *hadd*, in the sense "definition", with the word *ta'rif* parenthesis, since one of the uses of *ta'rif* is in fact "definition", although its meaning includes both description and name.[40]

In the term *hadd*, this implicitly deontological sense of the *horos* is made explicit, 'in theology, *hadd* in the meaning of limit, limitation, is an indication of the finiteness which is a necessary attribute of all created beings but incompatible with Allah.'

> Ibn al-'Arabî says that differentiation (*tafriqa*) is the root of all things. This is because through the process of differentiation limits (*huddud*) are set between things, and except for the limits knowledge would be impossible.[41]

In Ibn Sina, the difference between definition and the definition of definition concerns the essential being of a thing. *Horos* differs from *horismos* by antinomy; where the *horos* is *hadd*, the definition *horismos* cannot be separated from its essence, it is the thing itself. But does this mean that it is identical to the thing or a representation of the thing in

---
39 Kennedy-Day (2004) 51, 102.
40 Gibb (1979–2005) 'Hadd.'
41 Bashier (2004) 87.

speech? Al-Farabi provided a definition of definition as 'a signification (*dalla*) of the essence of a thing,' saying of definition that it is used 'in signifying (*dalala*) how to distinguish a thing,' but also that 'it is considered that there is no difference between a thing and its definition.'[42] This is what Aristotle meant by stating that the *horos* is the word that as *logos* means the essence, τὸ τί ἦν εἶναι, of a thing: *horos* is the divisive signification that unites the explanation, *logos*, with its essence, *ousia*. The *horismos* is this as activity. Essence enters as the divisive factor between *horos* and *horismos*, and yet, as Aristotle put it, *ousia* is the only definition or main term (*horos*). This ambiguity or ambivalence of the *horos* is exactly what joins it (συνάπτει) to the essence or being of a thing (οὐσία).

The big difference in translation is, however, the absence of the lithic in the Arabic *hadd*. Here definition is abstracted from the material, it might be materialised in a barrier, but it is not essentially identified with stone. Nonetheless, the lithic is never far away. In Arabic, *ousia* is translated as *jawhar*, and by Gibb *jawhar* is translated into English as 'substance.'

> *Jawhar* [...] (the Arabic word is derived from Persian *gawhar*, Pahlawi *gor*, which has already the meaning of substance, although both in Pahlawi and in Arabic, it can mean also jewel) is the common translation of οὐσία, one of the fundamental terms of Aristotelian philosophy. "Substance" in a general sense may be said to signify the real, that which exists in reality, *al-mawdjud bi 'l-hakika*.[43]

The idea of 'reality' is basically foreign to the Greek language, though if it is to be found anywhere, it is most certainly not in the word *ousia*. Even translating the word *hypostasis* as 'reality' is more than a stretch. Reality for the Ancient Greeks does not seem to be related either to being or to 'things' (the πραγματικότητα of modern Greek is a loan word coined in 1787, and inspired by the French *realité*.[44])

According to the entry on *jawhar*, we learn that there is one point upon which the Arabic philosophers 'go beyond their master' Aristotle, for whom being is predicated analogically, that is by degrees.[45] For the

---

42 Kennedy-Day (2004) 50–51.
43 Gibb (1979–2005) Djawhar.
44 Babiniotis (2010) 1148.
45 Lane (1968) 475.

Arabic philosophers, however, there is a supreme being and intellect, that is, Allah, the principle of otherness; he is the Real, Justice, Truth (*Haqq*).⁴⁶ In order to be translated into this context, the essence of being (τὸ τί ἦν εἶναι) is itself divided, between what is here in the material world, and this essence as the *Real*, that is to say, Allah. In Arabic, then, we cannot help but recognise that what is substantial in definition and what is defined as substance consistently points to what it is to be (τὸ τί ἦν εἶναι), the definition as signifying the Real which is God, Justice, Truth, *Haqq*.

This 'reality' is, however, also coindicative of *Jawhar*, 'any kind of jewel, precious stone, or gem [...] any stone from which is extracted, or elicited, anything by which one may profit.'⁴⁷ This is what I mean when I say that the lithic is never far away. The rock is more significant for Ibn Sina than it may immediately seem, and Ibn Sina's absorption with rocks affects the very definition of the future and the past. Alchemy, obviously, is derivative of a fascination with rocks or minerals and their potentially combinative and explosive relation with one another. And while Ibn Sina does expound the different healing properties of rocks, it is another aspect of his work that has come to play a significant part in the lithic drama of the earth, or at least the human interpretation of this drama.

Ibn Sina is known as the first to read into the rocks a story of earthly history, now known as stratigraphy, the writing of the rock strata. The idea is that we can read time into rocks by taking the deeper rock layers (strata) to represent time periods far in the past and the strata closer to the earth's surface to represent periods of time closer to the present. In geology, this is known as the Law of the Superposition of Strata, and it is a principle fundamental to the measurements that comprise the geologic timescale. The following is Ibn Sina's account of the principle of superposition.

> It is also possible that the sea may have happened to flow little by little over the land consisting of both plain and mountain and then have ebbed away from it. It is possible that each time the land was exposed by the ebbing of the sea a layer was left, since we see that some mountains appear to have been piled up layer by layer, and it is therefore likely that

---

46 Cf. Gutas (1998).
47 Lane (1968) 475.

the clay from which they were formed was itself at one time arranged in layers. One layer was formed first; then, at a different period, a further layer was formed and piled (upon the first, and so on). Over each layer there spread a substance of different material, which formed a partition between it and the next layer (perhaps implying unconformity); but when petrification took place something occurred to the partition which caused it to break up and disintegrate from between the layers [...] As to the beginning of the sea, its clay is either sedimentary or primeval, the latter not being sedimentary. It is probable that the sedimentary clay was formed by the disintegration of the strata of mountains. Such is the formation of mountains.[48]

This theory was adopted later and generated what we now call the geologic timescale. George Sarton in his *History of Science* stated that the translation of Ibn Sina's *Mineralia* (elaborated upon by Alfred Sareshal) 'was an important source of geological knowledge,' especially concerning the formation of mountains and rock strata.[49] Toulmin and Goodfield add that our understanding of the past is 'no longer restricted within the time-barrier of earlier ages, this is due above all to the patience, industry and originality of those men who, between 1750 and 1850, created a new and vastly extended timescale, anchored in the rock strata and fossils of the Earth's crust.'[50]

How time is measured in the geosciences provides the framework for multiple fields of study, from a cosmological reconstruction of the history of the earth to understanding extinction events and predicting climatic rates and processes. Although there are different conceptualisations of time in the geosciences, the stratigraphic record continues to be the most important method of measurement, or 'clock.' Here, information is contained within the layers, or strata, and can be used to reconstruct the history of the earth. The underlying principle to this method is that of superposition. This method of dating is often accompanied by biostratigraphy, the use of paleontological, fossil, content found within the stratigraphic record, correlating spatially separate and potentially very distant strata and providing something of a cross-reference between strata in order to come up with a relative age for each stratigraphic

---

48   Ibn Sina (translation and source unattributed) quoted by Munim al-Rawi in Al-Hassan (2001) 414. However, Alfred of Sareshal's *De Mineralibus* also comprises some of Ibn Sina's earlier tractate, see Sarton (1931) 515.
49   Sarton (1931) 515.
50   Toulmin (1982) 141.

unit. A biozone, delimited by biohorizons, where divisions are made according to the first and last appearance of a fossil taxon, is described both spatially and temporally, where the occurrence that is the deepest down coincides with the occurrence that is furthest in the past. Even in the geosciences, space and time work together as a temporal duality.

It is interesting to note that we see something that quite closely resembles Aristotle's conceptualisation of the 'now,' a temporally specific point that is bound on either side but that contributes as an inseparable part to a continuum. Here, we have the biozone, bounded by biohorizons and contributing to the idea of continuous sedimentation, and when added up these layers of sedimentation become the spatial representation of the temporal continuum. 'A boundary horizon corresponds to a geological moment—the moment when the horizon was deposited. The interval between two successive physical boundaries is thus the embodiment of an inferred interval of time, or "age".'[51] The word choice here, of the 'horizon,' cognate of *horos* (verbal *horizo*, and neuter participle of the verb to be -*on*) suggests to me that accidents are rarely devoid of meaning and that the history of a word remains embedded even after it has long been forgotten. The horizon in stratigraphy can be constituted of stone (lithohorizon) of fossils (biohorizons), there are (in this context seemingly synonymous) marker horizons, there are also event horizons. The word 'horizon' here functions simply to draw attention to an alteration in rock layers whose uniformity allows the geologist to abstract a determinate interpretation. This is the *horos* in its primaeval form, natural mark and marker of nature, but still read by us.

However, to bring us back to earth (or perhaps the opposite), in the words of Aubrey, 'should boundary definitions take full precedence in chronostratigraphy?'[52] How can boundaries (and this is a direct echo of Aristotle) be defined? Must a time boundary be instantaneous, or can it last for several centuries or millennia? For most geological boundaries the transforming event can last a long time, which makes giving a particular date of change very difficult, and it is always possible that not everything changed so that the boundary is not an absolute but a relative boundary, perhaps including some species while excluding others. Ager addresses this problem, in discussing the relation between

---

51 Aubrey (2009) 94.
52 Ibid.

sedimentation and 'breaks' in sedimentation. For example, if a column of earth is taken, not only can different layers be observed but breaks within those layers, and if another column of earth is taken from the other side of the globe, one might expect to find a vaguely similar column given that significant change tends to happen on an earth-wide scale. However, this is not necessarily the case. What was merely a thin layer in the one column might appear as several feet in the other. Continuous sedimentation is interpreted as meaning continuous without significant breaks. 'But what is significant?,' asks Ager, 'Obviously there are plenty of unconformities where the break is obvious, such as the splendid unconformity between the Upper Cretaceous and the Precambrian of the Bohemian Massif.'[53] As studies continue to be buried in ever more detail, more breaks become apparent. It would appear that the geologic record has as much difficulty in designating and verifying 'continuous sedimentation' as Aristotle had in proving the continuity of time.

These discrepancies pose a problem in the definition of a particular period of geological time because time appears to be relative to place but also relative temporally. Ager's response is to reformulate the stratigraphic record not in terms of layers of sedimentation but in terms of gaps interspersed with layers of sedimentation, where 'gaps predominate,' 'lithologies are all diachronous' and 'fossils migrate into the area from elsewhere' and then out again. In the words of Deleuze and Guattari, 'stratification in general is the entire system of the judgement of God (but the earth, or the body without organs, constantly eludes that judgement, flees and becomes destratified, decoded, deterritorialized).'[54] Ager uses slightly more mundane language to describe the relation between breaks and sediment.

> Perhaps the best way to convey this attitude is to remember a child's definition of a net as a lot of holes tied together with string. The stratigraphical record is a lot of holes tied together with sediment.[55]

Diachronous, rather than synchronous, measurement allows for flows, reiterations and intra-actions in the fossil record. So that evolution is no longer visualised as an arrow, or a climb upwards on the pyramid of being. Instead, we have infiltration and movement and flux, as

---

53 Ager (1973) 28.
54 Deleuze and Guattari (2014) 46.
55 Ager (1973) 34.

well as interruptions and one-way streets. As Ager puts it, 'this may be called the Phenomenon of the Gap Being More Important than the Record.'[56] On the one hand, the problem of the inconsistency between the gap and the continuum, outlined by Ager, has since resolved into relative time, with biostratigraphy and stratigraphy working together.[57] On the other hand, the concept of geological time is being increasingly funnelled into attempts to delineate absolute time through technological advances providing continuous and anchored methods of measuring time (radiometric, astrochronology, dendrochronology). The first is measured according to rocks that provide both the material basis for the continuum and for the gap. The second is measured as measurement abstracted from the material (or the attempt to do so): that is numerically.

> Chronostratigraphic ages and numerical ages thus differ in a fundamental way. One refers to a duration, the other to a discrete stratigraphic horizon. They also differ in their stability. Once a chronostratigraphic unit has been defined by physically fixed boundaries, its true duration remains unchanged. In contrast, numerical ages may vary considerably, even in measurements on the same material, let alone in different samples measured in different laboratories with different tools [...] For this reason numerical ages are often explicitly characterized by method, whether radio-isotopic, astronomical, or estimated.[58]

These methods of measuring absolute time are integrated, or synchronised, in order to construct a geologic timescale unfettered to the inconsistences of the material. However, where the stratigraphic record is bordered, bounded or limited by the origin of the earth and the present—that is, it covers the last 4.54 million years—the astrochronological record goes back 50 million years (and no further because of chaos). How on earth can any kind of isochroneity be established between things (beings, organisms, objects) that are simultaneously spatially and temporally distant? When they are literally worlds away, how can different strata share isochronous biohorizons?

> To restate the obvious, duration is an interval of time between two moments, i.e., two points in time. It follows that any consideration of time involves three parameters, a proximal point, an interval, and a

---

56 Ibid.
57 see *Stratigraphy and Timescales* Montenari (2016).
58 Aubrey (2009) 96.

distal point. The greatest duration for Earth sciences is 4.54 billion years, from the time of the formation of the solar system to the time of today. Intermediate points in this 4.54 billion years temporal continuum are necessary to comprehensively describe Earth history.[59]

There is something reassuringly banal about the fact that something posed as one of the great *aporias* of ancient philosophy is here treated as something that can be taken for granted. The assumption here that Aristotle's definition of time is not only correct but self-evident evades the interruption into the continuum of time of gaps, hiatuses, *stasis* or quantum discontinuity. All those gaps in the stratigraphic record that confounded Ager, what are they made of? Did nothing happen? Are they marks of an absence of change? Were they felt or sensed as a lapse in time at that time? It might be possible to say what this missing time in the stratigraphic record is composed of though that is not the same as knowing what it was when it went wherever, whenever that was. Does it not seem peculiar that a theory of geologic time is so dependent upon lapses or indeterminate breaks in time? On this at least it appears that the geologic timescale is, perhaps not based upon, but at least metaphorically and terminologically indebted to Aristotle's description of time as continuum interrupted by the sensation of movement or lapse thereof, forming a line marked by a series of points.

Although the tendency to resist metaphor in the sciences is strong, Gould states the difficulty of conceptualising time as so extreme that it can only be grasped metaphorically.

> An abstract, intellectual understanding of deep time comes easily enough—I know how many zeroes to place after the 10 when I mean billions. Getting it into the gut is quite another matter. Deep time is so alien that we can only comprehend it as a metaphor.[60]

Perhaps this is why descriptions of space, linear and circular, always arise whenever a new definition of time is attempted. Or what if time itself can only ever be taken as a metaphor, matter carried over spatial temporality, as Aristotle would seem to suggest when he says that it is 'of change'? Metaphor functions by drawing out similarities that might not otherwise be apparent. My suggestion is therefore that there is a

---

59   Ibid.
60   Gould (1987) 3.

deep conceptual relationship between our 'feeling' of time and our experience of solidity. The metaphor might be described by a phrase, such as 'all that is solid melts into air.' What if there is only floating time, and any attempt to bring time down to earth, to fix it to a particular point in time must of necessity employ metaphor? Given that stratigraphy is the act of reading what was never written, geologic time reads as poetry. For example, as Aubrey states, a 'chronostratigraphic boundary itself is comparable to a datum: a point in the rock (no thickness) that represents a point in time (no duration).'[61]

In response to the common belief that contemporary science is divorced from ancient mythical belief systems, Gould elaborates a series of metaphors used to envision time both within the biblical tradition and in antiquity, of the arrow, the cycle and the line, that have supported subsequent forays, scientific and literary, into conceptualising the passage of time. He argues that these metaphors are so deeply instilled in the psyche of researchers that they are fundamental even to the geological formulations of deep time. The result is that the founding theories of the geologic timescale (Hutton, Lyell) were primarily based upon these metaphors, and only secondarily based upon a familiarity with rocks. These scientific elaborations upon geologic time, 'deep time' as Gould says, might be called philosophy, metaphor, or organising principle, 'but one thing they are surely not—they are not simple inductions from observed facts of the natural world.'[62]

Concerning these metaphors that remain latent in the interstices of the project of modern science, Eliade argues that the linear version of history, with its overtones of progress and linear evolution, has more recently been invested with a rehabilitation of earlier, prehistoric cyclical versions of time, marked by periodic oscillations and fluctuations. While the theory of the linear progress of history may be attributed to the Middle Ages, the linear theory of time is as we saw much older and is also intricately linked with the notion of cyclical time.[63] Eliade highly valued the reappearance of cyclical theories in contemporary thought, obviously derived from archaic fertility myths (such as the Orphic myths, the reversion of the Dao, the repeated creation of the Enuma Elish, and

---

61 Aubrey (2009) 93.
62 Gould (1987) 9.
63 Eliade (1959) 145.

many more), since 'the formulation, in modern terms, of an archaic myth betrays at least the desire to find a meaning and a transhistorical justification for historical events.'[64] I agree with Gould when he says that deep time 'imposed a vision of reality rooted in ancient traditions of Western thought, as much as it reflected a new understanding of rocks, fossils, and strata.'[65] That said, I would rephrase the statement to include other traditions, in particular the Arabic philosophical tradition, as well as stressing that the vision of reality was firmly based upon a much older understanding of rocks, without which the notion of reality itself would not have been definable.

Horos, even in its stony presence, comprises a notion of the cyclical. The *horos*, as the definition of a thing, is also in a sense the reality or essence of a thing; it draws up the boundaries of a thing, defining it from and in reference to other things that are close but are not it. The limit of a thing is therefore its beginning, but it is also its end; *Horos* might also be translated as the limit in the sense of an 'end' or 'aim' towards which something drives. And that is a problem, because once things become metaphorical there is always the risk of determinism intervening in the guise of the supernatural or the divine, which is not necessarily the opposite of what is real.

Another boundary that dissembles the metaphorical presence of the *horos* on a universal scale can be found in Ibn 'Arabî's conception of the *barzakh*. As with *horos*, so here, *barzakh* is expressed in a relation of similarity with the 'now,' 'the now (*al-an*) is like a partition (*barzakh*).'[66] This *al-an*, 'now,' is a 'moment' or 'presence' that is given as the only real part of imaginary time, a moment that can also be expressed in the phrase 'Day of Event' or 'Day of Breath,' or in the single letter, *alif*, the initial vowel of the name of Allah. All letters (and this also holds for the world at large) can be broken down into this single letter and built up from it, though it does not break down into them.

> Time is a circumstance for an event just like meanings for letters, and space is not like a circumstance, so it is not like a letter. Time is confined through division by "now" and does not necessarily require the existence of objects, but space can not be comprehended without objects (that

---

64 Ibid. 147.
65 Gould (1987) 10.
66 Yousef (2008) 68.

occupy it), so it is a kind of (ontological) "home" (for what is created in it).⁶⁷

Barzakh is a 'boundary' that is inclusive 'in the sense that things participate in the limit not that the limit constitutes the final part of a thing.'⁶⁸ As the very possibility of defining, the *barzakh*, like *horos*, resists further definition in so far as it presents a common limit to all things. It is the separation between two things (definition) as well as the separating factor (that which defines) 'become manifest as one in entity.'⁶⁹

> So the reality about the *barzakh* is that within it there can be no *barzakh*. It is that which meets what is between the two by its very essence. If it were to meet one of the two with a face that is other than the face with which it meets the other, then there would have to be within itself, between its two faces, a *barzakh* that differentiates between the two faces so that the two do not meet together. If there is no such *barzakh*, then the face with which it meets one of the two affairs between which it stands is identical with the face with which it meets the other.⁷⁰

In an echo of the boundaries of stratigraphy, the *barzakh* is 'between-between, a station between this and that, not one of them, but the totality of the two.'⁷¹ Ibn 'Arabî puts it simply, 'the true barzakh is that which meets one of the things between which it separates with the very face with which it meets the other[...] It is in its essence identical to everything it meets.'⁷² This reflective otherness is essential to any notion of a boundary; no boundary can be double, and yet it remains the essence of duplicity. It is division, but undivided, and as such it remains as the common term or boundary of either side, even when either side have nothing in common beyond this boundary. The *barzakh* defines by relating what falls to either side of it to what is other to it, it is not a limit that draws something to an end, but a limit that defines by unifying relations between Other and its other. As Bashier states, the closest, as well as affectionate and unifying of all 'relations is one between Other (khilâf) and its other, from which it is differentiated. [...] Affection (mawadda) between differentiated things prevents each of them from

---

67 Ibid. 181.
68 Bashier (2004) 86. Ar.*Met*.1022a. tr. Ross.
69 Bashier (2004) 87.
70 Chittick (1998) 334–335.
71 Ibid. 333.
72 Bashier (2004) 87.

wanting the disappearance of its other from existence.'[73] The *barzakh* cannot be differentiated in thought; it is not entirely logical. Thinking about it is said to be comparable to threading a camel through the eye of a needle. In the canonical tradition of the Qu'ran *barzakh* is also the intermediate state between death and resurrection. It is the grave, in a temporal and spatial sense, where the dead linger for the time between death and judgement.[74] The experience of arriving at the boundary, *barzakh*, is described by Ibn 'Arabî in two comparable states, that of the 'greater death' which occurs to a person after death, and that of the 'lesser death' occurring to someone during sleep.

> Do you not see that, when he is transferred to the barzakh through the greater death or the lesser death, he sees in the lesser death affairs that he was considering rationally impossible in the state of wakefulness? Yet, in the barzakh, he perceives them as sensory things, just as, in the state of wakefulness, he perceives that to which his sensation is connected, so he does not deny it. Despite the fact that his rational faculty proves to him that a certain affair cannot have being [*wujud*], he sees it existent in the *barzakh*. There is no doubt that it is an affair of being [*wujud*] to which sensation becomes connected in the *barzakh*.[75]

The sensation that is located here realises the possibility of a presence, which Ibn 'Arabî calls the 'presence of the imagination,' this presence is other than that of perception. But that does not mean the *barzakh* cannot be conceived, imagined or real. It is no doubt the confrontation itself where what is logical meets what is imagined, and the boundary between the two is expressed by the *barzakh*, a boundary that exactly bounds upon the 'Real,' *Jawhar*. *Jawhar* is the stone, but it is also *Allah*.

Indefinite Human Time

Are we forced time and again to return to Aristotle as the originator of the myth of the returning circle of time? If the 'now' is, according to Aristotle, the determination or definition of time, but time is not without movement—that is, it is nothing other than indeterminateness—the 'now' is either not a part of time or time is both indeterminate and

---

73 Ibid. 88.
74 Ibid. 88. (Qu'ran 23:100)
75 Chittick (1998) 337.

determinate, with and without definition. This is the problem of the limits of time inherited from Aristotle's conception of movement as something indefinite (*aoriston ti*).[76] Here, Aristotle is responding to the theories of the pre-Socratics that nothing can come into or pass out of existence.

> οὔτε γὰρ τὸ ὂν γίνεσθαι (εἶναι γὰρ ἤδη), ἔκ τε μὴ ὄντος οὐδὲν ἂν γενέσθαι· ὑποκεῖσθαι γάρ τι δεῖ.
>
> [F]or what is could not come to be, since it is already, and from what is not nothing could come into being, since something must form a substrate.[77]

What remains in time is movement, as what is both same and other to time. If time is sense and consciousness according to determination, movement is necessary as the indeterminate continuity of time that is not sensed, that is not felt. In Book II of the *Physics* Aristotle had thus defined movement as *aorist*—'indeterminate,' literally 'unbounded,' *aoriston*, 'without *horos*' since 'when movement is determined, it ceases' (ὅταν γὰρ ὁρισθῇ, παύεται). Or, as Heidegger explains, 'Being-there is being-there-completed in its place, limit. If it is moved, it is something that changes its site; it is such a thing that is no determinate place.'[78]

What is the significance, in light of this, of the verb-form in Ancient Greek that poses a challenge to the Latinate tense system, the *aorist*? Because of the 'primitive' nature of its stem the aorist is believed to be the oldest Greek tense, and indeed requests to the deity are usually phrased in the aorist. Does this mean undefinability precedes definition, temporally speaking, that is verbally? The fact that its name is the *a*-privative-*horos* tends to lead toward definitions of this supposed tense via negative determination, 'without limit,' 'without time,' in variations on the theme of the occurrence as simple and undivided. However, that is not to say that it never happened or happened 'once for all,' 'final,' or 'completed.'

In fact, the aorist can imply that an event is in the past, without actually belonging to the past itself. The verb form can be used in association with other tenses to denote present or future events (hence its use in

---

76 Ar.*Phys*.201b23.
77 Ar.*Phys*.191a27–33.
78 Heidegger (2009) 215.

proverbs or gnomic sayings). As one study suggested, the aorist is punctiliar because it 'simply refers to the action itself without specifying whether the action is unique, repeated, ingressive, instantaneous, past, or accomplished.'[79] Therefore the aorist has been defined not as a tense but an *aspect*, rendering it a matter of perception, or a sense for the moment. It is, in short the tense of the verb that most lends itself to sensing time beyond movement.

One article on the 'abused' aorist's exegetical function decries the semantic interpretation that would take the aorist's punctiliar aspect to imply that the action of the verb is a point. Insisting instead on taking the name of this supposed tense literally, Stagg states 'the aorist draws no boundaries.'[80] The 'punctiliar,' or 'snap-shot action' of the aorist belongs to the writer's presentation, not to the action of the verb itself. In *Revelations*, creation is described in the aorist, which is certainly not to say that it is a single act, nor a completed one; 'that the aorist here covers a semantic situation which in itself is not punctiliar but clearly linear is as normal an aoristic usage as can be found. The aorist is simply a-oristic.'[81] Creation is indeterminate, neither a point nor a line. It is definitely a matter of interpretation, whether creation was something that happened or continues to happen. Whatever it is, it is neither momentary, nor a simple action, nor limited to the past. 'The main point [!] is that it cannot represent action as progressive,' or completed, thus the 'life eternal' is manifested every hour, in 'every word' and 'every deed.'[82] Mirroring creation in speech, the aorist is not a historical singularity, or definite occasion, but nor is it just one step in the linear march toward organised systems (*cosmos*).

The aorist 'represents the action denoted by it indefinitely.'[83] The distinction that must be drawn up is that between the form of the verb and the action it describes. This is more than a simple difference of syntax and semantics—it is not the act that is punctiliar, it is the verb, 'the tense stems indicate the point of view from which the action or state is regarded.'[84] But where is this spectral point if we are talking about

---

79   Carson (1984) 70.
80   Stagg (1972) 222–231.
81   Ibid. 228. *Rev.* 4.11.
82   καὶ ἡ ζωὴ ἐφανερώθη, John 1:2, ζωὴν αἰώνιον ἔδωκεν ὁ θεὸς ἡμῖν, 5:11. Stagg (1972) 225.
83   Stagg (1972) 229–231.
84   Ibid. 230.

indeterminateness? If movement is defined as 'indeterminateness,' the question remains how we are able to define something in the absence of determination itself.

Obviously, the problem is the 'point of view' or perception. When it comes to the aorist, it all depends on one's point of view, as Aristotle himself suggested when he stated that we feel the movement of time, we sense it. In the other tenses, one's point of view is defined by temporal relation to the verb at hand, whether one is involved in the action of the verb (present continuous), placed after the action of the verb (past perfect), before it (future/conditional) and so forth. But with the aorist, one's temporal relation is not at stake, that is, one's position is as actor or acted upon without further elaboration as to this temporal position (the determining factor for translation is therefore the context itself). If there is any verb that represents floating time, it is the aorist. The aorist is punctiliar, but it is not instantaneous; as Stagg says, the aorist 'presents' an action, 'of whatever nature, without respect to its nature' and the action itself is thus represented in the negative (*a-oriston*).[85] The aorist is change itself, only partly abstracted from nature, and undetermined because when it is determined, it stops.

What really matters is the position of making this indetermination present: *horos*. Movement, like the aorist, requires something else to transform it into time. According to Aristotle, nature is movement ἐν δυνάμει, in potentiality. And we should have sensed this contradiction, between nature and (human) time, with the first *horos*, the boundary or term from which the human marker has been obviated. The *horos* names itself so that determinateness, boundaries, definitions and so forth might be 'natural,' inscribed in nature, an already prescribed limit that leaves us free to go about the task of (re)definition.

We require the potentiality of the *horos* to determine even its negation; in which case the *horos* becomes exactly this, our 'point of view.' So, the *horos*, in the absence of the negating *a-* is what? Non-movement? A point, *stigmē*? Our bondage to our brief moment in time or the stigmata of mortal beings? *Horos* would appear to put in question the exclusivity of a linear boundary and the point of transgression. The opposition is not limited to that between *horos* and *aorist* but between the whole order of organic and nonorganic movement and this singular stone's immovability. But

---

85 Stagg (1972) 231.

the opposition is also there between our determination of ourselves in contrast to nature, inorganic and organic. Or is it the matter that marks our lapse of consciousness and the indeterminate 'continuity' of time? Levinas expresses the position as existential: 'the value of images for philosophy lies in their position between two times and their ambiguity. Philosophy discovers, beyond the enchanted rock on which it stands, all its possibles swarming about it.' [86]

Prometheus Unbound

Do the structures of language reflect a preconceived conceptual chronology or do the words we use modify our ability to recognise limits and agencies within or outside of time? The demiurge might be timeless or beyond time but does that mean that any consciousness of divinity also becomes extraneous to time? To reframe the problem from a secular position, is human reason capable of structuring a conception of time from any perspective but that of the human? Are we trapped within thought processes that constantly reenvisage time as an object of human thought despite epistemological advances or is there some way to escape the narcissism of human subjectivity when it comes to observing the sublimity of creation and the motion of the spheres?

There is a very similar structure of oppositions and play of metaphor undergirding the conceptual diagnosis of our age as the 'Anthropocene.' As DeLoughrey states, in 'recognising the history, present, and future of apocalypse, universalized temporality becomes parochialized and characterized by ruptures and an experience of "now-time," a marked shift from chronology to simultaneity.'[87] We have attributed the age with our name, and it is thus the name of the *anthropos* that presents the boundary of time. We are the 'now.' At once divisive and nominative, the Anthropocene reinstates humans as the determiners of time, this time not simply as subjects who sense time but rather as a major geomorphic force. As both dominators and denominators we are now masters of time, we make our own time. This hubristic denomination of an age should alert us to the true nature of the problem. The problem is only inadvertently given as the human use of natural resources, excavating

---
86 Levinas (1987) 13.
87 DeLoughrey (2019) 133.

and burning fossil fuels, mass deforestation, the enormous scale of chemical detritus we leave in our wake. The Anthropocene obviously points to all this and critiques it. But the deeper significance of the Anthropocene is the reinforcement of the egoism of humanity. The Anthropocene might be treated as a symptom of a more than material presence upon earth, where the 'diagnostic of the Anthropocene proposes a new geological epoch that designates humans as a collective being capable of geomorphic force, shaping Earth systems on a par with inhuman forces.'[88] The problem will be whether the attribution of the name, or rather our name, to an epoch serves to vindicate rather than hinder such egoism.

The scientific designation that poses the Anthropocene as the name of an entire age obfuscates the fact that we are not actually in control of the forces of nature; we are not in control of geomorphic forces nor should we be, and our continuing egoism in placing ourselves above 'nature' can only lead to our own destruction (in soul if not in body). More than anything the title 'Anthropocene' assumes a 'we,' a general humanity of actors who are in no way the 'we' who are in effective control of the detritus we leave in our wake. We might name names, but they should know already and that hasn't stopped them so far, on the contrary it has only spurred them on to greater acts of hubris.

But perhaps we can look at it from a different perspective. Rather than taking the human as a force that changes time, that insinuates itself as the lord and master of the nonhuman, we could think of this determination of the Anthropocene as a remineralisation of the human, putting us on a par with rocks. However, studies show that human activity is 'the most important geomorphic agent acting on the surface of the modern Earth, a conclusion that evokes several nontrivial consequences. It should be made clear, however, that anthropogenic and natural rates of erosion embody somewhat dissimilar measures of continental denudation.'[89] We might be a geomorphic agent, but we are not acting in any way similar or equivalent to the nonhuman forces that preceded us. If anything, the name of the Anthropocene is a pretence that permits us to reconfigure ourselves petromorphically, the scientific version of Adam and Eve's earthly and ostic origins. As Yusuff states, this 'immersion

---

88 Yusuff (2013) 779.
89 Wilkinson (2005) 163.

of humanity into geologic time suggests both a remineralisation of the origins of the human and a shift in the human timescale from biological life course to that of epoch and species–life.'[90] So which is it to be? Does the designation of the Anthropocene iterate human mastery over nature or does it reinvest us as mineral beings?

This passage back into mineralisation echoes the earlier mineralisation from the previous domination of soft tissue, 500 million years ago when bones emerged in organic bodies. De Landa describes it as 'if the mineral world that had served as a substratum for the emergence of biological creatures was reasserting itself, confirming that geology, far from having been left behind as a primitive stage of the earth's evolution, fully coexisted with the soft, gelatinous newcomers.'[91] In her *Allegories of the Anthropocene*, DeLoughrey describes the discourse of the Anthropocene as invigorating a 'geological turn whereby anthropogenic sediment becomes a sign of deep history, evidence of human minerality where the excavation of the "geos" reveals the "bios" and a merger between the human and the nonhuman nature.'[92] For DeLoughrey the Anthropocene also serves to restructure the belief systems of the past, such as that in developmental, technological progress. Given the fact that the new age is marked by a destabilisation of the elements, that essentially poses an existential threat to the previous pleasantly beneficial age of climatic stability of the Holocene, she suggests that this engenders a reinterpretation and revelation 'the enlightenment narrative of progress' as myth. She is probably using the word 'myth' in much the same way that Adorno and Horkheimer used the word in the *Dialectic of Enlightenment* to argue that a return of barbarism within advanced civilisation was possible.[93] Myth, of course, need not have this overtone of the barbaric/civilisation divide. Or, if it does, that divide itself should be the first item of study when investigating myths of civilisation. I would argue that the Anthropocene itself, as a concept, could be equally subjected to this critique, as myth.

Frodeman raises the possibility that a restructuring of thought might alleviate us of the burden of traditional methods of consumption.

---

90 Yusuff (2013) 779.
91 Delanda 26.
92 DeLoughrey (2019) 133.
93 Adorno and Horkheimer (1997) 44.

> The problems facing society today require us to question the intellectual taxonomy that has trained us to think ever more deeply within the same old ruts. Reordering the categories of our thinking and our institutions—even more, learning to think across categories—will help us create new conceptual and social spaces for addressing our environmental challenges.[94]

The call to break down the categories, to reconfigure the system, to spread out and dissolve all boundaries uses exactly the same language that got us here in the first place. The drive to transgress, break free, to exceed present limits, and to extend the limits of human thought and technology is the same as that which framed the scientific revolution. In the words of Bacon, what was desirable was 'the enlarging of the bounds of human empire, to the effecting of all things possible.'[95] In a similar vein, Latour claims that the time has come to 'develop *more*, not *less*' and in order to do so we must do away with 'the limits of the notion of limits.'[96] Not only are we forced to face our existence in a timescale that explodes our minds but Latour also tells us that accepting the paradigm of the Anthropocene is to accept that we are exiting the human drama and entering one on a planetary scale. Hence, all attempts at revolution are behind us since 'we have already crossed a few of the nine "planetary boundaries" considered by some scientists as the ultimate barrier not to overstep!'[97] Latour implies with irony that the Anthropocene brings in a new era of self-satisfied scientism, in which multiple disciplines collude in order to coerce us into obedience. The drama that science maintains is that of humankind's emancipation from Nature and 'the thrusting-forward arrow of time—Progress—characterized by its juvenile enthusiasm, risk taking, frontier spirit, optimism, and indifference to the past.'[98] While I agree with his critique of the Anthropocene as scientific megalomania, I think his resultant faith in technologies and political ecology as a force of intervention is not only theoretically dubious but also maintaining and giving power to exactly the same megalomania that characterises the Anthropocene. We might be able to observe the 'molecular machinery of soil bacteria,'

---

94   Frodeman (2003) 3.
95   Quoted in Neyrat (2019) 98.
96   Ibid. 95.
97   Latour (2014) 1.
98   Latour (2011) 21.

but that has not stopped us from doing our utmost to kill as much of it as possible with the use of agrochemicals.[99]

We live in an age where new technologies are created to confront new threats. The problem is that the new technologies and their demand on natural resources are so often the cause themselves of threats, such as deforestation, mineral depletion and contamination through mining, not to mention horrendously abusive labour conditions. It would appear that the solution is as much a problem as the cause. Perhaps this novelty that seems to be so desirable, in both thought, technologies and institutions, is itself the rut that we are trained to think with as well as believe in. It would appear that the designation of the massive boundary of the Anthropocene, separating us off from the Holocene that most of my friends were born in coincides or even permits the dissolution of boundaries elsewhere. Frodeman argues that this new age dissolves hard borders, so that 'processes flow across disciplinary boundaries. Life becomes lithic (e.g. limestone), while tectonics influences patterns of evolution. To put it differently, the terms "Earth sciences" and "environmental sciences" today represent a distinction without a difference.'[100]

It would appear that we live in an age where distinctions are breaking down, where flows and assemblages are transforming our world from one formed of categorical differences to one where technological interconnectedness and the rhizomatics of domination interrupt such autarchic desires as self-control and self-limitation.[101] That's not to say that life on earth is composed of entirely distinct, separate organisms, rather 'a sum of relatively independent species of flora and fauna with sometimes shifting or porous boundaries between them.'

Geology appears to be the core, even the substrate or bedrock, providing the junction for what was formerly thought distinct and separate. Frodeman continues his diagnostic with a prescription for the academy: 'To effectively grapple with our environmental challenges we must cross the boundaries that have separated the humanistic and scientific part of geology.'[102] Scientific facts cannot in isolation address the dead-end street that science has created, he says, so we must

---

99   Ibid. 21.
100 Frodeman (2003) 4
101 Deleuze and Guattari (2014) 55. 'Rhizomatics of Domination', see Mikulak (2007).
102 Frodeman (2003) 4.

'redefine the conceptual space of the Earth sciences.' The crux of the problem is 'philosophical and spiritual in nature.' While he surely does not mean it in this sense, I think it is not incorrect to interpolate into this diagnosis that natural spirit or the spirit of nature is lacking from scientific discourse. That the spirit of nature is to be found, as Frodeman suggests, in a nexus of scientific debate, democratic institutions, and humanitarian virtues, seems to me to reinstate power in the mire of the same old ruts.[103] As was the case with Latour, we see an advocation for change acting in the name of restoring the current systems and holders of power, albeit in a slightly different guise.

And yet, a limit is seen, floating around the edges, determinable within the bounds of the sciences, perhaps as the bounds of science: 'The Earth sciences are becoming the sciences of limit,' states Frodeman.[104] 'The scarcity we are facing will not be a matter of running up against purely physical boundaries. Scarcity in the twenty-first century will combine physical limits with a complex range of cultural factors,' these include everything from economics to theology.[105] The Earth sciences pose an 'ontological disruption,' the limit breaking into our everyday excursions from the pub to the supermarket, something like an earthquake opening up great chasms in the road and drawing up distinctions between the various exorbitant, consumptive activities we engage in on a daily basis and the enormity of geologic life. The Earth sciences are once again rising up as a soothsayer of catastrophism, as the old gods of the earth rumble in discontent below while the sea god creeps formidably closer and the god of fire wreaks havoc upon the land. However the Earth sciences do not call them 'gods,' they call them 'natural processes' disturbed and unbalanced by human activity, though that does not seem to explain the way these forces rage. But no, the absence of gods in the sciences is what has allowed science to progress in its mechanistic interpretations. At base I agree with Frodeman; we are confronted with a problem of limits, rather an absence of limits in contemporary scientific, technological and governmental development, in social and behavioural determinism too. It is this problem that the diagnostic of the Anthropocene should draw our attention to.

---

103 Frodeman (2003) 8.
104 Ibid. 16.
105 Ibid.

Neyrat, in *The Unconstructable Earth*, also brings our attention to the presence of limits in the discourse of the Anthropocene. Modern belief still has its consequences, he says, by 'believing that science had emancipated us from nature, we have believed in the existence of the Great Divide between us and the rest of the world.'[106] Neyrat quotes Hans Jonas's characterisation of the contemporary human as the 'definitively unbound Prometheus,' where he also calls for 'concerning ourselves with limits.'[107] Neyrat also criticises Latour for arguing against the existence of these limits or essentially the limit that divides humans from their environment. For Latour, the absence of limits does not mean only that we are one with nature but rather that all of nature has been anthropomorphised such that we have the ability, perhaps according to Latour the necessity, to totally remaster the environment in such a way as it suits us; 'more attachments, more mastery, more interventions.'[108] He gives the example of terraforming, which would be the opposite of recognising these limits.

Neyrat uses the word 'myth' to discuss the Anthropocene, but he does so with caution.[109] As the former section suggested, the word 'myth' in addressing geological timescales would not be inappropriate, based as they are upon archaic structures of belief that indeed required systems of mythical belief to support them. The Anthropocene is the 'myth,' the story that elaborates the mythology of human mastery and human dominance over nature, where the role played by today's humans is not unlike the role human beings play in the Promethean myth. And just like the Promethean myth, the intercedence of Zeus, father of gods and men is required as a heteronomous source of permission and legitimation for subsequent human activity. As Neyrat puts it, 'with the anthropocene, our winded postmodernity seems to have acquired a new breath and a means for resuscitating a grand narrative that [...] plunges us into the most distant past.'[110]

The grand narrative of the Anthropocene seems to justify an overwhelming dissolution of boundaries. More often than not these

---

106 Neyrat (2019) 92.
107 Ibid. 93.
108 Ibid.
109 Ibid. 34–35.
110 Ibid. 35.

boundaries pertain to the individual rather than states and corporations, as movement between corporations, banks and state systems of power is definitely becoming more fluid. Biotechnological control and surveillance of individuals is already being justified by necessities claimed to have been instigated by climate change. Similarly most environmental concessions are forced upon individuals rather than the corporations largely responsible for aggressively rapacious forms of resource extraction and use or the large stakeholders in such firms. With the Anthropocene, boundaries dissolve, and nature becomes subsumed into aggressively despotic human nature, or a few limited examples thereof.

Nonetheless, limits arise again and again in human discourse, and here specifically the consideration of the human relation to the nonhuman should recall us to our own limits and boundaries. While many boundaries are internal, or at least linguistic, they are also substantially present in our relations with the world around us, framing those relations, whether in transgression or symbiosis. Perhaps there are only absolute limits in nature, the limits that are even today becoming evident because once transgressed they produce unpredictable and perilous disequilibrium in the natural systems that support not only human but all organic and nonorganic life. Mining, an attack upon the deep sedimentary deposits of the earth is as destructive as deforestation, and personal technologies, such as phones and computers, are based upon the ongoing extraction of increasingly rare metals. Biotechnologies, along with genetic modification of plants, animals and humans, consistently cross the boundaries of what it means to be a plant, animal or human. And as these technologies show, there is always a price to pay, even if that is simply the ensuing dependence upon the industry that created you, or made you as you are. The resulting catastrophes of wildfires, pesticide poisoning, the disappearance of heirloom plant varieties, the human epidemic of allergies and pharmaceutical dependence are all as a result from human intervention claimed in the name of science, to improve upon natural processes and what we cannot help but recognise as natural limits, from the earth's crust to human skin.

Walter Benjamin's notion of similitude arrives via a redemptive theory of language where the principle has long been lost to the past (whether it ever *was* remains an issue in Benjamin's evolutionary messianism). Any similarity in word or letter can only act as a reminder/remainder or a brief moment of recognition of what language as such could have been or was. It is thus exactly what is lost that can be a subject not of knowledge but of recognition, something that 'flashes up' in the instant of similitude: 'The past can be seized only as an image that flashes up at the moment of its recognizability, and is never seen again.'[111] This illuminated image draws Benjamin's gaze beyond the horizon whereby 'allusion to the astrological sphere may supply a first reference point for an understanding of the concept of nonsensuous similarity.'[112] Not just because the form that similarity takes in recognition is that of a flash but because there is a very real possibility that the star you happen to admire tonight has ceased to exist many thousands of years before. In which case, how can we ever solidify our relation with the whole as anything but in loss, of the lost returning as a memory, an instance of eternity in the midst of life's brevity? What are stars but rocks reflecting light at a distance, exceeding extension and measurable by time? Is there a correspondence between human beings' tendency to place stones upon the land as marks of memory and the overwhelming eternity of rocks in the sky?

Since we are now standing in the place of the third term of astrological measurements, οἱ τρεῖς ὅροι, we must be forgiven for extrapolating without the hindrance of atmospheric pressure.[113] The definition of the 'now' has a 'non-sensuous similarity' with *horos*, in all its determinations, boundary and mark, letter and word, definition and stone. Or to put it otherwise, the 'now' is *horos* exactly because the singularity of identification is impossible. There is no opposite of the 'now'; it is not opposed to continuity even though in the vulgar concept of time it is the single moment, the exception that proves the rule. Just as there is no opposite of *horos* since once we start determining what is *a-horos*, we must have placed a limit from which to begin. It is a point that takes place at a certain distance from time. The point is that with the *horos*, this limit is none other than the raising of the question of definition. In conclusion, we can begin again with Aristotle's definition that time begins as a sense or, to rid this sense of its intentionality (*dianoia*), as a feeling for what is other than time, that is for something else that falls in between the 'now' that is past and the 'now' that is to come.

---

111 Benjamin in Löwy (2005) 390–391.
112 Benjamin (2005) 721.
113 LS: 1256 (IV.4).

Fig. 6. Gravestones. Photograph by M. Goutsourela, 2013. Rights belong to the Kerameikos Museum, Athens. © Hellenic Ministry of Culture and Sports/ Hellenic Organization of Cultural Resources Development (H.O.C.R.E.D.).

Fig. 6a. ΗΟΡΟΣ ΜΝΗΜΑΤΟΣ, in Lalonde (1991) [I 7462].
Fig. 6b. ΗΟΡΟΣ ΣΗΜΑΤΟΣ, in Lalonde (1991) [I 2528].

6. Geophilia Entombed or the Boundary of a Woman's Mind

ὁ ὅρος — metaph. [...] *the boundary* of a woman's mind, [...] *memorial stone* or *pillar*.[1]

Were women marginalised in Ancient Greek society? Was this a norm for the archaic period as well as the Classical? Are there traces in the Greek corpus of a system of matriarchy belonging to the late Neolithic, Iron and Bronze Ages? Are later seventeenth- to nineteenth-century AD interpretations as much to blame for the tone of misogyny that dominates scholarship of the ancient world as they are responsible for manipulating the primary sources into reflecting their own beliefs, rather than clarifying the beliefs of the time? Given the filtration of our sources through the monotheisms of Islam and Christianity followed by the fundamentalist hegemony of the scientific revolution, can we even trust what we read in order to weave some kind of a web to trace us through the truth of what it meant to be a woman in the fledgling Greek *polis*? The intervention of masculine hegemony between then and now as affecting the way we read the city may also have had the effect of obliterating any original documents that may have enlightened us as to the thoughts, the lives and the preoccupations of women. Or, if intervening misogyny is not to blame, then what were women doing— were they sleeping, were they so engrossed with providing a genetic inheritance that they forgot to supply us with an intellectual one?

This chapter will not answer these questions. But that does not mean we must not ask, perched as we are upon the boundaries of Greek thought trying to follow through with all these *aporias*. The archaeology of the *horos* might be traced via the cultic and into the philosophy and

---

1   LS: 1255–1256.

economics of the Athenian *polis*, but it has to go through women in order to arrive there. One of the basic appearances of the *horos* is as a marker of graves, and as a swathe of texts from archaeological remains to tragic theatre make clear, this realm remained the monopoly of women. Whether a preoccupation with the realm of death was an act of subjugation or whether it reveals the significant power that women held over the existential reality of the society's population depends on how willing the reader is to find an alternative model of freedom to our highly politicised, biologically determined, publicly limited freedoms of today. Here I present a discussion of boundaries and attempt, through something like a game of Go, to place women in relation to these boundaries, on this side, on the other or anywhere in between.

We have already witnessed the possibility that the *horos* described a face-to-face relation, a divisive mark that demands the bonds of hospitality and transgression in friendship alone, where either side embraces the very limit they share, the otherness they have in common or the definition of being whose immediacy is interrupted only by the definition itself. Then again, we have seen *horos* erupt into the continuum of time, as both time's limit and definition and as 'what it was to be' (*to ti en einai*). In all of these, the spatiality of the *horos* is related to a transgression of boundaries and to what is past as what is no longer but nonetheless provides the substratum for being present.

This substratum or what underlies is the topic of this chapter. It might be the earth, or the place of the feminine, that provides the substrate for existence. But it also might be what is past, done, gone and buried. The past of the *horos*, whether it is dead and buried, implicated in those who laid the boundaries or continues to be read in museums today, raises the question of the authority of the mark. Is the *horos* a sign, an intermediary mark drawing up the definitions between subterranean powers and the active imagination of human beings? Where does the *horos* get the power to define and determine from? Is it in us who read or from the dead who placed the stones and drew up the boundaries, or is the power essential to stone itself, emitted from the depths of the earth? In Ancient Greek society how someone was buried was as much the realm of women as was childbirth. And if anyone can be said to have spoken up for what lies underneath, it was Antigone. But there's plenty of time before Antigone enters the stage. In the meantime, there's another boundary to consider.

The Female Boundary

The Liddell and Scott lexicon provides us with a metaphorical example of the use of the word *horos* said to mean 'the boundary of a woman's mind.' It is taken from Aeschylus's tragedy, the *Agamemnon*, which tells of the hero's bloody fate at the hands of his unfaithful wife Clytemnestra upon returning home after ten years from the victory over Troia. Spoken by the chorus of old men, and after condemning Clytemnestra's extramarital affair with Aegisthus, they discuss the possibility of news of the return of Agamemnon. Here I quote several stanzas with a typical translation to provide the context. I then follow with a brief criticism and alternative translation that dramatically changes the meaning of the word *horos* in this context, which should prove the lexicon's entry here as entirely mistaken.

> ἐν γυναικὸς αἰχμᾷ πρέπει
> πρὸ τοῦ φανέντος χάριν ξυναινέσαι.—
> πιθανὸς ἄγαν ὁ θῆλυς ὅρος ἐπινέμεται
> ταχύπορος: ἀλλὰ ταχύμορον
> γυναικογήρυτον ὄλλυται κλέος.[2]

> It seems that a woman in temper
> grants consent to what is pleasing before it is apparent.-
> Too easily persuaded, the woman's boundary [*horos*] is encroached upon
> swiftly, but swift-dying
> perishes rumour proclaimed by a woman.

This sexually conservative reading obfuscates the libidinal overtones of these lines and seems to require a special manoeuvre in the translation of *aichmai* as 'temper,' rather than 'spear.' Another singular appearance is the *gunaikogureton* (γυναικογήρυτον) implied to be connected with *guros*, circle, as in 'what goes around,' something, I suppose, like how rumour 'gets around.' But I suggest the implication is to the word *gorutos* (γωρύτος), 'bow-case or quiver,' so the *gunaiko-gorutos*, would be the woman's quiver, the place where euphemistically speaking 'arrows' are put. Presumably a spear is in this case a particularly well-endowed 'arrow,' hence her easy persuadability. In this alternate reading, a woman gives consent to the pleasure of a spear, her easily persuaded

---

2 Aesch.*Ag*.483–487

boundary is broken, and the good name of her quiver dies. The 'female boundary' (*thēlys horos*) can then be interpreted as none other than the hymen. The subsequent lines play around the idea of a woman's consent, an interpretation that, if anything, is apt given the sexual basis of the tragedy and the old men's censure of Clytemnestra's sexual exploits.

And yet the lexicon described this instance as not only 'metaphorical' but also 'the boundary of a woman's mind.' It must be asked what a woman's mind has to do with it? And why is this particular meaning of the *horos* and this alone 'metaphorical'? All the other meanings suggested in the lexicon were unmediated identification but not this one. Woman yet again provides fertile ground for the exception of non-identity. No doubt this could be turned to her advantage. Nonetheless it is also interesting to note the shift towards the metaphorical the closer you get to the hymen.

There is another reference given by the lexicon for the same sense of the 'woman's boundary', again from Aeschylus's *Agamemnon*. But this time it is Cassandra, and the boundaries are questionable; they are the boundaries of her prophetic method, the origin of which is posed in terms of possession by the chorus: πόθεν ὅρους ἔχεις θεσπεσίας ὁδοῦ /κακορρήμονας; 'Whence have you the *horoi* of the ill-omened prophetic way?'[3] I have purposefully failed to provide a translation for *horos* as I think the ambiguity here is telling. Are these landmarks along the way to prophesy? Or is it the origin of the terms of the art that is being put into question? It is a question of method and knowledge as well as claiming possession (*horous echeis*). Cassandra, at this point, is literally possessed by her art. She is looking into the future at the murder of Agamemnon by Clytemnestra, as well as her own murder. It must be said that these 'boundaries' are if anything excessively expansive, and not at all suited to the senses of 'boundary of a woman's mind.' On the one hand we have the *horos* as 'hymen,' on the other, as the terms along the prophetic way. Either way there is nothing to suggest the metaphorically limiting implication of the definition of the boundary of a woman's mind. Perhaps what we are dealing with, then, is not the boundary of the ancient woman's mind, but the boundary of the nineteenth-century male mind, that is, the mental barriers of sirs

---

3   Aesch.*Ag*.1154.

Liddell and Scott when it came to addressing women's subjectivity as the purveyor of truth, not to mention women's sexual parts.

That the 'female boundary' (*thēlys horos*) should be none other than the hymen certainly agrees with the significance the ancient city placed upon virginity and the passage from the semi-sacred role of the virgin to that of the married woman; and yet in Greek 'hymen' as membrane is linked to the uterus, the stomach lining. Hymen is the god of marriages, and variations of the word signify marriage and the marriage song, all dancing around while obscuring the whole point of the matter (which of course is never whole, nor a point). It was plausible for a male physician to argue that the physical membrane of the hymen did not even exist in women.[4] But perhaps male ignorance about women's bodies was not so significant, given the segregation of the two realms of reproductive or domestic life and political or civic life. At least it may not have mattered until the political started to intrude into the private, subjecting both the woman and the household to a series of legal and religious interventions that focused upon limiting and controlling the sexual, as well as reproductive, activity of a young woman.

The obsessive compulsion to control women's sexuality and reproductive potential was strictly orchestrated within the institutional structures of the city-state. In her analysis of the role of rituals performed for the goddess Artemis, Cole suggests that state institutions introduced the presence of state boundaries into the lives of the people by mirroring biological boundaries in the transition from girlhood to womanhood. The goddess Artemis was often worshipped on geographical margins, close to territorial frontiers. 'The rites of young women at these sites marked important transitions in the female life-cycle, but signified more than the individual female's safe passage across a personal biological boundary. The community as a whole depended on ritual activities undertaken in border areas.'[5] The festival calendar required that both girls and young women perform public ceremonies at remote sanctuaries, such as at Brauron. Cole argues that these dedications and rituals demonstrate 'the centrality of women's religious role and the crucial part played by their offerings in securing the well-being and survival of the *polis*,' while the 'sacred space on a border defined the limits of a city's territory

---

4   Keuls (1993) 143 and Merchant (1990) 161.
5   Susan Cole, 'Domesticating Artemis' in Blundell and Williamson (1998) 27.

and protected the transitional area that divided one community from another.'[6]

The traditional claim is that sanctuaries were placed on boundaries 'as markers of territorial sovereignty'; however, I could venture another interpretation, given that many sanctuaries stretch back to the time preceding the institution of the *polis*, they may not have marked territorial boundaries at all, certainly not those of the city-state. Or if they did mark boundaries, maybe they did so in homage to the boundary itself, rather than as a mark of possession and dominance. Certainly, in the case of Artemis, the masculine dominance that inhered to the *polis* seems not only anachronistic but also antithetic to the older, more fearsome character of the goddess. That these sanctuaries and rituals were later adopted and reconfigured, as an apparatus beneficial to the propaganda of the *polis* should not be excluded. A reconstitution of the religious character of border zones in order to reinforce social and political dominance was certainly a possibility.

The idea that the security of the city's women mirrors that of the city's borders is a metaphor that could appear intrinsic to ancient political and religious thought. 'There was a recognisable correspondence between the vulnerability of a city's women and the vulnerability of a city's borders,' states Cole, where intrusion and violation on a border, especially one of ritual significance 'was a sign of ritual failure and indicated that the security of the *polis* was threatened by a war with its neighbours.'[7] Not only was 'lack of respect for the boundaries of another community' expressed in myth by 'lack of respect for the integrity of its women,' but it was also used as the basis for justifying violent acts of retaliation between states.[8] However, what if the metaphor worked the other way around? Rather than the sexual vulnerability of women representing the vulnerability of the state and therefore requiring the ritual activities of the women in order to secure the state, what if the vulnerability of borders was depicted in rituals of femininity in order to represent women as vulnerable and insecure? To pacify a potential enemy is a much surer tactic than simply disarming them.

If we consider the Artemis rituals from this inverted perspective, the situation as it stands becomes much more interesting. One example

---

6   Ibid.
7   Blundell and Williamson (1998) 28.
8   Ibid.

that became stock standard propaganda in the expansionist policy of imperial Athens was that of the Lemnian incursion at Brauron, which was then used as a significant part of the rationalisation for the violent Athenian attack on Lemnos as described by Herodotos.[9] The claim that girls and young women (particularly virgins) were at risk during the festivals and rituals on borders supported a nexus of ideas featuring the masculine assertion for control and domination, over the territory and its borders, as well as over its women (regardless of social standing, girl, mother, slave, etc). An assault upon territorial boundaries (*horoi*) was akin to the violation of the woman, the breaking of her *horos*, and these two ideas were mythically connected and reinforced through ritual performance. The subsequent mythical parity between the 'female boundary' and state boundaries, between the sexual control of women and the security of the *polis* emphasised how an entire community could suffer from untoward sexual license amongst the female population of the city. In contemporary analysis, women are often attributed marginal roles in the Ancient Greek city, and while on the one hand that is absolutely true, there they are dancing on the boundary, it almost seems too obvious, like hiding it in the open. Their marginalisation (as is the case with most minorities) plays a central role in the preservation of the constitution of the state. In religious festivals and liturgies, women literally put their *horos* on the line in support of the state.

My question, then, is whether these women were willingly acting for the benefit of the *polis* or whether these activities were in some way coerced. Were women putting their sexuality on the line in order to consciously reinforce the dominant political and religious framework of the city, or was the control of their sexuality a method of limiting the rebellious force of a considerable part of the population? We know that there was a certain degree of resistance amongst women in the face of the polity of men: Both Aristophanes' *Thesmophoriazusai* and his *Lysistrata* paint an image of women who are anything but passive in the face of the claim to male dominance in the socio-political and economic sphere. The men go off to war, redirecting state and private funds into these exploits abroad, only to return carrying stolen arms and stolen, foreign broads in their arms. No wonder in Aristophanes' comedies, women are willing to go to great ends to change their economic and social conditions, not

---

9 Hdt.6.137–140.

to mention the great heroines of tragedy who revolt against the various systems of power they are trapped within. Clytemnestra murders her husband in retribution for what she sees as the criminal sacrifice of her daughter, Medea also responds murderously upon her male children when faced by the abandonment of Jason, Helen simply walks out of the institution of marriage, and Antigone in her refusal to accept 'the way things are' is far from alone in standing up and resisting the status quo. Elektra is in the minority as contributing to the founding myth of a judicial system that reinforces the status quo. Everybody else seems to revolt against it. Might these be representative, not of women as willing contributors to the dominant political power, but as active participants in ongoing social dissent?

In the *Republic*, Plato claims to bring women into the machinations of the state. He permits them to engage in the sphere that was, according to the actual Greek polity, exclusively male. Given mental proficiency and reproductive ability, he grants them equality in some measure to the guardians of his mythical constitution.[10] Perhaps Socrates was aware of how dangerous a force women could be if they remained on the other side of politics. In Ancient Greece the other side is exactly where it is said that women were, the other side of the door, indoors where they belonged.

> The household constituted the nonpublic sphere within which the female was subsumed and which therefore defined her. Because the good at which the household aimed was a lesser good than that which was the end of the *polis*, the wife-mother achieved only the limited goodness of the 'naturally ruled,' a goodness different in kind from that of the naturally ruling.[11]

But that does not mean that the realm of the household was in itself lesser than the public realm. The word *economics* comes from household management, and we know, from the Homeric epics as from archaeology, that the household in the Bronze Age was the main productive and economic organisation, before cities developed and took over this role.[12] And if women were excluded from public life, they nonetheless

---

10 Elshtain (1993) 32.
11 Elshtain (1993) 45–46.
12 Austin and Vidal-Naquet (1980) 36–47.

remained essential, providing the preconditions upon which public life rests.

The assumption that participation in a particular form of representational government and free-market economics is the front door to social freedom and wholly constitutes public life is today so taken for granted that it actually starts to seem like inter-generational indoctrination. The question, however, should be whether social and political 'equality' within a system structured upon inequality is even desirable given the inherently corrupt constitution of the economy, politics, the law and the private sector. In any case, later legislation took Plato at his word and refigured the state such that it absorbs women within it, along with the requirement that women be subject to the laws, the economic system and the state's constitution even if that means performing roles as perniciously violent as those that were once directed against them. Meanwhile, the ability to even imagine any other form of organisation be that kinship, communitarian, communal or whatever, is becoming increasingly more difficult.

Is this absorption of women into the public realm, even if not entirely, what began to happen in the fifth century that changed the perception of women? For example, the earlier Bronze Age myth of the murder of Agamemnon is attributed to Aegisthus, while the classical *polis* put the weapon in the hands of his wife Clytemnestra. Why this shift in responsibility? Is this a demonisation and denigration of the woman who demands control within her household? Or is it a warning of what women do when they are unchecked and beyond the power of their husbands? That the role of women in myth elucidates the unconscious tensions, ambiguities and fears dominant in society seems obvious to us today.[13] However, a further question poses itself, especially given observations of contemporary media and the distortions of stories and facts to maintain corporate interests: to what degree were the representations of women purposeful? Or, who was controlling the images, attitudes and opinions portrayed, if anyone? And, consequently, what was gained by the renovation and potential modification of ancient myths as they were staged within the democratic *polis*?

The Ancient Greek *polis* was not so naïve that it did not reconfigure the facts in order to represent the city and its actions to its own benefit,

---

13 Gould (1980) 55.

nor was it unwilling to manipulate public opinion in order to maintain the status quo, as the great demagogues Perikles and Alcibiades are testament. The funeral oration of Perikles is definitely a fine piece of political propaganda, not to mention Alcibiades justification of the Sicilian expedition.[14] Another fine piece of propaganda may well have been the manipulation of the worship of Dionysus into a city cult and Artemis and girls' rituals celebrating the crossing over into womanhood into festivals securing state power. So, if these publicly sanctioned forms of speech, entertainment and ritual were performed in order to cover over an alternative world-view, what was that other perspective and why was it so threatening to the continuation of male hegemony?

I suggest (and this is merely suggestion, for the reasons outlined above concerning lack of evidence) that it was not only an attitude but an entire system of relations that threatened the behemoth of state authority, not necessarily exclusively matriarchal, though it certainly had room within for the generative power of birth and the degenerative power of death. In stark contrast to the civic representations of Artemis as protecting territorial borders, was Artemis as Mother Goddess, *Thesmophore*, goddess of childbirth and protector of the ancient laws or customs (*thesmoi*).[15] The Mother Goddess is well accounted for in statuesque form from the Palaeolithic until the Iron Age and is linked with matriarchy or at least the worship of a fertility goddess or the 'great mother.'[16] The problem is that although we have plenty of cultural artefacts that suggest that an overwhelming significance held to the mother goddess, any traces of this worship within the historical period are deeply contested and heavily overladen with the values of later patriarchally organised, economically constituted societies (that is to say state centralised, non-household economics). That said Benigni does succeed in deploying a plethora of evidential finds, so that it seems that this worship is coming to air, despite the incongruence of present socio-economic conditions.[17]

---

14   Basically the entirety of Thucydides' *History of the Peloponnesian War* and Herodotos' *Anabasis* can be read as state propaganda. The orators also generally engaged in some form of truth-twisting to the benefit of their cause, e.g., on the funding of martial affairs, the theoric fund and public versus private wealth, in Austin and Vidal-Naquet (1980) 340–358.
15   Detienne (1977) 79–81.
16   See Benigni (2013).
17   Ibid. 1–22.

The dominant cosmology of the classical era that has come down to us is one of mythical, cyclically patricidal, inherited power, where the feminine elements seem to feature only as the exceptions that prove the rule.[18] That said, I do not doubt that mythological narratives had at least two sources of dispersal, and therefore there are at least two versions of the same myth, although there are normally many more. There was the dominant, authoritative narrative deployed by men in the service of political and social allegiances (for example, Telemachos's dismissal of his mother Penelope with the statement that 'myth is the province of men').[19] But there were also the mythical cycles told by women, such as myths sung to pass the time while working, myths told to educate and entertain children and sing them to sleep, myths used to illustrate conversation during hours of leisure, bathing and dining, perhaps accounting for some of the less distributed versions of myth (such as that of Helen's duplicate following Paris to Troia, while the real Helen passed the war partying in Northern Africa).

The overwhelming presence of women in Greek myth should alert us to the fact that patriarchally dominant society never succeeded, if it ever aimed to do so, at obliterating the powerful position of women both in the family and in the community. Many women feature in the mythological canon of Greece, from the well-known goddesses of the first generations of the gods on into the Olympians (Aphrodite, Demeter, Hera, Athena, Artemis, etc.) and the lesser divinities as well as the plethora of nymphs and local deities, including a number of divine female collectives, (the Graces, the Muses, the Fates, the Pleiades). There was no lack of the female in the Greek mythological corpus. But there are also the mortal women famed for their misbehaviour or good behaviour, such as Clytemnestra, Helen, Hecuba, Medea and Penelope. Women from this class also extend over generations, such as Iphigeneia, Elektra, Hermione, Cassandra. For the most part they are from ruling families or that failing of the priestly caste (Chryseis, Briseis). As Blundell states, 'Royalty was one of the bits of traditional social baggage that Greek myth carried with it into the later ages.'[20] There are also the female monsters, whose purpose seems wholly to threaten and chastise

---

18 Ibid. 35.
19 Hom.*Od*.1.356–9
20 Blundell (1995) 17.

the little boys and girls into doing the right thing (Gorgons, Medusa, Sphinx, Furies: Erinyes/Eumenides). There are also plenty of examples of choruses of women within Greek theatre, where women *en masse* were not always represented straightforwardly either as victim or threat.

Symbolic associations of women, or the mythological female, put women on the side of the unbounded, men with the bounded, women with nature and reproduction, men with law and order. Although in the so-called *Pythagorean Table of Oppositions*, Aristotle aligns the unlimited, *apeiron* (ἄπειρον) with the feminine side, against limit (πέρας) on the masculine, we can certainly understand this opposition as having the opposite effect socially.[21] As Anne Carson argues, the fact that women were considered to be unbounded is perhaps enough to implicate them in the maintenance of common, social boundaries.[22] Zeitlin states that the 'boundaries of women's bodies are perceived as more fluid, more permeable, more open to affect and entry from outside, less easily controlled by intellectual and rational means,' and for this reason, as can be seen on stage, women were perceived within the *polis* as a physical and cultural instability.[23]

That women were passive may also have been an idea promoted within the city, but it was certainly not apparent upon the city's stages or within the city's myths. An example featuring the culture hero Herakles, a woman's arts and the *horos* appears in Sophocles' *Trachiniae*, where Herakles, drawing up the location, *horizei*, for altars and woodland sanctuaries, in the worship of Zeus (ἔνθα πατρῴῳ Διὶ /βωμοὺς ὁρίζει τεμενίαν τε φυλλάδα) receives the poisoned garment from his wife Dianeira.[24] That this hero of masculine strength withstood the twelve labours, facing off beasts and monsters, only to die at the soft touch of cloth from the hands of a woman, is telling of the power that adhered to women in Greek society. That power might not be very pleasant, but it is there all the same. It is a power that threatens because it is unbounded, falling beyond the bounds of civic authority, identifying women with everything that men are not.

---

21 Ar.*Met*.986a24. In these dichotomies evil, *kakon*, is also on the side of women, exemplified by Pandora. See also Carson (2000) xxxiv.
22 Carson (2000) 153.
23 Zeitlin in Winkler and Zeitlin (1990) 65.
24 Soph.*Trach*.743.

The dichotomy aligning men with civilisation and women with nature that was so popular during the enlightenment may find its origin within the Greek *polis* and even continues today to be a favourite mythology both of those supporting the hegemony of certain political forms and those desiring a return to wildness and a unity with nature. As Blundell states:

> Prominent among these is the identification of women with the wildness of nature- that is, with whatever exists beyond the boundaries of an ordered civilisation. It is generally assumed that it is women's capacity for child-bearing, and hence their alignment with natural forces beyond male control, that prompts these commonly envisaged relationships with trees, plants, springs, birds, and so on.'[25]

This nature symbolism operates within a nature versus culture model, a dichotomy presumably disseminated by men to demobilise women and women's power to the margins of society (for example the man-eating maenads in Euripides' *Bacchae*). However, this interpretation is presumably as much a result of the propaganda of the classical period as it is our own contemporary conventions still at work.

Considering that most social and economic powers today are based upon the use and abuse of natural resources, and the surplus of profit created by wage inequalities between workers and executives, that women should be separating themselves from the 'forces of nature' and relocating themselves within the workforce, whether as workers or executives, obviously does a great deal to maintain these already existing cycles of natural and labour resource extraction and profiteering. So, if women have also moved over to the side of law, capital and polity, who is left to speak up for the unbounded?

Authority's Attire: Body, Tomb, Sign

Conceptualise the *horos* as a simple lithic confrontation or even an apperceptive, perpendicular arrangement, outlining boundaries run horizontally in closure or are left open, the stone's upper façade points towards the heavens, its base planted firmly in the ground. The *horos* is buried, at least partly. Does it also transversally gesture below? If so,

---

25 Blundell (1995) 18.

the *horos* stands upon another boundary, the boundary that stands as a point of disjuncture and therefore also conjuncture between those in the 'now' and those below, inscribed within the earth, those who live no longer, the worm-feeders. The eruption of the *horos* in the continuum of time was also phantasmagoric, haunting the conceptual world of memory with an inscription of stone. *Horos* was a sign no less real for all its ghostliness; it was the material representation of the dead. The living engrave stones, and this is a reciprocal relation; sooner or later, the stones engrave us. In this grave subjectification we can catch a glimpse of what was at stake in the *horos* from the first. *Horos* was also inscribed upon gravestones, and this inscription separated the material world of the living from the spectral realm of the dead, a distinction that might be spooky and even petrifying but is not for all that unearthly.

They may not be the earliest examples of *horoi*, but the funerary *horoi* are at once plenteous and have the advantage of an additional inscription which serves to mark them out as different from other *horoi*. Some funerary *horoi* have been found during the excavations of the Athenian *agora*, even though burial ceased to be practised there from the end of the seventh century BC.[26] There are some special cases of burial until the end of the sixth century, largely limited to certain family plots. It is assumed that these were aristocratic families whose traditional tomb was maintained while the larger populace was excluded to burial sites elsewhere. This theory is supported by the high-quality pottery discovered in these tombs. The latest of the graves are those of two infants placed in the ancestral burial ground at the end of the seventh or beginning of the sixth century. In the absence of further information, one can only attribute the archaic extension of the spirit of death in the *agora* (such as the cult of the heroised dead) to proverbial idiosyncrasy, old habits die hard.[27] The majority of later classical funerary *horoi* have been found in the Kerameikos cemetery.

The lettering of the funerary *horoi* is rough and for the most part epigraphists propose only a vague date up until the third century BC. They are marked by six main inscriptional variations:

---

26 Lalonde (1991) 16–18; Thompson (1972) 10, 19.
27 Thompson (1972) 119.

ὅρος τοῦ δεῖνος
ὅρος μνήματος (μνημάτων, μνημείου)
ὅρος σήματος
ὅρος θήκης (θηκῶν)
ὅρος χωρίου
ὅρος χωρίου μνήματος

Each gravestone is inscribed first with *horos*, and then presented in the genitive there is a choice of inscriptions: a name (for example, *Xsanthio, Helikēs*), a memorial or remembrance (*mnēma*), a sign (*sēma*), a receptacle (*thēkē*) which could be either the grave as such or the receptive earth, or ground (*chōriou*), or even the determined place, as the place of memorial (*chōriou mnēmatos*).[28] Today, it would be more usual that a memorial (*mnēma*, the neuter noun of memory) of the name of the dead stand in its own right, where the name inscribed in stone is already in memory of the dead. It appears that the ancillary demarcation of the *horos* was, however, often necessary. It seems to me that the inscription of the word *horos* draws attention to the monument itself, rather than to whom the monument was there to serve, or what it was there to do. Perhaps the second word of the inscription served this second function. It is almost as if we were to go into a cemetery and the gravestones were all inscribed with the word 'gravestone of Jane Smith,' for example. Our gravestones tend to leave this word to context, but it is still there. A gravestone might read 'in the memory of,' but what is elided is 'this is a gravestone in the memory of.' So, in a way common usage today is not so different to the ancient inscription; except that they did not elide the reference to the monument, the memorial as object of memory.

The words *horos mnēmatos* and *horos sēmatos* offer an indulgent range of opportunities for translation, though I find it difficult to feel satisfied with any one in particular as conveying what was fully intended in the name of the dead. I could suggest another meaning for the *horos* and translate the first as 'gravestone in the memory of'; that would certainly be easier to understand, though not necessarily true to the original. The second part of the inscription, with the word for sign, *sēma*, is trickier. The lexicon glosses over the possibility of a more complex meaning by simply saying that *sēma* can also mean 'sign by which a grave is known.'

---

28 For examples, see IG I³ 1139; IG I³ 1138; IG I³ 1132; IG I³ 1134; IG II² 2587; IG II² 2594. Cf. Lalonde (1991).

But with the word *horos* this would be doubling up, something like the 'gravestone that is the sign of a grave.' Presumably not. Suffice it to say here that regardless of how we translate *horos* (term, limit, mark, boundary, and so forth), the real question the grave should pose is how memory and the sign stand in relation to the *horos*. In this question all the remaining genitives of the above clauses are brought into the same relation of correspondence.

Socrates claimed that there was a linguistic similarity between the tomb and the sign. In the *Cratylus*, he gives us a (dubious but interesting) etymology that would describe a relation between the grave or tomb, the body and the sign: 'are you talking about the body?' asks Socrates (τὸ σῶμα λέγεις;).

> καὶ γὰρ σῆμά τινές φασιν αὐτὸ εἶναι τῆς ψυχῆς, ὡς τεθαμμένης ἐν τῷ νῦν παρόντι· καὶ διότι αὖ τούτῳ σημαίνει ἃ ἂν σημαίνῃ ἡ ψυχή, καὶ ταύτῃ 'σῆμα' ὀρθῶς καλεῖσθαι. δοκοῦσι μέντοι μοι μάλιστα θέσθαι οἱ ἀμφὶ Ὀρφέα τοῦτο τὸ ὄνομα, ὡς δίκην διδούσης τῆς ψυχῆς ὧν δὴ ἕνεκα δίδωσιν, τοῦτον δὲ περίβολον ἔχειν, ἵνα σῴζηται, δεσμωτηρίου εἰκόνα· εἶναι οὖν τῆς ψυχῆς τοῦτο, ὥσπερ αὐτὸ ὀνομάζεται, ἕως ἂν ἐκτείσῃ τὰ ὀφειλόμενα, τὸ 'σῶμα,' καὶ οὐδὲν δεῖν παράγειν οὐδ' ἓν γράμμα.[29]

> For some say it [the body, *sōma*] is the tomb [*sēma*] of the soul, their notion being that the soul is buried in the present 'now'; and also because by this it signifies [*sēmainei*] whatever the soul wants to signify, therefore it is correctly called 'sign' [*sēma*]. However it seems to me that it is more likely that the Orphics established this name, as the soul has a penalty to pay, on account of which it has a cage, to keep it safe, that is like a prison: and this is, just as it is named, and until it pays up in full, the 'safe' [*sōma*] of the soul, and it is not even necessary to change a letter.

This proximity of the sign, body and tomb is also brought up in the *Gorgias*, where the scholia attribute the idea both to a Pythagorean scholar, Philolaus, and to the mystical Orphic religion.[30] Derrida almost quotes the sentiment exactly when investigating Hegelian semiology; he states that the 'tomb is the life of the body as the sign of death.'[31] In Socrates' explanation the convergence between sign and tomb is explained by the soul's 'burial' in the present 'now.' One cannot help but expect to find

---

29 Pl.*Crat*.400b-c.
30 Pl.*Grg*.493a.
31 Derrida (1984) 82.

the *horos* floating around here somewhere, and yet it remains unwritten, uninscribed within the text, materialised only as the gravestone marked out and defining in the interstices between all these words.

Etymology aside, what is the sign's relation to death? A sign unites a concept and a sensory perception, signified and signifier, however memory is the production of signs, according to Derrida, and is also thought itself: 'The body of the sign thus becomes the monument in which the soul will be enclosed, preserved, maintained, kept in maintenance, present, signified.'[32] In his study of gravestones, Sallis states that 'stone comes from a past that has never been present, a past unassimilable to the order of time in which things come and go in the human world.'[33] He continues, 'that nonbelonging of stone is precisely what qualifies it to mark and hence memorialize such comings and goings, births and deaths. As if stone were a sensible image of timelessness, the ideal material on which to inscribe marks capable of visibly memorializing into an indefinite future one who is dead and gone.'[34] The tomb is the sign of the dead, but it does not belong to the dead. It is the sign of the living, and the living investment in the dead. This is the beginning of what I call the economics of death. This sign that is both the monument of life-in-death and death-in-life, the 'sepulchre of the soul' and the 'hard text of stones covered with inscription,' is given by Hegel as the 'pyramid,' or as Derrida argues the 'semaphore' of the sign or the signifier of signification itself.[35] However,—and this is where a long history of women's rights resolve into a preoccupation with death—Antigone is desperate, and for her, any hole in the ground will perform the task, any covering of dust, as long as it is accompanied by the appropriate wailing, the dirge of the dead.[36] But it is not merely the funeral rites of her brother that Antigone demands, it is the immortality of the soul that she is fighting for, the maintenance of the sign and the continuity of its meaning within the entire system of semiotics that the burial of the dead is part of.

Antigone's infamy, in Sophocles' tragedy, is her obeisance to what she defines as the binding precedent of the unwritten and unfailing laws

---

32 Ibid.
33 Sallis (1994) 26.
34 Ibid. 26.
35 Derrida (1984) 83
36 Alexiou (2002).

that dictate the burial and mourning of the dead. The King, Creon, has decreed that Antigone's brother's corpse go unburied as a punishment for his belligerent claim to the throne. The problem that resounds, not only in the case of the disputed authenticity of the king and the dictates of burial customs, is that of authority. But in this case the question is not who has the authority to control, the authority of power; it is rather an oddly spectral authority, the jurisdiction of women, the mourning and ritualised burial of the dead. When it comes to the obeisance of unwritten laws, Antigone declares the authentic primacy of unwritten customs by means of negation, which does not mean that they are word-of-mouth or in some way give precedence to speech. On the contrary, that they are read despite being unwritten seems to be where the real issue lies, that is the serious issue for mourners and murderers alike of what to do with the body.

Antigone explains the origin of the laws by drawing attention to the gods who she claims did *not* authorise Creon's edict barring the sacred duty to bury the dead, because they already stand as authorities for the opposite.

> οὐ γάρ τί μοι Ζεὺς ἦν ὁ κηρύξας τάδε,
> οὐδ' ἡ ξύνοικος τῶν κάτω θεῶν Δίκη
> τοιούσδ' ἐν ἀνθρώποισιν ὥρισεν νόμους.
> οὐδὲ σθένειν τοσοῦτον ᾠόμην τὰ σὰ
> κηρύγμαθ', ὥστ' ἄγραπτα κἀσφαλῆ θεῶν
> νόμιμα δύνασθαι θνητὸν ὄνθ' ὑπερδραμεῖν.[37]
>
> Zeus was not the herald who gave me that [edict], nor did Justice, who lives with the gods below, determine (*hōrisen*) such laws amongst men. Nor did I believe that your decrees were so forceful, that the unwritten and steadfast laws of the gods could be overcome by a mortal.

The verb used is that of the *horos, horizō*; Creon's laws or customs (*nomima*) are not 'determined' or 'circumscribed' by the gods. In contrast, the laws that Antigone does recognise are placed within the horizon of men by the gods. A subterranean Justice earths them and presumably that is where their authority resides, in the earth, which is why the burial (earth to earth) of the brother belongs to their jurisdiction. But it is also a matter of time, for Antigone's customs remain in the

---

37 Soph.*Ant*.450–455.

present as a prescription whose origin belongs to the indeterminate past, or in Antigone's own words, οὐ γάρ τι νῦν γε κἀχθές, ἀλλ' ἀεί ποτε/ ζῇ ταῦτα, κοὐδεὶς οἶδεν ἐξ ὅτου 'φάνη, these customs are 'not something of now or yesterday, but live forever, and no one knows from whence they appeared.'[38] Here she seems to echo the chorus who asked Cassandra in the *Agamemnon* from where she had the *horoi* of divination. It is this indeterminate origin that makes these customs so secure, but it is also the fact that they are unwritten (*agrapta*). Perhaps it is not Antigone who needs these unwritten customs or laws to support her act but the unwritten laws that require Antigone's act: by marking out the grave, the sign of the burial gives form to the unwritten laws. There is no division between the laws themselves and their enactment; the enactment is the 'writing' or 'sign' (*horos mnēmatos/sēmatos*) upon the earth of the continued presence of the laws. This earthly enactment might be the only form these laws ever take. It could be that the laws require the sign of the grave in order to be read at all.

Death's Legal Signature

Antigone's authenticity, raising her up to the level of the legislator and giving her the strength to stand in opposition to legal power, is maintained by her 'right' to death's sign, a mark of authorship that she embraces in the absence of her brother by inscribing with the earth and upon the body of her brother those 'unwritten laws.' As Derrida states, 'the tomb is the life of the body as the sign of death.'[39] The tomb and sign of the dead is the 'written signature' that in the case of Antigone claims her presence in the past of her brother. The sign that Antigone writes upon her brother's body may be her own responsibility, but what remains, i.e. the grave (*horos*), cannot be claimed as hers, nor even her brother's. Both authors are eclipsed by the divine origin of the laws themselves, whether it was his tomb or her sign. The signature implies, as Derrida states,

> the actual or empirical nonpresence of the signer. But, it will be claimed, the signature also marks and retains his having-been present in a past

---

38 Soph.*Ant*.456–457.
39 Derrida (1984) 82.

> *now* or present [*maintenant*] which will remain a future *now* or present [*maintenant*], this in general *maintenant*, in the transcendental form of presentness.[40]

Antigone's claim is exactly that her sign breaks into the 'now' of human laws, interrupts them with the silent eternity of the grave, breaking into state-sanctified memory. This is why Creon must object to the burial, not because he wishes to punish Antigone (and Ismene) by deferring the materialisation of their memory of their brother, but because the burial of the brother inevitably becomes a memorial also of dissent and civil-war that contraindicates Creon's reformation of the city after *stasis*. Part and parcel of his post-war authority is the denigration of those who fought on the other side and the commemoration of martial heroes on his side. Similarly, Perikles funeral oration was as fundamental in instituting the concept of Athenian citizenship as it was in memorialising the dead.[41]

Antigone's signature is a demand addressed to others to remember the laws of the dead, and in doing so, they must 'read what was never written.'[42] It is a trope common to poetry that the act of writing tricks death. Horace says in his odes, 'I shall not wholly die' (*non omnis moriar*) and this is because his poems live on. This statement that puts off the fulfilment of death is explicitly in relation to what has been written, which remains a part of the author, even beyond the grave. Antigone stands somewhere near here, and her deed risks all because it (whether intentionally or not) rewrites the accepted history of the city. In the words of Benjamin: 'Only that historian will have the gift of fanning the spark of hope in the past who is firmly convinced that *even the dead* will not be safe from the enemy if he wins. And this enemy has not ceased to be victorious.'[43] For Creon, outlaws of the state are punished by legal means, on account of Antigone's act both the laws that permit such punishment and the history that defines her brother as outlaw come into question. In the Machiavellian book of power, this is not acceptable. Every system that is built upon the control and manipulation of its population engages in the twofold denigration and active eradication of dissent.

---

40 Derrida (1988) 20.
41 Thuc. 2.34–46.
42 Benjamin (2005) 722.
43 Benjamin in Löwy (2005) 42.

Agamben's argument that law is the sphere of signatures holds for the law of the state where the signature defers responsibility to a past that can in fact always be rewritten and retracted. Authority depends upon the unremarked past of dissent, the glorification of its heroes and mastery over the sign. The theory of signatures in alchemy is based upon the notion that similarities in form and language are not coincidental and that the signature draws attention to a relation between things, their powers, their forms and how we read them: 'Signatures, which according to the theory of signs should appear as signifiers, always already slide into the position of the signified, so that *signum* and *signatum* exchange roles and seem to enter into a zone of undecidability.'[44] Adoption of the theory of signatures into the law allows the law to extend beyond the secular domain into theology. A signature does not merely express a semiotic relationship between sign and signifier, 'rather, it is what—persisting in this relation without coinciding with it—displaces and moves into another domain, thus positioning it in a new network of pragmatic and hermeneutic relations.'[45] In short, whoever controls the signatures is in control.

Diogenes Laertius provides an explanation of the definition of *horos* and the subsequent definition of *hypographe*, which in Greek is literally 'written under' or 'underwritten' (and now means 'signature'), but here is probably used in terms of logic, meaning 'description.' In legal terms, it is also the 'accusation' or 'statement of liability.'

> Ὅρος δέ ἐστιν, ὥς φησιν Ἀντίπατρος ἐν τῷ πρώτῳ Περὶ ὅρων, λόγος κατ' ἀνάλυσιν ἀπαρτιζόντως ἐκφερόμενος, ἤ, ὡς Χρύσιππος ἐν τῷ Περὶ ὅρων, ἰδίου ἀπόδοσις. ὑπογραφὴ δέ ἐστι λόγος τυπωδῶς εἰσάγων εἰς τὰ πράγματα, ἢ ὅρος ἁπλούστερον τὴν τοῦ ὅρου δύναμιν προσενηνεγμένος.[46]

> A definition [*horos*] is, as Antipater said in his first book *On Definitions* [*horoi*], a phrase [*logos*], which according to analysis corresponds to what is said; or, according to Chrysippus in his book *On Definitions* [*horoi*], is the explanation of the word itself. Description [*hypographē*] is a phrase [*logos*] introducing the matters in outline, or a definition [*horos*] that deals with the authority [*dynamis*] of the definition [*horos*] in a simpler form.

---

44   Agamben (2009) 37.
45   Ibid. 40.
46   Diog.*Vit.Phil*.7.60.9.

Although the translation I offer here is not definitive, it is evident that in the Greek a nexus of terms is brought together. Unfortunately, all these terms, *horos, logos, hypographē, dynamis* vary quite significantly in meaning from any exact English counterpart. 'Description' here differs from *horos* insofar as it is definition in outline with recourse to the authority of the sign. The underwritten in Ancient Greek is thus already a synonym for the authority or power (*dynamis*) of a word or term (*horos*). The signature introduces the notion of authority but whether that is in speech or writing is unclear, despite the *hypographē*. As Agamben states, the sign 'signifies because it carries a signature that necessarily predetermines its interpretation and distributes its use and efficacy according to rules.'[47] As with the signed artwork, or the stamped coin (*signare* in Latin also means to stamp a coin), the signature denotes authority (who has money has power), authenticity, or a complex network of relations of authority. Thus, the signature denotes more than a relation between whoever signs and what is signed; it decides at its base what words mean.

Does this mean that the *horos* has authority implicated within it, without raising that authority as a question? No doubt this is what was significant about the *horos* all along, that the authority or power to describe boundaries, or the potential to define and determine was always already inherent and remains a power that fails to point elsewhere to some external authority. But that does not mean it is not subject to questioning. If we ask of the *horos*, like the chorus to Cassandra, from whence it has the *dynamis*, the power and potentiality to define, bound, determine and limit, it might answer thus: 'HOROS.' Does it say *horos*, or do we read *horos*? Of course, stones cannot speak. But we can read the word *horos*, or that failing the fact that the stone is placed on the boundary, in which case the *horos* insistently points back to us, the ones inscribing or even the ones doing the reading. So, the answer must be that the *horos* has no power to bind and define unless we attribute it this power. But then, to echo the chorus, from where do we have this power? That is for another time, or, in Antigone's words, it is 'not of now or yesterday, but always forever.'

And so, Antigone's act can be disputed not only within the text but outside of it as well, in the text of power relations that is alive and

---

47 Agamben (2009) 64.

well today, and that continues to bolster new readings of the *Antigone* in order to support new authorities, systems and new relations. Her insolence is not merely that she disobeys the edict of the king; the real insubordination lies with the fact that she challenges our hermeneutic position about what law really means or how law should be read. She takes us back to the ground of definition, where the customs and laws are defined. The play poses, even despite itself, the question concerning the authority of these definitions, it asks who the author is that defines the laws. Both Antigone and Creon claim to have insight into the real authorship and power of law, and on the boundary in dispute, the no man's land between the two where nothing is sacred, we see the problem brought into definition, the *aporia* at the heart of the law, or the *aporia* that brings us up short of following the law to the letter. Because they cannot both be right, can they?

The 'sign' of the grave of her brother is for Antigone the sign of justice, a subterranean justice, while for the king it is the sign of her revolt. But more than this, Antigone's act suggests that the grave itself must be read as the unwritten laws themselves, and that here the identification between law, written sign and deed should coalesce in a single interpretation, indisputable because although not legally signed, it is nonetheless read in the sacred laws of burial and mourning.

Foucault states that 'everything would be manifest and immediately knowable if the hermeneutics of resemblance and the semiology of signatures coincided without the slightest parallax.'[48] This gap is essentially that between semiology and hermeneutics. The gravestone does not fill in this gap, despite its solidity, but it does remind us that the body of habitation, and the 'dark space' of the dead amongst the living bears a certain similarity. Here, we can read Antigone as trying to situate herself in this gap. Her signature, which is really the entire system of those unwritten laws that she in both deed and speech is attempting to give expression to, is supposed to be and is read by the chorus, even though the authority of her own interpretation is constantly slipping away in favour of Creon's. The chorus, however, finds themselves in a dilemma, the only position true to form in the entire play.[49] They at least recognise the *aporia* in the text. They cannot say one way or the other

---

48 Foucault (2008) 33.
49 Soph.*Ant*.278, 681, 724.

which is the right interpretation of Antigone's act, at least up until a point.

Ambiguity rests with the grave itself, which necessarily evades an absolute identification with a name or any kind of authority, and becomes a matter of deep time versus present time. The sign, *horos*, is only that of memory, *mnēmatos*, and is associated with the name of the dead only so long as the living hold him and his place of burial in mind. The grave belongs to the dead only so long as he and his site of burial remain in living memory. While the deed of burial itself might be Antigone's signature, the sign itself has meaning only so long as it is read. In this case the grave and sign refer back to the initial problem of the *horos*; how is it to be read? Is it word or stone, and how can it be both? But the sign of the grave does not cease to be supported by *horos*, just as the stone lies under the chisel. It is appropriate that it is on the boundary between signature and interpretation that the *horos*, the gravestone comes, solidifying what remains of the 'unwritten laws' and putting into question any kind of possession particular to one time or another. With typical candour, Antigone asks, 'And yet how could I have gained greater glory than by placing my brother in his grave?'[50] The grave maintains the always in the 'now,' but if the 'unwritten laws' dictate burial, and the act of burial is the power of these laws in the 'now,' then the grave itself (*read: horos*) stands as the mark that also interrupts the continuity of any kind of law.

The unwritten laws that Antigone invokes would seem to have traversed the 'now'—a definition that interrupts into indeterminacy. And yet Antigone's insistence would suggest that there is only one way that these laws remain so secure, by giving definition to them in the form of a grave (*horos sēmatos*). Hence her repetitive need to act, to follow her responsibility to mark out the dead as buried until the laws are visible upon the body as earth, or written into the land as grave. As laws, they are unwritten, *agrapta*, but they must be read all the same. Likewise, the chorus is unwilling to speak about them, though they know them, until the laws themselves are recognised or read. In the words of Nietzsche, 'it is true knowledge, insight into the terrible truth, which outweighs every motive for action' until what is sacred about these laws becomes apparent in another's act (Antigone's, or with the ethical support of

---

50 Soph.*Ant*.502.

Teiresias, or with the help of Haemon as in Euripides' version), the sacred determination through which they make themselves known.[51]

These laws are perhaps none other than the limits of political power, the boundaries of secular power, (especially as defined by Creon) beyond which is the realm of the sacred and anyone who transgresses these boundaries without the appropriate ritual is none other than *homo sacer*, cursed to an unbounded death. Hence, as a figure of politics, as Butler suggests, Antigone, 'points somewhere else, not to politics as a question of representation but to that political possibility that emerges when the limits to representation and representability are exposed.'[52] But I would respond that once beyond the realm of these limits, there is no political possibility, and any attempt to politicise this region becomes tyranny, like Creon, the totalitarian ruler who can accept no limits to his kingdom. The will to draw attention to these limits is not political naivety on the part of the *Antigone*; on the contrary, it can be read as playing with the exposure and transgression of limits of the political institutions of the classical *polis*, which can be interpreted in turn as providing the framework for Creon's authoritarian rule. It is these limits that the city's legislature repeatedly attempts to drown out or flood with novel proscriptions and seemingly petty legislations upon the body politic, as well as the woman's body (which is purposefully excluded from the body politic).

According to Butler, 'the Hegelian legacy of *Antigone* interpretation appears to assume the separability of kinship and the state, even as it posits an essential relation between them.'[53] In Hegel's reading, the binary between kinship and state suggests the existence of a boundary distinguishing a system structured by bonds of loyalty to the household from the duty of the citizen to the state, it is 'the limit at which the self-contained Family' breaks up and goes beyond itself.[54] For Hegel, the *Antigone* stands first and foremost as a conflict over the boundaries between the laws of the Gods and the laws of the *polis*, between the divine law and the human law. This interpretation has now been realised (*aufheben*) and Hegel's separation seems to be the basis for

---

51 Nietzsche (1999) 40.
52 Butler (2000) 2.
53 Ibid. 5.
54 Hegel (1977) 275.

the crisis between private and public power today, especially in social welfare states where welfare and policing take on the dual role of carer and punisher (Mummy/Daddy), while the family's role/rule breaks off abruptly when a child comes of age, becoming a legal citizen, leaving family life flailing with the sudden negation.

This is our inheritance, not from Sophocles so much as from later interpretations of Sophocles. For Sophocles, the separation between kinship and the state is just another in a series of boundaries that are overstepped, both by Antigone and by Creon. As Butler points out, Antigone and Creon are chiasmatically related. Their language, their mode of argument, the laws and ethics for which they stand, resemble that of the other, but diametrically. Both Antigone and Creon transgress kinship norms in their relations with one another, while Antigone transgresses gender norms and Creon the norms of political leadership.

Readings of the *Antigone* that attempt to stress the ethical or sexual aspects of the play tend, whether they mean to or not, to place Antigone on the other side of politics, beyond the realm of the political. For example, Lacan's fascination with Antigone turns her into some kind of resuscitated virgin goddess of pure desire, while reviling her mother Jocasta as harbouring impure lust, and thus reiterating typical binaries of womanhood and down-playing the political reading of the play.[55] According to Irigaray, this version of Antigone is seductive precisely because she is beyond the political. 'It suits a great many people to say that women are not in government because they do not want to govern' states Irigaray, 'But Antigone governs as far as she is permitted.'[56] Irigaray's reading of Antigone seems to call for a new conception of the civic realm in which female sexuality is taken into account, as if a different kind of political power, a Creon more well-disposed towards the unwritten laws perhaps would arrest the tragic outcome of the play.

It might be seductive to simply invert the power relations and replace Creon with Antigone. This would automatically suggest that Antigone's position was initially the weaker of the two. But as we know from the end of the play, it is Antigone who emerges victorious, dead admittedly but triumphant. The strangest thing about the *Antigone* is how the tyrant

---

55 Miriam Leonard 'Lacan, Irigaray, and Beyond: Antigones and the Politics of Psychoanalysis' in Zajko and Leonard (2006) 130–134.
56 Irigaray (1994) 68.

Creon suddenly accedes to the recommendations of the chorus and goes off to free Antigone and bury her brother. But too late; the plot is in free-fall and the suicides, of Antigone, Haemon and his mother Eurydice, flow.[57] But Creon, having only just seen his mistake and changed his mind, suffers all the more for his wrongs, which also takes away the Schadenfreude we the audience might have felt witnessing his sufferings. The moral of the story, though ancient Athens was not what you'd call a moralistic place, all the same, the moral of the story might be that tyrants, or their democratic understudies must listen not only to the old men (the senate) but also to their Antigones (disenfranchised youth), if they are to successfully rule.

Does this mean Antigone, and with her the women of the city, should be included within the institutions of power in order to 'give them a voice' or does it mean that a smart tyrant will include women in order to suppress the possibility of dissent coming from the margins of society? While individuals may contribute to increased dissatisfaction in the structures of political authority, the alternation of sex within the same structures of power will not magically transform the political system into a more inclusive one. On the contrary, the more inclusively a political power presents itself, the more exclusive are its methods, until we arrive at a system where there is no conceivable valid alternative of political power beyond neoliberal corporate capitalist representative democracy. And anybody thinking otherwise is branded a fool, a dreamer or a terrorist.

Antigone, with her seemingly innocent obsession with her brother, her claim to follow the unwritten laws and her death wish, could be all three. Her act and her rebellious speech in the face of Creon's edicts refusing burial rites to her brother interrupt, if nothing else, the continuous flow of legal hegemony. Antigone asserts her responsibility for her insubordination three-fold; in the symbolic deed of burying her brother, by refusing to obey Creon's edict against it, and then testifying to her refusal to obey. Thus, as Judith Butler states, her claim 'becomes an act that reiterates the act it affirms, extending the act of insubordination by performing its avowal in language.'[58] In doing so, Butler argues, Antigone appropriates the voice of authority even while

---

57 Creon's about face begins and the suicides follow immediately, Soph.*Ant*. 1099.
58 Butler (2000) 10.

she refuses to assimilate her own acts to that same authority. She can do so only because she claims that she is following an alternative system of justice and has the language to do so having the privilege to be born into the royal house. Her defiance of the latter and reverence of the former is indicated in her authorial iteration of those unwritten laws, which she signs three times upon the body of her brother. This maintenance of the grave is by definition the sign and signature of her double act, her insubordination against the laws of Creon, and her self-proclaimed obedience to those other laws.

Economics of Death

Maybe the *Antigone* is a cipher for whatever interpretation most benefits the reader: for Hegel the play represents the separation between traditional kinship and later political systems, while the character of Antigone represents the nexus of the feminine (passive, unconscious, disobedience and guilt); for Lacan, the character of Antigone is pure desire; for Loraux she stands for the possibility of the politicisation of desire; for Irigaray, Antigone is the sexual difference of the unconscious; for Morales, she is rising up against gender discrimination; for me, the play draws attention to all those boundaries, in words and stones.[59] Underneath this cipher, Antigone is woman idealised such that she is whatever we want her to be. She moves at our bidding, changes sides with our whims. Here she is the other of masculine power, there she stands for universal ethics; here she supports the incestuous heredity of the royal bloodline, there she is revolutionary spirit; here she is subservient to the unwritten laws, there she is subversive femininity rising up.

Antigone might ask of this manipulation of herself and the play, 'is nothing sacred anymore?' and she would surely get a firm negative. The theatre is no longer an act of worship, a set of rituals presented in the name of Dionysus, the great trilogy of tragedy that followed the procession of the phallus through the city, and preceded the comedy that was, at least for Aristophanes, the institutionalised satire about the Athenian

---

[59] For a discussion on these interpretations, see Leonard in Zajko and Leonard (2006) 122ff. Irigaray on interpretations to suit the day (1994) 68. For Antigone as the symbol of challenging gender norms, see Morales (2020).

demos. That is where the *Antigone* was originally situated, and perhaps it is worth refiguring the play in its original setting, if only because our interpretations have become so saturated with contemporary biases, beliefs and political allegiances that to read something truly other into the play is becoming more and more difficult.[60] Which also means that the play is becoming less threatening, doing nothing other than reinforcing our present values. That said, how challenging the play was to its original audience remains an intriguing matter for speculation.

I mention the social and political setting of the play's performance to point out where Sophocles' inspiration was embedded and to what he would have been responding, opening to debate topics that the play's audience would have felt moved by or at least implicated in. Given that the *horos* stood as the boundary separating tribal regions or private lands, it can be seen to be intimately involved in drawing up the boundaries of kinship, especially in its role as marker of grave in the name of the dead. That both death and kinship rituals underwent significant change during this time, from the end of the archaic into the beginning of the classical periods, should alert us to a shift in significance of the *horos* as well. Within the classical period the *horos* becomes a tool for marking the boundaries of the Athenian market-place, abandoning its exclusive use in the sacred and the natural. The following will describe these shifting allegiances and existential alterations.

That the *Antigone* represents a conflict between a previous system based upon the ties of kinship (founded upon relations between wealthy and powerful households of royalty) and the institutions of the democratic *polis* is, I think, beyond doubt, particularly given the aristocratic leanings of its author.[61] That said, the dramatic festival was not an autonomous product of the author; it was a collective production in which, as Longo states, 'the concepts of artistic autonomy, of creative spontaneity, of the author's personality so dear to bourgeois aesthetics, must be radically reframed, when speaking of Greek theatre, by considerations of the complex institutional and social conditions within which the processes of literary production in fact took place.'[62] Longo

---
60 Osborne 'Competitive Festivals and the Polis: A Context for Dramatic Festivals at Athens' in Rhodes (2004) 18ff.
61 Rhodes (2003) 104ff.
62 Oddone Longo, 'The Theatre of the Polis' in Winkler and Zeitlin (1990) 15.

has also argued that the 'dramatic spectacle was one of the rituals that deliberately aimed at maintaining social identity and reinforcing the cohesion of the group' but that does not mean that there was exclusive agreement about the topics presented on stage.[63] No doubt the audience would have comprised both champions and critics of the democracy.

The theatre might also have comprised some women, whose presence in the democratic institutions was notably absent, though nonetheless essential and whose interactions with male citizens cannot have escaped have some effect upon those institutions. Loraux states that tragedy was the main genre that, 'as a civic institution, delighted in blurring the formal frontier between masculine and feminine and freed women's deaths from the banalities to which they were restricted by private mourning.'[64] It also allowed women to orchestrate the deaths of others, even if unintentionally. If only few women actually were permitted to attend the theatre I am not sure that this would help them much. The idea that tragedy allowed women to take death into their own hands is particularly interesting given the fact that death was already in their hands, insofar as it was the women in charge of the funeral rites. It would be very intriguing to read the unfortunately mostly lost Euripidean version of the same myth, given that Euripides was a little more sympathetic to the democratic system of the classical city or at least had a sense of humour about the shortfalls of citizen rule. It would be even more interesting still if Aristophanes had written a comic version.

That Antigone is the heroine of the previous system of aristocratic, inherited rule is, however, not without its problems. While she is the daughter of wealth, and her ancestry is (on both sides) descended from the royal household, she is however of the cursed house of Thebes, the mythic alter-ego of Athens, much as Sparta was the city's political alter-ego, though the representation of an enemy sympathetically was definitely within the scope of tragedy (*The Trojan Women, The Persians*).[65]

---

63 Longo in Winkler and Zeitlin (1990) 16.
64 Loraux (1991) 3.
65 Antigone states of herself that she is the sole survivor of the royal house of Thebes (apparently forgetting her sister and her surviving brother). The chorus compare her noble lineage and fate to Danae et al. Soph. *Ant*.940ff. On Thebes as 'the negative model to Athens' Froma Zeitlin 'Thebes: Theatre of Self and Society in Athenian Drama' in Winkler and Zeitlin (1990) 131.

As Zeitlin states, 'for the tragic poets Thebes represents the paradigm of the closed system that vigorously protects its psychological, social, and political boundaries.'[66] This over-protection of boundaries can be seen to be the downfall of the house of Thebes, given the cyclical incestuous tendency that finally brings it to its end. Antigone was the immediate offspring of incest, a big taboo for the Greeks given its saturation in myth, and she was also the descendant of a throne inherited by patricide and tainted by rape. She was unmarried, despite her age, a more serious transgression of the city's laws than may at first seem apparent. Meanwhile in the name of family bonds, she disregarded the distinction between sides of internecine war in her bid to bury the city's assailant. In her very person Antigone appears to break the boundaries in many directions, and for the original audience these original transgressions (but not 'sins' as they are forced upon her rather than enacted by her) are what make her a tragic, rather than heroic, character.

Irigaray describes Antigone's stand as a call to respect the 'economy of the cosmic order.' Antigone 'reminds us that the earthly order is not a pure social power, that it must be founded upon the economy of the cosmic order, upon respect for the procreation of living beings, on attention to maternal ancestry, to its gods, its rights, its organization.'[67] This cosmic order is also a matter of time. Aristotle's *horos*, the 'now,' linking past and future and permitting the continuum of time in tragedy must be maintained in the presence of the grave. For Thebes, burial or the lack thereof is a central problem that interrupts the proper flow of time (think of Oedipus as he searches for a place to die in the *Oedipus at Colonus*). Zeitlin suggests that the issue of the proper place of burial, under the earth and outside the city, problematises the very notion of time, where 'inside and outside, above and below, are factors that come to determine the most important boundary of all, that between before and after.'[68] Burial keeps time in joint, but has failed in Thebes so that 'no future time opens out in Thebes.' Antigone is both the end of the line and the recurring point; she is, as her name suggests, 'anti-generation,' or 'in place of the parent.' And in the *Antigone*, this distortion of time is played out, where 'the linear advance of the narrative events turn out in the

---

66 Zeitlin in Winkler and Zeitlin (1990) 148.
67 Irigaray (1994) 69.
68 Zeitlin in Winkler and Zeitlin (1990) 152.

end to be circular.'[69] In contrast, the healthy burial and ritual mourning of the dead comes to exemplify a harmonious cosmic economy because in the common entombment of family members, the household of death acts as a reminder of the continuation of the shared household of the living.

Because the economy of death has broken down in the household of Oedipus, for Antigone the grave becomes a desirable site, a site of reunification that in a sense conjures up bonds formed in the womb. The most cogent and challenging interpretation of Antigone's will to provide her brother's burial rites is the shift from attributing Antigone with some kind of incestuous obsession with her brother, when she should be thinking of her husband, to putting the stress on the matrix of generation that is shared in common between sister and brother. Antigone seeks to live out some kind of eternal return in order to feel at one with the family that she has lost. This interpretation offers an alternative reading that might not be what Sophocles had in mind, but it does provide the *Antigone* with an eternal significance, beyond quarrels over state boundaries and one that does link her to some kind of 'cosmic order.'

> Antigone clearly invokes the ground for her absolute obligation to bury her brother in their joint standing for, as well as having in common a space of co-generation not simultaneously with each other, as in the case of twins, but as a space of sharing that defines a primary ethical order of co-being, that is about connectivity and co-response-ability (Ettinger's term) and not the solitary, celibate individuality of the phallic order. Invoked, but waiting to be *heard* in Antigone's pathos, is this feminist heresy: that the condition of being humanly generated and born is an ethical ground *ab initio*, a form of linking, an already trans-subjectivity conceived as primordially, irreducibly relational—in a form that appears transgressive to a phallic autism when its archaic foundations are activated and invoked politically, ethically, aesthetically, symbolically as the basis for human thought and action.[70]

The gravestone is also an ethical marker of responsibility and care for the other, a mark of death shared within the family tomb, all the more significant if the matrical origin was also shared.

---

69 Ibid.
70 Griselda Pollock 'Beyond Oedipus: Feminist Thought, Psychoalanysis, and Mythical Figurations of the Feminine' in Zajko and Leonard (2006) 104.

What is at stake is not merely a distinction between two sets of laws, such as the Hegelian dichotomy of kinship versus politics. Burial is a marker that indicates how one is mourned; it is a very tangible sign of household allegiance, of love and friendship. The relation of hospitality itself drives toward this sign, since burial ceremonies appear repeatedly in classical literature as the highest duty that one undertakes both for friends involved in the relation of *philoxenia* and family (for example the importance of Achilles mourning Patroklos, and the funeral games that always follow upon the death of a respected warrior in the Homeric epics). Although in Antigone's case it is her immediate kin who requires burial, the problem is then inverted. By the time Antigone is facing her own death it is also she who is in need of and refused the rituals of burial. Both of these refusals are suffered by Antigone as a woman. To deny burial to a man is an insult to the women of his family who would lay out the body, adorn it and mourn. To deny burial to a woman is an insult to the woman whose rightful place is to be concealed, as when alive, within the familial folds of the household. Hence the challenge that the *Antigone* poses is also directed towards the place and function of women in relation to death.

In Athens, the economy of death belonged to the household, the *oikos*. The death of a woman was a private matter, something to be kept within the household. The death of women in tragedy is the opposite, often murder, more often suicide, these deaths are spectacular and out in the open. While they were no doubt exciting to watch, they mostly had the effect of reinforcing the need for maintaining the privacy of the women within the household. At least the period subsequent to Sophocles saw no women's uprising to prove otherwise. Plato stresses the self-willed nature of this privacy of women, when he states in the *Laws*, 'accustomed as they are to live in concealment and darkness, if one would drag them into the light, they would resist with all their might and be far stronger than the lawgiver.'[71] This dark concealment suggests that women were already entombed within the household. And, as Keuls shows, the symbolism of marriage was saturated with the same symbolism and rituals as those of death.[72] 'One of the motivations

---

71 Pl.*Laws* 781c. quoted in Keuls (1993) 128.
72 See for example, the nuptial vessel used as a tombstone and deceased women dressed as brides on funerary monuments, on pages 131, 136, 151 in Keuls (1993).

behind the strong drive toward the continuation of the hearth, or *oikos*, was the desire to maintain the ancestral tombs, and to have one's own tomb cultivated by future generations.'[73] The place of women in Ancient Greece, from marriage on was always on the side of death, and the household was intricately linked with burial rites and the maintenance of the tombs of the dead.

Keuls states that the preparation of bodies for burial 'a kind of reverse birth, was performed by women.'[74] The importance of burial seems to be a theme of some significance to Sophocles. Obviously, it is one of the topics, if not the main topic, in his *Antigone*, but it is also of key import in the *Ajax* and *the Seven Against Thebes*. I argue that it is the significance of burial rites that was Sophocles' main focus, perhaps on account of a barrage of laws that were brought in controlling the orchestration of such rituals and limiting them.[75]

The connection between women and death finds its acme in the monument of the Leokorion, the monument erected in honour of the myth of the sacrifice of the three daughters of Leos, situated in the corner of the ancient Athenian *agora* right beside the *horos* that marked the *agora's* limits.[76] The theory that this continued to be a site of the sacrifice of women within the classical *polis* (during the plague years 430–429) might be discordant with what most people would prefer to think of as founding democratic institutions and bloodless accountancy, though it does seem evident that in one way or another the ancient city was fundamentally structured around the use or abuse of virgins. This might be considered one amongst many institutionalising discoveries experimented with in order to subjugate and obliterate the gestational powers of women in favour of the autistic productivity of the market.[77]

Perhaps it is in this economic light that we should consider the second burial that takes place in Sophocles' tragedy, that of Antigone herself. Hers is a living burial, buried alive and provided with the victuals of life in death. It is also brought into direct relief with marriage. As a virgin promised in marriage to Haemon, the son of Creon, her fate

---

73 Ibid. 150.
74 Ibid. 149.
75 Discussed in more detail in Chapter Seven.
76 Keuls (1993) 137.
77 See Keuls on ancient biology, e.g. (1993) 142–147.

is reversed and, in her own words, she becomes the bride of death (ἀλλ᾽ Ἀχέροντι νυμφεύσω) a result that she almost seems to glorify in.[78] She greets her tomb with the ecstasy of a bride: ὦ τύμβος, ὦ νυμφεῖον, ὦ κατασκαφὴς/ οἴκησις ἀείφρουρος, 'Oh Tomb, oh bridal-chamber, oh deep-dug eternal prison-house.'[79] The tomb thus doubles up and reinforces the proximity that already existed in the social mores of Athens between the bridal chamber (*numpheion*), the household (*oikēsis*) and the tomb (*tymbos*):[80] This burial ordered by Creon also signifies his transgression of the laws of the dead as well as the household bonds of *xenia*. Even the chorus find that the situation has gone beyond all limits, νῦν δ᾽ ἤδη 'γὼ καὐτὸς θεσμῶν/ἔξω φέρομαι τάδ᾽ ὁρῶν ἴσχειν δ᾽, 'But now, witnessing this, I too am carried beyond the bounds of loyalty.'[81] Creon furnishes Antigone with victuals as if he is giving her a place to stay, a temporary residence, when he is actually burying her alive in an unmarked tomb. Creon did not have Antigone stoned, but he did hide her behind stone.

Her grave doubles as her home where the stone that Creon uses to block up the cave is a parody both of a door (that she will never open) and of a tombstone, his sign, this time, of her living-death. The stone is a door that accepts her entry but refuses her exit. It signifies her entrance into his own familial customs, a twisted rendition of the future that was to be but never will be, in which she was to become part of his household, more than a guest, married to his own son. And yet in the cave, he provides for her. She is neither daughter nor guest; she is, rather, condemned to living and dying in a house that will strip her of her familial connection to her own household, by depriving her of her family tomb. She is henceforth homeless, a stranger (*metikos*) even in death.

ἔμπας ξυμμάρτυρας ὔμμ᾽ ἐπικτῶμαι,
οἵα φίλων ἄκλαυτος, οἵοις νόμοις
πρὸς ἔργμα τυμβόχωστον ἔρχομαι τάφου ποταινίου·
ἰὼ δύστανος, βροτοῖς οὔτε νεκροῖς κυροῦσα
μέτοικος οὐ ζῶσιν, οὐ θανοῦσιν.

---

78 Soph.*Ant*.815.
79 Ibid. 891–900.
80 Ibid. 892. Also, 1069.
81 Soph.*Ant*. 800. Trans. Jebb.

> you, at least, will bear me witness how unwept by loved ones, and by what laws I go to the rock-closed prison of my unheard-of tomb! Ah, misery! I have no home among men or with the shades, no home with the living or with the dead.[82]

Her tomb is 'new' (*potaniou*), not the family tomb that her royal descent had promised her, and in a repetition of her brother's fate her death must go unmourned. For Antigone, what is 'homely' (οἴκησις) about her tomb is exactly the fact that she is not at home anywhere else, not just because her family are all dead (if not buried), but also because family, household, mourning and burial are a complex that must be enacted together in order for them to hold firm. Because these have been deprived her, she thinks of herself as a guest and stranger.

Her tomb is in fact no proper tomb, not only because she enters it alive provided for with the victuals that are to keep her alive, but also because she must go unwept. Similarly, the result of her unmourned burial is that she goes to her death as a stranger; she might be welcomed in Hades, but, unlike her parents, whom she washed and dressed with her own hands and poured offerings at their graves (ἐπεὶ θανόντας αὐτόχειρ ὑμᾶς ἐγώ/ ἔλουσα κἀκόσμησα κἀπιτυμβίους/ χοὰς ἔδωκα), she will never be at home there because of her lack of burial rites.[83] The gravestone not only takes shape in the gift of grief but as a demand made upon the living both to mourn and to die. The gravestone underlines and draws attention to the singularity of the repetitive alterity of death, a rupture that reduces all differences to a common limit.

The funeral rituals glorified in the Homeric epics were not limited to a family affair, and the archaic as well as classical city was strongly influenced by the prototypes of myth. Before Solon decreed a limit to the expression of grief over the tombs of non-family members (and the very fact that he thought this necessary would suggest it was a significant part of ritual grief) mourning was an extended matter for friends and loved ones. This is not a description of familial obligations within a nuclear family. It is not even limited to bonds of blood; it is extended within the obligations of *philoxenia*.

---

82   Soph.*Ant.* 845–852. tr. Richard Jebb.
83   Ibid. 891–900. tr. Richard Jebb.

A Stranger Tomb

Relationships of *xenia* would no doubt have formed a major, if not the major factor in inter-tribal, inter-household, and then later inter-city relations as well as in their dissolution (for example the Trojan war commenced because Paris had broken the rules of *xenia* by abducting his host's wife). *Philoxenia* is not, even if it once was, the essential factor in politics, but this is not the point.[84] *Philoxenia* in its ancient form was not merely a matter of being friendly to strangers, or being well mannered and behaving oneself in another's home. It can be defined along much more sombre terms, as care of the other not only unto death, but beyond it as well.

In what appears to be a *hapax legomenon* in Homer, the initiation of a relation of hospitality is expressed with the otherwise apparently formulaic ἀρχὴν ξεινοσύνης προσκηδέος.[85] To translate the meaning of the phrase, while leaving aside its syntax, would be something like 'the initiation and principle of care for the foreigner/friend until death.' And beyond death as well, for the *kēdos* (κῆδος) is the funeral ceremony. The word preceded by the relative *pros-* is said to express the notion of 'bringing into an alliance' or creating a relation of kinship. So, the word that describes being in a relation of kinship literally already has the funeral rites implied within it. The principle (*archē*) is that of *xenia*, where *philoxenia* begins with a mutual relation that promises care for the dead. At its simplest, the verb *kēdō* (κήδω) means simply 'to care' extending then to 'mourning.' So, this relation of caring with those who are not blood relatives, who are strangers in the Greek sense of the word (*xenos*) means that one accepts responsibility for the life of the other as well as undertaking to perform the rites required and outlined by all those 'unwritten laws' of the dead. But the noun κηδοσύνη, *kēdosynē*, means 'yearning,' so while the cognate verb κηδεύω (*kēdeuō*) is 'to tend to the dead, bury,' it also has the additional undertone of desire. Along with the rituals in the name of the dead there is also the living intensification of the bond of hospitality through the marriage ceremony; hence *kēdeuo* (κηδεύω) also means 'to ally oneself in marriage,' again bringing to mind the correspondence between death and marriage.

---

84 Seaford (2003) 18–19.
85 Hom.*Od*.21.35. Hesychius defines this as τῆς τὴν οἰκειότητα ἐμποιούσης. The more succinct ξενίην συνεθέκατο appears more frequently.

Here, then, a complex of love, grief and ritual meet in a single relation. And since both grave and boundary are marked by the *horos*, the beginning of the relationship with the stranger is bound to find its fulfilment in the same place, when crossing a boundary in friendship. This relation finds its expression, in what must have been the signature representation of burial rites and mourning, toward the end of the *Iliad* with the triple events of Achilles mourning for Patroklos, his vengeance upon Hector, the funeral games of Patroklos and the return and dressing of Hector's corpse. After Hector's death, 'they put him on the carved bed, and stood singers beside him, leaders of laments, who lamented in grievous song, and the women wailed. And white-armed Andromache began their wailing.'[86]

Lament, as Alexiou has illustrated, was essential to funeral rites within the Homeric epics and obviously was such a big deal for the society that it attracted all sorts of legislation limiting its practice within the classical city.[87] In the *Iliad*, Achilles is said to grieve for Patroklos with so much passion that he is heard by his mother in the depths of the sea, he covers himself with ash and tears out his hair.[88] Homeric lament must be understood as being intrinsically linked with burial, dressing of the dead, funeral games, all as necessary privileges due to the dead. Since these acts are constantly reinforced by the retelling of these burial rites immersed within myth, the actualisation of the rites within the household and the society creates 'the substantial unity of myth and ritual,' and this is what Benveniste calls the 'potency of the sacred act.'[89]

The interesting thing here is that this care unto death does not cease with death. The host or guest is not off the hook once the other dies; the care extends through the death rituals, burial and into grief and mourning and intergenerationally, in the maintenance of the tomb as well as in the inherited relation of *xenia* (one also plays host to the guest's children and grandchildren). A good example in the literature of this extension of the bonds of hospitality beyond the bounds of death is in Euripides' tragedy, *Alkestis*, which revolves around Herakles' reception as a guest, *xenos*, into the house of Admetos. Admetos is in mourning

---

86 Hom.*Il*. 24.720f.
87 Alexiou (2002) on heroic lament, 55; on legislation limiting lament, 14.
88 Hom.*Il*.24.513–514.
89 Cf. Agamben (2007) 22, 69.

for the death of his wife, Alkestis, and rather than revealing his grief to his guest, he tells the 'true lie' that she was a stranger who has died, in order to receive his guest with goodwill untainted by grief. The word for stranger, *othneios* (ὀθνεῖος), provides the pun and stands in opposition to someone who is a relation in the sense that they are 'of the household,' *oikeios*.[90] Strictly speaking Admetos tells no lie; it is literally true, his wife Alkestis is not of his house. She was from another household, introduced into the household of her husband upon marriage and then deeply involved in the generation of a new family, but she did not cease to be a stranger. On account of this white lie, Herakles accepts the hospitality and starts drinking and carousing, but it is not long before he learns the truth that it is in fact a woman of the house who has died. Herakles then confronts his host and accosts him for depriving him of the right to grieve and allowing him, albeit unwittingly, to offend the customs of grief: ἐγὼ δὲ σοῖς κακοῖσιν ἠξίουν/ἐγγὺς παρεστὼς ἐξετάζεσθαι φίλος, 'but I should show my worth as a friend in your grief, and stand right beside you in proof of my friendship.'[91]

By welcoming Herakles into his house and not implicating him in his grief, Admetos betrays the pledge (ἐγγὺς) of hospitality which should first and foremost be in the immediacy of giving and receiving, even or especially when this gift takes the form of grief. Therefore, Herakles' accusation is directed at the core of the hosts' claim to have granted hospitality, for all of the value or worth of the relationship is located exactly in this ἐγγὺς παρεστώς, 'being present beside.'

But it is more than a matter of presence, because while it is easy to recognise the offer of hospitality as a gift, in this ἐγγὺς παρεστώς there is encrypted a further indebtedness in which both host and guest are enshrouded: on the one hand we see the stranger assigning liability to the host for not recognising his guest's *value* (ἠξίουν, 'I was worthy'), on the other hand the very nature of *xenia* is to hold the guest safe, this is the security (ἔγγυος, ἐγγύη) the bond that hospitality offers. One might, as Derrida says, call the guest a voluntary hostage, and yet this does not exclude the possibility that the host is just as much hostage to the guest by whom he is temporarily substituted as master of the

---

90 Eur.*Alk*.530.
91 Ibid. 1010.

house.[92] In Greek, it is linguistically impossible to tell the host (*xenos*) apart from the guest (*xenos*), and the demand to substitute the one for the other is thus already inscribed in their names. The moment a relation of hospitality arises, a certain substitutability of the one for the other is supposed. And this substitutability of guest/host, rather than the exchange of gifts, is what makes *philoxenia* essentially a kinship economy.

The precedence of the *xenia* relation, even before an exchange of gifts shows that the economy of *philoxenia* is usually conceived of the wrong way around. That is, that the host gives the gift of hospitality, whereas in fact he is in the position of receiving it, in his reception of the presence of the other. Thus, the host receives the guest and the two are bound in a mutual relationship of strangeness, but estrangement from themselves, as they must share a name that simultaneously describes their bond and relation, *xenos/xenia*. Tending to one another's death is one, but not the final, act implicated in the *xenia* relation. The reception of the stranger as present includes making him a gift of the *pathemata*, the emotional involvement, of the host. In this doubling of the gift of hospitality, where reception is granted in the person of both host and guest, all the worth of the stranger-come-guest is in the proximity of presence, which as the resolution of dialectic of self and other cannot be evaded. In the receipt of this gift, host and guest become properly 'akin' (ἐγγύς).

Hospitality outlives the individual, enacted in death but also inherited in turn by descendants. While the relation is not written in blood, its inheritance is. It is, as Derrida states, a familial or genealogical pact that 'is not only a question of the link between birth and nationality; it is not only the question of the citizenship offered to someone who had none previously but of the right granted to the foreigner as such, to the foreigner remaining a foreigner, and to his or her relatives, to the family, to the descendants.'[93] The security or pledge follows the bloodline, while the relationship of *xenia* administers to the stranger as stranger, remaining in the house temporarily but as if he were a member of the family and no guest. That the guest's stay is temporary is the one sure factor that permits the host to defer to the guest. And yet the 'substitution' of guest for host reflects back upon the host, whose

---

92 'Hostipitality,' in Derrida (2002) 376; 'Word of Welcome,' in Derrida (1999) 57.
93 Derrida (2000) 23.

stay in the house is also subject to temporal limits. Both guest and host are bound to forfeit inhabitance; the difference is merely a matter of time. Thus, in the *oikos* that bears witness to the stranger, there is an enactment of the final *oikēsis*. It is not so much that the stranger places himself, his life and death, into the security of the host, whereupon the host takes upon himself the role of protector, custodian or caretaker. Rather, the guest stands as the marker for the host's future, in promise of reciprocal hospitality, by honouring the other's name from afar, in the proliferation of familial, social and economic ties through marriage as well as in mourning. In this sense the host is indebted to the guest first and can only repay the debt by putting himself on the line as stranger, as 'security' for needing security. The pledge in the person of the substitutability of the guest/host is dependent upon the principal of possession, of homely possession and the household as something that can be said to belong to the host rather than the guest.

Death in ancient Athens was not experienced as a private affair, and yet the nature of death is that it is irrevocably one's own and no else's. In this sense the uniqueness of the death ritual as a part of *xenia* also remains appropriate (and for this reason not entirely appropriable) as a proper beginning (*archē*) to give expression to what is uncommonly strange about the end.[94] Levinas described the problem of possession as resting with the feminine, that the house 'is possessed because it already and henceforth is *hospitable for its owner*. This refers us to its essential interiority, and to the inhabitant that inhabits it *before every inhabitant, the welcoming one par excellence, welcoming in itself—the feminine being.*'[95] Gestation or the womb, therefore, is the first experience of *philoxenia*, as well as the endogenous metaphor of the earth, where the problem of what is proper comes into being as self and the fracturing of self from place; the matrix of codependent, shared mortality and the origin of the debt of life. Heidegger states that 'mortals are they who can experience death as death. Animals cannot do this,' in fact 'nature' as a whole cannot.[96] Even Derrida reckons on this distinction, stating that animals may perish, but they 'can never properly die.'[97] Here death is twisted

---

94 Derrida (1993) 22.
95 Levinas (1969) 157.
96 Heidegger (1971) 107.
97 Derrida (1993) 35.

to be some kind of odd human privilege, the last chance to separate us from everything else, the entirety of the nonhuman.

Is this why the *Antigone* retains such power even today, because it stages the dissolution of a deeply indebted relation between the conceptualisation of matter, language and death that binds humans together in mutual responsibility and care for the other? Herakles' platitude in the *Alkestis*, βροτοῖς ἅπασι κατθανεῖν ὀφείλεται, 'for all mankind the debt of death is due,' and Antigone's preoccupation with death εἰ δὲ τοῦ χρόνου /πρόσθεν θανοῦμαι, κέρδος αὔτ' ἐγὼ λέγω, 'if I die before my time, still I say that is profit,' both frame death in economic terms.[98] How can death be considered cause for debt or profit? Is it because we owe ourselves to the earth in dying, but where's the profit in that? Is it because giving to the dead represents the gift in an absolute sense? Is grief a gift, from the giving of which one can gain no return?

Archaic death practices do suggest that reciprocity was a driving force in providing the dead with gifts. The dead were believed to be able to reciprocate.[99] They could always come back as a presence of pollution and disaster. Conversely, if tended well the dead might return with assistance and as beneficial presence to the living. Love might be the most beautiful form of the pure gift, but it is clouded by the presence of the other who can always reciprocate, giving love for love; it does not command the same degree of selflessness as the gift of mourning. It is by virtue of the rites of burial that, as Levinas says, 'the death of the other is the first death,' since 'it is for the death of the other that I am responsible, to the point of including myself in death. This may be phrased in a more acceptable proposition: "I am responsible for the other insofar as he is mortal."'[100] The responsibility for mourning the other is at the heart of kinship relationships and is essential to understanding ancient cultural practices related to death.

If we consider hospitality in the light of mourning, it is impossible to consign it, after Mauss, to the archaic precedent of a 'gift economy,' even if, with Herman we modify this as a 'debt economy' whose

---

98 Soph.*Ant*.460.
99 Josine Blok 'Solon's Funerary Laws: Questions of Authenticity and Function' in Blok and Lardinois (2006) 236–237.
100 Levinas (2000) 38–40. Cf. Derrida (1993) 38.

system is one of 'alternating disequilibrium' aiming at accumulation for de-accumulation.'[101] Gift-exchange, as Ricoeur recognised 'is neither an ancestor nor a competitor of—nor a substitute for—such commercial exchanges.'[102] On the contrary, commodity-exchange occupies the site of gift-exchange, and gradually forces gift-exchange into the margins that its victor abandoned. Today calculative rationality and evaluative exchange is so firmly invested within our social practices that it is profoundly difficult to imagine how a community could function in their absence.

---

101 Herman (1987) 10; Cf. Mauss (1967); Lévi-Strauss (1987); Derrida (1982) 2.
102 Ricoeur (2007) 235.

Fig. 7. ΟΡΟΣ ΚΕΡΑΜΕΙΚΟΥ *'Oros* of the Kerameikos' (4th c BC). Found outside the archaeological site in the area between Hippias Kolonos and Plato's Academy. [I 322] Photograph by M. Goutsourela, 2013. Rights belong to the Kerameikos Museum, Athens. © Hellenic Ministry of Culture and Sports/ Hellenic Organization of Cultural Resources Development (H.O.C.R.E.D.).

7. Solon's Petromorphic Biopolitics

ὁ ὅρος-*decision* of a magistrate [...] *standard, measure* [...] *end, aim.*[1]

ἐγὼ δὲ τούτων ὥσπερ ἐν μεταιχμίῳ
ὅρος κατέστην.

I stood between them like a horos in no man's land.[2]

Solon brought Athens out of a situation of *stasis*, or so he claims. In order to appreciate the further implications of Solon's intervention into the Athenian *polis*, the word '*stasis*' should be understood in both its political, and physical sense. That Athens was caught up in civil war (*stasis*) provides the justification for the intervention of legal reforms instituted by Solon. However, that a stable state of equilibrium where the equal strength of opposing forces cancels one another out (*stasis*) is not economically profitable or beneficial to expansionist political and imperial policies should be the key lesson learnt and adopted into the normal, everyday functioning and theoretical constructs of the city-state. To put it otherwise, deconstructing *stasis* becomes the main tenet of economic, political power.

Solon is often championed as the liberator of the poor, introducing the basic legislative structures that would eventually bring about notions of equality and freedom in the Athenian state. That this was not the case at all and that this is a reconstruction developed to the benefit of the later constitutional powers, keeping Solon on their side, is certainly possible. Solonic Athens is not normally understood as the beginning of a gradual institutionalised breakdown of human relations, but that does

---

1   LS: 1256.
2   Ar.*Ath.*12.5.

not mean it was not. As an economic and legal project sometimes called 'oligarchy,' other times 'democracy,' the city of Athens used multiple resources in its creation of a mythological political heritage: the myth of autochthony is one example and Solon may well be another. Although the name changed, with the numerical fluctuation of those present in the spaces of public decision-making, the structures that supported these systems remained the same, and have largely remained the same since. Law, economics, the dissemination of information and knowledge discourses from the natural sciences to the human sciences, all enforced limits that kept humans at an increasing distance from other humans and ensured the domination of some over the many, be this through rhetoric, demagoguery, legislative authority or the implementation of novel laws.

The ancient polis well deserves its fame, because here, perhaps exclusively at that time throughout the world humans had developed a political and philosophical justification and methodology for human autarchy and the domination of the human over the nonhuman. This permitted the almost total eclipse of the nonhuman in the intellectual and emotional life of the human. Humans were separated from all other beings, both practically and legally. And while the definition of the human might have been officially inclusive, in a practical sense the citizen was the active autonomous subject, responsible and dominant over excluded others, from women, children, slaves, sometimes foreigners, to animals, plants and land, as well as anything else falling in between these categories.

The development of the *polis* as an institution connected speech (*parrhesia*, freedom of speech of its citizens) with exchange (market-based valuation of goods, animals and people as objects to be bought and sold). And it did so under the umbrella of a politically organised community of consenting mature males of a particular mythically-based ethnicity and caste not only coinciding but providing the basis for the exclusion of other models of organisation, including religious, sexual, cultural and ecological. Rather than celebrating the Ancient Greek state as the origins of 'democratic' systems of government we should condemn it as the cause of the institutionalised conspiracy between economic interests, elite classes and political and legal structures of control over and against the animistic interactivity and cohabitation of all beings within the cosmic order.

In this chapter, I will provide a number of examples of the changes that occurred under the legislative authority of Solon restricting the movement of women in particular and their activity as the primary economic actors. I also refer to laws that intervened within the household, destabilising it and making it an area subject to the laws of the state, isolating it as the 'private sphere' as opposed to the 'public'; such as the law that recognised the frequency of the sexual act as constituting the basis of legally binding marriage, and laws that regulated the outcome of sexual reproduction. Human biological processes are made the subject of law, not just culturally organised by religious or ritual activities as they were previously, but legally and economically mediated by the state. Economic and biological productivity are defined as something that can be organised by the state and not left up to nature, instinct or mutual relations of communal life. With Solon's reforms, law becomes proscriptive, discriminatory and deeply invasive, and it could be argued has remained so since.

Is Solon's legacy not a legal code disseminating equality, but in fact the active desecration of former kinship relations, and in their place the institution of intrusive and aggressive policies that permit public bodies to increasingly encroach upon the private life of the family and the individual? Solon's reforms can be understood first and foremost as a problem of limits. Here I argue that Solon's reforms opened up a new set of relations between the human being, the human body and the earth, a relation that instigated a principle of unlimited productivity and use both of the body and of the earth for economic processes and purposes. Foucault argued that the analysis of power must take into account not only discursive practices but also how the materiality of the body is regulated through its movements and 'according to a system of constraints and privations obligations and prohibitions.'[3] Something analogous can be understood as happening here. The body of women, men and children is being used as the text of the law, through which law communicates itself. Merchant investigated how women lost ground in the sphere of production and reproduction during the transition to early modern capitalism.[4] Here I present the argument that it is possible to see a similar recasting of women's activities as early as the sixth century

---

3   Foucault (1991) 11.
4   Merchant (1990) 149ff.

BC. Not only was the development of an economic system of exchange coincident with the elision of the value of women's roles and bodies for and within the common space of the community, but it was also coincident with the development of autocratic systems of legislation and the shift to centralised government.

Market-based economic exchange and city-state institutions were founded upon the domination of novel notions of production over earlier systems of household production and reproduction. Foucault shows 'how the deployments of power are directly connected to the body—to bodies, functions, physiological processes, sensations, and pleasure.'[5] Following Foucault, this analysis seeks to make visible the systems of power in which the biological and the historical are 'bound together in an increasingly complex fashion in accordance with the development of [ancient] technologies of power that take life as their objective.'[6] The political use of the human body, both in a passive and active capacity as well as the reproductive capacity is subjected to the laws of the centralised state, so that reproduction also reproduces the enforcement of law. And as children are born into socio-politically constituted spaces, the laws become naturalised, passing from generation to generation the governed life comes to be taken for granted as part of the biological landscape, as much as of the political.

The language used during Solon's legal transformations is significant and casts his reforms as deeply involved with the breaking and making of limits, or determinations. Solon casts himself both as abolishing the ancient *horoi* and the customs bound to them, and presents himself as a new *horos* standing amongst the Athenian people.

In Bed with the Law

Up until now we've been balancing upon the boundary without actually assuming the position and certainly without having crossed over to one side or the other. Why? For fear of what lies on either side? Or is it because this is the very position/non-position from which differences are decided and definition given? The question that will draw this archaic example of a stone to a close is; what became of the *horos* in the politics

---

5   Foucault (1978) 152.
6   Ibid.

of the state and what were the economic repercussions of politicising the *horos*? The following laws referred to should all be thought of as intervening in the most basic functions of human social and biological life. They should also be thought of as potentially modified in practise, instituted in fact just not by Solon, or as not quite the same as the actual laws in effect.[7] The exact nature of the laws that are here discussed, and their implementation in the archaic *polis* is not always known, though their retention in the writings of classical authors suggests that they were in one way or another politically useful even if for later times and other authors.[8] That we today base our concepts of government upon those of Ancient Greece, should alert us to the ongoing presence of these kinds of interventions and their insidious character particularly given the fact that for the most part the Greek *polis* is celebrated as privileging 'freedom,' 'equality,' and 'justice,' rather than the oppressive legislative control and surveillance of social and biological functions, as we see here.

To begin with, the demonstration of mourning rituals was quickly clamped down on by Solon. Whether this was to the disadvantage of aristocrats or women or a heartless attack upon the dead remains unclear. Aristocrats doubtless exhibited grander funerals and could have been seen as presenting a threat to the state, while women are said to have been disorderly during such times, and so a crackdown on their expressions of grief would serve to remind them of their social propriety.[9] It seems to me that both these explanations miss the more sinister aspect of Solon's laws restricting mourning. Plutarch tells us that, amongst his reforms, Solon enacted a law restricting demonstrative mourning at funerals.

> ἐπέστησε δὲ καὶ ταῖς ἐξόδοις τῶν γυναικῶν καὶ τοῖς πένθεσι καὶ ταῖς ἑορταῖς νόμον ἀπείργοντα τὸ ἄτακτον καὶ ἀκόλαστον [...] ἀμυχὰς δὲ κοπτομένων καὶ τὸ θρηνεῖν πεποιημένα καὶ τὸ κωκύειν

---

7   Ruschenbusch's collection of Solonic laws remains the main compendium of fragments, and he discusses the plausibility of Plutarch's version, see Ruschenbusch (1966) 31–42. However, on the accuracy of the laws collected by Ruschenbusch, see Adele Scafuro 'Identifying Solonian Laws' in Blok and Lardinois (2006) 175–176.
8   For a discussion on the probability of Solon's laws, see Harris (2006) 3ff; and on the political motivation for altering Solon's verses, see Lardinois 'Have We Solon's Verses?' in Blok, J. and A. Lardinois (2006) 15–38.
9   'Women were apt to flock to the funerals and graves of people outside their own family.' Shapiro (1991) 630; 'the task of mourning the dead fell chiefly to the women, whose displays of grief, unless checked, might amount to a social nuisance.' Garland (1989) 5.

ἄλλον ἐν ταφαῖς ἑτέρων ἀφεῖλεν. ἐναγίζειν δὲ βοῦν οὐκ εἴασεν, οὐδὲ συντιθέναι πλέον ἱματίων τριῶν, οὐδ' ἐπ' ἀλλότρια μνήματα βαδίζειν χωρὶς ἐκκομιδῆς. ὧν τὰ πλεῖστα καὶ τοῖς ἡμετέροις νόμοις ἀπηγόρευται· πρόσκειται δὲ τοῖς ἡμετέροις ζημιοῦσθαι τοὺς τὰ τοιαῦτα ποιοῦντας ὑπὸ τῶν γυναικονόμων, ὡς ἀνάνδροις καὶ γυναικώδεσι τοῖς περὶ τὰ πένθη πάθεσι καὶ ἁμαρτήμασιν ἐνεχομένους.

He also subjected the public appearances of the women, their mourning and their festivals, to a law which did away with disorder and licence [...] Laceration of the flesh by mourners, and the use of set lamentations, and the bewailing of any one at the funeral ceremonies of another, he forbade. The sacrifice of an ox at the grave was not permitted, nor the burial with the dead of more than three changes of raiment, nor the visiting of other tombs than those of their own family, except at the time of interment. Most of these practices are also forbidden by our laws, but ours contain the additional proviso that such offenders shall be punished by the board of censors for women, because they indulge in unmanly and effeminate extravagances of sorrow when they mourn.[10]

Plutarch would have us believe that Solon enacted a whole spate of laws that restricted the movement and expression of women in public, the exhibition of grief, given the importance funeral rituals held in the lives of women, must have been chief one amongst them. On Attic and Athenian funerary plaques and vases, detailed pictures of lament are found of women acting as professional mourners, so evidence suggests that mourning was the traditional role of women.[11] However, the last sentence of Plutarch could also suggest the earlier involvement of men, which was however no longer condoned; by the time legislation was laid restricting mourning, lament was considered the role of women, otherwise men who indulged in what were deemed excessive forms of grief would not be required to be sent to the women's council.[12]

If, as argued in the previous chapter, women were caught up in a structure of ancient law that bound together responsibility and care for

---

10 Plut.*Sol*.21.4–5. tr. Rackham.
11 Horst-Warhaft (1992) 103, 113–114; Alexiou (2002) 6.
12 For men lamenting, see Creon lamenting the death of his son, *Antigone* (1261–1346), Theseus mourning the death of Phaedra, *Hippolytus* (811–873), Orestes, Electra and the chorus singing a kommos for Agamemnon in the *Choephoroi*, and the *kommos* that ends the Persians. Webster (1970) 114, 127; Arnott (1989) 34.; Pickard-Cambridge (1968) 86–91.

the dead with an economics of kinship rather than exchange, then the restricting of funeral rites and rituals may have gone to the heart of such a social structure. It is significant, here, that women should bear both the burden and the responsibility for representing grief in the community, and that expressions of grief were a communal, and not merely a private matter. The dead continued to belong to kin after burial, whether in a good sense 'as tomb cult kept kin and group allegiance alive' or in a bad sense, as death was a 'source of pollution, which, if not properly handled, could cause various disasters.'[13] For these reasons, Blok states, 'the early funerary laws reveal a common purpose, albeit with differences in details: they regulated the relations between the living and the dead. They did so in three ways: they regulated behaviour at various stages of the funeral, they restricted the (value of) goods put into the grave, and they regulated the sacrifices at the tomb.'[14] Mourning and the expression of loss was one of the most significant activities in the archaic community and one which, as the city develops into an economically productive state, above all else suffered restrictions and was limited. I suggest that these restrictions reduced the arena in which goods and actions were exempted from the economy, or went out of circulation, in order to raise the political to the main organising structure of economic affairs, and eventually permitted the exponential expansion of the economic and the administration of the realm of productivity.

There is without doubt truth to Denise Ackermann's suggestion that Solon's restrictions on, particularly women's, ritual mourning and lamentation were politically motivated: 'traditionally lament was expressed by pulling hair, lacerating cheeks and beating breasts. Such behaviour could amount to a social menace and disturb the public order. Although Solon did not do away with these gestures entirely, he restricted them.'[15] That funerals stirred up feelings that were not easily quashed or channelled into useful political or economic activities is surely one among the reasons motivating the reforms. But that it is merely a question of the political preference for 'order, not chaos, cooperation not vengeance,' is I think a serious oversight as to the insidious nature

---

13 Josine Blok 'Solon's Funerary Laws: Questions of Authenticity and Function' in Blok and Lardinois (2006) 230.
14 Ibid.
15 Ackermann, 'Lamenting Tragedy from "the Other Side"' in Cochrane (2000) 213–241.

of policy reforms within states when they begin to intrude into and censor culturally and religiously sanctioned behaviour.[16] Lament was indeed tamed by the state, though this is not something that happened overnight. But what was the political danger that appeared to adhere to mourning? What exactly was the core of the problem? Why mourning practices posed a political challenge to the status quo remains a matter of conjecture. I can only suggest that mourning rituals, and the focus upon the household that came with it as the main locale of ritual performance, challenged on the one hand the political dominance of the public sphere and on the other the drive to economic profit, where mourning meant the cessation or interruption of economic activities.

It is clear, however, that the political reforms of Solon were also motivated by the political advantage of controlling the different gender roles expressed within the city. Many of the reforms were undoubtedly sexually discriminative; though as regards mourning it is disputable whether the effect was the restriction of one sex more than the other. As I argue, however, this stress on the restriction of certain sexual activities and the suppression of particular social expressions of sexuality were not ends in themselves. Rather, the aim was (and still is) to modify and even curtail the social power of the different sexes in order to promulgate an alternative economics that was reliant upon productivity and profiteering taking precedence over other affiliations and identities. Henceforth, and in spite of its etymology, economics was not a household affair, it no longer came within the purview of women, and the exteriorising of economic effectively raised productivity into the arena of the state. All this was done under the auspices and often the nomenclature of the traditional religious institutions of the city, which were the main authorities and the centralised state apparatus of laws, procedures and offices, there to organise and 'oversee an increasingly monetized form of sacred wealth.'[17]

With Solon law enters the bedroom and I doubt this presence heightened libido. He ensures the legal imperative that an heiress be approached with sexual intent by her husband 'at least three times a month,' he publishes laws on prostitution and adultery, prohibits dowries amongst the lower classes, bans pederasty among slaves, and he limits a woman's

---

16 Ibid.
17 Bubelis (2016) 5.

excursion beyond the house at night with the qualification that she travel by lighted wagon and carry no more than three cloaks and a quantity of victuals to the value of one obol.[18] It is easy to read into these restrictions a policy that was intended to do no more than reduce a woman's (and a slave's) role in public affairs. However, given the gradual rise of market-based policies and productions over the last two thousand odd years, as well as the ongoing legislative attacks upon individual legal, social and economic autonomy all the while accompanied by a parallel discourse championing sexual freedoms, I think it is permissible to interpret Solon's laws as the beginning of a chronic manipulation of public and sexual discourse while negotiating new forms of political and economic control. As obvious as this may appear to me today, I work however under a dimmed light of interpretation, as the effects and reactions to such evidently sex-oriented legislation are still not commented upon in the literature, no doubt for good reason: either the laws had the desired effect, or unable to be properly enforced they remained a weak spot in the new regime.

As much as we might wish such debates were resolved or simply not an issue, these laws, regardless of their subsequent validity and enforceability, must not be permitted to recede into the background when we consider the novelty of the Solonian city-state. They are foundational for the democracy, as much at least as are Solon's economic and representative reforms. And yet, given the impossibility of privileging any one interpretation unreservedly over another, these laws will not be engaged with in order to present any steadfast image of the sexual relations in the ancient city and the question of the body's place in these reforms will remain for the moment as a tantalising morsel for later consumption. Instead, I will break with the typical categorisation of these reforms in order to bring a certain economic silhouette into outline, a boundary that might resonate with the previous chapters and draw us into a complex of questions, that far from being conclusive will actually provide the profile for a new method of questioning and provide the basis for the explosion of Athens onto the economic scene.

---

18 ἐξιέναι μὲν ἱματίων τριῶν μὴ πλέον ἔχουσαν κελεύσας, μηδὲ βρωτὸν ἢ ποτὸν πλείονος ἢ ὀβολοῦ φερομένην, μηδὲ κάνητα πηχυαίου μείζονα, μηδὲ νύκτωρ πορεύεσθαι πλὴν ἁμάξῃ κομιζομένην λύχνου προφαίνοντος. Plut.Sol.20–24.

Reframing Biological Boundaries

According to Aristotle's account, Solon resolved a state of civil war, *stasis*, in the city of Athens that had broken out between the aristocrats, or landed gentry and the rest of the population, including presumably, the disenfranchised poor.[19] As Aristotle presents him, Solon, in the grand tradition of political and legislative authority, did not belong to the latter party.

> ἦν δ᾽ ὁ Σόλων τῇ μὲν φύσει καὶ τῇ δόξῃ τῶν πρώτων, τῇ δ᾽ οὐσίᾳ καὶ τοῖς πράγμασι τῶν μέσων.[20]
>
> Solon was in his nature and in reputation of the first rank, but in wealth and position belonged to the middle classes.

He was, as Plutarch says, 'a man of the people and of the middle rank' (δημοτικὸς ὢν καὶ μέσος).[21] Solon is most famed for a reappraisal of representation based upon property in order to construct a class-system that, as the representative democratic myth goes, enfranchised a larger proportion of the populous while leaving the holding of offices within the jurisdiction of the wealthy. Although the labouring class was granted perhaps a degree of power by their permission to act as jury-members in the courts of law, the new system did not bring about the redistribution of property and universal equality that Plutarch suggests the lower class had hoped for (γῆς ἀναδασμὸν οὐκ ἐποίησεν ἐλπίσασιν αὐτοῖς, οὐδὲ παντάπασιν).[22] Aristotle also describes the people's hopes for a redistribution of land,

> καὶ πάλιν δ᾽ ἑτέρωθί που λέγει περὶ τῶν διανείμασθαι τὴν γῆν βουλομένων:"οἳ δ᾽ ἐφ᾽ ἁρπαγαῖσιν ἦλθον, ἐλπίδ᾽ εἶχον ἀφνεάν, κἀδόκουν ἕκαστος αὐτῶν ὄλβον εὑρήσειν πολύν,
>
> And again in a different place he says about those who wish to divide up the land: They that came on plunder bent, were filled with over-lavish hope, each and all imagining that they would find abundant wealth.[23]

---

19 For debate on these divisions and Solon's institution of the festival Genesia, see Bubelis (2016) 6; 92f.
20 Ar.*Ath*.5.3.
21 Plut.*Sol*.16.2.
22 Ibid.16.1; Ar.*Ath*.12.3.
23 Ar. *Ath*. 12.3 trans. H Rackham.

Stripping away the moralistic justification against a universal redistribution of land to all equally, Solon's refusal can be seen explicitly to support the maintenance of wealth and power in the hands of the wealthy and the powerful. As his own poem explains he cast this refusal to rule over the wealthy in reapportioning the land as his own refusal to act as king (*tyrannos*). The implication being, in the style of advanced propaganda, that he followed the peoples will, rather than his own, and as with election promises unfulfilled in the aftermath of an election, claimed to have done exactly what he promised he would do.

ἃ μὲν γὰρ εἶπα, σὺν θεοῖσιν ἤνυσα,
ἄλλα δ᾽ οὐ μάτην ἔερδον, οὐδέ μοι τυραννίδος
ἀνδάνει βίᾳ τι ῥέζειν, οὐδὲ πιείρας χθονὸς
πατρίδος κακοῖσιν ἐσθλοὺς ἰσομοιρίαν ἔχειν.

for the things I promised, those by heaven's aid I did,
And much else, no idle exploits; nothing did it please my mind
By tyrannic force to compass, nor that in our fatherland
Good and bad men should have equal portion in her fertile soil.[24]

The relative virtues and vices of the reforms' revolutionary potential are not at issue. What is significant here is that there remains a sinister edge to the method Solon adopted in his legislation, a suspicious presentiment of later alloys of power that is not merely that of the legislator come sovereign in a 'state of exception' who exiles himself perforce once he has brought about a new state of legal hegemony. But there is also the use of the message, that is, his own poems, to distort both the views of his opposition and the actions the legislator performed, but I will look at the poetry later.

Solon organised the representative rights of each man in accordance with a system of proportion that differed from the former constitution as well as the expectations and claims of the different classes:

λέγεται δὲ καὶ φωνή τις αὐτοῦ περιφερομένη πρότερον, εἰπόντος
ὡς τὸ ἴσον πόλεμον οὐ ποιεῖ, καὶ τοῖς κτηματικοῖς ἀρέσκειν καὶ τοῖς
ἀκτήμοσι, τῶν μὲν ἀξίᾳ καὶ ἀρετῇ, τῶν δὲ μέτρῳ καὶ ἀριθμῷ τὸ ἴσον
ἕξειν προσδοκώντων.[25]

---

24 Ibid.
25 Plut.*Sol*.14.2.

It is also said that a certain utterance of his which was current before his election, to the effect that 'equality bred no war,' pleased both the men in possession of land and those without land; the former expecting to have equality based on worth and excellence, the latter on measure and number.

And yet Solon offered a third option that satisfied neither party and which can be said to be the democratic principle of his reforms, where equality is measured neither according to aristocratic principles (value and virtue, *axia kai aretē*) nor *in utero* communist principles (measure and number, *metro kai arithmo*). He introduced a proportionate mean—he is himself after all described as *mesos*—based upon produce, or, more precisely income. Aristotle states that he divided the population into four classes, just as they had been previously divided, and he made the dividing measure economic (τιμήματι διεῖλεν εἰς τέτταρα τέλη, καθάπερ διῄρητο καὶ πρότερον),[26]

ἑκάστοις ἀνάλογον τῷ μεγέθει τοῦ τιμήματος ἀποδιδοὺς τὴν ἀρχήν[27]

giving to each a position [*archē*] analogous to the size of the payment [*timēmatos*].

It should be no surprise, then, that one of his first enactments was to augment the value of the measures and weights of coinage to the percentile, bringing weights into correspondence with the currency (ἐποίησε δὲ καὶ σταθμὰ πρὸς τὸ νόμισμα, τρεῖς καὶ ἑξήκοντα μνᾶς τὸ τάλαντον ἀγούσας, καὶ ἐπιδιενεμήθησαν αἱ τρεῖς μναῖ τῷ στατῆρι καὶ τοῖς ἄλλοις σταθμοῖς.).[28] On the one hand, then, he brought law into the bedroom, but on the other he made the economic and productive capacity of each man the principle of his claim to political representation and office-holding potential. What is evident in Solon is how the market, through market values and measures, not only provided the means but also became the means and method of political activity. Henceforth, it can be said even today that there is no such thing as pure political power, there is only economic power activated within the legal constitution of the *polis*.

---

26 Ar.*Ath.* 7.3.
27 Ibid.
28 Ibid.10.

How, then, do what I call Solon's 'bedroom policies' correspond to this economic reform of the political, or his politico-economic reform? Here an answer is already implicated. Productivity, both biological and economic, comes under civic protection.

For the most part the bedroom policies as they are recounted by Plutarch orient sexual activity towards the exclusive outcome of producing children. In Ancient Greek, it is worth noting, the word for 'interest' (money to be repaid at a rate for the use of money lent, or for delaying the repayment of a debt) in Greek is *tokos* (τόκος), and the word also means 'childbirth'; as well as the 'children' themselves.[29] In what sense childbirth and children are transformed into profit is perhaps not entirely savoury. Of course, we have no idea how accurate Plutarch's rendition is.[30] But we have to deal with something, and the mere fact that these laws were possible even as thought experiments is significant enough.

For example, the law that in the case of sexual dysfunction of some sort or in the case that the husband cannot perform at all entitles an heiress to 'consort' (ὑπὸ τῶν ἔγγιστα του ἀνδρὸς ὀπύεσθαι), not necessarily to remarry, but to have sexual relations with another kinsman. This law condones exogamous sexual relations but only in the case that a woman is wealthy enough to support the habit. The law also limited her choice of partner from blood relations of the husband, as Plutarch states, 'that her offspring may be of his family and lineage.'[31] So the legally prescribed production of children appears to be the main aim of such a law, and certainly not the satisfaction of woman's pleasure. Age was also a theme of law, insofar as marriage was condoned only between a man and a woman within the fertile years of age: the law did 'not tolerate untimely and unseemly intercourse, nor sex that has no result or aim' (οὐδὲ περιοπτέον ἀώρους καὶ ἀχαρίτους ἐπιπλοκὰς καὶ μηδὲν ἔργον γαμήλιον ἐχούσας μηδὲ τέλος).[32] Indeed, forcible removal seemed to be within the bounds of the law, as it is stated that

---

29 Seaford (2003) 218.
30 That marriage became a predominantly economic affair, see Michael Leese 'An Economic Perspective on Marriage Alliances in Ancient Greece' in Kehoe and McGinn (2017) 32–45.
31 Plut.*Sol*.20.2-3.
32 Plut.*Sol*.20.5.

if a young man is discovered living with an elderly woman, he will be removed and given to a younger, more fertile woman.[33]

> εἰς τοῦτο δὲ συντελεῖ καὶ τὸ τὴν νύμφην τῷ νυμφίῳ συγκαθείργνυσθαι μήλου κυδωνίου κατατραγοῦσαν, καὶ τὸ τρὶς ἑκάστου μηνὸς ἐντυγχάνειν πάντως τῇ ἐπικλήρῳ τὸν λαβόντα. καὶ γὰρ εἰ μὴ γένοιντο παῖδες, ἀλλὰ τιμή τις ἀνδρὸς αὕτη πρὸς σώφρονα γυναῖκα.[34]

> Conformable to this, also, is that the bride must devour a quince and then be confined with the bridegroom; and that at least three times a month the husband of an heiress shall have intercourse with her without fail. For even in the case that this doesn't produce children, this is the price a man should pay to a chaste wife.

Not eating the quince was probably not a punishable act. There were also varying fines given for rape, depending upon how it was performed; for example an adulterer caught in the act could be killed, and the rape of a free woman resulted in a fine of one hundred drachmas, while the same conducted through persuasion was twenty drachmas.[35] What appears to me to be the most extreme law is, however, presented as an aside, for 'no man is allowed to sell a daughter or a sister, unless upon intercourse it is discovered that she was not a virgin,' in which case sell away!—(ἔτι δ' οὔτε θυγατέρας πωλεῖν οὔτ' ἀδελφὰς δίδωσι, πλὴν ἂν μὴ λάβῃ παρθένον ἀνδρὶ συγγεγενημένην).[36] Such a law, with such high stakes, would certainly have the effect of limiting the activities of girls and young women, sexual or otherwise.

And to reinforce this novel situation that puts so much focus upon production and reproduction Solon enacts a law holding a father responsible for the lack of productivity of his son: he 'enacted a law that no son who had not been taught a trade should be compelled to support his father.'[37] The state has entered the household fully, to the extent that the basic indebtedness and obligation of care of one's parents, that correspondence in the archaic family between birth and death, between the shared womb and the shared tomb, has become optional, or at least

---

33 Ibid. 20.4.
34 Ibid. 20.3
35 Ibid. 23.1.
36 Ibid. 23.2.
37 Ibid. 22.1.

not obligatory for all. He also instituted a policy that sons born out of wedlock need not support their fathers.

> ἐξ ἑταίρας γενομένοις ἐπάναγκες εἶναι τοὺς πατέρας τρέφειν. ὁ γὰρ ἐν γάμῳ παρορῶν τὸ καλὸν οὐ τέκνων ἕνεκα δῆλός ἐστιν, ἀλλ' ἡδονῆς ἀγόμενος γυναῖκα, τόν τε μισθὸν ἀπέχει, καὶ παρρησίαν αὑτῷ πρὸς τοὺς γενομένους οὐκ ἀπολέλοιπεν, οἷς αὐτὸ τὸ γενέσθαι πεποίηκεν ὄνειδος.

> He relieved the sons who were born out of wedlock [from a prostitute] from the necessity of supporting their fathers at all. For he that avoids the honourable state of marriage, clearly takes a woman to himself not for the sake of children, but of pleasure; and he has his reward, in that he robs himself of all right to upbraid his sons for neglecting him, since he has made their very existence a reproach to them.[38]

The result is, of course, a policy that denigrates pleasure and seeks to ensure the productivity of its citizens (men and women alike) and the utmost economic potential of the city as a whole. The supreme legislative council is for the first time not merely permitted but commanded to manage the economic usefulness or serviceability of its citizens: καὶ τὴν ἐξ Ἀρείου πάγου βουλὴν ἔταξενἐπισκοπεῖν ὅθεν ἕκαστος ἔχει τὰ ἐπιτήδεια, καὶ τοὺς ἀργοὺς κολάζειν, 'and he ordered the council of the Areiopagus to examine into every man's means of livelihood, and punish those who had no occupation.'[39] These laws might be said to be an archaic version of the capitalist welfare state, where the status quo is maintained, supporting the wealthy classes, while subjecting the labouring classes to legislative controls and supervision. The reason given for the necessity of the productive 'examination,' the management and surveillance of the labourers, is that farming is longer sustainable and that those in the city must go by force into trade. What punishment meant for the slackers in practical terms is not made explicit. Later, the Athenians had recourse to the silver mines in much the same way as the twentieth century had work camps, perhaps they were sent there.

It is in this light that we should read Solon's restriction against mourning rituals, since mourning, the expression of loss as such, is in principle non-productive. With Solon we have a political and

---
38 Plut.*Sol.* 22.4.trans. Rackham.
39 Ibid. 22.3

economic climate that is increasingly forcing its gaze toward gain and the productive and reproductive procedures that such a directive requires. Mourning intervenes into such procedures by introducing non-productive, non-evaluative activity that is inherently opposed to the reproductive processes of city life. Mourning is shared; production is self-interested. Mourning is without value, work generates value. Mourning and the ritual care for the dead is not primarily political but that does not mean that it is not radical or does not have significant political consequences.

And then above and beyond all this, mourning breaks into (by bringing into definition) the continuity of a functional and hence utilisable measurement of time. In contradistinction, the very last law that Plutarch credits to Solon is the introduction of a new measure of time, in his attempt to regulate the anomaly of the month (τοῦ μηνὸς τὴν ἀνωμαλίαν) in relation to the sun and the moon.[40] Benigni, in her collation of studies into calendar and rituals, draws an outline of a feminine precedent of the calendar based upon regenerative cycles influenced by the rotations of the heavenly body of Venus.[41] I can only speculate upon the matter, but it is possible that the decrees introduced during this period impacted upon or deviated from an earlier feminine concept of time measurement.

My Boundary, My Choice

Solon claims to have succeeded in bringing about the end of *stasis*. That he used the situation of *stasis* as justification to bring in a whole spate of laws is not impossible. That his reforms changed the definitions, the limits and boundaries of the political and economic realm of Athens both materially and in the social imaginary of the city seems obvious, but how he did this and what changes were wrought will be the topic of this section. It must also be asked what measures he brought in under cover of his reforms and whether his *seisactheia* corresponds to the potentially metaphorical appearance of the *horos* in his poetry. Solon provides an

---

40 Plut.*Sol*.25.3.
41 On the associations between the worship of Venus and the cosmology of the sacred feminine, including archaeoastronomy and ritual calendars that reflect the cycles of Venus, see Benigni (2013) 1–48. Also, Barbara Carter 'The Astronomy of the Nights of Venus' and 'The Eight Year Cycle of Venus' in Benigni (2013) 83–96.

image of himself as raising the boundary-stones (ὅρους ἀνεῖλον), but whether this was an actual act of his where material stones were torn from the ground, or whether he meant to denote the removal of certain more nebulous limits or distinctions that separated the people, is up for debate. In a way it does not matter because under the auspices of the *horoi* what Solon really achieved was to alter the warp and weft of the social fabric of Athens, changing the relations between its citizens and noncitizens, or excluded others, as well as between the people and the land. Solon does this by explicitly assuming the position of authority in the middle. In his poetry he states that he stood as a *horos*, as both an end and a principle of the law, but also as the marker of boundaries and determinations as well.

Ἐγὼ δὲ τούτων ὥσπερ ἐν μεταιχμίῳ
ὅρος κατέστην.[42]

I stood between them like a boundary-stone (*horos*) in no-man's land.

This place of authority was in the middle of the people, he says, neither in support of one side or the other, no friend to any, on the contrary he presents himself as standing alone in the centre with the spears of the people pointing at himself. His claim or right to occupy this position is put figuratively by his appropriation of the place of the *horos*. Solon's use of metaphor when he assumes for himself the position of the *horos* accomplishes this manipulation in a particular way. By placing himself in no-mans'-land, *metaichmion*, literally the 'place between spears,' he subjects himself to the violence of the Athenian city, divided, but suddenly no longer distinguished into two camps mediated as the populous is by his presence.[43] Instead, the image transforms the division into a single hostile force that Solon's self-sacrificial assumption of the position in the midst confronts with the solid determination of stone, or *horos*.

What must be assumed in Solon's assumption of the position of the *horos* is that the *horos* in the archaic period before Solon's reforms bore a certain significance, such that this statement, even metaphorically, was comprehensible to all. *Horoi* must have been commonly known

---

42 Ar.*Ath*.12.5.
43 I agree with Loraux's etymology as discussed in Martin, Blok (2006) 165.

and visible as actual stone, or at the very least frequently employed as a metaphorical trope. As the previous chapters have shown, there were various forms of the *horos* extant throughout Attica, though the exact nature of any pre-Solonian *horoi* is unknown. Nonetheless they do appear in the Homeric epics a couple of times both as boundary-markers on the field of battle and as similes taken from agrarian life.[44] That said, the epics are hardly saturated with *horoi*, the references are few, could be later interpolations and hardly justify the use of the *horos* by Solon as a marker of a common metaphorical, poetic vocabulary.

Solon's reform as a composite achievement is known to us through his poetry. The other reference to the *horoi* appears in the longest remaining fragment of Solon's poetry, given to us both in Plutarch and Aristotle. It is worth quoting the poem in full, as a number of coincidences in terminology (between *horoi*, mother earth, time and freedom) become evident and require further discussion.

> ἐγὼ δὲ τῶν μὲν οὕνεκα ξυνήγαγον
> δῆμον, τί τούτων πρὶν τυχεῖν ἐπαυσάμην;
> συμμαρτυροίη ταῦτ' ἂν ἐν δίκη Χρόνου
> μήτηρ μεγίστη δαιμόνων Ὀλυμπίων
> ἄριστα, Γῆ μέλαινα, τῆς ἐγώ ποτε
> ὅρους ἀνεῖλον πολλαχῇ πεπηγότας,
> πρόσθεν δὲ δουλεύουσα, νῦν ἐλευθέρα.
> πολλοὺς δ' Ἀθήνας, πατρίδ' εἰς θεόκτιτον,
> ἀνήγαγον πραθέντας, ἄλλον ἐκδίκως,
> ἄλλον δικαίως, τοὺς δ' ἀναγκαίης ὑπὸ
> χρειοῦς φυγόντας, γλῶσσαν οὐκέτ' Ἀττικὴν
> ἱέντας, ὡς ἂν πολλαχῇ πλανωμένους·
> τοὺς δ' ἐνθάδ' αὐτοῦ δουλίην ἀεικέα
> ἔχοντας, ἤθη δεσποτῶν τρομευμένους,
> ἐλευθέρους ἔθηκα. ταῦτα μὲν κράτει
> νομοῦ βίην τε καὶ δίκην συναρμόσας
> ἔρεξα καὶ διῆλθον ὡς ὑπεσχόμην.
> θεσμοὺς δ' ὁμοίως τῷ κακῷ τε κἀγαθῷ,
> εὐθεῖαν εἰς ἕκαστον ἁρμόσας δίκην,
> ἔγραψα. κέντρον δ' ἄλλος ὡς ἐγὼ λαβών,
> κακοφραδής τε καὶ φιλοκτήμων ἀνήρ,
> οὐκ ἂν κατέσχε δῆμον. εἰ γὰρ ἤθελον
> ἃ τοῖς ἐναντίοισιν ἥνδανεν τότε,

---

44 Discussed in Chapter Three.

αὖθις δ᾽ ἃ τοῖσιν οὕτεροι φρασαίατο,
πολλῶν ἂν ἀνδρῶν ἥδ᾽ ἐχηρώθη πόλις.
τῶν οὕνεκ᾽ ἀλκὴν πάντοθεν ποιούμενος
ὡς ἐν κυσὶν πολλῇσιν ἐστράφην λύκος.

> But what did I leave unachieved, of all/The ends for which I did unite the people?/Whereof before the judgement-seat of Time/The mighty mother of the Olympian gods, /Black Earth, would best bear witness, for 'twas I/Removed her many boundary-posts [*horous*] implanted:/Ere then she was a slave, but now is free./And many sold away I did bring home/ To god-built Athens, this one sold unjustly,/That other justly; others that had fled/From dire constraint of need, uttering no more/Their Attic tongue, so widely had they wandered,/And others suffering base slavery/Even here, trembling before their masters' humors,/I did set free. These deeds I make prevail,/Adjusting might and right to fit together,/ And did accomplish even as I had promised./And rules of law alike for base and noble,/Fitting straight justice unto each man's case,/I drafted. Had another than myself/Taken the goad, unwise and covetous,/He'd not have held the people! Had I willed/Now that pleased one of the opposing parties,/And then whatever the other party bade them,/The city had been bereft of many men./Wherefore I stood at guard on every side,/A wolf at bay among a pack of hounds!⁴⁵

That the word *horos* in Solon's poetry refers to security-markers, rather than boundary-stones, as indicators of a debt or mortgage upon the land, is the interpretation given within the descriptions of both Aristotle and Plutarch.⁴⁶ On this interpretation, the *seisachtheia* is understood as being related to the removal of the *horoi* from the land, and the cancellation of debts.⁴⁷ Finley argued that Solon's reforms abolished debt-bondage, the practice of lending on the security of the body, and this remained the largely accepted interpretation of the passage used to explain the actual state of affairs before and after Solon's reforms.⁴⁸

In this interpretation, Solon appears as the champion of the poor peasants, 'in some fashion he lifted the encumbrances that were squeezing the small Attic farmers off their land.'⁴⁹ However, that *horoi*

---

45 Ar.*Ath*.12.4–5. tr. Rackham. Also in Plut.*Sol*.15.
46 Ar.*Ath*.2.2,4.4,6.1,9.1 Plut.*Sol*. 13.4,15.2.
47 For terminology and the difference between, 'enslavement for debt' and debt 'bondage,' see Harris (2002) 415–416.
48 Finley (1981) 62–66, 117–118, 122, 157, 166.
49 Ibid. 63.

were security-markers was not, as we have seen, the normal use either of the word or the stone as marker until the fourth century BC (or 363/2 to be exact). Before this period *horoi* were boundary markers of one sort or another, proscribing entrance to the Athenian *agora*, describing the borders of temple lands, or placed upon roads to outline the edge of counties, or of course, gravestones.[50] To ascribe the pre-Solonic *horoi* the same function as they developed within the fourth century, that is, roughly two centuries later, is, if anything, anachronistic. There is, as Harris states 'an insurmountable objection to this interpretation: the word *horos* in early Greek literature always means boundary marker,' or as has been investigated here, a number of variations on the theme.[51] That the pre-Solonic *horoi* were mortgage-markers in the same capacity as the later use can be ruled out. That there were *horoi* placed upon the land as boundary markers that also signified in some figurative or metaphorical sense a kind of relational bond between land and freedom is nonetheless possible.

Harris ventures that a literal reading of the poem must be ruled out, since Solon could not have actually torn out the boundary-stones, as their removal was considered a serious crime (as seen in Chapter Three). In which case Harris suggests a metaphorical reading. Here the suggestion is that there were boundaries separating the population into the divisions of civil war or *stasis*, and it is these metaphorical boundaries that Solon did away with. The language that is used is figurative, then, so not about land at all, nor about debt or freedom, purely about *stasis*. The argument is persuasive, especially given Solon's other comparison to himself as a *horos* that stands between spears, as on the dividing line of a battle.[52] It would appear, then, that the appearance of the *horos* in both these cases acts as a metaphor for the activities of Solon, the first in eradicating the differences or divisions that kept the people apart in a state of *stasis*, the second as representing the role of Solon as 'putting himself on the line' insofar as he became the legal mediator or the 'in between man.'

It must be acknowledged that poetry was an acceptable means of disseminating information about the political, legal and economic reorganisation in Attica, otherwise someone in such a position of

---

50 Jeffreys, IG ii (2)2654.
51 Harris (1997) 104.
52 Ibid. 105–108.

power would not have used the poetic form, whether it meant that the reforms slipped into an epic sensibility on account of their poetic form, or whether this gave them a religious legitimacy remains a question. Nonetheless, that poetry, or as Martin argues, 'the aesthetic' had a social role in Athens is convincing.[53]

Perhaps the importance of rhetoric for later demagogues also suggests the continuation of the importance of form in the political life of the *polis*. Just because the poetry is ancient and the *polis* is still in its early days does not mean that method by which the message was transmitted must have been naïve. Putting something modern in verse might have been the best way of naturalising radical content in a form that was tested by time and endowed the content with a formal validity.

Poetry, by giving voice to a common experience, through implication, metaphor and an embedded audience, has the potential of creating social cohesion and control in a way that the enforcement of legislation cannot. In the *Rhetoric*, Aristotle says that poetry is manipulative, 'for something that goes on in circles tricks the ears, and the audience suffer emotion just as most people do with prophets' (φενακίζει γὰρ τὸ κύκλῳ πολὺ ὄν, καὶ πάσχουσιν οἱ ἀκροαταὶ ὅπερ οἱ πολλοὶ παρὰ τοῖς μάντεσιν).[54] In comparison to today, we might say that government control over media outlets creates a soft platform of social and political manipulation and ideological, indeed even intellectual conformity. Of Solon we can make one generalisation, that everything can take the form of poetry— philosophy, morals, exhortations and rebukes to others, justifications of his own actions, even his actual legal policies are said to have been transferred though epic poetry. Should this fact alone not suggest that for Solon philosophy, morals, rebukes and laws are inseparable from poetic form? Plutarch explains that Solon's poetry began as a worthless diversion, κατ' ἀρχὰς μὲν εἰς οὐδὲν ἄξιον σπουδῆς, ἀλλὰ παίζων, 'he was playing a game with no serious value.'

> ὕστερον δὲ καὶ γνώμας ἐνέτεινε φιλοσόφους καὶ τῶν πολιτικῶν πολλὰ συγκατέπλεκε τοῖς ποιήμασιν, οὐχ ἱστορίας ἕνεκεν καὶ μνήμης, ἀλλ' ἀπολογισμούς τε τῶν πεπραγμένων ἔχοντα καὶ προτροπὰς ἐνιαχοῦ καὶ νουθεσίας καὶ ἐπιπλήξεις πρὸς τοὺς Ἀθηναίους.

---

53 Richard Martin 'Solon in Noman's Land' in Blok (2006) 157.
54 Ar.*Rhet*. 3.5.4.

> Then later, he put philosophic maxims into verse, and interwove many political teachings in his poems, not simply to record and transmit them, but because they contained justifications of his acts, and sometimes exhortations, admonitions, and rebukes for the Athenians.[55]

It is instructive as to how removed from the pre-Solonic setting Plutarch must have been to believe that poetry was little more than a diversion, rather than the necessary form of radical political and religious change. It should stand as a case in point that we might be dealing with something in Solon that is considerably different, even for the periods immediately following, to what we have come to view as the distinction between law, politics, economy, and aesthetics.

Presumably, however, he did not eradicate the state of *stasis* with his poetic use of metaphor. So, what exactly did he do that 'freed' the earth and 'brought the people together'? If we do not need to explain Solon's reforms as a new system of land tenure or mortgage repayments, Solon's use of the figure of the *horos* to explain his reforms is open to speculation, whether metaphorically or actually. Ober offers one solution, that the *horoi* may well have been boundary markers between counties or communities, and the retraction of these may have contributed to an idea of a unified state, or 'asserting the conceptual unity of a "divinely founded homeland",' though his consequent assertion that they were in any way symbolic of 'asserting the freedom and base-line equality of the Athenians' is I think doubtful.[56] Or if they were it was purely symbolic, with little actual reality of equality 'on the ground,' as Solon himself makes clear in his resistance to the equal redistribution of land.

Harris suggests the *seisachtheia* was more likely the abolition of a fixed, feudal tithe placed upon peasant landowners to secure their protection by the lord of the area. Examples taken from Homeric epics and Hesiod imply that the lords provided both protection and a certain glory to the area in exchange for money or gifts.[57] Such a reform would weaken these lordly households, and make them to some degree at least subservient to the *polis*: 'This corresponded to Solon's attempt to strengthen the powers of the elected officials and the formal institutions operating in

---

55 Plut.*Sol*.3.3. trans. Bernadotte Perrin.
56 Josiah Ober 'facts on the Ground in Ancient Athens' in Blok (2006) 451.
57 see Harris (1997) 108–109.

the center of Attica in Athens.'⁵⁸ While it makes sense that Solon's aims were therefore to obliterate the cause of instability in the region between feuding households in regional areas, it does not take away from the fact that he did so by reducing the economic predominance of these regional households in favour of a centralised legal and religious *polis* authority underscored by a penal code that enforced a centralised economic system. The authority of his reforms was thus based both upon the alteration of a previous economy of tithe systems and the institution of economic penalties (such as those for rape) and economic restrictions (such as the eradication of the dowry), such that the *polis* itself became the main edifice of (sacred) economic activity, with the power to give and to take away.

The reference to the *horoi*, in Solon's poem, regardless of whether it refers to actual stones lifted, or metaphorical boundaries raised, serves to show us that Solon is engaged in an act of redefinition. His reforms have to do with redrawing the limits, the definitions and distinctions of the city, as well as obliterating old definitions, distinctions, determinations and limits. As Ober says, 'in seeking to instantiate a new political/ethical order in Athens in 594, Solon confronted various facts on the ground. Prominent among these, not least in terms of their presumptive materiality and groundedness, were *horoi*.'⁵⁹ That these *horoi* are metaphorical is as speculative as is their presence as rocks. That said, the archaeological record does not show an abundance of archaic age *horoi* thrown into waste dumps, or acting as filling for walls in the classical period. But that does not mean they were not there.

As has been discussed in previous chapters, the *horoi* although they are often recognisable in the archaeological record on account of the inscription of the word ΗΟΡΟΣ, need not necessarily have been inscribed in order to be recognisable as a *horos*. In which case they might have just been appropriately placed rocks, that, as has again been discussed in Chapters One and Two, were read as *horoi* nonetheless because the boundaries they signified or marked were already known to the local population. However we read his removal and assumption of the *horoi*, Solon is the manipulator of markers and markets. Perhaps it is not necessary to choose between a socio-economic reading of Solon's

---
58 Ibid. 111.
59 Ober in Blok and Lardinois (2006) 446.

seisachtheia and a religious and political reading, because the definition between these different aspects of the city was exactly what was called into question and reframed by Solon's metaphorical or actual dealings with the *horoi*.

Maybe the removal of the *horoi* had the effect of changing the sites of exchange, bringing them in to the centre of the city; then again, maybe it changed the allegiances between counties allowing marriages and other alliances or prohibiting them; maybe it opened up the property market, allowing Athenians to buy, sell and rent land; maybe it changed the relations between the small landholders and the regional authorities; maybe it caused a massive centralisation of legal, economic, religious and social authority in the *polis*. That Solon's law reform was a catalyst for secularisation is not an argument held to here. That his reforms had an effect upon later efforts at secularisation I do not doubt. However, if Solon's reforms must be interpreted as some kind of forerunner spurring novel institutions within the Athenian *polis* into the future, I believe that catalyst is his economic policies rather than his legal ones: or rather, his legal policies were framed in such a way that they were for the most part enacted economically or had a significant economic impact.

Alienable Earth

That these reforms negatively affected or destabilised the household as the primary site of economic production within the city was perhaps paralleled with the maintenance of a religious economy as the principal site of the accumulation of capital.[60] That the democracy developed out of a predominantly religious system could explain the continuing import of the city's cults and ritual practices within the fifth century and the sacral administration of the fourth. The myth of Athenian autochthony for example provided the Athenians with their exclusive notions of citizenship, with the Parthenon and the Erechtheum as spatial representations of this myth. Among Solon's reforms, the reorganising of religious festivals and the cultic calendar is no small matter—for example the importance he placed on the festival of the Genesia was likely to have simultaneously put more focus upon the city cult while

---

60 On property and sacred offices, or the relation between state and cult, see Bubelis (2016).

retracting from other regional cults.⁶¹ 'Hence the reorganisation of the Genesia from private cults of the dead into a *polis*-cult with a fixed date in the calendar. The Genesia as *polis*-festival only makes sense if it subsumed the former commemoration of the dead by *groups*, such as phratries or extensive families.'⁶²

After Solon's law and into the classical period, the *polis* enforced all laws related to sacred affairs, since 'parallel to such exclusive power of the management of resources, the classical *polis* also possessed an absolute judicial authority such as would be necessary for the sacred treasurers to exercise the fullest control possible.'⁶³ The religious sector particularly within the city thus coincided, as Bubelis argues, with economic control, or rather even though there were analogous offices held both within the religious and political sector, it appeared to be the norm that the political offices were the ones that organised the funding of cultic practices and temple maintenance.

How Solon's reforms actually changed the landscape of the political and religious performance and the social imaginary of the city is not entirely clear. The main problem is that the exact nature of the situation that preceded his reforms is unknown, though it has engendered plenty of speculation, which, given the political predisposition of the speculators should only make us more suspect in believing these later interpretations from the classical period until now.

For example, there has been a strong tendency to romanticise Solon as the forefather of the democracy, as well as his reforms as the catalyst of secular politics. The implied assumptions are indicative of the position from which the interpreters come to the original texts, for example, the democracy was a site of freedom and equality, organised and originating in a patriarchy; rather than an exclusive politico-religious organisation that benefitted the few, designated as masculine adults of substance and a particular ethnicity and dependent upon the non-remunerative labour of women and slaves and the religiously sanctified use of children to support the cultic institutions and boundaries of the state. It might be worth reconsidering Solon's reforms from this perspective, especially as regards the importance placed upon freedom, both of the population and in regards to the land.

---

61 Bubelis (2016).
62 Blok in Blok and Lardinois (2006) 235.
63 Bubelis (2016) 12.

κύριος δὲ γενόμενος τῶν πραγμάτων Σόλων τόν τε δῆμον ἠλευθέρωσε καὶ ἐν τῷ παρόντι καὶ εἰς τὸ μέλλον, κωλύσας δανείζειν ἐπὶ τοῖς σώμασιν, καὶ νόμους ἔθηκε καὶ χρεῶν ἀποκοπὰς ἐποίησε, καὶ τῶν ἰδίων καὶ τῶν δημοσίων, ἃς σεισάχθειαν καλοῦσιν, ὡς ἀποσεισάμενοι τὸ βάρος.[64]

Solon having become lord of everything freed the populous both in the present time and for the future, by prohibiting loans secured on their bodies, and he laid down laws, and enacted cancellations of debts, both private and public, known as the *seisachtheia*, because the men shook off their burden.

Conventionally, as was said to begin with, the *seisachtheia* was perceived as describing a new relation between citizen and land. According to Finley, this was the eradication of the situation in which a citizen was enslaved on account of failing to repay a debt.[65] But the relation might be considerably different if Harris's alternative reading holds. In which case it might be worth asking whether the above quote meant that freedom was entitled to the citizen as the very meaning of the word 'citizen,' as it became later; or if freedom held to the land, in so far as a citizen was 'free' who owned land without indebtedness. Perhaps a free citizen designated anyone who owned land, as was the case in the classical period, where land ownership becomes a requirement of being a citizen. But in neither of these cases is the land itself 'free.'

Meanwhile Solon explicitly states that he 'freed' the black earth (πρόσθεν δὲ δουλεύουσα, νῦν ἐλευθέρα) but we know that he did not make the earth free in the sense of being freely available, or open on the free market, or free to acquire or dispose of. The reference to the earth's colour, 'black' (*melaina*), could possibly be in reference to the boundaries of Attica, where the ephebes went to perform their military service.[66] Why the boundary markers of the furthest regions of Attica would be implicated in this reference, is however entirely hypothetical: perhaps he permitted exchange to be conducted with other cities, opening up the boundaries of the region to increased interactions with other cities, and thereby expanding markets? Perhaps he allowed the use of lands that were previously thought to be beyond the realms of agriculture?

---

64 Ar.*Ath*.6.1.
65 'The Alienability of Land in Ancient Greece' in Finley (2000) 153–160.
66 See Vidal-Naquet (1986) 106f.

Finley suggests that the alienation of land in Greece was one of the most important changes in Athenian law, impacting what it meant both to be a citizen but also how property came to be subject to buying and selling. Finley proposed that the above lines of Solon be taken implying a means by which men could take out loans by placing themselves as security, as opposed to the later custom when they could offer property or land as a kind of mortgage.[67] As Harris states, 'in this arrangement the debtor pledges an object in his possession as security for a loan. If the debtor defaults on the loan, the creditor has the right to seize the security, over which he thereby acquires the rights of ownership.'[68] This is distinct to enslavement for debt, where a man who could not repay his loan would be sold into slavery until such a time as the debt was paid off. The situation of debt-bondage differs from enslavement insofar as the man retained his status as a freeman, meaning he could potentially be freed again, whereas a slave was a slave for life (unless his owner decided to grant him freedom).

And yet, as Solon's reforms suggest there must be considerable doubt about whether, given that a man might be sold into slavery and sent abroad, the subsequent release from enslavement could actually be achieved. According to Plutarch's interpretation the body of the debtor was 'reserved' as a security (ἐγγύς) for the loan; as he puts it, they were χρέα λαμβάνοντες ἐπὶ τοῖς σώμασι, 'contracting debts on [the security of] their bodies.'[69] The subtleties of the situation before Solon depend upon a comparison of different texts from varying periods and places and are a problem that has not been entirely resolved, nor is there any unreservedly conclusive argument that Solon effectively prohibited this situation.[70] Before Solon, it appears to be the case that it was impossible to acquire land except through inheritance. This explains why Solon changed the inheritance laws, to keep what he designates as unwanted miscreants and illegitimate sons from land ownership. If this was a way to keep objectionable elements of the society from access to land ownership, even after Solon's reforms, land could not have been available as a property open to exchange, because they could simply have bought into what inheritance refused them.

---

67 Finley (2000) 153–160.
68 Harris (2006) 255.
69 Plut.Sol.13.4–5.
70 But see Harris (2006) 249ff.

So, we end up again at the reading of Solon's poem as metaphorical—that the earth was metaphorically, not literally, freed. When he addresses the subject of the earth, Solon alludes to this subterranean power as a mother of the Olympians, at once witness to Solon's law and former slave (συμμαρτυροίη ταῦτ' ἂν ἐν δίκῃ Χρόνου/μήτηρ μεγίστη δαιμόνων Ὀλυμπίων/ἄριστα, Γῆ μέλαινα, [...] πρόσθεν δὲ δουλεύουσα, νῦν ἐλευθέρα). There is a correlation here with the *Antigone* of Sophocles.[71] Antigone, repudiating the decrees of Creon, invoked subterranean Justice (*Dikē*) and Zeus; Solon reiterating the justice of his laws invokes Time (*Chronos*) and Earth (*Gē*). In both cases a subterranean force is invoked, even though the two instances appear in every respect to be opposite. Antigone opposes the predominance of the laws of the city, Solon establishes them; Antigone covers her brother's corpse with a handful of earth, Solon limits burial rituals and expressions of mourning; Antigone upholds the laws of the gods, Solon reforms the legal relations between men and women. There is one other significant contradiction; Antigone stated that Creon's decrees were not determined by the gods, implying that the eternal laws of honouring the dead and mourning had been determined by the gods, and she used the verbal form of the *horos*. Solon, on the other hand states that he has removed the *horoi* and freed the earth from its slavish determinations. Solon might be said to have achieved what Creon mishandled. Solon, in the divinely inspired form of poetry, related how through his actions he had the earth on his side, taking this mother of all positions to stabilise his own otherwise volatile and precarious position as the giver of laws.

In this sense, Solon's call to the earth as witness is an expert work of publicity, turning the potential criticism of him as a tyrant disobeying the ancestral, subterranean laws to his advantage. The fact that his reforms were thus advertised through poetry also reinforces their sanctity, stressing the reverence for the gods even while doing the work of men. The pre-Solonic *horoi* may well be actual, material markers. And yet, there is no evidence in the archaeological record of any *horoi* that can be said to belong to the period during which Solon instituted his reforms. We therefore have no idea what these *horoi* actually were, whether metaphorical or material, except by assuming they bore a certain resemblance with other later examples within the classical era of

---

71 Sophocles' *Antigone* was discussed in the previous chapter.

Athens. Were they inscribed or were they mere stones? Were they even stone?

Essentially, an alternative has already been suggested. For we saw the *horos* erected upon the grave of the dead, supplemented with the inscription *sēmatos*, which in a liberal translation could be read the 'limit of the sign.' Therefore, the limit of the sign coincides with the marker of the tomb. On top of this we've also confronted the problem of deciphering exactly what, or who this marker is. Obviously, it is the stone itself, but it is also the inscription, and whoever it was who demarcated the site as (re)markable, be it Antigone or the body of her dead brother, not to mention those 'unwritten laws' prescribing burial and mourning. The legal restrictions that limited the gifts the living offered to the dead broke into the reciprocal relation between the living and the dead and as it were cemented the separation between the living and the dead. As Blok concludes,

> offerings to the dead, like those to the gods and heroes, would create a relation of reciprocity and exchange with the recipients. This must have been the attitude the early lawgivers wanted to restrict: the limitations on grave goods and sacrifices to the dead cut down the degree to which the dead had to reciprocate these gifts and had to act on behalf of the living.[72]

So *xenia* and death rituals are inherently related and posed a challenge to the development of the *polis* as an autonomous structure of economic and legal authority. And yet, what is most interesting in the debate is a relation often lost in the finer details between body and land. For, whatever the situation before Solon, it is significant that in the light of the later usage of the security-markers it was interpreted that when it came to debt a *horos* was placed upon the land to signify that the body of a man was in some way put into a condition of suspension. In this condition the payment of debt was deferred by holding the body as pledge for the land, inverting the former state in which the land was held as a pledge for the loan, and suggesting a certain substitutability between land, body and *horos*.

The question is that, if the debt was incurred ἐπὶ τοῖς σώμασι, 'upon the bodies,' why would this be represented with a *horos* placed upon the land? What is the relation between the debt and the body on

---

72 Blok in Blok and Lardinois (2006) 237.

the one hand, and its representation of *horos* and land? Further, is it correct to view the *horos* as a type of representation or signification, a 'sign' upon the land of a body burdened by debt? Does this not already suggest to us the nexus of ideas that adhered to the tomb as *horos sēmatos*, the sign of the dead? Is the relative correspondence between debt and *horos* that of signified and sign, or have we lost the actual relation that these four terms were supposed to describe by assuming a system of signification?

The *horos* would appear to consolidate stone, living and dead in a single term. In this sense the *horos* never functioned as a signifier, hence the addition of the sign in the genitive. It is the boundary, the stolidly material boundary that gives definition to either side, be this guest-host, letter-word, before-after, living-dead and so forth. And, it would appear, it shares this site with the body that remains and is yet different between life and death. It is worth noting another coincidence that refers us back again to the previous chapter and implies the collusion between the relation of *xenia*, and all these different ways of being indebted in the mark and the *horos*. Before Herakles was received as a guest in the house of Admetos, this household was the most unusual case of a god having fallen into debt-bondage.[73] In the prologue, Apollo tells how he came to work for Admetos. After Zeus killed his son Asklepius with his thunderbolt, in retaliation Apollo killed the Cyclops who forged the thunderbolt. In compensation for this murder, Zeus commanded that Apollo be enslaved in the house of Admetos, in order to pay off his debt to Zeus for his blood-guilt.

Is this what the pre-Solonian *horoi* marked then; that the body is the limit and that the incurrence of debt, which is also the pledge of increase, of production/reproduction, and of return and repayment finds its limit, finds its *horos*, in the body? Were these markers of the fact that we each of us are our (re)productive limit, we describe the boundary of our input/output, the boundary of our economic value is prescribed by the body? Perhaps. In any case, whatever the situation was in regards to this limit, it was prohibited by Solon.

After Solon, the traditional definitions where different customs and meanings collide were suspended. And the earth that he claimed was enslaved was made free. Men were free from their relations as defined

---

73 As discussed in the previous chapter.

by the earth, or a relation of *xenia* with other men; they were also henceforth free from the indebtedness to the great mother, as well as all those other women who believed that their role as primary producer had been eclipsed. Men were then free to work, to produce, to borrow, to repay and everyone, women, men and children alike were all freely subjected to the laws and economic penalties imposed upon them by the state—now that Solon had removed the limits (*horoi*). Is there, or was there once, an inherent relation between the human body and the earth? Just as men were henceforth free to engage in their transactions without the threatening limits of traditional customs, was the earth also free to be worked? Was there in pre-Solonian times a corresponding limit upon men's use of the land as upon the use of their own bodies? Did Solon do away with some very material limits that described a common boundary of 'use' between man and land?

It is feasible to imagine a time when the relation with the earth was modified by a structure of beliefs in which its utility in the productive life of humans was limited. As much as it might appear that it is the earth that is the subject of liberation in his poem, it is more likely that it was actually the relation between a man's body and the earth that becomes not the subject of liberation but the object of possession. Each (free Athenian) man, henceforth, was the indubitable possessor of his own body, his own land, any beings that inhabited that land, and he was consequently responsible for the productivity of all.

Death to the Speculator

If appropriation is death to the speculator, how does the masochistic potentiality of the *horos* resonate upon whomsoever would aspire to claim the boundary in his own name?

ΗΟΡΟΣ ΕΙΜΙ ΤΕΣ ΑΓΟΡΑΣ read the stones, 'I AM THE BOUNDARY OF THE MARKET,' and presumably the work of the market was limited to the confines of these boundaries. Not only did these boundaries signify who was to enter within the area, but they also restricted what would escape. In the classical period the *agora*, the 'market-place,' became the site of exchange of goods and of words. Here values could be discussed and challenged without posing a risk to daily life dependent upon the stability of such values. Well and good, but the boundaries did not hold. Socrates escaped the boundaries, raising his questions of the value of words and concepts well beyond the secure confines of the Athenian *agora*. He might have been put to death for it, but the borders had been broken; at least the matter of the boundary did not mean what it meant before.

The transgression and violation of boundaries are not necessarily a call to obliterate boundaries as such. Boundaries might be removed only to be displaced and imposed elsewhere, just as, when we approach the horizon, a further horizon opens up at a distance before us. Even Solon could not evade the necessity of placing new boundaries. His supreme act of hubris is that he believed he could be the one and common boundary for all (Ἐγὼ δὲ τούτων ὥσπερ ἐν μεταιχμίῳ /ὅρος κατέστην).[74] Solon's claim, and I do not mean necessarily the historical man but the absent signifier of the force of the law, is that opposition can be mediated by men, that men have the power to mediate what before was determined by gods or 'unwritten laws' mutually inscribed by the community as a whole, including women and children, the memory of the dead but presumably also the nonhuman as it imposes restrictions or interacts within the world shared with humans. In contrast, the Law asserts that there are no boundaries in nature beyond our control to mark, choose and enforce, and that human or more particularly masculine authority is master over the living, the dead, animals, plants, stones and whatever else comes within his dominion. By adopting the site and name of the *horos*, Solon presents this position of authority as neutral ground. Ironically, Solon recognised exactly the problem of this claim to neutrality, since if anyone else claimed this position it would put into question the very essence of his own position, his authority, his laws.

Positions of power are rarely appropriated for the sake of the common weal, and Solon's reforms should come under scrutiny as to what more subtle changes were brought about and to the benefit of whom. Solon himself, in his poetry, is acutely self-deprecatory; he asserts to never have claimed power for himself, and moreover, after instituting his reforms, he absents himself. After the laws were posited, they came under scrutiny, and Solon was subjected to a barrage of questions as to their applicability under different conditions:

---

74 Ar.*Ath*.12.5

ἐπειδὴ προσιόντες αὐτῷ περὶ τῶν νόμων ἠνώχλουν, τὰ μὲν ἐπιτιμῶντες τὰ δὲ ἀνακρίνοντες, βουλόμενος μήτε ταῦτα κινεῖν, μήτ' ἀπεχθάνεσθαι παρών, ἀποδημίαν ἐποιήσατο κατ' ἐμπορίαν ἅμα καὶ θεωρίαν εἰς Αἴγυπτον, εἰπὼν ὡς οὐχ ἥξει δέκα ἐτῶν, οὐ γὰρ οἴεσθαι δίκαιον εἶναι τοὺς νόμους ἐξηγεῖσθαι παρών, ἀλλ' ἕκαστον τὰ γεγραμμένα ποιεῖν.[75]

Because people kept annoying him about his laws, questioning here and criticising there, and as he did not wish either to change them or by his presence to become hateful, he went abroad to Egypt, at once both for the purpose of trade and to see the wonders, saying that he would not come back for ten years, as he did not believe it was right for him to stay and explain his laws, but for each to act in accordance to what was written.

Was this absence necessary in order to hinder attempts at further legal reform or modifications of his laws as he suggests, or is his absence the necessary displacement of the authority of the law? The law is always forced to confront the limits of its authority. As Agamben acknowledges, the 'paradox of sovereignty consists in the fact the sovereign is, at the same time, outside and inside the judicial order.'[76] What this means is that 'the sovereign, having the validity of the law, legally places himself outside the law.' Solon's absence becomes the absent origin essential to the maintenance of the law, the heteronomous authority that cannot be questioned because the origin of law is always elsewhere. Solon stands as the sovereign figure reassuring through his exception that there is 'nothing outside the law.'[77]

In a way Solon is the precedent, the legislative basis of this paradoxical state of exception in the law. As Agamben suggests, it is worth reflecting upon the topology implicit in the paradox of the legal reformer, 'since the degree to which sovereignty marks the limit (in the double sense of end and principle) of the judicial order will become clear only once the structure of the paradox is grasped.'[78] Hence, the name 'Solon' is attached to the law, which thereby gains in sanctity and authenticity, regardless of whether it was actually coined by him. In a way the name 'Solon' becomes the necessary signifier for the authority of law, all the more potent when the particularities and historical accuracies of his acts

---

75 Ar.*Ath*.11.1–2.
76 Agamben (1998) 15.
77 Ibid.
78 Ibid. 15.

are withdrawn. Before the name of Solon was absented, he claimed for himself the position of authority, on the boundary between men, the neutral ground of the *horos* from which he could ensure the immutability of his legislative reforms.

Ironically, before absenting himself from the city, he decreed that no other man could ever again claim the *horos* for himself, positing the law that no man was to remain neutral in a situation of *stasis*, that every citizen had to choose one side or another—with the exception, of course, of himself. Again, we could ask if this *horos* that Solon identifies with himself is metaphorical. Given that the claim of the law to inhabit neutral ground is still observed and has considerable, actual effect, the metaphor, if it was one, has no lack of material consequences. Can these be traced back to a material basis that the law has abstracted in order to claim the position? Is there any meaningful origin that matters but the material? The word itself, '*horos*,' is material, and its meaning is indivisible from the word, type-set on this page or inscribed upon stone. Is the read word, thought word, the spoken word any less material than the senses required to read it, with eyes moving, synapses firing, tongue forming and lips contorting? The *horos* is never fully abstracted from its material or its place. So, Solon placing himself bodily as a security and pledge between and against the restive population becomes the *horos*, the definition of the material foundation of the law, or the body of the law, his body and person belongs to the people as an investment and intervention. The task of the withdrawal of this bodily imposition is to keep the dogs at bay, separated when it comes to their disagreements but joined in one new polity. But no man can embody the foundation of authority absolutely. Despite what he says, man is not as solid as stone.

With the reforms of Solon, relations amongst the populous as a whole, between men and women, between parents and children, and finally between land and body became a subject of political economics. Perhaps metaphorically, perhaps actually, the removal of the *horoi* had ensured this. Is the result the expansion of economic limits or their abstraction, that is the removal of earlier limitations? Is the tendency toward an ever-expanding market paralleled by new economic determinations that make everything a potential object of exchange? If so, the problem that this expansion of the economic caused in the early classical society might be what prompted the placement of the *horos* markers of the *agora*. This may well be why the Athenian *polis* instituted a market with clearly defined boundaries, in order to keep the behemoth of free-market economic exchange within discreet terms, within human limits.

Do we mourn the dead alone, or do we also mourn the breakdown of our relations with nonhumans? It might be obvious to some that we mourn (with) animals, but what about our experience of loss of other things: an old house destroyed to make a car-park, a mountain valley dug up and sacrificed for a swathe of tourist villas, the draining of a swamp (swimming pools included), the ancient birthing tree cut down to make way for another highway, a faithful pair of shoes that finally gave up the ghost. The interventions and mediations that have arisen between us and the things to hand put us out of touch with the common boundaries of our interaction and the shared experience of living in a world where emotional investments are not limited to marriage vows or blood relations.

Nonetheless, we experience feelings of loss with the world around us as it changes and morphs into a world full of things and places and people that at first appear foreign and often antipathetic. In our ability to mourn the past and its inhabitants, of all walks of life and nonlife, organic and inorganic, human and nonhuman, we can make out the traces of a material embeddedness of language and thought, a non-mediated relation with the matter of meaning. George Steiner refers to a Kabbalistic speculation 'about a day on which words will "shake off the burden of having to mean" and will be only themselves, blank and replete as stone.'[79] Perhaps this is the reverse side of what Solon's *seisachtheia* ('shaking off the burdens') described. Perhaps in the *seisachtheia* matter shook off the burden of meaning. In any case we do know that from the end of the sixth century the language of the Greeks began to take a turn toward the speculative. Thales is the champion of economic speculation, and the story of his monopoly of the olive presses reveals that in form speculation is inherent to philosophical thought, while the result (increased profits) is foreign and undesirable.[80]

---

79 Steiner (1998) 313.
80 Ar.*Pol*.1259a.

After Solon's reforms, even words would be required to serve different purposes in different conditions; the classical era witnesses the gradual formalisation of a legal vocabulary, an economic one, a technical philosophical lexicon. How did this influence the *horos* and its swathe of meanings? To what degree was the material presence of the *horos* fractured throughout the classical period? It might still have implied a nexus of meaning and matter, however its use becomes increasingly context specific until within the fourth century it splinters into matter on the one hand and meaning on the other, signifying debt in its material form and philosophical term in its immaterial form. This could be said to be the logical conclusion of all those other meanings transposed and translated into the legalese of the democratic *polis*. The Athenians might be said to have had no particular terminology for law, economics and commerce, continuing to use a language largely inherited from earlier social conditions. And yet the adoption of this language may simultaneously have caused the linguistic eclipse of prior social conditions.

What was initiated by Solon was nothing short of a linguistic coup. It was not only the law, politics and economics that began to spread its tentacles throughout the region of Attica, but the economically enforced transformation and appropriation of language that supported his economic and legal reforms. Solon shakes up language: this language engendered a politico-religious, legal structure that insinuated itself into aspects of life that were hitherto unregulated by anything but those unwritten laws Antigone so desperately defended.

This coup worked by creating a new vocabulary within the epic structures of the old. Solon's poetry brought the novelty of his laws into relation with age-old, revered terms and determinations (*horoi*), all the while filtering in a new responsibility for the self and the other, for one's own and others' property, a new basis for production and reproduction, a new economy prescribed within a system that structured *polis* life into (increasingly more) distinct categories of possession. Above and beyond the separation of the dead and the living, we have all those new limits placed upon the family, denigrated in favour of the increasingly legal categories of the individual as woman, man, child, foreigner, slave.

Solon removed the *horoi* from the *polis*, but do the material limits remain to be read in the nature of the stone? In the absence of traditional *horoi* and in the absence of material limits, the work of politics, law and economics is supposed to be autonomous, but does this make it also automatic? It might continue in its own time, unwriting, rewriting, buying, selling, producing, trading, speaking, condemning, interpreting interminably in a process that has no natural end in sight. But has the *agora*, the market-place extended its boundaries so widely and furtively that it has obliterated every trace of our authorship in the materialisation of limits? Is the definition of the loss of such limits the final word and then also the common term or the grounding determination by means of which the presence of the stone can be read again in the fateful continuation of life?

Fig. 8. ΗΟΡΟΣ ΕΙΜΙ ΤΕΣ ΑΓΟΡΑΣ [retrograde] 'I am the *horos* of the agora.' *Horos* stone discovered in situ in the northeast corner of the Ancient Athenian Agora, by the Tholos. *IG* I³ 1088 [I 7039] Photgraph by M. Goutsourela, 2013. Rights belong to The Athenian Agora Museum © Hellenic Ministry of Culture and Sports/Hellenic Organization of Cultural Resources Development (H.O.C.R.E.D.)

8. I Am the Boundary of the Market

If I must read into this work any single aim, it would be that it provides a material foundation for, in Levinas's words, 'interpreting human resistance petromorphically.'[1] To begin with, I have elaborated upon the very real limits to economic growth and progress that have existed and continue to exist in the matter itself, the natural resources we make use of in order to go about the tasks of producing and reproducing. This will already be known to many of my readers, so I hope that this excursion contributes by providing a basis for further resistance to the forces that seek to make use of our common material, ourselves included, to the profit of a few and to the detriment of all. While the limits are no doubt material they are also conceptual and they depend upon us; they are recognised or read into the material itself but always by us, or that failing it is we who have forgotten how to read what the world around us, populated as it is by humans and nonhumans of every walk of life, so adamantly tells us. So, if we listen to stone even today, perhaps we can hear the echo of ancient wisdom and relay it back into our present conditions to help us make a stand, as the stone did so long ago, in an act, this time of disobedience, defiance or noncompliance to work within the tyranny of an economic system that is structured around stripping dignity, pride and soul from us and every aspect of the world, organic and inorganic, human and nonhuman alike: 'I am the boundary of the market,' let us say, 'and this stops here.'

Some fifty years after Solon's reforms and his removal of the *horoi*, a stone calls witness once again to a limit. It announces itself as the economic limit of all transactions, 'I am the boundary of the market,'

---

1   Levinas (1987) 78.

ΗΟΡΟΣ ΕΙΜΙ ΤΕΣ ΑΓΟΡΑΣ. In Ancient Athens the market-place (*agora*) was marked by the *horoi* which were engaged in drawing up the boundaries of this space. These stones mark the boundaries of any verbal and more than verbal exchange and they do this because not everything is exchangeable, not everything in short nothing—neither word nor thing, animal nor human—is essentially reducible to a single exchange value or substitutable by a collection of monetary units. Ascribing nonessential, nonesoteric worth to anything comes at a cost to the human soul. It should come as no surprise, then, that a limit was declared. And yet it was a limit that did not intend to stop these processes, but that took the need for marking limits onto itself in order that the processes could go on beyond such limits. As little as we know about the pre-Solonian *horoi*, we may make one assumption, that not one of them named itself. It is only within the boundaries of the late archaic *polis* that the stone rises up and gives itself a name, that the boundary (transgressed) reasserts itself, that the term enunciates its presence and the limit declares itself a place. In the shadow of the matter of self-proclamation, human works and deeds retire into the machinations of the market's forces because there is an external limit, a limit that takes upon itself the definition of the market. This limit is marginal, yes on the one hand, but it is also central to the *polis*. It frames the city and its work, which becomes increasingly powerful as it engages in the export and import of words, deeds and things, expanding the boundaries of its *agora* exponentially. Until, finally, it is the *agora* that comes to take precedence over the *polis*, Athens becomes an imperial city and philosophy is now taught and sold as a commodity all over the world.

Unlike an earlier boundary-stone inscribed with the words ΗΟΡΟΣ : ΔΙΟΣ (retrograde) '*Horos* of Zeus' (marking the extent of a sanctuary of Zeus), the boundary-stones of the market were not marked as belonging to any particular god.[2] In contrast, it states that it belongs to the market. Would we be correct, then, in assuming the *agora* was in the league of other sanctuaries? To some degree, perhaps, especially given the fact that at the central point of the *agora* stood the temple to the Olympian Gods among many other shrines and altars. And yet there is something that differentiates this stone from all the others, and that might give us a clue

---

2 Lalonde (2006).

as to why the *agora* is a space that simultaneously provides a sanctified place for exchange and evaluation and puts into question this very notion of the sacred. The *agora's* use as a place where exchange-value finds its home can be maintained only in the absence of any definitive terms of value. Indeed, when it comes to what is sacred about the *agora*, we are confronted before anything else by the name of its limits.

This *horos* does not merely describe the boundaries of the market; it is also inscribed as giving itself a name. It declares (to us) what it is in the nominative and where it belongs by virtue of the copulative 'I am' (EIMI). Why is the simple word *horos* not sufficient when it comes to the market? Why does this stone, of all stones, assume the task of speaking to us and of giving a name for itself, of telling us what it is and thereby making itself the subject of the market, a subject of belonging which however does not enter into the market, but remains on the edge for us to see before *we* enter? It tells us its name, and its name is 'boundary,' a boundary to be transgressed, and we transgress it. Upon this site where possession is always at issue, where everything is up for sale, the only thing that claims to belong there is the boundary itself, which remains nonetheless both marginal and defining. All the other meanings of the word *horos* are assumed in this single act of self-definition: it is there where we abstract the matter itself as an object of worth, where transgression between what is mine and yours is essential to the everyday functioning of the market, where language itself comes into question, and where time stretches in an eternal present suspended in the deferral of gratification (despite the copulative 'I am'). It is without doubt more than a fortuitous coincidence, this self-appellation of the stone on the margin of the very place where intercourse (*agoreuein*) is embodied by acquisition (*agorazein*).

Archaeological studies suggest that the agora was initially the place of social discourse and public speaking (*agoreuein* means 'to speak in public') and indeed the word *agora* on its own can be used to mean a place for public speaking. In any case, although by the classical period the *agora* was chiefly a site devoted to the exchange of goods, the etymological history of the *agora* was resurrected by sophists and philosophers alike occupying the site and putting into question generally assumed conceptions of goods and bads. Socrates himself frequented the *agora*, and in his trial claimed that he spoke nothing more than the language of the market-place.³ The Stoics also take their name from their tendency to loiter about the stoas of the Hellenistic *agora* and engage in their discussions in this public place. If we accept these later examples as indicative, we could say that the *agora* was a place that was devoted not only to public speaking, but to a common task of definition; where what was discussed but not resolved were questions of meaning and value, the question of the city's common aims, customs and laws. The *agora*, then, was the very site of legal and economic disputation, whether as with Socrates that meant questions raised about the Just and the Good, or with Diogenes the Cynic the ridicule of rife acquisitiveness and the defacement of the value of currency (or any transitory beliefs). The raising of questions as such could take this position because here questions (with or without answers) were at home. For these questions to even be possible there had to be the precedent that the site was not foreclosed to the potential dangers of raising questions: concepts and activities in practice were not already definitive. Definitions as such had to be dubitable and even destroyed, we might say put out of use, in order that new definitions be attributed.

So, within this clearly demarcated area, defined off from the banal duties of everyday life, what was up for grabs was definition itself. In the act of public discourse, intentions, laws and words themselves are in dispute. Outside the *agora* where people go about their lives, language had a determined value, it was used in the courts, the theatres, the assemblies, in both town and country. But within the *agora* this use-value of language as such was put on hold, undetermined as the possibility of conferring new meanings, new standards and new linguistic rules. The *horos* drew up the boundaries of this task of redefinition. It provided the definitive limits within which there are no limits to discourse, intercourse and exchange. Every time we try to define a word or reform a law the very act of definition requires a beginning, a basis or a foundation, a language within which to work. We must use other words to define the one that is at issue, and yet no other word is discreet in itself or absolutely definitive, so that in the process the structure of language itself comes into question, just as we countermand the foundation of Law as such when we consider the formulation and applicability of a new law.

---

3   Pl.*Ap*.17C-D.

For this reason, Solon the lawgiver exiled himself so that he would not be called upon to explain or change the laws that he had undersigned. He exiled himself, thus making himself the basis of the law, the absent principle, the unquestionable *archē*. But what Solon did for the political system from afar, the *horos* did to the economy from within. What is exceptional about the *agora* can only be maintained because there is a limit that simultaneously restricts what is exceptional about the *agora* and makes it central to the community. This limit is simultaneously declarative, self-appellating and, significantly, material. It is neither law nor man, it is stone. And as stone it takes on the burden of defining the market-place, drawing up the limits and marginalising matter from the processes of exchange and perhaps giving a taint of the ideal to those processes within.

It is said that this stone provided an outline of an area into which those who had perpetrated unforgivable crimes such as patricide were not permitted to enter.[4] These men were given the title *atimos*, they were dishonoured and were considered unclean in the ritual sense. Why criminals should thus be exiled from the market-place is a question that can be considered according to a conjunction between what we consider the sacred customs of the ancient world and the economic bias of the modern. That is to say that this extradition of the criminal cannot be explained away as an idiosyncrasy of ancient ritual and religion, unless we accept that the market-place itself is also a site of value for the sacred. But does this mean that the market itself is of sacred value, or that for any notion of value to take place within the market it must of itself have limits? What if, as the civic space closed off for the exclusive purpose of exchange (of words and things) it is deemed sacred insofar as it can be put to no other use? What can be seen is a co-determination between the stone '*horos*' and a boundary of social significance that, in a community without a clear cleft between sacred and secular, describes public spaces. Thus, the market can be understood as a site of holy value, which is however not wholly sacred.

René Girard has argued that traditional sacrifice was performed upon a substitute scapegoat.[5] In the case of Athens, this stone might be said to offer itself up, by assuming for itself a name that belongs to the

---

4   And.*Myst*.1.76.
5   Girard (1989).

market (*tēs agoras*, 'of the agora') and permitting the boundary to be redefined upon its person. Although it thus becomes the defining subject (*horos eimi*) of the market, and the one object that cannot be subjected to the procedures that it contains, it does not, for all that, sacrifice its base form as stone. In the *horos* of the market, stone, mark and margin all meet at exactly that point where they undertake to separate what is *agora* with what is not: infinite exchange and intercourse within, and whatever is other, whatever is limited, defined and of pre-determined value without. And yet *horos* remains stone, and its inscription must have been written and someone must read into both the inscription and the placement of the stone a meaning that preceded both the position of the boundary and the prohibition of the word. This problem, the materialisation of meaning cannot help but point to whoever it is that is writing and reading.

Somebody is obfuscated by the stone—somebody who took chisel to stone and assumed in this inscriptive work the assertion 'I am the boundary,' repeated again every time it was read, every time the boundary was crossed in recognition or defiance of what the stone said and someone entered the *agora*. Somebody drew up this boundary and in so doing permitted its readers to recede into stone. By making the stone the subject of the verb, the stone became an authority for human transgressions as well as limits. That original marker of the *I am horos* was eclipsed by the self-appellating stone, and the human subject returned to the nebulous priority of indefinability, an indeterminate cause that can introduce the work of the *agora* as accident (οὐκ ἀναγκαῖον ἀλλ' ἀόριστον, λέγω δὲ τὸ κατὰ συμβεβηκός).[6] Human responsibility is deferred by embedding the work of copulative naming in the soil and allowing the *agora* to go on by itself, unlimited by any more determinate human proscriptions. Nonetheless, we are included in these boundaries because we read and acknowledge a deferral of the limits of our actions. Today we have sacrificed our control of the market's limits in an infinite deferral of responsibility. We are not beyond the bounds of exchange, but are all bound up in exchange, 'everywhere in chains' and continue to be so as long as we let the market determine the limits for itself.

As conceptual as it might sound the problem of limits, or now the absence thereof, is a very real problem and can be seen in how the market

---

6   Ar.*Met*.1065a25.

has evolved today, expanding beyond all possible earthly limits, literally beyond earthly limits in more ways than one. Now the wealthy exercise no limits in their hubristic behaviour or their desire for control over and forced compliance of desperate populations. Corporations themselves have become responsible for the same bodies that are instituted to restrict and limit the overweening activities of those corporations: for example, the FDA is funded by pharmaceutical companies, the WHO by vaccine entrepreneurs, MPs in national governments have stocks in the corporations that fund them in turn, mass media outlets receive grants from the companies they're supposed to be reporting upon, banks create the crises they then step in to solve and war is declared to create a market, selling weapons to both sides manufactured by the warmongers themselves. This behemoth of stakeholder capitalism, a kind of debauched ouroboros, is a figment of human imagination. As Aristotle said, money exists by custom and can be withdrawn by custom.[7] Although it creates its own dependency, both addict and purveyor of toxic substances, nothing stands beside it, or underneath it except us and our willingness to enter into it or let it enter us.

The *horos* is, then, what drives us on to the task of finding limits and of raising the essential questions while simultaneously presupposing itself as the substantial limit that supports this task that had to start somewhere. Are we in a position to reject the market, to resist it? Can we hear an ancient voice calling us back to the matter of meaning? The copulative 'I am' takes the responsibility of its own marker, who merely inscribed what the stone meant to say. Even there where the limit and boundary are in question, deposed only to be replaced in a movement of ever-increasing momentum, where market forces, justice and philosophy work towards new determinations introducing new definitions, even there, on the margins an archaic limit remains, suspended by us and putting us in suspension, while it enforces its solid materiality and reminds us that matter does not cease to matter. Despite all our words and deeds, all those objects bought and sold there is a limit to the deferral of gratification encrypted in us as our nature, a

---

7   'But as a representation of demand (*chreia*) money exists by social convention. And this is why money has the name nomisma, because it exists not by nature but by custom (*nomos*), and it is in our power to change its value and to render it useless (*achrēston*).' Ar.EN.1133a.

natural end that should stand as a warning that like our rare metals we will be used up. If there are no limits or boundaries in nature, it is then our responsibility and ours alone that could claim to separate us from nature and permit us to abuse it. In doing so, we face no other limit but ourselves, and this limit remains in us as our bond to the material—the knot in the subject—which we may use and abuse freely but whose terminal point is by necessity a return to nature. For the (re)production of words and things will always come up against this, our primeval limit, the intransigence of stone, the brute matter that makes us what we are. As Levinas said, 'Resistance is neither a human privilege, nor a rock's, just as radiance does not characterize a day of the month of May more authentically than it does the face of a woman. The meaning precedes the data and illuminates them.'[8]

---

8   Levinas (1987) 78.

Bibliography

Addas, Claude. (1993) *Quest for the Red Sulphur*. The Islamic Texts Society, Cambridge.

Adorno, Theodor. (2007) *Negative Dialectics*, trans. E. B. Ashton. Continuum, New York. https://doi.org/10.4324/9780203479605

Adorno, Theodore and Max Horkheimer (1997) *The Dialectic of Enlightenment*, trans. John Cumming. Verso, New York.

Aeschylus. (1999) *Agamemnon, Libation-Bearers, Eumenides, Fragments*, trans. Herbert Weir Smith. Loeb Classical Library, Cambridge, MA.

Agamben, Giorgio. (1998) *Homo Sacer: Sovereign Power and Bare Life*, trans. Daniel Heller-Roazen. Stanford University Press, Stanford. https://doi.org/10.1515/9780804764025

— (1999) *Potentialities: Collected Essays in Philosophy*, trans. Daniel Heller-Roazen. Stanford University Press, Stanford.

— (2007) *Infancy and History: The Destruction of Experience*, trans. Liz Heron. Verso, London.

— (2009) *The Signature of All Things: On Method*, trans. Kevin Attell. Zone Books, New York.

— (2011) *The Sacrament of Language: An Archaeology of the Oath*, trans. Adam Kotsko. Stanford University Press, Stanford.

Ager, Derek. (1973) *The Nature of the Stratigraphic Record*. Macmillan Press, London.

Andocides. (1968) *Minor Attic Orators Volume 1: Antiphon Andocides*, trans. K.J. Maidment. Loeb Cassical Library, Harvard University Press, Cambridge MA.

Alaimo, Stacy. (2010) *Bodily Natures: Science, Environment, and the Material Self*. Indiana University Press, Indiana.

Alexiou, Margaret. (2002) *The Ritual Lament in Greek Tradition*. Rowman & Littlefield Publishers, London.

Al-Hassan, A. Y., ed. (2001) *The Different Aspects of Islamic Culture: Volume Four, Science and Technology in Islam, Part 1: The Exact and Natural Sciences*. Unesco Publishing, Beirut.

Antiphon. (1960) 'The Second Tetralogy' in *Minor Attic Orators, Volume I: Antiphon and Andocides*, trans. K. J. Maidment. Loeb Classical Library, Cambridge, MA.

Aristotle. (1932) *Politics*, trans. H. Rackham. Loeb Classical Library, Harvard University Press, Cambridge, MA.

— (1959) *Ars Rhetorica*, ed. W. D. Ross. Clarendon Press, Oxford.

— (1960–1963) *The Physics, in two volumes*, trans. P. H. Wicksteed and F. M. Cornford. Loeb Classical Library, Harvard University Press, Cambridge, MA.

— (1961–1962) *Metaphysics in 2 Volumes*, trans. Hugh Tredennick and G. Cyril Armstrong. Loeb Classical Library, Harvard University Press, Cambridge, MA.

— (1962) *The Categories*, with *On Interpretation, Prior Analytics*, trans. Harold P. Cook and Hugh Tredennick. Loeb Classical Library, Harvard University Press, Cambridge, MA, 1962.

— (1964) *On the Soul*, with *Parva Naturalia, On Breath*, trans. W.S. Hett. Loeb Classical Library, Harvard University Press, Cambridge, MA.

— (1966) *The Topics*, in *Posterior Analytics, Topica*, trans. High Tredennick and E.S. Forster. Loeb Classical Library, Harvard University Press, Cambridge, MA.

— (1967) *The Athenian Constitution*, with *The Eudemian Ethics, On Virtues and Vices*, trans. H. Rackham. Loeb Classical Library, Cambridge, MA.

— (1968) *The Nichomachean Ethics*, trans. H. Rackham. Loeb Classical Library, Harvard University Press, Cambridge, MA.

Arnott, Peter D. (1989) *Public Performance in the Greek Theater*. Routledge, London.

Aubrey, Marie-Pierre. (2009) 'Thinking of Deep Time,' *Stratigraphy* Volume 6 Issue 2 (January). Micropaleontology Press, New York, 93–99.

Austin, M. M. and P. Vidal-Naquet. (1980) *Economic and Social History of Ancient Greece: An Introduction*. University of California Press, Berkeley.

Babinioti. (2010) = Μπαπνιώτης, Γ. *Ετυμολογικό Λεξικό τής Νέας Ελληνικής Γλώσσας*. Κέντρο Λεξικολογίας, Κηφισιά.

Barad, Karen. (2003) 'Posthumanist Performativity: Toward an Understanding of How Matter Comes to Matter,' *Signs: Journal of Women in Culture and Society* Volume 28 Issue 3, University of Chicago Press, Chicago, 801–831. https://doi.org/10.1086/345321

— (2007) *Meeting the Universe Halfway: Quantum Physics and the Entanglement of Matter and Meaning*. Duke University Press, Durham.

— (2010) 'Quantum Entanglements and Hauntologogical Relations of Inheritance: Dis/continuities, SpaceTime Enfoldings, and Justice-to-Come,' *Derrida Today* Volume 3 Issue 2, Edinburgh University Press, Edinburgh, 240–268. https://doi.org/10.3366/drt.2010.0206

Bashier, Salman H. (2004) *Ibn al-'Arabî's Barzakh: The Concept of the Limit and the Relationship Between God and the World*. State University of New York Press, Albany.

Baudrillard, Jean. (2001) *Impossible Exchange*, trans. Chris Turner. Verso, New York.

Beeks, Roberts. (2010) *Etymological Dictionary of Greek*. Brill, Leiden.

Bekker, Immanuel, ed. (1814) *Anecdota Graeca. Volume 1.* G. C. Nauck, Berlin.

Benigni, Helen, ed. (2013) *The Mythology of Venus: Ancient Calendars and Archaeoastronomy*. University Press of America, Lanham.

Benjamin, Walter. (2002a) *Selected Writings: Volume 1, 1913–1926*, ed. Marcus Bullock and Michael W. Jennings. Belknap Press of Harvard University Press, Cambridge, MA.

— (2002b) *Selected Writings: Volume 3, 1935–1938*, ed. Howard Eiland and Michael W. Jennings. Belknap Press of Harvard University Press, Cambridge, MA.

— (2005) *Selected Writings: Volume 2, Part 2, 1931–1934*, ed. Howard Eiland, Michael W. Jennings and Gary Smith. Belknap Press of Harvard University Press, Cambridge, MA.

Bennett, Jane. (2010) *Vibrant Matter: A Political Ecology of Things*. Duke University Press, London.

Blanqui, Auguste. (2003) *Manual for an Armed Insurrection*, trans. Andy Blunden. Source: Auguste Blanqui, *Instruction pour une prise d'armes. L'Éternité par les astres, hypothèse astronomique et autres textes*, Société encyclopédique français, Editions de la Tête de Feuilles. 1972; Transcribed: for www.marxists.org, by Andy Blunden*Instruction pour une prise d'armes. L'Éternité per les astres, hypthèse astronomique et autres textes*. Société encyclopédique français, Editions de la Tête de Feuilles, 1972.

Blok, J. and A. Lardinois, eds. (2006) *Solon of Athens: New Historical and Philological Approaches*. Brill, Leiden.

Blumenberg, Hans. (1990) *Work on Myth*. MIT Press, Cambridge, MA.

Blundell, Sue. (1995) *Women in Ancient Greece*. Harvard University Press, Cambridge, MA.

Blundell, Sue and Margaret Williamson, eds. (1998) *The Sacred and the Feminine in Ancient Greece*. Routledge, London.

Bubelis, William. (2016) *Hallowed Stewards: Solon and the Sacred Treasurers of Ancient Athens*. University of Michigan, Ann Arbor.

Butler, Judith. (2000) *Antigone's Claim: Kinship between Life and Death*. Columbia University Press, New York.

Carson, Anne. (2000) *Men in the Off Hours*. Alfred A. Knopf, New York.

Carson, D. A. (1984) *Exegetical Fallacies*. Baker Book House, Michigan.

Castoriadis, Cornelius. (1997) *World in Fragments: Writings on Politics, Society, Psychoanalysis and the Imagination*, trans. David A. Curtis. Stanford University Press, Stanford.

Chittick, William C. (1998) *The Self-Disclosure of God: principles of Ibn al-'Arabî's cosmology*. State University of New York Press, Albany.

Christidis, A. (2001) *History of the Greek Language: from the beginnings until late antiquity*. Centre of Greek language, Institute of Modern Greek Studies, Foundation of Manolis Triantaphyllidis. [Χριστίδης, Α. Φ. εε. Ιστορία της Ελληνικής Γλώσσας: άπο τις άρχές έως την ύστερη αρχαιότητα, κέντρο Ελληνικής Γλώσσας, Ινστιτούτο Νεοελληνικών Σπουδών, Ίδρυμα Μανόλη Τριανταφυλλίδη].

Cochrane, James R. and Bastienne Klein, eds. (2000) *Sameness and Difference: Problems and Potentials in South African Civil Society*. Council for Research in Values and Philosophy, Washington D.C.

Colonel, Raucourt. (1821) *A Manual of Lithography, or Memoir on the Lithographical Experiments Made in Paris at the Royal School of the Roads and Bridges: clearly explaining the whole art, as well as all the accidents that may happen in printing, and the different methods of avoiding them*. 2nd ed, trans. C. Hullmandel. Rodwell and Martine, London.

Coope, Ursula. (2005) *Time for Aristotle: Physics IV. 10–14*. Oxford University Press, Oxford. https://doi.org/10.1093/0199247900.001.0001

DeLanda, Manuel. (2000) *A Thousand Years of Non-Linear History*. Swerve Editions, New York.

Deleuze, Gilles and Felix Guattari. (2014) *A Thousand Plateaus*. Bloomsbury Publishing, London.

DeLoughrey, Elizabeth. (2019) *Allegories of the Anthropocene*. Duke University Press, Durham. https://doi.org/10.1215/9781478005582

Derrida, Jacques. (1981) *Dissemination*, trans. Barbara Johnson. University of Chicago Press, Chicago. https://doi.org/10.7208/chicago/9780226816340.001.0001

— (1982) *Margins of Philosophy*, trans. Alan Bass. University of Chicago Press, Chicago.

— (1988) *Limited Inc.*, ed. Gerald Graff. Northwestern University Press, Evanston.

— (1993) *Aporias*, trans. Thomas Dutoit. Stanford University Press, Stanford.

— (1995) *On the Name*, ed. Thomas Dutoit. Stanford University Press, Stanford.

— (2016) *Of Grammatology*, trans. Gayatri Spivak. Johns Hopkins University Press, Baltimore.

— (1999) *Adieu to Emmanuel Levinas*, trans. Pascale-Anne Brault and Michael Naas. Meridian: Crossing Aesthetics, Stanford University Press, Stanford.

— (2000) *Of Hospitality: Anne Dufourmantelle Invites Jacques Derrida to Respond*, trans. Rachel Bowlby. Stanford University Press, Stanford.

— (2002) *Acts of Religion*, ed. Gil Anidjar. Routledge, London.

Detienne, Marcel. (1994) *The Gardens of Adonis: Spices in Greek Mythology*, trans. Janet Lloyd. Princeton University Press, Princeton.

Diodorus Siculus. (1990) *The Antiquities of Egypt*, trans. Edwin Murphy. Transaction, New Brunswick and London.

— (1888–1890) *Diodori Bibliotheca Historica* Volumes 1–2, ed. Immanuel Bekker, Ludwig Dindorf, Friedrich Vogel. B. G. Teubner, Leipzig.

Diogenes Laertius. (1964) *Diogenis Laertii Vitae Philosophorum*, 2 volumes, ed. H. S. Long. Clarendon Press, Oxford.

Dionysius of Halicarnassus. (1960) *The Roman Antiquities of Dionysius of Halicarnassus, in seven volumes*, trans. Ernest Cary and Edward Spelman. Loeb Classical Library, Harvard University Press, Cambridge, MA.

Diels, Hermann and Walther Kranz, eds. (1903) *Die Fragmente der Vorsokratiker, griechisch und Deutsch*. Weidmannsche buchhandlung, Berlin.

Donlan, W. (1989) 'The Unequal Exchange Between Glaucus and Diomedes in Light of the Homeric Gift-Economy,' *Phoenix* Volume 43, Ontario Classical Association, Toronto, 1–15. https://doi.org/10.2307/1088537

Eliade, Mircea. (1959) *Cosmos and History: The Myth of the Eternal Return*, trans. Willard Trask. Harper and Brothers, New York.

Elshtain, Jean Bethke. (1993) *Public Man, Private Woman: Women in Social and Political Thought*. Princeton University Press, New Jersey.

Encyclopedia of Islam, New Edition. (1979–2005), ed. H. A. R. Gibb, J. H. Kramers, E. Levi-Preovencal, J. Schacht. Brill, Leiden.

Euripides. (1964) *Alkestis*, in *Euripides: Volume IV*, trans. Arthur S. Way. Loeb Classical Library, Harvard University Press, Cambridge, MA.

— (2008) *Euripides Fragments: Aegeus-Meleager Volume VII*, trans. Christopher Collard. Loeb Classical Library, Harvard University Press, Cambridge, MA.

Falcon, Andrea. (2016) *Brill's Companion to the Reception of Aristotle in Antiquity*. Brill's Companions to Classical Reception, Volume 7. Brill, Leiden. https://doi.org/10.1163/9789004315402

Fine, John. (1951) 'Horoi: Studies in Mortgage, Real Security and Land Tenure in Ancient Athens,' *The Athenian Agora* 8, American School of Classical Studies at Athens, Princeton.

Feldstein, Richard, Bruce Fink and Maire Jaanus, eds. (1996) *Reading Seminars I and II: Lacan's Return to Freud.* State University of New York Press, New York.

Finley, Moses. (1952) *Studies in Land and Credit in Ancient Athens, 500–200BC: the 'Horos' Inscriptions.* New Brunswick, New Jersey.

— (1981) *Economy and Society in Ancient Greece*, ed. B. D. Shaw and R. P. Saller. Chatto and Windus, London.

Fletcher, Judith. (2012) *Performing Oaths in Classical Greek Drama.* Cambridge University Press, Cambridge. https://doi.org/10.1017/cbo9781139005272

Fodor, A. (1970) 'The Origins of the Arabic Legends of the Pyramids,' *Acta Orientalia Academiae Scientiarum Hungaricae* Volume 23, Akadémiai Kiadó; Budapest, 335–363.

Foucault, Michel. (1978) *History of Sexuality, Volume 1: An Introduction*, trans. Robert Hurley. Vintage Books, New York.

— (1991) *Discipline and Punish: The Birth of the Prison*, trans. Alan Sheridan. Penguin Books, London.

— (2008) *The Order of Things: An Archaeology of the Human Sciences*, trans. Alan Sheridan. Routledge, London.

Frodeman, Robert. (2003) *Geo-Logic: Breaking Ground Between Philosophy and the Earth Sciences.* State University of New York Press, New York.

Gadamer, Hans-Georg. (1999) *Hermeneutics, Religion anf Ethics*, trans. Joel Weinsheimer. Yale University Press, New Haven.

Gagliano, Monica. (2018) *Thus Spoke the Plant.* North Atlantic Books, Berkeley.

Garland, R. (1989) 'The Well-ordered Corpse: an Investigation into the Motives behind Greek Funerary Legislation,' *Bulletin of the Institute of Classical Studies* Volume 36, Oxford University Press, Oxford, 1–15. https://doi.org/10.1111/j.2041-5370.1989.tb00559

Gelb, I. J. (1952) *A Study of Writing: The Foundations of Grammatology.* Routledge, London.

Geniusas, Saulius. (2012) *The Origins of the Horizon in Husserl's Phenomenology.* Contributions to Phenomenology 67: Springer Dordrecht, London. https://doi.org/10.1007/978-94-007-4644-2

Girard, René. (1989) *The Scapegoat.* Johns Hopkins University Press, Baltimore.

Gould, John. (1980) 'Law, Custom and Myth: Aspects of the Social Position of Women in Classical Athens,' *Journal of Hellenic Studies* Volume 100, Cambridge University Press, Cambridge, 38–59. https://doi.org/10.2307/630731

Gould, Stephen. (1987) *Time's Arrow, Time's Cycle: Myth and Metaphor in the Discovery of Geological Time.* Harvard University Press, Cambridge, MA.

Gutas, Dimitris. (1998) *Greek Thought, Arabic Culture: The Graeco-Arabic Translation Movement in Baghdad and Early 'Abbāsid Society (2nd-4th/8th-10th C.).* Routledge, Oxford.

Hardy, Thomas. (2006) *The Collected Poems.* Wordsworth Editions, London.

Haraway, Donna. (2016) *Staying with the Trouble: Making Kin in the Chthulucene.* Duke University Press, London. https://doi.org/10.2307/j.ctv11cw25q

Harman, Graham. (2009) *Prince of Networks: Bruno Latour and Metaphysics.* Repress, Melbourne.

— (2018) *Object-Oriented Ontology: A New Theory of Everything.* Pelican, Milton Keynes.

Harpocration, Valerius. (1833) *Harpocration et Moeris*, ed. Immanuel Bekker. G. E. Reimer, Berlin.

— (1853) *Lexicon in decem oratores Atticos*, ed. Wilhelm Dindorf. E Typographeo Academico, Oxford.

Harris, Edward. (2002) 'Did Solon Abolish Debt-Bondage?' *Classical Quarterly,* Volume 52 Issue 2, Cambridge University Press, Cambridge, 415–430. https://doi.org/10.1093/cq/52.2.415

— (2006) *Democracy and the Rule of Law in Classical Athens: Essays on Law, Society, and Politics.* City University, New York.

Hegel, Georg Willhelm Friedrich. (1892) *The Logic of Hegel, translated from Encyclopaedia of the Philosophical Sciences*, trans. William Wallace. Clarendon Press, Oxford.

— (1894) *Lectures on the History of Philosophy vol. II.* trans. E. S. Haldane and Frances H. Simson. Kegan Paul, Trench Trübner & Co., London.

— (1969) *Science of Logic*, trans. A. V. Miller. George Allen & Unwin, London.

— (1971) *Hegel's Philosophy of Mind, Part III of the Encyclopaedia of the Philosophical Sciences*, trans. William Wallace. Clarendon Press, Oxford.

— (1977) *Phenomenology of Spirit*, trans. A. V. Miller. Oxford University Press, Oxford.

— (1988) *Aesthetics: Lectures on Fine Art, volume 1*, trans. T. M. Knox. Clarendon Press, Oxford.

— (2003) *Phenomenology of Mind*, trans. J. B. Baille. Dover, New York.

— (2006) *Phänomenologie des Geistes.* Felix Meiner Verlag, Hamburg.

Heidegger, Martin. (1962) *Being and Time*, trans. John Macquarrie and Edward Robinson. Blackwell, Oxford.

— (1966) *Discourse on Thinking,* trans. John M. Anderson and E. Hans Freund. Harper and Row, New York.

— (1971) *On the Way to Language,* trans. Peter D. Hertz. Harper, New York.

— (1977) *Gesamtausgabe Band 5.* Holzwege, Vittorio Klostermann, Frankfurt am Main.

— (1984) *Early Greek Thinking: The Dawn of Western Philosophy*, trans. David Farrel Krell. Harper Collins, New York.

— (1985) *History of the Concept of Time: Prolegomena,* trans. Theodore Kisiel. Indiana University Press, Bloomington.

— (1995) *The Fundamental Concepts of Metaphysics: World, Finitude, Solitude.* Trans. William McNeill and Nicholas Walker. Indiana University Press, Bloomington.

— (2000) *Basic Writings,* ed. David Farrell Krell. Routledge, London.

— (2000a) *Introduction to Metaphysics,* trans. Gregory Fried and Richard Polt. Yale Nota Bene, New Haven.

— (2001) *Phenomenological Interpretations of Aristotle: Initiation into Phenomenological Research,* trans. Richard Rojcewicz. Indiana University Press, Bloomington. https://doi.org/10.2307/j.ctvswx8nz

— (2003) *Plato's Sophist,* trans. Richard Rojcewicz and André Schuwer. Indiana University Press, Bloomington.

— (2009) *Basic Concepts of Aristotelian Philosophy,* trans. Robert D. Metcalf and Mark B. Tanner. Indiana University Press, Bloomington.

Herman, Gabriel. (1987) *Ritualized Friendship and the Greek City.* Cambridge University Press, Cambridge.

Herodotus. (1960–1963) *Herodotus, in Four Volumes,* trans. A. D. Godley. Loeb Classical Library, Harvard University Press, Cambridge, MA.

Hesychius Alexandrini. (2005) *Lexicon,* ed. Kurt Latte. Walter de Gruyter, Berlin.

Homer. (2001–2003) *Iliad in Two Volumes,* trans. A. T. Murray. Loeb Classical Library, Harvard University Press, Cambridge, MA.

— (2002–2004) *Odyssey in Two Volumes,* trans. A. T. Murray. Loeb Classical Library, Harvard University Press, Cambridge, MA.

— (2003) *Homeric Hymns, Homeric Apocrypha, Lives of Homer,* trans. Martin L. West. Loeb Classical Library, Harvard University Press, Cambridge, MA.

Horst-Warhaft, Gail. (1992) *Dangerous Voices: Women's Laments and Greek Literature.* Routledge, London. https://doi.org/10.4324/9780203333846

Inscriptiones Graecae, Volume II (1940), ed. Johannes Ernst Kirchner. De Gruyter, Berlin.

Inwood, Michael. (1999) *A Heidegger Dictionary.* Blackwell, Oxford.

Iriagary, Luce. (1994) *Thinking the Difference: For a Peaceful Revolution*. Athlone Press, London.

Jeffrey, L. H. (1990) *The Local Scripts of Archaic Greece: A Study of the Origin of the Greek Alphabet and Its Development from the Eighth to the Fifth Centuries BC*, rev. and ed. with supplement by A. W. Johnston. Oxford University Press, Oxford.

Kant, Immanuel. (1914) *Eternal Peace and Other International Essays*, trans. W. Hastie. The World Peace Foundation, Boston.

Kearney, Richard and Mark Dooley. (1999) *Questioning Ethics: Contemporary Debates in Philosophy*. Routledge, London. https://doi.org/10.4324/9780203450833

Kehoe, Dennis and Thomas McGinn. (2017) *Ancient Law, Ancient Society*. University of Michigan Press, Ann Arbor. https://doi.org/10.3998/mpub.9374271

Kennedy-Day, Kiki. (2004) *Books of Definition in Islamic Philosophy: The Limits of Words*. Routledge-Curzon, London. https://doi.org/10.4324/9780203221372

Keuls, Eva. (1993) *The Reign of the Phallus: Sexual Politics in Ancient Athens*. University of California Press, Berkeley.

Kisiel, Theodore. (1995) *The Genesis of Heidegger's Being and Time*. University of California Press, Berkeley.

Kuhn, Eduardo. (2013) *How Forests Think: Toward an Anthropology Beyond the Human*. University of California Press, Berkeley. https://doi.org/10.1525/9780520956865

Krell, David Farrel. (1990) *Of Memory, Reminiscence, and Writing: On the Verge*. Indiana University Press, Bloomington. https://doi.org/10.2979

— (1992) *Daimon Life, Heidegger and Life-Philosophy*. Indian University Press, Bloomington.

Lacan, Jacques. (1988) *The Seminar of Jacques Lacan, Book XX: Encore 1972–1973*, ed. Jacques-Alain Miller. W. W. Norton & Co., New York.

— (1991) *The Seminar of Jacques Lacan: Freud's Papers on Technique* Volume 1 Book I, trans. John Forrester. W. W. Norton & Co., New York.

— (2006) *Écrits*, trans. Bruce Fink. W. W. Norton & Co., New York.

Lalonde, Gerald V. (1991) 'Inscriptions: Horoi, Poleitai Records, Leases of Public Land.' with Merle K. Langdon, Michael B. Walbank, *The Athenian Agora* Volume 19, American School of Classical Studies, Princeton. https://doi.org/10.2307/3601987

— (2006) *Horos Dios: An Athenian Shrine and Cult of Zeus*. Monumenta Graeca et Romana Volume XI. Brill, Leiden. https://doi.org/10.1163/9789047417392

Lane, Edward William. (1968) *An Arabic-English Dictionary*. Librairie du Liban, Beirut.

Latour, Bruno. (2014) 'Agency at the Time of the Anthropocene,' *New Literary History* Volume 45 Issue 1. Johns Hopkins University Press, Charles Village, 1–18. https://doi.org/10.1353/nlh.2014.0003

Lenin, Vladimir. (1972) *Collected Works: Volume 14*, trans. Abraham Fineberg and Julius Katzer. Progress Publishers, 1972, Moscow. 'Marxists Internet Archive' (marxists.org).

Levinas, Emmanuel. (1969) *Totality and Infinity: An Essay on Exteriority*, trans. Alphonso Lingis. Dusquesne University Press, Pittsburgh. https://doi.org/10.1007/978-94-009-9342-6

— (1987) *Collected Philosophical Papers*, trans. Alphonso Lingis. Martinus Nijhoff Publishers, Dordrecht. https://doi.org/10.1007/978-94-009-4364-3

— (2000) *God, Death and Time*, trans. Bettina Bergo. Stanford University Press, Stanford.

Lévi-Strauss, Claude. (1987) *Introduction to the Work of Marcel Mauss*, trans. Felicity Baker. Routledge and Kegan Paul, London. https://doi.org/10.4324/9781315005102

Lewis, David and Lilian Jeffrey, eds. (1994) *Inscriptiones Atticae. Inscriptiones Graecae*. De Gruyter, Berlin.

Liebeschuetz, J. H. W. G. (1979) *Continuity and Change in Roman Religion*. Oxford University Press, Oxford.

Liddell, Henry George and Robert Scott (1968) *A Greek-English Lexicon*, Clarendon Press, Oxford.

Loraux, Nicole. (1991) *Tragic Ways of Killing a Woman*, trans. Anthony Forster. Harvard University Press, Cambridge, MA.

— (2006) *The Divided City: On Memory and Forgetting in Ancient Athens*, trans. C. Pache and F. Fort. Zone Books, New York.

Löwy, Michael. (2005) *Fire Alarm: Reading Walter Benjamin's 'On the Concept of History'*, trans. Chris Turner. Verso, London.

Marx, Karl. (1981) *Grundrisse: Foundations of the Critique of Political Economy* (Rough Draft), trans. Martin Nicolaus. Penguin Books, Middlesex.

— (1904) *A Contribution to Political Philosophy*, trans. N. I. Stone. The University of Chicago Press, Chicago.

— (1990) *Capital: A Critique of Political Economy, Volume I*, trans. Ben Fowkes. Penguin, London.

Mauss, Marcel. (1967) *The Gift: Forms and Functions of Exchange in Archaic Societies*. trans. Ian Cunnison. W. W. Norton, New York.

McNeill, Desmond. (2021) *Fetishism and the Theory of Value: Reassessing Marx in the 21st Century*. Palgrave Macmillan, Camden.

Merchant, Carolyn. (1990) *The Death of Nature: Women, Ecology and the Scientific Revolution*. Harper and Row, San Francisco.

Merleau-Ponty, Maurice. (1968) *The Visible and the Invisible*, trans. Alphonso Lingis. North Western University Press, Evanston.

Meritt, Benjamin D. (1939) 'Greek Inscriptions (14–27)' *Hesperia: The Journal of the American School of Classical Studies at Athens*. Volume VIII Issue 1, The American School of Classical Studies at Athens, Princeton, 48–82. https://doi.org/10.2307/146453

— (1940) 'Greek Inscriptions' *Hesperia: The Journal of the American School of Classical Studies at Athens*. Volume IX Issue 1, The American School of Classical Studies at Athens, Princeton, 53–96. https://doi.org/10.2307/146632

Mikulak, Michael. (2007) 'The Rhizomatics of Domination: From Darwin to Biotechnology,' in *Rhizomes: Cultural Studies in Emerging Knowledge*, Issue 15 (Winter) http://www.rhizomes.net/issue15/

Mills, Watson E., ed. (1997) *Mercer Dictionary of the Bible*. Mercer University Press, Macon.

Mitchell, Lynette and P. J. Rhodes. (1997) *The Development of the Polis in Archaic Greece*. Routledge, London. https://doi.org/10.4324/9780203440827

Montenari, Michael, ed. (2016) *Stratigraphy and Timescales*. Academic Press, Elsevier, London. https://doi.org/10.1016/s2468-5178(16)30015-6

Morales, Helen. (2020) *Antigone Rising*. Wildfire Press, London.

Narby, Jeremy. (2006) *Intelligence in Nature: An Inquiry into Knowledge*. Penguin, Putnam Inc., Los Angeles.

Neyrat, Frédéric. (2019) *The Unconstructable Earth: An Ecology of Separation*, trans. Drew Burk. Fordham University Press, New York. http://dx.doi.org/10.2307/j.ctv8jnzp4

Nietzsche, Friedrich. (1999) *The Birth of Tragedy and Other Writings*, trans. Ronald Speirs. Cambridge University Press, Cambridge.

Onions, C. T rev. and ed. (1962) *The Shorter Oxford English Dictionary: On historical Principles*. Clarendon Press, Oxford.

Ovidius, Publius Naso. (1967) *Fasti*, trans. James George Frazer. Loeb Classical Library, Harvard University Press, Cambridge, MA.

Owens, Joseph. (1978) *The Doctrine of Being in Aristotelian Metaphysics*. Pontifical Institute of Mediaeval Studies, Toronto.

Painter, Corinne and Christian Lotz. (2007) *Phenomenology And The Non-Human Animal: At the Limits of Experience*. Springer, Dordrecht. https://doi.org/10.1007/978-1-4020-6307-7

Pascoe, Bruce. (2018) *Dark Emu*. Magabala Books, Broome.

Pennick, Nigel. (1992) *Magical Alphabets*. Samuel Weiser, Boston.

Plato. (1921) *Theaetetus, Sophist*, trans. Harold North Fowler. Loeb Classical Library, Harvard University Press, Cambridge, MA.

— (1935) *Republic*, two volumes, trans. Paul Shorey. Loeb Classical Library, Harvard University Press, Cambridge, MA.

— (1963) *Cratylus. Parmenides. Greater Hippias. Lesser Hippias*, trans. Harold N. Fowler. Loeb Classical Library, Harvard University Press, Cambridge, MA.

— (1961–1967) *The Laws* [two volumes], trans. R. G. Bury. Loeb Classical Library, Harvard University Press, Cambridge, MA.

— (1962) *The Statesman, Philebus*, trans. Harold N. Fowler and W. R. M. Lamb. Loeb Classical Library, Harvard University Press, Cambridge, MA.

— (1972) *Pseudepigrapha I: pseudopythagorica, lettres de Platon, littérature pseudépigraphique juive : huit exposés suivis de discussions*, ed. Fritz von Kurt. Fondation Hardt, Geneva.

— (1996) *Lysis, Symposium, Gorgias*, trans. W. R. M. Lamb. Loeb Classical Library, Harvard University Press, Cambridge, MA.

— (2001) *Euthyphro, Apology, Crito, Phaedo, Phaedrus*, trans. Harold North Fowler. Loeb Classical Library, Harvard University Press, Cambridge, MA.

Plumwood, Val. (1994) *Feminism and the Mastery of Nature*. Routledge, London.

Plutarch. (2000) *Moralia, Volume VII*, trans. Phillip D. Lacy and Benedict Einarson. Loeb Classical Library, Harvard University Press, Cambridge, MA.

— (2005) *Lives, Volume I: Theseus and Romulus. Lycurgus and Numa. Solon and Publicola*, trans. Bernadotte Perrin. Loeb Classical Library, Harvard University Press, Cambridge, MA.

Powell, Barry. (2009) *Writing: Theory and History of the Technology of Civilization*. Wiley-Blackwell, Chichester.

Protevi, John. (1984) *Time and Exteriority: Aristotle, Heidegger, Derrida*. Bucknell University Press, Lewisburg.

Rhodes, P. J. (2003) 'Nothing to Do with Democracy: Athenian Drama and the Polis,' *The Journal of Hellenic Studies* Volume 123, Cambridge University Press, Cambridge, 104–119. https://doi.org/10.2307/3246262

— ed. (2004) *Athenian Democracy*. Edinburgh University Press, Edinburgh.

Ricoeur, Paul. (2007) *The Course of Recognition*. trans. David Pellauer. Harvard University Press, Cambridge, MA. https://doi.org/10.2307/j.ctv1dv0tv0

Roberts E. S. and E. A. Gardner. (1905) *An Introduction to Greek Epigraphy: II*. Cambridge University Press, Cambridge.

Roudinesco, Elisabeth. (1997) *Jacques Lacan*, trans. Barbara Bray. Columbia University Press, New York. https://doi.org/10.7312/badi16510

Ruschenbusch, E. (1966) ΣΟΛΩΝΟΣ ΝΟΜΟΙ. *Die Fragmente des solonischen Gesetzeswerkes mit einer Text und Überlieferungsgeschichte*. Historia Einzelschriften 9, F. Steiner, Wiesbaden.

Sachs, Joe, trans. (1999) *Aristotle's Metaphysics*. Green Lion Press, New Mexico.

Sarton, George. (1931) *Introduction to the History of Science Volume II: From Rabbi Ben Ezra to Roger Bacon*. The Williams & Wilkins Company, Baltimore.

Schmitt, Carl. (2007) *The Concept of the Political*. trans. George Schwab. Chicago University Press, Chicago.

Seaford, Richard. (2003) *Reciprocity and Ritual: Homer and Tragedy in the Developing City-State*. Oxford University Press, New York.

Senefelder, Alois. (1911) *The Invention of Lithography*, trans. J. W. Muller. The Fuchs & Lang Manufacturing Company, New York.

Shakespeare, William. (1996) *Titus Andronicus*. Wordsworth Editions, Ware.

Shapiro, H. A. (1991) 'The Iconography of Mourning in Athenian Art', *The American Journal of Archaeology* Volume 95 Issue 4 (October), Archaeological Institute of America, Boston, 629–656. https://doi.org/10.2307/505896

Shear, T. Leslie. (1939) 'The Campaign of 1938' *Hesperia: The Journal of the American School of Classical Studies at Athens*. Volume VIII Issue 3, The American School of Classical Studies at Athens, Princeton, 201–246. https://doi.org/10.2307/146675

— (1940) 'The Campaign of 1939' *Hesperia: The Journal of the American School of Classical Studies at Athens*. Volume IX Issue 3, The American School of Classical Studies at Athens, Princeton, 261–308. https://doi.org/10.2307/146481

Sheldrake, Merlin. (2020) *Entangled Life: How Fungi Make Our Worlds, Change Our Minds and Shape Our Futures*. Random House, New York.

Siewert, P. (1977) 'The Ephebic Oath in Fifth-Century Athens,' *The Journal for Hellenic Studies* Volume 97, Cambridge University Press, Cambridge, 102–111. https://doi.org/10.2307/631025

Sophocles. (1891) *Sophocles. The Antigone of Sophocles*, trans. Richard Jebb. Cambridge University Press, Cambridge.

— (1912) *Sophocles Volume 1: Oedipus the king. Oedipus at Colonus. Antigone*, trans. F. Storr. Loeb classical library, Harvard University Press, Cambridge, MA.

— (1913) *Sophocles Volume 2: Ajax. Electra. Trachiniae. Philoctetes*, trans. F. Storr. Loeb Classical Library, Harvard University Press, Cambridge, MA.

Sorabji, Richard. (1983) *Time, Creation and the Continuum*. Cornell University Press, Ithaca.

Sorel, Georges. (2009) *Reflections on Violence*, ed. Jeremy Jennings. Cambridge University Press, Cambridge.

Stagg, Frank. (1972) 'The abused aorist', *Journal of Biblical Literature* Volume 91 Issue 2, Society of Biblical Literature, Atlanta, 222–231. https://doi.org/10.2307/3263206

Steiner, George. (1998) *After Babel*. Oxford University Press, Oxford.

Suida. (1705) *Suidae Lexicon, Graece et Latine: Textum Graecum cum Manuscriptis Codicibus Collatum a Quamplurimis Mendis Purgavit, Notisque Perpetuis Illustravit; Versionem Latinam Aemilii Porti Innumeris in Locis Correxit, Indicesque, Auctorum et Rerum Adjecit Ludolphus Kusterus*. 3 volumes, in Greek and Latin, ed. Ludolf Kuster, trans. Aemilius Portus. Typis Academicis, Cambridge.

— (1854) *Suidae Lexicon*, ed. Immanuel Bekker. George Reimer, Berlin.

Sutton, Peter and Keryn Walshe. (2021) *Farmers or Hunter-Gatherers? The Dark Emu Debate*. Melbourne University Press, Melbourne.

Estienne, Henri, ed. (1572) *Thesaurus Graecae Linguae, Volume 2*. H. Stephani oliva, Munich.

Thomas, Dylan. (2010) *The Collected Poems of Dylan Thomas: The Original Edition*. New Directions Books, New York.

Thompson, Homer A. and R. E. Wycherly. (1972) *The Agora of Athens: The History, Shape and Uses of an Ancient City Center*. The American School of Classical Studies at Athens, Princeton, New Jersey.

Thompson, H. A. and D. B. Thompson. (1987) *Hellenistic Pottery and Terracottas*. American School of Classical Studies at Athens, Princeton.

Thucydides. (2003–2005) *History of the Peloponnesian War*, in three volumes, trans. Charles Foster Smith. Loeb Classical Library, Harvard University Press, Cambridge, MA.

Toulmin, Stephen and June Goodfield. (1982) *The Discovery of Time*. University of Chicago Press, Chicago.

Vardoulakis, Dimitris. (2010) 'The Ends of Stasis: Spinoza as a Reader of Agamben,' *Culture, Theory and Critique* Volume 51 Issue 2. Routledge, London, 145–156. https://doi.org/10.1080/03122417.2021.1971373

— (2009) 'Stasis Beyond Political Theology?' *Cultural Critique* Volume 73, University of Minnesota Press, Chicago, 125–147. https://doi.org/10.1353/cul.0.0050

Vidal-Naquet, Pierre. (1986) *The Black Hunter: Forms of Thought and Forms of Society in the Greek World*, trans. Andrew Szegedy-Maszak. Johns Hopkins University Press, Baltimore.

Walker, C. and John Chadwick eds. (1990) *Reading the Past: Ancient Writing from Cuneiform to the Alphabet*. British Museum Press, London.

Waltke, Bruce K. and Michael Patrick O'Connor. (1990) *An Introduction to Biblical Hebrew Syntax*. Eisenbrauns, Winona Lake.

Weber, Max. (1978) *Economy and Society: An Outline of Interpretative Sociology*, Volume 1, ed. Guenther Roth and Claus Wittich. University of California Press, Berkeley. https://doi.org/10.4159/9780674240827

Webster, T. B. L. (1970) *The Greek Chorus*. Methuen, London.

Wilkinson, Bruce. (2005) 'Humans as Geologic Agents: A Deep-Time Perspective', *Geology* Volume 33 Issue 3, Geological Society of America, McLean, 161–164. https://doi.org/10.1130/g21108.1

Winkler, John and Froma Zeitlin, eds. (1990) *Nothing to Do with Dionysus? Athenian Drama in its Social Context*. Princeton University Press, New Jersey. https://doi.org/10.1515/9780691215891

Yousef, Mohamed Haj. (2008) *Ibn 'Arabî: Time and Cosmology*. Routledge, New York. https://doi.org/10.4324/9780203938249

Yusuff, Kathryn. (2013) 'Geologic Life: Prehistory, Climate, Futures in the Anthropocene,' *Environment and Planning D: Society and Space* Volume 31 Issue 5, Sage Publications, Thousand Oaks, 779–795. https://doi.org/10.1068/d11512

Zajko, Vanda and Miriam Leonard, eds. (2006) *Laughing with Medusa: Classical Myth and Feminist Thought*. Oxford University Press, Oxford. https://doi.org/10.1093/acprof:oso/9780199237944.001.0001

Index

Aboriginal 2, 70
Abraham (Old Testament) 84
Achilles 228, 233
Ackermann, Denise 246
Admetos 233–234, 269
Adorno, Theodor 22, 24, 138–140, 188
Aegean islands 72, 90
Aegisthus 198, 204
Aeschylus 198–199
Agamben, Giorgio 34–35, 38, 97, 109, 111, 126, 216–217, 233, 272
Agamemnon 198–199, 204, 214, 245
Ager, Derek 175–178
Aglauros 108
agora (ἀγορά) xxii, xxxii, 1, 5–6, 9, 24, 32, 51–52, 92, 95, 138, 209, 229, 259, 270–271, 274, 276–277, 279–283
Alaimo, Stacy 40–41
Al-Aqsa Intifada xv
Alcibiades 205
Alexiou, Margaret 212, 233, 245
Alkestis 233–234, 237
Al Kutba 63
Allah 171, 173, 180, 182
Ancient Greece 71, 203, 229, 244, 252, 265
Ancient Greek xxi, xxvi, 76, 118–119, 183, 196–197, 202, 204, 217, 241, 252
Andromache 233
animal xx, xxiii, xxv, 21, 26, 28, 33, 35–36, 38, 42, 65, 70, 76, 110–111, 113, 137, 149, 155, 193, 236, 241, 271, 274, 279
animism xvi, 33, 51, 69–70, 241

Anthropocene xxxi, 88, 154–157, 186–193
Antigone xxxii, 197, 203, 212–215, 217–231, 237, 245, 267–268, 275
Antipater 216
Antiphon 19
aorist 124, 183–185
Aphrodite 206
Apollo 2, 269
aporia (ἀπορία) 16–18, 20, 22, 77, 89, 100, 105–107, 114, 131, 137, 139, 148–149, 157, 164, 167, 218
Arab 171
'Arabî, Ibn 83, 171, 180–182
Arabic 63, 73, 83, 87, 171–173, 180
Areia 108
Areiopagus 254
Ares 10, 108, 112
Aristophanes 202, 223, 225
Aristotelian xxi, xxxi, 19, 22, 83, 102, 123, 127, 130, 135, 142–143, 145, 170, 172
Aristotle xxx, xxxi, 11–12, 16–22, 31–34, 36–39, 42, 49, 51–52, 57, 74, 77, 100, 119–125, 127–128, 130–132, 135–137, 139–142, 145, 147–151, 155–168, 170–172, 175–176, 178, 182–183, 185, 194, 207, 226, 249, 251, 257–258, 260, 284
Artemis 200–201, 205–206
Asklepius 269
Athena 10, 89, 108, 112, 206
Athenian xvii, xxii, xxv, xxx, xxxii, 1, 4, 9, 12–14, 46, 55–56, 62, 70–71, 73, 75, 89–92, 95–96, 101, 108, 112, 140,

197, 202, 209, 215, 223–225, 229, 240, 243, 245, 254, 256, 259, 261–263, 266, 270–271, 274–275, 277
Athens xv, xxvii, xxxii, 2, 4–5, 9, 12, 14, 45, 48, 52–53, 79, 82, 88–91, 95, 97, 101, 110, 117, 202, 222, 224–225, 228, 230, 236, 240–241, 248–249, 256, 258–262, 267–268, 239, 195, 279
Attic 20, 245, 258
Attica xxx, 2, 14, 48, 257, 259, 262, 265, 275
Aubrey, Marie-Pierre 175, 177, 179
Augustine, St 54, 122
Australia 70, 97
authority xxvii, 35, 84–86, 92, 97, 99, 103, 131, 197, 205, 207, 213, 215–219, 222–223, 241–242, 249, 256, 262–264, 268, 271–273, 283
autochthony 146, 241, 263
autonomy 16, 59, 90, 115, 151, 224, 241, 248, 268, 276
autopoiesis 55, 63
Aztecs 84

Babel 63
Babylonian 83
Bacon, Francis 189
bacteria, archaea xxiii, 4, 14, 38–39, 155, 189
Barad, Karen xxvi, xxviii, 3, 15, 26, 43, 66–69, 166
barzakh 83, 87, 180–182
Bashier, Salman H. 83, 140, 171, 181
Bekker, Immanuel 56–57
Benigni, Helen 205, 255
Benjamin, Walter xxvii, 74, 77, 81–82, 193–194, 215
Bennett, Jane xx, xxvi, 3
Benveniste, Émile 148, 233
Bhaga 83
Bhagavan 83
Bhagya 83
Biblical xxx, 63
biohorizon 156, 175, 177
biozone 156, 175
Blanqui, Auguste xv, 114

Blok, J. and A. Lardinois 237, 244, 246, 256, 260–262, 264, 268
Blumenberg, Hans 25
Blundell, Sue 200–201, 206, 208
body—*sōma* (σῶμα) 22, 34, 108, 122, 156, 176, 187, 211–214, 218–220, 223, 228, 242–243, 248, 255, 258, 266, 268–270, 273
Bohr, Niels 26, 66, 68
bond xvii, xxii, xxx, 5, 17–19, 77, 103–104, 107–108, 113–115, 136, 139, 142, 151, 197, 220, 226–227, 230–235, 259, 285
boundary, boundaries xvi, xvii, xix, xxi, xxii, xxiii, xxiv, xxv, xxvi, xxvii, xxviii, xxix, xxx, xxxi, xxxii, xxxiii, 2–10, 13–16, 18–20, 22, 24, 28–29, 31–32, 41–42, 46–49, 51–55, 57–59, 61, 66, 68–70, 72–75, 78, 80–92, 96–109, 113–115, 120, 124–125, 127, 129–133, 139–141, 143, 151–152, 157–163, 165, 167–171, 175–177, 179–182, 184–186, 189–190, 192–194, 196–202, 207–209, 211, 217–221, 223–224, 226–227, 233, 243, 248, 255–259, 261–262, 265, 269–274, 276, 278–285
Brahman 66
Brauron 200, 202
Briseis 206
British Empire 87
Bronze Age 196, 203–204
Bubelis, William 247, 249, 263–264
Butler, Judith 220–222

capitalism xix, xxv, xxviii, xxix, 5, 7, 76, 98, 155–156, 204, 208, 222, 242, 254, 284
  cartelism xix, 156
  corporate xix, xxv, xxviii, xxix, 155, 204, 222
  stakeholder xix, 284
Capitalocene 156
Capitoline Hill 83, 120
Capitoline Temple 83
care 70, 221, 232, 255
  in death 227, 232–233, 237, 245, 253
  in *xenia* 233

Carson, Anne 184, 207
Cartesian 66, 68, 151. *See also* Descartes, René
Cassandra 199, 206, 214, 217
Castoriadis 35
Catholic Church 84
Celtic 2, 63
Chauvet 70
Cheth 73, 84
Chitragupta 63
Christian 83, 120
Christianity 83, 120, 196
Chryseis 206
Chrysippus 216
chthonic, chthulucene 155–156
Classical xxii, 53, 196
Clytemnestra 198–199, 203–204, 206
Cohen, Jeffery xxvi, 16, 50
Cole, Susan 200–201
communication xxi, xxii, xxiii, xxiv, xxxi, 2, 8, 13, 15, 47–48, 50, 70, 134, 143, 154, 157, 169, 172–173, 190, 208, 242
  interspecial 70
  lithic xxi, xxii, xxiii, xxiv, xxxi, 2, 8, 13, 15, 47–48, 50, 134, 143, 154, 157, 169, 172–173, 190, 208
consciousness 21, 29, 33, 38, 40, 43, 47, 58, 143, 163, 183, 186
Coope, Ursula 18, 158–161, 167
Corcyrean 72
cosmology 73, 174, 206, 255
cosmos xxiii, 23, 69, 184
Creon 213, 215, 218, 220–223, 229–230, 245, 267
Crete 72
culture xxiv, xxv, xxvi, 9, 14–16, 35, 50, 52–53, 59, 63, 69, 73–74, 88, 91, 99, 119, 154, 191, 205, 207–208, 237, 241–242, 247
Cyclops 269

Danaans 93. *See also* Greek
Dao 179
Dasein 36, 38. *See also* Heidegger, Martin
death xxxii, 3, 12, 23, 61, 64–65, 77, 135–138, 182, 197–198, 205, 207, 209, 211–215, 218–220, 222, 224–237, 244–247, 253–255, 267–271, 274
  burial xxxii, 209, 211–215, 218–219, 222, 226–233, 237, 245–246, 267–268
  rituals 231, 233, 244–247, 254, 267–268
definition xx, xxi, xxiii, xxix, xxx, xxxi, 2–4, 8, 11–15, 19–24, 26–28, 31, 33–34, 37, 42–43, 46–49, 54–57, 61, 66–67, 74–75, 78, 92, 97, 99–102, 104–107, 114, 118, 120–134, 137–152, 154, 157–173, 176–179, 181–185, 194, 197, 199–201, 212, 215–220, 223, 227, 232, 241–243, 255, 262–263, 273–274, 276, 279–281, 283
deforestation xxviii, 155, 187, 190, 193
De Landa, Manuel 188
Deleuze, Gilles 176, 190
DeLoughrey, Elizabeth 186, 188
Delphi 2
Demeter 206
democracy xxiv, 14, 90, 97–98, 113, 191, 204, 222, 224–225, 229, 241, 248–249, 251, 263–264, 275
Derrida, Jacques xxvi, 18, 58–60, 62, 64–65, 68–69, 74, 77–78, 105, 107, 127, 129–130, 136, 138, 148, 157, 162–167, 211–212, 214–215, 234–238
  Derridean xxx
Descartes, René 65. *See also* Cartesian
determination xxi, xxiv, xxx, xxxi, 2–4, 15, 20, 24, 30–31, 34–36, 49, 61–62, 66, 68–69, 92, 106, 122, 124–125, 130–139, 141–142, 144–149, 151, 160–161, 163, 166–170, 175, 182–187, 197, 210, 219–220, 256, 267, 271, 276, 281–283
determinative 30–31, 35, 133, 140, 169
Deuteronomy 81, 85–87
Dianeira 207
difference (*différance*) xxx, 8, 11–13, 33, 49, 56, 58, 60–61, 64, 72, 77–78, 81, 92, 94, 96, 99, 103, 110, 114–115, 118, 120, 123–130, 133–134, 136–137, 147, 158, 160, 167, 171–172, 184, 190, 223, 236, 258
Diocletian 83
Diogenes Laertius 5, 216
Diogenes of Sinope 5

Diogenes the Cynic 281
Dionysus 205, 223
dynamis (δύναμις) 35, 38, 216, 217. *See also* potentiality

Earth 13, 99, 174, 178, 187, 190–192, 258, 267
   Earth sciences 178, 190–191
   mother 257
   planet 174, 187
Easter Island 2, 63
ecological destruction 113
economy xvi, xix, xxiii, xxiv, xxviii, xxxii, 5, 7, 22, 50, 62–63, 70–71, 84, 90–91, 94–96, 98, 112, 115, 138, 146, 157–158, 202–205, 208, 226–229, 235–237, 240–244, 246–248, 251–252, 254–255, 259, 261–264, 268–270, 273–275, 278, 281–282
   cosmic order 226
   death xxxii, 212, 223–236
   debt 237
   gift 237
   household 146, 203
   kinship 235
   philoxenia 235
   state 197, 204–205
Ecuador 40
Egypt xv, 2, 63, 83, 272
einai (εἶναι) 121, 128, 165, 197
Elektra 203, 206
Eleusis 9
Eliade, Mircea 179
English xv, 10–11, 13, 98, 121, 160, 169, 172, 217
Enuma Elish 179
Enyalios 108
Enyo 108
epigraphy 5, 45, 52–53, 60, 71, 117, 170, 209
Erechtheum 263
Erinyes 207
essence (τὸ τί ἦν εἶναι) xxx, 11, 81, 121–123, 125–126, 128, 130–133, 137, 141, 164–165, 171–173, 180–181, 271

Euklides 71
Eumenides 207
Euripides 208, 220, 225, 233
Europe xxvi, 54, 65, 143
Eurydice 222
exchange xxii, 5–7, 22, 62, 95, 120, 137, 216, 235, 238, 241, 243, 246, 261, 263, 265–266, 268, 270, 273–274, 279–283
   gifts 235
   in *agora* (market) xxv, xxxiii, 5, 95, 270, 274
   on borders xxii, 5–6, 6–7, 19, 265

family 12, 103, 206, 209, 221, 226–228, 230–231, 234–235, 242, 244–245, 252–253, 275
festivals 94, 120, 200, 202, 205, 224, 245, 249, 263–264
   Genesia 249, 263–264
Fink, Bruce 59
Finley, Moses 9, 48, 54, 56–57, 90–91, 132–133, 258, 265–266
Foucault, Michel xxiv, 65, 96, 111, 218, 242–243
Frankenstein 29
freedom 35, 139, 150–152, 197, 204, 240–241, 244, 257, 259, 261, 264–266
French xv, 4, 48, 172
French Revolution xv
Frodeman, Robert 188–191
Furies 207

Gadamer, Hans-Georg 35–36
Genesia 249, 263–264
Genesis 54, 84, 87
geo-engineering 155
geologic; time, timescale xxxi, 154–155, 157, 170, 173–174, 176–179, 188, 191
German 98, 134–136, 145
Girard, René 282
God 54, 65, 83, 85–87, 122, 173, 176
Gorgons 207
Gould, John 178–180, 204
Greco-Roman 86
Greece xvi, 2, 47, 53, 70, 91, 206, 266. *See also* Ancient Greece

Index 306

Greek xxiv, xxx, 6, 10, 11, 19, 23, 32, 54, 58, 62, 63, 72, 73, 74, 76, 83, 84, 86, 87, 91, 93, 95, 97, 120, 121, 122, 132, 133, 135, 139, 142, 143, 145, 146, 158, 160, 161, 170, 171, 172, 183, 196, 200, 203, 206, 207, 208, 216, 217, 224, 226, 232, 235, 244, 252, 259, 274. *See also* Ancient Greek
Guattari, Félix 176, 190

hadd 171–172
Hades 231
Haemon 220, 222, 229
Haraway, Donna 156
Harman, Graham 41–42, 84–85, 122–123
Harpocration 48, 55–56
Harris, Edward 91, 244, 258–259, 261, 265–266
haunting, ghost xxxii, 165–166, 209, 274
Hebraic xxx, 65, 73, 84
Hebrew 63, 86–87
Hector 233
Hecuba 206
Hegel, Georg Wilhelm Friedrich xxx, xxxi, 20, 22–23, 31, 33–35, 113, 127, 130, 134–138, 141, 146, 151, 165, 212, 220, 223
Hegelian 82, 135, 152, 211, 220, 228
Hegemone 108
Heidegger, Martin xxx, xxxi, 30, 36, 37, 38, 39, 41, 42, 43, 96, 98, 99, 124, 128, 141, 142, 143, 144, 145, 146, 147, 157, 164, 165, 183, 236. *See also* Dasein
Hellenistic 14, 53, 71, 281
Hera 206
Herakleitos 29, 31–32, 35, 138
Herakles 108, 207, 233–234, 237, 269
Herman, Gabriel 237–238
Hermes xvii, 34
Hermione 206
Herodotos 202, 205
Hesiod 261
Hestia 108, 112
H (eta), letter xxii, 1, 45, 59, 71–75, 79, 84, 117, 135, 147, 153, 170, 195, 249, 239

Hill of the Nymphs 53
Hindu 63, 83
Hiphil stem 87
history xv, xvi, xx, xxiii, xxvi, xxvii, 24, 27, 41, 47, 50, 53–54, 60, 62, 67, 69–70, 73–74, 82, 91–92, 102, 109–110, 113, 119–120, 122, 136, 138, 155–157, 173–175, 178–180, 184, 186, 188, 205, 212, 215, 243, 271–272, 280
Holocene 188, 190
Homer 82, 232
Homeric 10, 52, 54, 93, 203, 228, 231, 233, 257, 261
horismos (ὁρισμός) 120, 124–127, 140–143, 145, 147, 171–172
horizon xxxi, 39, 50, 104–106, 127, 140–141, 143–146, 169, 175, 177, 194, 213, 271
Horkheimer, Max 188
horos xvii, xxii, xxiii, xxiv, xxv, xxvi, xxix, xxx, xxxi, xxxii, 1, 3, 5–6, 8–16, 19–22, 24, 30–34, 39, 41–42, 46–50, 52–59, 61–62, 67, 71–73, 75, 77–79, 81–83, 87–94, 96–97, 99–110, 113–116, 118–120, 123–136, 138–143, 146–148, 151–152, 155, 157–163, 165, 167–172, 175, 180–181, 183, 185, 194, 196–200, 202, 207–214, 216–217, 219, 224, 226, 229, 233, 240, 243–244, 255–259, 261–262, 267–271, 273–275, 277, 279–284
hospitality xxvii, 102–107, 109, 197, 228, 232–237
household xxii, xxxii, 76, 95, 146, 200, 203–205, 220, 225, 227–234, 236, 242–243, 247, 253, 263, 269
hubris (ὕβρις) xx, 70, 114, 187, 271
human xvi, xix, xx, xxi, xxiii, xxiv, xxv, xxvi, xxviii, xxix, xxxi, xxxii, 3–4, 8–9, 14–16, 18–19, 21, 23–29, 32–38, 40–43, 46–52, 58–60, 62–65, 67–71, 74, 81, 84, 87–88, 95, 99, 102, 106, 110–111, 113, 115, 132, 140, 142–143, 147, 154–157, 168–169, 173, 185–189, 191–194, 197, 212, 215, 220, 227, 237, 240–244, 270–271, 274, 278–279, 283–285
anthropos 25, 154, 186

humanity xxiii, xxix, 25–29, 155–156, 187–188
nature xxix, 29, 110, 193
human nature xxix, 29, 110, 193
Husserl, Edmund xxxi, 143
hyle (ὕλη) 150
hymen 199–200

Ibn al-'Arabî 83, 171
Iliad 10, 93, 106, 127, 233
imperialism 14, 90–91, 115, 140, 202, 240, 279
Indian 66, 83
Indo-European 54
Indus-valley 62
inscription xxii, 4, 5, 8, 9, 13, 14, 15, 22, 24, 46, 48, 53, 54, 61, 62, 71, 72, 73, 77, 100, 101, 130, 131, 169, 170, 209, 210, 212, 262, 268, 283. *See also* epigraphy
Ionic 72
Iphigeneia 206
Irigaray, Luce 221, 223, 226
Irish 136
Iron Age 196, 205
Islam 196
Ismene 215
Israel xv, 85

Jacob (Old Testament) 84
Japan 63
Jaspers, Karl 65
Jeffrey, L. H. 5, 9, 72
Jonas, Hans 192
Jupiter 83, 120

Ka'aba 82
Kabbalistic 274
Kennedy-Day, Kiki 171–172
Kerameikos 48, 79, 195, 209, 239
Keuls, Eva 200, 228–229
King James Bible 81, 86
kin, kinship xx, 102–103, 204, 220–221, 223–224, 227–228, 232, 235, 237, 242, 246
Kuperus, Gerard 38

Laban (Old Testament) 84
Lacan, Jacques xv, 47, 54, 59–61, 75, 221, 223
Lalonde, Gerald V. 5, 9, 48, 52–53, 91, 101, 195, 209–210, 279
landmark xxiii, xxx, 10–11, 46, 48, 61, 80, 82, 85–87, 129, 168
language xx, xxi, xxv, xxix, xxx, xxxi, 14, 16, 19–20, 22, 25, 27, 30–32, 35, 41, 46, 50, 53, 57, 60–62, 64–67, 75, 77, 95–96, 99, 102, 106, 109–112, 118, 120–121, 123, 126, 128, 130–133, 135–136, 140, 145, 148, 152, 172, 176, 189, 193–194, 216, 221–223, 237, 243, 259, 274–275, 280–281
Latin 55, 120, 122, 128, 135, 147, 217
Latinate 133, 141, 145, 183
Latour, Bruno 50, 189, 191–192
law xix, xxi, xxx, xxxii, 5, 11–12, 23, 26, 29, 35, 50, 65, 70, 76, 78, 83–84, 87–91, 97–103, 105, 107–110, 112–115, 124, 146, 204–205, 207–208, 212–216, 218–223, 226, 228–232, 241–249, 251–256, 258, 260–261, 263–268, 270–273, 275–276, 281–282
    Athens 12, 266
    marital 232, 242, 252, 263
    mourning 244, 246–247, 254–255, 267–268
Lebanon xv
Lemnos 202
Leokorion 229
Leos 229
Letter – in Derrida, in Lacan 47, 54, 59–60, 74–75, 127, 148
Leviathan xix
Levinas, Emmanuel xxvi, 106–107, 140, 150–152, 186, 236–237, 278, 285
lexical xxix, 48, 55, 81
lexicon 48, 55–56, 119, 168, 171, 198–199, 210, 275
Liddell and Scott lexicon 48, 55–56, 198, 200
limit xvi, xix, xxii, xxiii, xxv, xxviii, xxxii, 2, 6–9, 12, 14, 21–23, 25, 32, 38–39, 41, 46–47, 52, 59, 61, 70, 75, 77–78,

80, 83, 87–88, 104–106, 113–116, 125, 128–129, 133, 137, 139–140, 142–145, 147, 152, 154, 159–164, 168–171, 180–185, 189, 191–194, 197, 199–202, 207, 211, 217, 220, 229–231, 233, 235–236, 241–243, 247, 253, 255–256, 262, 267–270, 272–276, 278–285
lithography 80–81, 115
logos (λόγος), logic 11, 20, 23, 25, 30–35, 52, 54–55, 57, 81, 100–102, 109, 120, 123–131, 133–134, 136, 142, 145–150, 171–172, 216–217
Longo, Oddone 224–225
Loraux, Nicole 89, 97, 223, 225, 256
Lycian 93

Machiavellian 215
magic (of letters) 8, 66, 70, 73
man xxxii, 10, 17, 23, 25–27, 32, 54, 57, 61, 65, 81, 83, 86, 89, 92–94, 100, 108–109, 113, 139, 144, 149, 171, 174, 192, 198–199, 202, 206–208, 213, 218, 222, 228, 231, 240, 242, 245, 249–254, 256, 258–259, 265–271, 273, 275, 282
  death 228
  domination 213, 215, 218, 220–223, 229–230, 245, 267
  history 271
  in mythology 198–199, 204, 213–215, 218, 220–223, 229–230, 245, 267
  lawgivers 213, 215, 218, 220–223, 229–230, 245, 267
  mourning 228
Martin, Richard 256, 260
Marxist 67
Marx, Karl xxii, 5–6, 28
matriarchy 196, 205
mattering 61, 69, 122
matter, material xvi, xvii, xix, xx, xxi, xxiii, xxiv, xxvi, xxvii, xxix, xxxi, xxxii, 3–8, 11, 14–16, 18–20, 22–25, 28–29, 39–43, 46–53, 59–69, 73–76, 81–82, 87, 92, 95–96, 99–100, 102, 106–107, 113–116, 119, 121, 123–124, 128–129, 131–132, 134, 136–137, 139, 143–146, 149–151, 155, 162, 165, 167–170, 172–173, 177–179, 184, 186–187, 191, 200, 209, 213, 219, 224, 226, 228, 231–232, 234–237, 246–247, 255–256, 267, 269–271, 273–276, 278–280, 282, 284–285
Mauss, Marcel 237–238
Maya 62
Mecca 2
Medea 203, 206
mediaeval 143
Medusa 207
Megarian 72
memory (μνῆμα) 9, 26–27, 87–88, 194, 209–212, 215, 219, 271
Merchant, Carolyn xxvi, 27, 51, 200, 242
Mesoamerican 2
Mesopotamian 63
metaphor xxxi, 24–25, 27, 31, 37, 47, 50, 65, 75, 95, 143, 145, 155, 170, 178–179, 186, 201, 236, 256, 259–261, 273
Middle Ages xxvi, 179
Mizpah 84
money xxv, 6, 12, 61, 95, 97–98, 119–120, 149, 217, 252, 261, 284
monotheism 63, 196
Morales, Helen 223
Mother Goddess 205
motion 21, 29, 31–32, 38–39, 43, 50, 97, 102, 140, 160, 162, 166
movement xv, xxxii, 6, 21, 29, 31, 39, 82, 102, 140, 141, 152, 158, 159, 160, 161, 162, 166, 167, 168, 170, 176, 178, 182, 183, 184, 185, 193, 242, 245, 284. *See also* motion
mystery, mysteries (Eleusinian) 41, 59–60, 72
myth, mythology 23, 25–26, 39, 49, 63, 89, 97–98, 113, 179–180, 182–183, 188, 192, 201–204, 206–208, 225–226, 229, 231, 233, 241, 249, 263

nature xix, xx, xxi, xxiii, xxiv, xxv, xxvi, xxvii, xxix, xxx, xxxi, xxxii, 2–4, 8–9, 13–16, 20, 22–29, 32–34, 38–42, 46–51, 53–54, 58, 63–70, 72–73, 82, 84, 89, 98–99, 102, 109–113, 121, 129, 132, 139–140, 148, 155, 162, 166, 169, 175, 179, 183, 185–193, 207–208, 224, 228,

234, 236, 242, 244, 246, 249, 256–257, 271, 275–276, 278, 284–285
Neolithic 196
New International Bible 81, 86
Newtonian 66
Neyrat, Frédéric 189, 192
Nietzsche, Friedrich 138, 219–220
Nisaba 63
nomos (νόμος) 89, 284
nonhuman xxi, xxiii, xxiv, xxviii, 4, 7, 23, 27–28, 34–35, 40, 46, 50, 58, 69–71, 88, 100, 109, 154–155, 187–188, 193, 237, 241, 271, 274, 278
Northern Africa 63, 206
now (νῦν) 12–13, 124–126, 158–163, 165, 211, 214, 230, 257, 265, 267
Nuba 63

Ober, Josiah 261–262
object 7–8, 31, 34, 37, 40–42, 66, 68–69, 85, 122–123, 134, 143–144, 152, 159, 167, 170, 210, 215, 266, 270, 273, 280, 283
Odin 63
Oedipus 226–227
Ogham alphabet 63
Ogma 63
Old Testament xxx, 84
Olympiad 156
Olympian 13, 206, 258, 267, 279
ontology xx, 3–4, 15, 20, 25, 35, 41, 60, 66, 68, 133–134, 140–141, 144–146, 151, 165, 181, 191
organic, inorganic xix, xx, xxi, xxviii, xxxii, 27, 39, 51, 58, 69, 109, 112–113, 129, 137, 157, 185–186, 188, 193, 274, 278
Orphic 179, 211
Orphic myths 179
ousia (οὐσία) 12, 23, 77, 120–124, 128–130, 146–148, 172
Owens, Joseph 121–122

Padārtha 66
Pahlawi 172
Palaeolithic 49, 205
Palestine xv
Paramārtha 66
Paris 3, 206, 232
Parthenon 135, 263
patriarchy 86, 205–206, 264
Patroklos 228, 233
Penelope 206
Pennick, Nigel 73, 83–84
Perikles 205, 215
Persian 172
Petros 50
phallocentrism-logophallocentrism 134, 227
Phoenician 74
physis (φύσις) 32, 33, 137. *See also* nature
plant xx, xxiii, 14, 26–28, 38, 42–43, 65, 88, 108, 111, 155–156, 193, 208, 241, 271
Plato xxx, 11, 49, 66, 82, 95, 97, 100–102, 104, 107, 109, 124, 129, 168, 203–204, 228, 239
Platonic 11, 118, 129, 149
Platonists 152
Plumwood, Val xxvi, 32–33
Plutarch 23, 110, 244–245, 249, 252, 255, 257–258, 260–261, 266
Pnyx 9, 11
politics xvi, xxiv, xxvi, xxxii, 7, 12–14, 32–33, 52, 62, 76, 88, 90, 96–98, 100, 109, 155, 189, 200–206, 208, 220–224, 227–228, 231–232, 240–241, 243–244, 246–248, 251–252, 254–255, 259–264, 275–276, 282
potentiality 20, 34, 35, 85, 104, 111, 139, 145, 147, 150, 159, 169, 185, 217, 270. *See also dynamis*
productivity xxxii, 22, 24, 28, 127–128, 203, 229, 242, 246–247, 251, 253–255, 269–270
progress xvi, 15, 17, 29, 33, 39, 76–77, 83, 179, 188, 191, 278
Prometheus 192
Protagoras 95
Protevi, John 165–167
Proverbs 86–87
Pythagorean 207, 211
quantum physics xxiv, 3, 65, 166

Quaranic 83
Qu'ran 182

rationality xx, 22, 24–25, 27, 32, 35, 158, 182, 207, 238
reality 27, 41, 47, 49–50, 66, 172–173, 180–181, 197, 261
reason xxi, xxii, xxvi, xxviii, 26, 27, 30, 31, 32, 33, 49, 54, 65, 69, 73, 78, 102, 112, 122, 129, 134, 149, 177, 207, 236, 248, 254, 282. *See also* rationality
reproduction xxxii, 81, 134, 156, 200, 203, 207, 242–243, 253–255, 275
rhizomatics
  fungi 155
  of domination 190
Ricoeur, Paul 238
Rigveda 83
Roman 83, 86, 120, 133–135, 141
Romantics 134, 136
Rome 83
Ross, W. D. 17, 181

Sabine 83
Sachs, Joe 121
Said, Edward xv
Sallis, John xxvi, 67, 212
Sareshal, Alfred 174
Sarton, George 174
Saussure, Ferdinand de 74
Sausurrian 131
Scientific Man 65
script 8, 16, 46, 48, 49, 52, 54, 58, 60, 62, 63, 66, 67, 70, 71, 72, 75, 76, 80, 99, 135, 154. *See also* letter
Scythian 63
Septuagint 11, 86–87, 109
Seshat 63
Shelley, Mary 29
signature 70, 86, 114, 214–219, 223, 232–233
sign (σῆμα) 8–9, 25, 31, 46, 58, 65–67, 71, 77, 121, 123, 127–131, 133, 136, 188, 197, 201, 209–212, 214–219, 223, 228, 230, 268–269
Sina, Ibn 170–171, 173–174

society xxiv, xxvi, xxxii, 27, 52, 62, 113, 189, 196–197, 204, 206–208, 222, 233, 266, 274
Socrates xxii, 29, 61, 95, 124, 203, 211, 271, 280–281
Socratic xxv, 30, 61, 124, 151
Solon xxxii, 12–13, 52, 71, 97, 169, 231, 237, 240–276, 278, 282
Solonian 244, 248, 257, 269–270, 279
Solonic law xxi
Sophilos 72
Sophocles xxxii, 207, 212, 221, 224, 227–229, 267
Sorabji, Richard 31–32
soul xxi, 21, 24, 30, 32–34, 37, 40–41, 43, 49, 51, 61, 75, 78, 122, 130, 135, 160–161, 166, 170, 179, 187, 189, 191, 209, 211–212, 223, 278–279
  anima 21, 33–34, 51, 135
  psyche (ψυχή) xxi, 21, 32–34, 179, 211
  spirit 21, 24, 30, 33, 43, 61, 75, 78, 189, 191, 209, 223
  world soul (*anima mundi*) 34, 49
Spaniard 84–85
Sparta 225
Sphinx 207
Stagg, Frank 184–185
Steiner, George 274
Stoics 281
Styx 109
subject, subjectivity xix, xxi, xxv, xxviii, 3–4, 8, 15–20, 23–24, 34–35, 46, 49, 55, 65–70, 73, 89, 92, 94, 100, 106, 111–112, 115, 118, 134, 139–140, 147–148, 154, 164, 194, 200, 204, 217, 227, 236, 241–242, 266–267, 270, 273, 280, 283, 285
substance 8, 15, 20, 23–24, 29, 34, 47, 67, 76, 95, 110, 113, 120–122, 129–131, 134, 137–138, 147–150, 152, 172–174, 264
Suida 48, 55, 74
Sulawsi 70
Sumer 62
Sumerian 63
Switzerland 98

Tattva 66
technology xix, xxviii, 25–27, 29, 50, 65, 81, 115, 157, 177, 188–191, 193, 243
Teiresias 220
temporality xxxi, 12, 16, 31–32, 38, 58–59, 61, 72–73, 82, 86, 97, 144–145, 157–159, 165–170, 175–178, 182–183, 185–186, 236
Tenjin 63
term xxi, xxii, xxiii, xxix, xxxi, 10–11, 14, 29, 46–50, 52, 54, 57, 61, 69, 71, 75–78, 82, 87, 104, 106, 115, 118–120, 124–126, 130, 133, 135–138, 142–144, 146–147, 151–152, 155–156, 168–172, 181, 185, 194, 211, 217, 227, 269, 275–276, 279
terminology 61, 90, 99, 119–120, 123, 157, 165, 257–258, 275
Terminus 46, 83, 120, 133, 141
terraforming xxviii, 192
Thales 50, 274
Thallo 108, 112
Thebes 225–226, 229
Thoth 63
Thucydides 96, 205
tomb xxxii, 196, 209, 211, 212, 214, 227, 228, 229, 230, 231, 233, 246, 253, 267, 268, 269. *See also* memory; *See also* sign; *See also* woman
Toulmin, Stephen 174
tragedy 197–199, 203, 212, 221, 223, 225–226, 228–229, 233
Troia 10, 198, 206
Trojan 93, 225, 232
Trojan war 232
Troy 93

Vardoulakis, Dimitris 97–98
Venus 255
Vidal-Naquet, Pierre 108, 112–113, 203, 205, 265

virginity 200, 221, 229, 253
vitalism 3–4, 7

wall, barrier xvi, 7, 10, 17–18, 53, 73–78, 83–84, 89, 93, 97, 100, 106, 109, 112, 114–115, 139, 144, 172, 174, 189, 199, 262
Weber, Max 7, 85
Western philosophy xxxi, 32, 151
woman xv, xxiii, xxxii, 12, 22, 29, 76, 168, 196–208, 212–213, 220–223, 225, 228–229, 233–234, 241–248, 252–254, 264, 267, 270–271, 273, 275, 285
  death 228, 234
  in mythology xxxii, 197–199, 203–204, 206, 212–215, 217–231, 237, 245, 267–268, 275
  killing men 198–199, 203–204, 206
  status xxiii, 29, 196, 198–200, 202, 204, 207, 220, 223, 228, 234, 247–248, 252–254, 275, 285
wordplay 10, 29, 47, 121
world, worldless xv, xvi, xviii, xix, xx, xxiii, xxiv, xxvi, xxviii, xxix, xxxi, xxxii, 4, 7–8, 15, 24, 26–29, 32–34, 36–43, 49–51, 58, 60–61, 64–70, 73, 83, 89, 91, 99–100, 104, 110–111, 113, 115, 136, 139–144, 154–156, 166, 173, 179–180, 188, 190, 192–193, 196, 205, 209, 212, 241, 271, 274, 278–279, 282
xenia/philoxenia (ξενία, φιλοξενία) xxvii, 102, 103, 106, 228, 230, 231, 232, 233, 234, 235, 236, 268, 269, 270

Yggdrasil 63
Yusuff, Kathryn 187, 188

Zeitlin, Froma I. 207, 224, 225, 226
Zeus 9, 11, 53, 100, 101, 102, 103, 104, 107, 108, 192, 207, 213, 267, 269, 279

About the Team

Alessandra Tosi was the managing editor for this book.

Melissa Purkiss performed the copy-editing and proofreading.

Lucy Barnes indexed this book.

Anna Gatti designed the cover. The cover was produced in InDesign using the Fontin font.

Luca Baffa typeset this book in InDesign and produced the paperback and hardback editions. The text font is Tex Gyre Pagella; the heading font is Californian FB. Luca produced the EPUB, AZW3, PDF, HTML, and XML editions — the conversion is performed with open source software freely available on our GitHub page (https://github.com/OpenBook Publishers).

This book need not end here...

Share

All our books — including the one you have just read — are free to access online so that students, researchers and members of the public who can't afford a printed edition will have access to the same ideas. This title will be accessed online by hundreds of readers each month across the globe: why not share the link so that someone you know is one of them?

This book and additional content is available at:

https://doi.org/10.11647/OBP.0266

Customise

Personalise your copy of this book or design new books using OBP and third-party material. Take chapters or whole books from our published list and make a special edition, a new anthology or an illuminating coursepack. Each customised edition will be produced as a paperback and a downloadable PDF.

Find out more at:

https://www.openbookpublishers.com/section/59/1

Like Open Book Publishers

Follow @OpenBookPublish

Read more at the Open Book Publishers BLOG

You may also be interested in:

Plato's *Republic*
An Introduction
Sean McAleer

https://doi.org/10.11647/OBP.0229

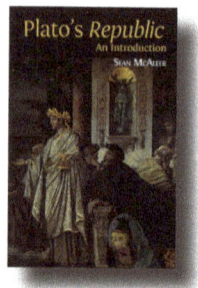

That Greece Might Still Be Free
The Philhellenes in the War of Independence
William St Clair

https://doi.org/10.11647/OBP.0001

Ancient Greek I
A 21st Century Approach
Philip S. Peek

https://doi.org/10.11647/OBP.0264

www.ingramcontent.com/pod-product-compliance
Lightning Source LLC
Chambersburg PA
CBHW041731300426
44115CB00022B/2974

A Spectacular Life

Mary Lopez AM
Hon DLitt(UWS), FFCSME, B.Mus.Ed, DSME, A.Mus.A,
Emeritus Director Schools Spectacular
Emeritus AD Talent Development Project

A Spectacular Life

First published in Australia by Mary Lopez AM 2025
www.marylopez.com.au/

Copyright © Mary Lopez AM 2025
All Rights Reserved

 A catalogue record for this book is available from the National Library of Australia

ISBN: 978-1-7644380-0-1 (pbk)
ISBN: 978-1-7644380-1-8 (ebk)

Typesetting and design by Publicious Book Publishing
Published in collaboration with Publicious Book Publishing
www.publicious.com.au

Cover images:
Author portrait by Nathan Thomas ©
A vast field of sunflowers basking in the warm sunlight - Bogdan Pigulyak © (shutterstock)

No part of this book may be reproduced in any form, by photocopying or by any electronic or mechanical means, including information storage or retrieval systems, without permission in writing from both the copyright owner and the publisher of this book.

Dedication

To Kate, Andy and Rob

To all the dedicated and passionate teachers of the
Performing Arts in NSW Public Education

The Mary Lopez Story – Summary

Mary Lopez's story, a tapestry woven from the threads of dreams, determination, and familial bonds, unfolds in the quiet, wide streets of Merriwa, a small NSW country town that nurtured a young girl with big aspirations.

Born Mary Feneley, 8 months after her father's death, her journey from the daughter of a female publican to the architect of the world's largest classroom – the Schools Spectacular – is a narrative of overcoming adversity, embracing one's passions, and the power of unwavering family support.

In 1968, at 14, Mary walked up Bettington Street, Merriwa, transforming it into her personal runway, yearning for the stage and a sense of belonging.

Living above her mother, Irene Feneley's hotel, her home life was unconventional, marked by the absence of a traditional family structure and the constant presence of hotel guests instead of neighbours and friends.

Despite these challenges, Mary found solace and expression in performance. Her talent shone brightly in school concerts at St Joseph's Catholic School, where she played a leading role in almost every item. Her family supported her passion with love, encouragement and moral support.

Mary's dreams were vivid and multifaceted. Mary longed for a normal family life, something she observed in her peers but found elusive in her own experience. The constraints of living in a hotel meant privacy and normality were luxuries she didn't have. Yet, this young girl's resilience shone through as she adapted her environment, using her sewing skills to create a semblance of a typical family home.

Mary's aspirations weren't limited to Merriwa; she dreamt of being an actress, a dream that seemed distant due to her lack of exposure to city life and theatre. Yet, it was the very foundation of her education in Merriwa and Maitland, under the guidance of nuns, that laid the groundwork for what was to come. The cultural knowledge and love for performance she gained there were instrumental in shaping her future endeavours.

In her teenage years, Mary's desire to fit in and be part of the "cool scene" was evident in her fashion choices, reflective of the trends of the '50s. She engaged in the popular activities of her peers, such as starching petticoats and sewing flower medallions on skirts, despite the limitations of living in a small town.

Her journey took her to the Conservatorium of Music, where her love for performance and fashion flourished. She sewed her evening dresses for the many balls she attended, thanks to her cousin Anne Feneley, who owned a school of speech and deportment, and who played a significant role in her student life.

Fast forward to 2009, the year of her retirement as the director of the Schools Spectacular. This moment was a culmination of her lifelong journey, a dream realised on a scale she'd never imagined. The arena at the Sydney Entertainment Centre became a symbol of Mary's achievements, filled with thousands of performers, exceeding the population of 1,000 in her hometown.

This event was not just a professional milestone but a deeply personal one, attended by her family, including her son Andy, daughter Kate, and partner Rob. The surprise performance of *The Town I Love So Well* was a poignant reflection of her journey, a life lived in pursuit of dreams, underpinned by the love and support of her family.

Mary's reflections on her career are interwoven with memories of her mother, whose sage advice: "You'll never get a big head, will you Mare?" and unconditional love were her guiding stars. Her mother's words, emphasising humility and recognising Mary's potential, resonated with her throughout life. This unconditional love was a constant source of strength, especially in dealing with the loss of her siblings and the longing for a father she never knew. Her father's absence was a void in her life, influencing her relationships and her understanding of family dynamics.

Mary's narrative is also a testament to the societal challenges she faced. Growing up as the publican's daughter brought its own set of prejudices and judgments, teaching her valuable lessons in social tolerance, inclusiveness and the fight for equality.

As she reminisces about her childhood, Mary acknowledges the selective nature of memories, often centred around dramatic events. Yet, it is clear that her family – her mother Irene, siblings Cecil, Shirley,

Geraldine, Shane, Widge (Ian) and Dot – provided a foundation of love and support that was crucial in shaping her character and aspirations.

In her reflections, Mary does not shy away from the grief and loss that have marked her life. The passing of her young husband, mother, siblings, and the never-known brother Peter are poignant reminders of the impermanence of life and the enduring impact of familial love. Her mother's wisdom about the irrevocable loss of a child resonates with Mary, highlighting the depth of maternal love and the complexities of family relationships. Her daughter Kate's strength in dealing with her physical disabilities, inspired Mary to give a platform to these marginalised performers.

Mary's story culminates in the realisation of her childhood dreams through the Schools Spectacular and her massive productions of indoor and outdoor concerts and spectaculars in Sydney and national locations. What started as a vision to provide a platform for young talent grew into the world's largest variety show, a testament to her perseverance, creativity, and dedication. Her son Andy creating and co-owning one of Australia's leading entertainment and motor sports events companies fills her with great pride.

The Schools Spectacular was more than just a show; it's a reflection of Mary's life, her struggles, her victories, her travels and most importantly, her unyielding belief in the power of dreams, her respect for human beings and her love of Australia. It's a stage where everyone can be a star. A world where neither disability, nor cultural differences defines a person. It's the biggest and most inclusive family in the world! The Talent Development Project (TDP), the training program co-created by Mary, has turned out another family – a family of stars and wonderful human beings who have realised their dreams.

In conclusion, Mary Lopez's journey is a compelling narrative of a girl from a small town who dared to dream big. Her life, interwoven with the fabric of her family, her community, and her passion for the arts, demonstrates the transformative power of ambition, resilience, and the human spirit. Her passion and leadership changed the face of the Australian entertainment industry.

Her legacy through the Schools Spectacular is a beacon of inspiration, showcasing what can be achieved when one holds onto their dreams and is bolstered by the love and support of family.

Preface

Upon my retirement from the NSW Talent Development Project (TDP) in April 2018, I was flying Emirates to Spain to walk the Camino and I made a note in my diary called Reflections.

> *First point: I owe it to Kate and Andy to record this. They sacrificed so much and they're the two people I love and admire most.*
>
> *Second point: Rob, my partner for 19 years, encouraged me and particularly enabled me to fulfil my dreams and complete my career. He now seems to think it's important for me to write about it all. As usual, in his tender, encouraging manner, he has convinced me to do what I need to do.*
>
> *Third point: I want to explain myself and why I was such a "crusader."*

As I review the timeline of my life, I see how each step I took was activated by excitement and passion. I didn't consider any consequences, so sure was I that I could pull off any event. Also, I was brave enough and confident enough to grab hold of each opportunity and never doubt myself that I could carry through the big idea. My mother gave me that self-confidence. She always told me how lovely I looked, how clever I was and that I could do anything I wanted. She believed in me and made me believe in myself.

My background, work ethic and passionate dedication brought about many changes in the Education Department's performing arts and contributed richly to the music and entertainment industries. I never stopped to consider the personal or financial costs. Ask me now if I'd do it again and my answer was a resounding "no". The cost was too great in missed time with my beloved Kate and Andy. My two children are by far my greatest productions. However, at the conclusion of my memoir I do change my mind because of the love and appreciation that has come my way from the Department, teachers, TDP graduates, SS performers, and the mums and dads.

I travelled constantly to find the talent rather than expecting it to find me. I was passionate about levelling the playing field for country kids. I wanted to showcase Australian music and themed shows to have a distinctive Australian content as well. My aim was to show off the Aussie spirit which I'd identified in "To Be Australian" in 1999.

My sense of social justice drove me to include those who were not usually included in mainstream entertainment, like disabled performers and Indigenous children. I was also determined to encourage boys to participate much more in the performing arts.

My extensive travels overseas, motivated by my late husband, Manuel, I believe gave me the broadness of life and knowledge to pass on to the thousands of teachers and children who came into my life. I encourage everyone to travel because it is such a great educator. Often the Schools Spectacular reflected my most recent travels.

So, let's start at the beginning!

Contents

1. **Family matters in Paterson** 1
   The Paterson incident, 1953 9
2. **The road to Merriwa** 10
   My dreams 24
3. **Foundations laid for the future** 28
   Life in Lithgow 32
   On to the big smoke 36
   Another school, another choir 40
4. **Motherhood** 43
   Kate begins her medical journey 45
5. **Choirs by the score** 52
6. **The travel bug bites** 63
7. **Professional progress and profound loss** 68
8. **The Schools Spectacular** 75
   Schools Spectacular No. 2 85
   Australia Week at World Expo '85 88
   Back to the second Spectacular 89

9. New year, new productions 95
    The SS opens for talent from over the Great
    Dividing Range 97
    The Bicentenary year and a move to Walker St,
    Lavender Bay 102

10. Mary Lopez Productions 107
    Mary Lopez network 108
    Manuel's lung cancer diagnosis 115
    Schools Spectacular Nos. 6 and 7 117
    The big stage – Talent Development Project (TDP) .. 122
    The network expands 125

11. A turning point and a SS for reconciliation 131
    More travel and more shows 138

12. Death and survival 144
    Fight to hold on 154
    Survival my way 155
    On with the job 163

13. Mary Lopez AM 170
    Culburra 178
    A burst of spectacle 180

14. The Rob years 191
    Dismay 206
    Turning 60 209

15. The Robyn years 213
SS comes of age, more travel and moving house again 217
TDP goes international 221
Outreach 224

16. Family expansion 229
Keeping the playing field level 231
Personal milestones 232
I am finally on stage 238
Reflection 241

17. A lot to be happy about (Kate's story) 245
Starting school 261
Afterward 264

18. Life wasn't ordinary, it was extraordinary (Andy's story) 265

19. Picking up life again 272
TDP steps out and the accolades keep coming 277
The 20th Reunion Graduation Concert 283

20. Family changes 295
The Kimberley dream is over but the TDP goes on ... 297
TDP 2013: the network strength in numbers 302
This is Australia 306
Lifetime Achievement Award 309

21. The end of an era 311
Goodbye Walker St 313
Goodbye TDP 316
The Camino 320
EBHS to the rescue 325

22. Australia All Over 329
Country music 331
Culburra, Covid and a book 332
Thirty years of TDP 337
Free again in 2022 339

23. The book 341
After Japan 344
The 40th Anniversary SS 346

24. March 22, 2024 – A grand age 352
Mary's 80th party speech 352
Mary's 80th – By Anna Rose 354
80th birthday messages from TDP graduates 355

25. Successful TDP Graduates 2024 363

Acknowledgements 367

1
Family matters in Paterson

It's a girl! That was the joyful news shouted around the bar of the Commercial Hotel, Paterson, on March 26, 1944. Seventeen-year-old Cecil Feneley, who ran the hotel with our mother, was delighted to announce the arrival of his eighth sibling, baby sister Mary – me.

It was somewhat of a miracle I came into the world, considering my father, Gerard Lesley Feneley, died just four weeks after I was conceived. I'm lucky to be here, really. All that follows almost didn't happen.

The Commercial Hotel, Paterson

The Commercial Hotel was a typical Irish pub, with a cedar wraparound bar. You'd often see the Catholic priest enjoying a glass of his favourite drop in the cosy parlour. He used to come down to have a drink after Mass and the drinkers there were treated like family. I was horrified when I went back to Paterson in my 20s and found that the cedar had been ripped out and burnt.

From the moment of my arrival in the world, I was much loved and always encouraged by my doting mother, Irene Clare Feneley (nee

Buxton). As small-town girl, born in Nurse Hanks' Private Hospital in East Maitland, I grew up without hoping I was destined for a life of excitement although my mother led me to believe I was capable of being successful at anything and everything. I often wonder how my poor mother felt giving birth with no husband and seven children to support. She must have been so lonely.

Nurse Hanks' Private Hospital in East Maitland

At that time the family consisted of Cecil, the oldest, who took over the role of father; brothers Shane and Ian (always called Widge), who attended St Joseph's College, Hunters Hill; and sisters Shirley, nursing at St Vincent's Hospital in Sydney, Geraldine, who worked on the Paterson telephone exchange and Dot who was about to start boarding at St Joseph's College, Lochinvar. It must have been so hard for Mum to have a new baby with no husband and six other children. Our other brother Peter, died at 11 months. Mum told me that she'd never have let me give away a child if I'd become pregnant before marriage, because you never ever recovered from the death or loss of a child. It's a pity she didn't tell me that in my single days, as the reason I stayed "pure" was to prevent pregnancy out of respect, fear and love for my mother.

My brother Shane once built a cabinet style radio in the hotel storeroom. It was wooden and at least a metre tall. He used to sit me in front of it and talk to me through it. He was completely hidden behind it and he completely fooled me, but that was my first taste of talkback radio.

Mum and me

Widge remembers

Mary was born in 1944 at Nurse Hanks' Private Hospital in Maitland. She was the youngest child and was born into a loving family.

In 1942, our father Gerard Leslie Feneley, signed up to the army, having previously been the Captain of the Civil Defence force at Paterson. We believe that Dad did this to avoid our eldest brother, Cecil, having to be conscripted into the army.

Following Dad's death in 1943, our whole world changed. Mum and Cecil, assisted by the older members of the family, took over the running of the pub in Paterson. Shirley was training to be a nurse and Geraldine was working in the Postmaster General's dept. The four younger children were all later able to attend boarding schools because of the work of the older siblings and our mother.

Let me tell you of the moral police of Merriwa, namely Mary and her friend, Marie Byfield (aged about 12 years). When the local theatre had advertised forthcoming movies, some of the women were wearing scanty swimming costumes. Mary and Marie were offended by this overt display. They both descended upon the theatre and tore up the posters that advertised this outrageous spectacle!

I can recall another little incident about Mary. I asked her how she managed a situation where she was in the backseat of a car, with two boys (both keen to become her boyfriend). She replied that she sat in the middle of the two boys, holding both of them by the hand.

Dorothy and Mary were both the first Talkback radio audience in Australia. Shane and one of his best mates had taken a large wireless, big enough to sit in, and Shane got into the back of the radio, pretending he was Santa Claus. Both the girls were very happy to tell Santa what they wanted for Xmas. I was in the background, enjoying every moment of it.

After training at the Conservatorium of music at Newcastle, Mary commenced teaching at Lithgow high. She later taught at Epping boys HS and by then, she was directing school musicals and involving the male rugby team players in her choirs. From here, of course, Mary went on to great heights with the Schools Spectacular. Mary recognised and appreciated so many talented colleagues and students in the realm of the Arts.

Even though Shane and I were so envious for many of our younger years of the seeming indulgences given to our younger sisters (eg pianos, whilst I had a stick for a rifle) it is still true that we were so fortunate to be part of such a loving family. Mary is such a gracious and wonderful sister.

My sister Dot and I used to have a little stall outside the fence from which we would occasionally sell lemonade. That's about as much work I can ever remember doing as a child. Dot was in boarding school at Lochinvar from the time she was three years old. Imagine that now.

I played with my friend Robbie Stedman most of the time. He lived just up the street across from the post office and telephone exchange where my sister Geraldine worked after she returned from New Guinea.

Geraldine

As a child I was already into dressing up myself and others. Poor Robbie Steadman, my best friend. Dot and I used to dress him up all the time – usually as a girl. One time we painted his face black, put him into a barrel of chook feathers and sent him home through the main street of Paterson.

Robbie Steadmand and me *Dot and me* *Me*

Life was carefree in Paterson although it was a confusing time in my life. I remember thinking I must be adopted as I didn't have a father. I ran around barefoot and had the freest childhood roaming around in that beautiful Hunter Valley town. I loved the river where the big kids could go and swing off ropes into the Paterson River or paddle along on tyres down the river at Allynbrook and Martins Creek. I don't think I did because I couldn't swim then. In those days the Paterson River was flowing and healthy. The park was always an attraction with its great big trees and slippery dip. Just behind the park was the cemetery with its very interesting history – but I was too scared to go in there.

My brothers and sisters gave me the best time. I remember one time Shane and Widge sat us down in the store room and pretended to be Father Christmas on the radio. Shane actually climbed into the body of the wireless and I was convinced it was Santa Claus talking directly to me! Shane would often laugh about that in later years. Another strong recollection is the day my sister Dot and I were riding the new family bike down the hill from the bank corner. Dot fell off and I ran home to report her for breaking the bell. Poor Dot had actually broken her arm.

The picture show and School of Arts played an important role in my brothers' and sisters' lives, but I was bit too young. It was only a hundred yards away and I was very impressed when my sisters sometimes went to the pictures.

The lounge room was the place where all the music, singing and card playing happened. The piano was the centre of attention and there was always singing in the air. The kitchen was where we all ate at the big table. My favourite food was bread and butter with black sauce (Worcestershire) on it. I also enjoyed tripe in white sauce, rabbit in white sauce and cauliflower in white sauce. We didn't often all sit around the table for family meals because my brothers and sisters lived away from home. By the time I had any early childhood memories Dot was already at Lochinvar boarding school, Shirley was nursing at St Vincent's, Geraldine was in Port Moresby on the telephone exchange and Shane and Widge were at Joey's (St Joseph's College, Hunters Hill, Sydney). There was only Cecil around most of the time.

Cecil married Clare when I was six and I used to be very much in their lives, most likely making a pain of myself while they were trying to conduct their courtship. Nevertheless she kindly put up with having me as Cecil's baby sister constantly around.

I started kindergarten at Paterson Primary School in 1949. One vivid memory of this time is when they were casting the Christmas concert. I was so anxious to be given the role of the Mary the Mother of God. I still remember feeling so important because I was chosen although the reason given later was that my name was Mary. Regardless, this production began my love affair with Christmas and all the traditions surrounding it as well as my love affair with extravaganzas and staging.

I later spent a term at the Catholic school in Largs before being enrolled at St John's Catholic Dominican Convent in Maitland, which involved a daily steam train ride from Paterson to Maitland. I would arrive at Maitland station and walk through the back streets past my Aunty Verlie's house to the school. Pretty brave for a nine-year old. Auntie Verlie White was also my Godmother and sister to the famous Marist Br. Liguori, who was a great mathematician and crucial in solving the meeting of the two scans on the new Sydney Harbour bridge. There's a resources centre named after him at St Joseph's College, Hunter's Hill, Sydney.

Mum

Throughout my childhood my mother loved to take me to Allynbrook, where the relatives on my father's side lived, the Whites. An ancestor, Sarah Therry had married Will White and their daughter was my grandmother. Sarah was related to Father John Therry, who was the first Catholic chaplain of NSW and built St Mary's Cathedral. Father Terry was a great champion for convict rights and I'm very proud of my association with a civil rights campaigner in the early days of colonisation in Australia.

Another of those early relatives, Jack Feneley, was a co-founder of rugby league in Australia and a foundation member of North Sydney Bears. Jack was a life member and founder of the Balmain 10-Footers Sailing Club and the Royal Sydney Yacht Squadron, which is nearby where I live today. In fact I overlook North Sydney oval, the home for years, of Jack Feneley's beloved ARL team the North Sydney Bears.

We'd sometimes travel 25km from our hotel in Paterson to "Mingpose" at Allynbrook. It seemed such a long way. We'd then spend days talking, eating, swimming in the river, riding horses, exploring the old dairy and going over the hill and out the back. Sometimes I simply played games on my own.

All the relatives I knew, and there were plenty, would eventually make their way to Allynbrook. Goodness me, it was so quiet and peaceful. I was shattered years later when it was sold, even though all the blood relatives had died. The Allynbrook rellies were such a fascinating and eccentric mix of characters, and they told such wonderful stories. They had beautiful manners, were staunchly Catholic and most drank a lot of sherry and rum. I was devastated when the property was sold in about 1992. At the time, my husband Manuel and I were interested in buying it but it was sold out from under our noses, even though we'd expressed an interest in purchasing to Bridgie White, the then-owner. I so wanted to hold onto those wonderful memories.

I often wonder how I got from being a child growing up in a place of such peace, love and contentment to being the adult who created what has become the show with the largest cast in the world and has helped start the careers of so many people in the music and entertainment industries.

L to R Shirley, Geraldine, Widge, Dot, me, Shane

Family through the years

The Paterson incident, 1953

One of the disadvantages of being so free as a child growing up in a tiny country town was that I became prey. I was sexually assaulted when I was nine years old. And while that incident has haunted me all my life, particularly throughout my teens, it didn't define who I became.

I think I must have been about nine because I was still going to Paterson Primary School, and he was about 13 (he might have been a bit younger). In these days, when so many people are being prosecuted for historic crimes committed many years previously, I do understand how their victims can clearly recall incidents from childhood, which have had a profound effect on their lives (more than 70 years ago for me).

We were playing near the railway line, and he had intercourse with me. I felt no guilt at the time, because I don't think I knew what guilt was, although much worse emotional effects were to come. I do remember him trying for sex another time, because I was wearing a long white dress-up frock. I wonder about my predator to this day. This boy was definitely not one of the kids my family would have wanted me playing with as he was from a pretty rough background. I can see still see the old, wooden, falling-apart house he lived in. No one in my family ever knew about what this boy had done to their precious little girl. It was too embarrassing to write about it until now. My advice is to teach your children to talk to you, to tell you of unusual behaviour.

After I went to the Dominicans when I was about 8, I came to realise that his behaviour was wrong, in fact, sinful! I was introduced to sin while I was being prepared for First Holy Communion. I don't know why but that is when I began the process of denial. I wanted to be a virgin like everyone else. All through the years of my education at Catholic schools – and beyond – I was haunted by this secret. In fact, the whole quest to protect my virginity was blown way out of proportion because I was living with that terrible memory. I wonder how many other young girls have experienced this kind of traumatic episode in their lives?

I eventually lost my faux virginity in my early 20s, to the lovely young man I'd been going with for a few years. I'd just come back from my first visit to the snow. Fighting off the young men was so hard that I decided if it was inevitable that I would "lose my virginity", I was at least going to have sex with someone I really liked. I was terrified he'd find out I wasn't a virgin. He didn't mention that aspect after it was all over.

2
The road to Merriwa

My first stint at boarding school was when I was nine and Mum was selling the Paterson Hotel and moving to Merriwa. The nuns would tell me about my handsome, debonair father who used to hang over the fence and flirt with the nuns. They said he looked like Errol Flynn.

Dad. I never met him

I felt very lost at boarding school. I had a photo my sister Geraldine had sent of children in Port Moresby and got into terrible trouble when I proudly showed everyone, because the boys' penises were exposed. I was mortified and have never forgotten that feeling of humiliation.

I vividly remember the day my brother, Cecil, collected me from the Dominican Convent, Maitland, where I'd been boarding for a few months and drove me to Merriwa. It was on my 10th birthday and we drove on a gravel road for the last 27 miles. The view of sleepy Merriwa from the hill on the way in, is still the same to this day. Warm and inviting. While I was at boarding school Mum and Cecil had been busy relocating from Paterson to the new hotel, the Royal, in Merriwa. I wore a white organza dress with red spots and a charming frilly neckline, as remembered by Marie Byfield, who became my best friend. And so I started at St Joseph's Convent, Merriwa, which was just a short walk from our hotel to school.

At St Josephs, we used to have big outdoor school displays because we'd been taught marching and Irish dancing by the late, effervescent Peg Shannon. Her daughter Patsy is still a cherished family friend. This period of my life was about school friends — especially Marie — school concerts, and loving sports because the new central school headmaster, Geoff Falkenmire included us convent kids. Looking back now, I think how incredibly tolerant and insightful this man was, bringing together the warring factions of the Catholics and "publics."

It wasn't just Mum, Cecil and me moving to Merriwa, my siblings Shirley, Shane and Geraldine were also around at the time. Dot was at away boarding school and Widge was teaching but Cecil's wife Clare, with two of the six children they would eventually produce, completed the family picture.

Growing up in hotels meant that I never had birthday parties because other kids' parents didn't want their children going to a pub. Plus, it was hard to have friends come round to play. The exception was my best friend, Marie. On the plus side, I never washed up, cooked meals or made beds.

When the circus came to town I was in my element. We all loved the animals. Of course, there were the grand parades of animals and performers to add to the excitement. The circus was not at all popular with Mum, but I was fascinated every year with the variety of it all — jugglers, clowns, tightrope and trapeze artists, animals, costumes, whip cracking and the fabulous make-up. The risk taking, excitement, adventure, romance and the mix of performers made the circus an annual highlight for me. I still love circus acts and am in awe of their skills. My second Schools Spectacular (SS) featured a three-ring circus! The circus was certainly part of the fabric of my small-town knowledge as I headed from the Big Top to the Sydney Entertainment Centre.

Being country kids, we tended to make our own fun — out of necessity — Luna Park and the zoo were too far away for entertainment.

We'd meet after school at cafes and on Saturday night we'd go to the pictures. I recall with fondness drinking milkshakes in cafes after school. Then there are those memories of sitting in the back row of the front stalls of the picture theatre with boyfriends. I can still remember those arms creeping over the shoulder towards the boobs. It was all innocent fun. As well as the circus, the annual show and rodeo were pretty high on the list of fun things to do, exposing me to sideshows, freaks, rough riders and quite a few clowns.

Going swimming under the bridge was a favourite pastime. We would jump from the bridge and dive off the big rock. There certainly wouldn't be any of that now because there's never enough water in the river. We had secret clubs and built club houses in the sheds out the back of the hotel. We were very unpopular after we managed to cut out a window in one tin wall. Going on picnics was always fun. I can still see our small gang walking along the banks of Smiths Rivulet with the wind-up gramophone (record player) and a few vinyls, plus the first aid kit (in case of snakes). We would walk beyond the weir where the river seemed to us to be flowing strongly. That same poor old river is now looking sad.

Our forebear, Jack Feneley's passion for rugby league certainly travelled down the generations. My family was obsessed with the game, but I couldn't really whip up the necessary enthusiasm – I didn't quite get it. My brother Shane was a coach, club president and an administrator of Group 21. My sister Shirley even used to wash the team's footy jerseys. Now that's dedication. And my son now owns a company specialising in sporting events.

I vividly recall the men playing two-up in the Royal Hotel's back yard, the ANZAC Day marches and ceremonies, and the enormous respect shown to veterans and those who served. It certainly captured my imagination as I won a newspaper competition back then for an essay about the ANZACs. As school kids, we used to march behind them to the cenotaph. Afterwards many of them would come to the hotel for a drink and a game of two-up. I have been inspired throughout my life by the stories of bravery and sacrifice from our men and women who served.

And then there are always the memories of singing around the piano at home, first at Paterson and later at Merriwa – these were great family times. Either Dot or myself played the piano and all of us would sing favourite songs of the day. In Merriwa, the forerunner to the big ballads was *Jerusalem* and songs from current musicals like *South Pacific* were family favourites.

I remember my days at St Joseph's were very active. In fifth class we would play games, skipping, hopscotch, rounders, tunnel ball and do Irish dancing.

Returning to boarding school in my first year of high school, I recall Saturday nights were spent in the chapel learning beautiful choral music for Sunday mass. Particularly on these nights, I'd cry my heart out as I was so homesick. My older sister Dot, who was also boarding, was very comforting and nursed me through my sadness and homesickness, but I only lasted one term before the nuns advised Mum to take me home – so it was back to St Joseph's in Merriwa. I mentioned earlier that my dear sister Dot had been in boarding school since she was three years old. Imagine that today. But these were decisions based on my stoic mother's desperate way of caring for her seven children and ensuring they were well educated.

Merriwa 1956 – me in the middle – Marie back row on the end

Unfortunately, when I returned to Merriwa the subjects that were on offer weren't the type to set me up in an academic sense – no more Latin, French, chemistry, history, or maths 1 and 2. Instead, I had needlework, business principles and general maths. We had the enthusiastic and bubbly Peg Shannon come regularly to the school to drill us in physical culture and Irish dancing which we all loved.

The needlework came in very handy then and was a great help in later life. I was always top of the class so that was encouraging, and I got to do lots of acting in school concerts. I tried very hard to fit in with the other girls and boys at school, but I nevertheless felt everything about my life was so different. I was very good at sport. I loved anything athletic – broad jump and high jump were my strengths. My sister Geraldine taught swimming in Smith's rivulet at Merriwa, where I was awarded an intermediate star in lifesaving. At one time I even fancied I might become a famous athlete. That dream finished when I returned to Maitland and boarding school (my third attempt) in fourth year of high school.

The main street in Merriwa 1958 was wide and open, and it was my stage. I remember being 14 years old, strutting along, heading towards the tennis courts, trying to walk like a model. I passed the war memorial – with its cenotaph and gravel pathways – the scene of so much of my inspiration later in life. I remember thinking, maybe if I were a model people would notice me.

I loved to sing and dance and had been given lots of parts in school concerts. I was obsessed with performing on stage and my dearest wish was to become an actress. I was in pretty much every item in school concerts, with so many costume changes involved. At the last concert at St Joseph's when I was 14, I was in 23 of the 25 items. I thought it quite reasonable that my sister Shirley and Mum provide all the costume changes required, so sister Shirley was my wardrobe mistress. I was desperate to be a performer.

Me in the grounds of the Dominican Convent, Maitland – aged 16

After three adventurous years in Merriwa, I returned to St Mary's Dominican Convent. From 1959 to 1960 I was once again a boarder before gaining my Leaving Certificate in 1960. Things really changed from this point on. I think I'd grown up a little. I was trying so hard to become a lady, and the Dominicans were very much about making ladies of us. I think I became a bit of a poser and I'm ashamed to admit it but, during that period, I thought I was a bit too good for my old school friends from St Joseph's!

As I mentioned before, I wasn't homesick this time and I think my love for choral music came out of these years. How incredibly lucky was I to have been exposed to and learned the music which would feature prominently in the repertoire of my Epping Boys' High School choirs in later years.

One morning in 2023, I was listening to Ben Fordham on 2GB. He played *Every Day*, a Buddy Holly song, which sparked a memory. I must have been about 14 years old. Radio reception was terrible in Merriwa so there was no pleasure in listening to songs on the wireless. However, I was trying to be cool, so I rang the local radio station at Muswellbrook to request a song by Elvis Presley. I knew Mum wouldn't approve, so I put the request via the local telephone exchange where the sister of my best friend, Marie, was working. Imagine my shock when I heard a call on the radio for me to phone back because they didn't have the song I'd requested and would I request another. I really didn't know another and thought I'd be in such trouble, so I didn't dare. I just wanted the whole experience to stop. That was the last time I attempted such cool behaviour.

My only exposure to music was the songs we sang around the piano and those we learnt at school, and of course, hymns. Thank God for the nuns. I learnt piano and violin at St Joseph's Convent in Merriwa from a very lovely and kind young nun. Contrary to what many people say, I never got smacked on the knuckles. Does anyone remember the Boomerang songbooks which used to have the words of popular songs? I knew the words but didn't get to listen to the music because the radio reception was dreadful. The purchase of Mum's first radiogram, when I was about 12, and a few records of musicals like *Oklahoma* and *The King and I*, opened up a whole new musical world full of colour and drama.

Louise, who is more like a sister to me than a niece, came to stay at the hotel in Merriwa when she was five so she could attend school.

The eldest child of Cecil and Clare, Louise was enrolled at St Joseph's, Merriwa and lived with Mum until her family sold their farm in Clarence Town many months later.

This began a practice which continued for the rest of Mum's life. She and my eldest sister, Shirley, provided accommodation and school fees to ensure the grandchildren all had access to a Catholic and university education. It's a little ironic when you consider she never converted to Catholicism. Her reasoning was she liked the structure of the Catholic Church and education system, particularly the framework. Mum was of the belief you had to give kids a very firm framework and teach them boundaries. She lived by that belief. Rightly, or wrongly, I think I did, too.

After Mum sold the Royal Hotel, Merriwa, and moved to Lane Cove, some of Shane's, Geraldine's and Widge's children lived with her and Shirley whilst completing their secondary and university education. There were always grandchildren living with Mum and Aunty Shirley and this was accepted as the norm. Aunty Shirl (Bub to her brothers and sisters) was much loved by us all and extraordinarily generous with her time and money. She never married or had her own children but instead dedicated her life to her nieces, nephews and family.

In the laundry, out the back of the Royal, we had a coke-fuelled machine called "the Donkey" for heating water for the hotel. Marian Hunt was the washerwoman who worked in the awful heat of that room, stirring the boiler with the sheets. She was a very impressive woman despite living in very poor surroundings by the river. I was amazed when I visited her house to see that the wallpaper was made of newspapers. My mother was very fond of Marian and was always very respectful towards her. Marian had a quiet dignity and made a great impression on me. She was intelligent and very kind. She told me lots of stories – including one about how in the drought the rabbits used run up the trees to eat the leaves.

Next to our hotel was a big mixed retail store called Campbells. I thought it was huge. Campbells had other shops in Muswellbrook and other Upper Hunter towns. Out the back were storage sheds for grain. One year a rat plague brought those despised vermin to the hotel. They died inside the walls and created great difficulty for Mum who had to remove them. My stomach still turns at the thought of that hideous smell!

Then there was the dunny carter who lived across the road. He came from a very poor family. It was a dreadful job, but essential to the town.

I wasn't allowed in the bar and certainly was never allowed to serve drinks but I nevertheless got to know many of the hotel's customers. There was "Hipshot" who used to wear flares with a huge waistband. He was murdered by a young man (I think mentally incapacitated) with whom he'd allegedly been having a sexual relationship. It was a huge scandal for the town. Back then no one would accept a homosexual relationship as being in any way acceptable. Just imagine what it would have been like to have to keep that secret liaison hidden from everyone.

When we first moved to Merriwa the accommodation was always full, mainly with commercial travellers, men who used to sell products out of suitcases and their cars. There were some permanent residents like Sandy, a shearer. I know that living with a constantly changing population of travellers and all the other hotel customers has given me a lifelong ability to appreciate and mix with all types of people.

Marie, my best friend and I used to get up to mischief. One thing we enjoyed was occasionally short sheeting the beds, just for fun. One day it backfired on us, and I can recall to this day the dark looks we received at breakfast from the guest in question.

Marie and me as children and then as adults

How lucky I was to have Marie. She lived just up the road, and we were inseparable, although our lives were so different. She had lots of jobs to do at home and I couldn't understand that because I didn't have any. I thought her mother was cruel because Marie was made to cook and clean. Both Marie's parents worked in Campbells and were absolutely delightful and kind parents.

Me – I did nothing. All my meals were prepared for me, and I would go into the dining room and the waitress would serve my meals. I certainly didn't learn how to clean or cook. When I went to Newcastle to study, I was suddenly faced with cooking and cleaning and somehow I managed to survive. However, to this day I'm not the slightest bit attracted to cooking or housework – and I'm no good at either.

My mother didn't have a social life at all. Her only friends were women who worked in the hotel like Amy Aldwell. My three brothers and three sisters were always coming and going. Cecil lived up on the hill in Merriwa with his wife Clare and their six children and he ran the hotel. Geraldine married Les Bailey, a wonderful horseman, and lived out of town with their four children although she would visit often. So I guess Mum didn't really need any more company. I once asked her why she didn't remarry, and she said: "Who would take on anyone with seven children?"

Among Cecil and Clare's children was Stephen John. Steve was born with the umbilical cord wrapped around his neck, depriving him of oxygen. This left him with a mental disability which taught all of us about acceptance and about loving people outside the mainstream in terms of mental ability. In fact, what I learnt from Steve was that disability is normal and I still have a desire to share that truth with everyone. He was a central part of our family and went everywhere with his parents. Yet again, exposure to something different gave me an early insight about life. I also learnt about respect for those parents who have to shoulder such huge responsibilities. That's why when I created the SS I made sure disabled people were given a chance to shine.

When I gained my Leaving Certificate, I couldn't decide what course to do and so I followed my sister, Dot, into the Music Diploma course at Newcastle Conservatorium and Newcastle Teachers' College. I really wasn't that committed to it all, but the course gave me the skills and disciplines for what was to become my second career (after music teaching). The two As and three Bs on my report card weren't exactly what I was hoping for but Mum, as usual, was very happy with my efforts. Mind you, studying was not my forte – I didn't like to study at all and did everything I could to avoid it.

Having decided I'd follow my sister and become a music teacher I headed off to Newcastle Teachers' College and Conservatorium.

I thought I was free at last – from boarding schools and a protective mother, my sister Shirley, the staunch Catholic and director of manners and social awareness, and three big brothers. After an unpleasant episode as a boarder in a private house in Glebe Road for a few weeks, I moved into a flat in Perkins St with my sister Dot and Cathy Gould, another Conservatorium student and a very pretty girl. Dot had previously spent two years at Sydney University on a Commonwealth scholarship studying arts. She didn't do any work though so decided to transfer out and do something different. She found the music course in Newcastle. She was a very gifted pianist. Because she was so good, I always felt inadequate and lived in her shadow. I found my own special strengths in acting and producing.

My 21st birthday with extended family – Anne second from right

With our cousin, Anne Feneley as our benchmark, we set out to be the hostesses with the mostest. Anne was a social queen (the local equivalent to June Dally-Watkins). If you were to go to the corner of Watt Steet and Reserve Road in Newcastle, you'd find yourself at the plaque dedicated to Anne Feneley at the Lookout! She really was somebody special and the life she introduced me to was filled with fabulous occasions, with an emphasis on polite behaviour and ladylike deportment. I absolutely loved it all. Being able to sew certainly came in handy, making long evening dresses to go to all the balls I attended.

Student days wearing my creations and with my brother-in-law – Robert McCormack

We lived in a constant round of party throwing and entertaining. We gave the conservative, studious music students something to think about. However, I partied so hard at that Perkins Street flat that after only one term, I had to go home for the rest of the year to recover from what was diagnosed as chronic non-articular rheumatism. All my joints had swollen up. The doctors had initially thought it was rheumatic fever, so I was confined to bed in Merriwa, but it was later correctly diagnosed.

My darling mother used to walk all the way up the stairs with a tray laden with bacon and eggs and tomato, lots of white bread toast and tea in a teapot. I used to have wonderful sleep-ins till 11am. How absolutely treasured are those memories.

Mum

After I was let out of bed, I took the opportunity to really get to know a new group of friends in Merriwa, some of whom had been away to school and were now home looking for things to do. I really got to know the local country boys and had such a fun time.

I remember one highlight of that year was the visit of a pilot friend of my cousin, Anne. The town was buzzing with excitement about the plane arriving. He landed on Kevin Shannon's airfield which was on the Shannon's property a few kilometres out of town. Patsy, the daughter of Kevin and Peg (that same Peg who taught us Irish dancing at Merriwa) has become a great friend and is still welcomed at all family functions as a member of our extended family. The three Shannon brothers, Ted, Kevin and John were part of the Catholic landed gentry in the district. They were gentlemanly and dignified, and their wives and families were respected and admired by all in the district.

The rest of the year is a little hazy, but I remember spending a lot of time with Karen, the daughter of the bank manager across the road. I also remember trying to develop a relationship with Kim Black. Kim's one of the nicest men you'd ever meet but his mother was a staunch Presbyterian which made it hard for him to mix with the Catholic girl. This is when I became aware of the terrible religious bigotry that existed in country towns. Although this wasn't the first time I'd had to wear this bigotry, it was made all the more ridiculous as my mother actually belonged to the Church of England. We had only been brought up as Catholics because she liked the firm frames surrounding Catholicism.

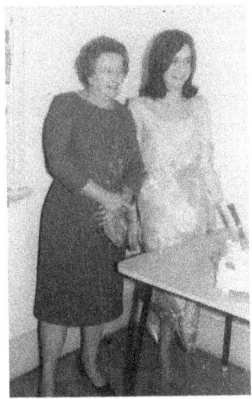

With Mum at my 21st

But there were plenty of fun times with the Wright brothers and James Furze (now deceased) whose family owned the picture show. I went water skiing on Glenbawn Dam and attended a couple of bachelor and spinsters' balls in woolsheds around the district. This was the year I discovered B&S balls. All I really wanted was to be a part of that culture. Unfortunately I wasn't and it's taken me more than 50 years to accept that fact and be satisfied. I was a girl full of longing and sensitivity who was looking for my place in the world.

I attended one ball with Ted O'Brien wearing a dress I'd made like one I saw Shirley Bassey wearing at Princes nightclub in Sydney. It was cut out from hip to underarms. I remember we left early to go to midnight mass and so, of course, I had to change outfits!

One again I practised what I'd learned and made great use of my school sewing lessons. Because there was nowhere in the pub to entertain my new batch of friends I decided to cover the old lounge suite in the upstairs loungeroom. It was a marathon effort and I'm afraid it didn't really get much use anyway because we usually finished up around the kitchen table. Our entertainment food was mostly cheese and tomato on toast (modern day melts).

There were never any cakes or home-cooked biscuits. Mum didn't do any cooking, so I grew up without any exposure to sweet things. To this day I still don't know (and I don't want to know) how to cook cakes and biscuits.

I became more friendly with an old school friend from Merriwa, Gail Ashton, who later that year married a young man whose family had bought a property just over the bridge. I thought knocking around with that Sydney group was very swish. I was a bridesmaid at her wedding at Riverview. I was excited to be taken to a Sydney beach and bought a skimpy yellow bikini to wear. That was very risqué for the prudish country Catholic school girl. Unfortunately we lost touch when I returned to Newcastle and my studies the following year.

Bridesmaid with Mum

During those eight months back in Merriwa I used my scant musical experience of one term at the Con to stage a musical for the town – *The Flower Drum Song*. Irene Gleeson's unscripted "Chinese language" shouts still make me laugh. The performance was going really well but I suppose Irene thought her attempt at improvisation would enhance the excitement.

That year the Christmas production in the church for midnight mass was wonderful with huge and enthusiastic Catholic community involvement. The choir was great. Dot was on the organ, so the quality was really good. I found I loved conducting, and we created a robust and very good choir including the five Shannon sisters and other local Catholic identities. It really brought the Catholic community together and was a truly wonderful occasion. It was a memorable event and everyone got so much pleasure from the rehearsals and from being in the show.

My love affair with Christmas shows, which begun in kindergarten at the public school in Paterson, was reignited by the big Christmas musical extravaganza productions my sister Dot and I continued to put on at the local Catholic church on Christmas Eve. This gave rise many years later to the wonderful Darling Harbour Christmas pageants I created – with a cast of 1,000 costumed characters, a massed choir and symphony orchestra with camels, horses and farm animals – which ran from 1989 to 2001.

Marie, my best friend, was left out of all of this because she was living the traditional Merriwa town life. She started working after she left school after the Intermediate Certificate. In a couple of years she was married to the handsome Barry Scott and appeared to be very happy and contented although her social life was very different to mine.

On reflection, that was the year that I started to lose my perspective on what was of real value in the men I would want in my life. At the time I thought boys on the land were to be sought after.

I had a loving childhood and always felt the freedom only country kids know. As the baby of the family, I had a mother, three brothers and three sisters who all spoilt me. Mum always told me how lovely I looked and convinced me I could do anything, but never once did she push me – it was her gentle encouragement I remember most.

So much of my character, which was to shape the themes for the SS, was formed by my life, first in Paterson and then in Merriwa.

By the time I retired as director of SS, there were 3,500 performers – that's 2,500 more people than live in my home town of Merriwa. It's the longest running and biggest variety show in the world. Not a bad sized cast and statement from the girl from the country. How ironic is it that the girl from Merriwa who didn't know the name of another song by Elvis Presley finished up with the Ted Albert Award for outstanding contribution to the music industry!

My dreams

Memories are selective, aren't they? My childhood memories seem to be based around dramatic events and I find with a prompt they come from many different quarters. I have a clear recollection of what my dreams were.

I wanted to be famous. I wanted to be noticed. I wanted to be someone. In truth I was a lonely girl. I spent so much time alone because Mum was preoccupied with the hotel and I wasn't encouraged to have friends around. Living in a hotel there was nowhere for friends to go anyway – there was only a lounge room that housed a lounge covered in a bright shade of floral yellow that I had measured and sewn.

When I was old enough to be going out with boys, I sewed new covers for the lounge chairs so I'd have somewhere decent to take visitors. Luckily I'd learnt sewing at school in Merriwa. It was a constant source of embarrassment not to have anywhere to take friends except the kitchen. Even the piano was in the dining room.

I always wanted to be accepted. This was harder than you would imagine being the daughter of a publican. I was already incredibly sensitive, as I now see. I was aware that some of my school friends' parents didn't think I was the best company. This may have been because their fathers spent too much time at the hotel, or it may have been sheer snobbery or even religious bigotry. I think this is where I learned the importance of social tolerance and the desire to fight for equality of opportunity. However, at the time, it just hurt. I particularly longed to have friends from within the landed community but there was little hope of that because they saw themselves as a definite cut above the townspeople.

I wanted a normal family – as I saw it then. I wanted what I saw all my friends had – mother, father, a few kids living in a house. When I was a child, all my brothers and sisters were either away at boarding school or, later, teachers' college or nursing. The Merriwa kids all seemed to have regular houses where their families sat down for meals. I didn't have any of that growing up in the hotel. I was never allowed to have friends in for meals. I had no idea what it would be like to have that "normal" set-up – and so, of course, I so badly wanted it.

I wanted to be an actress – I had no experience of live theatre, not living in the city, and so I couldn't really see myself going anywhere as an actress. In this instance I am particularly grateful for the opportunities I had at the various schools I attended. The nuns, whom everyone seems to be discrediting these days, did a great job for me. They taught us everything they knew, however limited that might have been. The Josephites in Merriwa and the Dominicans in Maitland educated me. The culture I learned through those women created the building blocks which formed the foundation which has educated hundreds of thousands of public-school children. My love of performing and music background and repertoire also came from them. The Gregorian chants and Latin motets I learned from the Dominican sisters have always enthralled me.

I wanted to be popular, to fit in, to be part of the "cool crowd." I always felt I missed out because I didn't have a father who was around. I so wished I'd had a father because I think I would have been less fanciful in my relationships, particularly the expectations I placed on boyfriends and my late husband. I really didn't have any idea of how fathers and husbands behaved. I had a few boyfriends, but my main companion through my student years in those days was John Truscott.

In the 1950s, my friends and I got into starching rope petticoats. We also used to make the big, gathered skirts with medallions of flowers on them. It was a bit hard trying to be modern in such a small town with nowhere to go except the local picture show (theatre now sadly pulled down). I remember we tightened up all the legs of our slacks so much we could hardly sit down in them.

My Mum, Cecil, Shirley, Geraldine, Shane, Widge, Dot and me … how incredibly fortunate was I to be so loved as a child. Mum loved all her children. I know she never stopped loving Peter who died when he was 11 months old (in-between Geraldine and Shane). My mother and brothers and sisters always treated me as if I was special and loved me to bits. It hurts so much still that I've lost Mum, my sisters Geraldine and Shirley, and brothers Shane and Cecil. I was full of grief when Mum died. She was concerned and overwhelmingly unselfish to the end. When I came rushing to see her in hospital the day she died, her words to me were, as always, concerned: "You've had a busy day, have you, Mare?"

I only have Dot and Widge now, and I cherish them. When you have such a solid family it's difficult to fit in with the new, very different ideas about family, responsibility and loyalty.

Cecil, Shane, Widge

My three brothers

Lessons learned
- Mother's love
- Family support network
- Music is the food of life
- Pageantry and performance is good for you
- Respect and tolerance for everyone
- Pride about country life
- Love of Australia
- Respect for sacrifice of ANZACs
- Acceptance of difference

3
Foundations laid for the future

After that year off, I moved back into the Perkins Street flat with my sister and our friend, Cathy. She left not long after I returned, making way for another flatmate. These were years filled with parties, balls, concerts and learning the discipline required to achieve success. When you want to be good at playing an instrument you have to be consistent in your practice. Last-minute attempts to pass exams for the piano, violin and singing are not a good option. I learned that you get as much as you give in effort and that lesson became a constant teaching tool for me. I can now see how those four years were not only fun but provided the groundwork for the many streams of the career that was to follow.

But it wasn't all study and partying. We made our own fun. One afternoon, two young men came knocking. Dot, Cathy and I had a great time trying to "corrupt" these good-looking and charismatic Mormons, Bud and Bliss. We could not believe that they were so committed; although at the same time we were committed church-going Catholics. I couldn't believe it when I got a bit close and found they wore a "onesy" undergarment. That put paid to any further exploration. We still had many hours of fun with them and they remained "pure."

I continued to attend many balls, often with my friend Robert McCormack, and continued to draw on my dressmaking skills. Robert recalls how I'd often be sewing the finishing touches to my newly made outfit as he arrived to pick me up. We loved to dance and have been through a unique relationship as friends. He married and later divorced my sister, Dot, and is father to my delightful nieces Madeleine and the late Juliet, as well as Dominic, my nephew. He became a lawyer and looked after my legal affairs when my husband Manuel died. He also became a big contributor to the TDP I developed. Here we are today, both in our 80's, one month apart and still, hopefully "kicking up our heels"!

One incident from those years still disturbs me. A girl we knew became pregnant. In those days we didn't think it was an option to keep the baby. I remember how we helped her find St Joseph's Home on the Pacific Highway, Waitara. She had her baby there and it was given up for adoption. We didn't see her after she had the baby and I've often remembered her sad predicament and considered how society now views single mothers so differently.

I continued to spend a lot of time with my lovely cousin, Anne. Everyone knew her as she had a school of speech and deportment. She was so eccentric and used to have meals delivered to her in a taxi. How far ahead of her time was she? The 1960s version of Uber Eats! Like me, she didn't cook either.

I was so unsophisticated. Anne told me to come to her flat in Derby St, Newcastle. As a 16-year-old, I caught the train from Muswellbrook to Broadmeadow station and hopped into a cab. I asked to be taken to Flat 4, Derby St. I'd no idea that Derby St was (even then in January 1961) full of apartment blocks! Fortunately, since Anne was very well known and loved in Newcastle, the cabbie knew exactly where to take me.

On the beach in Newcastle with niece Louise and in the newspaper!

Anne introduced me to restaurants, reporters and a world of fashion and fantasy. This world was a huge contrast to my student life and I began to see a much bigger picture than I had grown up with. Photos of me were sometimes featured in the local newspaper. One photo of me in a bikini resulted in a letter arriving from a nun who'd taught me in Merriwa. She was so disappointed I was showing off my body in what she thought was such a scandalous way. However, I didn't give it a second thought. This was the time of beatniks and duffle coats, but I didn't hang out with them. Instead I was attracted to Anne's world.

Life in Newcastle was so much fun – not the course, but acting in plays, singing in concerts and having parties. I used to claim my very distant Spanish (from Irish) roots. I was the best and most enthusiastic Spanish dancer at parties in Newcastle. Gosh, I had a good time. I really wasn't a good student because I was much too busy enjoying myself with this amazing new life in the city. My good friend, Margaret Ross, whose parents ran the People's Palace, used to take notes for me when I missed lectures, and her parents provided a haven for me when I was exhausted. Newcastle Con was a very sociable place although the students were all quite serious.

I always felt like I was an outsider because I just wasn't seriously interested in music or playing instruments like the other students. When I arrived and met the other students I felt I really had only had a superficial background in music training. All the other students seemed to be more advanced and were very much keener than I was. Certainly I was not a good student because I had too many serious interests in socialising, acting and producing. I knew I wasn't much good as an instrumentalist but I managed pretty well by putting on a great emotional performance in exams. However, the classical repertoire, my love of opera and the discipline required to pass exams nevertheless prepared me for what was to later become my methodology for training young performers in the TDP.

I only chose the course because my sister Dot was doing it. I really wanted to study social work. However, my brothers didn't think that was a good idea and I was fairly easily convinced not to pursue it.

I was, however, seriously interested in the social and theatrical side of the Con and Teachers' College and produced a couple of music revue shows and acted in several college plays. This was a completely new area for me, stretching my creativity. While I'd put together musicals in Merriwa, I'd never attempted anything on this scale. I played Hansel in the Conservatorium's production of the opera, *Hansel and Gretel*. I also played the lead in a couple of melodramas.

Dot and me

Me as Hansel

The discipline, music training, drama activities, revue productions and English literature knowledge gained from this four-year period in Newcastle was to set me up for a different type of teaching career. I graduated with a Diploma in Special Music Education (DSME). This diploma was later converted to a Bachelor of Music Education degree.

Mum (second from right) with her mother and sisters. Noting the amazing likeness to me.

Life in Lithgow

I began my teaching career at Lithgow High School. When I arrived there was a girls' choir directed by Marie Gow, and I set up a separate boys' choir. It never occurred to me that it might not work. In my view of the world at that time, anything was possible. My Lithgow Boys' Choir went to the Sydney Eisteddfod and won. We knocked out Fort Street Boys High School which been unbeatable up until then. We were shown through the Sydney Opera House, then under construction, and the choir sang down there in the bowels. It was unbelievable, although I didn't think that at the time.

Lithgow Boys' Choir outside Sydney Conservatorium

It was also at Lithgow that I set up my first spectacular type variety production called *Viva Sonido*. It was a huge success. Even though it was my concept, and I was the driving force, I was shocked when a person in higher authority took the credit. That was the first time I had experienced such a thing.

During school holidays I would always go home to Merriwa. On one occasion Mum and I visited our special place. It was in the loungeroom of the old farmhouse at Allynbrook where I received some pearls of wisdom from my dear mother, words I've carried and lived by to this day. I'd been excitedly telling Mum and the three old aunties about *Viva Sonido*, the variety show I was producing at Lithgow High. We were all watching snowy TV, which was very new at the time. Mum quietly turned to me and said: "You'll never get a big head, will you, Mare?"

This was also the Mum who was always telling me how beautiful I was, and that I could do anything. She unconditionally loved all her children and made us each feel especially cherished. She taught us all how to love and respect all people no matter what race, social position or what they looked like.

My son, Andy and daughter Kate also have very happy memories of Allynbrook, particularly swimming in the crystal-clear Allyn River. One unforgettable incident involved our huge Doberman/Rottweiler-cross dog named Paddy. He'd been happily swimming in the river when he decided it would be a more comfortable ride to be in the canoe Andy and Kate were paddling. It was hysterical watching the dog's attempts and the children's laughter. My husband Manuel and I sneaked back to the property after it had been sold to collect river stones which finished up as a border in the garden of our first Walker St home in Lavender Bay. I wonder if they're still there?

I loved my two years in Lithgow. It was the beginning of my fascination and love of introducing boys to the joy of singing. I had a choir of about 100 boys there. Frank Murphy and his brother "Spud" were the major musicians from that period at Lithgow High School.

There was also a sensational theatre group in Lithgow directed by the English master, Des Davis, who later moved to the University of Wollongong. For me, Lithgow was a significant training ground, where I broadened my skills base and knowledge of theatre. I acted in plays including Berthold Brech's *The Good Woman of Szechuan*. Others Plays we staged were by Chekov and other great playwrights. I also starred in musicals like *The Boyfriend*. I immersed myself in the town culture as much as possible and generally had a ball.

Lithgow 1967

Lithgow 1968

Me as Polly in The Boyfriend

The local Greek café was owned by a very handsome family who introduced us to Katoomba's Carrington Hotel and Guest House. It was rather rundown but that was where I discovered Greek dancing. I danced those Zorba steps for years to come. Another time, a lovely chemist took me on a couple of trips to the Hydro Majestic at Medlow Bath where I was so impressed by the rundown grandeur of the building. It was pretty dangerous and scary driving down the mountains through the hairpin bends and fog.

I did have some hair-raising trips back to Merriwa at all hours across dirt roads. One night I left Lithgow about 7pm and was travelling through the river into Poggy Scrub. I slid off the road into the scrub near the O'Brien's property.

During my second year at Lithgow I was completely swept off my feet by a man who claimed to be a German count. I was living in a flat across from the hotel in the main road in Lithgow. One night I went into the bar where I could hear opera music playing. I met a charming German man who was working in Lithgow. He was responsible for the music. Over the next weeks he bought out the local florist shop and flooded my flat with flowers – unheard of at the time in a town like Lithgow. I took him to Merriwa to meet Mum and even caught up with him in Sydney. Things went swimmingly until he announced he was leaving town.

Liz, my flat mate at the time, insisted we drive to his house to investigate further. We arrived at his home and knocked on the door. It was opened by a very attractive woman who said: "You must be Mary!"

I was completely shocked, as I could hear him singing in the shower. She appealed to me with words I can still remember: "It's very much easier for you to leave than it is for me." Liz and I took off and that was the end of that.

And then there were others... one night across a crowded room (yes, really), I spotted this very handsome fellow at a dance in the Merriwa School of Arts. He was there with his Danish friend (who in fact was a real count). We got to hold each other closely in the progressive barn dance, which neither of us minded at all. We had a marvellous fling for a couple of months although Mum was uneasy about this new relationship. One time while driving from Merriwa to Newcastle to attend an event his car broke down. We had to spend the night in a Kurri Kurri motel, which did nothing to allay my mother's concerns.

All the while I was seeing these other chaps in Lithgow, I was still officially keeping company with my long-term boyfriend from Newcastle. He possibly got the rough end of the straw before I eventually set him free to pursue someone who would be more in love with him than I was.

It was only a year after that I met my tall, dark, handsome Spaniard in Sydney.

On to the big smoke

My next posting was in 1968 to Punchbowl Boys' High School. I moved to Sydney and lived with my sister Shirley in Double Bay. At that time PBHS was predominantly a white, Anglo-Saxon school with a very strong academic record. I was very enthusiastic and quickly became involved with the school's music theatre productions. *Oliver* was the musical produced that year and three strong performers came out of it who went on to be extremely successful in their chosen careers: Brett Johnston was Arts Advisor to NSW Premier Bob Carr; Trevor Walsh became a professional musician and Geoff Flick had a distinguished legal career, finishing as the Honourable Justice Geoffrey Flick in the Federal Court of Australia.

Although I was now living in Double Bay and teaching in Punchbowl, it was through the Lithgow theatre group that I met my late husband, Manuel. The theatre group members had come to Sydney and gathered at a party arranged by Paul Hackett, involving a

Sydney theatre group, the Genesians. During the party I spotted this very handsome man, and we spent the night eyeing each other off. Unbeknown to me he was there with his girlfriend whom he quickly dispatched home. We arranged to meet the next day for a picnic. Not being much of a picnicker, I bought a couple of pies and sausage rolls from the bakery in Double Bay and thought that was a treat. Manuel must have been very shocked but didn't say so. Three weeks later he asked me to marry him.

Three months later, on October 19, we were married in Merriwa and had the reception at the hotel. It was a huge affair with guests travelling from Newcastle, Sydney and Lithgow. Most of those wedding guests who'd travelled for the occasion were accommodated in the family's hotel while the overflow bedded down in all sorts of places. We made sure everyone had somewhere to lay their head. Since Merriwa is a small town, the guests walked happily from the hotel to St Joseph's Catholic Church, as did Manuel and his groomsmen. I had turned 25 in March and Manuel was turning 25 in November.

It was a lovely wedding and I was delighted that my two nieces, Louise Feneley and Bronwynne Bailey were included in the bridal party. I still love the company of both of them.

On the morning of the wedding I had a panic attack and suffered from a stiff neck all through the nuptial mass and reception. You can see it in the photos. I had to go to bed well before the reception had finished after taking a couple of antihistamines which I think knocked me out. Perhaps the stress was as a result of me realising it was all too soon, and fearing I was possibly making a huge mistake.

One of the guests at the wedding was Geoff Flick, then a Year 12 student of mine. Geoff's parents offered to bring the flowers from Sydney knowing that flowers in Merriwa would be in short supply. The Hon Geoffrey Flick, a Federal Court Judge, was the first of my many famous students and I maintained my friendship with him for many years. I was so proud to see his amazing legal career unfold. Many of my ex-students continued to enrich my life for the following 60-plus years.

After my marriage, I moved further away from being "Merriwa Mary" and basically began a whole new life trying to become someone else. I was on the pathway to fulfilling my dreams although I had no idea how to plan a career and no network upon which to draw. I now know how impossible it is to get anywhere without a network.

I had no idea how to pursue my desire to become an actress. For example, that year I attempted to join a theatre group at Hunters Hill. Dramatically I received my first rejection – "too qualified" for the company was the director's reason. Rubbish! However, there was no one to advise and guide me.

On the marital front, Manuel and I were just getting to know each other. He had told me he was an experienced horseman. Les Bailey, who was then married to my sister Geraldine, was well known for his horsemanship. In 1970, he was competing in the Tom Quilty 40-mile endurance ride around the Windsor area and he asked us to be his strappers. We were supposed to be ready with hot drinks and sustenance when he rode in at 6am. Unfortunately we slept in and so were embarrassed to be woken by Les long after 6am. A couple of years later Les won that race and is recognised in the Stockman's Hall of Fame at Longreach, Queensland.

Over time I gradually learned the true story of Manuel's mother and father and his life in the Philippines and Spain. He was a very proud Spaniard with a mix of Filipino and Spanish blood. He was very fond of the Filipinos but as I found later in our married life, he was happiest and felt most like himself when he was in Spain.

When Manuel initially told me his father was a Dominican priest, I was absolutely dumbfounded! Both Mama and Papa were remarkable people with an incredible story.

Isidro Lopez Alonso (Papa) was the brightest boy in the village of San Esteban, Spain. As was the custom for the smartest boy in the village, at age 13 he was sent to study in the prestigious university in Avila, Spain, where he became a Dominican priest. After he finished his lengthy studies, the already highly educated priest took on further studies at the University of California where he gained a degree in civil engineering.

At 27, he was posted to teach at the highly regarded University of Santo Tomas, in Manila, founded by the Dominicans. There he met a beautiful and intelligent 18-year-old student, Maria Navarro (Mama). She had a very difficult childhood, although she never complained about it. Her father, she said, was a doctor of Spanish descent who died in a shipwreck. He was apparently the black sheep of his Spanish family so there was no help for the newly widowed Filipina. Her mother was unable to support three children, so Mama was raised in a Catholic orphanage. Mama had nothing but praise for the nuns who loved her and were very kind to both her and her mother.

After the relationship became known, Father Isidro was quickly dispatched back to Spain. After such a huge investment in his education, the Dominicans in Spain were not about to let him go. But Isidro jumped ship in Singapore and returned to Manila where he set up house with Maria.

Their life together produced six children who were all educated at the best Catholic schools and universities in Manila. Life was not easy for the Lopez children with their father being a lapsed priest in such a strongly Catholic country. I can only imagine how difficult life would have been. There were many instances when they were humiliated by their peers and some of their teachers. Yet, according to Mama, they were also emotionally supported by some of the clergy.

Papa worked as an engineer, overseeing the building of dams in the mountains and the Clark Air Force Base in Manila. He was very much loved by the Filipinos because he was so kind and respectful to them.

The family spent the war years hiding from the Japanese who occupied Manila and didn't like the Spanish. For the rest of his life Papa sported a huge scar on his leg where he'd been kicked by a Japanese soldier early during the occupation.

Some years later, Manuel, Kate and I visited the rural village where they lived during that time. I have some remarkable memories, picturing Manuel in those surroundings, and later so stylish in his Zenga suits, fine cotton shirts and designer silk ties wining and dining in Sydney's top restaurants.

Mama and Papa remained absolutely committed members of the Catholic church until the day they died. Papa did not initially receive a dispensation from the priesthood from the Dominican order or the Catholic church. That came much later. He always remained proud of his relationship with the priesthood. Through our friendship with Father Ted Kennedy, Manuel and I began the process of securing a dispensation from the priesthood for Papa so he and Mama could marry. The dispensation had to come from Rome. Eventually it was granted, and Mama and Papa were married at St Mary's Cathedral behind the altar in the early 1970s.

Because Papa was Spanish and wished to retain his Spanish citizenship, the family could not own property in the Philippines, so they decided to migrate to Australia, paying their own way. Papa had been promised work as an engineer in Australia. However, it was 16-year-old Manuel who planned their travel and arranged the finance for the whole family to be brought out to Australia. He told me about how he approached family members and friends to assist with money for the airfares.

When the family arrived and settled in Neutral Bay, Manuel began his HSC at technical college while working at Woolworths to supplement the family's income. Papa's promised work didn't eventuate, and he ended up working at the North Sydney Post Office, where he was very happy and content.

When I came into Manuel's life, he had just started his legal studies. I encouraged him to continue, even though at the time he was considering giving up.

Another school, another choir

My second school appointment was to Balgowlah Boys' High School (BBHS), where I had wonderful theatrical experiences, especially being involved in *The Royal Hunt of the Sun* by Peter Shaffer. I learnt so much from this experience and really threw myself into the musical challenge. I was newly married when I arrived at BBHS and joined a mostly male staff with three other young women and a couple of older women.

Paul Kelly was an inspired, wonderful drama teacher, who was very influential in my career, especially with regard to directing large-scale productions, including *The Royal Hunt of the Sun*. Paul died a few years later – an early AIDS victim. He seemed to recognise right from the beginning of our association that I was always up for a challenge.

Paul wanted to produce and direct the play which had a tricky and unique musical score with manufactured musical instruments and majestic staging. Instruments included a lion roar drum and a musical saw. The plot was about the Spanish conquest of the Incas and fascinated me as I was already in love with Spain. The fact that it was set in Peru opened the whole new world of South America and the Andes to me.

I'd never attempted anything like this before and the challenge with the whole production inspired me to think big. Katie French and two other young female teachers joined the cast. Funnily enough, I hadn't seen Katie French since that time. Then I ran into her at Kim's Resort at Toowoon Bay on New Year's Day, 2024. It's quite extraordinary really, as I was wearing a piece of gold Inca-inspired jewellery I'd purchased in Machu Picchu, where the original play was set. I hadn't worn it for years.

The impact of this play on my future life was quite extraordinary. It not only gave me a taste for staging majestic productions but it influenced my travel plans to visit South America later in life. It also brought out a curiosity within me to learn more about these ancient civilisations.

Papa attended opening night and absolutely loved it. I think he saw some similarities in the small village setting, while his Spanish pride provided him with a solid reminder of his culture and upbringing.

We also staged an opera, *Amahl and the Night Visitor*, which challenged to take on a completely different style of music and drama. I had already performed in this opera at Newcastle Conservatorium so I understood the difficulty of the score.

I taught Phil Scott for two years at BBHS in 1969–70. He was clever, a very good pianist and comedic character even then. Now he is widely celebrated, and best known as co-writer of the 25 annual Wharf Revues. Phil is an extraordinarily talented singer, pianist, writer and comedian whose name is everywhere in the world of Australian theatre. I guess you say he is the second member of my HSC Elective music classes to hit the big time! (Remember Hon Geoffrey Flick, retired Federal Court Judge – HSC Punchbowl Boys HS 1968). I had a dilemma that year at BBHS, in choosing between two very musical students, as to who would receive the BBHS music prize. I didn't choose Phil as the other music student showed slightly more attention to detail. Fortunately, I was supported by the Department of Education because of the final scores for the NSW Higher School Certificate result. My two students gained first and second in the whole State, with Phil being in second place. Decisions like that have stayed with me over the years because I really was so dedicated to doing the right thing by my students. I have felt very proud watching Phil's career explode after my small part in his early path.

With Phil Scott and Trevor Ahsley

4
Motherhood

Another year passed and Manuel continued studying for his law degree. We had bought and were living in a unit in Neutral Bay. We were on the third floor with no lift, so it was a real slog carrying everything up those stairs.

I remember I was pregnant with Andy when the Springboks played their last game for many years in Australia at Moore Park. As I was standing silently in line with the Women from the Black Sash Movement (a peaceful women's anti-apartheid group introduced to me by Mem, who would later become Andy's babysitter) a few BBHS students walked past me. Mem, who was further along the line, heard them say: "Did you see who was there? Mrs Lopez – that's disgusting!"

Australians were not so aware of the dire situation in South Africa for black people. I was absolutely in awe of Nelson Mandela for his leadership, courage, vision and sacrifice. His messages have inspired many themes and items in SSs which were to form such a huge part of my life in the years to come, beginning with the quote "Education is the most powerful weapon which you can choose to change the world". But it was his inauguration speech in 1994 that I completely related to: "who am I not to be brilliant, gorgeous, talented and fabulous. Actually who are you not to be … as we let our own light shine, we unconsciously give other people permission to do the same." This is how I thought about creating a level playing field for all children and I set out to do just that.

Andy was born on July 6, 1970, at the Mater Hospital in North Sydney. He was a beautiful, healthy baby with a huge amount of black hair. Papa adored Andy and addressed him as "Don Andres." Both grandmothers were equally besotted with the new baby.

Having a child was so foreign to me and I don't think motherhood came naturally to me. I found it confusing. I had always been the baby of my family. The first two years of Andy's life were a shock. My expectations of how it would be having children didn't turn out. I was so surprised to find that I was expected to continue working, returning to work after only three months. My sister Dot had taken over my position at BBHS when I went on maternity leave and Manuel was in no way open to the idea of financially supporting me to stay at home with a baby. I understand now that he was not up to taking on another responsibility after all the effort of bringing his family out to Australia and continuing to support them.

So, there I was just a few months after Andy's birth looking for a babysitter so I could go back to work. I was appointed to Epping Boy's High School. Dot began minding Andy. She would arrive to pick up Andy and off he'd go in the back compartment of her VW. We thought that was a very cosy place for him in his baby basket – now you'd be arrested for child abuse for not having a baby correctly restrained.

Although Dot loved looking after her infant nephew, we knew we had to find a more permanent arrangement. Our salvation came in form of the God-given gift of Meyrick (Mem) Young, whom we had met through our Neutral Bay parish priest, Father Ted Kennedy.

We first met Father Ted in most unusual circumstances. I was a very committed Catholic in those days and insisted that Manuel go to confession with me at Neutral Bay. Manuel took himself into Father Ted's confessional and said: "I don't believe in this at all and I'm in here only to keep my wife happy." Ted loved that comment and after I could hear laughter they arranged to meet outside the church. That was the beginning of a great friendship and the source of my awareness of politics and issues of Indigenous and social justice.

Ted later became famous for turning the Redfern Presbytery over to the Aborigines as well as his incredible work trying to bring about justice for them. It was through him that I first began to understand something of the Indigenous way of life. These were wonderfully exciting, liberating years. The girl from the country was in the thick of the movement for social justice for Indigenous Australians.

Father Ted hosted Friday night dinners at the Neutral Bay Catholic Church hall. Parishioners organised the food and we took along bottles of wine and then listened to some great speakers. One of them I remember was the inspirational Jack Mundy. These gatherings created an opportunity for a very interesting group of socially aware people to band together.

I also became more politically aware at this time. Gough Whitlam became Prime Minister in 1972 and we demonstrated against Australian involvement in the Vietnam War and against apartheid in South Africa. Led by icons such as Germaine Greer, women were into liberation, and we joined in.

Andy went to Anti-Vietnam War demonstrations in his pram with Mem and her baby, Duncan, while I was teaching. Mem and her then-husband John used to host parties in Cammeray where I remember sitting in the garden with her Aboriginal friends enjoying political discussions as well as consuming flagons of wine. It was such an exciting time in politics, and we were all full of grand ideas about social justice for everyone. We thought we would now have a much better chance for reforms and social justice under a Labor government.

Manuel and I were already having marriage difficulties at this time. Well, why wouldn't we, after marrying having known each other for only three months. At that time Manuel had only been in Australia for nine years. I was also new to Sydney, and coping with shattered dreams and a tempestuous husband.

One night Manuel's father had to come down from his third-floor apartment to stop Manuel yelling at me in the street. Manuel had been drinking and I had been out marking HSC papers. I came home early, and he wasn't there so I went looking for him. On another bad-tempered occasion he kicked the porridge bowl from Andy's highchair, and it splattered all over the ceiling. What lightened that rather distasteful episode was watching Manuel cleaning that porridge from the roof of our apartment. I remember that argument was over him talking about pulling out of his law degree. I was shocked and distressed by this behaviour, never having witnessed anything like it before. Remember, I was an innocent girl from the country who'd never been yelled at in her life.

Kate begins her medical journey

Kate was born at 10pm on June 3, 1972, at the Mater Hospital, North Sydney. It was a breech birth and Kate subsequently suffered a cerebral haemorrhage.

From the first moment I saw her I was in love – she was gorgeous, cherubic and perfect. I was so happy. A few short hours later it was a very different story. She had tubes coming out of everywhere and was being wheeled off to Camperdown Children's Hospital. It was devastating!

Sister Beatrice, the Mater's sister in charge of maternity, came in around 6 o'clock the next morning to tell me she couldn't work out what was wrong with my baby, but said she had a feeling things were not right. Kate wasn't crying properly, so Sister Beatrice called in John MacDonald, the paediatrician. My obstetrician, Frank Thong, was also summoned. I've always thanked God for the intuition which came from Sister Beatrice, a woman who had selflessly devoted her life to caring for other people's babies. Both doctors visited me and were very kind, but the nightmare was just about to begin.

There was no counselling available, as was the norm in those days, and hence I had no preparation or support for the emotional and medical disasters which were about to confront me. As for poor darling Kate, she was in another hospital miles away and I didn't get to see her for a week. Manuel visited her every day, but I was in a spaced-out dream world. It was so awful and terribly confusing.

All the natural conditions after giving birth came along – my breast milk came in, and unfortunately, a curette was also needed. I was given a drug for the procedure, which induced what I now know was a terrifying psychosis, which recurred for some 12 months. I was in "eternity" – I would just drop into that void without any warning. One time I was travelling down River Road, Lane Cove and thankfully, was able to pull over as it came on me. However, I told no one.

The guilt and shame I suffered when we brought Kate home from hospital after a couple of weeks soon overwhelmed me. I had not bonded with her. Of course, no one warned me about that, and I was terrified about her health. We would monitor her fontanelle to check for fluid build-up and had to measure her head continuously for growth in circumference to check if it was increasing.

Then, only a few months later we were all whisked off to Canberra when Manuel had received a promotion with the Australian Taxation Office. This was another blow, as it effectively removed me from my support network that was Mum and Shirley and Dot. The Canberra move was exceedingly difficult. I not only had a baby with worrying medical conditions but the whole situation was further complicated because we did not really know how serious the condition was. Not only was I constantly monitoring her head circumference but there were the constant flights to and from Sydney for Kate's medical appointments. I was isolated in Canberra and was scared and lonely. I felt I really had to grow up then, coping with the awareness and shock of Kate's enormous medical problems, which have now followed us all our lives.

Eventually, because we were spending more time in the air than on the ground, it became only logical for us to return to Sydney. All up we only lasted about six months in the national capital. It was just too hard to manage without family support and all that travelling.

Manuel had found us a very nice house in Canberra (all by himself as I had to stay with Kate in Sydney until she was safe to move). I was living with my sister Shirley in her apartment in Epping Rd in Lane Cove while he was house hunting. We settled into a ranch style house in the then relatively new suburb of Aranda in the Belconnen district. Manuel did very well whilst working in the Taxation Department and made friends with a coworker, the charismatic, John Tannhauser.

John has become a lifelong friend and had a close relationship with both our children. He remained a great friend to Manuel during their working lives and was a loyal, loving friend through Manuel's illness. He was with us when Manuel died. John and his late wife, Libby continued to love and care for us all after Manuel's passing. John eventually became a business mentor to Andy and has always been a great friend and advisor to me and Kate. I still enjoy John's company, along with his partner, Joan Keating.

Where was Andy in all of this? My dear little boy was being looked after by everyone except his mother. I still miss those years. I felt I was losing my relationship with my little boy. Family and friends were generous with their care of him because my focus had to be on Kate. I was terrified of her falling over as she could damage her brain, even though she didn't walk until the age of three. Losing that connection with my beautiful little boy is a loss I have regretted and mourned all my life and I have fought hard to regain that bond in the years since then.

So, by 1973, we were back in Sydney. I was appointed to teach at Ryde High School. I only returned to work on Mum's advice. She insisted I would go mad if I didn't have some outside stimulation but I lasted just one term at Ryde HS.

Kate was 11 months old when she was diagnosed with hydrocephalus and had the first shunt inserted. At that time we joined the New South Wales Spastic Centre where Kate was treated for athetoid spasticity. We were told the centre would become central to our lives but neither Manuel nor I were interested in that prediction.

Kate was a beautiful, alert baby but she couldn't sit up or roll over. Mum would say: "There's nothing wrong with her brain, Mare." She would prop Kate up in the highchair and put tasty bits of food onto the tray, trying to tempt Kate to pick them up. It was Mum who taught me how to love Kate and to teach her.

Andy and Kate

I remember I read somewhere how the brain could be repatterned, so I'd come home from school each afternoon and work with Kate. First I'd work out how I would naturally go through the movement required to, for example, move from lying down to a sitting position. Then I'd do that movement with Kate over and over, day after day. I desperately missed Andy during this time but I knew I had to give nearly all of my attention to Kate.

I returned to Epping Boys' High School (EBHS) in 1974, as the headmaster was keen to have me back on board. And behind all the passion and excitement of building the EBHS choirs, staging productions and developing lifelong friendships, I lovingly and studiously taught Kate over the next two years to stand up, walk (then back to crawl) and skip, all based on repetitive patterning.

Manuel and I gave up going to the Spastic Centre for treatment because my method was working. I had read that it was important to cover all the processes of learning to walk so that's why we did a crash course in crawling, too. There is no doubt in my mind that teaching Kate to walk is by far my greatest achievement. Kate was so determined to keep up; she was a magnificent, dedicated and passionate student – the best I ever had.

It seemed like we spent the next four years in and out of Camperdown with Kate, fighting for her life. I don't know how I managed to stay teaching. And I wasn't just teaching regular hours. I spent lots of time as a volunteer, producing mediaeval pageants, and working with my beautiful choirs and school musicals. I loved that part of my life.

During this period, things on the home front were full of worry and stress about Kate's health. The next few years were all about upheaval and desperation at home. As a couple, Manuel and I were ill equipped to deal with this completely unexpected tragedy. No young people can ever be seriously prepared for the arrival of a baby with health problems, let alone serious ones. We moved to Cabramatta Road, Cremorne, Sydney where we rented for a year before buying Frank Hyde's house in Lane Cove. Frank was a famous ARL footballer, coach and broadcaster. As I've been writing this memoir I see how I was following the trail of Australian Rugby League as set up by my forebear, Jack Feneley.

It wasn't all that long before my mother bought a house around the corner in Lane Cove, where she lived with my eldest sister, Shirley. It must have been so hard for her as a country woman to make a new life in the city. I know that feeling of being a country girl in the Big Smoke and never really feeling at home. What a huge sacrifice she made.

Mum and Shirley taught me so much about dealing with Kate's slow physical development. It's true that I didn't consider her development unusual, probably because I was just intent on making things work. Having a mother who had eight children and a sister who was a baby health clinic sister ensured that not only did Kate have all the attention she needed, but I was also given the love and attention to deal with her issues. Thinking back, I don't know how I did it – going back to work and doing a juggling act between work and home life. It was really tough, but thank God for Mum, Shirley, Dot and Mama and the rest of our fabulous families who were always around us to fill in the gaps.

The girl from Merriwa was growing up. In a real sense I was learning about the genuinely tough side of life and dealing with it in the only way I knew how. My way to cope was to believe I would do wherever it took to give my daughter a normal life. I did not accept that she had any permanent disability because I knew I could make it right.

Kate herself was incredibly determined and she has a beautiful nature. She never complained. Andy was the same. He was such a beautiful little boy, never resenting the time I gave Kate and always loving and protecting her. However, I'm still sad that I missed so much time with him.

I followed my heart and my gut in terms of Kate's physical training routine, working hard with her so she could lead a normal life. I lived by the instincts that have guided me throughout my whole life. I had no counselling or support in the hospital when the drama unfolded and I was told by Kate's surgeon that "she'd never be normal." Instead, I followed my intuition and I believed my daughter would be normal.

My beautiful daughter again experienced the same desperate heartache when her daughter Eva was born. Kate again had numerous medical problems including a tumour on the pituitary gland which has left her dependent on artificial cortisol for the rest of her life. So many traumas for Kate. I love and admire her so much as she continues to take each new physical problem on board with great strength. I do wish, however, that her problems were shared more equally with me, so others could understand just how much she has been through.

Manuel with his favourite people and Paddy the dog

5
Choirs by the score

The years I spent at EBHS (1971–1987) were wonderful and full of energy and excitement. I threw my passion into my work, looking for the satisfaction that was lacking in my marriage. The foundation for producing and directing that had been laid in Merriwa, and built upon by my time at Newcastle Teachers' College and Conservatorium, had been enhanced by the superb teacher I had in Paul Kelly at BBHS.

At EBHS, through the many musicals and *The Royal Hunt of the Sun* I produced, the concerts and eisteddfods in which my choirs performed, I know now I was looking for something like the SS. So many teachers and students at the school were extraordinary and it was important to give them a bigger stage.

My colleague in the music department, Rod Heard, was sensational. He was in a rock band and was an exciting, vibrant force. The instrumental music at the school was his passion but he was very available as an accompanist for my choirs. He also produced a recording of my special choir. Rod was largely responsible for introducing me to the world of popular music. Up until then, I'd really only been immersed in classical music and musical theatre. For this I'm extremely grateful.

At work I couldn't stand administrative duties, lesson plans, etc. I was a pain to the "special masters", as they were called then, who were in charge of music, art and, I think, manual arts. My dislike for writing is exactly why it's taken me so long to pen this biography. Anyway, here I am now and finding the frantic life I've led now making some sense.

When I started my music room was in the manual arts block. Later I graduated to the music block close to the assembly hall which was much more convenient. The manual arts teachers were lovely though, and very helpful to me. Dot often wrote program notes for me because she was really good at that type of organisation and was a very kind sister.

The EBHS years were full of wonderfully exciting times for me with my five choirs and choristers ranging from Years 7 to 12. Rod and I created a musical scene probably unequalled in any state school in terms of the performance opportunities we gave hundreds of boys each year.

Rod and I with the passionate choir members – some are still friends today

When I first arrived at the school, there was an immense respect for music already in existence, albeit in a smaller way. My vision was to involve everyone at the school in music because it was my passion.

Each year we would stage specific events: a Gilbert & Sullivan or a musical of some description, and regular concerts showcasing the band and choirs.

By working hand in hand with the sports teachers and coaches, we were able to give EBHS students the rare opportunity to be fully engaged in both music and sport. I can't emphasise enough the importance of the ties I made to the sports leaders and coaches at EBHS. The school had a very proud rugby tradition and was also building a reputation as a soccer force.

I knew that I needed the support of these teachers to make my programs work – and they were magnificent. Without their support, I'd never have had the numbers in the choirs I had. Ian Dundon led the charge with Noel Fitzgerald, Jim Bennett, Dave Glasson, Col Harris and Geoff Wing. These teachers then became the "power behind the throne" when SS launched. They were there as stage managers and cast control. I felt secure knowing they'd make it work.

Ian Dundon was the one who decided that, following the Welsh tradition, we would set up the Rugby Choir. Now that was a real challenge, but we had so much fun with those rugby players. *The House of the Rising Sun* became their catchcry and theme song.

Ian's main aim for supporting the choir was to foster team spirit while mine was to stop the bullying of my regular choir members. In doing so we built up the numbers and I ended up with five choirs, plus the Rugby Choir. Pretty soon, the school's reputation for producing award-winning rugby players was matched only by its multiple choirs' success in eisteddfods, musicals and concerts.

Little did we know that forming the Rugby Choir would open up a vast new network in the rugby world. None of us could ever have imagined this when we began. It even led to me being asked to teach the Australian School Boys rugby team to sing the National Anthem in 1983. I later used those same Rugby Choir books when Alan Jones, in 1984, asked me to teach the Wallabies to sing.

The coach's rule at EBHS was if you wanted to play rugby, you had to join the Rugby Choir. EBHS had two students in that team who later both became Wallabies – Ian Williams and Brett Papworth.

The Rugby Choir worked its socks off and it was so effective, the school's first grade soccer team coach, Geoff Wing, wanted in on the action. The culmination of our musical success was an invitation to sing at the Sydney Opera House for one of the Education Department's choral concerts.

However, it was an outstanding achievement when, among all the elite choirs in the Opera House Choral Concerts, our EBHS Rugby Choir performed *What Shall We Do With The Drunken Sailor* and *Oh, Susanna* on the Opera House stage. We were so proud of them. Of course, the exquisite EBHS Chamber Choir also featured and our tenors and basses, as usual, were the force in the Combined Choir.

A great incentive to attend choir was the annual choir picnic at Lane Cove River. It was such fun for the two hundred or so choir and band members. It's hard to believe now we did that but no one was injured and everyone had great fun swimming and canoeing. Choir numbers swelled and practices were very well attended towards the end of the year.

I was very proud of my choirs and very fond of the boys I taught. I loved that I'd been able to introduce them to singing, having always believed singing truly frees you and helps form indelible bonds and friendships.

EBHS won every section of the Sydney Eisteddfod we were eligible to contest, for many years, including the Open Male Choral Championship for four years prior to the inaugural SS in 1984.

EBHS Chamber Choir 1984

EBHS choirs and trophies

The parents were also incredibly supportive and encouraging. I had such rewarding and friendly times with so many of them, especially Maureen and the late Ian Simpson, parents of John Simpson, and Jacquie and Mal Pearce, Grant Pearce's parents.

John, Grant and many of the boys became lifelong friends.

John Simpson has had a long and rich career as an actor and film and theatre producer. He gave the most wonderful speech at my 80th birthday party, which I share with you here.

> *It was the mid-1970s, the place Epping Boys' High School – 1000 boys. The school motto was "strive to achieve", which reflected the school's total devotion to sport.*
>
> *The reception foyer was lined with trophy cabinets boasting of sporting prowess. The school's culture was hypermasculine, very intimidating ... and then something amazing happened ... Mary!*
>
> *Mrs Lopez strode into school with her curly hair and leather boots, bringing with her a love of music and a heart full of enthusiasm.*
>
> *Changing the culture of a boys' school in the 1970s was no small task.*
>
> *Realising that, she enlisted the help of sports master Ian Dundon, who, having been born in Wales, knew the value of a male voice choir, so he made a new rule: to be in A grade rugby you had to be in the choir!*
>
> *I was recruited as a Year 7 lad by two Year 12 front-rowers who dragged me to the music room by the collar barking: "You're now in the choir!" That's where it started, where Mary shared her passion and her ambition for us.*
>
> *There were so many milestones due to Mary's selfless dedication to us – endless before-school, recess, lunchtime and after-school rehearsals. Mary had set her sights on Sydney's largest male chorale championships.*
>
> *Every year the same choir won the Sydney Male Chorale – it was suggested that it couldn't be done, that we would never win. Well, we did, thanks to Mary, and the trophy was enormous ... too big for the cabinet ... so it was displayed in the middle of the foyer, a vision of shining silver.*
>
> *The music room was a place of inspiration and a safe space, as were the music room staff. Mrs Lopez became Mary, our teacher, our coach, our friend; she believed in us and expected our best.*

Mary's vision kept expanding. There were multiple award-winning choirs and endless concerts and shows, all staged by Mary and then a total school extravaganza calling on all departments – The Royal Hunt of the Sun, *a magnificent Peter Shaffer play.*

Never doing anything by halves, Mary organised the original costumes and special instruments to be sent from the Adelaide Festival Trust. It was nothing short of spectacular. At 17 years of age, being entrusted with the role of Pizzaro, was the greatest gift I had ever received.

It's one thing for a teacher to encourage students with uplifting words, and quite another to create and build experiences that allow them to grow into their potential.

Mary opened her life and her home to us …

Parties at the Lane Cove house were filled with great fun, food and where some of us may or may not have had our first glass of wine!

Mary and Manuel honoured us by treating us like young adults, taking us seriously, having real conversations about our dreams, our lives, and first relationships, crucial life advice.

For many of us, Epping Boys is just where our friendship with Mary started. Nearly 50 years later it has been such an inspirational journey with so many adventures along the way. The list of artists and events, productions and opportunities she involved us in are far too numerous to mention now.

Thank you, Mary, for your wisdom, your generosity, your integrity, your passion, your loyalty and your faith in us.

Grant Pearce arrived at EBHS in Year 7 and went on to have a wonderfully successful life in fashion. He was one of the many excited young choristers who taught me as much as I taught them. He, and many others became part of our family life.

Grant is now a renowned fashion industry expert with over 25 years working in Australia and overseas. His roles have included Editorial Director of Conde Nast Asia Pacific overseeing publications like *Vogue Australia*. He continues today in creative and commercial advisory roles as a creative director for magazines *Esquire Australia* and *Harpers Bazaar*.

In the Public Education magazine, *Inform*, Grant wrote:

> *Mary transformed EBHS into an arts-driven, creative environment that included sport … Mary and the sports director at the time (Ian Dundon) developed a strong relationship and worked in tandem in terms of merging the cultural and sporting aspects of the school. It was a great time to be there.*

Making music creates a bond which breaks down all barriers, including age. There are so many more of my ex-students I'd love to mention.

In terms of my life outside school, I have no idea how difficult it must have been for Andy and Kate to have a continuous flow of my students in and out of our home but they tell me now it was all ok. They just accepted it as normal.

At this point, I especially want to thank my mother for her unwavering belief in education, especially for women. She was ahead of her time and driven by the belief that a wife needed to have a job that could ensure she was not dependent on her husband's income. This could only be achieved through education.

I was particularly lucky to have family, Mum, Shirley and Mama, living close by during these hectic years. They were aways happy to mind Andy and Kate, and so I was able to follow the pathway which would open up to the SS and my future career. Without them, my passions and dreams would not have been fulfilled. I see this fact so clearly now and can't stress enough how fortunate I am to be born into such a wonderful family.

Shirley was working as a baby health sister working at the Lane Cove clinic. Andy and Kate, who were attending St Joseph's Catholic primary school just down the road, would call in on the way home from school for treats. Shirley was always willingly on call for baby sitting and attendance at all family functions. There were even occasions when she was called in to sort out problems with our neighbours over our huge Doberman–rottweiler cross dog named Paddy, who sometimes escaped and terrorised the neighbourhood. He was big but not at all aggressive since his size was enough of a deterrent.

Rod Heard and I also created a lovely Carols by Candlelight production, presented by my choirs at Channel Seven Epping over a number of years. This was my first venture into the professional world of entertainment. Wow! What fun and infinitely enjoyable for all.

Carols by Candlelight at Channel 7 Epping

And, of course, there was the professional production of *Joseph and the Amazing Technicolour Dream Coat* at Her Majesty's Theatre, which I will talk about in more detail later. I was initially refused permission by the Education Department to have the EBHS choirs perform in the show. They claimed it was against departmental policy to have students participate in a commercial production. So I got around this by creating a new name for the choir: the Epping Boys' and Girls' Choir. I invited Cheltenham Girls' High School, EBHS, Loreto Kirribilli and Aloysius College, Milsons Point to form a combined choir, which really expanded our ranks!

I then came to the attention of the ABC, who in 1982, invited me to adjudicate the Hunter Valley Choral Festival. This festival comprised about 40 choirs and was funded by the Joint Coal Board as a way to help re-establish the choral tradition in the region. I had already felt the urge to expand my horizons so the invitation was timely indeed.

Out of this festival emerged the wonderfully successful and legendary Waratah Girls' Choir in Newcastle, founded and directed by Wynette Horne OAM. I clearly remember when I was introduced to this newly formed tiny choir at the Waratah church hall. Wynette's passion and the purity of her aim to create a choir with such a spiritual and social focus fascinated me and filled me with admiration.

I helped Wynette with repertoire and choral training techniques, as I knew them, along with a heap of encouragement. This choir has since performed all over the world, including Carnegie Hall. The choir is the pride of Newcastle and I feel Wynette is a kindred spirit. Waratah Girls' Choir is now under the inspired leadership of Wynette's daughter, Lindy Connett. They're still charming audiences with not only their outstanding, glorious tone but with their unique joyfulness in singing together.

Wynette and I became very close and her grandson, pianist and composer, Jacob Neale was a graduate of the TDP, securing the Bound for Broadway scholarship in 2013. He later became the brilliant Musical Director for TDP workshops, graduations and many other performances. Sadly, he passed away in December 2023.

At the time, I didn't really feel that the inner clique, who controlled the music-teaching scene, accepted me as a genuine musical talent. However, I was too busy, encouraging as many boys as I could to discover and relish the joy of singing, to be bothered by them. I really didn't have the time or energy to be bogged down by such narrow-minded and resentful characters.

Thankfully, the headmaster, as well as fellow music teacher Rod Heard, and so many other teachers at EBHS were up for the challenges I threw their way. They were passionate about creating opportunities and supporting the boys and they all worked way beyond normal school hours. Their efforts were far and above what they were paid for. These were heady years indeed.

The school's principal, the late Joe Regan was incredibly supportive. He realised what a great thing it was for the school to have a dual culture of excellence in music and sport in addition to academic prowess. For me, it was great knowing someone in authority had my back.

I feel that somehow through spending so much time on the SS and the TDP I lost who I actually am and where I started, so it has been wonderful to relive all those happy memories. From the mediaeval pageants staged with Jan Bailes when I first arrived at EBHS, through all the musicals, the huge annual school variety concerts, and the choirs that featured in Education Department choral festivals at the Sydney Town Hall and the Opera House, I really crossed all genres. And the successes were numerous: winning so many sections at Sydney and Canberra Eisteddfods and performing at countless public events. EBHS was a rich training ground for me as well as the students. I know I became a much more rounded person because of my association with the sports teachers and coaches.

In writing this, I feel so grateful for those years. It was particularly special to be reminded about these fantastic years by Garth McDonald during his pre-COVID reunion for the class of 1972–76. The boys were mainly from the Rugby Choir. Mind you these "boys" were now close to sixty year old men! One unexpected but delightful surprise was that I was presented with a record saved from a garage sale by one of the boy's parents. The prized record was of my chamber choir which was produced by Rod Heard for us when we were at the height of our Eisteddfod winning years

Towards my final years at EBHS I even had an ex-students' choir named Eklipse. The senior boys loved singing so much, I guess we all wanted to keep going with such wonderful camaraderie and musicians. Jill Wran became our patron and we gave some memorable performances including at Government House. We also won the Open Championship at the Sydney Eisteddfod and featured as Toreadors in the first SS.

Olivia Newton-John with the senior choristers from the EBHS choir

By the time I'd started the SS in 1984, I felt I'd really pushed my students and choirs as far as they could go. The demands on them were becoming unreasonable. I know now I was pushing them too far because I needed to take on a bigger world.

Behind the scenes of those exciting and energetic years teaching at EBHS, I was struggling with Kate's difficult life caused by her physical problems while Manuel's legal career was powering along. Remember the 1980s and the tax benefits that could be had for long lunches and entertaining? They were great for the lawyers and their assistants but could be damaging for marital relationships. Many a solid marriage became victim to those excessive times. Manuel and I were struggling with our lack of intimacy. He didn't feel a need for physical closeness and that made me feel rejected and frustrated.

In contrast, I used to love Sunday night Mass with Andy and Kate. I felt comfortable and contented with the time to myself and the children. I remember the hugs I gave them.

6
The travel bug bites

My love affair with travel began in 1975 when Mum and I went to Hong Kong and the Philippines. Before that my love of Australia was what I thought life was all about. Travel later became my enrichment and my escape.

Looking back on the enormous amount of travelling I've done over my lifetime I can confidently say travel stretched my imagination and has been an influence on every creative idea I had from that point onwards. I've always told my students that travel is the best education you can have.

My early trips were not really holidays in the popular sense of the word – they were travel adventures which educated me and added and understanding of multiculturalism, tolerance, inclusiveness and splendour to my portfolio.

When Andy was six and Kate four, Manuel and I decided it was time for my first European trip. We planned to go to Spain and Italy. In our naivete, we felt it would be ok to leave the children with Missy (Bronwynne) Bailey, our niece, during our overseas adventure. Missy was just 18 at the time. Mum and Shirley were living just one street away and Manuel's mother was close by, another couple of blocks. I was so lucky and privileged to have such a loving, generous and caring family living so close and I couldn't see the problems that might arise from such an exercise. Missy had the children on weekdays, and they were with Mum and Shirley at weekends. Prior to this Missy had been a frequent babysitter, as she was living with Mum and Shirley whilst studying at Loreto Kirribilli and then attending university. She was yet another beneficiary of Mum and Shirl's generosity in providing accommodation so the country grandchildren had access to the best education available. So, onto the disaster that was about to unfold.

As it turns out, Missy and the kids had a miserable time. Missy coped by inviting some of her friends over for the weekends whilst Andy and Kate were with their grandmas or Aunty Shirl. Andy and Kate thought it was outrageous that Missy's friends used their beds. They packed their bags and ran away around the corner to Nanny's house in Southerland Street. I can't believe we thought it was acceptable to expect an 18-year-old to be able to cope with such a responsibility, but she did and they all survived! We all laugh about it now, however, I think it took Missy, Andy and Kate quite a few years to recover from the experience.

I had romanticised Spain as a country of small medieval villages, whitewashed with flowers hanging from pot plants on window ledges. With rose-coloured glasses, I envisaged all the villages and cities in Spain as being like the El Greco painting I so loved, *Toledo In A Storm*. Shirley had also visited Valencia many years before and had brought me home a gorgeous hat, which just added to my romantic view of Spain.

Spain was not at all what I expected. I found San Esteban to be grey and quite muddy with small houses and very dark interiors. The huge city of Madrid and its modern development was a shock to me, as were the unattractive hamlets we passed through on the train trip to Leon. Of course, I know now I was confusing Northern Spain with the much more colourful Southern Spain. And it was winter time in Spain.

The trip was an eye-opener for me, to say the least, when I met Manuel's Spanish family. Imagine my surprise to hear Manuel's auntie Antonina talk about the Granville train disaster that had just happened on January 18, 1977. What a huge shock to the system that was, to hear Australian news discussed on the other side of the world! Manuel's relatives seemed to be poor, but hospitable, and lived a basic farming life.

During another part of the trip we were robbed, and our suitcases were stolen from our car while it was parked outside the cathedral in Sevilla. We never did get our suitcases back, although our insurance covered the purchase of new clothing and luggage. Despite all this, I still love Spain.

In 1979, Manuel and I went to London and Ireland. At one point in the trip, I took a bus to Stonehenge on my own and met Martin, a young German who was studying law. He convinced me to travel to East Berlin when the wall was still in place. I recall going into East Berlin through security along these tiny corridors, with unsmiling humourless guards that frightened the life out of me. Once we got through Checkpoint Charlie, there was absolutely nothing to buy anywhere. The imposing buildings were all intact as they had not been bombed like those on the other side of the wall. I was very impressed with the architecture, but it was a scary experience regardless.

We went to an art gallery where there were people lined up, stretching for hundreds of metres outside. We thought that this was the queue to enter the museum, but as it turned out, it was just the queue to buy the exhibition catalogue. When we discovered this, we gave up and resumed sightseeing in West Berlin.

Martin and Manuel got along famously, both being legal eagles. He remained friends with our family for many years.

A few years later, before the Wall came down, Manuel, Kate and I joined Martin on another trip to East Berlin. What a strange place it was. I remember Manuel got into trouble in a restaurant for removing his coat and hanging it on the back of his seat. Apparently, coats had to go in the cloak room and putting your coat on the back of your seat was a definite no-no. He was roundly told off in German, as if he had broken the law, and yet he couldn't respond because he didn't speak the language. We laughed about it afterwards but, at the time, it was no laughing matter.

One of our first overseas family holidays was to South East Asia, Kuala Lumpur and Ubud just after Christmas in 1980.

I'd been told by a fellow teacher at EBHS about how lovely Fraser's Hill was. So we went there as part of our trip and what an adventure we had. In the '70s and early '80s we were first introduced to the squatting toilet. One night we took the kids to a local eating place. I was busting to go to the toilet and was directed to an outdoor room with a few very large pottery pots full of water. I assumed that this was the toilet! I urinated and then realised to my horror it was actually the water supply! At least I had the decency to try to own up to the café owners … but then I threw the kids under the bus and told the owner it was them who did it!

In Ubud, Bali, we found a very beautiful and welcoming place that I've never forgotten. I revisited it twice after our first visit. Sadly, the tiny village of Ubud has now changed beyond recognition. When we first visited, there was only one street where you could shop and eat. These days, it's so over-commercialised and there are shops and eateries everywhere you look. Oh, for a return to that simplicity!

When we stayed at the then hotel Tjampuhan I discovered one of my favourite fruit combinations – papaya and lemon juice. This fabulous delicacy was delivered every morning after we struck the cowbell outside our very clean but rustic villa.

Another memorable family holiday was to America. We were looking forward to Disneyland for Andy and Kate and to the beauty of Niagara Falls. In Disneyland we stayed at the Howard Johnston Hotel. Our two day stay there was memorable because the four of us were disappointed and horrified to find turds floating in the pool both afternoons after our Disneyland fun. I'm sure you've all experienced a similar horror!

The only problem was we missed the Falls… We began our journey in San Francisco, travelling through Death Valley to Las Vegas. Joining us on part of our trip was our great friend, and then brother-in-law, Robert McCormack. Robert was in San Francisco at the time on a conference but realized when we contacted him that he'd missed his flight. Manuel, Andy, Kate, Robert and I hired a big American Limo and set off for Yosemite National Park where we rented a cabin overnight. Yosemite was really beautiful and we'd have loved to stay longer, but we had Death Valley to look forward to. We were very much aware of the dangers of the heat and holdups if we stopped. We felt as if we were in an American Western Movie. We could see the bright lights of Vegas from miles and miles away as we were (unwisely) arriving in the dark. We had been booked into the Pink Flamingo Hotel but when we arrived there was no sign of our booking. The Las Vegas Hilton rescued us. We were all amazed at the size of it. Walking through the gaming tables was a real eye opener for us all. However, the next morning seeing the poker machines in the Post Office shocked me.

After Vegas, we went to Tucson, Arizona, and came across storms and lightning, the like of which I've never experienced before or since. It was terrifying, but we did get to spend some time with a couple of American girls, Rita and Tex, who had stayed with us in Sydney in the 1970s. But we didn't get across to the East to see Niagara Falls.

When Andy was nineteen years old, he and Manuel took a grand tour full of surprises and adventures in the USSR. While they were in Russia, Manuel was physically removed from the train they were travelling on. He was wearing only a lightweight woollen,

Italian-designed overcoat. Apparently, he was carrying too much cash, so the Russian authorities wanted to get to the bottom of it. Andy slept on oblivious to his father's predicament. Several hours later, after being interrogated by the most charming Russian officer (Manuel's words!), a little more subdued Manuel was returned to the train to find a still sleeping Andy. They went on to have a wonderful holiday exploring Russia and Czechoslovakia.

7
Professional progress and profound loss

In May 1980 I had my first glimpse into a professional future when I took my EBHS choir to perform as part of a massed choir for the Royal Charity Concert at Sydney Opera House. In the audience were Her Royal Highness Queen Elizabeth II and Prince Phillip, the Duke of Edinburgh. It was screened via the Nine Network and seen by viewers all over the world. The legendary Peter Faiman was the producer, and it was an honour to be included in such a gala event.

Hosted by Bert Newton, the concert itself was certainly memorable, featuring a luminary cast which included Peter Allen, Paul Hogan, Helen Reddy, Julie Anthony, John Farnham, Roger Woodward, Olivia Newton-John, Maestro Tommy Tycho, the Sydney Dance Company, the Australian Ballet, and an assortment of jugglers, acrobats and ventriloquists. I clearly remember thinking how much I'd like to produce a variety show like that, blending all genres of music.

I had a policy of taking my choirs outside the school to perform as often as reasonable. "Performance, performance, performance" was my motto. Again, I was acting purely on instinct. I firmly believed there wasn't any point just singing to ourselves inside the classroom and school hall. As a result we had the most wonderful years, always having exciting and challenging goals to work towards. Mateship, discipline and music education were the lessons learned both by myself and by my fabulous choir boys. They enjoyed enormous success wherever we went.

I was then contacted by Channel Seven, Epping. The CEO Ted Thomas had heard about my boys and wanted them to perform. We were asked to present carols for the locals at Epping. Channel Seven created the tallest Christmas tree in Sydney at that time. And newsreader Ross Symons was the host of this huge outdoor production.

My boys presented a full program of carols and were outstanding. Scanning the printed program notes I remember how I smiled as I read Ted Thomas' description of the EBHS choir as "the best in the state." I always thought they were anyway.

Then, suddenly, the light went out of my life on April 4, 1981, with the death of my beloved mother. When she died I lost the one person I felt who loved me unconditionally. I remember sitting and crying in my bedroom alone, not knowing how I would cope. She was the one person who had been there for me my whole life. She gave me strength and was always there to support me. She taught me how to love my children. I am so grateful I had a mother who knew how to give love and, perhaps more importantly, how to show it. After she died I used to think I could see her, that she would just pop up randomly in my everyday life. You know how that happens when someone you're so close to dies.

In March of that same year my nephew Doyle was killed in a car accident. His mother, my sister Geraldine, was in Sydney preparing for a St Patrick's Day party at our home when she got the phone call with the tragic news. She never fully recovered from losing her eldest son, and lost much of her exuberance and joy for life. When I think back now, how terrible must it have been for her then to lose Mum not long after. How awful not to have Mum there to comfort her through her grief, which never ended. Mum was the one person who would have most understood her tragic loss. That was the year we stopped singing around the piano as a family. Since that day we have never celebrated St Patrick's Day. It just brings back so many dreadfully painful memories. I took some EBHS singers to Merriwa to sing at Doyle's funeral.

But it wasn't just our family who suffered. That was also the year the AIDS epidemic became scary. Everyone we knew was losing friends.

Kate and Andy were then in early high school and now, when I look back, I do feel sad that I gave so much time, attention and energy to other people's children. I was a crusader for boys singing and I put all my energy into my work. I wonder now whether I should have also found time to give something to Andy and Kate's schools. I was always very nervous when seeing my children in their school concerts and musicals, and we didn't attend many secondary sporting events because neither of them showed any interest or skill in that direction.

May 1, 1983, was a significant date in my story. It was the official opening of the Sydney Entertainment Centre. The NSW Premier

Neville Wran officiated. The Sydney Entertainment Centre was a multi-purpose arena located in Sydney's Haymarket precinct. It replaced the Sydney Stadium, which had been demolished in 1970 to make way for the Eastern Suburbs railway line. At the time I had no idea Sydney Entertainment Centre would become my "office" for the next 30 years!

Sydney was certainly growing up. We had a new entertainment centre, there was soon to be a new Darling Harbour precinct and Australia's Bicentennial was only a matter of years away.

Barry Manilow was the first artist to put on an entire show at the new venue on May 7, 1983. A highlight of that concert was the finale. I brought together 200 singers in a massed choir to join the star singing his big hit, *One Voice*.

Tony Chapman (journalist) wrote at the time:

> *The high point for me was the work that had been done with a choir of local schoolboys to make One Voice the finale. Very few concert moments, before or since, have given me goosebumps the way that song did on the night.*

I don't doubt it gave him goosebumps! The boys looked amazing in their robes and the sound was out of this world. They really did us proud that night. We were all thrilled to be involved in such a huge celebrity's concert. Thanks to Kevin Jacobsen for inviting us to be part of it. I was also so pleased to have Andy, my son joining the singers.

Barry even came to the dressing room to visit the boys, and we took some Polaroid photos to mark the occasion. I entrusted these photos to Andy and sadly they never made it home. They were lost somewhere between the Sydney Entertainment Centre and Walker Street, Lavender Bay where we lived at the time. He was not too popular for that little episode!

I was then introduced to James Thane, CEO of The Really Useful Company. My choirs at EBHS were becoming well known in wider circles although I didn't know that at the time. James asked me to be children's choral director and coordinate the choirs for *Joseph and The Amazing Technicolour Dreamcoat*. This was to be staged at Her Majesty's Theatre, opening the following year on March 15, 1984.

I asked Joe Regan, the ever patient and encouraging principal of EBHS, for permission for the boys to be involved. Imagine my surprise and shock when he regretfully informed me it was against Education

Department policy to involve the students in a commercial production. I was outraged. I saw this as a fabulous opportunity not just for the boys but for the school. Everyone would gain so much from being in a professional production and working closely with music industry stars.

Devastated at having to say no to me, Joe arranged a meeting for me with the Education Department's community relations unit manager, the late Frank Meaney. I went into that meeting absolutely furious! In an effort to calm me down, Frank told me "something was in the air." He hinted that I'd be very excited by a new project that was in the pipeline. Little did I know then that the late Doug Swan, Director-General of the Department, had already set in motion a plan for me to create a public relations showpiece for the Education Department.

Not willing to take no for an answer with regard to *Joseph*, I found another way to involve my boys in the show. I simply created a new name for the choir: the Epping Boys' and Girls' Choir. Under this name, we appeared with choristers from Loreto Kirribilli, where Annie Power oversaw music, my sister Dot's school, Newington College, Cheltenham Girls High School and Aloysius College, Milsons Point. The real bonus was that I was now able to include both Kate and my niece Madeleine who were pupils at Loreto. It was an exciting experience for the young singers and a solid lesson for me about professional standards and discipline.

Joseph cast and Kate (far right)

Even though Andy wasn't able to be included in that choir, he was still there, mainly alongside me, watching my every move. He was part of the whole thing whether he wanted to be there or not. Now, years later, running his own production company, I do wonder if he maybe thinks back to that time and realises it wasn't all that bad being dragged along by Mum.

That's when life really started getting hectic, not that it hadn't been before. After the school holidays, rehearsals started for *Joseph* and we were all insanely busy. It was a marvellous experience for all the kids and gave them all something to remember for a lifetime. And while it was hard work for me, there were great rewards. I learned so much and met some great performers including Peter Casey and Angela Ayers. I didn't really have anything to do with the male lead, Darryl Cotton.

Peter continued to have a highly successful career as one of Australia's leading musical directors. Angela and I kept in touch. She stepped away for a time to have babies before returning to the stage. Of course she had to come back; it would have been such a shame to not hear that fabulous voice and her great range again. She even came into TDP a few times as a voluntary consultant. We came full circle in the 2023 production of *Joseph*, when two of my TDP graduates, Paulini and Trevor Ashley, had leading roles. How wonderful!

Through the production of *Joseph* I met the late Brian Walsh. Brian, who wound up as the boss of Foxtel, died suddenly in April 2023. When we met he had a PR and media company with ties to the NRL. He was a generous man and gave me some very worthwhile and valuable opportunities to produce big shows in the world of rugby league. I'm a huge admirer of Brian's well-deserved success and his passing was a great loss to the industry.

I was then approached by Alan Jones, coach of the Wallabies, to teach them to sing for their upcoming British Isles tour. Of course, the players were far more interested in the game than music, but I believe they enjoyed the experience. Alan felt it was important for them to sing the National Anthem properly. He also felt that singing together would help build team spirit, so they could match the Welsh, Scottish and Irish players they would face on the tour.

Not being particularly sports minded, I didn't know anything about Alan or the Wallabies. Manuel, who loved sport, said he thought

I should take up that invitation. So I gathered my EBHS rugby song books and went into St John's College. There they all were, Alan and the Wallabies – waiting to sing. It was time for another life lesson: believe in yourself. Although I never doubted that I could get them to sing. It has always been that way with all the choristers and hundreds of boys I've taught over the years. I remember we only had the one session and then there was the farewell for them at The Rugby Club in York Street, Sydney. The team went on to famously win the 1984 Grand Slam in England and Europe.

One of my teaching techniques was to point to an individual and shock them into singing solo. I got a surprise when I pointed to a player and asked him to sing *Waltzing Matilda*. I started with the very easy "one, two, three" and received an absolutely blank response. The player was Topo Rodriguez, and he'd only arrived in Australia from Argentina just a couple of days earlier!

They were a mighty team and I've kept contact with some of them over the years since then. People often take a step back in surprise when I tell them I taught the mighty 1984 Grand Slam Tour team, which included Andrew Slack, Mark Ella, Topo Rodriguez and David Campese, to sing.

That contact was also the beginning of a lifetime friendship with Alan Jones. Alan was a great friend of the SS and would voluntarily promote it at every opportunity on his then-2UE radio program. His station CEO, John Brennan, was also a great supporter. When they moved to 2GB a couple of years later, the SS went with them.

But what were Andy and Kate doing during this frantically busy time in my career? I was about to embark on the project which was going to fulfil my dreams and completely change my life and theirs. I now regret that I was so distracted and working so hard, that I wasn't around to experience and celebrate their accomplishments. I ache when I think of what I lost in those years.

Andy was already beginning to show his entrepreneurial side. At age 14, he established a rock band, appeared in school musicals and co-organised a rock concert at St Aloysius, Kirribilli. The band used to rehearse at our home and, although I wasn't often around, his father was happy to play roadie when they performed at school and other venues. It was only when he left school that I found out he had managed to avoid sport throughout his whole secondary education.

Interestingly, shortly after he left school, he joined a rugby union team. However, his sporting career was short-lived thanks to a knee injury. He was carried from the field in the first game of the season, as his very proud father watched on, shocked, and that was that.

With Cecil, Manuel and Clare at McDonalds prior to a family wedding

Meanwhile Kate was dealing with her physical disadvantages. She was frustrated because she couldn't finish her exams. So, together with her school, we tried to work out ways for her to handle examinations on an equal footing with her classmates. The first thing we tried was for her to be allowed extra time. This didn't help, however, because her hand wasn't able to cope after an hour of writing. We did some more research and eventually found a solution through Education Department resources. Just before her HSC year we realised that the only way to level the playing field was for Kate to work with a scribe. Kate dictated her exams to a student scribe who was always one grade lower, so as to not be able to assist her with the actual subject material. After many years of looking for a solution, imagine how thrilled we were when she went from the bottom of the class to the top.

Musical activities played a big part in Kate's life. She has a melodious and rich voice. During these busy years she appeared in the professional production of *Joseph* and had many happy times in the Australian Children's Choir under the direction of Sean O'Dea.

8
The Schools Spectacular

John Foreman talks about Mary
I auditioned John when he was 14 years old at Kotara High School. He is now one of Australia's leading TV hosts, musical directors and events producers.

***

A visionary is a person who can see what others don't see – potential. They can imagine a future and bring it into existence.

Mary Lopez is a visionary whose foresight, and insight, has forever changed the face of Australian entertainment and, in so doing, has transformed the lives of tens of thousands of Australians.

Perhaps most remarkably of all, Mary's ability to shape the future has manifest itself both on the grandest – and most personal – of levels.

In 1984 Mary was asked by bigwigs in the Department of Education in NSW to stage a concert to showcase performing arts in public schools.

Me and John Foreman

Mary took this relatively simple idea and saw an opportunity: she transformed the concert into an extraordinary entertainment event that has, so far, endured for more than 40 years, become a major live and television extravaganza and has provided an unforgettable learning experience for tens of thousands of young Australians: the NSW Schools Spectacular.

Arising from the Schools Spectacular was another opportunity that required Mary's visionary skills to bring to fruition: the Talent Development Project.

Mary saw the career potential of some of Schools Spec's featured performers and realised that they needed career guidance; she dreamed TDP into being and, in so doing, provided another great legacy for Australian performers: a not-for-profit organisation whose aim and objective is to help talented, young Australian performing artists have a sustainable career in the music industry.

And, on a personal level, Mary has maintained a rare ability to see potential. Through her leadership and mentoring work at TDP and Schools Spectacular, Mary has been able to unlock the potential talents of many performers, helping them to find skills they themselves may not have realised they possessed.

Mary would encourage a singer to develop their hidden songwriting skills; a dancer, their acting abilities; a musician, their singing or arranging abilities.

In my case, Mary could see something beyond my piano playing – she was the first person to provide me with a platform to learn how to MC an event and encouraged my abilities as a musical director.

But I am just one of many, many Australians whose skills have been encouraged, discovered and unlocked by Mary.

Mary Lopez has received numerous awards, accolades and honorary citations; but amongst her many achievements, perhaps the most enduring will be the quiet, personal and profound impact she has had on the lives of so many Australian performers and, by extension, the audiences they continue to entertain.

I was teaching full-time at EBHS when I became producer and director of the first SS. On reflection, I see now that the very first one was such a hit and miss event. All I knew was it was a fantastic opportunity to put on an amazing show involving all the things I loved. It was so exciting and I allowed my heart and gut to lead me.

My friend, the late Ian Skilton, a bookkeeper from Newcastle, had incredible musical theatre knowledge. Together we worked out the program for SS No. 1. Ian and I worked out the huge Australian flag finale in a coffee shop in Chatswood. Who else had ever unfurled an enormous flag in a schools variety concert? A really lovely man working in the community relations unit, Rob Foulcher, found the flag and we were under way.

Rod Heard, my colleague at EBHS, was the music arranger and musical director, while Graeme Russell, a music inspector, conducted the orchestra, which came from Sydney Conservatorium High School. Frank Meaney and the Education Department's community relations unit coordinated and marketed the show. The Department's publicity and marketing director, the vivacious Irina White, chased media and coached me in TV and radio interviews – an invaluable skill.

I would bounce ideas off my close friends, Ian and Rod. We spent hours planning the program's content. Meetings all happened after school hours and of a weekend. It was an enormous job, but we were so excited and passionate about the idea and absolutely committed to making it happen.

It all started when I received a call from Frank Meaney. He was working on a plan with Jack Neary, vice-chairman of Arena Management, and Bruce Harris, retired Australian managing director and chairman of SSC&B: Lintas Worldwide Advertising. This was the "something in the air" Frank had mentioned in our previous meeting.

Frank, Bruce and Jack worked together on a children's television commission committee. Jack, a director of the Sydney Entertainment Centre, had been inspired by the school choirs and instrumental ensembles that had performed at a pre-opening event to test the acoustics in the new venue. Aware of my passion and ambitions for my six EBHS choirs, Frank invited me to a meeting to discuss the idea of taking this concept to another level.

The Education Department's music branch had already produced a concert to test the acoustics of the Sydney Entertainment Centre with massed choirs and an orchestra. It has been claimed by some that this was the beginning of the SS, but I can tell you it wasn't. It was, instead, the music branch's regular style of concert, with no dance. And it was far from a spectacular event.

Behind the scenes, Doug Swan, Director-General of the Education Department, had been doing his own research. His grandson was a student at EBHS and Doug wanted to create a public relations flagship event for the Department. At the time I was unaware Doug's grandson was a student, so I didn't realise he'd attended some of my musical events. These were variety concerts, not the Gilbert & Sullivan-type musicals that seemed to be prevalent in most schools back then. Doug liked the variety and inclusiveness of the EBHS concerts and understood the direction they could go with support.

I knew the choir world because I was in the thick of it and I firmly believed I could create massed displays by utilising the choir members to their full capacity. This was the beginning of giving choirs activity and movement to make the performing experience more visually stimulating.

Having originally been approached to "put on a concert" I seized the chance to create a show that was really all about making dreams come true. Looking back on it all now I realise the scope of the cast and the spectacle was extraordinary. This new type of show was indeed a "spectacular" of song, dance and display, colour and entertainment not seen before in education. Because of my upbringing and my social conscience, I also saw this as a chance to create something magnificent while teaching some really strong lessons. I'm proud to say I was the creator of what I named the Schools' Spectacular.

There were 40 schools involved in the first SS, most showcasing their choirs. EBHS was the main performing force and the backbone of the event – the students, parents and teachers. The EBHS teachers stage-managed the 1,700 performers, taking a lot of the strain off me. Most of the other student performers were taught by teachers whom I knew through the choir network and many came from performing in other massed choir concerts.

Wendy Tierney from Tower St Public School brought her choirs to perform in that first SS and has been contributing ever since. Later she later watched as her own children, Andrew and Michael, who went through the SS and TDP, blossoming into Human Nature. Her daughter Margaret, another high achiever, became Miss Australia in 1995.

Cheltenham Girls High School was also a key contributor.

We needed to think big. We required big numbers and we had to find anything big to create a spectacle. When I first walked on to the arena to inspect the site for the first SS, I thought: "I'm never going to be able to fill up this space." That's where the idea of using the massed choir as a "moving choir" came from. I realised I could fill that massive space with vibrant young choristers.

The *Carmen* segment came together in my lounge room at Lane Cove. I loved the opera *Carmen* and my choirs at Epping had sung the Toreador song before. It was familiar and I felt I could make it look good. The moving, massed choir provided the cast spectacle I envisaged. We filled the floor with the massed choir secondary members who were costumed to look and move like Spanish gypsies. My ex-students' choir from EBHS, Eklipse, performed as the toreadors to give some power and depth to the choral sound and add to the spectacle. They looked magnificent in their Eklipse costumes with red capes swung from their shoulders.

The choir members loved being such a vibrant part of the show. That was literally the start of the concept of choir not only singing but being more actively involved with appropriate and good-fun body and hand movements. The ribbon twirlers and acrobatics came later in the show.

Kate recalls how as a 12-year-old she was taken to the SS rehearsals conducted by me and Ian Skilton in the EBHS assembly hall. She remembers us choreographing the choirs to perform the Spanish segment. She thought that was great fun.

The late Ross Milne came on board with the massed display concept, bringing great ideas which involved more props for the choir and enhanced the spectacle. I have wonderful memories of both him and the late Laurel Barranikow, working tirelessly to calculate the incredible mathematical exercise with hundreds of cards for the massed choir. Laurel went on to become the magnificent SS costume designer for the next 25 years.

Wendy Tierney (mother of Human Nature), Laurel and me celebrating 30 years of service

Rolf Harris was the first major artist associated with the SS. I always saw Rolf as a gentleman, respectful to the young performers, despite the revelations in later years. He was maybe a little daggy and a bit over the top with some of his comments, but at that time he appeared to be a complete professional.

The SS executive producer was Rolf's brother, the late Bruce Harris. He was very keen to see Rolf in the spotlight. Bruce created the printed programs, naming every school included for every show, a practice that has continued to this day.

Bruce saw the Spectacular as a way of reviving Rolf's flagging career. He really was the best big brother anyone could hope for. I believe he fell in love with the SS from the beginning. He couldn't do enough to help the students, all of whom he admired and considered to be enormously talented. He was so soft hearted and could be relied on to shed many tears throughout each show. We shared some wonderful years until his retirement in 2002. That was about SS No. 18. Thanks to Bruce's hard work in writing extensive program notes for each show I am prompted to remember many contributors and facts which otherwise would slip by me.

1985 SS production Team

As I now look through that first program, I am reminded of the trailblazing teachers who took the risk and brought their students to participate in this new type of show. They brought their choirs, drama groups, cadets, acrobats and dancers. They gave their students an opportunity to showcase all their performing skills. I just had to convince them that this new Spectacular was something they'd love. They came on board and stayed for many, many years – all of them.

I called on all the teachers I knew through my choir network. Anne Ratty, a drama consultant, provided circus acts, acrobats and jugglers, and the item from Farrar School for the Deaf. Sue Rix (who later worked at the arts unit and became dance director), Debra Mann and Bob Pritchard also presented solo items.

Dance was limited at that time, because dance programs had just started in public schools. The legendary Betty Barnes was the Education Department's dance consultant and she recommended Judi Joy and John Mullins to me as dance teachers. John and Judi were major players in establishing dance in public education and the SS was a great vehicle to inspire this type of performance. They came on board and subsequently choreographed dance items in every show for about 30 years.

For this first Spectacular, each segment was inspired by passion. The magic of Spain shone through the *Carmen* section while the third segment was Songs of War, which was obviously a tribute to the ANZACs and those who paid the ultimate price defending our country.

My passion for respecting the sacrifices made by the ANZACs so that we could have a life of peace led to a segment being developed for the show. I've spoken earlier about my respect for the ANZACs and the other men and women who have fought for served our nation. I believe we need to acknowledge how lucky we are to live in the most peaceful country in the world. At the time of the first SS there was some reprehensible behaviour and attitudes around with people showing a lack of respect for our Vietnam veterans and especially ANZAC Day. I was even criticised for "warmongering" by some. I disagree entirely. I know I used the Schools Spectacular as a forum to teach the lessons of respect for those who sacrificed much for our country.

Minnie the Moocher was Bruce Harris's contribution and was choreographed by Sue Rix. *Cats* was the theatre show of the time and we just had to include it. *The Gloria* from *Misa Criolla* (a South

American Mass inspired by my productions of *The Royal Hunt of the Sun*) was another song the choirs at EBHS already knew and we were sure we could make it look good if we added a group of dancers.

The finale segment – an Australian tribute – was the beginning of my commitment to presenting Australian music and moving away from the American influence on our local entertainment scene. In later years we would proudly present our own shining stars, like John Williamson. The Australian section was highlighted by the inclusion of Farrar School for the Deaf signing choir, which proved they were as capable as those who were a part of the mainstream entertainment scene.

Although regional representation was light on in the first Spectacular, it quickly grew once word got out about the show.

A tiny but "magician-like" team of volunteers pulled off the first SS on 20 August 1984. The production team of four people and 45 magnificent, dedicated teachers opened the door to what has become the flagship for public education. EBHS teacher, Jim Bennett, remained the overall stage manager for 17 years. A young woman by the name of Trudy Dalgleish, an electrician at the venue, was asked to light the first show. She has done so ever since and is arguably now Australia's finest lighting designer. I didn't know much then about the technical support needed to stage something like this, I just had the grand ideas. The staff at the Sydney Entertainment Centre came to the rescue and provided the staging, technical skills and equipment to make the performances come to life. It must have been an absolute nightmare for those responsible for creating quality sound in a venue as massive as the Sydney Entertainment Centre – particularly having to accommodate so many microphones for the huge cast and orchestra.

It is a constant source of wonder to audiences how the SS appears to be a seamless production. It's thanks to the dedicated team of teachers, who are prepared to remain in the background, shepherding thousands of performers as they wait in the wings for their turn on stage. They take on this huge responsibility year after year and fulfil their task with love and care.

After the finale of that first SS, the audience erupted with a standing ovation. It was then that the SS was confirmed as an icon on the Australian entertainment scene for the next 40-plus years. It truly was a spectacular night and a huge relief for me when it was over. So successful was the first Spectacular that the green light for the next show was given almost immediately. In future it would be seen as the launching pad for not only performers but creative and technical personnel across the entertainment industry. Doug Swan, the Director General, treated the EBHS music and sporting staff to dinner to celebrate the remarkable success of SS No. 1.

Then it was straight back into the classroom with no time to dwell on feeling excited or proud. I was just too busy to enjoy it. I was still teaching fulltime at EBHS with all my choirs and elective music classes including HSC students. We continued to enter and win Sydney Eisteddfod Championships and of course, at the end of the year had Carols by Candlelight for Channel Seven at Epping.

Because the Spectacular concept was completely new, the children were not generally confident, and so the smiles were not so forthcoming as they were in later shows. The talent was always there but the performing skills were not. It took quite a few SSs before we saw the emergence of talent combined equally with performing skills. Even so, the SS had opened the world of entertainment for me.

Frank took a huge risk with me and my big ideas, and I think he was the person most relieved when the SS was a success. He said to me later that night he felt that his job was on the line.

With Bruce Harris and Jack Neary

When I first took the ideas for a Spectacular concept to a meeting of the executive committee (Frank, Bruce and Jack) everyone thought it was fabulous except for Jack. He said: "Who do you think you are – a bloody entrepreneur?." I possibly should have been intimidated by this but I wasn't. I was too caught up in realising my dream. Jack eventually became very supportive of the big vision and used all of his very powerful network to ensure I had everything I needed. I credit him with introducing me into the entertainment industry. He knew just about everyone in it and loved and admired talent. It was because of Jack that we had the magnificent Sydney Entertainment Centre (SEC) as our venue with all the personnel and resources it could supply. Kevin Jacobsen, who stood alongside of Jack as a director of SEC, was equally enthusiastic and supportive of the new idea.

Over Christmas that year, Manuel, Kate and I travelled to Italy, Spain and New York, where we were joined by our American friend, Rita. Manuel and I had separated the previous year. I could no longer cope with his drinking, his awful behaviour towards the kids and me, and his anger. The lack of intimacy was also still there. Manuel was devastated. Through counselling we both learned about our destructive behaviours. I know now that one of the issues was that we didn't know each other very well, because we married only three months after we met. Neither of us had any intellectual maturity. We should have been friends first and not rushed into marriage. Thankfully we did become great friends over the next dramatic years.

The trip was an attempt on his part to reconcile us. However, we weren't ready, and I made it very difficult for anyone to really enjoy the trip. I was too angry and what should have been a glorious overseas trip turned into what Kate still refers to as "the fighting trip." After one of our famous blues, Kate, Manuel and I were walking together back towards our hotel, the famous Algonquin on 42nd street, about 11pm. We were then warned to get off the streets by a security guard at a nightclub we tried to visit. He made it clear it was unsafe and ordered a cab for us. New York was clearly a dangerous place to be at night in those days.

On the flipside, our holiday did introduce me to a whole new world of performance – the sophisticated world of cabaret and New

York musical theatre. We heard celebrated cabaret artist Julie Wilson, who was singing at the Algonquin. Since we were staying there, we had nightly access to her performances. This exposure and education became the inspiration for the TDP Broadway scholarships which I initiated some 30 years later with Michael Kerker, in 2006.

Regardless, the fighting during that trip must have done Manuel and me some good because we got back together the following year. I realised I had no right to deprive the children of their father although I was upset by Manuel's lack of physical interest in me. It was a revelation to me that they loved their "often angry" Dad as much as they loved me.

Schools Spectacular No. 2

When it came time to plan for the SS No. 2 in 1985, I knew the lessons I wanted to teach alongside providing great performance opportunities and entertainment. The concept was to keep it very Australian, hence all the Australian folk songs. I also saw this as a chance to pay respect to our Aboriginal culture, create a level playing field and show disability as the norm.

Two fabulously dedicated principals, Colleen and the late Phil Hayward were huge contributors to the SS. Colleen was a champion of Indigenous people, while her husband Phil was passionate about involving students with disability in performance. Both have since won the Mary Lopez Medal for their outstanding work as teachers in the SS. They would do anything for their students and both were excellent role models, way ahead of their time. Colleen also joined me in preparing Indigenous children being taken to dance at World Expo '85 in Tsukuba, Japan.

Their son, Peter, is a passionate musical theatre guru, still actively involved as a producer and director of theatrical and large-scale productions both in education and the professional theatre. Peter takes himself off to productions at the drop of a hat anywhere in the world, but especially New York.

Rob Foulcher joined the team in 1985 and came up with the practical solution to my idea of having a three-ring circus tent as the focus of SS No. 2 (a bicycle wheel).

The circus in 1985 SS

Jan and Barry Foster, who were then teaching at Dubbo South High School, fell in love with SS and trained gymnasts and dancers for the second production. They became dedicated contributors and supporters and led me to open the SS to schools from western NSW and isolated communities. Jan and Barry took me to four public schools at Ivanhoe, Tilpa, Bourke and Wanaaring, and introduced me to pupils studying via School of the Air.

My aim was to showcase these children just as they were with the inherent belief that everyone is a performer. It was so important for me to show city people that culture existed over the sandstone wall of the Great Dividing Range. To me that was where the true Australia existed.

We brought many of these kids to Sydney and opened their eyes to the world of entertainment. These children certainly educated many of the "city slickers" on the SS team about the reality of talent outside the confines on Sydney.

Jan and Barry uncovered some extraordinarily talented youngsters including livewire singer and actor Tracey Case, as well as nationally acclaimed musical director and conductor Kelly Dickerson. They nurtured these performers through the music and dance programs at Dubbo South High School.

The trips were extraordinary adventures for me, and I loved being back in my beautiful country. We also visited two darling children from the School of the Air, whose idol was Nadia Komenich. They had their own gym bar set up in the yard on their property.

The second Spectacular was used to launch the International Year of Peace the following February (1986). Prime Minister Bob Hawke joined the cast on the floor of Sydney Entertainment Centre for the finale, *We Are The World*. Eleven-year-old Andrew Tierney made his first appearance on that second show. We then had another win when Australian businessman Dick Smith was so impressed he opened his wallet, giving a substantial contribution to the production.

Bob Hawke with me and some of the SS cast members

Over the next few years several guest stars were invited to participate, to encourage children to aspire to professional levels of performance. This included jazz musicians Billy Burton and Andrew Firth, opera singers Robert Allman and Amanda Thane, the Sydney Dance Company, the Aboriginal Islander Dance Company, John Williamson and Ricky May.

Australia Week at World Expo '85

In May 1985, I was invited by Jack Neary and Kevin Jacobsen to direct the Australia Week concerts in Tsukuba, Japan at World Expo '85. What an opportunity for a girl from the bush! After just one SS, I'd been recognised by some of the biggest names in the entertainment industry. The Education Department granted me leave to direct the entertainment in Japan. I was still a full-time teacher at Epping BHS.

In Tsukuba, I met the Tourism and Sport Minister John Brown when he visited the expo site. He was so friendly and handsome. This was the beginning of our lifetime friendship. John became a support for me throughout the rest of my career and we're still the best of friends to this day.

Kevin was promoter of the concerts in Japan, and I seized the opportunity I was so lucky to have been given. He gave me several chances to work on shows which very much took me outside my comfort zone. I'm so grateful to him for the chance to learn and broaden my network. Kevin was one of the most generous and enthusiastic men in the entertainment industry. I learned a lot about professional production meetings, and I threw myself into the unknown. I grabbed hold of this chance with both hands, even though I'd previously had no experience of such a momentous production. But remember, I'd always been convinced by my mother that I was capable of anything.

I attended production meetings and was able to advise on the cast. This cast included James Morrison, the late David Gulpilil with the Indigenous component consisting of the pupils from Darlington PS and the Aboriginal Islander Dance Company, pianist Roger Woodward, opera singer Rosamunde Illing and the Sydney Dance Company. Rolf Harris was employed to compere and perform. Another of my dreams had come true.

I recall there was one particularly memorable night when we were celebrating in a café after we'd finished our shows. I found myself sitting in a booth with World Expo '85 concert production manager Christine Dunstan and lighting designer Don Byrne. We were listening to James Morrison and David Gulpilil improvising and creating magical music. It was certainly an unforgettable evening.

My love for blending all genres of music and showcasing Indigenous Australians was clearly evident in the cast I advised for those Australia Week concerts in Japan.

I had learned about variety in Kevin's previous productions such as the 1980 Royal Charity Concert in the presence of the late Queen Elizabeth II at Sydney Opera House, and again in the Sydney Entertainment Centre opening in 1983. My EBHS choirs had been included in those gala concerts and numerous other major events. Kevin's productions featured international and Australian stars in all genres of music and entertainment.

Directing the Australia Day concerts World Expo '85 was pivotal in my future direction.

Christine Dunstan, the acclaimed production manager of the concerts schooled me in the technical and production world which in turn lifted me and the SS onto the next level. Christine brought home to me the importance of having professional technical experts like Don Byrnes, and later Michael Scott Mitchell, who designed the set for the Incas. Christine not only educated me but very generously donated her service to production manage Spectacular No. 2. She returned for further Spectaculars, offering her services for mate's rates. She was always very patient and tolerant.

I also met Tony Moffat, Chris Kennedy and Meri Took, who owned companies that were very free with their technical advice and expertise for the SS over the years I was leading the team. As I look back now I see how the SS provided opportunities for many technical and staging suppliers, quite a number of whom are now giants in the entertainment industry.

Back to the second Spectacular

After the first SS, we set up a creative team composed of a few teachers who were motivated to give their students the thrill of performing in such an exciting venue, plus the small group of us who'd pulled together the very first SS.

The teachers who joined us were Lyndall and Greg Bowman, who were young and enthusiastic members of the production team. Greg Bowman has since become famous on the international scene through his music for Olympics' ceremonies and creating other huge events. He was always full of energy, passion and big ideas. Greg soon left education to set up his own company called Great Big Events. I was very touched to receive a beautiful bunch of flowers and a congratulations from Greg on the 20th anniversary of the SS.

Ian Skilton, Rod Heard, John Mullins, Judi Joy, Laurel Barranikow and I would meet either at my home at Lane Cove, or at other team members' homes. Those creative meetings were sensational and went until all hours of the night. Remember that this was all voluntary and after hours work at this stage. We were all teachers holding down full-time jobs. How on earth I ever had the energy or time to lead and inspire, I now find impossible to imagine. But I did. We all did. Over a little food and wine and lots of laughter, the show came together seamlessly.

When I look at the photos of the fabulous teachers on those early productions I experience such a wave of affection and respect for them all. They look so young and passionate, and I remember how much fun we all had. The camaraderie that grew from those early days has continued and it is that that has kept the SS going. Everyone who came near the SS was injected with a shot of energy and optimism.

The SS was able to survive because each team member took a responsibility for his or her role, and I stopped micro-managing. It was the only way to go. The show has always been built on trust and the teachers involved are amazing individuals who give up so much of their time to educate and enhance the lives of their students.

The cast for Spectacular No. 2 soon grew to 2,000 after I conducted auditions in Dubbo, Albury, Lithgow, Gunnedah and the South Coast, enticing additional bands and schools to participate. I knew we needed to take the message directly to the teachers whom I knew would be as passionate as I was about this new and exciting performance opportunity.

In August 1985, I produced and directed a pageant in historic Parramatta Park for the opening of Education Week on behalf of Metropolitan West region. This was a very tricky location and a huge spectacle. The show was amusing with the inclusion of trainee chefs from the Ryde TAFE catering course, who proceeded through to the amphitheatre surrounded by 200 children from public schools, costumed as pieces of fruit. The whole program was joyful and went off with a bang.

Of course, in my "spare time" I still organised the Carols by Candlelight, performed by EBHS choirs and soloists that year for Channel Seven.

Below is an excerpt from a letter by Doug Swan the Director General for Education in 1984. He outlines his rationale for the creation of public education's flagship performance. He wrote it after attending the 25th Anniversary of the SS and gave it to me when he invited me to lunch.

The Schools Spectacular

Amidst the myriad of issues confronting the Department of Education during the 1980s was the constant concern about the image of public education being presented by the media. were constantly under the microscope with standards in literacy and numeracy alleged to be falling, despite clear evidence to the contrary. Good news regarding schools and their achievements did not really interest readers or viewers.

While Education Week focused on each school and its immediate community where the feedback was positive, the sum of these views did not equate with the view of the education system.

Choral and artistic efforts such as Art Express and the Choral and Instrumental concerts in the Sydney Town Hall and Opera House for both primary and secondary pupils were well supported by the parents and schools involved, yet never received mention in the media.

The scene at the local, district and regional level was very positive in relation to these educational activities, with the media willing to cover these events.

While the orchestral performances in the Opera House and Sydney Town Hall were of a very high standard, and I regularly attended these, I had a concern that these reflected only one aspect of the music being encouraged in our schools, the programs reflecting an emphasis on classical or "highbrow" music.

This was the perception of many in the schools and of many of the music consultants attached to regional directorates where they were *endeavouring to broaden the scope to reflect the popularity of bands and folk music, of dance and other activities.*

I was well aware of the diversity of music being developed in our schools as my wife and I were constantly attending the evening performances of musicals in schools throughout the state.

In addition to the aforementioned central focus in music, the department annually participated in the Sydney Festival, held in January of each year. Among many activities during this month, we presented a week of Gilbert and Sullivan operettas.

In education, money for such activities was always tight, so the Commonwealth Bank generously sponsored these performances, providing $20,000 annually.

January was not an ideal month in which to assemble school students for practise or performance, venues in the city were costly to hire, so the performances were usually scheduled for the TAFE hall at Darlinghurst or facilities at Andrew Mackie Teachers' College. In January 1984 we had a real breakthrough when the Conservatorium of Music allowed us to use their music hall at no cost. On that occasion we presented The Pirates of Penzance *for one week. On the night of the official performance, where I had invited a number of special guests, among them David McNicholl, the editor of* The Daily Telegraph, *we discussed at the interval the performance. He expressed the strong view to me that Gilbert and Sullivan was not really suited to teenage voices which were still not mature enough to have clarity, hence much of the dialogue on stage was not appreciated by the audience.*

His observations reflected my own views on such operettas, but on this occasion, I was an interested listener who kept my views to myself, not wanting to be quoted in the media the following day.

No review of the performance appeared in the media, even though many of the reporters attended as my guest.

The following morning, I had a lengthy discussion with Frank Meaney, the Director of Public Relations, in which I canvassed my unease about those matters in music which I have mentioned above. I indicated that I had attended a musical evening at Epping Boys' High School in November 1983 which produced a diversity of musical performances consistent with those I had observed in many secondary schools.

The person responsible for that evening's program was Mary Lopez and I asked him to visit the school to discuss the possibility of presenting in a central venue a musical program over one week which would reflect the diversity of music education in our schools, this adding to the orchestral and choral performances being held in the Opera House and Sydney Town Hall.

Such was to be held during the school term. I indicated I would provide additional staffing at Epping High School if she were willing to accept the challenge to organise such an event in a venue such as the Entertainment Centre.

Fortunately, Mary Lopez agreed to work with Frank Meaney to develop a proposal for a Schools Spectacular, as the proposal was named, when I met with the state manager of the Commonwealth Bank, Jack Brighton, to discuss a possible funding of this concept. Frank accompanied me, also present being Major-General Gordon Maitland, in charge of public relations at the bank. Our proposal was to replace the musical performances held during the Sydney Festival and funded by the Commonwealth Bank with a major spectacle for which we needed $100,000, a not insignificant amount.

Within a week I was invited to a luncheon at the bank where it was announced that the Commonwealth Bank would sponsor the Schools Spectacular.

So we were on our way, never realising that it would prove such a resounding success and provide a real window of what was happening in music education in our schools.

I then set up a committee composed of Sydney metropolitan people working in public education, and with expertise in music to assist Mary Lopez to bring the concept to fruition.

Already the staff and headmaster at Epping Boys High School had indicated their willingness to be involved. I often wonder if they realised initially the immense burden it would place on them in terms of time and effort.

At an evening following the 1984 performances where I hosted a dinner for the Epping group and their wives, they were elated at the success of the performances and I heard no murmurings about the workload; maybe murmurings might have been kept to the staffroom but their role became central to the Spectacular over many years.

The rest is history. The Spectacular has gone from strength to strength as a showpiece of music and dance in public schools throughout New South Wales, its participants including small schools in remote areas.

It receives media coverage on national networks. In 2008, Bob Winder and his wife Marion and I were guests at the 25th anniversary of the Spectacular where we admired the splendid production, this still in the hands of Mary Lopez, the outstanding director for so many years.

Doug Swan
Director-General
NSW Department of Education

9
New year, new productions

The year 1986 was a very important year for me because it was the year my political network began to develop. A public performance group was formed within the Education Department's community relations unit. I was engaged to produce an enormous body of work, including four huge cast spectaculars – Overture for Peace for the Federal Government, a production featuring 2,000 performers as part of the Queen's Official Opening of Parramatta Stadium, the Education Expo at the Whitlam Centre, and of course the SS No 3. I had a team of three part-time consultants assisting me, Rod Heard, Lyndall Bowman and Denise Smith.

At that point I was working two days a week in the Department's Community Relations Unit and three days a week at EBHS.

Frank Meaney (back row left) and Rob Foulcher (grey suit) from DOE Community Relations unit with PM Bob Hawke, Hon Bill Haydn and the team who pulled the SS together

The year opened with a February production to launch the International Year of Peace, which was a recreation of the 1985 SS. The Overture for Peace at the Sydney Entertainment Centre served as the Opening for the International Year of Peace. A highlight of the event was the moment when Bob Hawke (then Australian Prime Minister) spontaneously joined the thousands of kids on the arena for the finale. He hoisted one of the kindy dancers onto his shoulders. The Prime Minister must have surprised his security officers. I don't know such a thing could happen now, when we have the threat of terrorism looming over our heads. Premier Barrie Unsworth and other NSW government members and public servants also attended. They loved the talent and the spectacle.

April Pressler, who was at that time first secretary in the Hawke Government, was the one who set it up. We became very good friends and Manuel and I enjoyed some hilarious times with April and her partner, the Archibald prize-winning artist, Keith Looby. She was a very important influence and her recommendation saw the SS move into another realm. We were now nationally recognised.

I then produced and directed the entertainment for the Official Opening of Parramatta Stadium. The event was of course all about speeches by politicians and local dignitaries and sportspersons. The entertainment included some solo items from SS 1985 and a cast of 2,000 in a spectacular display on the new arena. The stadium was opened by Her Majesty, the late Queen Elizabeth II, and was thrilling for the people of Parramatta, in particular ARL Eels supporters, who were at the top of their game in that year. Dubbo South HS dancers came nearly 400 km to be a part of the display and Barry and Jan Foster, their teachers, became a crucial part of the SS team from then onwards.

Later that year I advised on the production of Education Expo at the Whitlam Centre in Liverpool. It was at a rehearsal for this production that I met a teacher who had a group of disabled children who were performing in the show. One of the children, who was in a wheelchair, had had a similar health background to my daughter, Kate. My conversation with the teacher had a profound effect and reinforced my conviction to always include children with disabilities in the SS. The teacher said to me that the difference between the child in the wheelchair, who was only able to do very little, and my Kate, who was then leading a "normal" life was that "Kate has a mother like you." It broke my heart while also proving to me that my determination and patterning of Kate had been right and had worked in the long run.

To conclude the International Year of Peace, the SS No. 3 was titled Performance For Peace. The late Ricky May and John Williamson joined the cast, which featured strong Australian content and big spectacular items. Performers from Papua New Guinea International HS were visiting so we invited them to join us. I remember how this created much consternation within the Education Department because the dancers were bare-breasted. However, we managed to overcome the hysteria and the item was very well received. The dancers delighted in the experience of performing in such a huge venue.

The SS opens for talent from over the Great Dividing Range

In 1987, I was appointed full-time into the Community Relations Unit. Frank Meaney told me it was important to branch out and to include a broader reach into the regions of NSW. Andrew Bee took over my role at EBHS as music teacher. He was a young, enthusiastic and extraordinarily talented musician. His mother was a noted music educator and, as a schoolboy, he'd learned some valuable lessons working in productions with his mother and Ross Milne, then a teacher at McKellar Girls High School. He quickly embraced the busy music scene at EBHS and the SS that year. Andrew was to become a leader in the creative and technical development of the SS in the years that followed. He was my right-hand man in both the SS and TDP until my retirement. He left the Department to join my son's company a few years later. He and Andy are now business partners in the highly successful Out There Group.

I threw myself into work, leading the Public Performance Group and we created some huge cast spectaculars in some unusual and tricky locations. For example, I was advisory producer and director for the Moree Spirit of Youth Outdoor and Indoor Spectacular for all schools in the Western Region for Education Week. This involved travelling to Moree to advise the enthusiastic team of teachers on how to stage their massive show using two venues, the new large, multi-purpose hall and the attached oval. The result was a very successful and memorable

Education Week opening involving pupils from all over the north-west region. I do have to say that it's more enjoyable for me now that I'm writing about these productions than it was at the time … now there's no stress involved!

The SS was opened up to Western NSW and SS No. 4 included, for the first time, students from remote country areas. I achieved my goal to break down the barrier and sandstone wall of the Great Dividing Range when 51 children from the outback schools performed that year. They had an experience of a lifetime and *March To Australia*, sung by John Williamson, showcased their outback lives. Ricky May joined the cast, while magnificent musicians and arrangers, Maestro Tommy Tycho and Arthur Greenslade (Shirley Bassey's arranger) were now helping out with music arrangements for the orchestra and choir. The cast now numbered 2,500 performers.

Working with Ricky May

I actively set out to level the playing field for country kids. I applied and was given permission to take trips into the country to unearth and develop country talent and give country kids equal opportunity to perform. The trips became extraordinary adventures for me and it was wonderful to be back in my beloved country towns and open spaces. Over the next couple of years I made more time to visit outback schools to provide access to SS for isolated schools. I was a country girl and proud of it so I wanted to show it off. I became insistent that we reach into the isolated country towns, not just the big centres like Orange and Dubbo. The Education Department were not all that interested in reaching out to the regional areas and actively supporting rural participation, but neither did they stop me. To this day I believe many of the people involved in the management of SS have barely crossed over the Great Dividing Range.

Barry and Jan Foster were two amazing teachers who were then teaching at Dubbo South High School. They became extremely dedicated contributors and supporters of the SS, leading to the participation of schools from the Western and outback regions of NSW. They took me to tiny schools and communities way out west and we brought those kids to Sydney and introduced them to the world of entertainment. The Fosters never ceased to source new talent throughout their entire association with the SS and later, the TDP.

My first outback trip organised by Jan and Barry was to Louth, Tilpa, Ivanhoe Bourke and Wanaaring. This is where we came across unusual acts like gymnasts from the School of the Air. These amazing students had studied gymnastic techniques via television. I even auditioned performers in their lounge rooms. One of whom was the now famous Musical Director the late Kelly Dickerson. Another find was Drew McAlister, who made a tape of himself singing. The Fosters played the tape to me over the phone, demonstrating his amazing voice and his ability to hold long notes. This tape became Drew's audition for the SS. He went on to be a Golden Guitar winner at Tamworth and has a huge profile in Australian country music.

Barry and I also visited schools like Nyngan, Bourke and Cobar. It was so moving to walk into the bar of a hotel and see a sign and a collection box: "Help send our kids to the Schools Spectacular." I felt like a crusader who was introducing city folk to the world I had come from. Thank God for people like the Fosters who shared my passion.

On a later visit to Weilmoringle Public School in 1990s we were accompanied by the celebrated journalist, Jennifer MacDonald with an ABC team. All the kids in that school were Aboriginal and the school was like an oasis in the outback.

I travelled about 30 times into regional and outback areas during my years with the SS and TDP, seeking to give young Australians from outside city areas the best opportunity to share the stage – to have an equal opportunity to perform, to give them the opportunities that I missed as a country kid. On my trips I met some amazing teachers who created new and exciting Spectacular adventures to perform in

Sydney for their isolated pupils. I'd love to see them again and to hear their recollections. For example, there was the sensational Principal at Hermidale PS school (just outside Nyngan), Anne-Maree McAnaulty. She coordinated five one-teacher schools (Hermidale, Louth, Engonia, Nymagee and Wanaaring PS) to perform an hilarious item about the Todd River Dry bed race in 1999. I honestly don't ever remember meeting anyone more dedicated and passionate.

Alongside this was the wonderful "Ascott Gavotte" and the first appearance of John Deacon's brilliant horse puppets from New Lambton Primary School. Also in this segment were dancers from Bathurst High School, Kelso High School and Orange High School. It was always a joy to walk through the outdoor carport at the back of the Sydney Entertainment Centre and be welcomed by John and his bubbly wife Julie. They would set up their production workshop on site, and create a fun-filled bustling environment.

In 2001, when I was on a 4WD car rally, I was able to visit Tibooburra PS. The rally organisers arranged to have the children sing for us. It was thrilling for everyone there when I offered them a spot in the SS, where they sang the National Anthem. They sang-shouted, barefooted, with such enthusiasm that the audience was brought to tears. Imagine how hard it would have been for the families of Tibooburra to raise the money needed to bring those children to Sydney. I even held a fundraising dinner for them at my home and invited the drivers from the car rally to donate to the school fund raising fund. I was in an hotel in Tibooburra some years later, chatting to a local father of one of the kids. He told me it was a wonderful and unforgettable experience for them all.

In the SS printed programs up until 1994, Bruce Harris charted the steady inclusion of all the Education Departmental Regions. Through this we were able to see the steady levelling of the playing field and to acknowledge the wonderful work of public school teachers throughout the state.

On the other hand, I used to get so irritated when some members of the Department's music scene used criticise me for what they saw as "token inclusions." Comments such as "country kids weren't talented enough" infuriated me. I knew the only problem was that they weren't experienced enough because they didn't get the same opportunities as the city kids. I knew the potential of those country kids because I was one of those kids.

Already the backlash against my style of production was being felt in music circles in the Department and amongst conservative school principals and departmental administrative personnel. I honestly couldn't believe that they would not embrace such an exciting opportunity for their pupils to perform. I know the teachers loved what we were doing but I fear it envy and jealousy were driving the detractors.

My brother, Ian, was a great educator. He was a highly thought of Inspector of Schools and worked with many school principals. He encouraged me not to give up and to ignore the disparagers of the Spectacular. I really appreciated the celebratory and congratulatory functions he held for me and the family at his home at Kenthurst. No-one else in departmental circles thought to say "well done." His acknowledgement and encouragement gave me the will to continue and the strength to ignore the negative comments.

On the family front, Andy graduated from St Aloysius College, Milsons Point. His HSC year is amusing in retrospect. He was not a dedicated student. He had unlimited access to a car and he and his mates spent hours in Tom Fletcher's father's office at Sydney University. I can only imagine that what went on there was what you'd expect from 17/18 years olds.

I'm saddened to say that I feel I missed some important years of my own children's lives by being caught up in the establishment of the SS. These were enormous years for me in my new career. First taking over the full-time role coordinating events for the Education Department and visiting so many country regions to open up the SS. The following year was the 1988 Bicentenary year and there were so many productions.

Australia Day 1988 at Kirribilli house

The Bicentenary year and a move to Walker St, Lavender Bay

The year began with Manuel and I being invited to Kirribilli House for the announcement of the Australian of the Year, John Farnham. In those days the winner was from the previous year. Bob Hawke was most impressed with the choice and was effusive in his compliments to the singer who was at the height of his fame then. Then we celebrated with many thousands of others on the forecourt of the Opera House. I couldn't take it all in and enjoy it as I should have, because I had never expected anything like that to happen to me. We were very excited to be on that invitation list. We'd recently made a move from Lane Cove into an Edwardian Terrace house in Walker Street, Lavender Bay, so we were able to walk to Kirribilli House for the event. I was to move in and out of four properties in the street over the next 50 years.

Frank Meaney died that year and was mourned by us all. He'd been incredibly brave and entrepreneurial in activating the SS and his support was important through those early years.

I transferred to the Schools Directorate with a new Performance Team in order to produce a massive number of Spectaculars. It was a very exciting and invigorating year until right at the end.

I was given permission by the Department to join the production team for the Royal Bicentennial Concert in January, which was to be held in the presence of Prince Charles and Princess Diana. I worked with Kevin Jacobsen Television Productions as a segment producer. Once again Kevin gave me an opportunity to upscale my knowledge and skills. I worked on a team with expert production people for both stage and television. I was in awe of the big names involved especially with the hugely talented television producer, David Mitchell. The cast was made up of talent from all musical genres. including iconic Australian names and international stars, all under the musical direction of the legendary maestro Tommy Tycho. The amazing cast showcased consisted of:

- Air Supply
- Dave Allen
- Peter Allen
- Angry Anderson

- Don Burrows
- Barry Crocker
- John Denver
- Jon English
- Marcia Hines
- Rolf Harris
- Icehouse
- Col Joye
- Jeanne Little
- Little Pattie
- Jackie Love
- John Paul Young
- Kylie Minogue
- James Morrison
- Olivia Newton-John, and
- Cliff Richard.

I was now observing and mixing in much wider entertainment circles. This would change my career forever and bring to the SS, a vastly developed network as well as an enhanced understanding of professional production.

Barrie Unsworth was the Premier of NSW and the late Gerry Gleeson was Chairman of the Bicentennial Council. Both of these men were familiar with my work and supported me in growing my skills and career.

I produced the Work Skill Olympics Opening Spectacular Ceremony in February with the team I'd been working with in the Department of Education. It was early days in the promotion of the importance of education in trades. although even then we could see the need for more tradies.

SS No. 5, staged in September 1988 and entitled "Spectacular for the Future", was a major turning point. The production team had grown for this very busy year and included for the first time Annie Whealy as Musical Director. Annie returned from an auditioning search and raved about this group she had seen at Boorigal Primary School. The purpose of her trip had been to see the choir, but instead she found John Deacon and his puppets. John, with his wife Julie, were major contributors to the SS with their brilliant puppets from then onwards. John later went on to produce and direct Star Struck, a SS satellite production in the Hunter region.

The massive gala production used mostly Australian music. We aimed to open up the SS to a broader performing world and also to celebrate the Bicentenary. It featured Australian icons of all genres including:

- John Williamson
- Rolf Harris
- Sydney Dance Company
- opera singers Amanda Thane and Robert Allman
- trumpeter Billy Burton
- Aboriginal Islander Dance Theatre and Stephen Page
- clarinettist Andrew Firth, and
- Michael Tierney (Human Nature).

Deaf Signing Choir and Robert Allman. One of the girls in the choir said it was the first time she had heard a sound. That was Robert Allman's huge bass vocal tone!

In December, we were at it again with another two huge cast productions – the Pacific Schools Games Opening and Closing Ceremonies. The Gala Closing Concert at the Sydney Entertainment Centre was the official closing for the NSW Bicentenary. Tim Webster compered the true Australian program which inclued Aussie iconic performers and friends of the SS: John Williamson and Aboriginal

Islander Dance Theatre. Cobar Public School also featured. I remember vividly how Barry Foster took on the role of coordinating the parade of thousands of athletes from the Sydney Entertainment Centre through Darling Harbour.

However, I sensed trouble was coming. Director-General of the Education Department, Fenton Sharp, and others (including Monica Miland) who were my superiors, apparently did not want the SS to continue. The SS had become a big story over the past five years and now it had all become too much for the Department. Jealousy and resentment from the bureaucracy had started setting in. No "tall poppies" were to be allowed and I was to be sent back to teaching. I was handed my letter of "appointment to a school" before the last night of the 1988 SS. There was no conversation and no discussion. I was devastated. It had been a huge and challenging year, producing and directing, providing marvellous experiences for hundreds of pupils and teachers, and then it only took a couple of people to decide it was all over.

My "SEO1" position as producer of Public Performances had been cancelled. I had given up my music teaching position at EBHS in 1986 and now I was to be appointed to Hornsby Girls High School. The SS had generated publicity, credibility and excitement as a huge cast spectacular. Invitations were routinely issued to NSW State Government politicians and celebrities and it was a wonderful vehicle to publicise public education to the wider general public. Doug Swan's vision was well established. I had produced and directed eight major productions in 1988 alone, but that was clearly not enough. In response, I decided it was time to resign as a teacher. I created the concept of the SS in 1984 and I directed them until my retirement, after 25 years, in 2008. I remained as an Artistic Consultant until 2015.

Helen Pain, who was a member of the production team, was there when I received the notice. She worked tirelessly and passionately for 20 years across many areas including in the "tunnels." The tunnel teachers ensured performers made the show a seamless success, always getting them all to the stage on time. Helen became choir director later Associate Director before her retirement. Her late husband, principal Dave Pain, was much loved by us all and provided invaluable advice on repertoire as well as overseeing tunnel entries himself for more than 20 years.

1989 SS production team – look how we have grown in numbers!

Just hours after I'd handed in my resignation, I called into John Trevillian's office. He was then Director of Australia Day and was responsible for building the Australia Day program for some 30 years. He'd been a huge supporter of mine and encouraged me to keep going when I was being undermined by Department administrators.

Australia Day was then run out of the Premier's Department which was under the leadership of the much-respected late Gerry Gleeson. John suggested I have a talk with Gerry and seek his advice, In his other roles, including the Bicentenary committee, he had been able to observe my leadership of the major events I had produced and directed since 1984. On hearing what had happened Gerry asked me what I wanted to do now. I said "produce concerts and spectacular events." He said "I know a man you should meet. I've just come from a meeting with a man whom I think would be interested in employing you." The next day I found myself in Tom Hayson's office. Tom was my saviour and was to become my mentor for the next phase of my career.

10
Mary Lopez Productions

Early in 1989, I created Mary Lopez Productions which in the 1990s became a successful and profitable company, specializing in the production of large-scale productions for indoor and outdoor venues. Major clients and major productions and spectaculars included:

- NSW Government (Australia Day Concerts and Ceremonies)
- Merlin (Hayson Developers of Darling Harbour) – Opening of Manly Wharf and SkyGarden shopping complex Pitt St Mall
- ARL (arena spectaculars for major sporting events including Finals and State of Origin)
- Catholic Church (Jubilee 2000, Mary McKillop Beatification, Hyde Park Pageant for the Papal visit)
- Wesley Mission (10 huge cast Christmas Pageants in Darling Harbour).

In January, I was employed by the Tom Hayson to be the Manager of Entertainment Harbourside, Darling Harbour. The dynamic Tom Hayson was to become my mentor.

I was introduced to Tom, the legendary man who came up with the proposal to develop Darling Harbour, by Gerry Gleeson, Head of the Premier's Department, after a meeting with the Director of Australia Day, John Trevillian AM. Tom was the person who introduced NSW Government to Baltimore idea for the development of Darling Harbour. Tom offered me a job at our first meeting. The salary was twice the rate I had been receiving in my SEO1 position in the Department. I couldn't believe my good fortune. Moving out of the toxic education environment to one of huge energy gave me the encouragement and confidence to keep my dream alive. Tom knew no boundaries. He was such a driving force. He called me "Legs" and taught me to think BIG. From 1989 to 1992 I was the Director of Entertainment for Tom at Darling Harbour. Tom's company, Merlin, was the private enterprise manager of Darling Harbour. We used to affectionately call Tom "Poppy Hayson" behind his back. I always called him Mr Hayson to his face and loved and respected him.

I'm forever grateful to those three men, John, Gerry and Tom for opening the door to the next exciting 30-year chapter of my career.

In February, I negotiated with Graham Drayton, CEO of the Community Relations Unit, to continue to produce and the direct the Schools Spectaculars as a contractor. Graham had suggested this as a way forward, otherwise that would have been the end of the SS. And so began my first year as a contractor and not a teacher, producing and directing the SS. While my vocation as a teacher remained intact I undertook the challenge I was offered. If I hadn't, this book would be pretty empty.

I was told two truths by Gerry Gleeson: "if you've got a talent, you'll always have work" and "when the timing's right the work falls into place." This was so true of my quest for football contracts and then my association with Brian Walsh.

In 1989, I was busy concentrating on establishing my company, Mary Lopez Productions. In Kate's graduation year, 1990, she had to deal with the aftermath of her father's diagnosis with lung cancer and my frantically busy year as Director of Entertainment for Tom Hayson in newly opened Darling Harbour precinct. My children are very forgiving.

Mary Lopez network

My role as Entertainment Director for was a major turning point in my career and an incredible education in the importance of networking. It was during the 16-year period from 1984 to 2002 that I built my very strong network of politicians, entertainers, music industry and business contacts. These people continued to encourage me throughout my career. This network was the reason the SS continued to gain public attention and provided the basis for the development of the young artists who would be accepted into the TDP. I'm quite sure the Department of Education has never appreciated the importance and value of the power of the contacts I created for it, although the Director-Generals knew it and valued my network. Without this network, I would not have been able to give the SS and the developing artists the professionalism and introductions that they now all benefit from.

As a producer, I employed innumerable stars, emerging stars and musicians which later stood me in good stead when asking favours for the TDP volunteer panel of consultants. I worked with the cream of producers, musical directors, talent managers and associated technical production personnel in stage and television. Throughout all my productions, as well as the SS, I always worked closely with business leaders and sponsors as well as public relations companies and the media. So many of those people became invaluable TDP supporters.

Because of my fearless approach for staging grand productions, Tom encouraged me to think outside the square to create large one-off events to market Harbourside and Darling Harbour. Sydney became my stage. I created the Darling Harbour Christmas Pageant, which ran for 10 years, and such events as the gala openings of Manly Wharf and SkyGarden Shopping complex in the Pitt St mall. They were two exciting events to open Tom's new shopping centre developments. The SkyGarden opening featured jazz trumpet virtuoso, James Morrison and a super sophisticated abseil-type presentation by the Police Rescue Squad. It was a very classy event.

For the opening of Manly Wharf, Tom convinced marathon swimmer, Susie Maroney to swim from Darling Harbour to Manly Wharf. I produced a pyrotechnics display and a music festival for the opening by Premier Nick Greiner. A street parade led to the multiple stages set up for performances around the wharf. We had an anxious moment when sparks from the fireworks landed on the new awnings on the wharf restaurant, because it was an incredibly hot day. It was embarrassing to see the minute holes scattered around on the blinds. However, I was too busy with so much going on to concern myself with that detail.

Tom was a master in public relations and finance and was great teacher for me in the art of networking. He was fearless in approaching whomever he thought would be a draw card to his centres. I wish I'd been able to hold onto the confidence he had in me, to stand against the sniping that was often directed towards me as the SS and TDP developed.

Tom wanted a stage to hold performances on Cockle Bay (outside Harbourside Shopping Centre) so he created a floating stage called the Aquashell. I was to organise the entertainment with Bobby Limb as host. Bobby was a favourite of Tom's and Bobby was generous to the core in encouraging new talent.

Bobby Limb and Maria Venuti with TDP Graduate Melissa Preston

I remember Bobby gave me great advice one day when I was feeling nervous about leading a huge meeting set up to coordinate Tom's big ideas for the opening of Manly Wharf. The meeting involved security, road closures and more. I was wondering where I should sit in this 20 person production meeting that included Sydney City Council and Premier's Department personnel. "Mary, wear the hat and sit at the top of the table", he said. I did.

Tom asked me to create a Chinese Festival to sit with the annual Dragon Boat races held on Cockle Bay, Darling Harbour. He was an ever encouraging and public relations mastermind. A Tulip Festival was set up in the Harbourside Galleria which involved flying in tulips from Holland and familiarising myself with the Dutch community in Sydney. I produced an International Buskers Festival, a massed Band event called Bandemonium and many other promotional events, all intended to increase the interest in shopping in Harbourside Darling Harbour. Sitting on top of all the promotional events, was the huge "An Australian Christmas at Darling Harbour" Pageant.

The Reverend Dr Gordon Moyes loved the Christian theme and saw the potential to promote the work of Wesley Mission and thereby attract funds to the Mission.

This pageant was to run every December from 1989 until 2001. The first year was funded by Tom Hayson's Group and afterwards from 1990, by the Wesley Mission. The Wesley Mission, under the leadership of Gordon Moyes, were great people who were enthusiastic, respectful and dedicated. They were very different to the people I was working for in the Education Department. Paula Duncan was employed by Wesley as their marketing consultant, and we formed a lifelong friendship. Paula was, and is, an inspirational woman who has played a big part in my life over the years. It was a fortunate 1990 meeting that in 2001 brought about my meeting with Rob Bail and the adventurous and love filled life that continues with Rob today.

I absolutely loved that show. I called it an Australian Christmas and modelled it on the Passion Play performed in the village of Oberammergau in Bavaria. This play is performed every ten years by the villagers. I wanted a community of participants who loved the Christmas tradition and enjoyed being on the stage. We would act out the Christmas story on the Tumbalong Park stage and parade the people of Bethlehem and all the animals, from the Pyrmont bridge through Darling Harbour. This production was of course inspired by my Paterson PS appearance as Mary as a 5 year old, and the Merriwa church choir at Christmas as a teenager.

Christmas Pageant Manger scenes. Margaret Tierney as Mary on donkey

The first year had a cast of around 1,000 performers, and included a symphony orchestra, massed choir, celebrity performers, 40 animals including sheep and lambs, three camels and three horses. People loved performing in that show and everyone enjoyed working on the pageant. In the beginning many of the soloists roles were sung by the extraordinarily talented graduates of the TDP. Julie Anthony and footballer, Wayne Pearce, were special guests. For most of the years of the pageant's life, the symphony orchestra was conducted by the pageant's Musical Director, Maestro Tommy Tycho. Two other notable Musical Directors were Steve Watson and Andrew Bee. The size of the cast remained about the same for the next 12 years, and gradually more and more entertainment celebrities generously came on board and donated their services for the charity, including:

- Francine Bell
- John Paul Young
- Mark Williams
- Graeme Connors
- Caroline O'Connor
- Bachelor Girl
- Eric Bogle
- Jackie Love
- Peter Cousens
- Darren Coggen
- Felicity Urquhart
- Jane Rutter
- John Simpson
- John Foreman
- Col Buchanan
- Anne Kirkpatrick
- Maree Montgomery
- Maria Venuti and
- Kamahl.

The atmosphere surrounding this pageant was one of sheer joy. The on stage narrative was the heartwarming story of the birth of Christ. The pictures were painted through Christmas Carols and led by celebrities and stars from the entertainment industry.

Jackie Love

Preceding the stage performance was a 500 metre parade through Darling Harbour, made up of groups we imagined to be a cross section of the people of Bethlehem at the time of Christ. There were many hundreds of colourful characters. The singers, dancers and actors included a large group of everyday people from the Wesley Mission congregation. The costumes were owned and organized by the Wesley Mission. The hundreds of characters who received these costumes gathered with much excitement under the Pyrmont Bridge near the Maritime Museum in Darling Harbour. These ranged from simple styles like groups of shepherds, lepers and fisherfolk to elaborate and grandiose costumes for the Angel Gabriel and the three Wise Men.

McKillop nuns (twins Christina and Lucy) with right hand man Ian Skilton

Mary and Joseph's costumes were the traditional robes we are used to seeing in Christmas Christian pictures. One beloved group were the 40 farm animals comprised of sheep, lambs and calves provided by Rhonda Hall from Richmond. There was friendly competition to be in the cast to be a shepherd to mind these animals.

I really regret that I never got to witness the vibrance and energy of the Parade, because I was always too busy and occupied up my end of the production at Tumbalong Park. However, the photos show the imagination and enthusiasm of this overall great event.

Bjelke-Petersen Physie Angels courtesy of the late remarkable Judy Spence

The massed choir was drawn from many wonderful established choirs, the general public and the Wesley Mission. From the first pageant, where the beautiful Australian Opera Children's chorus and 23 schools from the Broken Bay Diocesan Schools Choir led the carols, the choir numbers swelled to include the Willoughby Symphony Choir, Waverley Philharmonic, Sydney Male Voice Choir, the Carlson Chorale, St Mary's Cathedral College and so many others. For a few years we were also able to feature Wynette Horne's glorious Waratah Girls Choir that I had discovered and nurtured way back in the early 80s.

We always finished the event with fireworks and Handel's *Hallelujah Chorus*. I note that Carols in the Domain soon adopted that glorious music and exciting idea with fireworks to conclude their Channel 7 very commercial Christmas show.

We had very warm and enthusiastic hosts including Kathryn Greiner, Sandra Sully and the Reverend Gordon Moyes.

Manuel's lung cancer diagnosis

I was now working out of the Old Darling Harbour Wool Stores building that Tom's company had restored, when Manuel asked to meet me at a café in Harbourside for a meal. I recall the horror I felt when he told me that he'd been diagnosed with lung cancer. The statistics were dreadful in those days and the survival rate was only 1 in 5. My typical reaction though was to be the optimist and say "Well why wouldn't you be the 'successful' statistic?" I promised God that I would make a huge effort to contribute to homeless youth if he fixed Manuel up. Very soon after that I came across the legendary Father Chris Riley, recently deceased, and tried to follow through with my promise.

Father Chris established YOTS – Youth Off The Streets. I met him not long after he started YOTS, with the aim of championing vulnerable youth. His charity looked after the youth that no one else was prepared to give time to. I was inspired by him. His legacy is immeasurable and lives on in the 50,000 young people his programs have rescued. He established safe houses and schools, as well as support for those in need of professional support for legal, psychological, drug and alcohol problems. We teamed up for quite a few years in which I attempted to help build self-esteem in his young charges through performance and a choir. The choir lasted a few years but it was very hard to have continuity of commitment. Father Chris and I became firm friends.

The next six years after Manuel's lung cancer diagnosis were the best we had as a married couple. We finally learned to appreciate each other, and life moved smoothly along. I had my new production company (MLP) to escape to and fill the gaps in my life, and Manuel bravely set out to keep himself alive. He threw himself back into the law firm where he was a partner and continued to drive himself with an incredible work ethic in spite of the underlying dread of an early death.

One problem we had was finding a surgeon prepared to take on the operation Manuel needed, because it was in a dangerous part of the system very close to the aorta (I think). Alan Farnsworth from St Vincent's came to the rescue. He had a reputation for taking on the impossible. The operation was a success and Manuel taught the doctor to communicate. (You know how surgeons have a reputation as poor communicators). I remember a beautiful scene when Manuel gave Alan a hug, which really surprised the doctor, although he was delighted with it. Men didn't do much hugging in those days.

Two years later Manuel had a pneumothorax, which was a dreadful discomfort for him, but because the operation involved the lungs it confirmed that the lung cancer was gone. Dr Peter Corte, then came into our lives and looked after us after Manuel contracted stomach cancer through to his death. He's a marvellous and compassionate human being.

One of the pleasures of writing this is reacquainting with the enormous amount of kind and generous people I was so privileged to meet along the way. I sent Peter a text in 2023 to say thanks again for managing Manuel, Andy, Kate and me through all those dreadful years and afterwards. It's so lovely to hear he's happily retired with Pippa and now has 13 grandchildren. A mighty man.

Schools Spectacular Nos. 6 and 7

In 1990, we saw the emergence of another unit within the Education Department which would take over the running of the SS. The formation of this Performing Arts Unit (PAU) was the most important Education Department initiative to grow out of the SS. The PAU was to become the engine room of the SS and the leader of the newly formed unit was Alan Suthers. Over the next 40 years masses of talented performing artists/teachers increased the quality of their disciplines in the performing arts of music, dance and drama. As a result of their exposure to the commercial world of entertainment with performance, staging and technical professionals the teachers' horizons began to be vastly expanded.

Some of the volunteer teachers from the first few SS took up positions in the PAU. This small and talented group of ex-teachers played an important role in future SS developments. However, it was the end of the small volunteer SS production team comprised of generous and dedicated practising teachers. Thanks to Bruce Harris' amazingly learned program notes for every SS, the pathway of the PAU is drawn clearly. Bruce used to often say how the SS gave birth to a new broader direction for performing arts in public education. By the 1990s, an enormous change in direction had taken place from the unit's forerunner, the Music Branch in Blackfriars St, Chippendale. From its original brief in 1972, which only developed music programs, the new PAU was responsible for expanding music, dance and drama programs in public schools.

That same year, Steve Williams, an outstandingly talented band leader and music teacher then at Forestville HS, took over the conducting of the orchestra for the SS. He continues to conduct the orchestra in 2025. He is an inspirational man and his contribution to the lives of thousands of young people is immeasurable. Over the years while we worked together, we had sometimes strong differences over musical choices, but we always reached a satisfactory compromise because we had such respect for each other's integrity and creative intentions.

Andrew Bee appeared on the SS production credits for the first time as "Technical Assistant." Two years later he became Musical Director and later also became Technical Producer. Andrew, affectionately known as "Mr Bee", became the creative and technical driving force for the SS for the next 25 years. He became my most skilled, loyal and trusted adviser throughout my career and remains a cherished friend.

The participation of schools from regional NSW was increasing and it gave me great pleasure to see how country performers were being given a showcase. I understand what dedication and love was required from the teachers and parents in those schools to bring those performers to Sydney. They had buses, accommodation, meals and supervision for four days now ahead of them. Bravo!! Schools from the Hunter, North Coast, North West, Riverina, South Coast and Western Regions joined their fellow metropolitan performers to perform with a huge and diverse cast of 2,500.

The SS is like a huge jig-saw puzzle. The concept or theme is set by the Creative team with music and songs chosen to fit the theme. Once they have been selected to be in the SS the soloist or performing group is invited to take on a particular piece of the "puzzle." It all comes together with just one full dress rehearsal at the performance venue (in my case the Sydney Entertainment Centre). The teachers, performers and technical staff make it work based on trust, skill, good humour, dedication and remarkable team spirit.

On the family front, Kate graduated from Loreto Convent, Kirribilli with a very successful HSC and no immediate plans for academic studies.

To keep myself healthy and sane I started visiting the Kurrajong Health Farm, which sadly doesn't operate anymore. I'd been a few times already and thought it would be good for Kate leading up to her HSC. Whilst we were there we met the charming and eccentric Ellie and her husband, Solicitor, John Picone. They became lifelong friends and Kate spent a couple of years working for John after she studied law. John is still my solicitor to this date.

I had several hypnotherapy sessions while at the Health Farm, where I went in search of memories. During one such session I was at my father's funeral, at the graveside. It was raining and there were only a few people there. I felt sorrow and desolation. When I asked my sister Shirley about his funeral, she told me that's how it had been – raining and just a few people there. I've since wondered: can a foetus feel? Mum would not even have known that she was pregnant at the time of my father's funeral. I can still see that picture in my mind. The unfortunate suicide of the therapist a few years later made me wonder at the strain and complexity of that type of career.

Over the next two decades we engaged a range of comperes who were entertainment and TV celebrities like the late Bobby Limb and Mike Hammond and importantly, SS soloist alumni (nine in fact). In SS No. 7, with the very first SS alumni Tracy Case engaged as compere, we were delighted to see very young performers Nathan Foley (aged 12) and Felicity Urquhart (aged 14) make their performance debut at the Sydney Entertainment Centre. Tracy had been a student from Dubbo South HS and had been a favourite singer from the first three SSs. John Foreman, another SS alumni famously hosted the SS for over 20 years as well as now mentoring and co-hosting with current students.

Felicity Urquhart – Country music star

I first met Mary Lopez when I was 14 years old in my Year 9 sky blue tunic at Tamworth High School.

It was exciting getting to sing and play one of the music room school guitars for some important people from Sydney. It seemed like the perfect reason to be excused from maths class.

I remember the moment I was introduced to a very stylish and well-spoken lady and gentleman, Mary Lopez and Jack Neary. They had flown up from Sydney especially to hear me sing.

Both Mary and Jack greeted me with smiles and lots of questions about my love of singing and country music. It was organised through then-THS principal David Hicks as he believed it would be worth their trip.

I later found out Mary's personal connection to the country influenced why she felt strongly about giving children in regional areas the same opportunity as kids in the city. Little did I know her trip to Tamworth was going to be the beginning of new possibilities opening up for me and a wonderful friendship to follow into adulthood. Sydney became an exciting place I would soon frequent thanks to Mary and Jack selecting me to perform at the Sydney Entertainment Centre for the Schools Spectacular.

I performed as a soloist every year till I finished high school. It was through that opportunity I went on to join the Talent Development Project.

I didn't know what was ahead but it exposed me to talented high school kids across the state. It was in this time I learnt the value of respecting other's unique talents and music styles.

Mary's encouragement made an impact on me during those teenage years as she passionately instilled how important it was to be proud of my country roots and the genre I loved.

Mary encouraged me to stand up and be counted and take pride in what I do in every area of life, both on and off the stage.

Since graduating from the TDP I've stepped into different roles in the entertainment scene. Working in television for 15 years on Channel Seven's **Sydney Weekender** *lifestyle show and ABC TV's* **Back Roads** *special feature host and I spent 11 years broadcasting ABC radio's flagship program* **Saturday Night Country***.*

It's been a journey recording six solo albums over the decades playing some big festivals and stages. Being awarded 16 Golden Guitar Awards, ARIA nominations and feeling blessed to be touring with Josh Cunningham working on our third album together as the story keeps unfolding.

I've been very grateful to see many parts of Australia and the world throughout my career whilst raising a family.

From the very beginning I was encouraged by Mary to be proud of who I am, where I'm from and my love of a country song.

As Mary said: "You can do it all!"

Jim Beam Mo Award for Female
Country Performer of the Year 1997

Felicity in concert and with her family

In July 1991, Andy's 21st gave us a challenge. Andy was proving difficult to pin down regarding a venue suited to his style of living which was not to his parents understanding. He was not going to be dictated to by what he considered his ultra conservative parents. In the end the crowd who attended was a good mixture of family and his friends and we were very relieved that the party worked. I convinced Manual to give Andy the Alfa Romeo (which he owned) for his birthday gift. That went over very well. However, a few months later the engine burnt out for lack of something (oil or water) and like so many young drivers, Andy learned how to look after a car.

Kate took a year off to study in Perugia and travel in Europe. Her travelling companions were two friends from Loreto, Gaby Carney and Mad Heatherton. We were so proud of Kate with her adventures and her studies. Her sojourn to Morrocco with a rock band we only found out about when she returned to Australia!

My company, Mary Lopez Productions Pty Ltd, operated out of our first house, 35 Walker St, North Sydney. Remember this street, reader, because I move in and out of Walker St four times over the years to come. The delightful and enthusiastic Jean Jenkins (then Jean McLeod) applied for the position of my personal assistant with a unique and memorable application. She said she would be the "best assistant in the world." She certainly was that for me. She built such a fine reputation that later in her career she became marketing manager for Radio 2GB and Channel 9.

I moved into the 1990s with a well-developed set of production skills and an impressive network, which now included leaders in the entertainment world and influential business and government personnel. The world I inhabited was vastly different to that in which had I lived during my teaching career. Unfortunately, the majority of people with whom I'd been working in the DOE Administration in setting up the SS could neither acknowledge nor happily accept my achievements. They preferred me when I was a classroom teacher.

In contrast, Tom Hayson encouraged me to see a much bigger stage than the Sydney Entertainment Centre. Now I was about to further take on "open air" Sydney. I needed all the experience and knowledge I had acquired to take on, and be effective in, what was to bring great change to the face of the Australian music industry – the newly established TDP. Nevertheless, as always, I didn't plan the next decade or consider what it would bring, I just continued my forward pathway and followed my nose.

The big stage – Talent Development Project (TDP)

The Darling Harbour Harbourside job with Tom Hayson finished after three years, as the focus of the company business changed. However, with the experience I had gained through my association with Tom, I felt I was now equipped to run my own company, Mary Lopez Productions, and explore new horizons. We were now living in our second house at 17 Walker St, Lavender Bay. It had been a brave and optimistic financial move on Manuel's part to purchase another property while living with looming lung cancer diagnosis.

Since the first SS much bigger new horizons had opened for me. I had been involved with NSW Government productions and ceremonies through the Premier's Department. David O'Connor had taken over as Head from Gerry Gleeson. He was so generously supportive to me and enjoyed my style of work. John Trevillian remained Director of Australia Day during much of my career. They were two men who gave me both encouragement and wonderful opportunities.

Importantly, 1991 saw the formation on the Talent Development Project (TDP) which would conduct its workshops at the Sydney Entertainment Centre. The co-founders were Jack Neary, Bruce Harris and me. The aim of the TDP was to help the outstanding talent which appeared in the SS, find a way into the entertainment industry. We were to assist them to make the transition from school to active employment in the industry. The successful applicants were to be advised, coached and nurtured by professionals currently working in the industry. The idea was to develop stagecraft, presentation, voice craft, musicianship, record production (remember this was the still the time of vinyls), publicity and communication (mobile phones were just in coming into use).

You will read, as this story progresses, from many graduates who are now household names. They will tell you how the TDP helped them to have an introduction into the "business." The first class of 1992 included the highly successful John Foreman, Darren Coggan, Human Nature, Vanessa Corish and Jenny Davis.

The first TDP graduation was held in the Green Room at the Sydney Entertainment Centre. It was attended by music and entertainment industry leaders from Jack's network. I remember how I was pulled into line sharply after I made a speech about how our performers were to be trained as performers singing known repertoire. I received firm advice and correction from Fifa Ricobonna, who discovered ACDC and was then CEO of Albert's Music. I was to learn that to be successful in the contemporary music scene you had to sing original songs. I spent a great deal of my time and energy from that time onwards trying to convince Jack and the board that song writing was essential to success.

Our connection with Albert's Music was important. TDP students were to benefit from being recorded for many years in Albert's studios at Neutral Bay. David Albert even donated a stunning grand piano to the TDP which was still used when I retired.

Sony Music, under the CEO, Denis Handlin, came on board as a sponsor through the Sony Foundation. While the annual cash injection was wonderful, the experiences the students had in Sony's recording studio were invaluable and something they never forgot.

Wendy Purdie and Elaine Horsfield were the first TDP coordinators. We travelled to country towns to advertise the new Program and audition talent. I knew that it would be difficult for the talented students, their parents and teachers to understand how this new project could change their lives and make their dreams come true. I remember Elaine coming back very excited after seeing Darren

Coggan at Wagga Wagga High School. Darren was selected to join the first TDP class and has had a long and successful career as a singer, composer, actor, teacher and producer in the music industry.

I was extremely busy juggling a double career with the Education programs of SS and the TDP as well as MLP events.

As SS producer and director I had a very large platform from which to observe talent. I seem to have been given a gift for talent identification. The talent that appealed to me always had to be unique and honest. I was not attracted to performers who seemed to me to have been "over-cooked" at dance and music studios, and had too often lost their uniqueness.

Darren Coggan talks about Mary and the TDP

I will be forever grateful to Mary Lopez and her family, for their support and friendship over my entire career.

Mary has been a constant source of encouragement and a facilitator of opportunities for me since I was 18 years old, always championing a belief in my abilities to strive for greatness.

I shall never forget the day in 1991 when Mary, along with Elaine Horsfield, drove down to my beloved hometown of Wagga Wagga, to Kooringal High School, to audition prospective country kids for an exciting new initiative called the Talent Development Project.

I'm not sure what it was that captured her imagination in me, but that day changed my life, for the first time, out of my immediate family circle, here was someone from the Big Smoke, Sydney, recognising raw talent and offering a pathway to the possibility of a career in the entertainment industry.

I was successful in graduating the very first TDP in 1992, and two years later my sister, Naomi, would also graduate from this incredible initiative, that would become undoubtedly the finest program in Australia for nurturing and developing young artists of all genres.

It provides them with a safe platform in which to grow and learn from the best in our industry, with the objective of developing well rounded skills that would sustain a career in the performing arts.

Since those first steps for me in TDP, I have enjoyed an incredibly rewarding and diverse career on stage and screen.

My professional career kicked off in 1995 when I won the inaugural Trans-Tasman Entertainer of the Year on Norfolk Island and then went on to take out the prestigious Toyota Star Maker Quest in 1996, charting a course as a successful recording artist within the Australian country music industry with a swag of Golden Guitar and Independent Country Music Awards under my belt.

I have been equally as comfortable in musicals and on screen having toured Australia extensively playing roles including Richie Cunningham in **Happy Days the Arena Mega Musical** *1999, Teen Angel and Vince Fontaine in* **Grease – The Mega Musical** *2001–2002, Col Joye in* **Shout – The Musical of the Wild One** *2003, understudied John Farnham as Teen Angel in* **Grease – The Arena Spectacular** *2005 and the lead role of Dad in the world premiere production of John Williamson's musical* **Quambatook***, 2008.*

My on-screen credits include the award-winning Channel Seven drama **All Saints** *2001/2004/2005 and I am currently presenting the lifestyle TV program* **Sydney Weekender** *for the Seven Network.*

My touring productions celebrating the songbooks of John Denver, James Taylor and the critically acclaimed portrait of Cat Stevens have inspired audiences in the grandest theatres across the globe including sellout seasons at the Sydney Opera House Concert Hall, Glasgow Royal Concert Hall and Liverpool Philharmonic.

The network expands

Manuel and travelled again to the Philippines in 1992. Because Manuel grew up there, we made good friends with his childhood relations and family friends. It was an enriching and educational experience as well as very enjoyable and I regret that we do not see them anymore. From the resorts to the mountains we loved it all and saw much that was well off the tourist trail.

My own children were moving towards adulthood and I was drooling over the house down the road in Walker St. I used to sit on the now defunct church parking lot wall and dream of living in the lovely big Victorian terrace across the road. We eventually bought the house while keeping the Edwardian one up the road, which became my office. I was a bit overwhelmed at the time by Andy as he was growing into himself. I really didn't have a clue how young men became adults.

Over the next six years whilst my business grew, Andy and Kate became adults, travelled, gained university degrees, drove cars into the ground, and worked in a call centre and Manuel's legal firm.

Kate's Bachelor of Arts Graduation

They always earned their own money and were very independent of us. They were great travellers and adventurers. I know I was controlling whilst they were young adults and I still thought they were children. It was hard to give them their freedom.

Andy grew into himself when he found creativity and stopped trying to be a sportsman, and Kate found compassion and loyalty when she later gave up living in Japan to come back home during Manuel's last year. By the time of Manuel's death they were responsible human beings. I was comforted by them, and so proud of them when we sat with their father, on the night he died.

Sadly, my lovely sister-in-law, Pat Feneley, died suddenly on 1 November 1992. Manuel received the phone call and was quick to say we must go to Kenthurst right away. She left behind a shocked husband, Ian and four children, Mark, Merise, Adrienne and Damien. They're an incredibly close and loving family.

By now my network and reputation had expanded from my educational projects of musical and talent development to encompass the professional world of Sydney and national television productions.

However, I felt I was still lurching along and not planning any career moves, not really believing it was all happening. I was fearless though. My mother had told me I could do anything and it seemed to me as if the world had jumped on board my career. I was working hard and happily taking on these exciting new offers. I loved it.

I'd built a positive reputation as a creative producer and director of large scale performances. I'd directed the Australia Day Concerts at World Expo 1985 in Japan. I'd produced and directed Australia's televised "Performance for Peace" for the Commonwealth Government at the beginning of the International Year of Peace in 1986. I had designed and produced the gala opening extravaganzas for the SkyGarden Shopping Complex in the Pitt St Mall, Sydney, and the newly renovated Manly Wharf Complex. I'd had a bumper year in 1988 with eight huge cast extravaganzas, all with casts numbering in the thousands, and produced and directed the Closing Ceremony of the Bicentenary at the Sydney Entertainment Centre. All of this alongside producing and directing the last eight SSs as well as the Darling Harbour Christmas Pageants, which I created in 1989. I had also shouldered the work load for the newly established TDP, all while being Entertainment Director for Tom Hayson's Harbourside at Darling Harbour. Whether it was performances in the Opera House, the Town Hall, concert halls, shopping centres or churches, and even Eisteddfods, all of my experiences were enlightening in so many ways.

All of this experience should have been received by the Education Department as a bonus, a way to improve performing arts education. But no, I think envy was at work amongst those in administrative positions within the Performing Arts. I've always believed, throughout my whole teaching career, that it is so important to take the students outside the school walls to broaden their education. It's a shame that too many people within education seem to confine themselves to very narrow worlds within "walls."

In March 1992, I produced and directed the Gala Premier's Concert for Senior Citizens week "Everything Old is New Again" at Sydney Entertainment Centre. The program was youth based and the soloists were mostly "stars" from the SS. Jenny Davis, The 4 Trax (Human Nature), Nathan Foley and John Foreman were the stars of the show. We also presented a large cast of beautifully costumed dance items reprised from the SS1991. The seasoned performers included

TV presenter, Beverley Gledhill, soprano Rosalind Keene and three Baritones: John Brosnan, Graham Sattler and John Simpson. Andy Lopez was stage manager while Andrew Bee coordinated the orchestra, cutting their teeth as very young men on their first Premier's Senior Citizens' Concert. After Rob and I attended a Premier's Senior Citizens' Concert produced by the two Andy's in 2022, I wrote in my diary:

> I'm proud to see that my son's and Andrew Bee's company Out There Productions, has been producing The Premier's Concerts for Senior Citizens for quite a few years. Their productions have seen audiences enjoying seeing many of the now very well recognised TDP Graduates amongst their celebrity casts. Human Nature presented one whole Program recently which Rob and I and the rest of the audience enjoyed enormously.
>
> It only occurred to me now, how unusual but fulfilling, for me, to have my son and Bee who was my most important creative and technical colleague, also employing technicians who had honed their skills in SS. How far is the influence?

Another of their Premier's Concerts was cast with TDP alumni who are now celebrated artists: Paulini, Lorenzo Rositano, Julie Lea Goodwin and Trevor Ashley.

Since the first SS my network had grown to include NSW Premiers and their Department, politicians, and leaders in the music and entertainment industry. I was so busy I didn't really have time to consider how my life was so intensely being enriched and my horizons expanded. I didn't have time to focus on the excitement of it because I was too busy coming up with the next big event.

In July and August the World Expo in Sevilla, Spain, beckoned and it seemed like a good idea to go and observe. Doug McClelland invited me to the Aussie Reception. I travelled with my friend Graeme Stroud, with whom I had worked closely when he was the marketing manager at Harbourside.

In Spain, I was astounded by the colour and extravaganza with the World Expo in Sevilla and the Olympics. I saw what I consider to be the best-ever lighting of the Olympic flame when my travelling friend,

Graham Stroud, and I were in a bar in Toledo. Watching the TV with a bar full of passionate Spaniards was unforgettable. The drama and tension of the archer lining up and firing the bow to light the Olympic flame was sensational.

Manuel surprised and delighted me by turning up unannounced in Santiago de Compostela where we had finished our trip.

About this time I met Antony and Janelle Kidman at a dinner party at the Picone's and they become lifelong friends. I learnt to work an Apple laptop computer through a Tom Cruise birthday gift to Janelle, plus taking lessons. A special by-product of this introduction to Tom was that a few years later, I was able to arrange for my friend Bonita Mabo to be invited by Tom to visit the *Mission Impossible* film set. She was a fan of Tom. I was so impressed that Tom and the producer knew all about Mabo land rights and were most respectful to Bonita.

The Kidmans and their acting group soon joined the cast in the Darling Harbour Christmas Pageants. The Jan Cairns acting group were great fun and used to sneak the odd drink and ciggie along the way in the "People of Bethlehem" procession from Harbourside to Tumbalong Park. Janelle and Antony both became volunteer consultants for TDP. Janelle was able to bring much wisdom to the students about dealing with public acclaim having brought up a daughter, Nicole, who became a famous actor and film star. Antony was a renowned psychologist who gave his professional advice to the students in handling pressure. In my holistic approach to educating my students I tried to give them experiences and a network that was about so much more then performance.

Alan Jones had asked me to recommend some TDP students to perform at his Christmas party at his warehouse home in Newtown that year. I saw this invite as a great opportunity for whomever I chose, as they would be performing to a group of Alan's powerful and influential friends who would open doors for them. Denis Handlin from Sony was most impressed with the boys' performance and the managing director of the London Ritz, also a guest, invited them to perform at the celebrated New Year's Eve concert at the Ritz. This was the first step to stardom for Human Nature. I understood the power of networks and never forgot the words of Jack Neary: "always be respectful to those around you when you're on the way up – because they'll all still be there when you're on the way down."

Mary believed in us ... she nurtured us, developed our talent. The Talent Development Project and Schools Spectaculars gave us great opportunities and an awesome network. She's always there for us and we'll always be there for her.

Human Nature
Phil Burton, Michael Tierney, Andrew Tierney & Toby Allen

The PAU coordinated the SS in 1992, with the theme "Discovery." Mike Hammond was the compere with the acclaimed Michael Scott Mitchell the set designer. I had travelled to Peru early in the year and visited Cusco and other Inca sites with Manuel.

Andrew Bee joined the PAU Coordinators. Andrew was to become the major driving force behind both the quirky and humorous segments in SS as well as the technical development of the productions. He also became responsible for the development of an extraordinary range of contemporary singer/song writers to emerge from the TDP in the years from 2005 and onwards. I have always thought of Bee as my most important adviser.

Ken Boston was appointed Director-General for the Department of Education. Ken was very supportive throughout, until he retired in 2002. He was a breath of fresh air and made me feel welcome and acknowledged for the skills and the network I had brought to the SS and the TDP. Unlike so many others within Education, he didn't see me as a tall poppy needing to be pulled down.

11
A turning point and a SS for reconciliation

In January 1993, my sister Geraldine died from bowel cancer. The previous year had been so busy and I had found it hard to get to Merriwa to see her, but I had done my best. I was in Melbourne attending an opening night (of all things), instead of being with my sister. All my brothers and sisters were there with her when she died, and Manuel was with her and the family, for me. You don't forget occasions that you should have prioritised.

We celebrated Kate's 21st in June with a very smart party at a restaurant at SkyGarden, in the city. We chose that venue because our friend was maître d' at the time. I tried so hard to buy what I thought was a delicious Italian icecream cake from Leichardt, in keeping with her Perugian experience. It was a bit of a fizzer because it was too pink, too sweet and too sloppy. There was also a memorable quarrel between Manuel, and Andy over Andy's then girlfriend, of whom Manuel was not a fan.

Bonita

I met Bonita Mabo in 1993 and our friendship was a major turning point in my life, career and reconciliation journey. We became sisters and shared our lives until she died in 2019. Andy and Kate and my brothers and sisters were all embraced into her family and were equally embracing.

Bonita and I discovered each other on Australia Day, the January after the Mabo legislation was decreed. We have loved and respected each other since our first meeting, and we have been crucial to each other's lives. We have helped each through the healing of grief over our husbands' deaths and have led each other to explore further our place in the lives of many Australians. Bonita and I became firm friends and over 25 years became family.

On the way to the Australia Day Ceremony, Manuel, told me about Eddie and how he felt Eddie should have been "Australian of the Year." Eddie was *The Australian* newspaper's Australian of the Year. I said, "Who's Eddie Mabo?" Manuel told me about the Mabo case. He was passionate about social justice. I saw Bonita receive a posthumous award for Eddie during the ceremony and was moved by her dignified presence. Later, at the reception, I saw she was standing unattended. The people who'd invited her didn't take any responsibility for looking after her at the reception and I felt I should do something. Manuel encouraged me to introduce myself and that was the beginning of our friendship. Her daughter, Maleta, was excited to meet Manuel "a real Spaniard." We looked after Bonita and Maleta at the reception and took them back to their hotel that night.

One month later I was driving to Newcastle. The radio on my car had not worked for ages, but as I had two hours of driving ahead, I thought I'd have a try at getting it to work. I turned the radio on and a voice said "Eddie Mabo" and then dropped out. I pulled over to the side of the road to tune in and tried to find the reception again, but there was nothing. By the time I arrived in Newcastle, I knew I had the theme and concept for SS 1993. It was to be called "One Spirit" and was to be both a reconciliation spectacular and a tribute to Indigenous Australians. I invited Indigenous guests to be honoured on the arena in "One Spirit", including

- Bonita Mabo
- Mum Shirl
- Linda Burnie
- Bob Morgan.

I have to say that I was not aware of any push from the Education Department at this time to acknowledge the need for reconciliation lessons. The reconciliation segments in the 1993 SS were at my direction and were fuelled by my own sense of social justice. I hoped I was educating audiences and teachers.

It was in the early days of my marriage to Manuel, through our friendship with Father Ted Kennedy and Mem Gilchrist in 1972, that I was introduced to Indigenous Australia. But it was through meeting Bonita that I began to really know it. The night after the Reconciliation March 2000, (over the Harbour Bridge) Bonita talked about the pain of her people and shared her suffering with me. I felt the sorrow and pain that night – the loss suffered not only by Bonita but by all Indigenous Australians. I felt a terrible emptiness and was humbled and deeply ashamed.

I share some knowledge of how discrimination feels. I suffered minor religious and social discrimination in my country town. It makes me aware of how appalling those attitudes, experienced on such a magnified level, must have made the lives of Eddie, Bonita and their family so turbulent and hurtful.

We compared the environments in which we grew up, our differences in fortune and education and how that has affected our lives and the lives of our children. We both grew up in small country towns. Bonita's father was a cane-cutter in northern Queensland and my mother was a publican in the Hunter Valley. We both had wonderful mothers and had love showered on us as children. We are both so proud of our children. We both believed that life is good and how fine is the human spirit.

Our husbands both suffered racial discrimination – Manuel as an immigrant and Eddie as a black Australian. They were also both victims of lung cancer, from which Eddie died and Manuel survived. Stomach cancer eventually killed Manuel. The differences in the medical care available to our husbands were preposterous. Manuel was outraged by the lack of medical treatment available to Eddie and examined ways of taking legal action for negligence on Bonita's behalf. Manuel and Eddie both had wonderful legal brains and were great litigators. Had they met on earth, I know they would have been great friends. In death, Eddie joined Manuel in cementing the friendship between Bonita and I.

Bonita and I both played roles in influencing the lives of so many Australians: Bonita through her life with Eddie and the public profile she developed afterwards, and me in the development of young talent through my creative input in SS, An Australian Christmas, and the TDP. We were both teachers: Bonita in an Indigenous school she and Eddie set up in the 1960s, and I through my music teaching career of 20 years, the TDP and the SS. Throughout my teaching career I have attempted to instil attitudes of tolerance and social justice in my students. I am proud to see such magnificent role models emerging from the programs I helped create now influencing the entertainment industry, including Human Nature, John Foreman, Nathan Foley, Emma Pask, Felicity Urquhart, Blake Ralph, Paulini and Darren Coggan. Bonita and my dreams have come true and we have helped others realize their dreams. We are both proud of our work.

Before I met Bonita, I was already passionate about Indigenous Australians and had made sure each SS since the first one included an Indigenous item. I'd been switched onto the cause by our good friend Father Ted Kennedy, the priest of Redfern. We spent some unusual times as a family in that presbytery in the years from 1972 onwards. Ted insisted that all helpers had to be physically involved. My labour included peeling potatoes, but more significantly I used my musical skills to build a singing group with the children and I had some lovely times sharing songs. I met the legendary Mum Shirl during those days.

Manuel and I attended Eddie Mabo's tombstone opening in 1995 in Townsville. It was then I realised how ignorant Sydneysiders, and most of the people I knew, were about the depth of Indigenous pride and culture that exists. Bonita was very keen for us to attend and she referred to the event as involving much dancing. In my ignorance, I had envisaged the dancing to be like the dancing I knew such as barn dances, the Pride of Erin and the foxtrot. Instead, we were treated to waves of colourful and exciting Torres Strait Islander groups proudly dancing to honour Eddie. I was incredibly impressed by the sheer numbers of Indigenous guests, including the dancers. I remarked to Manuel at the time that most Sydneysiders had no idea that this culture existed, let alone with such large numbers, and I was determined to make a change.

I think I helped bring Bonita out of her shell. I encouraged her to make speeches, and to believe in herself and her strength. She gave a powerful Australia Day address at my 1994 Australia Day Ceremony production in Darling Harbour. A strong message she delivered was "black fellas – we have to clean up our own backyard first."

I introduced her to my circle of friends, some of whom were doctors who tried to sort out her serious diabetic and sight health problems. I realised most people I knew had never socialised with Indigenous Australians. They loved and respected her. My friend, ophthalmic surgeon Frank Cheok treated her deteriorating eye conditions, and introduced her to other medical clinicians to help sort out her diabetes. Then there was the excitement of her meeting Nicole Kidman and Tom Cruise, through my friends Janelle, and the late Antony Kidman. She loved being on the set for Tom's *Mission Impossible* film, and was treated with great respect by Tom and the film's producer. They knew all about Mabo Land Rights.

On the set of Mission Impossible with Bonita, Tom and Janelle

Bonita and I travelled to Alice Springs together when I was searching for Indigenous talent for a proposed Qantas commercial. Wherever I went with Bonita she was treated like royalty amongst Indigenous Australians. I tried to have her in the audience to as many SS as I could over the years, because it gave the Indigenous performers such a boost.

She was with me soon after I bought my holiday house in Culburra. We stood at the beach looking up and she loved it. She could still see then. We holidayed there when I took possession, and on one visit we recorded our conversations, intending to write a book. We sang and danced together. I was steeped in her history and in awe of her incredible life story and I wanted her to be recognised for her remarkable contribution to furthering the cause of support for Indigenous Australians.

Bon stayed with me in Walker St many times. One powerful and unforgettable occasion was when she led the Sorry March across the Harbour Bridge. We spent a lot of time talking that through after the march and I felt her pain. I know all about her life with Eddie and the high spots alongside the humiliations and deprivations she endured. I have those memories recorded. I loved spending time with Bon in her Queensland territory too, especially her beloved Halifax. I have those memories to cherish.

When Gail first rang me to tell me my friend was dying, I was on the Camino. I said goodbye to her through the phone with my son Andy visiting her. I asked her to wait until I came home. She was only expected to last for a few days and we were so relieved to have another year.

We have been so good for each other. Life without Bonita in it is diminished.

I felt she was ignored and neglected by an ignorant Australian Government.

The 1990s were rich with new exciting concerts and events for Mary Lopez Productions.

I continued to produce Australia Day Concerts and Ceremonies which were held in the beginning in Tumbalong Park and later the Sydney Convention Centre for a few years.

A new private school production was the Edmund Rice Centenary concert which MLP staged at the Sydney Town Hall for the Christian Brothers Centenary. Annie Whealy directed the shows for MLP and was assisted by an ex-EBHS student, Grant Pierce, who is now an established icon in the Fashion Industry. Annie and I also had another school production under our wing which we'd enjoyed. The concert for the opening of the new music centre for Kinross Wolaroi College at Orange suited us perfectly, with very good musicians performing at the school which was the located in lush rural surrounds.

The late Brian Walsh gave me some very interesting contracts over the next few years. I was to produce pre-entertainment for many major ARL and ARU games. The style of entertainment included big names from the Rock industry and always featured a huge cast display of children. The teachers and I saw these events as a further opportunity for the school children to perform, widen their view of life and have a good fun experience. The stage managers required to manage the cast were drawn from the talented and enthusiastic team of mainly teachers who worked on the SS. We all have such great memories of these mostly hugely successful events. I really don't want to remember the infamous Billy Idol chaotic performance, or lack of it, when we could not get his microphone to work.

The World Indigenous Day, part of an International Conference was held in Wollongong. MLP produced a parade of 3,000 international Indigenous participants, and a Gala concert at Wollongong Stadium. Ernie Dingo hosted and the concert included the first appearance of Women from the Central Desert. It was an amazing production although incredibly difficult because we couldn't have a rehearsal. The Women from the Central Desert couldn't be seen before their performance and no one from the International Indigenous contingents turned up for rehearsal. My team did an almighty magical job in stage managing to get them all out on to the arena for the concert. Ernie held the concert together, hosting with humour and skill. It was a wonderful show to produce and further cemented my reputation amongst Indigenous Australians. –But more importantly, it confirmed my commitment to be a voice for change.

This very challenging stage management project was led by Jim Bennett and his expert team of teachers from the SS. I knew if any individuals would be able to manage the parade of the 3,000 delegates from so many different nations it'd be those same teachers who managed 3,000 performers each year in the SS.

Noel Pearson was emerging as an Indigenous leader. I loved his ideas and his writings. I believed he would be a great person to enter politics. His manager, at that time, visited me in my office to talk over including performers in a platform to promote him. I was really keen to support Noel, but I didn't hear anything after that from his manager.

SS No. 10, entitled "One Spirit" was very significant for the future involvement of Indigenous performers. It also showcased some more now household names, including 17-year old David Harris, who gave a stunning performance of Peter Allen's *Don't Cry Out Loud* and is now a star of Broadway. Twelve-year-old Simon Tedeschi played piano accompanied by the symphony orchestra *Rhapsodie on a Theme of Paganini* by Rachmaninov. Simon is now an internationally renowned concert pianist. And finally there was Felicity Urquhart, who is now a multi–Golden Guitar winner at the Tamworth Country Music Festival. Special guest were The Four Trax boys who went on to become the international boy band wonder Human Nature.

In this year, 1993, the Year of Indigenous Peoples, we certainly paid tribute to the Aboriginal and Torres Strait Islanders. They inspired us with their intense spiritual relationship with this magnificent land, Australia.

More travel and more shows

Manuel and I proudly watched Andy graduate with his Bachelor Science/Psychology degree. Truthfully speaking, Andy was not a diligent student and he filled his years with the usual experimentations that are a worry to all parents. You realise how comforting were those school days where there were at least some restrictions and parental supervision. Our way to maintain contact as a family was to offer travel so we could share some overseas experiences. We had some memorable trips to the Philippines during these years with both Andy and Kate.

Manuel and I walked the Inca Trail in Peru in July with Manuel being minus half a lung. This was a magnificent adventure. Manuel hired a group of five porters to carry our tents and supplies, and we set off after a few days in Cusco where we sucked on coco leaves to protect us from altitude sickness. Having staged two stage productions of *The Royal Hunt of the Sun* about the Spanish invasion of Peru and the destruction of the Inca Empire, I was eager to visit the monumental Inca ruins of Machu Pichu and walk the four-day trail. Our Peruvian porters even carried a stove. One night our guide recommended we have a reading session with an Indian who connected with spirits. He told us someone close to us would die. As Manuel had been cleared of lung cancer, we thought we were safe. Two years later Manuel died of stomach cancer.

The trail was truly a wondrous experience. The scenery was too awesome to put into words. Manuel bravely rode on a small horse upwards to the greatest heights, because his lung capacity was so severely limited after his surgery to cut out the cancer. I also tried a horse but was terrified when the horse lurched from side to side on a path with deathly drops to the side. I can still feel the magnitude of this walk. It was certainly a huge challenge but it was the best walking experience of my life. I'm so glad Manuel led me to Peru.

I was notified in La Paz, that I had secured an interview for 2000 Olympics Director of Ceremonies. I was on a short list of five to be interviewed. We rang from La Paz to be reassured that it was a level playing field because we would have to return early. We were assured it was. No way was that true. As soon as I was interviewed, I knew they weren't interested. The people interviewing me didn't ask enough questions. I assumed correctly that the Olympic "gravy train", under the internationally recognised and admired Director of Ceremonies, Ric Burch would be appointed.

As I was the only female and one of only five people interviewed I was still hoping to have some contribution to the Ceremonies. I wanted to have some involvement, but Ric ignored any approach I made. It was worse for the very experienced and admired producer, Andrew Walsh, who introduced himself to Ric at a function only to have the response "so what." Andrew was so stunned and shocked he had to retreat to the bathroom to wash his face. Andrew has since been the creative and technical brain producing huge inspired global events. Amongst his triumphs are the Ceremonies and Spectaculars for the 2004 Athens Olympics, Melbourne Commonwealth Games, London Millenium and White Night Melbourne as well as many other unforgettable events.

I managed Jenny Davis for a few years throughout this period. Jenny became the face of NSW Tourism for a four-year period which led her to perform at Atlanta and record *Sail Down to Australia* to sing at 1996 Announcement of Sydney's successful bid for the Sydney Olympics 2000. Jenny was an outstanding performer with a voice like velvet and had featured in early SSs from the age of 14. The association with NSW Tourism increased my government network and broadened my knowledge.

Channel 10 televised the SS No. 11, which was themed to match the International Year of the Family. They wanted as Brent Myer, a young reporter for Channel 10, to co-host with John Foreman. The Performing Arts team this year became the powerhouse behind the SS and is still managing all these years on. Vanessa Corish was co-compere for this show. She co-wrote the song *Dare to Dream* which was then performed at the 2000 Olympics Opening Ceremony by Olivia Newton-John and John Farnham. Also appearing in this SS was the amazingly talented Shaun Rennie, then in primary school. Shaun, TDP graduate in 1999, is now one of Australia's leading theatre directors and a director of major operatic, musical theatre, and theatrical productions for the Australian Opera and a myriad of other theatres. He is the currently the Associate Director of Australian Opera and is spreading his immense talents to France in 2025 where he will revive a production of *The Tales of Hoffman* for Opera Lyon.

A young Shaun Rennie

In January 1995, I staged the life of Mary McKillop in a Pageant in the Sydney Domain. I was contracted by the Sisters of St Joseph to produce an event which would provide a welcome to the Pope, who had been invited to visit Sydney for the Beatification of Sister Mary McKillop. I came up with the idea of a costumed pageant which would depict the life of Australia's first saint. It had a celebrity line up and a huge cast, which included a symphony orchestra under the musical direction of Maestro Tommy Tycho. There were also a massed choir (including the famous Waratah Girls Choir and Carlson Chorale), actors, and hundreds of dancers from John Mullins Newtown High School of the Performing Arts, as well as many McKillop schools from Interstate and NSW. It was hosted by Bobby Limb with letters read by Geraldine Doogue.

I loved creating themed shows and this story was fascinating and perfect for dramatizing. There were seven segments depicting the life and influence of Mary McKillop. The Sisters were very grateful to the stellar cast who donated their services so the production could happen. They included:

- Julie Anthony
- Peter Cousens
- Genevieve Davis
- Grace Knight
- Normie Rowe
- Vanessa Corish
- Felicity Urquhart
- Human Nature (then Four Trax)
- William Bartton (didgeridoo) and
- Manuel, who acted as the Pope.

The late John Fahey was Premier of NSW at the time. He attended the performance and was very enthusiastic. He appreciated the big dramatic enactment of Mary's life.

Andy had graduated the year before with a Bachelor Science/Psychology and was considering doing further studies in 1994. He'd done well at Uni that year and had a position to study Honours in Psychology. He'd worked on other shows before but this time I could see that he would be very good in the events industry. He had his eye on all aspects of the show from soloists' direction, backstage and technical management, through to crowd management and security. I offered him a job at MLP which he accepted. It was a wise choice he made, which has led to an extraordinary career in the entertainment and motor events industries. My niece Madeleine McCormack also joined MLP later that year, while my amazing Kate found herself a job in Japan and set off on her adventure to teach English in a Japanese high school.

I look back on those three months and wonder how in heaven's name I managed to produce and direct three massive shows – the SS in November, the Darling Harbour Christmas Pageant and then the Mary McKillop Pageant in January. I had finally learned to delegate and trust the staff, although I kept my eye firmly on the big picture and quality control.

But there were very much more difficult times to come.

Through the years from when I upended my career in 1988 to 1995, where were Andy and Kate? They had both left school and completed university degrees. Andy had had an unforgettable adventure travelling with his father through Russia and Czechoslovakia, studied psychology and worked part time at Reark, a tele-marketing company. He behaved like most young men of that age and gave his father and me a few worrying years. But he came magnificently to the rescue later in 1995 and took over the running of all the MLP events when Manuel and I were given the grim diagnosis of Manuel's stomach cancer. Kate was teaching English in Japan. When her father was diagnosed with stomach cancer in September, she gave up that wonderful experience and came home to live with us for the last seven months of his life. They grew into adulthood very quickly and painfully. I thank them from the depth of my heart for the loving and generous way in which they both managed our lives through the terrible months that were to come.

During this time Manuel worked to release Jenny Davis from a recording contract with Robbie Porter. It was through seeing how Manuel was such a successful negotiator that I was later able to manage the legal fight with his partners in his own law firm that was to come after his death.

In September 1995, Manuel collapsed in the street. I received a phone call at lunchtime to tell me he had collapsed and been rushed to St Vincent's Hospital. The doctor told us he hoped it was a stomach ulcer. He was operated on late that day and I feel the terrible wait all over again as I write about that night. It was after midnight when the doctor rang with the news that it was stomach cancer – a new cancer with a grim prognosis.

Andy and I were in contact throughout the night. At some stage he was with me. Neither he nor I can recall exactly what his movements were that night. It was a terrible night. We had the ARL Grand Final pre-match spectacle and entertainment to produce just a few days later.

The next seven months were dreadful. But, thank God, Andy was working with me. He took control of MLP and enable me to be with Manuel all the time. During those seven months Andy and Madeleine, travelled the country and New Zealand pulling off displays for sporting events. Manuel made a huge effort to go to Madeleine's wedding on 9 December. We left from St Vincent's Hospital and he returned there after the reception.

MLP was very busy producing around 10 sporting pre-match spectaculars. Among them were the Sydney Kings' season opener, the soccer Grand Final Series in Melbourne and Adelaide, the ARL State of Origins in Sydney and Melbourne and the ARL Grand Final.

In 1995, it was also 50 years since the end of World War II. MLP, was honoured and very keen to produce a concert, which we held in Tumbalong Park at the end of the commemorative Anzac Parade through Sydney. "Australia Remembers" was a moving gala concert held on the Tumbalong Park stage in Darling Harbour. My passion for the honouring the sacrifice of service men and women was as strong as ever and I was honoured to be able to make a statement about it.

The SS program that year was built on Australian themes and music and was a very strong show. We also presented a powerful Anzac segment "Australia Remembers." Gavin Lockley sang *Bring Him Home*. We invited Vietnam veteran, Normie Rowe, to read the *Ode of Remembrance*. It was a segment intended to pay respect to our service men and women. Andy filmed a message from the then President of the NSW Returned and Services League, the late Rusty Priest, which was screened during the show and school cadets emphasised the respect we have for our serving men and women. Andy says he found that in researching the material he learned how very young were so many of the service men and women. No one who was in the audience that night will ever forget the magnificent performances by a thousand young Australians.

Can you imagine what it was like trying to manage and direct this SS followed by "An Australian Christmas" at Darling Harbour, with what was going on in my life with Manuel's cancer treatment and terrible prognosis? Thank God Andy had come to work for MLP and was able to take over the responsibility for ensuring all our events were professionally produced. The talented and loyal team I had built around me for MLP, the SS and the TDP continued to take great responsibility for their roles as they had always done. They knew how tough it was for me and my kids.

12
Death and survival

On 26 January my company staged the Australia Day Ceremony for the NSW Government at Tumbalong Park, Darling Harbour. The Governor of NSW, the Lord Mayor, members of the Australia Day Council, entertainment celebrities and government officials made the occasion a gala event. The event was a mixture of music and ceremony on a grand scale, accompanied by a symphony orchestra and the Waratah Girls Choir. I really enjoyed combining the solemnity of the occasion with music to reinforce the emotion of the occasion.

But life was about to change. Kate and I attended the Good Friday service at McKenzie St on 5 April 1996. I cried and cried that day as the reality of what was to happen set in. It was as if Manuel had already died. On the days afterwards I thought that that would be the end of the grieving. Little did I know what was about to happen and what grief was all about.

Stomach cancer is an awful way to live and die. Manuel kept busy with his work through the seven months right up until his last two weeks. I gave up work during this period to be with him.

He wanted to be at home even though he was suffering excruciating symptoms. He didn't want to receive visitors because he felt so wretched. Kate and I appreciated the warmth of friends and family, and entertained them downstairs. Andy kept my business running and came every night for months to spend time with his father. Eventually, the vomiting became unbearable, and Manuel spent the last two weeks of his life in the Sydney Adventist Hospital in Wahroonga. He received extraordinarily wonderful care from the hospital staff and his doctors, especially the brilliant Dr Peter Corte.

He wanted to see his home for the last time. We drove from the hospital to Lavender Bay and parked outside No 17 Walker St, where we had shared such happy years with family, parties and music. We had bought that house in 1991. Many people thought we were crazy to buy a new house at that time because of Manuel's tenuous hold on life, but it was the right move to live life as if you are going forward, not standing still. He loved the house.

It is painful to write about this day and remember how I had to pretend it really wasn't happening. I had to be strong for Manuel. Always putting on a brave face.

Whilst we were driving back to the hospital, we listened to the CD, *Barcelona* and settled on *Guide me Home*. He also requested the Kyrie from *Misa Criolla* and *The Wind Beneath My Wings* to be sung by and EBHS alumni, John Simpson. He knew my ex-choristers from EBHS from 1980–85, with Grant Pearce and Michael Spencer as soloists would sing the *Kyrie* from *Misa Criolla*.

Andy, Kate and I sang to Manuel throughout the night before he died on April 26, 1996. Our dear friend, John Tannhauser, was with us when Manuel died. Manuel was born in the Philippines on 30 November 1944.

I wrote in my diary a couple of weeks later: "My Popsy left his body behind". On 30 April a Requiem Mass was held at St Francis' Church at Lavender Bay. Andy and Kate organised it all because I seemed to have been defeated. But they certainly weren't." In the front of my 1996 diary I found: "And Time remembered is Grief forgotten. Blossom by blossom the Spring returns" – unknown author of this quote.

The church was overflowing with a congregation that had gathered to show respect to a man who had come to Australia with nothing just 30 years previously. He achieved success based on high intelligence, hard work and high principles. He was respected and loved by his friends, family and legal colleagues. I believe the Workers Compensation Courts even closed that morning to give his colleagues time to attend the Mass.

The Mass was concelebrated by three priests. Manuel had chosen the music for his funeral during the last drive we had together. The music was wonderful, provided by choir members and ex-students from EBHS choirs, as well as Jenny Davis. It was such a warm and loyal gesture by my EBHS choir and soloists. I've never forgotten them. Jenny Davis was a young performer we had enjoyed and helped in her career, and she sang *Guide me Home*.

I was involved with the Lavender Bay Parish and was grateful to my nun friends from the parish and the Mary McKillop Beatification team, who ensured this Mass was a fitting farewell and a celebration to be remembered.

Kate and Andy were front and centre with all the organisation because, to tell it truthfully, I felt finally defeated and exhausted. They did it all. We had a wonderful wake at home and followed his instruction "No cheap grog." Andy and Kate chose quote below to describe their father on his Funeral Mass program.

A fertile mind, deep understanding and a cultured taste lend a flavour to all of life THEN

Three things make for the superior man: a fertile mind, a deep understanding, and a cultured taste. There are minds that radiate light like the eyes of a lynx, which in the darkness see more clearly. Then there are those for the occasion. Guided by an uncanny understanding, they always strike upon that which is most beneficial. And good taste lends flavour to all life. A good imagination is another great advantage, but even greater is the ability to think clearly, for clear thinking is the sweet fruit of reason. The shoes of the superior man may not be for all, but all should make every attempt to walk in them.

Baltasar Gracian, 1658

Within a month of his father's passing, Andy hastily arranged a visit to Spain to retrace the steps he'd taken with Manuel years previously. While he was undertaking this pilgrimage of sorts Kate and I received regular letters detailing his progress. He speaks lovingly of his relationship with his father and gives an entertaining travelogue of his adventures.

Here are his first three letters after arriving in Spain:

18/5/1996

Dear Mum.

I'm sitting in the airport lounge in Madrid, waiting for my flight to Marseilles. It's about 10.45am, and I am having an orange to wash down the taste of a dubious looking and even more dubious tasting bocadillo.

I had a pleasant drive from Toledo this morning, waking up about 7am and I was here in the airport by 8.15 – the roads are great, and little Opal (my little black, steel margarine tub on wheels) is actually quite a nice drive. The weather has varied from freezing cold in Granada, to boiling hot in Cordova, wet in Toledo and now cool and temperate in Madrid.

For a trip planned at the last second, it has been remarkably hassle-free. I've had no huge problems, or gaps in planning, well, apart from one minor detail.

Imagine my horror this morning when I discovered that my return flight from Monaco was booked to leave during the actual bloody car race! I don't know whose fault it was, mine or STA's, but I'll be sure to have a little chat with them when I get back.

And of course, they'd booked me a ticket that was not changeable in any shape or form, so I had to get another one! (Don't worry. I didn't put it on my AMEX!) Anyway, now that I am a Buddhist as I'll take it all in my stride as I'm sure the travel agent will suffer duly in their next incarnation!

(This is all silliness, in case you're worried that I've freaked out and gone saffron, especially in light of our conversation last night).

Speaking of, it was lovely to get to chat properly last night, and I hope you are doing as well as you sound.

(I'll switch to capitals – my writing really is illegible otherwise).

I won't deny that it is difficult being here – I realised I haven't spent even one day in Spain without Dad. In January 1989, I tore through the country in another little rental car especially so I could pick him up at Madrid Airport, not stopping anywhere at all so I could make it on time.

Everywhere I go reminds me of him, and sometimes it gets a little bit too much for me. I <u>will</u> make that feeling a positive one though. I <u>won't</u> waste the opportunity you and Dad have given me here.

I'm beginning to sense the increasing familiarity of Spain, the sense of origin that I felt when I was here with Dad. When we travelled here together, Dad would be so proud of his country, his roots, and he became more settled, more relaxed, more his complete self.

He loved the way his language changed and adapted to contemporary Spanish, and the way he knew where everything was. And I feel that too, obviously not with the language, but a small sense so far of belonging. Being in Spain makes me even more proud to be Dad's son, because he chose to be with you, to raise us in Australia, to have the best that the New World and the Old World had to offer us.

When I return, let's look at learning Spanish together, and Kate can fill Dad's spot by being his Spanish voice at home and help us. It would be something he'd love and also something I know we could have done with Dad, had there been more time.

Read "The Tibetan Book of Living and Dying." It's helping me, Mum and I thank you for it. Remember, my religion is to live – and die – without regret.

I love you both.
Your son, your brother,
Andy xxooxx

22/5/96

Dear Mum and Kate.

I'm in Avila at the moment, scarfing down a flan in a restaurant a couple of blocks away from the main cathedral – which happens to be closed at the moment for restoration!

I've had a lovely day today, starting at Escorial, onto Valley of the Fallen, and arriving here about 3pm.

A lot of the monuments here are closed for restoration at present so I think I'll head straight onto Segovia tonight. It's about 1 hour from here. First, I'll pop out to La Encarcion Convent, pay my respects to St Theresa of Avila's finger (which I still don't understand how it came to be separated – too gruesome) and then wander the walls for a bit.

Madrid was sensational. I'm sad I only got to spend a couple of days there but I had an excellent time. So much to do and see – and eat! My hotel/hostel was lovely, and I just walked and walked the whole time I was there.

In Madrid restaurants they usually have a menú del día which is 3 courses and a drink of vino or cerveza. I thought 'what the hell?' so I had one beer and felt so pissed I had to have several coffees before I would allow myself to walk home!

The weather is stunning at the moment, thank goodness, as it is still generally a bit sad being here. I simply can't stop thinking about Dad and you guys, but that's why I'm here, I guess. I couldn't find that crucifix anywhere and I'm beginning to think it may *not be Spanish!* The search goes on but I'm thinking maybe this is something we should all do together. But if I see things that seem right, I will grab them.

As I said in my fax, Monte Carlo turned into a bit of a debacle, thanks to our somewhat dodgy tour operator. Poor Maddie *[Andy's then-girlfriend]*, her bus blew 2 tyres only 50km from the hotel, and they had to wait 5 hours for repairs. I was fine as I'd arrived at the hotel. albeit in some nowheresville town, and ensconced myself in the room watching a 24-hour English-speaking sports channel on the TV. Maddie and the rest arrived at approximately 6.30pm and we had a nice night.

The next morning, the bus was trapped in the parking lot by some cars and it took just over half an hour to get out of the bloody hotel, Then the bus developed some problem with the accelerator and it took us until 12.30pm to get to Monaco – four hours, including the parking lot scenario to go 200km on a motorway.

Of course, our tickets to the race were of such a position that we really should have been there at 9am to ensure getting a spot where we could see. Then it poured with rain. Mad and I couldn't find anywhere to sit and so wandered around Monte Carlo just listening to the cars go around. It actually rained so hard that only 3 of 22 cars actually finished the race, which Maddie and I watched through binoculars just where the bus was parked!

Oh, the other thing was that the bus people overbooked and I didn't have a seat although I had paid for it so Maddie and I took turns at sitting on the toilet (not in it). So, I got dropped off at some nowheresville place in France at 11pm on Sunday (which was preferable to sitting on top of the toilet block for another 20 hours).

Isn't it hysterical! Absolute madness. Anyway, Maddie tells me she has managed to secure a refund and they may even pay for my air ticket.

It's a good story and not too tragic in the end. It certainly took my mind completely off things for a few days.

Anyway, I'd best sign off for now. I'm growing a beard and mo at present, but it's a tidy one. I looked at some fellas in the Guernica Museum and decided that I'd copy it, so we'll see how this little fad goes. I hope all at MLP is okay at present, and that Kate has been taken into the partnership at Connery's. I love you both, and of course, wish we were all here together. I stopped by the Ritz Hotel last and took a photo.

I didn't try to go in as I felt a little bit scuzzy for the place, even sporting my new beard, etc.

I guess with things like that, I'm used to having you and Dad around to add a little class to the act. It's a beautiful part of the world here. I just wish I was here under very different circumstances.

I really better go, I have a fair bit of sightseeing to do and get to Segovia, all before the sun goes down. I lost my glasses, yes, and I won't drive unless I can wear my sunnies as they're prescription.

Again, love to you both. I'm lighting candles at every opportunity for Dad and us all. It is sad and strange here, but don't worry, I'm okay and hope you both are too.

Love, Andy.
PS Love to Shirley and Mama

25/5/96

Dear Mum and Kate,

You'll be sick of getting these letters. I can't think of any other trip I've written so frequently – no coincidence that I'm travelling on my own at present and need to look occupied while at dinner (not the only reason, of course!)

I'm still alive and surviving the driving – Spain is really quite easy to drive around; small; good, straight roads; and a mostly laissez-faire approach to speed limits. I'll admit I've been sailing around the countryside at a fairly good pace, but have never been stopped, or had the slightest attention paid to me as yet.

The police do pull people over though; maybe I'm just not going fast enough! Oh well, it leaves the holiday budget unharmed by incidental speeding tickets.

Segovia was lovely, as expected. The aqueduct appears to be holding itself together well in the absence of mortar or cement, but I'll admit I didn't want to stand around underneath it for too long. With our luck the bloody thing would have elected to fall down whilst I was leaning against it!

I spent a very pleasant couple of days simply wandering around the town – the cathedral is particularly magnificent and I discovered a new fear of heights standing at the summit of the Alcazar (palace) with only a two-foot-high wall between me and a 700 foot (or so it seemed) drop and about 300 hyperactive, running, jumping, screaming schoolchildren on the tower top with me.

All through Spain I've been followed (or in the presence of) thousands of school kiddies, all on their first visits to the same monuments I happen to be at. I must say I'm impressed with the importance placed on visiting sites of national importance by the Spanish Education Department, but my previously academic dislike of young children is turning into a desire to cause them actual harm (a joke, of course).

I also took myself on a big drive out into the surrounds of Segovia province. First stop was one of the summer palaces built for Filipe V (?) in about the 16th century, which also features a stunning garden with the most over-the-top series of fountains and man-made waterways you could imagine! The gardens were probably half the size of Sydney's Centennial Park but fully landscaped with hundreds of these interlinked fountains and waterways. Beautiful!! Then I simply tooled around through some pueblos and back leafy roads for a couple of hours. A most relaxing day indeed.

I spent a good couple of hours the first night in Segovia hunting for the restaurant where I ordered brains by mistake (well, actually, by insisting in spite of Dad's rather abstract warning), and, of course, where Grant [Pearce] fell down the stairs.

Speaking of, I've put a letter to Grant in this envelope so that (A) you'll have to see him to pass it on, (B) you can read it as there's a bit at the end of it I'd like you to see, and (C) copy it for me. You'll see I found the restaurant and thanks to a recently introduced English menu, got what I wanted. I really must learn Spanish! I don't think I'm going to have the same luck in Santiago (where I am at present) finding our New Year's restaurant.

The story behind that is at New Year's in Spain it's traditional to give everyone 12 grapes, to be devoured as the bell strikes at midnight. We had New Year's at Santiago and went to dinner about 10pm. Dad sent not one but three bottles of wine back in this restaurant, and the staff were so embarrassed by their obviously low-class wine, they gave us a bottle of good French champagne with our 12 grapes.

Not to be outdone by the restaurant's lack of class, Grantles shrieked about not possibly being able to eat the grapes with the skin on and even perhaps seeds in them! So, to the amazement of the onlooking waiting staff, not to mention Anna, Dad and myself, he squawked and panicked and desperately tried to peel these grapes and eat them, as all the bells were chiming away!

Dad was paying out on him something shocking and calling everyone's attention to Grant, which of course, only made matters worse. So, while I'm sure they'd remember us, even after 12 years, I just cannot find the place (as yet).

Also, today was San Esteban de Nogales Day. I'll write about that another time, I think. Suffice to say it was a very moving and unusual experience.

A couple of things: I've included a family tree for Kate and Mama to sort out – I thought it might be a nice thing to have. I stayed there for more than five hours and drove around and sat with Antonina all day. Thanks to the good people of Berlitz we actually communicated reasonably well. Finally, everyone came across, not just the relatives but all the townsfolk, expressed their regret and told me about the special Mass they held at the pueblo church "por Momo." There's a lot more tell you.

Anyway, I best go – it's well after midnight and I should finish my dinner and get out of this smoky restaurant and get some rest. It's been a long day and Maddie arrives here in Santiago tomorrow.

I've figured out (partly) what makes the whole holiday so strange for me. I am doing this for Dad mostly, not me, and I need to do this for myself because no matter how important this would be to Dad, it's more important that this journey resolve things for me somehow. Does that make sense? I'll have to think further upon it.

So take good care of your selves – I'm thinking of you always, and I look forward to an opportunity for all of us to do something like this together in the future. I hope all is well at MLP, and that you're [Kate] enjoying your new job at Connery's!

All my love
Andy

Just in case you missed it, a great song for Genny – I think is "Power of Love", Frankie Goes to Hollywood, and it's on the CD we own (either at MLP or Les Goch's)

As I read over these letters I realise what an amazing journey my son took and how lucky I was to have such letters to awaken memories of Manuel and of the country both he and I loved. Also I am mightily impressed with Andy's gift for language, the written word and punctuation. He has the great educators, the Jesuits, to thank for those skills. His father would be so proud to see these letters. He was absolutely determined that Andy have a Jesuit education.

Bonita Mabo came to stay for three weeks after Manuel died. I remember very little of her being with me through that period. She was like a spirit being there to comfort and support me, as only she knew how to do. Andy and Kate had arranged for her to come to me. I always felt I had to manage on my own. Ever since Mum had died I had never felt that I had anyone who would love me sufficiently to support me and take some responsibility for me.

Over the next eight to ten years we saw each other quite often. She was able to travel then and was in demand as a guest and speaker. I tried to get her some financial support since she was always poor. Then her health issues got in the way.

It was a strange coincidence that both of our husbands had suffered with lung cancer. It was tragic that Eddie died with such poor diagnosis and treatment. Manuel was looking at legal issues surrounding Eddie's poor treatment when he died in 1996.

Andy set up his own company in September and Kate graduated with her first degree in Arts in October. My two amazing children showed their strengths as they moved their lives forward,

Throughout these years, Jean had been my untiring and loyal PA. She went way beyond the call of duty. Her skills and experience were rewarded when she left me for another career as the Marketing and Promotions manager for 2GB and later CH9.

In August 1996, I travelled to Atlanta, Georgia, for the Olympics with Jenny Davis where she performed at an Australian delegates function. I met Dawn Fraser who was part of the Olympic Delegation. Dawn became a lovely associate over the years to follow and graciously appeared in a dancing role in a SS years later.

In September, MLP produced "Youthquake", which was a huge youth concert sponsored by Foxtel and held in Tumbalong Park, Darling Harbour. Brian Walsh was the Executive Producer.

Fight to hold on

The following years were difficult for me as I struggled back after the seven terrible years of Manuel's cancers. I became aware some people I had worked with for many years in the Department of Education in administration, as well as some TDP Board members, were undermining me. I don't know why, because I was still working hard. I guess they were not understanding of the immense pressure I had borne because of my husband's ill health and death. I can only put it down to envy. Instead of embracing my strengthening network and experiences those people wanted to own what I had created and crusaded for and dismiss me. How it hurt to know this undermining was happening.

After Manuel died I lost interest in the commercial world of production and decided to concentrate on my core business: the SS, the TDP and the Christmas Pageant.

Andy was working with me and took over the reins of MLP. He worked with my niece, Madeleine, to pull off the entertainment at sporting events my company had committed to around Australia and in NZ. They have told me hilarious stories about them having to find the display casts on their arrival in both Perth and Auckland. At very late stages they had to approach dance studios and virtually train them on the day of the event. I envisaged dance students on the loose, almost, on those football fields.

I know I took my eye off the ball during this time and for the following couple of years. I was completely emotionally and physically exhausted after Manuel's death and seven long years of his illness. At the same time as I continued to feel not wanted by the Performing Arts personnel and the Department of Education. I also had the most horrendous situation to deal with through Manuel's law firm.

Manuel had meticulously written out all his assets, insurances and work in progress. He wanted to ensure that I knew what my financial situation would be without him. It was this document that made it clear to me and the lawyers what his financial position was. Two months after he died his partners informed me that they would dispute the agreement he had with them regarding the insurance policy and his work in progress understanding. Kate, Andy and I were gutted. The shock was too much to bear. Andy rang and spoke to one of Manuel's partners, whose comment was: "It's nothing personal. It's business."

Could you believe it? These were our friends, and had been for some 20 years. One of the partners had even been mentored by Manuel and his successful career was largely due to Manuel's direction and guidance.

So, instead of grieving and learning to live without a husband and a father, we spent two years fighting a law firm. I thought about representation and asked a lawyer from a rival litigation firm, who had often opposed Manuel professionally. Manuel had always spoken very highly of the skills of Amando Gardeman. He was marvellous, both as a person and a lawyer. Thanks to Kate's great support in gathering and recording of all correspondence we came up with the evidence needed to settle the case.

The firm, to which Manuel had given so much of his incredible brain and time to develop, no longer exists. I no longer feel anger, but I am still shocked by the behaviour of certain persons. I thought they were friends.

When time came for the SS following Manuel's death, I was deep in the trauma of legal problems and I dreaded arriving at the rehearsals, which were held at Homebush. However, I was met by Judi Joy and other team members with great kindness and sensitivity. It was like I was returning to family. Even so, I could not concentrate at rehearsals as I was still in shock from the tragedy of that year. At the actual production in the Sydney Entertainment Centre, Meri Took, the Production Manager, complimented me and made me feel very special in the red dress I wore. The dress had been made for me by Merima Karat's mother, whom I had befriended. The Karat family were Bosnian Refugees and TDP provided direction and guidance for Merima as she pursued her musical career. Funny how those moments remain with you.

Survival my way

In 1997, my American friend Scott Stoner encouraged me to join him in South Africa and Madagascar. Scott was at the time Director of Dance and International Programs at the Kennedy Centre, Washington DC. Alicia Adams was leading the delegation which was auditioning performing artists in South Africa and Madagascar to potentially book for the future, to present at the Kennedy Centre. They would perform in the African Odyssey Festival. What an eye opener and education it was for me to see such "left of centre" performing groups in drama and music, including from the "township" outside Grahamstown, South

Africa, and in Antanarivo, Madagascar. During the trip we were invited to the American Consulate for a reception which the consul himself was unable to attend. He'd been attacked and left for dead by thieves who stole the push bike he was riding, although he did recover.

I produced the Australia Day Ceremony 1997, which was held indoors at the Convention Centre at Darling Harbour. It starred David Helfgott, Marina Prior, Don Burrows and Maestro Tommy Tycho. Barrie Unsworth, then-Premier was very generous in his praise for the ceremony and concert. David Helfgott's life story came out in year film that year with David being played by Geoffrey Rush. David absolutely charmed everyone especially the Premier.

I was kept busy producing the pre-match entertainment spectacles for the ARU Grand Final and numerous other sporting leagues. Andy was on top of these events and was soon ready to branch off with his own company.

"An Australian Christmas Pageant" continued. By now the Pageant was attracting names to perform who were household names in the entertainment industry. This year the strong and immensely talented women, Leah Purcell, Jackie Love and Sandra Sully, all appeared. These live Christmas Pageants were filmed and edited by Martin Johnson for Wesley Mission and screened a few days later on Channel 7 and again on Christmas Day.

Andrew directing Christmas Pageant stars

Family affair on the job – Andy, me, Kate

Tania Doko (Bachelor Girl), Maria Venuti, Caroline O'Connor, Maree Montgomery, Francine Bell, Felicity Urquhart

Jonathan Welch, Francine Bell, Graeme Connors, Darren Coggan

From Left Jacke Love, Vannessa Amorosi, Tania Doko, Francine Bell, Leah Purcell, Caroline O'Connor, Felicity Urquhart

During these years of the Darling Harbour Christmas Pageant, an amazing young 18 year old Michael Cassel briefly worked in my office and borrowed Christmas scores to stage his own Christmas Pageant in Kiama. Below is a reference I wrote for him some years later:

> *I have worked in the entertainment industry as a Producer and Director for over twenty-five years and I have never witnessed such a spectacular rise of a theatrical practitioner as Michael Cassel. As a teenager he showed outstanding talent and a unique ability to bring together huge casts for his very successful productions. His powerful communications skills have been largely responsible for the meteoric development of his career.*

> *Over the years, I have witnessed Michael's talents develop as a producer and creative director of special events, concerts and theatrical productions to the point where he has now risen to a position in the international arena that many would not achieve in a lifetime. His peers respect him for his extraordinary work ethic, good humour and generosity towards others in the entertainment industry.*

In April, my dear departed friend Sister Kay Fennel (a Dominican Nun) encouraged me to take a healing program at the Blessed Sacrament, Saint Mary's Towers Retreat Centre at Douglas Park. I was having a hard time finding space to grieve because of the legal dispute and my heavy workload leaving me no time to think or feel. I was emotionally drained and physically exhausted. I needed time for me, so in April I took a week of leave. I was to spend seven days without talking. Sister Joan Fisher, the spiritual leader of the retreat, was inspirational and the peace of the silence of the retreat worked wonders for me. Joan gave me a piece of advice I've always remembered. I told her I couldn't pray in a church. She asked me: "Where do you feel God?" I answered: "In nature." Her reply was: "Clearly, pray where you CAN, not where you can't." It's been very much that way for me ever since. I find peace in the country without the concrete, cars and buildings suffocating me. Give me trees and grass and I'm happy.

At the time, I also made lists of the people I had in my life whom I thought I could reach out to in my depressed state. When you are lost it's so hard to pick up the phone because you don't feel that anyone is there for you. But if you have a list than you can see there's a hand you can grab onto. I divided my contacts into three groups: 1 – Family, 2 – Friends of both of us; and 3 – My friends. Group 2 have since disappeared from my life. I was lonely because I found I really didn't have many close friends because we had mostly mixed with Manuel's friends who were associated with his career in law. They disappeared quickly. The lesson I learned is to be sure to hold on to your family and girlfriends because they'll always be there for you.

Sr. Joan insisted that Manuel would send me a sign. I was to talk to him and he would let me know that he heard me. I can still picture myself sitting in the sunlight in the garden asking for a sign. I knew he was there when a galah landed just behind my chair. Manuel was always amused by my serious attachment to galahs.

The retreat leader asked us to do some drawings about the way we felt. I drew myself shackled to a bed. I wrote about feeling manipulated. When I look at what was going on behind the scenes in my career, I was in fact being seriously manipulated. I wrote all of this down at the time and have since read it all over again. The memories are less painful, but they are remembered.

Annie Whealy, who was working with me as Musical Director for the Darling Harbour Christmas Pageant had been on the lookout for a harmonica instrumentalist for the song *I am Australian*. She excitedly announced she'd found one playing at the Riverview College Music Night, Frank Cheok. I didn't know it at the time, but he was not just a harmonica player. He was also an esteemed and leading ophthalmic surgeon. After appearing in the Christmas Pageant, the caring and thoughtful Dr Frank Cheok sensed my grief and suggested to me that it would be beneficial and enjoyable for me to join his Saturday morning walking group. I followed his advice, joined the group and am still walking 3–4 times a week.

Dr Frank Cheok and Maree Montgomery in cast of Christmas Pageant

They also invited me to join them on a safari to Broome and the Kimberley the following year. His wife Mee-Na and their best friends Pam and Graeme Johnson rescued me from a lonely life and invited me to share many social and walking activities. From here-on I rediscovered my Australian life and learned that walking had enormous physical and mental health benefits. These amazing friends truly did rescue me. They set me up with a strong foundation and knowledge for the busy years ahead. They kindly propped me up during those very tough and lonely years. I think that's the reason I'm still healthy at 80+ years.

In the Kimberley

Thus began a love affair with Broome and the Kimberley, which has enriched my life forever. The lessons I learned from this wonderful group of people, the travels in which they included me, and their goodness and decency educated me in family matters and gave me a solid friendship base which I still value.

I arrived at the airport with my suitcase and plastic bags ready for the Australian adventure which would, in so many ways, influence the next phase of my life. We were a group of about 20 travellers on a bus which sometimes worked and other times did not. Two inexperienced young fellows were our guides. Our walking group leader organised this Kimberley adventure which was a combination of staying in fixed tents like El Questro and pitching our own tents, as well as luxury resorts like the Cable Beach Club in Broome. I had never been camping or shared accommodation so it was a very enlightening experience.

I loved the magnificent scenery and the company of my friends. The majesty of the gorges reminded me of the great monuments and cathedrals I had seen in Europe, except these were natural wonders. The colours were extraordinarily bright, and my fascination with Indigenous culture was further ignited. I staged a couple of funny productions in our campsites featuring my fellow travellers acting generally to the words of a song. My "productions" became a fixture of the tours and rallies over the years to follow.

Our arrival at the swish Cable Beach Club was to be by sailing boat, which promised to be an especially memorable one. It certainly was, as we were dropped off amidst unexpected rocks and swirling tides. We arrived looking wet and bedraggled and feeling lucky to have made it without cuts and bruises. It was an hilarious end to our tour of the Kimberley. However, we did hear about the Kimberley legendary couple, Peter Murray and his late wife, Anne. We determined to return the following year for another trip with an experienced guide.

On the second Kimberley trip we travelled with Peter and Anne. I learned about Lombadina, an Aboriginal community up the "Corrugated Road", 200km north of Broome. Peter introduced me to Bill Reed, the extraordinary pearl farmer and co-founder of Linney's Jewellery and Pearl Business. I asked Bill what the best thing was to do in the Kimberley region. He said: "When I'm asked that question by clients and business people who can afford to do anything in the world, I advise them to visit Lombadina." I tucked that bit of information away and acted on it when I was a very deep low some months later in Sydney.

I rang Lombadina, to see if I could spend some time there to try to recover from the pain of Manuel's death and the subsequent drama I was living. I had no idea what to expect or how to get there from Broome. I asked if I could be picked up. Robert Sibasado (son of Basil and Carolyn) turned up in Broome to meet me. I hadn't realised I was supposed to take all my own food so we went shopping. He then drove me the 200kms of corrugated road to the community of Lombadina. That corrugated road was made famous by the musical written by Jimmy Chi, entitled *The Corrugation Road*. I had enjoyed his first musical *Bran Nue Dae*.

I was booked into accommodation in the half of the community which was run by Basil and Carolyn. After being taken to my cabin (a donga like a construction workers hut) I was told the Sibasado family would see me on Monday (it was then Friday). I was shocked because had no idea what I would do with myself.

It turned out to be a time of reflection and healing. I wrote to Manuel with my heart and in floods of tears. The family decided I was an ok guest and invited me to join them in a family picnic and fishing activities over the weekend. I found great comfort in being there with them and my respect for Indigenous Australians was reinforced. It's just sinking in as I write this now, that this was the second time I was looked after by Indigenous Australians after Manuel died since Bonita was there with me immediately after Manuel died. They understood my pain and were able to heal my sadness and trauma.

I've been back to Lombadina many times since then and have taken quite a few of my friends to that unique place. These off-the-grid relationships continued to shape me and influence the way I dealt with the young people I helped develop along the way as well as influencing the content of the SS.

When I met Rob in 2001, I introduced him to Lombadina. I told him that I didn't have time to educate him about Indigenous culture and I needed to have him understand my passion to help Australians respect the Indigenous Australians. He had to pass the test. Rob, like most Australians, had not had any opportunity to get to know any Indigenous Australians and it was essential for me if he was to be my permanent partner, that he accept and respect them and in return be accepted and respected. He passed with flying colours. He and Basil bonded over the community's watering system. Basil was a giant of a man who created a showcase community which is to this day almost my favourite place to visit. Sadly this giant of a leader and father died not long after. I'm so pleased that Rob got to know Basil.

On with the job

The Hon John Brown AO, the retired Minister for Arts, Sport and the Environment was so impressed with the performing talent and skills of the TDP graduates that in 1997 he began offering $10,000 scholarships through the Sport and Tourism Youth Foundation (STYF) Awards he had set up.

John Brown AO with volunteer TDP Consultant Little Pattie

John ran the Foundation with passion and had enormous respect for talent. He believed students needed money to move forward with their dreams. These scholarships and performance showcases at the fundraising dinners continued until 2014. John had the final say on the recipients after I gave my recommendations to him. The first recipient was Felicity Urquhart in 1997 then Trevor Ashley in 1998 and Jedd Hughes in 2000. The scholarships were integral in helping to kickstart the careers of over 50 TDP graduate recipients. These included such diverse musicians as:

- Trevor Ashley
- Lorenzo Rositano
- Roshani Priddis
- Julie Lea Goodwin
- Kirby Burgess
- Brendan Boney
- Harry Ward
- Christie Lamb
- Melanie Dyer
- Robert McDougall and
- Nicholas Gentile.

Lorenzo Rositano, a TDP graduate in 2005, was an outstanding tenor and was much admired by John. He was the recipient of several scholarships which enabled him to complete his Conservatorium and University studies. Over the years ahead all of us who had worked with him would marvel at his dedication and hard work. He was always available to show his appreciation by performing whenever he was asked for the SS or TDP. Lorenzo has become a treasured friend to both Rob and me.

Over the past 14 years I'd auditioned and run workshops for the SS in around 50 country towns and outback schools. We weren't even into the 2000s. I'd covered all country regional centres and even an off-shore school at Norfolk Island, whose excited singers and dancers appeared in the SS later that year.

In late December 1997, Andy, Kate and I travelled to Manila in the Philippines for Christmas. We were all a bit dazed after such an horrendous year. I don't recall much about the trip, but it was a commitment we all made to connect with Manuel through his connection to Manila and the Philippines. I do remember the fireworks at New Year which were a concern, seeing how there was no regulation and fires broke out easily. Kate remembers how I just cried my eyes out as the year ended.

I can't believe I was doing all this work whilst battling a law firm, but in May 1998 we went to mediation, and we won. Amando Gardeman skilfully guided the case, and Barry Toomey QC represented us. We were thankful to our expert and sympathetic lawyers and were satisfied with the outcome. Manuel's previous law firm had to pay costs and that says it all. It was finally over.

After the mediation I made up my mind to move forward. The past three years had been very bleak, sad and stressful for me personally. Dealing with Manuel's death and the ensuing legal battle had taken all my energy and emotions. Thrown in were tough neurosurgeries for Kate and the death of our ever-loving Auntie Shirl.

Then along came my old friend, Maree Montgomery, with her optimism and great resilience, and we set off to support each other in our personal recoveries. Maree was trying to hold herself together after a distressing divorce, which left her financially destitute and without the home in Lane Cove that she had bought. Kate, who was living with me after returning from Japan to support her dying father, suggested it might be a good idea for Maree to have a roof over her head and for me to have company. Kate had also been through so much with her professional legal research and support in the fight for Manuel's claims against his law firm. Kate's legal career had really begun in 1996 when she left her father's law firm after his death. She moved to Dexter Healy after being offered a job by the kind and sensitive partner, Peter Burston

Maree needed accommodation and I had plenty. I needed company and she was perfect. So, in between building her career as a jazz singer, nationally and overseas, she stayed with me on and off. She says she never knew who would be in for dinner and she spent much of her time at home "wearing rubber gloves." I had many catered dinners and lunches around my beautiful King William table for 12 (often stretched to 18). These were heady days and were full of colourful and energetic people. The following years were exciting and crowded with corporate and government lunches and dinners, many of which provided opportunities for young performers to showcase and practise their performing skills. My network increased the profile of the SS at the same time as introducing the young performers to a world they could only have dreamt about knowing. Just like the young girl from Merriwa all those years ago.

My career grew. Overall, I worked under seven Premiers of NSW: Neville Wran (1976–1986), Barrie Unsworth (1986–1988), Nick Greiner (1988–1992), John Fahey (1992–1995), Bob Carr (1995–2005), Barry O'Farrell (2011–2014) and Mike Baird (2014–2018). I had little to do with Wran and Baird but found all the Premiers in between to be very supportive and interested in the young performers and the Spectaculars I was producing.

Bruce Harris had told me about creating three and five year plans, and how if you write down your dreams, they come true. Maree and I wrote out our five year plans. Mine included a holiday house by the sea although I didn't plan what was to happen next. Maree had a childhood friend who had bought a house at Culburra Beach NSW so we decided to visit her. We set off on the wrong highway didn't realise until we stopped to ask for directions to Culburra Beach at a roadhouse near Goulbourn which is on the Hume Highway. We should have been on the Princes highway. We were way off track so we had to backtrack and get to the coast via the beautiful Kangaroo Valley. Anyone who knows that road will agree it's a difficult road with all the sharp curves and steepness leading to the coast.

When we eventually arrived, three hours late, Maree's friend Cathy immediately treated us both with the loving care and consideration we both so needed. I fell in love with Culburra and immediately went in search of a house to buy. When I contacted the local agent, I was shown one that was about to come on the market. The view was sensational and after a little negotiation the property on the water was mine. More about that later.

As a jazz singer, I asked Maree to give a young jazz pianist an opportunity to play with her and a group of fabulous musicians. The schoolboy, John Foreman, turned up dressed in a suit and played like a professional. The polite and extraordinary talented John made a lasting impression on Maree and those other great musos including pianist Ray Alldridge, bass Dave Ellis and drums Harry Rivers. John Foreman AM is now a household name with an Australian Medal awarded to him in 2024.

Maree and me

Kerry Vanslambrouck became the part-time TDP Coordinator, a position she held until 2004. Kerry was very nurturing, extremely experienced in marketing and events and thought outside the confines of performing opportunities formerly available in education circles. She was used to dealing with television because of her previous marketing work. It was natural that under her watch the four-part ABC series about the TDP was filmed and screened.

Kerry Vanslambrouck, Helen Pain, me and Andy

I continued my crusade to find talented performers from the country and in 1998 I auditioned musicians in many regional towns including Dubbo, Coonamble, Tamworth and Kingscliff. I also visited Gail Mabo, daughter of Bonita and Eddie, who was living and teaching in Coonamble. Gail was a creative choreographer, and it was an ideal chance for me to ask her to choreograph an item for both Indigenous and non-Indigenous dancers in the SS that year. The result was a truly inspired creative dance item which bought the beauty of Indigenous culture to the SS and was the inspiration for more Indigenous inclusion to follow.

Roshani Priddis putting her best foot forward

I'll be honest. Mary Lopez scared the shit out of me as a teenager. Just as well though, because she had the ability to make us all pull up our socks and put our best foot forward.

Whether it be the workshops for TDP or the many and varied performance opportunities that the project and Schools Spectacular provided for us public school-educated kids, she was always able to draw the best out of us ... because she led by example.

Mary had a presence about her – the distinct feeling that she meant business. She would walk in the room and you could feel her focus, her love and her passion for what she was doing.

It was palpable because TDP and Schools Spec was her life's work and she proudly wore that passion on her sleeve.

Mary created a space for performance education that had never existed before. She dreamed the impossible and then pulled up her sleeves and got to work to make that dream a reality.

Not for herself either. This was in service of the young creative community. This was about giving kids an avenue to pursue their wildest dreams and the education to back it up.

I was a kid from Tamworth – bright-eyed, bushy-tailed, full of gusto and slightly too arrogant, probably a teenager thing (or not, haha!)

Every month heading down on the CountryLink train to Sydney Entertainment Centre to spend two days with industry professionals from all parts of the music business, all coordinated by Mary, with the help of the wonderful TDP team was nothing short of astounding!

The opportunities I had in my early years set a foundation to bounce off and a safe space to come back to whenever I've needed guidance.

I look back at TDP and Schools Spec and see more than 20 years have passed. But it feels like yesterday.

Each year I grow as a person and as a musician I gain an even deeper appreciation for the early experiences in the project and for Mary Lopez and what she created.

A true-blue Aussie icon of the arts community in this country and a pioneer of performing arts education for our youth and beyond.

Mary, we thank you and salute you.

Roshani

13
Mary Lopez AM

At Government House with family

In the Australia Day Honours 1999, I received an Australian Honour: the Order of Australia for Services to the Performing Arts and to the Australian Entertainment Industry. I was overwhelmed with gratitude to be honoured in such a way, although it didn't really sink in until I retired. Some years later I was even more grateful when I found out that Andy had set up my nomination. I look back on my huge body of work and know that I was too busy getting on with the next project to appreciate what was right in front of my face. Andy's production and creative skills were in full flight as he and Kate staged the most wonderful surprise for me with my own special fireworks.

Andy, Kate and Me at my AM party

We'd been gathered for drinks and nibbles for an hour before we were told two buses were waiting outside my house in Walker St, Lavender Bay. We weren't told the destination, but it turned out to be a trip for all guests to celebrate with fireworks off Blues Point Park. When the bus arrived at Blues Point Park we were greeted with champagne, hors d'oeuvres and a stage for a few celebratory speeches. I'd love to do that party all over again.

Widge's speech

Most people here today have a pretty good idea of why Mary has received her "gong". That really is the end of the story and I thought you might be interested in the beginning of the story that has produced our kind, generous, loyal and creative sister Mary.

I'll talk you through from pig tails in infancy to outrageous hairdos during her conservatorium years that would have embarrassed Carmen Miranda, and give you an insight into Mary's first thirty years.

The last of eight children, Mary was hopelessly spoilt, particularly by Mum and Shirley. She even had shoes to wear to primary school, an indulgence that Cecil, Shane and myself were spared. even today Mary has only to mention that she's a bit peckish and Shirely will fluff her feathers and project herself into a frenzy of sandwich making and starvation prevention cooking. Dot might smile, but I also know she wore shoes to primary school.

With Mum and Cecil, the chief providers at well, small Paterson, flat out in the pub, Shane and I were often coerced into a bit of babysitting. I have memories of two barefooted boys, Shane and myself, racing madly their mentally modified turbo charged prams containing two wild-eyed sisters, Dot and Mary, around Mrs Williamson's corner and doing an Evel Kenevel leap over the storm water gutters. Wind conditions that hot afternoon were against us and the two girls fairly flew out of those prams when they bottomed in that paspalum matted gutter. Fear always brought out the best of compassion in Shane and myself – "Shut up, Stop that crying. Don't tell Mum." "I will." "I'll buy you a lolly." Shane, being older, was always a whiz with words in these situations. "Widge, go and pinch three pence out of Cecil's room." Cecil, the local S.P. bookie) had a tin of threepences which were a constant source of joy and wealth to Feneley family children. The sixpenny tin was for more important occasions, and no matter how hard that little squirrel worked, he never managed to fill those tins.

Mary at Paterson Public and the Dominican Convent could run like a rabbit and was the athletic champion.

Mary's love of costume and style was apparent at a very early age for, with Dot's assistance, half of the kindergarten boys in Mary's class would frequently be dressed in babies' clothes and asked to play in the backyard of the Paterson pub. I sometimes ponder as to what ever became of those cross-dressing boys.

At one of the Paterson public school concerts, Mary performed in every item, and at St Joseph's Convent at Merriwa she performed in 17 of the 19 items at their annual concert. At each appearance of Mary, Shane would call out, "Bravo, bravo" and Mary would respond with feigned annoyance and glowing delight.

At a rugby league match in Merriwa, when she was 13, Mary staunchly supported one of the local family friends. Ted, a solid drinker in his mid-forties and probably still hung over, was hanging about in midfield, waiting for the play to come back to him. The referees usually disregarded Ted as he did no one any harm and only occasionally came into contact with the play. At one match the opposition fans were beside themselves when Ted took out the fullback from behind. "Off side, off side, he's been off side all day – he's off again." Mary's loyalty came to the fore and she screamed back/ "He's off side because he wants to be off side – you stupid people." Mary's always been loyal.

Following Mass of a Sunday, be it in Paterson or Merriwa, it was always a good time for singing around the piano. The Feneley line had produced some magnificent musicians well before we had been thought if and the tradition of singing together carried on. Our late sister, Geraldine, was always the most enthusiastic and voluminous of the clan. As Mary matured, church choirs and school concerts all took on a much more upmarket beat to the tune of a young country girl's enthusiastic conducting and directing. At the keyboard or with the strings was the virtuoso Dot. Of interest, Dot had passed all of her letters in music by 14 years of age and had to wait until she was 16 to have them conferred. Mary, by this time was putting her print on the entertainment industry at a very early age.

When Mary was a Teachers' College, Shane recalls her coming home for the holidays to sleepy old Merriwa sporting an unbelievable beehive, platters of fruit or other outrageous hairdos. She frequently visited the Central School and would take the kids on singing journeys they would remember for the rest of their lives.

Talking of inventiveness and originality, a trademark of Mary, I can recall my late wife Pat's wonderment at Mary's capacity to quickly make a dress an hour before a dance, and I guess, her audacity to then wear it. These revolutionary creations, eye catching though they may have been, were a mass of safety pins, steel pins and metal staples. A too amorous squeeze of the waist would usually evoke both blood ana a small expletive.

Dux of her secondary school, then Newcastle Conservatorium, her impact at Lithgow, Balgowlah and Epping Boy's High Schools, outstanding school choirs and musicals, students topping the HSC in music were achievements along her teaching career. Her transfer from public education into private enterprise seemed to logically follow and I'm sure all here are aware of Mary's achievements in the performing arts, but more importantly in the development of artistic worth in young people.

A trusting, very naive Mary has, at times, found the opposition in the entertainment industry very puzzling, for she has never lowered her own personal standards to achieve her own cause. She has always given quality, commitment and energy to whatever project she takes on. If she choose I'm sure that in the performing arts the best years are still ahead of Mary.

And that's our baby sister!

In January 1999, my great friend Ian Skilton died. Ian had been a major creative contributor to the SS since 1984. He could always see the big picture and had a knowledge of films and music theatre that was encyclopaedic. Hundreds of teachers were challenged by his imagination and set about bringing his concepts to life. Ian had a wonderful sense of humour which we all found irresistible. He made us all laugh. I missed him terribly.

Ian and Me

In reading the program for the SS later that year, I was reminded about the tiny team from 1984, of which Ian was a crucial member. The team had ballooned enormously since then. The Arts Unit Production Team and stage management had trebled since 1984. The Department of Education via the PAU leadership had always seemed reluctant to give Ian the acknowledgement or credit he deserved. They resented paying him the small amount he eventually received. He was very much more crucial to the creative content than any other person on the team. The team loved and respected Ian.

My work with young talent had brought me to the attention on Les Goch. In May, I was contracted by Les, formerly of the 70s rock band, Hush. He was now the owner of the leading Australian marketing production company, Song Zu, which had engineered the incredibly successful, "I Still Call Australia Home" campaign. Les was an exotic mix of rock musician and marketing guru and was always dressed in designer black. He contacted me to lead the search for new young talent for a proposed new marketing campaign for Qantas to be run by Song Zu. Les had been asked to carry out a talent search for a new Qantas commercial. This was to feature special young unknown solo singers including Indigenous singers. I spent quite a lot of time getting to know Les' wife, Margaret who managed the business of Song Zu. Margaret also always wore designer black and was a calm but fiercely intelligent woman. We connected immediately.

I drew up a plan for a national Talent Search Australia-wide for the proposed new Qantas promotion. Geoff Dixon was CEO at time and was keen to include Indigenous talent. That was right up my belief alley too. The search for young talent took me as far as to the far reaches of the country, from the far north of Western Australia to the centre of Australia and Far North Queensland. I auditioned in the Gold Coast, Brisbane, Townsville, Cairns and Broome, among other places. In Broome, I spent time with the sister of the girl who played the lead in the film *The Rabbit Proof Fence*. I tried hard to bring her out of her shell, because she had a very nice voice, but didn't succeed in making her confident enough to come to Sydney.

Of special importance was my trip for talent search to Alice Springs with Bonita Mabo. We were driving in from the airport when we spotted a sign for the sign for the Baptist School for Indigenous children. Because of her presence we were able to audition students from the school at very short notice. The Aboriginal TV/Media television and media outlet Imparja television were also very helpful. We auditioned some students, two of whom I brought to Sydney to audition at Les Goch's Song Zu studio in Lavender Bay. The whole experience was eye-opening for the young Aborigines from Alice. I wonder where they are now?

I saw the respect with which Bonita was held throughout Australia. Everywhere I travelled with her, she was treated with love and admiration. It's a pity the government didn't show the same respect. She was a natural leader, dignified and intelligent. I look at many of those Indigenous leaders now in the spotlight of politics and wonder what Bonita would have thought of it all. Her wisdom is needed now.

I needed some extra staff to coordinate the itinerary and employed a recent TDP graduate, the now famous director of opera and theatre, Shaun Rennie. Unfortunately, the project didn't get off the ground because Qantas had a re-think about the project when there was a restructure or some internal reshuffle. However, I learned a lot. Shaun was a very professional coordinator, showing from those very early days his variety of skills and his perceptiveness. I loved this project and was very disappointed when it didn't proceed.

I had been introduced to the Kimberley legendary musicians the Pigram brothers. One of the brothers, Alan, and I met up and found we shared many common interests and beliefs. We were both keen to develop young talent and find further horizons. Over the following years we tried several times to activate a program to take talented youth from the Kimberley to attend TDP workshops. Unfortunately it proved too expensive because everyone had to be paid. I was finding people were not prepared to give their time freely, as I had for many years.

It was in 1999 that I created my best SS with the theme "To Be Australian." I happily handed over one half of my 15-year role as Producer/Director to Barry Foster, so I could concentrate on being a Director.

I was in Culburra by myself to work out the concept for the show. I used sit by myself overlooking the ocean and let the feelings flow in, and the skeleton of the show just fell into place. I wanted to define the Australia that I knew and loved. I wanted to stir hearts and remind the performers and the audience that we are lucky to live in the best country in the world. I'd been impressed by Mark Day's article about defining the Australian spirit. So, I went in my own search of the Aussie Spirit and I discovered characteristics that define the Australian character.

This was the most important lesson that I wanted to teach and it summarised for me all that I wanted to say about Australia. It was not an easy task. After brainstorming with a special creative group I'd brought together, we came up with the fact that there is not one spirit which defines an Aussie but a combination of eight spirits. Tap beneath the surface of any Aussie and you'll find some, if not all, of the following characteristics:

- Indigenous
- Explorer
- Settler
- Immigrant
- Women
- Digger
- Larrikin and
- Mate.

My friend, Janelle Kidman, reminded me to include "the woman" spirit to make up eight spirits. Janelle was a true feminist for all of her life and I see that same strength and integrity in her two daughters, Nicole and Antonia.

In July, I attended my dear friend Paula Duncan's wedding to Steve Mason. This event was significant because it led to my meeting with Rob Bail in 2001. Steve was the coordinator of the 4WD car rally in outback NSW where Rob and I began our life together.

The wedding was held at Peppers Milton Park near Bowral and was a memorable occasion. Steve and Paula also invited a friend, Dianne Ball, and I to visit them at Steve's property near Bourke. Dianne was someone with whom I'd worked for some years on Wesley Mission's Darling Harbour Christmas Pageants. We set off to join the honeymooners. We drove from Sydney and had special catch ups with school principal, Anne Maree McAnulty, whom I'd met through a previous SS. We also took in Cobar and Brewarrina Central schools. We met Paula and Steve in Bourke and they guided us out to the property, which was about two hours away. Steve's property was pretty wild and just as you'd imagine a "fair dinkum" property would look like with a few sheds and a manager's residence. Steve showed us over the place and told us how goat farming was on the rise. Sadly, the marriage only lasted a few years.

Dianne and I called in to see Anne-Maree McAnulty at the tiny Hermidale PS (around 30 pupils) where we were treated to a concert and saw the children singing as well as some action, riding their ponies. This experience inspired my vision for the opening segment of the 1999 SS which would include horses. One of the young riders became the star of the opening segment. Can you believe they went to all that trouble to bring a horse to Sydney to appear in the show? The opening segment featured a rider on horseback, wearing an Akubra hat and a Driza-Bone coat. She rode, (maybe walked for safety reasons) onto the arena to the overture from *The Man from Snowy River* theme with an Australian flag.

Does this sound familiar? Yes. The following year we saw the same idea with horses and riders in Driza-Bones and carrying Australian flags, just multiplied. That was the first segment of the Opening Ceremony for the 2000 Olympics. Maybe members of the AOC who attended SS '99 were inspired by the segment? It was at this time I was ready to resign from the SS because of being overlooked for any role in the Olympics Opening and Closing Ceremonies by the Education Department. The feelings of rejection by both the Department and the Olympic committee are still a painful memory.

Culburra

When I bought Culburra after Manuel died, it became my "safe place" as well as my safe haven. Culburra in the 1990s with its two beaches, a lake and a river was relatively unknown, but its beauty and friendly and nurturing neighbours became my protective haven in the years to come. The next-door neighbours were the best you could possibly hope for, Ron and Betty Fagan. They were a delightful older couple with three sons and a loving extended family and a group of life-long friends. They showed me the "Culburran ropes" and helped me both heal and find a new way of life. Sadly, they've both passed away, but we still have their fine sons and their wives in our lives. Rob and I later exchanged my first house to move across the road when we bought a house together in 2005. Ross, their son, and his wife Terry bought my original house many years later, pulled it down and built a stunning new one. They have been such good neighbours and it has been a joy to see their family grow and the arrival of their grandchildren.

Bonita Mabo came with me to Berry where we stayed in a friend's bed and breakfast. We took a trip to Culburra and I have a beautiful memory of us standing down on Lake Wollumboola looking up at the house on the cliff face that I had purchased. She said to me that I should never move out of it. Although I eventually moved across the road to a north facing aspect, when I bought a house with Rob, I'm sure she's ok with that. She came to Culburra with me and we planned to write our book together, entitled *Sisters*. I'm sorry I never found time to write it with her. We danced around in the lounge room because she loved music and loved to dance.

There is a definite turning point in my personal and working life from the beginning of the 21st Millenium year onwards. As I've written about my life, I define the next two decades to come as the "Rob Years." Kind, humble, extremely energetic and always busy, Rob set about loving me and enjoying life with me. He supported me absolutely in my career and helped me finish it. He looked after me and never resented the attention I received.

We built a life and a beautiful house together at Culburra Beach. Culburra was always to me a haven and when Rob entered my life the place was perfect for both of us. Rob absolutely loves boating and fishing and I wanted to have a life free of the city.

Rob and Culburra

Rob and I had so much fun entertaining our Sydney friends and getting to know the locals. One photo I have is of quite a big group of us dressed in our ski gear emerging from the rocks at the beach side of our house. We'd been evacuated from our shared ski lodge at Charlotte's Pass after a sewerage outage. We had a Christmas in July party not long after Rob and I met. The catering was supplied by a local woman Sylvia and her daughter, Nettie. Only there was a problem – Nettie was missing her front teeth and was reluctant to be seen. I paid the dental bill, and all was well. It was a memorable night with a gale blowing outside and a local male quartet providing the lead to our carol singing. In 2009, we moved across the road on the peninsula, to a north facing house which we named "Horizon." We carried out a great renovation and turned it into a perfect house for both relaxing and entertaining.

I always breathed a huge sigh of relief as we drove into Culburra. It was my escape from my never-ending work. Culburra energised me and gave me the spiritual strength to stay strong. You cannot encourage and motivate young performers to believe in themselves without giving an enormous part of yourself.

A burst of spectacle

In May 2000, Jack Neary, the founder of the TDP died. This lovely man who was apply nicknamed "gentleman Jack", left a legacy that helped changed the face of the entertainment industry. The mourners at his funeral included celebrities from his vast network of friends. Human Nature sang their own very moving rendition of Danny Boy – it had always been Jack's favourite. Jack loved Human Nature and had vigorously encouraged them to stay together as a group. Now here they are, years on, still together with a starry international career and a reputation Australia is proud to own.

In the year of the Sydney Olympics I could not join in the enthusiasm because I was so disappointed when I was excluded from the Education Department's involvement in the Olympics. Imagine how I felt. The joy and passion I had for the SS was severely tested. I felt that my effort in developing the performing arts in public schools was overlooked and dismissed.

The leadership team of the PAU knew that I'd been on the short list to direct the ceremonies for the 2000 Olympics. My late husband and

I had cut short our holiday in Peru in 1994, to return for an interview in Sydney, alongside four other Australian producers. Ric Burch had already made sure he kept me right away from any involvement and now I suffered another rejection.

Manuel had been so warm in his support and encouragement. We had received an urgent notice regarding the interview while we were walking the Inca Trail in Peru back in 1994. Manuel rang from La Paz to try to ascertain whether there was a chance I would be successful and to find out if the playing field was level. He was assured that there was a chance and it was worth returning for the interview. I can still see him pacing on the terrace of my sister's house in Surfers Paradise when we were waiting to receive a phone call to tell me the result of my interview. He didn't know I could see him. He had his fingers crossed behind his back. No, I wasn't successful.

I had created the concept of the huge spectacle of performing arts which was the SS. I had an established reputation in the corporate world as a Producer/Director with spectacular ideas and displays. So, when Ric Burch approached the Department to involve thousands of PS school children in displays for the 2000 Olympics, one would naturally assume I would be part of the team. The management of a huge number of participants required diplomacy, sensitivity and respect. These are angry words from me because I was bewildered, hurt and disillusioned when I was excluded.

The SS grew out of my life story. The extraordinary talent, creativity and passion of individual teachers made the SS possible. They were and still are honest individual teachers who work in the SS world for the absolute good of the children. I've never understood how people can be incapable of giving credit where it's due. I've always found it invaluable to acknowledge and surround myself with talented people because they make you look better anyway.

As the year progressed, I observed as some 20,000 children and their teachers wasted so much unnecessary time with badly organised rehearsals. There was also a huge financial cost to the Department of Education. It was extremely frustrating not to be able to assist in managing the participation, as I had done for the past 16 years of the life of SS. However, it was a wonderful and unforgettable experience for the children and hopefully for their supervising teachers. I choose to now focus on the joy and excitement it gave the children.

However, the ache of rejection did not diminish the pride and excitement I felt in our talented TDP graduates who were featured in the Olympic ceremonies. Human Nature performed their own acapella arrangement of the National Anthem, John Foreman's song *Carry The Flame* was performed by Tina Arena, and Vanessa Corrish's song, *Dare to Dream* was performed by Olivia Newton-John and John Farnham.

I had wonderful seats for the Olympic Opening Ceremony. They were at the invitation of Janelle Kidman and were Nicole's seats because she was unable to attend. I was so nervous for Human Nature but they were spot on. I watched (and received supporting phone calls throughout from friends) beautiful segments unfold that might have been inspired by scenes from past SSs such as *The Man from Snowy River* segment and the beautiful unfolding native flowers which covered the arena.

At Opening Ceremony with Janelle and Anthony Kidman behind me, and friends

In June 2000, I directed and produced "Jubilee 2000" for the Broken Bay Diocese. I partnered with my son's company, Out There Productions, and we created a wonderful and inspirational event together. I was introduced to the leadership team of the diocese by Chris Brown who is John Brown's son. It was so satisfying to be working with such a positive and appreciative team from the diocese and the teachers of the Broken Bay Catholic schools. It was particularly comforting for me as I was feeling so let down by higher officials connected with the Olympics and public education.

The cast of 20,000 came from 50 Northern Beaches Catholic Schools and also 27 State Schools. I thought that was a strong and brave statement of inclusiveness for those state schools. The massive choir filled most of the audience seats. They had the liturgy songs with fun movements and joined with the action on stage. The headline artists and celebrity presenters were chosen because they were all role models. All performed for a minimum fee, appreciating the importance of the message of Jubilee 2000:

- A Time for Land
- A Time for Rest
- A Time for Justice
- A Time for Reconciliation.

The role models and headliners were:

- Bonita Mabo
- Father Chris Riley
- John Maclean
- Matt Shirvington, Olympian
- Pria Cooper, Para-Olympian
- Peter Garret
- John Williamson
- Bachelor Girl and
- Darren Coggan.

Gail Mabo choreographed the Indigenous Dance for Djapana, sung by Indigenous TDP Graduate Peter Riley. It was one of many highlights in this joyful Celebration.

This was a very significant and satisfying production for me and was the culmination of my era as the producer of commercial huge cast events. I loved the theme and having the opportunity to create a show built on such important messages. I had tried to inculcate all my SSs with these same messages.

The Broken Bay Diocese who employed me were respectful and grateful for the effort and result. I had always hoped that I'd be given the opportunity to work in the Catholic school system because I wanted the children in that education system to benefit from my work too. After all, I was educated extremely well by the Josephite and Dominican nuns and my children attended Catholic schools specially chosen by Manuel and me.

I met Robyn Philpot through this production, because she was directing a school dance group who appeared in the production. She joined me a few years later in the TDP, as coordinator, and helped me lead the TDP to become a powerhouse and perhaps the "Real Fame School" until my retirement.

Christine, Robyn and Kate

In July, Andy and I produced the Anthony Mundine pre-fight "entertainment" for Anthony's first professional fight. This was a new challenge for my team in combining the ring, screens and special effects. It was a completely different style of production for me. We turned it into successful combination of dance and live performances by Indigenous musicians Troy Caser-Daly, Archie Roach, and other up-and-coming Indigenous singers/dancers.

The SS 2000 featured several successful alumni from previous SSs and the TDP. It was called "The Entertainers." However, after being rejected for any position in the Department's preparations for the Olympics I realised I was in a vulnerable position. I felt like an outsider in the show that I'd created, especially after reading the credits for the Olympic ceremonies in the SS program, where everyone was involved except me.

Nevertheless, I was encouraged and reminded that I was valued by the TDP graduates we brought back as guest performers, including John Foreman, Felicity Urquhart, Sharon Millerchip, Trevor Ashley, Nathan Foley, Emma Pask and Darren Coggan. Nathan helped restore my confidence by telling me how much I was appreciated by the young entertainers. I was so grateful to him. I enthusiastically looked forward to the entry of Dianne Duff, who was about to take over as Manager of the Arts Unit for Education Department.

Nathan Foley giving 100% – reflects on 30th birthday of TDP

I first met Mary Lopez when I was 11 years old in the Coca Cola Schools Spectacular auditions. I was a boy soprano just starting my career when I saw this strong and driven woman walk into the room who knew exactly what she wanted in a show and just how to achieve the best.

She was kind and nurturing and gave me an opportunity to sing a duet in the 1991 Schools Spectacular. This lasted for seven years of my life singing solo every year with great orchestras and bands. Mary was always on the mark when it came to producing shows and always so supportive of the talent she worked with.

Our professional relationship didn't end there, as I was accepted into TDP for the final two years of my schooling with great advice from industry pros and Mary along the way.

Mary Lopez, The Coca Cola Schools Spectacular and TDP definitely gave me my groundwork and cemented me in this music biz with a professional mind and outlook.

After TDP, I went onto being a TV presenter/singer on Channel Nine's Hi-5 for 10 years, airing in more than 80 countries, winning 5 ARIA awards and three Logic awards to recording my own original music and dabbling in theatre from **Mamma Mia, Jerry Springer The Opera** *and* **Grease on the Beach.**

I have achieved so much in my career, and I'm still working my butt off today, and it's all because of the foundations that Mary and the shows she produced bestowed on me.

The simplest thing I learnt was to show up on time and give 100 per cent, which I still do today.

Nathan had a very successful career as a singer, dancer and actor in musicals and his own cabarets and shows. He is one of most dynamic and energetic performers I've ever seen.

About this time Wendy Tierney and Helen Pain, who were great contributors to SS thought it would be a good idea to start up a program like the TDP in the Bankstown area for talented students. We were happy to help and invited Wendy to a TDP workshop to see how we operated. I was pleased to see her taking notes through the sessions. They've since run a very successful program in the Bankstown area called TAP which continued it's marvellous work for 25 years.

By the end of this decade and into the twentieth Millennium, I'd produced as many sporting spectaculars as I ever wanted to see. It had been an enlightening and exciting period crossing over so many different sporting leagues but I was ready to move back to my love of talent. And my son Andy was so much better operating in this sporting world than I was, so I was happy to hand the reins over to him. The 1990s had been an exhilarating career ride for me and had given Andy a solid basis in terms of production knowledge, experience and a strong network. He was well equipped to establish and lead, alongside his business partner, Andrew Bee, the very successful events company, called Out There Productions. Andy has gone from strength to strength in the events industry and is now also a huge name in motor sports events.

There were many major entertainment events we'd produced through the last decade, while also directing the TDP and SS. We created and produced huge cast pre-match entertainment for the following sporting events:

- 2000 Olympic Soccer Opening
- 1999 ARL Grand Final
- 1997 ARU International test matches
- 1996
- Rugby Super 12s Australian Launch and Finals series
- Australian Boomers vs NBA legends
- Golden Slipper Carnival
- 1995
- ARL Grand Final

- ARL Grand Final Series
- ARL State of Origin series in Sydney and Melbourne
- National Soccer Club Grand Final Series in Melbourne and Adelaide
- 1993 ARL Grand Final
- 1990 Coca Cola water Classic

By the end of the 20th century, many TDP graduates had begun to make their mark in the entertainment world, amongst them:

- Human Nature
- Shaun Rennie
- Drew McAllister
- Darren Coggan
- Emma Pask
- David Harris
- Nathan Foley
- Felicity Urquhart
- Glen Cunningham
- Trevor Ashley
- Jenny Davis
- Justin Smith
- Jed Hughes
- Gavin Lockley
- Vanessa Corish
- The McClymonts
- Anthony Snape
- Belinda Wollaston
- Paulini
- Dianna Rouvas, and of course
- John Foreman, who is now Australia's musical maestro extraordinaire.

I've followed the careers of these talented young Australians who are still going strong in the entertainment and music industry and it's now only the year 2000 in my memoir!

Shaun Rennie, a 1999 graduate is now one of Australia's top directors of both theatre and musical theatrical and operatic productions.

Amanda Harrison, Justin Smith, David Harris and Belinda Wollaston, who are all now stars of musical theatre in Australia and overseas, graduated in this decade. Paulini graduated this year and was soon to become a household name after being runner up on Australian Idol.

Jack Neary had predicted the success of the training program back in 1998 when he said: *"I know we are building a future not only for the participants but for the entertainment industry."*

The volunteer consultants played an invaluable and essential role in TDP. The structure for TDP two-day workshops under my training program was divided into three performing sessions. The young performers usually performed three different pieces over the two days to panels of volunteer entertainment industry specialists. I look back in amazement at the generosity of these esteemed performers, managers, theatre and recording producers, and career professionals from business and the law who donated their time to "give back." We asked them for just a few hours once a year. Jack was sure the entertainers would help, and they always did.

Over 250 volunteer consultants, including many celebrity names, are listed on the back of the 30th Anniversary TDP Graduation booklet. Amongst them were:

- Tommy Tycho
- Don Burrows
- Bobby Limb
- Jimmy Little
- John Williamson
- Angry Anderson
- Martin Bedford
- Ken Laing
- Michael Cassel
- Stuart Maunder
- Tony Grace
- Jackie Love
- Caroline O'Connor
- Les Goch
- Anne Maree McDonald
- Maree Montgomery
- Gretel Keneen
- Fifa Riccobona

- Normie Rowe
- John Paul Young
- Marc Williamson
- Kyle Sanderland
- Simon Moor and
- David Albert.

The diversity of the consultants was both vast and unique. A number are now deceased but they will never be forgotten by those lucky TDP students.

And of course, the growing list of TDP graduates headlining on stage, in concert halls, at festivals and on TV always supported us at workshops when they were asked. This simple structure worked for me until I retired as CEO and Artistic Director in 2017. I reflect with great pride on the graduates who were by then household names, still loyal and helping when they could.

> **A New Home for TDP**
>
> In July 2025, we saw TDP relocate its workshops and auditions to its new venue in the Walsh Bay Arts Precinct. Under the new enthusiastic and passionate CEO appointed this year, Amy Curl, TDP is forging ahead to develop a new generation of potential stars. So much has changed in the requirements for a career in the music industry since my days in this wonderful project. So I'm thrilled to see Amy, supported by the TDP Board, continue to react to the current trends in the music and entertainment world. I can't wait to see them all flourish.

On 12 December 2000, Kate underwent major surgery to remove a growth on her spinal cord. Peter Bentevoglio, her surgeon removed a growth from her upper spine which had developed probably from childhood and was threatening to block the spinal cord. She, as always, was stoic in the way she dealt with pain and her rehabilitation. We used the piano quite a bit to encourage the brain to remember fine motor functioning. In 2001, I remember seeing Kate run for the first time since primary school, and the exhilaration in what we hoped was a new normal.

After the initial elation at the improvement to her physical posture she then had a very tough return to normality as she basically had to learn to walk all over again, and I was happy to teach her. One positive moment out of all of this was the reappearance of her first love, Ivan Glavinic, who came to visit her in hospital.

Another huge invasive neurosurgery was performed just a few years later when Kate decided to have it done prior to her marriage to the devoted Ivan.

14
The Rob years

There is a definite turning point in my personal and working life from the beginning of the 21st Millenium year onwards. In January 2001, I wrote this New Year's resolution in my diary:

Time to develop me. No new projects for this year. Me. Kate. Andy. Work – SS / TDP.

I was trying to have a personal life. It was a forecast for the new stage in my career and personal life.

The next decade was about Andy and Kate sorting out their careers and them living their own social lives. Thirty-one year old Andy was well on the way to establishing himself as a leader in event production. He followed in my interest in production and events, although not in the area of the development of young talent. Kate was 29 and finding out that although she didn't get satisfaction from practising as a lawyer she could use her legal skills working in Andy's company. They were both late starters in finding their marriage partners but by the next decade all that had changed.

These decades saw an increase in my commitment to developing talent and giving young Australians a chance to realise their dreams. I had behind me a vastly increased network of influential personalities from the entertainment and music industries as well as sympathetic political figures from all sides of government.

Andrew Bee left the Department of Education and joined Andy's company fulltime. He'd been working with Andy since 1996, mainly on shows for MLP. Together their company, Out There Productions, became a powerful player in the events industry. Over the next 25 years they became one of Australia leading event management and sports presentation agencies. I'm extremely proud of them both.

The 4WD car rallies named "Desert Duel" began and, in May 2001, I met Rob Bail. Our many 4WD adventures over the next eight years culminated in an all-around Australian trip for us driven by Rob in 2019. The first of these "discover Australia" 4WD rallies, the Desert Duel, raised funds for the Paralympics and continued to do so for eight years. The drivers were small group of mostly highly successful self-employed businessmen. In March 2001, I was invited to accompany the 4WD "survey" which was to be mapped out by Pat Cole and Steve Mason.

The invite came about because I was a guest at Maria Venuti's 60th birthday party. Also attending were Paula Duncan and her then husband Steve Mason. Steve and his friend, Pat Cole were about to head off on the first of the 4WD Desert Duel rally's to raise money for the Paralympics. But first they had to do the rally survey, and so Steve invited me along. He suggested I bring a friend, so I invited Janelle Kidman. What an adventure we had. Neither of us had had experience of such rough dirt roads and extreme weather conditions. We were caught in a flash flood along the dingo fence out from Maree and got to stay overnight at Santos because Pat Cole (who had powerful connections everywhere) talked our way in. This all led to the actual rally a few months later where I met Rob. Our meeting was thanks to my friendship with Paula Duncan, forged through the Darling Harbour Christmas Pageants. As I wrote in my diary:

> *I met Rob Bail on the 4WD car Rally at Woolshed near Lake Cargelligo, 100km from Broken Hill, in the NSW Central West region. A different chapter began in my life. It seems too much of a coincidence that this fine man who entered my life has his birthday on 19 October on the same day that I married Manuel. It was the fulfilment of my "diarised wish" in January this year!*

It wasn't a very romantic way to meet. I was camping in a tent and Rob was camping in the wool shed. We both left to urinate behind our respective vehicles in the dark. As it turned out the cars were together. From my position I called out "Excuse me, I'm here"! Rob likes to exaggerate that I was so impressed with what I saw that I immediately snapped him up. It was actually pitch black! Anyway, we've been together ever since that unusual meeting and I have had encouragement and support from Rob enabling me to go full swing into my career.

Rob says: "at the start of the rally in the morning at Roselands carpark, I spotted this lovely lady standing near her car and I took a photo of her and their 4WD. I met her at the fence line later that night."

Rob's first rally photos

I arranged the entertainment for the rally. Felicity Urquhart and David Sanders, both TDP graduates, flew in to entertain us that night.

Kate and Andy were very encouraging and supportive of this new man in my life. I rang Kate from the Palace Hotel in Broken Hill and told her about the very nice man I had met. However, when we returned to Sydney after the rally, I got cold feet and decided I should end the relationship. It took a visit from Andy to assure me that he and Kate thought the relationship was a good thing and worth pursuing. How lucky was I to have such a caring and perceptive son and daughter. The next 20 years would have been very different for me as well as the tens of thousands of children and fantastic young solo performers. If Andy and Kate had not been so understanding and supportive of my relationship with Rob I might not have had the spirit to continue my hard work. I was impressed with Rob's business which was a wholesale nursery at Galston on the outskirts of Sydney. It so suited his warm and gentle nature. His love of nature was his work. Early in our relationship I met some of his family. His daughter Sharon arrived with Rob's two very cute, young granddaughter's, Toni and Demi. Today they are both happy and proud mothers of Rob's great granddaughters. Where have all the years gone?

With Rob, my love of country Australia was nourished as we spent time over the next five years driving on many 4WD car rallies through the outback and remote regions. We drove with a group of self-made businessmen unlike any I had encountered in my previous life, which had been amongst lawyers, doctors, teachers, entertainers, musicians and production personnel. These outback adventures all helped in continuing my crusade to find country talent and give children from country NSW the opportunity to share the excitement of the SS.

Rob's 4WD

I had really needed a hand along and that someone was Rob. He understood how hard to was to be heard if you lived over the Great Dividing Range and supported the time it took me to search for talent over the next fifteen years and to continue to level the playing field. I'm very proud that I persisted with my drive to give a voice to the kids from the country.

Dianne Duff was now manager of the PAU and producer of the SS. I breathed a sigh of relief at this appointment. Dianne was a powerhouse and we worked very well together. The next few years were extremely happy working years. The country and Indigenous participation was growing as well as the numbers of boys dancing, which we were both keen to foster. We asked the dance director to create a hip hop boys group which we hoped would appeal and it certainly worked. In June 2001, we toured country NSW to audition new talent and refresh the SS. Dianne was very enthusiastic and supportive and we were a great team.

An important development for the TDP was the screening of a four-part series on the ABC TV called *Rising Stars*. It followed the dreams and aspirations of a few of the students in the TDP and was great publicity for our training program. The most well-known student showcased is the now extremely successful musical director, composer and academic, Shannon Brown. I was asked by the television producer, Bruce Best, to be post-edited in to host the program. Frankly, I found the whole experience intimidating, but I did my usual coverup of faking confidence.

Although 2001 was an incredibly busy and productive year, and a turning point in my personal life because of my meeting with Rob, underneath it all I was also seeing and dealing with the effects of serious surgery on my daughter's life. My days were fully booked between the TDP and the SS with workshops, auditions, meetings, rehearsals and country trips, and then of course there was the Graduation Production in July and the SS itself in November.

Alan Jones' Christmas parties were always an opportunity for TDP performers to showcase themselves in front of influential business and political personalities including Prime Ministers. This year it was held at Edna's Table, which was then a smart restaurant in the Sydney CBD. TDP graduate, Travis Collins performed and as a result was invited to perform on Australia Day 2002 at the Lodge in Canberra by the then Prime Minister, John Howard. The PM and I spoke about hosting the first Australia Day function to be held that following January and I suggested he use Travis, who sang a wonderful version of *I Am Australian*. Travis was from public housing in Campbelltown and was only 17 years old. Imagine my surprise and the thrill of receiving that phone call with and invitation for Travis to sing. Travis, now a household name in the country music scene, always remembers the excitement he had as "the boy from public housing Campbelltown singing at the Lodge":

> *My memories of TDP, its staff, panellists and my fellow students are among my most cherished. Without doubt TDP was the first few steps in my professional life. I was a kid from housing commission, south west Sydney. I had no career plan or dream. Prior to TDP I was busker in Campbeltown. Shortly after TDP, I performed for the Prime Minister at the Lodge. Mind blown. It inspired thoughts, unveiled pathways and simultaneously challenged and supported creativity*

and encouraged a kid to think bigger. It identified the fuel that drove each one of us (creatively and mentally) and then ignited it. For the very first time I was observing, learning and being instilled with the fundamentals of music creativity and business professionalism – most importantly through the brand new lens of believing I could have a career.

John Brown's Sport and Tourism Foundation's Dinner and Christmas parties were also exciting and important showcases for the participants in the TDP. Between 1997 and 2014 over 50 scholarships from $5,000–$10,000 each were awarded to TDP graduates.

Alongside the above events, students performed at many more gala charity dinners, functions and concerts. They were always in prestigious venues and were accompanied by the current TDP coordinator who ensured they were presented professionally. I thought it was valuable for the young performers to not only have exposure to these classy venues but also corporate audiences, before which to practise and to perform. It was an opportunity to network in a world they would most likely not have otherwise experienced.

Both Alan Jones and John Brown have been encouraging and supportive throughout my career with young talent. John since meeting with me at the World Expo '85 in Japan and Alan since his invitation to me to teach the 1984 Wallabies to sing.

I came to the realisation that working with talented young people in developing their talents and then helping them find a pathway into the industry was what I now wanted to concentrate on. So, the next stage of my career was centred on building up the effectiveness of the TDP.

Those productive and exciting years from 1984 to 2000, working outside the Education Department in the professional world had equipped me with invaluable experience. With my greatly developed production skills and particularly the rich and varied network I now had in the entertainment and music industries, I thought I'd really make the TDP work very effectively. I now had a network of influential leaders in entertainment, music, media, government and business and I felt empowered with that network and experience to contribute it all to the TDP and SS. I was therefore astounded to find that there was no understanding or appreciation of what I now had to offer. It was as if the MLP professional and commercial production era had not happened as far as SS administrators and some members of the TDP Board were concerned.

Nevertheless, for the following years the TDP, under its tiny dedicated, talented and hard working team, continued to produce many of the next generation of remarkable young Australian artists. The team consisted of coordinator Kerry Vanslambrouck, followed in 2004 by Robyn Philpot, Musical Director Andrew Bee and myself. With the generosity of volunteer TDP Board members and consultants from the entertainment industry we created a unique training program.

In my dual roles as SS and TDP director, I continued to cover the regional areas of NSW. We stepped up our search to incorporate even more performers from the country into the program. I continued to crusade to level the playing field for genuine young talent from all over NSW. We were in the thick of the new TV Reality "big voice" shows such as *Australian Idol*, and I could see how artificial the process was in developing talent.

This was to be the final year of the Darling Harbour Christmas Pageant (2001) and I am glad that Rob was able to experience it. The dress rehearsal was washed out. We so often had a bad time with rain, but we always managed to have fine weather for the actual show. I can't tell you how nerve-racking it is to stage an outdoor production with no proper rehearsal. We didn't know at the time that this was the farewell to a very satisfying and successful production, but the following year Wesley was unable to sponsor us and by the time they pulled the pin it was too late to find another sponsor.

The City of Sydney Council was never interested in the Pageant. I assume it was because the Christian-based subject material was unsavoury for them. It is such a pity that Australia has felt it necessary to almost abandon this beautiful tradition. However, I notice that the Sydney Carols in the Domain adopted the finale music we always performed – Handel's *Messiah* – as their finale.

SS, No. 18, "Celebrate", featured performers from the "Teach your Children Well" TV campaign. Barry Foster, who was now a Director in the Department of Education, led a very successful public education campaign, and we were off to a good start in this new Millennium. Dianne Duff was the producer and we were a happy and highly motivated leadership team. I was inspired and motivated to be working with ABC to televise the SS again, especially with the highly respected Bruce Best as producer. Bruce introduced another level of expertise. He matched our passion for the performers and the concept. The whole country became our audience.

The SS now had a very large creative team which continued to grow in numbers. I personally found it difficult over the next 16 years of first Direction and then Artistic consultancy to be managing this creative team because they were such a diverse group, all having their own agendas. I don't disagree with talented individuals looking after their own performing interests, but it was very difficult negotiating with a very large group of up 20 people.

Paulini (runner-up in *Australian Idol*), Tonino Speciale (working in musical production in London), and Diana Rouvas (*The Voice* winner) who appeared in this SS, are now household names in the world of entertainment. They all spent a few years benefiting also from the TDP training program.

Bruce Harris retired as executive producer this year after providing an invaluable contribution and overwhelming generosity to public education. I was aware that underlying Bruce's original motivation was the desire to rekindle his brother's career. He had passionate belief in Rolf's talent.

Throughout this time, I stressed the importance of networking to my students, and I practised what I preached. I'll give you some examples of how my networking all the time benefited the careers of my students. I never attended a function without networking and taking some connection from it, which would sooner or later benefit the students. Opportunities would present themselves in many unusual situations. For example, as I have already mentioned, I visited the tiny school of Tibooburra while on a 4WD rally in 2001. I then invited the school to perform in the SS. To assist them with fundraising I hosted a dinner party fundraiser for people I met on the rally. I paid for the dinner. The guests donated money to help the kids come to Sydney. Years later, two of those same people, Gary Rush (PicPacnPay) and the late Gary Johnston (owner of Jaycar Electronics) gave considerable sponsorship money to the TDP after Alan Jones and I hosted them at AJ's apartment in 2012.

I spoke before about Travis Collin's appearance at the Lodge. Importantly, at that same Australia Day function we met the Austrian

Ambassador and his Madagascan wife. I had travelled in Madagascar so had stories to share. Shortly after befriending Otmar and Jeanine Kohler I was introduced to their Austrian friend Franz Donnhauser, the General Manager of the Shangri La in Sydney. So, of course, I approached Franz to see if there were opportunities for performances at his hotel. As a result, in 2008–09 TDP students such as Jessica Hitchcock, Robert McDougall, Sabrina Batshon and especially Shannon Brown, all had fabulous performing experiences in the beautifully sophisticated Shangri La hotel lounges. This only happened because I followed up with people I met. That contact was also important when it came to asking for accommodation for Michael Kerker when he first visited Australia and also for other TDP personnel, for example, John Foreman.

Another networking occasion occurred when Rob and I were on a Windstar cruise around the Caribbean in 2015 and we met and Evan and Barry Freid from Boston. Two of my very young TDP graduates had enrolled in Berklee College of Music in Boston. I introduced Nina Baumer and Alex Riordan to Barry and Evan, and they became the girls' "family" in Boston.

After Kate's Admission to Law ceremony
L to R   Rob, me, Supreme Court Judge George Palmer (Kate's friend's father) Kate, Andy, Ivan

In 2002, Kate graduated with her law degree and began two years at the College of Law. She explored the legal world for a few years, I think trying to maintain a connection with her beloved deceased father. She persevered for five years but didn't find the law satisfying.

In July, Jan McClelland was appointed Director-General of the Education Department and Chris Ryan was her Executive Assistant. These were very strong appointments and they were supporters of the flagship that was now the SS. Chris, in particular, protected me from the undermining and efforts of those within the Department who sought to remove from me from the role. He advised and guided me through the what I called the "shark-pit."

Andrew Bee was invited to take up the position of TDP Musical Director, a position he held from 2002–2016 when he retired because of his work commitments as a director of Out There Productions. He had generously donated his services to stage manage TDP graduations and consult in workshops since 1995. Throughout that early period, Andrew worked with me to identify, train and encourage many of those early emerging stars, such as:

- John Foreman
- Human Nature
- Darren Coggan
- Felicity Urquhart
- Emma Pask
- Shaun Rennie
- Paulini.

Andrew led the development of song-writing in the TDP until his retirement. Under his musical direction over the next 16 years, we developed some well-known heavyweights now in the music industry including:

- Kurt Bailey
- Katrina Burgoyne
- Jack Carty
- Imogen Clark
- Travis Collins
- Brad Cox
- William Crighton
- Melanie Dyer
- Morgan Evans
- Sam Fisher
- Nicholas Gentile

- Max Jackson
- Christie Lamb
- David Le'aupepe
- Cameron Little
- The McClymonts
- Joe Mungovan
- Roshani Priddis
- Angus and Julia Stone
- Angel Tairua
- Lily and Grace Richardson "Crew", and many others.

He guided the young performers to collaborate with each other and brought in expert consultants to develop their skills. He took up the offer from Albert's Music and Sony to use their studios and resources for producing and recording the music of these young performers. He had enormous respect for talent and the ability to select the best of the best from the many aspiring TDP applicants.

> **Where are they now – Sam Fischer**
>
> *Based in LA and recently in Australia doing publicity tour and sold out shows. Sam has toured internationally and co-writes with Guy Sebastian, Niall Horan and Demi Lovato. His most popular song to date receiving millions of downloads is* This City, *released in 2017 it was nominated for Song of the Year at the Aria Awards in 2020.*

Musical theatre/cabaret graduates benefited from the New York scholarships and the network we were now able to bring them. Graduates who received this very helpful training in New York include:

- 2006: Belinda Wollaston, Luke Dolahenty
- 2007: Kirby Burgess, Erin James, Lucy Maunder
- 2008: Roshani Priddis, Carly Champion
- 2009: Laura Herd, Brendan Irving, Lincoln Hall
- 2010: Adam Rennie, Jessica Hitchcock
- 2012: Miriam Waks, Robert McDougall, Natasha Hoeberigs
- 2013: Nicholas Gentile, Jacob Neale, Jessica Pollard

- 2015: Stephen Madsen, Nathan Allgood, Alex Gibson-Giorgio, Ashleigh Rubenach
- 2017: Matilda Moran and Jessica Rookeward.

Unfortunately, the scholarships are no longer awarded.

With Opera graduates such as Lorenzo Rositano, Julie Lee Goodwin, Jeremy Boulton and Emily Dwyer, as well as musicians and extraordinary instrumentalists such as violinist Harry Ward and guitarist Joshua Meader, we didn't interfere with their training for voice or instrument. Instead, we concentrated on developing communication with the audience, performance technique, networking, sponsorship and other skills required for longevity in their careers.

> **Where are they now – Harry Ward**
>
> *Harry is a highly respected and in-demand violin soloist and chamber musician around the world. As a young adult Harry was selected as an Emerging Artist of the Australian Chamber Orchestra. In 2021, Harry moved to Berlin to take up a position with the Karajan Academy of the Berliner Philharmonic. Harry has won countless awards both in Australia and Europe and has studied in Vienna and Austria. During his time in Europe he has had the opportunity to collaborate with some of the world's finest musicians.*

Andrew Bee's legacy is enormous. The now nationally and internationally acclaimed young performers, especially the song writers Andrew mentored, will be forever indebted to him because of his skills, talent, passion and dedication.

Mr Bee and I complemented each other in our different interests, knowledge, and experience in musical tastes. Together, we auditioned, trained, and then selected those who would graduate. We also considered the wise advise from coordinators, like Kerry and Robyn, who had so much to do with nurturing the talent. To graduate we had to be confident that the talented performer had the skills to survive in the area of interest they chose in the industry. Outside of the monthly Sydney workshops, we also conducted many workshops in regional NSW.

As mentioned before, Mr Bee joined my son Andy at Out There Productions and they've been long term friends and business partners ever since. Over the years until 2024, Out There Productions made extremely generous contributions to the TDP. These included providing an office space for us at their headquarters during the early 2000s, as well as providing innumerable wonderful performing opportunities for TDP graduates at their productions including Australia Day Spectaculars, opening ceremonies, rock concerts and gala concerts. The company also sponsored the last 2023 and 2024 $10,000 Mary Lopez scholarships for an outstanding TDP alumni.

Max Jackson talks about the impact of the TDP

I want to thank you again for having me as your scholarship recipient.

You've no idea how much I still draw upon the lessons I learned and the encouragement I was given all those years ago.

My time in TDP was truly invaluable. Being equally encouraged and challenged is the combo that a lot of young artists never get ... The "you can do this" and the "you can do better, here are the things you can improve.. OK, now, let's see it.". That's what makes TDP, what YOU founded, so unique and what made it so good for me at such a young age.

Seeing you and being there at the grad concert always brings back so many great memories of my time. It's so cool that, even 15 years after my time at TDP, this scholarship is going to help me so much in moving forward.

It will really help me to connect with REAL fans ... and will shape the audience I tour to for the rest of my career.

Max Jackson and Me

Max Jackson, receiving the Mary Lopez TDP scholarship

Thank you will never cut it! And I'm definitely keen to catch up for a coffee when we can make that work. Big love and gratitude.

– *Max Jackson*

The volunteer TDP consultants continued to be a major influence on our young artists through the next decade. I knew it was important for them to be guided by successful music and entertainment celebrities who were making a living in the industry. There were too many teachers who were advising and educating performers who were not practitioners in the industry. I also learned from these consultants, I listened to them and became so much more knowledgeable. I called on my network of wonderfully generous and highly skilled and talented household names, from all areas of show business expertise, to donate a few hours of their time to TDP workshops. Ours was an industry-supported talent school you couldn't pay to get into – you had to apply, audition, and have the potential to have longevity and a successful career. And of course now we have our own TDP alumni who are storming through the industry and always willing to support the TDP.

Denis Handlin, head of Sony Music was a strong supporter and an important help. Through the Sony Foundation we had ongoing financial support. The association with Sony also helped give the TDP participants access to studios, music producers and A&R personnel and elevated the program's standing within the music industry.

Simon Moor, who was an ex-student of mine from EBHS, was the A&R Manager at the time and is now Manager of Kobalt Music. He was incredibly helpful and taught me a lot about contemporary song writers and singers.

Tony Grace, head of Harbour Agency, gave me advice and support and educated me in the essential need for young performers to be song writers if they are to have a career in the music industry.

SS No. 19 was an absolute cracker of a show. With Barry Foster as producer, and Dianne Duff heading the PAU, we had a desire to refresh the show. We had toured the countryside to audition students and remind country schools that the SS was open for them. The soloists' cast included many who now have very successful careers in the entertainment and music industries. We could see the amazing impact that the TDP training was having on soloists in this SS. There are too many to list, but they included:

- Shannon Brown
- Erin James
- Travis Collins
- Lorenzo Rositano
- Brooke, Samantha and Mollie McClymont
- Scott Ryan
- the Baileys
- William Crighton
- Blake Ralph
- Kirby Burgess, and
- Lucy Maunder.

Unfortunately, within the TDP my style of managing was being questioned by some members of the Board. I think I had become too much of a public figure and I was resented for that. The relationship had in fact become toxic (although this was unknown to me). I think there was also a lack of sympathy for the fact that I was searching to have more time to have a personal life. And I think that my hosting of the ABC four-part program *Rising Stars* probably antagonised the old members of the TDP Board. I think it was this combination of factors that drove some of the TDP Board members to act in the way that they did the following year.

Dismay

I was invited to go on a walking trip to Italy in June 2002. I wanted to take recovery time out with my new love interest, Rob, and the dear friends who had helped me re-shape my life. It had been a tumultuous period from the time of Manuel's death from stomach cancer. Kate's serious medical issues, the legal battle with Manuel's law firm and the hurtful exclusion from the Olympics had all been great hurdles with which I had had to deal.

It was the first time Rob had been to Europe when we joined a Gourmet Walkabout Tour with friends, including the Cheoks, Johnsons and Messaras. We walked through countryside in Piedmont, Tuscany and the Cinque Terra. The wines we tasted in the Piedmont area and the five villages of the Cinque Terra remain as a solid and warm memory. We were so lucky to be able to walk through all the villages because I believe some walking paths are now not accessible. One amusing situation occurred in Sienna, when Rob and John Messara vanished, tired of the walking and the heat. They'd both reluctantly tolerated the walking for two weeks but on this occasion escaped to the comfort and sustenance of a luxury hotel they found, while our group persevered with our tour of a very hot Sienna.

However, I was unaware of what was waiting for me when I returned home. I took my eye off the ball and the sharks came circling again as they had in 1988 with my dismissal from the SS and a notice to take up a school appointment.

I'd put a proposal to the TDP Board for an increase of my contractor fee, as I had begun the process of extending the scope and reach of the TDP. Also, I had assumed there would be an appreciation of the highly enriched skills and network I was now bringing to the TDP after my 12 years in the commercial events industry. I no longer had the income I had received from my events career and I needed to plan for the future.

When I returned from the walking trip, I received a notice from TDP Board member, Bruce Harris, on behalf of the Board stating that my salary was not only not to be NOT increased, but was actually to be halved! I was flabbergasted, insulted and outraged.

Fortunately, I had the trust and support of two Board members, Tim Worton and the then chair, Matt MacDougal. They backed me up and helped me sort out the situation. Jan McClellan who at the time was the Director-General for the NSW Education Department appointed the brilliant and diplomatic Chris Ryan to represent the Department on the board. Jan had been very supportive of me and my work and was shocked by the TDP Board's decision. A number of changes were then made to the TDP Board membership.

I reflect on this now and wonder whether resentment was there because I now had a personal life with Rob. I understand that many of the personnel in the Department and TDP Board were dismissive of my career achievements after I left the Department. They couldn't accept that I wasn't a classroom teacher anymore.

There was no acknowledgment of the fact that I had any intellectual property ownership of SS or the TDP. Legally I didn't, but in my heart, I felt passionately that they were my babies. I felt this way because I created both the concept and the program content for the first SS. Dance teachers whom I knew were invited to contribute items. I motivated and led the team of teachers who gradually joined the team from 1985 onwards. For the TDP in 1991 I had created the formula, topics, training and process. All of this was documented and formed the core and basis of the unique TDP training system until I retired as Artistic Director in 2017. The success of my practical and holistic training program is demonstrated in the hundreds of graduates who are now living contented and successful lives as well as the 50 or so who are household names in the music and entertainment industries.

I was supported by almost every Director-General for Education right through until I retired. Only one didn't understand me or my motivation. It seemed to me to be the Directors who were distanced from the SS who had the greatest problem with acknowledging my right to lead the show which I had put years of blood sweat and tears into establishing. I was hurt and frustrated and carried constant stress because of this attitude.

The personnel I dealt with in Education seemed to be looking for hidden agendas with me and didn't accept that people with a passion for something don't have hidden agendas.

There was no appreciation of the importance of my network. They didn't understand that it was because of my personal background and my career outside of education that had helped to showcase the SS as the Department's flagship. It was my new network which helped make possible the careers of so many talented young people from NSW Public Schools.

As I look back over my career since 1989 when I resigned from safe education employment, I appreciate even more the opportunities I was generously given to upscale my skills and be introduced to a whole new and exciting world. Those who supported me were all powerful men you will notice: John Trevillian, Gerry Gleeson, Jack Neary, Bruce Harris, Kevin Jacobsen, Tom Hayson and Bruce Best. On a side note, Kevin Jacobsen actually contacted me in 2023 to remind me of his involvement in offering the Sydney Entertainment Centre for the first concert. I feel for Kevin as he has become a forgotten soul in the entertainment scene despite being a powerhouse for decades.

Despite all this wheeling and dealing behind the scenes I was very busy with the twentieth SS entitled "20 Years On." My auditioning trips took me to the Hunter region and also Wilcannia where I continued the search for talent from the regions.

As I have mentioned before, I had been moved by the great work that Fr Chris Riley was doing with his YOTS program. He invited me to visit his farm in the Southern Highlands to meet some of the young people and learn more about his program. I figured I could be helpful by starting a choir. Fr Chris had a belief that it would help his young students to be involved with both the joy of singing in a choir while also presenting a stylish image. We were given a base by Colleen Haywood, the Principal at Erskinville PS. I asked volunteer TDP consultants, like the delightful and generous Jonathan Welch, to join me in engaging with and enthusing the YOTS youngsters. Jonathan later formed the famous Choir of Hard Knocks in Melbourne.

For a few years Kate and Andy and Out There Productions continued the initiative, but it was difficult. The attendance by the YOTS young people was pretty haphazard and everyone eventually gave up. However, we had a few years of contributing a choral performance to the YOTS graduation Ceremony at Bankstown Sports Club. It was a very worthwhile learning experience for all of us. Andy and his OutThere Production company continued to support YOTS for many years by producing the graduation nights and the gala fundraising dinners.

The TDP had already made a difference in the entertainment and music scenes by the early 2000s. It was becoming even more effective, and I was dedicating most of my time to finding ways to enhance the training program. I had given up my events career although I still had many connections in the entertainment and music world who were generous in supporting the talented young TDP students.

In SS No. 20, we showcased some of most amazing and exciting talent which had been developed and nurtured through the TDP and previous SSs. These young performers are now household names in the Australian and international music scene, in musical theatre and the entertainment industry. They included:

- Lucy Maunder
- Morgan Evans
- Tim Power
- Nick Perjanik
- Allegra Giagu, and
- Luke Dolahenty.

> **Where are they now – Morgan Evans**
>
> *ARIA winner, Morgan, has sold-out shows whether local or global, and now has the status as one of Australia's top country music Artists. His power packed performances and powerful and emotional song writing establish him as a true star in the international music industry.*

It was a real honour to have the past Director-Generals in the audience namely, Doug Swan, Bob Winder, Fenton Sharp and the then current Director-General, Jan McClellan.

After a long and invaluable contribution to the SS, Barry Foster was transferred out of performing arts and into another administrative role within the Department of Education. I was sorry to see him leave and will never forget how he and his wife Jan opened up Western regional NSW to the SS.

Turning 60

Kate graduated as a lawyer LLB, in 2004. Andy and I proudly attended the graduation ceremony and thought what a great achievement it was for her. This was her second degree and gained with all the underlying medical problems she had encountered through the years of study while also working full time. After graduating she went to work for our great friend the lawyer, John Picone, for three years until she joined Bull, Son and Schmidt lawyers in St Leonards, Sydney.

I wrote in my diary 15/06/2004:

> *So much has happened in the past three years. Tonight, I need to write down that I must stop all the work that I am doing. It is ruining the lovely life that I have built with Rob. I feel like an empty shell and I don't feel any warmth or passion. It is time to make changes to suit ME.*
>
> *This city life is sapping me up. I feel so good with Rob – safe, loved, calm and content.*

My 60th birthday was celebrated in Vanuatu with Rob, Andy and Kate. I felt very special to have my children and new beau with me for a week. We also took Bonita Mabo with us. She took the opportunity to stay with relatives but celebrated my birthday with me and the family.

We had a scary time on the flight from Sydney and were diverted to Noumea because of driving rain and wind. There was a shocking lack of communication from the pilot both during the flight and when we landed. I had to become a spokesperson for the passengers in order to find out what was happening after landing as we were left to our own devices for hours in the middle of the night at Noumea airport. Eventually we were taken to an hotel where we had about two hours sleep before being transported back to the airport and back on our way to Vanuatu. It was really scary flying, for what seemed like hours, as we tried to land during the bad weather and were not told what was happening.

Rob and I had adventurous travels in Africa later in 2004. After doing the usual safari and visit to major animal viewing in Kenya, we flew to Il Ngwesi, a Maasai community built and run eco-lodge in Kenya. This travel experience cemented the fact that Rob and I were on the same page when it came to "off the grid" holidays. A flower grower from Kenya had visited Rob's wholesale nursery in Galston on business. In conversation Rob had told the Dutch businessman about our intended trip. He then insisted that we contact the travel company he used in Nairobi because they would provide us with professional service and a unique itinerary.

The agency certainly gave us an exhilarating African travel experience we'll never forget. The highlight was our five-day stay in the remote eco-lodge Il Ngwesi. On one of the days, Kip Olo Polos, the Maasai chairman, asked if we'd like to join in an elephant tagging. Kip was one of the most charming and attractive men I've ever met. We set off on the open jeeps with the Maasais in their brilliant red attire and the professional game reserve wardens with their guns, pith helmets and knee length boots. I felt like we were on a movie set.

These colonial-attired men were employed on Ian Craig's massive holding, Lewa Ranch, next door, much of which he had converted into a conservation game reserve. Ian had advised Kip and his community about the tourism benefits of converting some of their land to be environmentally healthy again. Out of that advice grew the eco-lodge. Because of Ian's connections wealthy tourists would visit and finance the improvements to the Maasai lives.

We raced through the bush before coming to an area where a massive elephant with enormous tusks was lying on the ground. It had been sedated to enable the game wardens to place a collar around its neck to track its movement and protect it from poachers. There was a great deal of activity and photos taken as they worked quickly. We then heard a loud bellowing and were rushed back into the jeeps because the sedated elephant's mate was about to arrive. Gun shots were fired into

Me resting on sedated elephant

the air to hold him off. The sedated, and now safe elephant, was given injections to revive it and we were quickly driven to safety. All in a day's work for these guys!

During our stay we arranged to visit a village for dinner. We didn't realise that young warriors had been summoned from surrounding villages to entertain us. It was exhilarating watching them bounce through the village with their shouts and enthusiastic whooping. Rob was invited to drink blood directly from the neck of a newly slaughtered goat. Rob did but I couldn't come at that one.

I loved Il Ngwesi and felt so privileged to have experienced it.

This trip set the tone for future adventures for Rob and me. One night while eating dinner in the bush I told Kip that we wanted to come back next year and to book the same open room. "You like that one?" asked Kip. "So does William, who always likes to stay in that one." That was Prince William. We returned a year later to follow up with sneakers for Fred, one of the Maasai.

In 2004, we met a couple who would become great friends for us both, and wise counsel for me. Debbie Hockings and Peter Lorking were both in Department of Education in administration roles and like us, owned a holiday house at Culburra Beach. We had many entertaining occasions with them. Debbie, because of her experience as a Director in public education, was very helpful in advising me about navigating my way through the intricacies of departmental policy.

It was a year of significant change and progression for the TDP as Robyn Philpot's long running role as coordinator began. We also set up the new TDP office at OutThere Productions, thanks to the generosity of Andy and Mr Bee, who donated the office space.

15
The Robyn years

I see Robyn's years from 2004–2017 as TDP Coordinator/Talent Manager as an era of extraordinary development. Her background as a professional dancer, teacher and events coordinator brought a diverse range of skills to the project. Her warmth and nurturing of all the students gave heart to the program and helped make the workshops safe and welcoming for young people from very diverse backgrounds. Her capacity for hard work was legendary. She is one of the most dedicated and compassionate women I know. This, I believe, was due in no small way to the fact she was raising three boys and had a keen understanding of teenage behaviour.

During the 12 years in her role Robyn led some remarkable developments including:

- regional workshops
- Indigenous outreach programs in some of the most remote areas of NSW
- TDP's steps onto the world stage through the Broadway ASCAP scholarship
- A mentoring program for TDP graduates.

Robyn found her way into the complex world of travel and accommodation in New York and enabled the invaluable experience which was to enhance and change forever the lives of all Broadway scholarship winners. She continued to increase the status of TDP through many high-profile public and government performances, organising and accompanying all the young performers to events to ensure they were presented in a professional manner and were safe.

She worked hard connecting many of our young performers to scholarship opportunities, including coordinating their performances at the John Brown Sport and Tourism Foundation scholarship presentations. This gave so many of our young performers the opportunity to impress high-profile audiences who in turn opened up a new business, corporate and government world to these public school students.

In 2011, Robyn helped reunite the TDP family of graduates by coordinating a reunion for the TDP 20th birthday celebrations. She had been managing our past graduate mentoring programs, which included employing alumni to perform at corporate events, and creating performing opportunities such as the Shangri La Hotel music events. She knew every single graduate and consultant and played a vital role in assisting TDP with employment and networking opportunities. She was always looking out for opportunities for employment for graduates to help them along the way with their careers.

In 2004, Alan Jones joined the board and he facilitated an immediate injection of sponsorship, eventually leading to the establishment of the TDP/Broadway scholarships which would lead the TDP to New York.

The 2004 Graduation Ceremony, which was coordinated by Richard Spiewak, became a milestone event in the training program, because Richard facilitated the first full studio recordings of the TDP graduates. That year, instead of just being presented with a certificate at their graduation, they left the TDP armed with a full media kit consisting of a bio, media release, professional photographs, certificate and a demo recording. Richard was the TDP Coordinator for a short period in 2004 before he left to take up a position in the Department of Education Arts Unit. He's now the Executive Producer of the SS.

This year also heralded the rise of the big solo singer in Australia. TV shows such as *Australian Idol* became popular. TDP reacted with a further increased focus on songwriting and recording. Musical Director Andrew Bee led the move to take the graduating class to Sony studios to produce professional quality recordings for each student, mixed by high level audio technicians and backed by professional musicians.

Regional auditions and outreach also grew. We took our workshops to Tamworth, Dubbo, Coffs Harbour and the Riverina, where some great talent was unearthed.

Milly Petriella from APRA came on board as a volunteer consultant, connecting us even more closely to the industry.

She remained a valued adviser to me during my directing years and mentored many of the aspiring graduates for TDP who were finding their way into the industry.

With a change in government, Andrew Cappie-Wood was appointed Director-General and Jan McClellan was unceremoniously dismissed. I was sorry to see her go as she'd been so supportive and fair in that role. However, I was relieved to receive a phone call from the new Director-General inviting me to meet with him. I was anxious that my troubles with the Department of Education might begin again. He assured me that all was fine for my relationship with the SS and I enjoyed his short stay as Director-General.

Jan, when Director-General, with young TDP graduates now with successful careers: Erin James FL, Travis Collins (front), Sam McClymont (back left), Scott Ryan (back right), Julia Stone (front next to Jan)

Through the TDP and SS I had always tried to find ways to include Indigenous talent and this year I made an extra special effort. We had some great finds plus some very disappointing receptions from what seemed to us to be lazy staff in some outback schools. For example, we arrived at Walgett to find that the principal and music teachers weren't even there. Chris Ryan CEO from Department was travelling with us, hoping to add serious weight to our mission. He was shocked by the general lack of enthusiasm shown by the staff of these country schools and disappointed by the lost opportunities for their students.

We staged a TDP Arena Concert at the Sydney Entertainment Centre, which we called "A Big Night In", featuring TDP stars on the Sunday night. We were able to use the production and staging from the SS which was held the night before. This show was an initiative of Out There Productions proposed by Andy and Andrew to be a marketing tool for TDP. The then Chairman of TDP, Alan Jones, and I were so nervous as we peered through the backstage curtains and hoped there would be a substantial audience.

The talent was coordinated by TDP graduate, Darren Coggan. Stars of the show were all TDP alumni including:

- Nadia Ackerman, who flew out from New York
- Morgan Evans
- Brendan Irving
- Lucy Maunder
- The McClymonts
- Robert McDougall
- Roshani Priddis
- The Baileys, and
- Lorenzo Rositano.

Naturally, Human Nature was the headline act and performed the second half of the show. They were extremely generous with their time and support given their intensive international commitments.

With Human Nature in Vegas

SS comes of age, more travel and moving house again

Bonita Mabo was a special guest for the 21st birthday SS. She sat in the audience with Andrew Refshauge, the Deputy Premier of NSW. Dianne Duff AO, with a total of 23 years' enthusiastic involvement as choir teacher, tunnel manager and choral conductor, became the SS producer from 2004 until her retirement in 2007. She had been very actively involved since 2001, when she had taken over the management of the Arts Unit. Peter Cook was the Dance Director and Steve Williams continued as Musical Director and conductor. The performance featured outstanding talent who've now made names for themselves in the music industry, including:

- John Foreman (as host)
- Julie Lee Goodwin
- Morgan Evans
- Brendan Irving
- Lucy Maunder
- Mollie McClymont
- Robert McDougall
- Roshani Priddis
- The Baileys (Kurt and Charlene)
- Lorenzo Rositano, and
- Katrina Burgoyne.

> **Where are they now – Julie Lee Goodwin**
>
> *One of Australia's most dazzling Australian sopranos. Her impressive career has seen her singing music across all genres including musical theatre, opera, operetta, and classical cross-over. Included in her starring roles were Maria in* West Side Story, *Grace in* Annie, *Christine in* Phantom *and the merry widow in* The Merry Widow.
>
>
>
> Me, Rob and Julie (when she played Christine)

This was the year that Rita and Richard Slingsby brought their school rock band, Brittle EFX from Ballina High School to SS. I had met Rita and Richard in a very brief stint I had teaching at Ryde HS back in 1973. Rita clearly outlined the important educational and life lessons that the SS gave some members of her band. She noted that they had never seen or heard a symphony orchestra before and now they were playing on the same stage. They were being exposed to a much broader cultural world as were so many of the SS performers.

Children who participated in the SS experienced the magic of hearing vastly different musical genres as well as being given the opportunity to perform with students from all socio-economic backgrounds and cultures. They had fun, without knowing they were also being educated through the story telling themes. Just participating was an invaluable educational experience for thousands of public-school children.

In 2005, I sold my home at 17 Walker St, Lavender Bay, and bought an apartment in Glen St, Milsons Point. My friends, and Rob especially, will tell you how I'm always moving house. Rob says during our 24+ years together he's packed up and moved eight properties for me, some in the middle of the SS. I enjoy the change, but Rob doesn't. I lasted one year in that Glen St apartment because I didn't like feeling so detached from the ground living 26 stories high.

I put my restlessness and penchant for constantly moving down to my childhood. As an eight- and nine-year-old I travelled 14km by bus from Paterson to attend my first Catholic school at Largs, then my next school, 17km by steam train to the Dominican Convent Maitland. I walked through the back streets of Maitland each day to the convent. In addition, during these two years Mum sold the Paterson Hotel and we were staying at a farm we had at Clarence town. I was also sent to boarding school at the Dominicans while we relocated to Merriwa. Thus began the saga of my frequently moving house and, I think, my passion for travel.

Rob and I travelled again to Nairobi, via Dubai. Here's my diary entry for that time.

> *Arrived in Nairobi at 1830 on August 14 to return to another fascinating African adventure where we had a hair-raising car trip with a guide who didn't know where we going. We ended up in what appeared to be a swamp!*

> *Fortunately some locals came walking in the opposite direction and helped us out. We were trying to reach a luxurious resort which we found out when we arrived was occupied by English people, mostly honeymooners.*

We were excited to return to Il Ngwesi with sneakers for Fred the Maasai. Fred had told us on our last trip how he ran 40km to home at the weekend in his sandals. He tried to fit into Rob's sneakers but they were about five sizes too small. Even so Fred had a good try.

This time around Rob organised an "Olympic" games on the airstrip which was going well until we were quickly moved off because of approaching elephants. Rob had even taken prizes which the staff enjoyed very much. The "games" held on the small airstrip included spear throwing and rolling tyres.

Under advice from TDP board member and Sydney Entertainment Centre General Manager, Tim Worton, we took a huge step and moved the TDP Graduation Concert out of the Jack Neary Room and onto a stage in the main arena. We took our workshops and auditions (Indigenous and mainstream) to several regional centres: Lismore, Dubbo, Tamworth, Moruya, Wagga Wagga and Woolgoolga.

It was at an audition in Wagga where I met an extraordinary young musician, Brendon Boney. He joined the TDP and graduated in 2005. Brendon has progressed from his successful band "Microwave Jenny" with wife Tessa Nuku, (also a TDP graduate in 2005) to an alt hip-hop outfit. He has a very successful career as a song writer and composer and has an influential role in consulting on Indigenous music panels as well as acting. He currently is a composer and sound designer for the Bangarra Dance Theatre.

Bill Anderson was appointed manager of the Arts and Sports Units with the Education Department and became Executive Producer for the SS. I enjoyed working with Bill. He was very supportive and encouraging. Having come from a background in television, he was aware of the requirements of staging and marketing such a production.

In "The Face of Australia", SS No. 22, we presented the most powerful of all ANZAC segments. Paul Viles, the very talented drama consultant from the PAU, directed the whole segment for the soloists, musicians, dancers, actors, massed choir and orchestra. It became a benchmark for all statements about "respect" as a lesson taught in the SS.

My son, Andy was contracted to research and supply video footage for SS 2005. He was surprised and saddened to see the faces of the soldiers and commented to me "they were all so young." And that's the truth, looking back as an 80-year-old, even the older Anzacs were young! An actor even stated that fact from the Sydney Entertainment Centre stage, as part of the powerful dramatisation created by Paul Viles. The show highlighted the tragedy that is the loss of lives and the grief of those waiting at home for their sons to return. We all wondered if we were worthy of such a sacrifice. Now well-known featured artists included opera singer Julie Lea Goodwin and musician, Brendon Boney. We also invited Dawn Fraser to be a special guest in a segment about Aussie icons. She was such a good sport and danced with a professional dancer to *Love Is in The Air*.

In 2006, I travelled to New Zealand on a bus trip with my sisters, Dot and Bub. It was the first and only time we travelled together. We had a memorable fortnight. Upon our return I sold our apartment in Peninsula Towers. We were moving again – back to Walker Street!

In late June I'd returned from visiting schools in Bourke, Walgett and Dubbo on the usual talent search for TDP and SS, in time to attend the wedding of the daughter of good friends, the late Janelle and Antony Kidman. Nicole Kidman and Keith Urban were married in the historic St Patrick's Estate in Manly. Of course, it was exciting to be a guest at such a precious occasion. Nic has always been so warm and down to earth, despite her fame, and she and Keith looked gorgeously in love. Keith singing his song for Nicole was a highlight. The décor, music and location were perfect. And of course being there with such a celebrity crowd gave us talking points for years to come. One memorable moment was Rob's encounter with Rupert Murdoch. As we walked through a pathway spectacle of thousands of candles and rose petals we were almost brushed aside by Rupert rushing in the opposite direction asking "where's Wendy?" (at that time, he was married to Wendy Dang). He slipped and fell amongst the candles and rose petals and had to be fished out by my hero, Rob Bail. Rupert took off without a word of appreciation and left us all wondering where indeed, was Wendy? Later during the reception Rupert caught up with Rob and thanked him for his help. As I'm now writing the final chapters in my memoir in 2025, Nicole and Keith have just announced their marriage breakdown. I'm sad that the long relationship and years of happiness together has not survived.

TDP goes international

In January 2005, my friend Scott Stoner, working for the Kennedy Center for the Performing Arts in Washington DC, introduced me to Simon Heath, who months later introduced me to Michael Kerker, the ASCAP musical theatre director for USA. This is how we began the exciting trail to the Broadway TDP/ASCAP scholarships in New York. The TDP was becoming international.

I always talk about the incredible importance of networks and knowing when you're meant to follow through a connection. This story goes to prove the point of the power of networks, and also demonstrates that when someone tells you "you should meet so and so" you should certainly take that advice.

I had a tiny window of opportunity to become Scott's friend. He was in Sydney leading a delegation from the Kennedy Centre in Washington in 1987. Irina White (then Marketing/PR manager for the Education Department) was hosting the delegation and suggested I meet Scott, who was setting up the Kennedy Centre Educational Arts Program. He only had half an hour available for a breakfast meeting before flying back to the USA that day. I seized the chance on Irina's advice and Scott and I remain life-long friends. Scott later introduced me to his friend Simon Heath, who visited a TDP workshop and become enthusiastic about the training program. This association and friendship which grew into the TDP ASCAP/Broadway scholarship has provided many invaluable opportunities for the scholarship winners and has changed their lives. Nowhere is the power of network more in evidence.

Through Simon I had the most amazing phone call in 2006 with Michael Kerker. Simon and I were on a call while he was sharing a New York taxi with Michael and so he introduced us over the phone. Simon grew up in Bourke NSW before living and working as a music producer for Paramount in Los Angeles for many years. Michael became a great friend to me, and a powerful influence on the professionalism, network and profile of the TDP and me.

In Michael I found myself talking to a person from the other side of the world, with the equal passion, drive and desire to nurture talent. I was again in unchartered waters, having little idea of how to go about this new project but I knew I was on the verge of finding my entry into a very exciting new opportunity.

Following this completely unexpected phone meeting with Michael, the annual TDP Bound For Broadway scholarship was founded. Belinda Wollaston and Luke Dolahenty were the first talented recipients and travelled to New York to be immersed in the Broadway music theatre scene. TDP Graduate, Nadia Ackerman, who was successfully marking out a singer/songwriter career in New York assisted Robyn Philpot in finding suitable and affordable accommodation for our students.

Michael wrote the following letter to me for inclusion in the TDP 30th birthday program in 2021:

As TDP celebrates its 30th year I have the opportunity to personally celebrate you as someone who has helped change my life in significant ways. I am the VP of Musical Theatre for ASCAP... (the US counterpart to APRA) and I had never received a call from anyone from Australia.

That initial contact took place 15 years ago. You had heard about our ASCAP Musical Theatre workshop headed by the extraordinary composer/lyricist Stephen Schwartz (Wicked, Pippin, Godspell etc.). You asked if it would be possible to send three recent grads of TDP to NY and observe these workshop sessions. This would give these young performers the chance to be in the room with, get to meet and to learn up close from the most important creators of American musical theatre. They also had an inside look at how musicals are created and how the collaborative process works.

I know that this opportunity you provided for the TDP grads was life changing. In addition, under your guidance, I worked closely with the young talents so they could also make their debut in a cabaret concert in NY. I set them up with a noted musical director, an established cabaret performer who offered coaching and a cabaret director. I also made certain that some of the composers whose songs your grads were to sing would be in the audience for the performance. Again, what an amazing opportunity and how this helped expand your vision of the TDP program.

It should be noted that your TDP grads were not only exceptionally talented but also extremely gracious and had acquired the social skills you no doubt help instil in them.

Fifteen years later I am still friendly with and are in constant touch with many of them. Over the years I have even invited some of them to participate in my ASCAP concerts at such venues as the Kennedy Center in Washington DC.

One final but very important note ... because of TDP I have made a lifelong friend in Mary Lopez and for that friendship I will be eternally grateful. We've shared travel adventures, dinners in our respective homes and the mutual love and respect for gifted young musical talents.

I am sending much love to my friend on this special occasion.

Michael Kerker.

With the TDP now 15 years old, the program was truly coming of age. It was time to spread our international wings with the ASCAP/TDP Bound for Broadway scholarship. The program was big enough to necessitate Robyn Philpot's role becoming full time. Anne Fitzgerald from Clubs NSW joined the board and was a valuable contributor. Clubs NSW was a major sponsor for the TDP from these early days and through all the years until 2025. In a change of career in 2020, Anne became the CEO for the TDP from 2020–2025.

The scholarship was to provide airfares and accommodation in New York for outstanding TDP graduates. As Michael's letter notes, they would meet and potentially work with some of the best American MT songwriters. As well as attending the ASCAP workshops conducted by Academy Award composer/lyricist Stephen Schwartz, Michael arranged training sessions, singing and interpretation sessions with celebrated musical directors, culminating in a 45-minute showcase. The showcase was to be presented in one of New York's favourite cabaret venues, "Don't Tell Mama." There were also performances by graduates at other established New York cabaret venues like Birdland, as well as the chance to attend famous cabaret performances and live theatre productions. These were all tickets that were only available because of Michael. Our scholarship recipients received introductions to celebrities within the music and entertainment industry that, as young performers from public schools in Australia, they could only have dreamed about.

So, how can the TDP, a charity, afford the cost of accommodation, airfares and expenses? Alan Jones found the sponsorship money to ensure the scholarship would be ongoing. He called on his network to give young Australians an opportunity beyond their wildest dreams. A real chance.

Two or three students were selected for the scholarship each year. Suitable candidates were then invited to audition, and a panel selected the winners. I learned so much about professionalism and the big picture through my association with Michael. I know what a gift he bestowed on our young Australian hopefuls. Michael was insistent that I come to a workshop in New York and observe Stephen Schwartz and he was right. I realised how important it was to expand my horizons and knowledge on musical theatre and cabaret performance and composition to be of greater assistance to my students. My network kept growing.

We asked for assistance from a TDP graduate, Nadia Ackerman, who had moved to New York and was making a name for herself as a singer/songwriter. Nadia's a fantastic woman and it gave me immense pleasure to catch up with her in New York. She was a comforting mentor for the young graduates.

The value of this scholarship to all of us involved in its initiative, for our individual development and management skills, is incalculable. The world stage door opened, and we had to find our way through it.

Sadly, I have since learned the Bound for Broadway Scholarship ceased to exist after my retirement. This is such a shame, as it was an unbelievable opportunity for these young people.

Outreach

I was determined try even harder to reach Indigenous performers. We had a great friend in Bev Baker, working for Macquarie Bank as an advisor on Indigenous educational programs, who introduced our program to Bill Moss, who was then the financial senior executive guru of Macquarie Bank. With their sponsorship we were able to take TDP workshops especially targeting Indigenous performers to Bourke, Walgett and Dubbo. Through these workshops we discovered Bruce Carr, a remarkably talented dancer and a gifted young singer, as well as 12-year-old Nathan Lamont. Nathan was so keen he stood outside the toilet waiting for me to make sure I heard him sing. Such a talent! It is such a joy to see him with his awards, scholarships and overall success being acknowledgements now by being chosen to represent Australia at Americana fest in Nashville in 2025.

Nathan Lamont on meeting Mary
Yiradhu marang, Mary (Good day in Wiradjuri).
It has been far too long since we have spoken! I just wanted to express how grateful I am for your generosity in offering a donation to help toward my music. It truly brings tears to my eyes.

I am in the process of paying instrumentalist and producers for costs associated with future single releases so this truly will go a long way.

I feel compelled to express how grateful I feel for having had you as part of my development as a young person and throughout my TDP years.

I can still remember my very first interaction with you at the indigenous TDP workshop at Wagga when I was around 12 or 13 years of age.

I was determined to steal your attention as I saw the opportunity the program would bring and I really had nothing to lose.

In hindsight, meeting you was a major turning point for me in music and firmly believe I couldn't have gotten as far as I have if it weren't for the opportunities that stemmed from you and the program from that point on forward.

I just want to thank you for everything that has blessed my life as a result of music since that time and hope that I can catch up with you again sometime in the future.

I'll be sure to forward you an update on my next single release which your donation will help in funding. This will be released on October 21, 2024, and is called **Disaster**.

Mandaang guwu (Thank you).

We also visited Tamworth in July with a workshop. The very enthusiastic and effective music consultant Di Hall was instrumental in making this happen. A further workshop was conducted on August 31 on the North Coast.

My relationships with Father Chris Riley continued and the TDP received sponsorship from YOTS to support TDP participants in need. Father Chris provided these $5,000 scholarships for several years to create opportunities for his YOTS students as well as current TDP students in need. I recently met up with one of these recipients at Fr Chris' Memorial, Jason Mobbs-Green, who graduated in

2014. I was delighted to hear of this outstanding young man's life and career success as a high school music teacher. Jason had very challenging circumstances as a child when he was for years his beloved grandmother's carer. My heart swelled with pride to hear what Jason has achieved and to know the TDP helped him along the way.

The year concluded with SS No. 23 – "Shine." The following is my message in the program.

> *Our deepest fear is not that we are inadequate. Our deepest fear is that we are powerful beyond measure. It is our light that most frightens us not our darkness. We ask ourselves, who am I to be brilliant, gorgeous, talented, fabulous? Actually, who are you not to be? And as we let our light shine, we unconsciously give other people permission to do the same.*

This quote was taken from the 1994 inaugural speech of Nelson Mandela, four years after his release from prison. That speech truly inspired me and supports the philosophy on which my life's work has been built.

Telstra came on board as the major sponsor of the SS, way back in these early 2000s, opening a new world of technical assistance and communication for this huge event. It's hard to believe that at this stage of my story the SS had been in production for over twenty years.

During the year I had auditioned kids from Lord Howe Island and practically the whole school performed at that SS. It must have been mind-blowing for those youngsters who'd possibly never left the island up until then. They performed alongside some very talented featured artists – all of whom were TDP trained:

- Jack Carty
- Melanie Dyer
- Tonino Speciali
- Michael Viasini
- Alex Gibson-Georgio
- Miriam Waks.

These performers from diverse musical genres are now internationally renowned with successful careers around the globe.

Chris Ryan reflects on Dr Mary Lopez AM – The Educator

Spoken at Mary's 80th birthday party:

Mary and I first met more than 20 years ago through my role as Executive Director of the Department of Education. Before long I somehow found myself on the TDP board and involved in the management group responsible for the SS.

The first thing you find when you look up Mary Lopez on the web is a statement that Mary is arguably Australia's most awarded female in the music and entertainment industry. The significance of Mary's awards and honours is not in their number or status ... but what they are built on.

From humble beginnings as a child in the Upper Hunter Valley, Mary pursued a career as a music teacher at a time when secondary music teaching, particularly in boys' high schools, was very challenging. Mary was hugely successful as a teacher and much of what she experienced was to underpin her future career. Not least was her commitment to unearthing talent and providing opportunities for students from less advantaged backgrounds.

Mary was always looking at ways of doing things better. Not only in the classroom, but also as an educator on a broader stage. There are two particular memories that come to mind.

The first relates to Indigenous participation. Mary knew Indigenous students were not getting enough opportunities and argued to me along the following lines:

- *that more needed to be done to support them to audition;*
- *that more needed to be done to provide performance opportunities;*
- *that more needed to be done to ensure teachers were encouraging them;*
- *that more needed to be done to ensure students were supported when coming to Sydney for rehearsals and performances;*
- *and that Aboriginal elders ought to be involved with the process.*

Having raised these issues with the appropriate Regional Director I found myself touring schools in central NSW with Mary and leader of the Aboriginal Education Consultative Group, Cindy Berwick, to encourage Indigenous kids to have a go in a nurtured and supported audition process. The outcome – a significant increase in the number of Indigenous kids in SS, suitably supported. Also, more Indigenous students successfully auditioning for the TDP.

Another insight into Mary, the educator, was clear to me at a milestone celebration dinner related to the Schools Spectacular. To mark the occasion Mary gave a speech that focused on what she had learnt from every person present. Displaying an in-depth knowledge of each person's expertise and what they had done to help Mary, not only as director of SS, but as a person.

I later found that almost everyone in the room had a personal story about how Mary had helped them, sometimes as a mentor, sometimes as a counsellor, sometimes as an adviser and sometimes by telling them what she thought they needed to hear.

In both SS and the TDP, Mary worked hard with both students and adults, providing opportunity, helping to build hope and managing expectations, engaging with industry experts, striving for excellence, and ensuring extra support was provided when needed.

Mary, while it is important to acknowledge you as Emeritus Director, Dr Mary Lopez AM ... for many of us it is your enduring friendship that we value most.

Be proud Mary ... and keep on rolling.

16
Family expansion

In 2007, we were living back in Walker St, Lavender Bay. The Glen St apartment had proved very disappointing for several reasons. I felt disorientated living 26 floors in the air. The air-conditioning for the building was also on top of our unit and the constant hum drove me mad. The last straw was when I heard a man passing wind in the kitchen next door. I was not yet ready for apartment living. I had already spoken to my former next-door neighbour in Walker St about my misery and asked her to contact me if she was ever going to move. Luckily, she decided she was on the move and contacted me. I was soon back to my beloved Walker St, living in a sister Victorian Terrace house.

With Andy and Kate

There was great excitement at Prince of Wales Hospital in the very early hours of July 12. My first grandchild, Mani Lopez arrived with a shock of long, black hair. An absolutely beautiful and perfect baby boy. Prior to our arrival at the hospital, I had the most unusual experience of getting to know my daughter-in-law Christine whilst she was taking a soothing soak in the bathroom of their home, before she went into full-on labour.

We had some more exciting travels this year. Rob and I had an idyllic trip though France with French friend, Odile Mayet, who'd become a friend after we met on the Tiwi Islands north of Darwin of all places. It was quite a change from outback travel and chasing elephants in Africa.

An unexpected accolade came to me out of the blue in October when I was presented with the Variety Clubs Humanitarian of the Year Heart Award for "helping thousands of children experience the magic of show business while learning discipline, hard work and attention to detail." This was indeed a thrill and one which I will always treasure.

With family, Robyn Philpot, Kirby Burgess, Andrew and Megan Bee

John delivering the tribute speech

Since the establishment of TDP in 1991, we had conducted monthly workshops at the Sydney Entertainment Centre. During 2007, it also became the administrative headquarters of TDP.

In May 2007, I took a trip to New York and Washington for my first face to face meeting with Michael Kerker and to attend the New York workshops. I realised the enormity and opportunity that this scholarship was giving our students. How I would love to have had such an opening when I was that kid from Merriwa. Nobody I knew then (or even in 2007) dreamed they could be a part of such a life. Through Michael we were able to secure good seats for *Wicked, Spamelot, Hairspray, Grey Garden* and a tribute night for Gerry Herman. Wow!

The ASCAP scholarship in 2007 was awarded to three TDP graduates instead of two because the girls were equally talented. They were each so strong although very different and I'm pleased we did that because they've all been very successful in their careers. Kirby Burgess, Erin James and Lucy Maunder all made the most of their Broadway experience. Kirby was invited back to perform at the New York Town Hall at a show called the Rising Stars of Broadway after the producer saw her cabaret show at Don't Tell Mama. Kirby was the first and only Australian in this show. The TDP provided the funds for Kirby to return and perform at this prestigious concert and to have a lifetime memory.

Keeping the playing field level

We held another Indigenous workshop in October at the Sydney Entertainment Centre for students coming from 10 city and country high schools. Bonita was the patron and attended the workshops. Tutors included:

- opera star, Deborah Cheetham
- award winning actress, Ursula Yovich
- 2004 *Australian Idol* winner, Casey Donovan
- country artist, Travis Collins
- Indigenous dancer/choreographer Albert Davis
- Francine Bell
- hip hop artists, Rival.

It was another invaluable proactive effort on the part of the TDP to provide opportunities to level the playing field for talented Indigenous students.

In SS No. 24 entitled, "My Spec", I was rewarded when I met up again with an Aboriginal mother from Woolgoolga, Wendy Dalton. She was with her performers in the Sydney Entertainment Centre back car park. Wendy told me what it had meant to the children all those years ago in the early years of the SS, when I first visited their school. "Look how far we've come," she said. No one conversation fills me with more pride and satisfaction than that.

Some new names, all TDP trained students, appeared in "My Spec":

- Lincoln Hall
- Bruce Carr
- Robert McDougall
- Angel Tupai
- Michael Viasini (Lombardi)
- Joel Newman
- Emily Edwards
- Richard Bloomfield
- Alex Gibson-Giorgio
- Daniel Gordon
- Shane McGrath.

Personal milestones

Looking back at this year, it was one full of personal sadness and loss, a family operation and a wedding, and my retirement from the SS.

On Monday, February 11, the third year of Broadway scholarship, a panel of highly qualified professionals auditioned the graduates. The prestigious panel included:

- John Robertson (Director of Cameron Macintosh)
- Kevin Jacobsen
- Justin Smith – TDP Graduate (*Billy Elliot*)
- David Harris – TDP Graduate (*Miss Saigon*)
- Peter Cousens (*The Hatpin*)
- Mary Lopez AM
- Andrew Bee (TDP Musical Director)
- the Hon John Brown.

The TDP/Bound for Broadway scholarship winners that year were Roshani Priddis and Carly Champion. As Roshani notes:

> *The Talent Development Project has been one of the most consistent supporters of my career in my two decades as a performer. From scholarships and trips to New York, to the supportive community that is always there for us all. As a 15-year-old, they helped fan the flame that would lead me onto experiences I will cherish forever.*

Roshani

Later in the year we held another Indigenous workshop in Taree, in partnership with the late Gavin Jones and VIBE Australia. Gavin was the producer for many years of the Deadly Awards which was staged at the Sydney Opera House and celebrated Indigenous performers.

Robyn and I attended the first joint venture workshops in Taree. We'd engaged Indigenous TDP graduates Tessa Nuku and Brendon Boney as consultants, accompanied by Indigenous singer and *Idol* winner, Casey Donovan, who is now one of Australia's most loved talents. This was our first association with and introduction to the

VIBE program, so it was very much a case of "learning on the job." Tessa and Brendon sang at the launch the night before and conducted very effective workshops with Casey. Our affirmative action in giving a fair go to Indigenous talent was paying off.

Sadly, Manuel's mother, known to us all as Mama, died on April 1. Before Mama had died, one of her sons had caused problems between Mama and me. It all stemmed from a promise I gave Manuel that I would give our children the proceeds from the flat in which Mama lived when she no longer needed it. He couldn't accept the fact that Manuel owned the apartment and not Mama and wanted to have "his share." He even engaged a lawyer at one stage to write to me and threaten to expose me as I had "a high profile." Desperate people do not act rationally. The other brothers initially shared his belief and thus had not had any contact with us since Manuel's death. They did, however, realise just in the year before Mama died the extent of his bad behaviour towards his mother. I received an apology from Manuel's brothers at the funeral.

It was in this year I took up aqua aerobics and met the aqua girls from the North Sydney pool. These "Aqua Belles" have become an essential part of my life. Joc Ibels was keeping an eye on me and invited me to join the girls for coffee. I was shy about becoming involved because I hadn't ever been included in any girls' groups before. Joc reminds me I was always dressed up. That's because I was in the thick of my career. Thank heavens for these warm, hospitable and loyal women who still meet a couple of times a week for coffee. The conversation bounces around grandchildren, fitness, solving the world's problems and women's issues. It's like a Maeve Binchy novel with the variety of characters offering support to each other. These friends and their husbands have become the solid base of Rob's and my life together.

We took a flying visit to Sarina, Queensland in the early part of the year to celebrate Bonita's 65th birthday. She'd been keen to show off her town and for me to meet some of her South Sea Island family members. I gained a clearer understanding of her life as child and her meeting with Eddie and their marriage. Her childhood days were poor, but they were happy and contented and surrounded by music. It was a privilege to be given this insight.

In May, Rob and I travelled to China to visit Shanghai, Beijing and the Great Wall. It was all so interesting. The history and grandiose buildings and spaces were unforgettable. We had so much fun and so many adventures exploring the unique tailors and fabric markets of Shanghai along with the food and memorable monuments and history.

Dot, Shirley, Widge and me

My eldest sister, Shirley, died in June. The leader of our clan was gone. This was a devastating loss for the whole extended family. We all called her "Bub", the name by which she'd been known since she was a child. She was kindness itself and never missed a birthday for any of us, including most of her nieces and nephews. Her role in the lives of my two children was loving, supportive and generous. I, to this day, feel the gap in my life.

Bub had always been there for me. As a child I would always receive postcards and gifts when she was travelling. There's so much to remember about her. I am so blessed to have been a part of my loving and respectable family. As I'm losing them all, I'm valuing them more every day and trying so hard not to regret lost moments. My brothers and sisters all tried hard to keep our big family together. It's a testament to their success that the family of nieces and nephews are all still very much in touch and turn up for family functions and funerals.

Bub's funeral was held on 5 June. However, I didn't really have a chance to feel this loss at this time, because Kate's needs became paramount. She was admitted to hospital on the Saturday – the day after her birthday and two days after Shirley's funeral. Her operation was scheduled for 11 June. I know Shirley would have been such a support for Kate and would have been at the hospital every day. I'll let Kate explain in detail in a later chapter the intricacies of the major spinal surgery she underwent.

The joyful highlight of this year was Saturday, 30 August. Andy and Christine Wu were married. Thank God for an occasion to now celebrate. The wedding was held at the Officers' Mess venue at Middle Head. Christine was a beautiful bride as were her bridesmaids and there were some very funny speeches. Mani was a little over a year old and was so cute. My family was growing.

There were many other family shining years to follow with Kate's wedding and the arrival of another two grandchildren, Izzy Lopez and Eva Glavinic.

Andy's wedding and my three grandchildren

Andy's wedding

Kate's wedding

I received a welcome invitation to open the Merriwa Show in September from the President of the show. Ed Shannon is the brother of my good friend, Eve Shannon. I felt very special as Merriwa had given me the life that had fuelled themes and passions for the career that I had enjoyed.

Michael Kerker visited Australia in November to see the TDP program in operation firsthand. Rob and I proudly showed off Culburra to Michael and his partner, Gene. They were impressed with the awesome beauty of Culburra and loved being able to get so close to the kangaroos on the side of the roads in the south coast towns of Sussex Inlet and on the Callala golf course! These were certainly good photo opportunities for the Americans.

Clubs NSW, who were a major sponsor of the TDP supported a new mentoring initiative and offered venues to TDP to showcase the students and graduates. The first of these was held at Campbelltown Catholic Club with Marty Rhone as host. The ever generous and multi-talented Marty had often provided his services as a volunteer consultant. Through this initiative Christie Lamb, a vivacious and talented country music performer, gained much valuable experience which helped lead to her now very successful career.

I am finally on stage

On the last night of SS No. 25, 2008, I walked onto the arena at the Sydney Entertainment Centre to say goodbye to all the SS family. This family had made my dreams come true. John Foreman called me onto the arena with the people I love most in the world –Andy, Kate and Rob. Andrew Bee had secretly rehearsed with the thousands of soloists, choirs, teachers and production team, as well as the orchestra, to perform my special song – *The Town I Love So Well*. How he managed to do all of this without me knowing anything still beggars belief. Bee walked beside me for 20 years as Spectacular Technical Producer and Associate Director, and had been my indispensable right hand, keeping me energised and inspired. I was enthralled by this gift from Bee and the SS cast and crew.

Waving goodbye to my beloved SS Family, on arena with my loved ones, Kate, Andy and Rob

At the matinee, I watched my whole life fall into place. My brothers were there in the audience, with many of my nieces and nephews and great-nieces. They were there for me as they always had been. My eldest brother, Cecil, had hired a bus to bring his family from Nelson Bay to Sydney for the show.

My memory is sketchy about my emotions on retiring, as I was quite stressed by all the activity behind the scenes prior to my retirement. It felt like I was being hurried to give up what had been my life's work. But I do agree, it was time for me to let go. My job as a teacher had been done and I was very satisfied that my lessons had been learned. I summarised those lessons in the printed program for that silver anniversary concert:

> *This glorious entertainment event sees the Spectacular family continue to grow and spread its messages about the Spectacular Spirit: the Spirit of Australia, Respect, Tolerance, Inclusiveness and Teamwork.*

I hoped now I would have plenty of time for Rob and me to continue our adventures across Australia and the world, and for me to share in the lives of my son and daughter and their families.

At the last performance, when John Foreman called me onto the stage, it was truly confusing emotionally and at the same time, shattering. I was saying goodbye to my wonderful SS family. How could I ever give them up? And it was devastating because I was giving up my creation. It was also a recognition of the fact that I'd been trying for 25 years to find a slot in the SS for my favourite song. Such is Bee's sense of humour.

John is still hosting the SS and is now sharing his expertise by mentoring young would-be hosts each year.

The SS was a model for several other school-based spectaculars throughout NSW, Victoria and Queensland. The most notable and long-lasting being "Starstruck" in Newcastle, "Creative Generation" in Brisbane and "Southern Stars" in Wollongong. The talented and dedicated teachers leading those three productions all learned their lessons from being major contributors on the team leading the SS. The original Victorian team were given their "notes" by the late Graham Drayton and sat in on several SS rehearsals. It now gives me great pleasure to see how far this concept has travelled and how many young Australians have felt the SS magic.

In the 25th anniversary SS program, I wrote my reflections on the growth of the production since day one, and all those who made it into the mighty event it now is. Here are a few excerpts from that program:

> *The DET is proud of its flagship and provides support and encouragement from the very top. John Foreman has been hosting the SS for eight years and has contributed so much to the enjoyment of each show with his wit and extraordinary memory for both the performers and the sponsors.*
>
> *The Schools Spectacular is a testament to the magnificent performers and their talented teachers from NSW public schools. We now have choreographers and conductors who performed as students in the show. Famous names in show business willingly acknowledge that the Spectacular gave them their taste for the thrill of an audience and the opportunity to develop as performers. They are out there, all over the world, in dance companies, orchestras, bands and the celebrity circuit.*
>
> *The Spectacular has provided opportunities not previously offered in mainstream entertainment. The Deaf Signing Choir has been part of the show since the beginning. Students with disabilities have performed alongside their able-bodied peers. Indigenous students, students from culturally diverse backgrounds and students from remote regions have all thrilled and delighted audiences year after year.*
>
> *The 25th show is my final production, and I am happy to retire as director to spend more time with my family and friends. I leave the Schools Spectacular confident that the robust spirit of camaraderie will continue to carry this remarkable success story on to further exciting adventures and dizzying performance heights.*
>
> *Above all, the Spectacular journey for me has been great fun. For allowing me that privilege, I thank you all.*
>
> *Mary Lopez AM*

Reflection

What an honour it was to lead such a dedicated and selfless team of public-school teachers through the journey of the SS. A destination that is now a shining beacon to how the world could learn many valuable lessons.

There are five very important streams I haven't written about in detail elsewhere but which have been a constant force behind every show. They are, of course: foyer performers, the stage management team, the technical team, the TV and video teams, and marketing personnel.

Foyer entertainment was introduced in 1986 as a showcase for outstanding acts that could not be accommodated on the arena. In that first show they were mainly bands of different musical genres from Denistone East PS, Toronto HS, Irrawang PS, East Hills Boys HS and Lithgow Chamber Orchestra. The practice continued until 2009 when, under Sandra Henderson's direction, the foyer exploded into an expo of the arts which now gives many more children the chance to show off their talents.

Stage manager Jim Bennet and his five EBHS teachers who were assistant stage managers in 1984 have long since left the team. Jim led the practice of involving the students behind the scenes by recruiting many EBHS students on the ever-growing stage management crew. I find it an amazing fact that two EBHS graduates who had first-hand experience with the SS become General Managers/Acting Deputy General Managers of the two great venues in which SS has been staged – Steve Romer at the Sydney Entertainment Centre, and Michael Cox at Qudos Bank Arena.

At the 25th anniversary Spectacular, Rebecca Cowen led the huge team of 60 teacher stage managers. All 60 have donated their time for SS, some since the beginning. These unsung heroic teachers are the army who are responsible for the seamless flow of SS. I've always been full of admiration for their dedication as they stand patiently in the tunnels, keeping the excited masses of dancers happy and quiet. I can feel the energy and throb as I write this now. The joy on the children's faces, being so thrilled to be performing "out there", is unforgettable. They're a very happy group these stage managers and there's a wonderful mateship that's evident each year as they make their pilgrimage every November to Sydney.

Since the first SS in 1984, the technical professionals have taught me everything I know about staging and technical requirements. In those first years, the patient and very clever Sydney Entertainment Centre production and technical staff, namely John Thompson, Ruth Catlin, Trudi Dalgliesh, Arthur Carruthers and Steve Hevern (who later became General Manager of Qudos Bank Arena) brought the SS to life. We always had sound "issues" and the lighting wasn't always spot on, but that was because this show was breaking new ground. The difficulties arose out of the sheer size of the venue, the huge numbers of performers requiring microphones. The combination of a massed choir, symphony orchestra, soloists and bands had not been experienced anywhere in a production in Australia before the SS.

Over the years, the SS has employed many fine sound companies who have grappled with the requirements and given their best to solve the problems. They've all been thoroughly professional and a joy to work with. We were all equally frustrated in those early years when microphones weren't switched on, squealed or were not balanced. Lighting designer extraordinaire Trudi has been leading the lighting team since 1984 and, in 2025, she's still there!

The TV channels always brought an air of added excitement, and it was always a matter of negotiation for the additional layer of cameras to be accommodated. The editing of the show by the TV channels was always a matter for me as director to deal with. I had to negotiate for as many schools to appear on the TV version of the show as possible. Our agenda was about inclusion, not just showing the best items. Doug Swan's dream for maximum PR for public education could only be realised through TV. I was bitterly disappointed when the ABC wouldn't broadcast the whole show and gradually cut down the slot to one hour only, by the time of the magnificent 25th anniversary Spectacular. For the past few years, SS has been televised in full by Channel 7 and I applaud the respect the channel has given the SS by broadcasting the complete production.

The marketing of the SS was the focus of Doug Swan's original brief. He wanted to create a flagship event to publicise public education. Thanks to the great publicists over the years including Penny Stevens, Stuart White and Amanda Buckworth, that aim has certainly been achieved in NSW. With the addition of the televised component, the SS has become a household name across Australia.

In the years preceding the 25th anniversary event, I was asked to write a succession plan to follow my retirement. It made sense to me that Andrew

Bee and Andy Lopez with their company, Out There Productions would take over. As well as the practical and financial benefits of this proposal, there was also the wealth of experience these two men had in producing huge events on a national basis. Firstly, there was Andrew Bee's nearly twenty year professional contribution to SS and his long-term association in developing young talent through the TDP. Then there was the fact that Andy Lopez had spent his teenage years growing up with the SS. It appeared to me to be a no-brainer. However, I failed to consider the investment of the Department in wanting to completely own the SS.

I remained as consultant in the role of artistic advisor for the next six years. My final involvement with the SS was in 2015. Bill Anderson was the executive producer and manager of the Department's sponsorship unit. He kept renewing my contract as he wanted to ensure continuity while the PAU found its management "feet" for SS.

On 6 Jan 2009, I had lunch with Doug Swan, who was the Director-General of Education in 1984, for the first SS. He invited me to lunch at the classy Aria restaurant near the Opera House. He gave me the letter I which I included way back in the beginning of my book where, from his perspective, he tells the story of the beginning of SS. It is a very important letter both for the Department of Education and for me.

I repeat his last paragraph:

> *The rest is history. The Spectacular has gone from strength to strength as a show piece of music and dance in public schools throughout NSW. Its participation including small schools in remote areas. It receives media coverage on national networks. In 2008 Bob Winder and his wife Marion. and I were guest at the 25th anniversary of the spectacular where we admired the splendid production, this still in the hands of Mary Lopez, the outstanding director for so many years*
>
> *Doug Swan*

Doug, I know you are proud of us.

Lessons learned
- A leader is only as good as the people standing behind him/her
- Know when it's time to move on and be a generous mentor

17
A lot to be happy about (Kate's story)

Kate wrote these following pages in 2009 and has kindy allowed me to share her story.

It's February 2009, and I am sitting with Mum on my check covered couch in my cosy apartment in Crows Nest. My little home is north facing, with a view over Willoughby of blue sky reaching above a church steeple to the right, and a mishmash of smallish buildings to the left. My patio fronts on to a curious squat like building hosting an elaborate roof garden, complete with an Australian flag billowing in the wind, shouldered by two other flags of unknown origins. During the last months I have watched with curiosity the people that venture on and off that roof, wondering what business is undertaken there and why on earth they would bother putting such an elaborate garden on such on a non-descript building.

Mum has just come back from a week down at her home away from home in Culburra on the south coast, I've met her after finishing my work for the day solving the world's problems as a lawyer. It's not been a long commute, I work just 200 metres from my front door, so it's easy to organise a catch up with Mum who just lives around the corner in Lavender Bay. She cuts a fine figure of a woman, particularly today I think. She's dressed in a black and white ensemble and has a dash of red lipstick on which offsets her soft green eyes, and spiky light brown hair. Over our hot tea with milk, we get onto discussing the serious issues of being women, the recurring lament about our soft bellies and the like, poking our stomachs as if doing so will make them go away.

We muse about everyday goings on – Mum's partner Rob is constantly amazed by how much, how often and what we can talk about. I suppose it really is an endless stream of chatter that throws up anything from the silly to the rarely profound, given the particular minute of the day. I guess men just don't get the female ability to gas bag. At this minute Mum is asking how work is going and, I tell her it's OK, but that I'm pretty tired by Wednesday, and Thursday represents a welcomed reprieve so I can gear up for Friday and the weekend. I tell her that recently when I've thought about the last eight months I can't quite believe that it all really happened. It's not only those eight months but the seven months building up to it, when everything seemed to be taut with uncertainty, that was the time that nearly brought me to my knees. I don't need to explain this to her, she knows what I mean.

Let me introduce myself to you, I am Kate Lopez, a 36-year-old lawyer with a great life. I am also an athetoid spastic with a cervical fusion from my second cervical to thoracic vertebrae, and I have water on the brain, otherwise known as hydrocephalus.

I have a great deal of metal works and tubing in my body, akin to a construction site and I think I could be forgiven for feeling that I've been in some sort of crazy negotiation with it since the day I was born, in an attempt to get it to behave in a reasonable fashion. Sometimes I compare my vast smorgasbord of medical eccentricities, and the havoc they wreak, to the ordeal of coping with inappropriately behaved guests … you know the sort of guest that turns up to your oh so sophisticated party knowing only Imogen's friend's brother Tom, and then proceeds to get hideously drunk, crack onto your beau and sob inexplicably for all her lost loves, whilst her mascara is running the river Nile down her face. All this, of course, is accompanied by her declarations of lifelong friendship to anyone with the misfortune of being nearby and is usually capped off by some sort of collapse or incoherent drunken breakdown. What you thought was going to be a relatively non-eventful evening has suddenly transformed into a chaotic turn, where you feel like you are part of a theatre skit in *Thank God You're Here* flailing around without any idea of the overall plot, putting up with the embarrassment, the reactions from other people, hoping for the end to it all, and a return to normality.

It's quite a good analogy really except that in my life, for whatever reason, I have never really been a sure-fire bet on the "return to normality" part of that equation. Nonetheless, when my inner drunken dinner guest turns up to party with me I like to explain things in simple terms to people, and just apologise for my body made in Bangladesh, which usually brings about a laugh, and a need not to elaborate further. Quite frankly it's a bit of an insult to the Bangalese considering my medical history, which is as chequered as my couch. I am not your cookie cutter mould of a person, but I know for Mum, my brother and I though quite different, are just as we should be.

Mum's now clear green eyes fixate on the view as she admits she was scared by it all. It was so hard for me, after the operation and it was like I was three again and she wondered was I going to give up this time? I could see how painful it must have been for her to watch as I endured the at times unforgiving hell-ride, knowing there was no way she could change it. She admits she felt completely helpless, to which I can only respond that I knew even when it was really appalling that I wouldn't give up trying. I believed that even if things didn't shake out as I hoped they would, I had made the right decision.

Before you conclude that this is a story about sugar cream, inspirational endings, I'd like to forewarn you that it's not. Mum says the starting point was when I met with my doctor in 2007, but the story I want to tell is different. I guess it's about family, living with a disability, moments of jaw-clenching, audacious love and sadness, and the unexpected crevices where I dealt with life's extremities, during what turned out to be 15 months in the wilderness.

To understand what comes, you have to know what's been.

If you pick up *Good Weekend* or the like, you'll see a section called "Ten Minutes with …." Occasionally one of the questions asked of the interviewee is along the lines of "what is one of the most significant/greatest moments that changed your life?" This offering promotes an unpredictable array of responses from meeting my partner, being with my parent when they died, climbing Mount Everest, holding my baby for the first time, holding my baby for the first time on top of Mount Everest (just joking). You can never really tell the moment or the quality of the moment that is going to change a person.

If I ever had the chance to answer that same question my responses would undoubtedly include meeting my tall, dark and handsome husband, living through the death of my father, seeing my brother become a father, watching my mother help my father through his final illness and the way she put herself into the world again after he went, learning to sing, and becoming a lawyer. Along with all of these milestones, the day that undoubtedly set my life on its tilting table was June 3, 1972, the day I was born.

I know I was born in the Mater Hospital in Crows Nest one day early, and I can imagine my wild parents Mary and Manuel, 28 years old at the time, making the hair-raising journey from their Mosman home to the hospital once I'd notified them of my intention to emerge. At some stage during the delivery, it became apparent that I was going to dive into the world backside first, or breech as they put it. This would be the first of what must be thousands of bum landings in my life. Mum says it wasn't a difficult birth, but for whatever reason my father decided to stage a hostile sit-in, arguing with the doctors intermittently so he could maintain his position near the action. Whether or not he was in the delivery room I can't tell you. Dad passed away from stomach cancer 13 years ago at the ripe old age of 51, and Mum said that she was dosed up to the eyeballs to cope with my splendid landing.

So, there I finally was, and Mum said I looked absolutely beautiful – a perfect child. She got to hold me, and it was the stuff of magic. Some time after, an elderly experienced nurse, Sister Beatrice observed that there was something wrong with my eyes and that I wasn't crying normally, but said not to worry she would keep a watch on me. Thankfully she kept more than her word, calling my mum's obstetrician Dr Thong and the family paediatrician, Dr John McDonald back to the hospital to watch for developments. It was this concern and decisiveness that meant immediate help was at hand when I suffered what is now referred to as a neurological event, thought at the time to be a cerebral haemorrhage. Sick, I was baptised on my birth date and within about eight hours transferred to the Royal Alexandria Hospital for Children in Camperdown.

My parents didn't receive the customary congratulatory presents to celebrate my birth, no-one sent flowers – bar one couple, the Hewsons – and my mother kept those and gave them to me on my 21st birthday. This lack of flowers or other soft stuff, however, was no measure of the binding metal of support that would flow through the years. Mum and Dad had many witnesses, aiders and abetters to the highs and lows of my childhood, and that of my brother, Andy.

Anyhow, back to me and one of the most important days of my life. My thinking is probably the first thing we do, being born, is one of the most dangerous expeditions we ever embark on. So you could argue that our default position is that of risk takers, which some people hold on to and others barter away unconsciously in favour of security. I can imagine that from the outside my life looks fairly ordered and probably staid, but in my mind there is little doubt that my rather shambolic inaugural landing on this earth left a permanent imprint which has served me through life, allowing me to take risks to achieve and reclaim abilities, when my body has faltered for another time, that are part of the everyday ho-hum for many.

I believe this is probably the same for the millions of other people that stamp through life with a disability. It can appear from the exterior to be a limited journey, but quite often the road is more dense and meatier (much like the shiraz beef pie I was reading about the other day). There are many unusual experiences you've had to bite off, taste and savour, whether you want to or not, to stay on your path.

I was aware from a pretty young age that I was a different little kid, something I don't look upon as necessarily bad, it was just the way life was. I definitely gave Mum and Dad a run for their money. And, I have to say, it's only really in the last few years, as I have seen my own friends become parents, that I think I may have an ability to comprehend how stressful and scary it must have been for them. In saying this I don't have children myself, so my understanding of all of that is watered down at best.

But, for all the chaos, uncertainty and stress that my predicament brought, the constant thing that I was aware of is that my parents showed up for it. You might think this of course is natural – isn't it Woody Allen who says that half of life is just showing up? Well, OK, yes sure, but when it's a protracted period of watching one of your children struggle, the theatre on offer can be somewhat turgid. From what I understand, my first five years were an exercise in bloody mindedness on their part that I was going to have my life.

The neurological event at birth was accompanied by excess cerebral spinal fluid which failed to drain placing pressure on my brain, a condition known as hydrocephalus. The doctors said this affliction would need to be dealt with, by way of inserting a shunt, if it did not resolve itself by the appropriate time. A shunt is a tube-like hose attached from the ventricles at the base of the brain to the heart. The appropriate time for this blessed event was not until I was 11 months old, so when I was eventually sent home from the Children's Hospital my parents had instructions to measure the circumference of my head daily, as this would indicate a negative change in my condition.

"Negativity" arrived for my young father in some doctor's office in the bowels of the Children's Hospital, who bluntly informed him while considering a film of my water-logged skull: "Mr Lopez, your daughter's brain is disappearing. I suggest we do something about it." Not nice words for a parent to hear, and I muse now that it's a moment that planted a pick axe in any hopes that I was to escape unscathed from the turbulence of my birth. This was going to be a long haul.

The short story is that at 11 months the shunt was inserted and the pressure on my brain was relieved. The longer version starts from the premise that the shunt, which remains in place today, was my life raft to survival, although sadly its presence could not rectify the damage done during the birth process, which would only become more obvious as I failed to reach those developmental milestones that mark our progress as babies. The clean-up from this was going to be my first Waterloo.

Hydrocephalus occurs in about one in 500 births and can also develop later on in life in adults. Not so rare, on my calculations that's 2000 people in every million. A human's ability to cope with the condition is like many things in life, usually down to a mixture of the correct knowledge, good teamwork and luck, which I definitely had in spades. Although my hydrocephalus has never resolved itself as it can do, upon arrival at the Royal Alexandria Children's Hospital I was placed under the care of an eminent surgeon, Dr Marcel Sofer Schrieber. Mum said he and his wife made themselves constantly available day or night for the care of his young patients and strongly steered them through the very scary terrain in a way that made them, and other frantic parents, feel supported. The doctor and his wife were unassuming people, so unassuming I am told that one day when my paternal grandmother, Mama, was visiting me at hospital she became concerned about who appeared to be a workman hovering around my bed, it was only after the requisite phone calls were made was this stranger identified as Dr Schrieber, who had come in to check on me from "afar."

One of the problematic aspects of implanting shunts in infants is that quite often the small size of the baby's ventricles prevent it, they are simply not large enough, and "forcing it", I understand, increases the chances of blockage, infection and other complications. Without doubt, having the hydrocephalus and neurological event were enough to deal with. However, by sheer luck the anatomical constitution of my already frazzled head favoured my predicament. I was born with large ventricles that could accommodate the intrusion of the shunt apparatus without too much drama. It was not unusual to hear of babies and young children who simply could not take shunts easily, their bodies repeatedly rejecting them and having replacements that reached into the double digits. I, on the other hand, escaped relatively scot free, my shunt rarely blocking. I say this with absolute sincerity because the symptoms that accompany a shunt blockage are extremely unpleasant. I did not need a shunt replacement from the age of four to 14, by which stage I had literally outgrown it, my teenage growth spurt causing its end point to dislodge from my stomach.

I understand that when the shunt blocks, symptoms can include disorientation and clumsiness, which I was spared. However, I will never forget the indescribable headaches, akin to the pressure of a shuttle launcher taking off in my head. Then there was the uncontrolled vomiting, so fierce and unrelenting it became safer for me to sleep half the night in the bathroom with my brother watching over me, than to make the 10-metre trip back to my bedroom.

Throughout my childhood I did experience other complications as a result of having hydrocephalus, such as contracting a golden staph infection during surgery, a couple of cardiac arrests due to my weakened system, and a bit of bad luck in acquiring a form of bacterial meningitis which proved to be quite perilous for someone housing a foreign object in their body. The bacteria clung to the shunt which was of course unable to sterilise itself thereby allowing the infection to become more rampant.

The doctors made it quite clear to my parents that I would never be normal. Full stop. By all accounts my outward appearance fell neatly into line with this diagnosis – my everyday preference was to be propped up, because I was very floppy and had no tone (part of the athetoid condition) with my arms flexed upwards and hands at shoulder height.

You can imagine that this would have been a heartbreaking and distressing condition to see day in and day out for those who got to watch. However, among that crowd was my maternal grandmother, Nanny. Now long gone from the world, my memories of her are as a refined woman with soft, pale skin and musky perfume, wearing twin sets and pearls to complement her frosted hair (a changing array of beige, dark blue-grey and pink as I recall). As a little girl I would spend my afternoons with her after school drinking milky tea with sugar, eating Sao biscuits, jam-packed with butter on flowered plates and watching *General Hospital* and *Search for Tomorrow* together as we waited for Mum to finish work. Having brought eight children into the world she was possessed of an unquestionable knowing wisdom, to which I was a golden recipient.

Nanny was a publican, and at the time of my birth she lived in a small town called Merriwa where she ran the Royal Hotel, otherwise known as "the top pub." A mother to eight, she had raised Mum as a single mother, due to the early passing of her husband Gerard from a heart attack four weeks after Mum was conceived. Gerard was a handsome man, a law clerk who at times bore an uncanny resemblance to Errol Flynn. As mothers did, after my birth Nanny came down to help my Mum, the youngest of her brood, with the new addition to the family. The circumstances, however, were very distinct to the norm; what should have been a joyous time was nothing of the sort.

Mum was skating on thin ice with the guilt that she did not innately love or feel connected to me as her child. I had been yanked from her eight hours after I was born, while she had stayed trapped in her Mater hospital bed for days, during which time her body changed and the milk arrived. While my paediatrician John McDonald came to see her every day at the hospital and her sister Dot sat by her side in the afternoons, she received no counselling to deal with the after-effect of what had gone on. Her way of coping was to build a protective wall around herself to insulate her from the feeling of hollow loss. In fact, I think the only thing that happened to Mum after my birth that was objective proof to her that there was actually a child was the fact she underwent a curette before she left the hospital to deal with the afterbirth.

The next time Mum saw me I was lying in a baby's hospital bed at the Children's Hospital with tubes and foreign instruments protruding out of me as my closest companions. I was small, frail and untouchable. In that environment I wasn't anything special, I was a sick child surrounded by sick children, I was waging my own battle while there were desperate wars going on around me. I guess in this picture my Mum and Dad were not any different from other young couple, devastated, lost, wanting hope and feeling wretched and helpless.

There was never any doubt in Mum's mind that she was going to make the best out of it, but inside she built her fortress as a way of coping with the trauma and brutality of the situation.

It was a few months before I was allowed to come home, and when I did Nanny provided Mum with an indestructible anchor. She spent every day with my mother, tending to her and me, all the while steadfastly pushing, "There's nothing wrong with her brain Mare, it can be fixed …" Apparently, she never retreated from that position.

There really has never been any end to the fix, but at some point Nanny showed my Mum how to start. Over months she would sit me up and put food in front of me, enticing me to break free from my prison, looking for the connection. I have always held a great love of food and I often wonder if it's because of this period in my life, Mum says I was quick to respond, recalling my little hands edging out of their cheerleader stance towards my feeding tray. This was really all she needed to witness to know that my world could open up, outside of what the doctors had predicted. It was this that was the greatest gift. Nanny's presence and unconditional love for Mum taught Mum how to love me. Nanny coddled her daughter's pain, which allowed Mum time to heal and the feelings to come back in. This is an exemplification of the simplest but most profound luck any child can have – motherlove.

The first few years of my life saw Mum and Dad firmly take hold of the baton for my development and care. By now they were dealing with two problems, the hydrocephalus and cerebral palsy (or spasticity), each condition being characterised as a brain injury. The question as to how each condition developed, whether the hydrocephalus caused the neurological birth event or the neurological event caused the hydrocephalus and the cerebral palsy seemed to be without reason, although the genesis of the problem would be discovered decades later. Getting back to the problem at hand though, whilst hydrocephalus occurs in one in every 500 births, your chances of being born with cerebral palsy drop to one in 400. Again, not so rare.

Every day my life was filled with "exercise therapy" to jolt my sleepy anatomy and brain into action, the exercise encouraging the pristine components of my mind to compensate for the damaged parts and find new pathways that would allow me to function in the physical world. My Mum called it patterning, over and over (and over and over – you get what I mean). For weeks and months she would repeat actions and sequences that would come naturally to other babies such as rolling onto their tummy and sitting up until the connective spark came. My "innate" instincts had to literally be created by design. To walk, she knew I had to make the progression from rolling onto my tummy and then to crawling, I never crawled in the conventional way though, preferring to shuffle forward on my backside. Apparently, it was after I took to my feet aged three, that my Mum made me crawl, as she had heard it was important for babies to do achieve this, whether they were walking or not.

And so the adventure of walking began. For those of you who glide from your bed into the world every day with grace (unlike moi), I have to tell you though the art of walking is a fine and beautiful skill, it's not simply about being able to stand up; it is a combination of complex components that need to come together to allow you to move dynamically in a world that is not always static. From a layperson's perspective (mine, in case you hadn't guessed, people) you need muscle control, balance and a sense of where your joints are in space. Otherwise, you can find the "road coming up to meet you" more often than you would wish – not in metaphorical sense, but a literal one, as your whole body descends to be slapped in the face by the earth's unkind surface. So, learning to walk was a slow process for me due to the fact that I was very challenged on all fronts. I hardly had any natural balance, very weak spatial perception and little muscle control – all by-products of the neurological event that resulted in my second and more challenging (to this day) condition of cerebral palsy. Luckily for me, muscle control has always developed slowly through the patterning. However achieving balance and maintaining spatial perception has been consistently more challenging, and has only been gained through risk taking once an appropriate level of muscle control has been achieved.

When I finally got on my haunches as a jaunty three-year-old, Mum said I started to move around by grabbing onto the furniture. Eventually I let go in my impatience to get into the world. I must tell you, the walking was not pretty. I continually fell for years due to lack of balance and everything else ... this became quite concerning because I did not have embedded into my system the natural inclination to protect myself. I was covered from head to toe in bruises and sore, scabby skin nearly all of the time, particularly on my forehead which seemed to bear the full impact of my adventures. In fact, the only part of the patterning process I really remember is my Mum teaching me how to fall and save myself. I do recall asserting proudly to one of my aunties, after mastering the process and falling (yet again), that it was all okay because "I put my hands out."

Amongst all these challenges I also had the advantage that comes with just being a child: I was completely without fear. No matter how many times I knocked myself about, Mum has always said it was me who didn't shy away from the chaos that came with walking. I kept going the extra round, largely oblivious to my physical state. It was this attitude that helped her and Dad let me go, as it was so clear I wanted to do it despite any calamity that would ensue. Mum also didn't want me for any reason to become afraid of learning to walk. While I don't think any of my family could have foreseen at the time, this really was the prelude act to a lifetime learning process. Mum and Dad's attitude of putting their own concerns on the backburner in that respect has meant I have largely remained open to facing risk and chaos throughout my life.

When I think about my early childhood I cannot escape the fact that many of the pictures in my head are associated with hospital. To this day I have very strong memories of the large, open wards, corridors and other children whose faces I can see clear as day. I am aware that some are probably not alive today, because they were so sick at the time; in that respect I am lucky. I remember where we all used to eat down the bottom of the ward and how the eating room was moved off to the side later. I clearly remember the separate rooms where you would be taken for treatment – needles, to have stitches removed and the like. I remember the faces of the kind nurses as they did what they needed to do while I would scream and cry for the discomfort of it all. I remember the deep baths we would have if we were able to get out of bed …

There are some very uncomfortable feelings that as an adult I still wrestle with today, feelings of being left alone in long corridors on hospital beds, the entrapment of objects being strapped to my head in the dark. Even now, I don't like things being placed around my head. I remember waking up to the faces of Mum and Dad after operations, and the first thing I would say to them is "no headache." I also remember at the age of 14, when my shunt blocked for the last time, being more aware of my mortality and asking Mum and Dad if I could die during the operation. I was really asking permission, because I was feeling pretty sick, and I didn't want to let them down. Although the procedure is quite simple, it does require someone to cut into your head, which is no walk in the park, leaving you post-operation with half a head of hair. I still remember their faces when they uttered a restrained "yes."

I recall a time I was in hospital when I was about six or seven, and meeting a young boy who was a paraplegic called Richard. He was a chatty young fellow with sandy hair and I remember him knowing that my brother Andy was coming in to see me after school. He asked quite innocently: "Is he a cripple, too?" presuming every boy in the world was just like him.

My childhood landscape is littered with slideshow experiences of the hospital, the stinging smell of sickness and antiseptic, the sounds of the dinner trays, the feeling of the first morning when I would be out of bed and allowed to sit in a beanbag while I waited for Mum and Dad. The never quiet that would descend over the ward as the day closed off. Yet, all those difficult feelings that run though me have left a quite asymptomatic result since I view hospitals as safe places, and I don't fear or dread them at all. I dislike the experiences that can occur within their walls, but my time in them when I was little has taught me to deal with pain, sickness and discomfort in a fairly objective way. I would never allow it to be an obstacle in my path to getting better. This has been a powerful weapon that I have engaged throughout my life to get me through curly times.

Earlier on I referred to the importance of teamwork and knowledge in not only learning to cope with my disabilities but to thrive and live with them. The Royal Alexandria Hospital for Children was undoubtedly a part of this. It sent to my family, Dr Schreiber, a man who was at the forefront of treating hydrocephalus in infants in Australia. The hospital was the place my parents turned to repeatedly during my younger years. There is little doubt that without his knowledge, expertise and care my experience would have been direr. I was also blessed with my paediatrician John McDonald, who never, despite my parents begging, sent them a bill for my treatment, repeatedly telling them they had "bigger things to worry about."

My innate luck flows from the blessing of being born to parents who never failed to advocate for me, to ask questions and make courageous decisions based on knowledge and gut intuition. As I sit and write this tale in my middling 30s, I can only look back at my younger parents and wonder how they spun through those years and came out relatively sane. But spin and dodge we all did, like any family, and though the rides on offer in the "amusement" park that was my health would have been sufficient to turn most clear minded people balmy, we kept moving forward.

Mum and Dad were great parents, but their ability to breathe energy into my rag doll body would not have been as possible except for the many aiders and abetters that make up my larger family, whom I referred to before. Because, you see, I must state a simple truth – my sickness had an unfair domino effect on the people closest to me and it was a corrosive influence in my older brother's life in terms of the amount of time it took Mum and Dad away from him when he was young. Like me Andy was (is) loved beyond belief by my parents although both of them, particularly Mum, was never able to be with him as much as they wanted because they had to be with me – the time hog. While I moved forward in those years protected by their embrace, Andy was cocooned in a much larger fold of individuals including my Aunty Shirley, my grandmothers, Aunty Dot and my renegade godmother, Merrick Gilchrist.

Much time has been spent on this ditty so far talking about me, so I'd like to turn to my brother for a moment. Not long ago, I had the fortune of meeting up with a very close friend of my Aunty Shirley for afternoon tea by the name of Kathleen Kennedy, a Scotswoman possessed with a gift of the gab, a cackling laugh and a dry wit. Kath and Shirley had enjoyed a 40-year friendship bonding as nurses from the time they trained together at St Vincent's in Sydney's Darlinghurst. She contacted me because she had made some red socks for Andy's two-year-old son Mani, similar to a pair she had darned for Andy when he was growing up. Sitting over afternoon tea on Blues Point Road, Kath, responding with excitement to the fact that Andy was also able to come and meet us with Mani, recounted the first time she met my gorgeous brother in her apartment in North Sydney in the early 1970s:

> *holding on to your Aunty Shirl's hand as if his life depended on it. He's always been such a happy, dear little boy, Kate, you know, with that black curly hair of his. He was with Shirley, you see, because you were in the hospital again, but Kate, he never complained you know. He only ever seemed to be concerned about you and what was happening as far as he could understand it, as little as he was.*

As true as that statement is of Andy as a toddler, it encapsulates who he is and how he has been with me all my life – my great friend and protector. Whilst I am comforted by memories of him as a little boy telling doctors to "stop hurting" me and encouraging my legs to move in my green tricycle, "Kate, pretend that dad is chasing you with a wooden spoon", they evidence the way sickness changes not only the person's life, but those around her or him. Andy had to a step back and take second position to cater for my calamities, which he did as though born to it and because of the gentleness of his character. Loving people consumed his life, but Mum, the lady who loved him most, did not get to hold his hand as much as she would have wished. "Kate, Andy was with everyone but me; I had to be with you."

In times past when I have talked to Mum about having children, she has said that she and Dad never really considered prior to my birth that there would be any problems. I was expected to be a healthy, normal baby, just like her first. Perhaps not now so much, but back then couples did proceed under the illusion of a guarantee of good health for their newborn and didn't consider the alternatives. The reality of my birth not only shattered this fiction, it also had the consequence of fracturing other promises my parents hoped to maintain with their first child, the promise of equal time and attention and love on tap. The love on tap certainly flowed, but the time and attention lost is a lament my mother still feels today.

Chaos reigned in our household far beyond what one would expect for a couple with two young children, trying to build a life. My parents were only married for four years when I was born, and having married each other after a short, 12-week courtship, were within the coupling discovering aspects of each other that quite honestly would have been better to know before slipping a ring on to each other's finger and saying "I do." For example, there was the fact that my father expected my mother to continue her job as a high school music teacher, even though they had two young children and she wanted to stay home with us. This expectation, which my mother met, only increased the stress of an everyday life that was far from ordinary.

If parents with healthy children spend their day sleep-deprived and juggling everything bar the kitchen sink, a sick child in the mix is often akin to that kitchen sink not only being up in the air, but often crashing down, wiping you out and flooding your house unexpectedly. Mum and

Dad simply never knew what they were coming home to. A trip to the hospital after me taking a turn was never out of the question; there was always a serious concern that the shunt could be blocking and putting me in danger. That technology in the 1970s was a relatively new treatment, and therefore it was not unusual for shunt recipients to experience adverse transient effects like the physical turns I would take. Too many times to remember Mum and Dad found themselves with me in the casualty department at the Children's Hospital, waiting to for someone to see me as I was in the throes of pain.

On one particular occasion, the desperation and sheer frustration of my parents overcame them after waiting for what seemed like an eternity. Dad turned to Mum and said: "That's it. We're out of here!" and ran with me and her through the grounds of the general hospital to the private doctors' rooms. He barrelled into the office of my neurosurgeon, sat me on his desk and, with force, informed the good doctor that I would be seen to now!

Mum and Dad had their differences, but instances such as these exhibit their fairly united approach to managing my health and not being afraid to deal with things head on. Not that they really had any choice in the matter, it was like a daily Darwinian test of survival of the fittest and expectations were adjusted accordingly.

Through all of this though Mum said she never got bogged down in the "seriousness" of my condition, it was just important to keep going forward. Yes, there were big names attached to my conditions, but at the end of the day after the initial trauma had dissipated and she had mothered me as her child, I became merely her little girl who couldn't sit up properly or get to her feet. I was not a medical diagnosis but rather someone who needed a lot of help, which she was going to provide. It was never really a question of "if" I could improve. For Mum the glass is always half-full. If something didn't work, she and Dad evaluated it and made their next move without looking back, all the while continuing to work hard with me on my physical therapy.

They made brave decisions at every turn. After a time of treatment at the Spastic Centre my parents resolved to withdraw me out of concern that my life, and importantly Andy's, would become entrenched in my disability. My sickness had already isolated us as a family. Dealing with it became the overriding extracurricular activity similar to a father's regular basketball game with his son after work.

The bottom line was whilst Mum and Dad were in no way ashamed to have a spastic child, the reality that it would become what identified us as a family was a barren prospect. Nobody wants to feel like they should just settle for a sheltered existence because the alternative is too hard. Comments that would be made along the lines of: "Don't worry. You'll soon understand that all your friends will be parents of spastic children," rankled them. Quite simply, it's fair to ask in those circumstances, what's to become of the rest of us? What about my child who is well? What about his life? Is it all just going to be about being sick from here on in? No one wants that.

So, we kept struggling forward and it was hard work – and there were hard lessons. In my first three years I spent too much time in hospital, with sickness surrounding me, being confronted by obstacles most people my own age still hadn't had to consider. My darling brother learnt too early in life about uncertainty, that your parents can't always be with you, and sometimes you have to simply be second. Mum and Dad learnt the lesson of what it is to have a sick child and to live your life in the brace position.

On the flipside, there was simple joy. With all the hard work came great achievements. Mum, Dad and Nanny's devotion to my struggling body through the patterning, resuscitated my limbs, which allowed me an unsteady freedom. And I finally walked on wobbly feet. Andy was a much-loved child, not only by my parents but the wider family who held him and cuddled him when my parents could not. And then for my young parents, in their imperfect marriage, I think it was simply enough that the glass had become more than half-full. They had gotten through a major storm intact.

While I was waiting for Mum to bring Mani over for a play date at her house the other day I had the chance to look through some photo albums and came across pictures of us all during those three years I have been meandering through with you on these pages. There were photos witnessing shocking fashion – my Mum in her Jacki O's, comically staring down the camera; me blonde-haired and pigtailed in my red dress, giggling away; Andy, tanned, round-cheeked and studiously wrestling playground equipment; and my father hanging about, slim, dark, and big-haired, looking as if he hadn't a care in the world. A picture tells a thousand words and there was a lot to be happy about ... many good days.

Kate through the years

Starting school

For me, starting school was the same as for any child – the beginning of a great adventure. I still remember my first day, dressed in my green checked uniform, long brown socks and brown shoes, sitting with my classmates in Mrs Carroll's class at St Michael's in Lane Cove, ready for the entertainment to begin. I remember Mum being in the classroom with me on that first day, slim and big-haired, but not being too concerned at all when she left.

Over time we settled into a routine. We used to watch *Play School* in the mornings, and I recall a great deal of time was spent on show and tell, clamouring and competing over the wide array of items that could be brought in for the interest of our classmates. Other than this there was the beginning of learning and making friends, which I enjoyed quite a bit.

I remember the enthusiasm with which I considered how I would learn to write my name, would it be Kate, Catherine, Cathy,

Kathryn, Kathleen ... oh, the possibilities were endless. I just loved being given that card with my "name of the day" written on it so I could trace it until I lost interest and then moved onto the next option. I must have driven Mrs Carroll mad. I can still feel the absolute mystery that my shoelaces provided every morning as I embarked on the battle to tie them, and the sense of accomplishment I felt when I finally managed to remember the process and wrap my pudgy fingers around those uncontrollable laces to make that bow. The day I passed my shoelace tying test was without doubt one of the highlights of kindergarten. Absolutely every child wanted their gold star up on the wall signifying their entry into the Shoelace Tying Hall of Fame – it was the absolute Mecca.

Little lunch and big lunch was where the real action took place, however. All the children from Mrs Carroll's and Miss Verzi's (the other kindergarten teacher) class would tumble out onto the front part of the quadrangle, facing closest to Longueville Road and run riot. In the playground I learnt to make friends with girls just like me named Justine, Samantha, Maree, Rebecca and Emma, and I learnt to run away from the Robbies and Glens of this world, who had boy germs. Whether you were a boy or girl from Mrs Carroll's class, the one thing you absolutely didn't do was cross the national divide and make friends with the youngsters from Miss Verzi's – that was just not on! Big lunch and little lunch were the times that really tested my mettle. Like any little kid I wanted to be part of the action that was tag or skipping, or even playing house with the girls. It seemed whatever I did I would always land smack down on my face at some stage and Andy, my older brother, who was in Year 2, would be called from the big boys' quadrangle to oversee the repair of his little sister.

About halfway through the school year it became necessary for me to go to hospital for a shunt replacement. Although this wasn't a happy time, I remember the excitement with which I received the colourful cards and gifts from the children at school and my teachers. It made me feel special. I guess around that time it also started to dawn on me that I was different. It didn't take me long to get back to school, my kindergarten friends and the motherly influence of Mrs Carroll, but I was not the same little girl. I wore a beautiful blue-and-green dotted scarf to mask my bald head. I had endured a big operation and that was very important. It was the most important thing about me. My big operation meant every time there was a school excursion, the red team, of which I was a member, had to have Mrs Carroll as a leader, and not one of the other mothers. This caused no amount of dissatisfaction with my fellow red people. Secretly, I felt the same way, but daren't say a thing for fear of what might happen.

The fact I was different also spilled onto the quadrangle and the machinations of playtime. As before, I would routinely play dodgem cars with my classmates and always come out the loser. Now, whenever real war broke out, I had a secret weapon in my arsenal – no one could really touch me because I had had my big operation. I was quite forthright in reminding my classmates of this as justification for all the woes and sins of which on my part, there were plenty. Sometimes in response they were equally forthright in excluding and teasing me because "Mrs Carroll, Kate thinks she's special because she had that big operation, and we don't want to play with her ..." It's true that little kids don't hide behind political correctness to navigate through difficult moments, and the way those situations played out were emblematic of this.

As a four-year-old, having walked the earth for no more than 1,460 days, the only way I felt that I could really show anybody that I was as good as them was to holler about my big operations – it was my show and tell and calling card. Beneath this lies the sadder truth that being sick at this early stage of life meant that it was very much a part of my identity. I thought it was the main reason other children would like me and should like me, much the same way as they liked Jimmy because he was a good runner.

To this day, I think how I felt was not completely separate to the truth of the matter. I believe the school and the parents of the children my Mum and Dad knew, protected and helped me by encouraging their children to become my friends. Looking back this was a tough call for all the four-year-olds involved, including me. I was an awkward little kid, who walked funny, fell over, was a little cross-eyed and frequently walked about with her hands half-flexed up in the air. I did not look like part of the crowd, so hanging out with me wasn't necessarily cool, because hey, you could get teased as well. Equally, because I was used to having more attention focused on me than the average child, and I was not accustomed to the survival of the fittest regime that permeated the quadrangle, when I didn't get my own way, I would resort to relying on the fact that I was different as a way of protecting myself. So really, at an early age I started seeing myself as someone who couldn't measure up in the normal world and was not good enough. I relied on being different to get me through because it was the only real thing I knew about myself. This had the not unforeseen result of being repellent to some. When you are a kid, being part of the group is the desired thing. No one really has any appreciation of someone or wants to be around someone who might always be pointing out that they are different as a basis for being included, "Mrs Carroll says you have to be nice to me because I'm sick ..."

My poor self-esteem, due in part to an inability to fit in, would become increasingly problematic through the first half of my schooling, and reach its peak in about Year 7, when I was made to repeat. I think the fact that I felt so awkward about the fact I was different and couldn't raise my identity above those factors, meant I was vulnerable to bullies. Bullies are interesting specimens. They so easily locate vulnerabilities to exploit in people who they perceive to be weak, all for the purpose of making themselves indistinguishable in the crowd.

When I first went off to St Michael's I had with me the person who is my dearest friend in life, my big brother, Andy. His presence in the playground took the sting off any offensive that could be launched against me, and made the world seem a safe place. However, his departure to St Aloysius College when he was in third grade meant that I continued solo from first grade and had to make my way on my own two feet. This was not an easy task, and I met my first two bullies pretty quickly in grade one.

To tell you the truth I don't remember how it all started, but I would go to the ends of my very small world to avoid these two lanky boys, who seemed to appear by unhappy coincidence wherever I was, chanting horrible names and making my life a misery. I can still recall running all the way around the school so I could get onto the playground undetected, only to have them intercept me and verbally beat me down with their mean names and awful dances. This went on for some time, although those lads did eventually get theirs in the form of my glamorous, warrior-like mother. I can still recall how they spotted me and started their routine in Lane Cove Plaza one day, only to scamper off when they saw Mum on approach from her shopping at Flemings. She, cluey as ever, knew immediately what was going on, and gave immediate chase. I am positive those young fellows had no idea about the scuttle launch attack that was about to befall them both. The image of my mother in her high wedge heels, shorts and singlet top with her hair tied back in a scarf on that summer day, reprimanding them amidst the GI Joes in the toy shop, as I cowered between her legs, has stayed with me to this day. Needless to say, that problem was immediately solved, and in the future, I was allowed access to the playground unhindered.

Show me a child who wasn't teased at school, and my bet would be that they were home educated. So no, I don't think it's anything remarkable there was a target on my head, and further, I am quite sure when I was in infants and primary at times I also engaged in teasing to make sure I was not the one being singled out. Over time I also remember quite clearly learning to fight back, and with the absolute inhibition of infancy, clawing and more particularly biting my way out of attacks.

Afterward

Kate wrote that story in 2009 and in ensuing years she would marry her partner, Ivan Glavinic, and have a baby, Eva. With her heroic, valiant and intrepid outlook on life, Kate continues to inspire me daily.

Meanwhile, Andy's career took a new turn with his venture into motor sports when he purchased Summernats, a huge event produced annually in Canberra. Andy has made a tremendous success of this business taking the concept to Alice Springs (Red Centre Nats) and Rockhampton (Rocky Nats). His interest in motor sports and car shows has expanded and he now co-owns many businesses which have grown out of this one entrepreneurial venture. This new venture of Andy's was particularly exciting for Rob, who has always had a very keen interest in anything that goes fast – on land or sea. He continues his successful business partnership and warm and trustworthy friendship with Mr Bee to this day.

18

Life wasn't ordinary, it was extraordinary (Andy's story)

To describe the Lopez house as an interesting household to grow up in would be an understatement. With a lawyer for a dad and a teacher mum, it could've been an ordinary life.

Nothing could be further from the truth.

67 Finlayson Street in Lane Cove was our home, the house we spent most time as a family. Life was usual and unusual, mundane and extraordinary, with love, conflict, fun and despair. At different times, sometimes all at once.

It was also the place where Mum and Dad's very separate worlds smashed together in what I remember as an endless series of parties. Solicitors, educators, judges, musicians, artists, students, they were in our house having a great time. At different times, often all at once.

It wasn't all fun and parties, far from it. Our parent's relationship was complex. They had a great love for each other, but conflict, jealousy and resentment were often present. That spilled over on Kate and me, as often happens in household where parents fight.

We were loved and valued, but it was hard going at times.

On occasion, I'd go to Dad's office in town after school or on a weekend to study while he worked. He'd proudly trot me around the office, and his team welcomed me with love. I'd muck around on the typewriters, play on the switchboard at reception, make prank calls, move stuff around and occasionally do filing (quite poorly). As a child, having Dad work at night and on weekends sometimes made me feel he thought his work and those people were more important than us. He seemed to spend a lot of his goodness and humour for others, and didn't have much in the tank when he came home.

Mum's life was super busy too. As the Head of Music at Epping Boys High School, she was a full time teacher, ran a number of choirs and produced a musical every year. This meant rehearsals, choir shows, musicals, all of which consumed a lot of her evenings and weekends. Kate and I would go to the Lane Cove Baby Health Clinic most days after school where our much-loved Aunty Shirl was nursing director. We went to independent schools, so our school holidays were usually longer than Mum's. This meant in our holidays we'd often go with her to work, mucking around, begging for pies from the tuckshop, playing in the school hall, that kind of thing.

Sometimes seeing Mum spending so much of her time with other young people made me feel she thought the kids she was teaching were more important than us. It occasionally felt like Mum gave her students so much attention and affection that sometimes she didn't have any left for us.

In the early 80s, some really exciting things began to happen for Mum professionally. Through her supporters at the Education Department including the wonderful Frank Meaney, Mum was given the opportunity to create a show to test the acoustics of the Sydney Entertainment Centre prior to its official opening. The show had a huge cast of singers, dancers, a massed choir … and Peter Allen.

Mum charged fearlessly into the project, and it was a great success. It was the genesis of the Schools Spectacular (SS), an education performing arts showcase that is still running over 40 years later. Every year it gives thousands of school kids and teachers an opportunity to collaborate and create in what Mum and I later called "the world's biggest classroom".

The SS has been replicated around Australia and internationally, and was Mum's springboard to eventually leave the Department for a world of producing major creative events. Mum's career is well documented here and in other places so I won't go through it in detail. But what Mum won't say about herself, or sometimes even recognise, is that creative arts in Australian education and our event industry itself were both fundamentally changed for the better as a result of her energy, innovation and bravery.

Mum made music a big part of my life by encouraging (forcing) me to learn the piano, which I resisted, but eventually enjoyed. One of her ex-students Alan Crackles McCracken was my teacher. I wasn't that committed and frustrated the life out of him. but he stuck with me because of Mum.

I wanted to join a band, so Dad bought me a Korg Poly 800 five octave synthesiser and Mum convinced a couple of her Epping Boy High School students let me join their band. I fell in love with the band thing and eventually formed one myself with school mates. We put on a few concerts at our school and other places. I was an average keyboard player, but above average at organising rehearsals, negotiating with school venues, budgeting, contracting production and promoting the shows. I'd get a few other bands to play, put up posters in schools around the area, and somehow we'd get a couple of hundred kids to come along and buy tickets.

At school and during university, Mum got me to work with her, first as a performer which wasn't my forte, then as a stagehand, then finally helping actually put shows together. She tells me that she saw something when we did a big show in the Domain for the 1993 Papal visit that made her think I might actually have a future in the industry.

It wasn't just me that Mum involved in her shows, she roped in Dad, Kate, her wider family and her friends. That all came together in a show Mum created called the Darling Harbour Christmas Pageant, later known as An Australian Christmas. The Christmas Pageant was based on the traditional story, with a grand parade, wise men, camels, performed by a cast of leading Australian artists, a live orchestra, a massed choir, and hundreds of costumed characters.

I finished university after taking six years to complete a four-year psychology degree in 1994 (another story entirely), and Mum convinced me to forgo a job offer I'd received to work for the Head of Psychology at Sydney Uni and take a gap year working for her at Mary Lopez Productions. She told me she thought I'd be good at it and to see how it went.

Graduation

It was 1995. Internet and emails were barely a thing. Mum charged me with business development – whatever that meant. We bought a computer, fax machine, proper mobile phones and a photocopier. Working alongside my awesomely talented cousin Madeleine, we set up lunches with important people in her network, and new work came. I convinced her to charge people for services she had previously just given away. We got contracts for the Australian Rugby League Grand Final pre-match entertainment, Super Rugby, Australia Day shows and others.

Then Dad's cancer, first diagnosed and treated with success against all odds in 1989, came back in 1995 a month or so before the Rugby League Grand Final. Mum had to step away from the business to be there for Dad, and when I was just 25 years old, she told Madeleine and I that she trusted us to look after the business.

Going back to psychology after my gap year was not a thing that was ever going to happen. After six months, the cancer got Dad and he passed away in April 1996. Mum wasn't ready to go back to work full time in any sense, and rather than ask me to maintain her business, she told me I was ready to open my own. So, I started Out There Productions. I named it for Dad to remind me he was always out there, but the very possibility of it happening only ever existed because of Mum.

Mum's primary objectives have always been to identify and nurture talent, give opportunities to people who might not otherwise get them, celebrate both the individual and the team, create shows with meaning, and combine great people to make magic together. She given her experience and expertise to others with great generosity throughout her career, and she's both inspired and been inspired by other people's talents.

I've watched her humbly share accolades she's earned with others. She stood in front when times are tough and stood back in good times do others can stand in the light. I've also watched her rise above it all when other less well-intentioned people would try to marginalise her for their own small-minded reasons.

Complicated, challenging and bugger all budget was a common theme in Mum's work. But more so was creativity, meaning, innovation and excellence. Mum's unwavering faith that it could be done came because she believed in herself and everyone around her. She led, she trusted, she supported, she empowered. And everyone believed that if

Mary said it could be done, and that we were good enough to make it happen, then it was true. Mum has spent her working life breaking rules and smashing ceilings, and she made everyone around her feel they can do the same thing.

When I try to encapsulate what her impact on my career has been, I go back to the Darling Harbour Christmas Pageant as the best example of the experience she gave me, something I'm still learning from 30 years later.

The Pageant was pure Mum. It was joyous, complex, professional, and full of the weird and wonderful. Central to the show was the massed cast of bible characters that included people from the homeless community through a partnership with Wesley Mission, and the rest coming from Mum's family and friends. It was run by Australia's leading production professionals every year – for a lot less money than they'd earn elsewhere – because they loved her way of doing things. Mum loved involving her family and her friends in the show. Dad was a wise man on a camel, Kate and her husband Ivan walked the Parade, and the cast of misfits often included Mum's brothers and sisters, her nieces and nephews, and great friends like the Cheoks, the Kidmans and the Piccones. It meant something to everyone in the show, and to everyone watching it. That was what made the Darling Harbour Christmas Pageant magic.

Fast forward 30 years. The details of where I am and how I got there aren't that relevant, but things are good. I'm still with my first business partner and dear friend Andrew Bee, and, no surprise, it was Mum who brought us together.

Mum has always told me that owning your own show is the only way to control your own destiny. So, when an event called Summernats came up for sale in 2009, Andrew Bee and I (managing a small event company that meant we were the go-to guys for high-profile events with mid-level budgets), did the least amount of due diligence you could imagine and just jumped right in.

That business has been extraordinary for us, and making the decision to buy it changed our lives for the better. I'd love to say there was a strategy behind it all, but that wouldn't be true. But I like to think that Bee and I are good people who genuinely care for what we do, love the people we do it with, and respect the audience we do it for. The universe has a way of working things out.

When I think about it, the Summernats is basically the Darling Harbour Christmas Pageant. The Summernats brings together a community every year to do something that means something to them. It has meaning and joy. It is full of family, and not just mine. Our team and the people who come to the show do it across generations.

And there's a big bloody parade that starts it all off.

Wu, my wife, has encouraged, supported and challenged me throughout our marriage. She even got me through some very tough times when I made some very bad decisions and nearly blew our business to pieces. She's also raised our boys to be fabulous young men of principle, kindness and humour.

In January 2023, my oldest son Mani worked his first Summernats with a bunch of his friends. Watching him work, being independent and valuable, gave me an insight into how Mum must've felt when she brought me into her world. When Izzy joined Mani at Summernats in 2025, the pride I felt standing with my two boys, and their friends, as part of my separate world, was overwhelming.

When I was starting out, Mum told me "you need to wear the hat". That means if you want to be a leader then you bloody well have to behave like one. Surround yourself with great people and trust them to be their most excellent selves. Celebrate your team because without them you are nothing. Develop and elevate everyone around you. Success stories are rarely linear, and success is never experienced without failure. We have succeeded and failed and succeeded again. Principles and ethics are important, but they will always be challenged by your own self-interest. It's how you respond that matters.

I said that growing up, I sometimes felt that Mum and Dad's separate lives and the people in them were more important than us.

Nothing could be further from the truth.

Writing this, it has actually dawned on me how much Mum and Dad included us in their lives outside of 67 Finlayson Street and how much that actually taught Kate and I compared to what we felt we might have lost. They brought us into their worlds, and brought their worlds into ours, openly and honestly. The way they cared for the people in their working life has taught me to care for the people in mine. The relationships I have built professionally are based on how they built theirs.

No matter the challenges around growing up, we are a family that loved each other, enjoyed being with each other, and always celebrated each other's success. I wouldn't trade the fun, mayhem and hard times of 67 Finlayson Street for anything, and I hope Mum has no regrets about the mum she has been to us and how we grew up.

Life wasn't ordinary, it was extraordinary.

The most important thing Mum taught me is that when you get a chance, put your family and friends in a silly costume and make them part of the show. And Dad, a high-flying lawyer riding a camel wearing a bedsheet and a turban, taught me that family will always want to be part of it.

Manuel the King in white robes

19
Picking up life again

In 2009, we had an enjoyable visit from a delightful young couple, Camille and Michael Cassel to our Walker Street home. A SS participant from years gone by, Michael is now one of the leading producers of music theatre in the world. They were about to move to New York to further their careers in the music theatre world. It has been wonderful to see their passion, skills and incredible hard work pay off. The Michael Cassel Group now has offices in Sydney, Melbourne, New York and Singapore. It's been many years since he sang in the choir of SS and borrowed my musical scores to produce a Christmas pageant in Kiama. Despite their success, they are still very grounded and never forget where they came from.

Rob and I continued to explore Australia on our four-wheel drive car rallies, this year having fun closer to home in Gulgong and Sofala. For something totally different, we ventured much further afield in June by going to Norway. We joined friends there for a walking trip organised by the Australian company, Gourmet Walkabout Tours. We met up in Bergen and walked through magnificent scenery.

We were having a wonderful time until Rob received a call from his brother, Phillip, who was in a state of panic, and Rob's daughter Sharon. They were both convinced Rob's lovely mother, Kate, was close to death, so we had to hastily rearrange our plans to return quickly to Oslo for the return trip home. Because we were in an isolated area our first job entailed rescheduling all flights, then securing a taxi, a boat and finally a light aircraft flight to Oslo. Predictably and happily, his mother was fine and only needed transferring to another facility where she would have additional nursing care.

It was quite the year for reunions as we had a delightful and memorable catch-up with Andrea and Tom Hayson in Manly. I owe so much gratitude to Tom who lived until the age of 97, passing away in 2017. He took me from the Sydney Entertainment Centre stage and opened the whole of Sydney and its glorious harbour to me. He was extremely encouraging and supportive of my career after I left the Department. He was the man and mentor who believed in me and reinforced in me the concept of thinking big.

In October, with the insistence of friends, the late Janelle and Antony Kidman and my GP, I made an appointment to see heart surgeon Rupert Edwards. I hadn't experienced any symptoms but Janelle was adamant that at my age I should have my heart checked out. I had accepted an invitation to attend a Sony Foundation Gala fundraising lunch on the same day as my stress test was scheduled, but there was no lunch for me. I was admitted to hospital that very day for observation and further tests when it was revealed I had an irregular heartbeat. After three days in hospital and a small procedure, I was discharged with a diagnosis that said my particular heart wiring caused the rapid heartbeat – and that it was adrenalin activated. My whole life up until that point had been adrenalin activated!

I'm exhausted just writing down how busy I was throughout my working life from when I first started teaching at Lithgow HS in 1966. As a high school music teacher I was relentless in providing extra-curricular activities for my beloved students. Then I had constant appointments, workshops, auditions, meetings, country auditions, and rehearsals for second career with TDP and SS. My twelve or so years in the corporate world were full of exciting and rewarding challenges with my company producing major events all over Sydney and some interstate. Then there were the TDP Graduations and the actual SS productions … plus gala fundraising dinners for networking and TDP performances, Culburra escapes, walks, travels within Australia and internationally.

The 2009 TDP graduates were a very talented and diverse group of individuals. I know many of them have very successful careers in the music industry including David Le'aupepe, lead singer of Gang of Youths, opera singer Emily Edwards, and music producers Ricki Bloomfield and Nicholas Gentile. Nick sums up the feeling of so many TDP graduates:

> *It is impossible for me to imagine where I might be without the consistent support from the TDP. From the moment I graduated 12 years ago they have provided a network so vast that no*

matter what aspect of the entertainment industry I'm involved in (performance, composition, producing), there is someone from the TDP family there providing guidance and making everyone feel important, valued, respected and esteemed.

These are the characteristics of a true family and values that were instilled in me from my time throughout TDP. There isn't a major project I have ever worked on in my professional career that wasn't full of TDP graduates.

Where are they now – Nicholas Gentile

Nick is now an international composer, orchestrator, singer, producer and educator. His original cinematic opera was a Paris Film festival winner. He is currently creating performance development programs throughout Vietnam as a Director of Future Nest. Recipient of Bound for Broadway and the Mary Lopez scholarship he continued his involvement with TDP as a tutor and then TDP Board member. Now he is a TDP artistic leader and remains a valued mentor to its students.

This was a year of tremendous growth for TDP. David Albert from Alberts Music very kindly donated a grand piano, which was certainly put to good use in every workshop and performance by our students and graduates. It was also becoming apparent to Robyn and I that we needed more staff. Lara Campese and Kristen Prescott came on board for a short time to help develop marketing strategies. But really, our great problem always was that we did not have the money to grow as we wanted because we were not a commercial entity.

The original training program was still our core business but many other strands were running including international scholarships, Indigenous workshops, regional outreach workshops, recording studio sessions at Sony and Albert's studios and numerous public performances at corporate and government events. These types of performances for graduates were invaluable as they exposed them to a landscape of what the future could hold for them, depending on the work they put into it.

Such was the wealth of talent that the size of graduating classes was increasing, requiring more and more hours of mentoring and individual support. The TDP was now attracting enough funding because of the Clubs NSW sponsorship, to be able to offer employment to past graduates who returned as mentors and tutors, and also to increase our administrative staff. Conscious of the generosity of all the volunteer consultants and the increasing demands on their time, we introduced an honorarium in recognition of their generous services.

Michael Kerker returned to Australia to sit in on the Bound for Broadway scholarship auditions and to host a concert at Angel Place featuring multi-award-winning music theatre composer and actor, Stephen Flaherty (composer of *Ragtime*). At that time it was decided that we would send three hardworking graduates with exciting potential to the States: Lincoln Hall, Laura Herd and Brendan Irving.

Their first meeting in the US was with Michael in Washington DC. They performed at the Australian Embassy to staff and guests at the invitation of Ian Whitney, Cultural Project Officer of the embassy. They then attended the Stephen Schwartz workshops for new musical theatre compositions in New York, working with celebrated musical directors and attending amazing cabaret performances organised by Michael, one of whom was the fabulous Julie Wilson, still performing after I'd seen her 25 years previously at the Algonquin. At the Sheldon Harnick Tribute Night (composer of *Fiddler on the Roof*) which was hosted by Michael Kerker, at the Kennedy Centre, Washington DC, they shared the stage with celebrated Broadway performers and received a standing ovation.

We saw how the international stage was opening for TDP graduates when Rob and I dropped into Hong Kong in May and caught up with three very talented TDP graduates appearing in the musical *Cats*: Shaun Rennie, Erin James and Brent Dolahenty.

As part of our mentoring program for TDP graduates, Franz Donnhauser, general manager of the Shangri-La Hotel in Sydney, came on board with a wonderful opportunity. He provided the hotel's famous venue, Blu Bar on level 36, for Shannon Brown and his band to do a series of performances. He also opened the lobby lounge for other TDP graduates.

TDP stepped up our efforts to sponsor country and Indigenous talent with workshops in Dubbo, where we met the charming and loving, Joan Wylie. Her daughter, Evelyn Wylie graduated from TDP in 2010. We also attempted to involve students from Walgett High School. Unfortunately the school made little or no effort to prepare for our arrival so, consequently, we came home empty-handed from Walgett.

> **Where are they now – Gang of Youths (David Le'aupepe lead singer)**
>
> *Gang of Youths have been touring consistently since the band formed in 2012. Relocating to the UK in 2017 they gathered a massive fan base and continued to write chart busting songs. Their breakthrough hit Magnolia cemented them as a hugely popular band. Their third album, Angel in Realtime, released in 2022 debuted at No 1 in Australia and No 10 in the UK.*

TDP graduates performed at some fabulous functions this year, including the annual Australia Day lunch in Sydney held at Darling Harbour Convention Centre, with 1,000 people in attendance, as well as the Steve Waugh Foundation launch. The very talented graduates included Brendan Irving, Alex Gibson-Georgio, Lincoln Hall and Jess Hitchcock, who continue to enjoy extremely successful careers.

At the end of this year, SS No. 26, "Reaching Out" was the first following my retirement. Bill Anderson, the new leader of the Arts Unit directorate, appointed me as artistic consultant to the production team to provide a safely net and continuity. Peter Cook was my successor as SS director and created the next two joyful Spectaculars. I was immensely proud of Peter and the spectaculars he directed and he always made me feel welcome and appreciated.

TDP steps out and the accolades keep coming

The year 2010 began with the arrival of a new grandson, Isidro (Izzy) Lopez, born on January 25. He was extremely considerate of his father, arriving the day before the huge spectacular Andy was producing with his business partner, Andrew Bee, at Darling Harbour.

It was also a year of academic recognition when the University of Western Sydney (UWS) conferred on me an honorary doctorate of letters for contribution to public education and the arts. I was absolutely flabbergasted but honoured. The degree was recommended by then Vice Chancellor, Janice Reid. UWS had been a sponsor of SS and Jan had attended performances and seen the value of it to public education. She acknowledged my initiative and leadership role. To celebrate my doctorate, we held a party at the Shangri-La Hotel where I thanked and showed my appreciation to the many people in the room who had supported me during my career.

Dr Mary Lopez

I was especially grateful to be appointed Emeritus Director for the SS, by the then-Director-General, Michael Coutts-Trotter. Michael was a keen supporter of SS and I found him personally most approachable and encouraging.

In May, we invited Bill and Eve Walter to accompany us to Norway following somewhat in footsteps of the tour Rob had had to abandon the previous year. I now had some contacts who were able to help with a fabulous itinerary and guide us in exploring the coast through the Hurtigruten boats. We loved the Lofoten Islands and made our way to Kirkenes in far north-eastern Norway where Rob drove me on a quad bike to the Russian border.

Later in the year, we travelled to Shanghai where we met friends Terry and Ross Fagan, and Pam and Gradie Johnson. Kate and Ivan joined us in Shanghai where Ivan asked Kate to marry him. They became engaged the following year.

To develop the TDP marketing process, Robyn Philpott and her husband Paul went to New York to oversee the making of a documentary following the paths of Bound for Broadway scholarship winners Jessica Hitchcock and Adam Rennie. With so many young artists auditioning for the TDP, we began a new program to provide workshops for juniors. This was designed to nurture their skills with a view to them joining the graduating class when they were older. It would also serve to prevent them from developing bad performance habits. In retrospect it was not a good idea in that it kept some youngsters in the course for too long so they felt they were in a holding pattern.

We partnered with Campbelltown Club to present a TDP production highlighting outstanding new talent such as Christie Lamb. As Christie wrote in the TDP's 30th birthday program in 2021:

> *I graduated TDP in 2010 and I am grateful for so many things this program brought me. TDP really encouraged me to hone in on my skills as a writer. They provided me with support and scholarships that allowed me to further my writing over in Nashville. TDP really helped me with the transition from student to a professional working musician in the real world. I will always be so grateful for the opportunity to have been a part of this program.*

This year Aussie businessman and philanthropist Dick Smith provided sponsorship for TDP to run Indigenous workshops in Wilcannia, a place close to Dick's heart. Dick also took me to Wilcannia in his private jet. There was excitement in the town when we touched down and everywhere we went, Dick was treated like a rock star by the local Aboriginal people. Dick is loved and appreciated for his contribution to the town. The workshops he sponsored were conducted by TDP graduates Brendan Boney, Tessa Nuku, Roshani Priddis and Felicity Urquhart. The project was a great experience for them. Robyn Philpott coordinated this entire, quite complicated project. She was a real perfectionist and dedicated to her role in my dream team.

This year was a classic example of how far the TDP reached with a swathe of recent graduates making an impact in music theatre, pop charts, songwriting and even heavy metal! These amazingly talented graduates included country music star Brad Cox, *The Voice* winner Anja Nissen, much awarded singer-songwriter Imogen Clark (now living in Nashville), and the late Jacob Neale, a gifted musician and pianist from Newcastle, who was taken far too young by an insidious disease. In the TDP 30th birthday program, Brad Cox wrote:

> *TDP, both directly and indirectly, introduced me to a lot of people I still collaborate with today, the most fundamental being the guys in my band. All of them either went through TDP or were involved with someone who did. I hope to be making music with these guys for a long time to come.*

In June, ASCAP's Michael Kerker returned to Australia at the invitation of APRA to present songwriting for musicals at the APRA Song Summit, involving TDP graduates. This is yet another example of the ongoing support TDP graduates received over the years.

While on an overseas flight I was reading through my 2011 diary and I wrote plans for a book. So this has been coming for quite some time. In my diary I asked myself the question "why?" with the answer: "Because I don't want the lessons to end."

This year was huge for Kate with her marriage to Ivan. It was a lovely occasion with the ceremony at St Francis's Church, around the corner in McKenzie St, Lavender Bay. The reception was down the road at the Kirribilli Club. It was super special with guests being able to call in to the Walker St house on their leisurely stroll to the reception. My only granddaughter Eva came into the world in December. Rob and I were excited to attend Sydney's Royal North Shore Hospital, with Ivan of course.

Kate's wedding and Eva as a toddler

Rob and I travelled to Broome in May hoping to arrange a connection between performers from Broome and the TDP. We stayed a couple of nights at a resort then owned by Marilyn Paspaley, of the famous Broome pearling family. She was producing Polo on the Beach and invited us along. Only in Australia would you find such a unique event. There was the added difficulty of the huge, 15-metre tides to contend with when timetabling and mapping out the course.

We were sitting in a marquee when a car came across the polo course on the beach, mid-game, ploughed straight into our tent and crashed onto the stage. Thankfully, nobody was hurt but we were rather surprised, to say the least. It was a memorable day and I'm very grateful to have had such a wonderful "only in Australia" experience. I successfully bid on a holiday in four villas in Bali at a silent charity auction held at the event. I offered it to Andy and Kate and their families.

In another unexpected accolade, I was on the receiving end of the Sydney Entertainment Centre Diamond Appreciation Award for 20 years contribution to the venue. I was thrilled, and somewhat amused, to join entertainment luminaries whose photos were on the wall of Sydney Entertainment Centre, like Sir Elton John!

We welcomed Michele Bruniges, the newly appointed Director-General for Education in NSW, onto the TDP board. She replaced

Chris Ryan, who had been a tremendous supporter of TDP in previous years. Michele was only able to be with us for six months before she had to resign because of her very busy job. Debbie Hockings, Director of School Operations, replaced Michele, so we had continued support at a senior level. It was important to have this level of governance for the public-school students for whom the TDP exists.

Matt McDougall retired as chairman and that was the end of our association with Jack Neary's legacy. Matt was Jack's godson, and he very kindly took over on the board when Jack died. Matt's work commitments brought about his retirement and Alan Jones AO replaced him as chairman of the TDP.

Robyn Philpot continued as coordinator and amongst all her other responsibilities, she began to develop a more formalised mentoring program for graduates of the program. It was a feature of our training that alumni continued to be assisted after they graduated. We were proactive in finding them work, looking for networking opportunities and scholarships, and even creating work for them.

Christine, Robyn and Kate

The TDP was now extremely busy with many new projects for our students and alumni. We were flat out with new scholarships, international travel, and more and more regional workshops. Remember at this stage it was only Robyn and I running the whole show. The board agreed we needed support, and the vibrant Kim

Lemke was appointed to a newly created Marketing Manager's position. She immediately set out to re-brand the TDP and our students with a sharper and more contemporary image. Her passion and enthusiasm helped bring about both a more contemporary profile for the TDP and styling for our vastly diverse talented young musicians. A special sponsorship was born this year when Jands/Shure joined our TDP family. Each of our graduates was presented with a top-quality Shure microphone as part of their graduation pack.

The much-loved Mr Bee took the songwriting program from strength to strength. TDP produced its own album, *Young Scribes*, which was released on CD and iTunes. Graduate Nathan Lamont's single, *Cinderella Chasing* met with some pop chart success. Christie Lamb also released her debut album that year at Rooty Hill RSL.

Christie Lamb on believing in yourself

I attended the Talent Development Project from 2006 until I graduated in 2010.

Since graduating from TDP, I have performed at Encore of HSC and received a four-year scholarship to WSU. I completed my Bachelor of Music whilst touring nationally with Jon English during the final year of my degree.

I have also toured nationally with The Girls Of Country – Amber Lawrence and Aleyce Simmonds. I have toured for four years with Lee Kernaghan as his opening act and as a part of his band playing keys, mandolin, guitar, as well as singing with Lee.

It was a huge thrill to be selected to perform a duet in front of tens of thousands of people with Keith Urban at the Deni Ute Muster and I have performed on all of Australia's major country festivals, as well as toured under my own name.

I have won a Golden Guitar for Best New Talent and two CMC Awards for New Talent of the Year and Female Artist of the Year.

My following and most recent album, **Truth,** *also charted at #1 on the ARIA charts and was announced as one of the top five highest selling albums in Australia at the Country Music Association of Australia (CMAA) Golden Guitar Awards in 2023.*

Mary Lopez was one of the first people who believed in me and gave me the confidence that I could pursue this as a career after TDP. I will always be thankful for her guidance and support.

TDP staged a live-in workshop in Coonabarabran in another initiative to engage Indigenous performers. The young performers spent two days in workshops where we hoped to find and nurture Indigenous talent. Two young teenage boys were selected to attend the Sydney workshops. Anne Fitzgerald sprang to the rescue and accommodated the boys when they came to Sydney for workshops. They had already had some valuable experience working with Desert Pea Media, a small company doing sensitive and worthwhile music production with Indigenous and outback talent. Michael, tragically, committed suicide some years later, a victim of a seriously troubled childhood, I think.

The 20th Reunion Graduation Concert

Now that I was retired from SS, I concentrated on leading the TDP team through the required development and growth for the next 10 years. With Kim now on staff, Robyn's new projects and Mr Bee continuing his remarkable success with his songwriting direction, the TDP soared. Our Graduates were to be given international opportunities and new scholarships.

Wow! It was now 20 years on and a big year for the TDP. To mark the occasion, we hosted a special reunion event at the American Club in Macquarie St. It was attended by many past graduates, consultants and sponsors. Some of the graduates travelled from interstate and even overseas to join us ... what a night of nights – I was so proud.

The TDP's 20th Anniversary Gala Graduation in August 2011 also clearly demonstrated the impact it was having in the entertainment and music industries. I thought it would be an enriching experience for our students to engage two current stars in the entertainment industry to be guest directors. I had directed every graduation since the TDP began in 1991 and I realised I was no longer contemporary! Mark Williams (Dragon) directed the singer-songwriters and Peter Cousens (*Le Miserables* etc) directed the musical theatre/cabaret performers. It was a real bonus to have such expertise and experience guiding the students. These two generous artists had already volunteered their services on many occasions previously at TDP workshops.

Former TDP graduates who were by then household names performed. They were:

- John Foreman (1992)
- Drew McAlister (1992)
- Emma Pask (1994)
- David Harris (1994)
- Trevor Ashley (1997)
- Paulini (2000)
- Lorenzo Rositano (2005)
- Julie Lee Goodwin (2006), and
- Jack Vidgeon (2011).

I'm often asked how I determine who will make it in the business. To me, what makes a TDP graduate are the following specific qualities: spark, talent, ability to communicate, uniqueness, motivation, drive to succeed, and industry readiness. They will always be making eye contact as they engage you. They won't hide behind their eye lids. You'll always find them interestingly dressed on stage. They will have tried to enhance their unique style of music by how they are dressed. Throughout their training, I constantly reminded our TDP graduates to respect the fact that their audiences would expect them to be more interestingly dressed then if they were just participating in everyday-life activities, such as shopping. To have a successful career they will then need to be driven by passion and hard, hard work.

In 2011 we graduated the largest group ever. There were so many talented performers among them, and they were all ready to take the next step towards a professional career. These graduates were from musical theatre and other genres and were standouts in their field:

- Declan Egan
- Cameron Little
- Stephen Madsen
- Chris Rose
- Ashleigh Rubenach
- Jack Vidgeon.

Stephen Madsen had this to say in the 30th Anniversary TDP program:

> *What really sets TDP apart from any other program for artists is the continuation of that support. The performance and scholarship opportunities we continue to receive are truly mind-blowing. Graduation was only the beginning. I credit a great deal of my current success to the lessons I have learned and people I have met through my involvement with TDP. I'm excited to think that others are having a similar experience as the project continues.*

The SS introduced a new initiative this year called the World's Biggest Classroom Project. Sandra Copeman, who for many years contributed remarkably creative dance items in previous SSs, developed and managed this huge display of artworks and crafts. Hundreds of students were able to share the excitement of being a part of the SS by filling the spacious foyers of the Sydney Entertainment Centre with their imaginative creative visual arts. This addition gave many more students an opportunity to experience the Spectacular magic and has since evolved into "Specfest" now filling the forecourts of the Qudos Bank Arena before the performances of SS. Previous foyer performers, since the first SS, have gone on to do great things. One such foyer entertainer was young pianist John Foreman, who is now a household name in the world of entertainment and a regular host of the SS.

Sandra Copeman remembers

> *I'll never forget the day I received the call from Mary, inviting me to choreograph an item for the 1990 Schools Spectacular – Singing in the Rain. Having seen the event only once and never having choreographed in an arena setting, that call changed my life. It launched my career on an unexpected trajectory, leading to creative involvement in world-class events such as Olympic ceremonies in Australia and beyond, and a specialisation in mass choreography for arena performances.*
>
> *From 1990 to today, I've embraced various roles within the Spectacular team: choreographer, dance director, media liaison officer, World's Biggest Classroom coordinator, and now, sponsorship manager. Each role was a testament to the trust placed in me to create a positive impact on and contribute to the continued development of the Schools Spectacular.*

Between 2011 and 2016, the World's Biggest Classroom expanded the event beyond just the performing arts. Students from across the state created audio-visual, graphic, and literary projects inspired by the theme of Spec each year. These projects were showcased in the foyer at the annual event and were also displayed in Westfield centres and train stations throughout Sydney, bringing the Schools Spectacular and the outcomes of public education to the general public at street level.

Working under the leadership of someone like Mary, who believed in my potential and allowed me the freedom to explore it, was a rare gift. While working with the usual limitations that both challenge and power creativity, her unwavering faith always pushed me to deliver. Mary fearlessly guided us all to elevate our work, to transform the ordinary into the extraordinary and to continually lift our students, teachers, and the event itself. What an amazing legacy Mary has gifted to us all.

2013 – Our Sporting Spirit segment – "Absolutely Everybody"

2013 – Our Sporting Spirit segment – "The Flame"

Ross Milne and Sandra Henderson (Copeman)

You can turn on the TV or open the newspaper and read all about the success of TDP graduates – Musical Theatre stars like Trevor Ashley, Lucy Maunder and Ashleigh Rubenach; *The Voice* winners Anja Nissan and Paulini; Golden Guitar winners Darren Coggan, Felicity Urquhart, Melanie Dyer and Max Jackson; opera singers Julie Lee Goodwin and Jeremy Boulton; singer-songwriters Travis Collins and Brad Cox; and stunning instrumentalists such as guitarist Joshua Meader and violinist Harry Ward. And again, so many more. In my dual role as TDP and SS Director I was in an enviable position. From 1984 until 2016, when I retired as Artistic Advisor to the SS, I could see and assess so much more talent in auditions, rehearsals, and performance than I would have seen solely through TDP auditions. As Director of the SS (for the first 25 years) I could also choose suitable material for the soloists in SS and monitor the presentation and performance of the soloists. With Andrew Bee, my trusted advisor, also heavily involved with auditioning and selecting students for both those projects, we were able to select outstanding and exciting talent. With our TDP team we could then prepare them for a career in the entertainment and music industries using our holistic method.

In March 2012, I travelled to New York for a brief catch-up with Michael Kerker and attended the ASCAP workshops to see how the TDP scholarship winners were benefiting from their experience in New York. Miriam Waks, Robert McDougall and Natasha Hoeberigs were that year's winners and have made significant careers for themselves in cabaret and music theatre respectively.

Andrew Bee on Mary

Mary Lopez is a remarkable person. I have had the good fortune to work with her over many years, and over that period she has become a lifelong friend. She has given me some wonderful opportunities and, if not for her, I would not have the career I enjoy today.

Mary is passionate about giving people opportunities. The SS show she developed was designed to give students and their teachers, particularly those living beyond metropolitan areas, performance experiences they would not normally have. Her shows provided life lessons for all involved: to cooperate, to be inclusive and tolerant and to be proud of being Australian. So many of us are so lucky to have been a part of this journey.

She also involved Indigenous communities in the production long before society decided that was the right thing to do. She showcased the abilities of special needs students and gave them the means to express and present on a professional stage to thrilled audiences

In 1992, Mary, alongside Jack Neary and Bruce Harris, launched the Talent Development Project to develop the best talent in NSW schools. Mary developed the curriculum and the training methodology. I joined Mary as Musical Director in 2000. It quickly became a heavy hitter in the Australian Music Industry.

TDP Alumni include: Human Nature, John Foreman, Darren Coggan, Drew McAlister, Amanda Harrison, Felicity Urquhart, David Harris, Justin Smith, Emma Pask, Nathan Foley, Trevor Ashley, The McClymonts, Shaun Rennie, Jedd Hughes, Diana Rouvas, Paulini, Travis Collins, Angus and Julia Stone, Kurt Bailey, Lucy Maunder, Morgan Evans, Julie Goodwin, Kirby Burgess, Brad Cox Max Jackson, David Le'aupepe (Gang of Youths)

Melanie Dyer, Jessica Hitchcock, Imogen Clark, Declan Egan and Brad Cox. And I stopped at 2012. There's so many more.

Through her work at the TDP Mary has inspired a generation of talented students to have careers in the Entertainment Industry. Her exceptional eye for talent and her workshop program structure for learning gave so many students their leg up to careers within the arts and education field. So many graduates of this program are now working in our industry in Australia and beyond.

Over the years Mary and I have become dear friends. She has always encouraged me to be the best that I could and she gave me endless opportunities and experiences over many years. Perhaps the greatest was an introduction to her son Andy.

I became part of Andy's production company "Out There Productions" and now I'm a co-director of "The Out There Group" a large event production company which manages a large calendar of events for lifestyle car enthusiasts held annually in Canberra, attracting around 130,000.00 people over four days. We are also still involved with performances. We are currently contracted by the NSW Government to present their annual Premier's Gala Concerts, by the NSW Department of Education to provide technical production for their StartStruck Spectacular in Newcastle and Creative Generation in Brisbane (The Queensland incarnation of Mary's SS model). The Out There Group provide musical direction, technical production and creative input for this annual show.

Mary was a recipient of the Ted Albert Award for Outstanding Service to Australian Music, as presented by APRA, in 2012 and thus stands alongside some of the biggest names in the industry:

- *1991 – Allan Hely*
- *1992 – John Sturman*
- *1993 – Peter Sculthorpe*
- *1994 – Ian Meldrum*
- *1995 – Harry Vanda and George Young*
- *1996 – Ron Tudor*
- *1998 – Michael Gudinski*
- *1999 – Slim Dusty*
- *2000 – Triple J*
- *2001 – Charles Fischer*
- *2002 – Barry Chapman*

- 2003 – Angus Young, Malcolm Young, Bon Scott
- 2004 – Don Burrows
- 2005 – Michael Chugg
- 2006 – Bill Armstrong
- 2007 – Michael McMartin
- 2008 – Roger Davies
- 2010 – Jimmy Little
- 2011 – Paul Kelly
- 2012 – Mary Lopez
- 2013 – The Seekers
- 2014 – Lindy Morrison
- 2015 – Fifa Riccobono
- 2016 – Cold Chisel
- 2017 – Archie Roach
- 2018 – Midnight Oil
- 2019 – Rob Potts
- 2021 – Helen Reddy, Joy McKean
- 2022 – The Wiggles
- 2023 – Colin Hay, Colleen Ironside
- 2024 – Bart Willoughby
- 2025 – Kylie Minogue

I am so grateful for all the time I have spent with Mary. She has been my biggest advocate, always supportive and always so positive. Mary Lopez you are remarkable and have had a huge impact on modern Australia.

Andrew Bee and me

Ministerial Statement 23 June 2011

Mr Adrian Piccolo (Murrumbidgee – Minister for Education)

It is with pleasure that I acknowledge and congratulate Trevor Ashley, who is the lead in the musical *Hairspray*, which opens tonight in Sydney, and who is a graduate of the Talend Development Project in New South Wales. The Talent Development Project is Australia's most successful music industry training program and has operated for 20 years. It is the only program in Australia that is free and solely directed towards public school students. It prepares these fine young performers from New South Wales public schools for careers in this highly competitive industry. The Talen Development Project and its brilliant staff help the young students develop their entertainment skills and provide them with the opportunity to network with others in the industry.

The Talent Development Project is largely funded by the Department of Education and Communities and also receives support from ither organisation such as the Sydney Entertainment Centre, Clubs NSW, Club Keno, Sony Foundation Australia, Sony Music, the Australasian Performing Right Association and Radio 2GB. On behalf of the New South Wales Parliament I take this opportunity to congratulate and thank those supporters of the Talent Development Project.

The Talent Development Project has a strong history of discovering and nurturing the talents of Indigenous students. It also has a particular emphasis on rural and regional New South Wales public school students and on Western Sydney, which I particularly commend it for. Workshop programs have been conducted in Tamworth, Moruya, Bourke, Dubbo, Mouth Druitt, Wagga Wagga, Lismore and Coonabarabran. Graduates from the Talent Development Project have been very successful in their chosen careers, and New South Wales should be proud of this program that has put our performers on the world stage. The Talent Development Project has an esteemed list of graduates including: Golden Guitar winner, the McClymonts; renowned musical direct John Foreman; and *Australian Idol* contestant Paulini.

> **Where are they now – The McClymonts**
>
> *The McClymonts are three sisters, Brooke, Samantha and Molly, originally from Grafton, NSW. Molly was the last sister to graduate from TDP in 2004. They have won fifteen Golden Guitars and two ARIA Awards.*

> **Where are they now – Paulini**
>
> *Paulini rose to fame in Australian Idol in 2003 and has been a household name since then. She is a singer, songwriter and musical theatre actor. She made her remarkable MT debut starring in "The Bodyguard" and is in constant demand as a diva in concerts and gala events.*

As I said, the lead actor in *Hairspray*, Trevor Ashley, is a recent graduate from the Talent Development Project. *Hairspray* opens tonight at the Lyric Theatre at Star City. Trevor honed his impressive cabaret skills at the Talent Development Project. Trevor has written, produced, directed and starred in countless musicals and cabarets such as *Priscilla Queen of the Desert, Jerry Springer: The Opera, I'm Every Woman* and *Showqueen*. He received the honour award for 2010 for his work, and was also named one of the 25 most influential gay and lesbian Australians.

Trevor is one of Sydney's best drag performers, and has an incredible ability to hear a piece of music and play it back immediately. The Talent Development Project should be congratulated on its well-designed and successful program for students. I wish the Talent Development Project well for its twentieth anniversary concert on 23 August at the Entertainment Centre and urge all members to attend. I am sure all members agree that nurturing and supporting our young performers in New South Wales Government schools should be continued. On behalf of the New South Wales Government I wish Trevor Ahsley well tonight in his role as Edna Turnblad in *Hairspray*.

Ms Carmel Tebbut (Marrickville)

I support the Minister and congratulate the Talent Development Program on its twentieth anniversary and pay tribute to its substantial achievements. I particularly congratulate Trevor Ahsley on his success and his role in *Hairspray*. The Talent Development Program grew out of the Schools Spectacular which is that wonderful annual event that showcases the talents of students in New South Wales public schools. The program identifies talented students who show a real interest in making popular entertainment a career. It gives young people who have the drive and talent, skills and knowledge to help them succeed in the often cutthroat work of entertainment.

In this day of *Australian Idol* and *You've Got Talent* it may not seem so exception but the program long predates those programs. Importantly, it encourages students to compose their own original works. When it was first set up it was truly groundbreaking. It is impossible not to talk about Mary Lopez, the original artistic director of the Talent Development Project. Mary developed the teaching program for the Talent Development Program and uses her vast network of contacts within the entertainment industry to constantly review the program. Mary Lopez was the director of every Schools Spectacular from its launch in 1984 until she retired in 2008 and she remains involve with it. The Talent Development Program is supported by some very eminent people, including its patrons Margaret Whitlam and Kevin Jacobsen, the board chair Matthew Macdougall, and board members such as the broadcaster Alan Jone who are all very passionate about the program.

Most importantly, the Talent Development Program works. If we look at the list of graduates, it is like the *Who's Who* of the Australian entertainment industry. As the Minister said, it includes the McClymonts, Human Nature, Nathan Foley, Angus and Julia Stone, Trevor Ashley and Julie Goodwin. Hearing their child say they want to pursue a career in the entertainment industry no doubt brings about a sense of apprehension, if not impending doom, for so many parents. But thanks to the Talent Development Program children from across New South Wales, irrespective of their background, have been able to pursue their dreams and a make a success of their chosen career in the entertainment industry. It is a great tribute to the strength of our public education system and the wonderful people within it that this program has been as successful as it has. I wish it all the best for the future. I wish Trevor Ashley the best for his performance.

http://www.parliament.nsw.gov.au/prod/parlment/hansart.nsf/V3Key/LA20110623046

20
Family changes

Over the next 10 years my son and daughter brought me immense satisfaction and happiness. They had both found their life partners and were producing delightful grandchildren for us all to adore.

With marriage comes a whole new world. First, I had to learn that I was no longer the focus of Andy's and Kate's lives. They needed the time to cement their partners' position, and that takes diplomacy and sensitivity. When their own children came along, I believe it was only then they realised the depth of love I have for them. You really can't fathom that until you are a parent yourself. School days can be all consuming and keep parents so busy with all that entails – yet those days pass so quickly as your children grow up to create their own path in the world.

However, this was for Kate the beginning of further health problems, following the birth of her daughter Eva the previous year, in 2011, I employed a nurse to be a help with Eva for a few months because I knew I could not be there due to TDP commitments. In April, Kate was hospitalised due to low sodium levels and then in May she had her cerebral shunt removed following an appendicectomy, which led to peritonitis. Being a foreign body, the shunt would not sterilise itself. She took the opportunity to see if she could function without it, but that was not to be.

I'm not one to display emotion but Kate recalls me flooding with tears as she was wheeled back to surgery for the second time to replace the shunt, saying: "If only I could have your pain." I think I read once something that stopped me in my tracks – "a baby forces you to live in the present tense … learn to do that." That's probably the hardest thing to do when people are constantly focused on what's ahead or what's behind – not what's right in front of them.

Kate displayed her incredibly strong will as she battled after setbacks with her health. Ivan was always a loving support for her, but it must have been very hard for them both so early in their marriage. I admire them both. Ivan demonstrated how loyal, loving and responsible he would be as a husband and father. By August, Kate's stamina was compromised which led me to suggest she live with me for two weeks so I could help her rehabilitate while Ivan concentrated on looking after Eva.

In August, I accompanied Kate to see her doctor Rory, for her post-operative check-up and future treatment. I noted in my diary: "low sodium, pituitary enlargement, hormonal imbalance." What a dreadful sentence for my long-suffering darling daughter to hear. While continuing to work, network and travel, I tried to accompany Kate to doctor and hospital visits as much as I could. If only I could have taken away her worries and pain. However, I was able to remain by her side and continue being supportive and encouraging because I gave myself space and diversions. My mother established this mindset when Kate was born and she was adamant that I return to work so I could have balance in my life. As a result, I had to keep up the strength required to help her.

Kate battled her way through the year with rehabilitation and determination. No one could pretend it was anything but painful and awful for her. She was determined to make sure that she'd do whatever was required for Eva. I used to marvel at her patience and ability to be down on the floor playing with Eva for hours each day.

We made a quick trip to Bali in June to take up the auction prize I had bought at the polo event in Broome the previous year. The intention was to have a family holiday. Andy and Christine and the boys made their plans and I travelled there a few days after them, as I wanted to be around for Kate's surgery. What I was doing there with Kate in this mess I really don't know! The Balinese holiday changed the lives of my family as it introduced Andy and Christine to the idea of an exotic new way of living. They loved Bali so much, they went back the following year and lived there for three years. I must remind myself that I introduced them to the country that they soon made their home.

I was still trying to ski, so in August we went to Charlotte's Pass. I'd begun my skiing career in 2001 and returned annually to the slopes. My efforts were not what you could call graceful, but I was steady in my resolve not to fall off the skis. I was blessed to have a wonderful coach and friend in the late Larry Adler, a legendary ski instructor and widely known for his sports and outdoor shops in Sydney, Japan and Jindabyne. When he died at age 97 his wife, Nan, told me Larry (a pharmacist by profession) had never taken a tablet. That's not hard to believe of a man who went heli-skiing for his 90th birthday!

In September we travelled to Vietnam. This was a holiday that saw me ride a water buffalo and a pushbike through the rice paddy fields. We made quite a few trips to Vietnam over the ensuing years. We enjoyed the law and order and found the culture and lifestyle very interesting. The contrast between Ho Chi Minh, Hanoi and Hoi An drew us back about five times over the years. Hoi An was our favoured location and I really contributed to the fashion industry by having many garments made to order. Brad Cox, then a recent graduate from TDP, was a keen traveller to Vietnam and gave me some very useful tips on South Vietnamese must-see locations like the Marble Temple near Hoi An.

The Kimberley dream is over but the TDP goes on

Midyear I spent a week in Broome in a bid to set up a combined program for the TDP with that Kimberley coastal city. Legendary local musician Alan Pigram was enthusiastic about the idea and introduced me to some locals who might help. The Pigram Brothers are local heroes in Broome and much further afield. They've stayed true to themselves and their musical style and never wavered from their love and passion for the Kimberley and for their people. The distinct flavour of their music is instantly recognisable and immediately conjures up the beauty of the Kimberley, for me at least.

Alan Pigrim very kindly agreed to facilitate a TDP workshop for me in Sydney. However, over the next few years I found out that the TDP could not attract the funding required for that bold idea. The truth I had to face was that no one was prepared to work just for the love of it anymore – they needed the money to go with it, which really is a fact of life. Not many of us do things for love these days. Sadly, the days of volunteering are almost gone.

Rob and I attended a moving performance by singer, songwriter and actor Darren Coggan, from the inaugural TDP class of 1992. His show, *War Stories* is a collection of his original songs and music.

He was accompanied by his sister Naomi, also a TDP graduate (1993). His parents were on the door selling tickets and merchandise, still proudly supporting their talented offspring's careers in 2012 all those years later. The Coggans are a wonderful family and I was reminded of the sacrifices made by countless parents and families who support their aspiring children to follow their dreams.

Towards year's end, things always geared up for the SS. Although there had been many staffing changes this year, I remained the constant as Artistic Consultant. The Arts Unit was powering along with many initiatives which had grown out of the Spectacular. They were things like the writers' program for multicultural students, formation of the Public School Aboriginal Dance Company and a boys' choral program. Workshops were designed for dance specifically for urban, disabled, rural and remote students. There were now also the industry and vocational workshops which trained students and teachers in stage management and technical skills.

The 29th SS showcased a strong contingent of TDP-trained outstanding musicians and singer-songwriters who would over the next 10 years create strong careers for themselves. They included:

- Anja Nissen
- Harry Ward
- the late Jacob Neale
- Brad Cox
- Joe Mungovan
- Benny Nelson
- Jackson Beasley
- Chris Rose
- Bernie Van Tiel.

Sonja Sjolander, now the SS Director, created an unforgettable segment, "From East to West", starring Menindee Central School and the Menindee Ladies Choir – all because she took the time to visit and reach out to this distant community. They performed with dancers from Norfolk Island. You can understand how thrilled I was to see that the 25 years I'd spent travelling to remote and rural areas, so as to include those students, was still very much on the current SS Leaders' agenda. At this point Bruce Best was still producing the SS for ABC Television.

2013 was a significant year for TDP with us cementing relationships through a very important networking trip to Western Australia. I met with Western Australian Academy of Performing Arts (WAAPA) music theatre course head Patricia Price. We discussed the continuing relationship between our organisations and it was a good chance to introduce myself after so many meetings over the phone. She'd been accepting students from the TDP for several years so it was excellent to consolidate this relationship for the good of the students.

One of the important outcomes of the TDP is to prepare students for that first step away into the area of their choosing. Some go straight to auditions and get chosen. It's a fact that the TDP has a reputation for excellence that is widely accepted in the industry. We also help prepare graduates to study and teach them how to get into festivals and other events. We didn't give them their careers; we just gave them a hand up to do what they were destined to do.

The TDP only took in outstanding talent. It wasn't about "giving kids a go." It was about developing careers for talented performers. These talented artists sometimes had to go to interstate to further their careers and their parents had to make sacrifices so their children could pursue their dreams. The TDP had many graduates go through to WAAPA with two shining examples being leading ladies Lucy Maunder and Ashleigh Rubenach, who've both gone on to have stellar careers in musical theatre.

Lucy Maunder

Ashleigh Rubenach

Ashleigh Rubenach on achieving her dreams

I was lucky enough to join the TDP when I was 14 years old. Little did I realise that meeting Mary Lopez would change my life irrevocably.

I'm writing this on the opening night of **Sunset Boulevard** *at the Princess Theatre in Melbourne where I'm playing Betty Schaefer.*

The opportunities I was given and the lessons I learnt through Mary – through her kindness, grace and unwavering encouragement – had a direct impact on my being here tonight.

Mary taught me to be ambitious, to always lead with heart, and to dress for the job you want!

An incredible mentor, leader and now dear friend, Mary and the TDP made me believe that I was enough.

She made me believe I could achieve the things I'd always dreamed of, and for that I will be forever grateful.

Lucy Maunder on the TDP

I was lucky enough to be accepted into the Talent Development Project when I was in year 10 and studying at North Sydney Girls High School. I always loved the TDP workshops and found the experience invaluable for me, not to mention the lifelong friends I made from the program. What a phenomenal initiative this was to foster and nurture young talent – the opportunity to meet and work with industry professionals and was led by someone so indomitable in Mary.

I adored my time there and took it incredibly seriously, but as a performer with 20 years professional experience I now truly look back on that time and am floored by what was on offer to us kids in Government Schools; the passion to give those opportunities to those who wouldn't otherwise have them and how incredibly lucky we were.

Mary was at the heart of it all, and I always wanted to make her proud. I auditioned and was successful in a place for the Bound for Broadway Scholarship in 2007, the year after I had graduated from WAAPA where I went to study a Bachelor in Music Theatre the year I finished school. This opportunity was one I will never forget. We were flown to New York for 5 weeks, attended countless shows, worked with and met several legends of Broadway Music Theatre and ended the trip doing a cabaret performance at the iconic Don't Tell

> *Mama with Christopher Marlowe at the piano whose work I had admired for years previously. It was a dream come true. It shaped who I am as a performer today.*
>
> *At times it was tough and I had a lot to learn. But I truly believe the experience I had at the TDP, Schools Spectacular and the Scholarship were incredibly instrumental in the tapestry of my now nearly 20 year career in commercial musical theatre.*
>
> *I have played many roles since graduating, and Mary has been a constant support. It was so special to have her in the audience recently to watch me as Roxie in Chicago, a dream role, with the amount of history we share.*
>
> *I owe so much of my resilience and determination and work ethic to her. I feel very lucky to be a part of the TDP alumni and cherish my time with everyone who worked there and made it possible for us.*

In March, we bid a sad farewell to Andy and Christine, who made the decision to move to Bali after their idyllic holiday the previous year. It was only going to be for a year, but it stretched to three years. Andy spent much of that time travelling back and forth to Australia with his ever-increasing work commitments as his entrepreneurial career was developing. I behaved like a typical mother, wasting my time giving advice about concerns regarding the grandsons' education and my son's business and his health with all his travelling. However, Andy, Christine and the boys had the time of their lives, created their own lifestyle and made lifelong friends. Rob and I visited a few times over those years and heartily enjoyed ourselves.

In August, I fulfilled a lifelong dream by visiting Anzac Cove. The ANZAC spirit had inspired me in every SS I'd directed, so this was one of the most satisfying experiences of my life – I'd finally connected the dots. The bleakness and waste of lives was apparent everywhere and I still feel the senseless loss of those brave men. I had made a point of trying to educate people from the very first SS. While the cruise itself, from Venice to Istanbul, was an enjoyable holiday, it was also a learning experience. Visiting Ephesus and Cappadocia in Turkey was an awakening revealing the great history of Christianity.

Lessons learned
- Importance of continued support after graduating
- Family sacrifice

TDP 2013: The network strength in numbers

By now our network of graduates was massive, and keeping track of them was becoming a task. But big as it was, I knew it was so important to maintain those friendships and to keep the team together. A common theme amongst graduates was their willingness to give back to the program which had been a stepping stone to their own careers. So, we formalised the mentor program, specifically to manage the network of graduates. Robyn Philpot had seen so many students pass through the TDP by this time that it was a natural progression for her to manage this.

We therefore needed a workshop coordinator. Meredith Burton who, as a teacher, had a long association with the SS and had facilitated one of the early regional TDP workshops in Lismore, was by this time working at Out There Productions and was contracted. Our workshops continued in the tried and tested vein with masterclass sessions, movement and vocal coaching, songwriting and business sessions.

We latched on to the internet, with every participant setting up an artist page on Facebook which they used for self-promotion and networking. In the months prior to graduation, we introduced individual programs where each student was offered support in an area identified in an interview. These ranged through vocal coaching, songwriting mentors, producers, drama lessons and even equipment. We also established a relationship with the Whitehouse Institute of Design where each graduate was connected to a design student who worked with them on their individual style and image. Kim Lemke led all this new emphasis on image and marketing.

The graduation concert moved from the Sydney Entertainment Centre to the International Convention Centre. We delivered a full production cabaret with spectacular lighting and vision effects and a wonderful variety show hosted by John Foreman. Produced and directed by OutThere Productions, the TDP graduates felt very comfortable in the hands of the two Andrews.

Singer-songwriter graduates continued to make their mark and on the advice of Milly Petriella, who was then working with APRA-AMCOS, we decided to put these artists in front of the industry movers and shakers who needed to hear them. Having the contemporary songwriters in the graduation production didn't showcase them enough so we decided to separate them and it proved a winning formula. As the director of member relations with APRA-AMCOS, Milly was invaluable as a volunteer TDP consultant from 2004 to 2021. I learned so much from all the consultants. People criticised me because I sometimes changed my opinions, but it was because I listened. Milly taught me so much as did the other consultants. The industry was changing and technology was taking over.

Milly Petriella and Kim Lemke

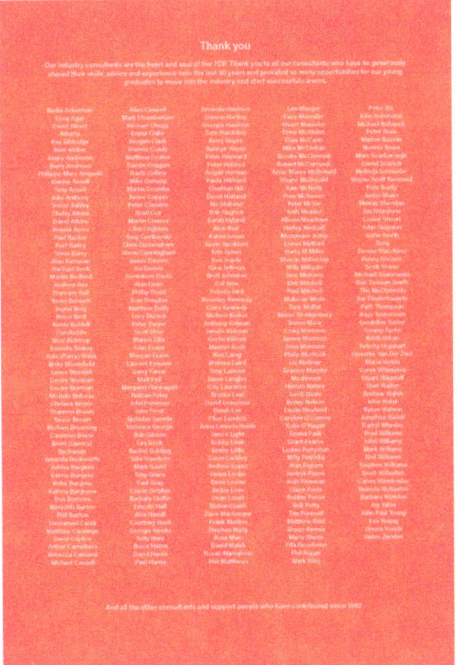

List of consultants over the first thirty years

We held the Rising Stars concert at the Seymour Centre, specifically to showcase some of our best recent contemporary graduates. Every song performed was an original and the audience included some bigwigs in the Australian recording industry.

Simon Moore, then A&R manager at Sony, became Managing Director of Kobalt Music. He was an ex-student of mine from the football choir at EBHS. The roles were reversed when this former rugby choir member became a trusted and invaluable advisor to me and TDP students for many years. Very early in the piece, he cautioned me that "bands don't fit into the TDP, so let it go …" While I agreed with this concept, there were exceptions to the rule, like Morgan Evans, for example. In the 30th TDP birthday program Morgan had this to say:

> *More than anything I'm grateful for the community TDP and Schools Spectacular introduced me to. I met some of my best mates in the world to this day through those organisations and I'll always be grateful for that. Mary and her team are such passionate supporters of young talent. That kind of belief, during that time of life, is really important and goes a long way.*

I found the best way to give these kids the confidence they needed to step out into the industry, was to treat them as individuals. We worked to identify the qualities that made them unique and so would earn them their place in the TDP. Then we would tailor a program to suit the individual. In most workshops we'd have one session where all the performers sat down together, and maybe a businessman, lawyer, community leader, marketing or fashion professional would pass on general information and guidance.

The program was constantly changing to adapt to industry requirements.

My personal emphasis was on performance, performance, performance. In the workshops the students would perform in front of a panel of two or three industry experts. Renowned performers like Jackie Love or Mark Williams, for example, were on the panel. I figured if the students could cope with the challenge of the discipline of preparing three songs as well as the close-up performance, then they would have a chance in the *real* music industry. Imagine you're standing less than 10 feet from one of your musical heroes, and the expectation is you will give a full performance such as you would deliver to an audience of 1,000. It could be quite daunting for some but it was excellent training for all.

Always I stressed that it was their individual, unique talent that they must hold onto. My advice was to "be who you are and be proud of where you come from. Don't copy anyone else and keep your Australian accent. Then you can communicate with the audience by singing from your gut. Keep your eyes open so the audience can see into your soul."

With Andrew Bee leading the charge for original works, we encouraged and turned out some great songwriters. I was constantly having to reason with some members of the board about the value of students performing their own original work.

I was privileged to attend the Tamworth Musical Society production of *Phantom of the Opera*, starring one of our graduates, Rob McDougall. Education Department music consultant for Tamworth Region, Di Hall was the director, and Rob McDougall was convincing and powerful in his role as the Phantom. I watched Di work passionately and with dedication to support talent and the growth of music and the arts in the Tamworth region over 30 years. She had passion, drive and energy to burn. Robert had been mentored by Di throughout his school years and beyond. We tried both in the TDP and the SS to connect with the Education Department's regional arts consultants who demonstrated the same commitment. It's gratifying to see Robert giving back to aspiring artists while lecturing at the Sydney Conservatorium of Music and tutoring for many years with TDP.

The voluntary contribution to the TDP and SS of professional artists from all spheres of the entertainment industry can never be understated. Their generosity in choosing to give back to the TDP in such a magnanimous fashion was absolute gold to the rising stars we were developing. You could see the lightbulbs switch on as the youngsters soaked in every word and phrase from these people who were working and succeeding within the industry to which all participants aspired.

Sonja Sjolander, as Director, and her team created a memorable and celebratory SS this year – "30 Spectacular Years." Sonja Benson (as she was then) came to my attention when she was a high school teacher contributing dance items to the Spectacular many years previously. She stood out to me as she always directed fascinating and interesting dance items. As a choreographer her contributions were always innovative and stretched creative boundaries. She was uncompromising in ensuring her dancers were given the best possible opportunity to shine. Rehearsal time was extremely limited but she always managed to stay on schedule in spite of the often-tricky staging her items required. She was an all-round professional.

With Sonja at the 2023 Launch

In the magnificent printed program for 30th SS I said: "Thank you to all those who have given their skills, passion and dedication who turned the SS into the masterpiece of show business it has become." Returning artists included internationally acclaimed singer-songwriter Morgan Evans, diva and songwriter Diana Rouvas, jazz singer and recording artist Darren Percival, and virtuoso trumpeter and recording artist Simon Sweeney.

Lessons learned
- Horses for courses
- Giving back

This is Australia

2014 was a year of primarily Australian travel with holidays to Cape York in a T-van – not my favourite form of accommodation on the road. There were other trips also to Broome, Palm Cove, Lizard Island

and my 70th birthday treat to Bali and The Oberoi Hotel, Hoi An. It was also a year of change for the family with Andy and Christine returning from Bali and buying the first of their properties at Kingscliff, a place that would become a home also to me and Rob 10 years later.

Up until this point the TDP was only offered to public school students but there was a great interest shown by young people across the board from public schools, private schools, universities, TAFE colleges and the general workforce. The TDP identified an opportunity to offer a version of the program to a wider audience so the Open Talent Workshops were born. These week-long intensives were open to all young people and were a truncated version of the main program designed to give young performers a boost.

Open Talent Workshops were fee-based so we were able to offer payment to our wonderful consultants and workshop leaders. As a result, several students moved from the private system into public schools so they could audition for the main TDP program. Following on from the success of the Rising Stars Concert we decided to trial a separation of our graduating streams for their finale. Our music theatre graduates presented a cabaret evening in the Qantas Lounge at the Sydney Entertainment Centre while contemporary and singer-songwriters presented an evening of great music at Lazybones Lounge in Marrickville.

This year we also began the implementation of our own TDP scholarship program, with Nicholas Gentile the first recipient of the $5,000 scholarship. Kim was able to secure sponsorships for over 30 scholarships during her years at TDP.

The 31st SS wasn't without its challenges for several reasons. Director Sonja Sjolander commenced maternity leave but we were fortunate to have the highly talented Peter Hayward stepped into the role. With the theme "This Is Australia" it was a real thrill to reintroduce some of the highlights from previous years and create a truly Aussie program.

One of the real jewels for me was my association with the wonderfully creative and famous producer-director with Channel Nine, the late Adrian Dellevergin. Adrian was producing the SS for the Channel 9 TV broadcast. I loved having such an enthusiastic and experienced director to work with. Adrian inspired and challenged me. He introduced me to many things I didn't know about in the world of television. I really admired his knowledge of individually great performers, and how he wanted to showcase the individuals who stood out among the past graduates. I loved his creative ideas and feel he had as much respect for what my experience taught him about youth and performance as I learnt from him. The standards of excellence which he demanded for his Channel Nine television gala specials was injected into our team and we all benefited from our too brief association and collaboration with him. Unfortunately, he didn't get to see the live performance as he had begun treatment for the long battle with melanoma that would claim his life in less than 12 months in 2015.

It was also the year of the inaugural SS Mary Lopez Medal, initiated by executive producer Bill Anderson. I was so grateful to Bill for this extraordinary honour which was to be an annual medal awarded to an outstanding teacher contributor to the SS. The inaugural recipient was Judi Joy, a thoroughly dedicated dance choreographer and a pioneer of the SS.

John Deakin, Me and Judi Joy at the 2023 launch

In successive years the recipients were:

- 2014: Judi Joy
- 2015: Colleen and the late Phill Hayward
- 2016: Wendy Tierney
- 2017: John Deacon
- 2018: the late Ross Milne
- 2019: Lynne Halpin
- 2022: Kay Taylor
- 2023: Kaz Levi
- 2024: Jillian Bradford.
- 2025: Michael Coleman

These teachers are the real story of the passion and dedication of teachers to the new big chance for their young performers to develop and shine, that was the SS from 1984 onwards.

By year's end Rob, who had suffered with deafness from childhood, miraculously got his hearing back, thanks to the modern concept of cochlear implants, and the expertise of Dr Chang at St Vincent's Hospital, Sydney. It has opened a whole new world for him, being able to hear just about everything.

Lessons learned
- No matter what your age – there are always new things to learn
- Acknowledge and reward dedication and integrity

Lifetime Achievement Award

In November 2013 I received another accolade.

Media Release – Three Australian Greats to be recognised with Lifetime Achievement Awards

Three Australian greats behind some of Australia's most iconic events will be recognised with Lifetime Achievement Awards at the 2013 Australian Event Awards next Tuesday night. Di Henry, Sandy Hollway and Mary Lopez have made a significant contribution to events in Australia and in so doing have done much for the way Australia is perceived overseas.

Founding producer and director of the Schools Spectacular Mary Lopez; and Di Henry, owner of Maxxam International, will join Sydney 2000 Olympic mastermind Sandy Hollway on stage in Sydney at the Industry Night of Nights, where the trio will be presented with Lifetime Achievement awards for their incredible creativity, innovation and dedication to Australia's iconic events culture....

Mary Lopez OAM directed the Schools Spectacular celebration of public education for 25 years and continues to be involved as Emeritus Director. In 2013 Mary is delighted to be asked to return as Artistic Director of the show's 30th birthday celebrations.

Ms Lopez's passion for nurturing talented young people led her in 1991 to co-found the Talent Development Project (TDP), which prepares exceptionally gifted young performers for careers in the music and entertainment industry. Mary has been Artistic Director of this unique program since its inception. She was instrumental in creating TDP's "Bound for Broadway" scholarships in conjunction with the American Society of Composers, Authors and Publishers (ASCAP).

In 2007 Ms Lopez received the Variety Humanitarian of the Year Award and in 2010 her contribution to public education and the arts was recognised with an Honorary Doctorate of Letters from the University of Western Sydney. In 2012 Mary received the prestigious Ted Albert Award for outstanding services to Australian music.

21
The end of an era

After I retired as SS Director in December 2008, after 25 years' service, I stayed on as a consultant at the Department's request until 2016. Rob and I were planning a full year of exciting travel to make up for what I felt was lost personal time.

In January, we were invited by good friends Wynette (founder of the Waratah Girls' Choir) and the late John Horne to join them in their condo for skiing in Whistler, Canada. Spending time with them was such a treat as they are very giving friends. We were all the better spiritually and energy wise for the enriching time spent in their company. Sadly, John passed away a few years later and in a tragic postscript, their grandson, Jacob Neale, a gifted TDP graduate and musical director, died of brain cancer in 2023.

Something quite peculiar happened on the way to Whistler, aboard a Japan Airlines plane. While Rob was in the toilet, a baby change table fell from the wall unexpectedly, knocking his cochlear device from his head into the toilet bowl and out into the universe! What an expensive exercise that was! The staff from Japan Airlines were very helpful in the situation and made us aware of the only doctor in Vancouver who could replace it. Several thousands of dollars down the drain, we resumed our holiday with our wonderful friends.

In April, Rob and I flew Barcelona where we cruised the Mediterranean then took a river cruise from Budapest to Amsterdam. I was so sick with a flu virus during our cruise along the Danube and Rhine rivers, I hardly had time to appreciate their beauty, and I have been rather reluctant to do another river cruise ever since. We stayed at the Shangri-La Hotel, Hong Kong on the way home and caught up with Franz Donnhauser, the hotel's general manager at the time. Years before (in 2010), Franz had been kind enough to offer performance opportunities in the majestic Shangri-La in Sydney for TDP graduates.

Staying true to our plans, Rob and I travelled to South America in October, a first for Rob although not for me. Our itinerary took in Santiago, Iguazu, Peru, Machu Picchu and the Galapagos Islands. The most magnificent sight I've ever seen are the Iguazu Falls between Brazil and Argentina. I am still as in awe of the force and power of the waterfalls as I was on my previous two trips. We had a train and bus ride to Machu Picchu on this trip and as ever I was mesmerised by the incredible engineering mastery of the Incas, which inspired me to include a segment in one of the first SS productions (choreographed by Sandra Copeman). *The Royal Hunt of the Sun*, to which I was introduced by Paul Kelly at Balgowlah BHS back in 1970, was my first exposure to the Incas' culture and the Spanish connection.

We finished our South American travels in the magic and quiet serenity of the Galapagos Islands. It was altogether an unforgettable journey. Rob often talks about snorkelling with baby sea lions coming right up to his goggles. I can still picture the masses of giant turtles and iguanas by the thousands. What a privilege it was to have such an experience. While writing about these travels with Rob, it occurs to me that I enjoy the memories of my holidays more then I enjoyed the holidays. I think that's because I was then almost manic with fitting my many lives into one life!

December 2015 was a sad time for those of us with long-term associations with the Sydney Entertainment Centre. Personally, I'd been there from the opening production in 1983, presenting events there right throughout its lifetime. SS No. 32, "This Is Our World", was the final major event held at the centre. Remember I was still actively involved with SS, though as an artistic adviser to Sonja and the team. The doors closed a week after that production with a final Elton John concert. The Sydney Entertainment Centre had been the home of the SS and the TDP for all of their lives and with its final curtain call came the end of a fabulous era.

In amongst all the upheaval the TDP remained a strong force in talent development. The TDP career scholarship program was fully up and running with Miriam Waks, Nathan Allgood, Harry Ward and Lincoln Hall each awarded $5,000 to further their careers. Graduation this year was held at Monkey Bar in Darling Harbour. We were on the lookout for a new place to call home with Kim Lemke leading the search.

I was by now completely exhausted with the TDP and trying desperately to retire but was at a loss to find a successor. I wanted to have the time to give to Rob, my family and grandchildren. I felt as if I was missing out again because of this workload and being responsible for other people's children as well as my staffing concerns. I was going at a hundred miles an hour and resenting the time away from those I loved. My brother Shane had suffered a stroke and was in a nursing home. I was frustrated, struggling to find the time to visit him as much as I would have liked. My grandchildren were growing up so fast and I was still missing out.

Lessons learned
- Find balance

Goodbye Walker St

2016 was the year of my final goodbye to Walker St, where I had lived since the 1980s. By the time I left I had lived in three houses in the very lovely, quiet street in Lavender Bay, with a heritage listing on the terrace houses. In February, I sold 11a Walker Street and bought an apartment in Cavill, in Milsons Point. Our stay in Cavill was only for a few years. The noise from nearby Luna Park was too much for me so we sold up and moved to a quieter area and an apartment in Kirribilli. I'm not one for screaming and spruikers with loud hailers!

I think the most significant fact about Walker St was that the four Victorian terraces (I had owned two of them) were part of Mrs McKenzie's estate from the 1870s. She was obviously a strong, clever businesswoman who had succeeded in real estate. I seemed to following in her footsteps with all my moves.

In December, we decided on a Caribbean cruise on the gracious Windstar sailing yacht over the Christmas period. Cruising with Windstar was a new and exotic experience. Early in the voyage we met a younger, flamboyant couple from Boston, Evan and Barry Freid. They made the trip so much more memorable by taking us to the resorts where the "rich and famous" frolicked. When we docked, they knew to hire a vehicle and driver and off we'd go. They were seasoned Caribbean travellers, while Rob and I were newcomers to the colour and beauty of the many ports we visited. I'd love to revisit but it's such a long journey to get there from Australia.

Kim's search for new digs for TDP was over. Philanthropist Tim Sims AM became a major sponsor and gave us a new home. We set up our new office at the International Screen Academy in Waterloo. The premises and facilities were a great fit for the program with a permanent theatre space to hold workshops, performances and, of course, our grand piano.

The International Screen Academy CEO Simon Hunter was warmly accommodating towards all the TDP staff and students. He went out of his way to ensure our situation was mutually beneficial, including us in many endeavours.

Kim Lemke (now Stevens) and Joff

Kim Lemke by now had become Kim Stevens (after marrying the handsome and charming Joff Stevens) and was negotiating more and more sponsorships. Her efforts in securing sponsorship meant TDP scholarships of $5,000 continued to be awarded while she was leading the Project.

After years of seeing the TDP grow from strength to strength, coordinator Robyn Philpot retired and moved to Queensland. I've written about Robyn's passion and dedication to her young charges but I also need to comment on her diligence, tenacity and often back-breaking work, as she took equipment from one venue to another. She is a truly amazing woman.

By October, demolition of our old home at the Sydney Entertainment Centre was well under way while down the road in Darling Harbour the major renovation of Sydney International Convention Centre was complete. It seemed so natural that the TDP were the stars of the Gala Opening of the Sydney Theatre within this new complex, with a roll call of stars who were now major, established artists. Long-standing TDP board member Tim Worton, then group director of ASM Global, controlling venues all over the world, including Darling Harbour, was the one who offered the TDP the opportunity to stage a gala opening of the International Convention Centre.

Tim Worton

Keith Urban staged the first concert in the newly built International Convention Centre. This gala opening saw the return of major successful graduates and showcased the validity of the training program I had created all those years ago back in 1991. Backstage and on stage the affection the graduates had for each other was clearly demonstrated, as was the network of support that now existed for those fortunate participants in the program.

This was effectively my last production for TDP. It was a memorable celebration and line-up of TDP graduates. I sat in the audience with the TDP Chair, Alan Jones, and we were like the "grandparents" – so proud of our wonderful young performers:

- John Foreman
- Felicity Urquhart
- Darren Coggan
- William Crighton
- Ashleigh Rubenach
- Steve Madsen
- David Harris
- Amanda Harrison
- Robert McDougall
- Anja Nissen
- Trevor Ashley
- Nathan Foley
- Lorenzo Rositano
- Christie Lamb
- Emma Pask
- Sam Fischer, and
- Miriam Waks
- with special guest Delta Goodrem.

The concert was produced and directed by the two Andys – Lopez and Bee. It had all the elements of a slick and thoroughly entertaining contemporary event as only they know how to stage, produce and direct. After her very recent retirement, Robyn Philpot graciously agreed to return, and stage manage the cast for this special occasion. Only Robyn could have done it. The line-up really was remarkable. There were also just as many sensational alumni unable to accept the invitation due to performing commitments both nationally and internationally.

Lesson learned
- The power of the mateship that is formed when like-minded and creative talents gather

Goodbye TDP

"If someone throws you the ball, you don't have to catch it." I took the advice I'd written in my diary in 2017 and was trying to separate myself from TDP. It must have been frustrating for those who were trying to forge ahead whilst developing programs. But this year was the beginning of my health problems and of the death of a precious friend, Meena Cheok. I still didn't register seriously my own mortality. That didn't happen until years later in 2023 when I had a mini-stroke (TIA). I think I finally stopped running then.

The work-life balance was finally levelling out and Rob and I were enjoying attending Grandparents' Days and seeing our grandsons playing rugby and Eva singing in her choir. I appreciated that Andy and Kate included us both in their family's activities.

In June, I made an appointment to see a heart specialist, Dr David Roy, as I was always tired and not so strong walking up hills. He'd booked me in to have the usual tests and by that afternoon I had had a stent inserted. The offending artery (the widow's artery) was 95 per cent blocked. A close shave. I asked the doctor if it was OK for me to continue with plans to visit the Kimberley in 10 days. His rapid response was: "It's a lot safer than it was two days ago."

I have to say David looked more the age of my students rather than the very eminent surgeon he is. He comes from a family of heart surgeons, so I knew I was in good hands. Four days after having the stent implanted, the TDP graduation was held at the Monkey Bar Theatre, Darling Harbour. I'd invited Peter Cousens to direct the graduation with Andrew Bee as the producer. My TDP team were not used to me having the same frailties as other humans and it went unnoticed that I'd had a *big* health scare and wasn't my usual strong self for that evening. It was a happy occasion for me as I was supported by quite a number of my friends, including Evan and Barry Freid from Boston and my loyal aqua aerobics girls.

This was the last TDP graduating class under my training system and guidance. A couple of hardworking and successful graduates to come out of that class are Angel Tairua, a talented contemporary singer-songwriter and Jeremy Bolton, who studied opera in Vienna after receiving a TDP scholarship. Shortly after the graduation, Rob and I took Evan and Barry to the Kimberley. They still haven't recovered from the frogs in their toilet at my beloved Lombadina on the corrugated road to Cape Levique.

In August, we returned to explore more of beautiful Vietnam, travelling up to Sapa this time. After 10 days in Hoi An, we had a fascinating holiday in Laos. We found a charming French-owned resort on the banks of a river in the village of Muang La. We went by car from Luang Prabang, which was an eight-hour uncomfortable journey. The bungalows were tastefully furnished and overlooked the clean and fast-flowing river. The hotel had an agreement that the villagers had access to a river pool where they cleansed themselves. Everything about tranquil Muang La, from the food to the excursions available, was first class in our book. I call it understated sophistication but one of the excursions took us into three primitive mountain villages where we saw people living a subsistence way of life who nevertheless appeared to be very healthy, unlike South-East Asia.

Kim Lemke was rightfully waiting in the wings and had done a most professional job managing new projects since she joined the TDP in 2011. Among her many contributions she had found the TDP's new headquarters at Waterloo in 2015 and had raised $175,000 in sponsorship to fund the scholarships which helped 30 recipients realise their dreams. Upon my retirement Kim was appointed CEO. She continued to provide professional management and administration to the TDP until her resignation, in 2020.

This was a big year for me, after 35 years of working with Schools Spec and TDP, it was time for me to retire. I was exhausted and desperately wanted to live my own life. I wanted to spend time with my grandchildren. It was very difficult preparing a succession plan for retirement, and I was talking to my lawyer about a compensation package for handing over the licence of my TDP training program. I had had no benefits from superannuation, holiday pay, office costs, sick leave, car allowance, etc throughout my career since leaving the Education Department in 1988.

The TDP created another big scholarship at this time for our successful country music alumni. AEG Ogden chairman and CEO Harvey Lister initiated and sponsored a $10,000 Nashville scholarship for contemporary songwriters to enable them to get to Music City USA to engage with writers over there. Imogen Clark was the first recipient, and she was followed by Travis Collins, then Brad Cox. They are now household names in the Australian country music scene.

> **Where are they now – Brad Cox**
>
> *Brad has toured extensively in Australia gathering a loyal fan base. His 2024 UK tour delivered sold out shows in Manchester and Glasgow. At the Country Music Awards in 2024, Brad won Male Artist of the Year, Contemporary Artist of the Year and Top Selling Country Album of the Year. Brad and his band (several are also TDP graduates) continue to write chart busting songs.*

After his many years of dedication Andrew Bee made the decision to retire from the TDP. This was the end of an era. Mr Bee had given so much to every graduate and the number of successful singer-songwriters who were now well and truly established in the industry are testament to his skill, musicality and unwavering support.

Between us we were proud to have fostered and developed some outstandingly talented Indigenous performers. They proudly represented their culture and we were so pleased to help them find their own voices in many areas of the music and entertainment world. Amongst the Indigenous TDP graduates are:

- Peter Riley
- Blake Ralph
- Brendon Boney
- Tessa Nuku
- Bruce Carr
- Evelyn Willie
- Nathan Lamont
- Googoorewon Knox
- Gemma Summerhayes
- Jessica Hitchcock

It's important to note here that our passionate and dedicated TDP Coordinator, Kerry Vanslambrouk, was the first and arguably the most successful Indigenous member of the TDP family. We love you, Kerry.

Lesson learned
- Know when to let go of the reins and call it a day

The Camino

Although I had officially retired from the TDP and SS in my dual roles of Artistic Director and CEO, I remained on the TDP board for another three years and looked forward to that continued association with "my baby." I swapped my career for a new life which was, I hoped, about grandchildren's birthday parties, concerts and sporting activities, my extended family, friends, and, of course, travel.

Upon my retirement, Peter Cousens was employed as Artistic Director, with Kim Lemke now the CEO. A new era was beginning for TDP. The new leadership team gave me confidence our program, which had grown from a small volunteer organisation way back in 1991, was in good hands. Peter had a new approach which saw the establishment of a small team of regular consultants. Gradually the TDP alumni consultants and volunteer consultants disappeared. I think that is a shame because it was because of those volunteers, that the TDP was able to graduate uniquely prepared students. They had been given firsthand advice and direction from very successful industry professionals who were then currently working as performers, producers, directors, lawyers and in many other careers who could help.

Our travels began in earnest for the year in January, with not much happening on my part with the TDP because I felt I was not wanted. We began with a visit to dear friends, Wynne and John Richardson, in New Zealand, followed by several other enjoyable jaunts to Broome, Vietnam and Laos. We also squeezed in quite a few trips to Kingscliff to visit the family.

However, the overseas venture that changed my life occurred in April 2018, when I spent four weeks alone walking the Camino de Santiago in Spain. I had dreamed of this pilgrimage since the 1970's when I first visited Santiago de Compostela with my late Spanish husband. Then I was captivated by the pilgrims I saw arriving at the grand historic cathedral. I've never forgotten the solemnity, spirituality and joy of the pilgrims and the drama of the interior of the cathedral. I loved the intense spirituality I experienced and was mesmerised by the drama created by massive swinging incense burner which sways across the length of the huge naves.

Flying to Spain with Emirates, I made the following notes in my diary 2018, which I titled "An outsider":

You wouldn't believe it but I've always felt like an outsider. Now that I've retired, (just six days ago) I'm facing the reality of who am I?

I never planned to have such a public life – with so many people it – I just wanted to be on the stage and be noticed.

I always wanted to sing and dance but had no idea how to get there from Merriwa.

Reflecting – it's no wonder I was an outsider – the youngest of eight children and born eight months after my father died.

As a little girl I wondered if I was adopted. My brothers and sisters never spoke about my "father" or "Dad" and Mum didn't mention him either.

I had no "father" or "husband" as a role model. I personally made a made a complete mess when married because my fantasy expectations were so off track.

I married my Spanish husband after knowing him only three months. He was so not what I expected as a husband and father. Mind you, he had a very tricky and dysfunctional family to deal with himself.

For a start, his father was a Dominican priest. There was a lot of deception in Manuel's story to me before we were married. I was shattered when I found out how it all really was. I married an "outsider" too.

I was swept up in my career as a teacher, producer and director and then, in 1984, I conceived the Schools Spectacular which totally consumed me.

Now I've retired I'm trying to work out how it happened and how I went from a town of 900 to creating the show that went from a cast of 1,700 cast in the first SS to a cast of 5,000.

I'm thinking about and excited to remember all the gorgeous people I've met and worked with over my 74 years. I've been driven by my intuition and passion. (Please note I was so young when I wrote this! – 10 years ago)

I don't know where I got that energy from – and the time – how did I fit everything in? Certainly, by never counting the hours I put in – or calculating an hourly rate.

You see I was fortunate to meet these men, from Jack Neary, Alan Jones, John Trevillian, Gerry Gleeson, Tom Hayson and John Brown, and followed my intuition – my gut feeling. I was always telling my students about singing from the gut.

The solo journey from Leon to Santiago is one I savoured, walking slowly and purposefully, while considering my life to date and taking in the historical vista. My life had been so full of thousands of people so to have this solitary time in such a setting was a luxury I'd never been able to afford until then. This was the first time I'd been back to Spain since Manuel's death. I had never really faced the reality and tragedy of his premature passing and of our marriage. Mama (his mother) said it took her 20 years to recover from Papa's death. At the time I found that impossible to believe but I now know she was right.

Rob and I departed Sydney on April 6 for a small group tour of Southern Spain. We flew into Madrid to meet up with the group. The bus tour was great because it encapsulated so much of what was colourful and interesting about Southern Spain. I'd visited places like Granada, Sevilla, Madrid and Toledo before but never Trujillo. This was the birthplace, in 1478, of Francisco Pizzaro, who conquered the Incas and brought about the disintegration of the mighty Inca civilisation. I'd been so inspired by that story, told in my involvement in two productions of the play, *The Royal Hunt of the Sun*, my two journeys to Machu Picchu and finally, a segment in the SS.

After the bus trip, Rob returned to Australia and I began my pilgrimage on the Camino de Santiago. I loved every step I took. The Camino helped me heal and sort out my priorities. It is such a privilege to have the time to reflect. The birdsong along the way was company and the scenery was constantly changing. Around every corner was another beautiful sight. There were many farm animals to see both on and off the Camino. I chose to walk by myself but there was always company if I wanted it. I made some very memorable companions along the way and found every pilgrim had a story to tell. The common factor that united most of us was we had an underlying problem we were hoping to resolve. I had quite a few issues and needed time alone.

My eldest brother, Cecil, died while I was on the Camino. I was in a lovely, small village when I received the devastating news. I didn't know whether or even how to fly home for the funeral, and my Spanish was too limited to ask advice and assistance from the hotel staff who didn't speak English. I rang my Spanish tour consultant who suggested I ask the Camino what to do. I walked outside my tiny hotel and heard a voice with an Australian accent coming from within a store.

Cecil and me

Somehow, we got to speak, and I told him of my tragic loss and dilemma. He said: "Come with me to my wife. She'll know because she has special connections to the spirit world." She was waiting just 10 metres away in a café. When I asked if she thought I should leave my Camino for the funeral, she was emphatic in her reply. "No, your brother is here with you." And you know, from that minute I felt Cecil was with me. I talked to him all along the way and felt at peace with the decision I'd made. I also talked with Manuel, whose Spanish roots were in this region. I loved and appreciated him more during that quiet time than I had when he was in my life.

I spent four weeks on the Camino, completing half the journey, with a plan to return the following year to walk the other half of this amazing pilgrimage.

It was a sad but fulfilling time as I finally found closure. During my pilgrimage, I also received the worrying news from Gail Mabo that my dear friend, Bonita Mabo was near death. I was anxious to make sure I got in touch with her as soon as possible. Being able to talk with her on the phone while on the Camino was a joyous experience. We laughed and reminisced and I'm delighted to say, I did get to see her later in the year.

Note my Camino emblem on my T-shirt

When I visited Bonita in July, I experienced one of the greatest thrills of my life. I was dreading it, expecting to find her in a wasted condition but she was up and about. Due to the extraordinary loving care of the doctors and nurses at Canossa Private Hospital, Brisbane, Bonita left hospital and was able to go home. Rob and I took our grandsons, Mani and Izzy, to visit her. How wonderful to see her happy and healthy. It'll be a memory those boys will treasure and appreciate when they are older. Sadly, she died in November and I lost a treasured friend.

Rob, Bonita, Me, Mani and Izzy

EBHS to the rescue

There was a huge void in my life for the next few years after retiring from TDP, and I felt something was missing. Then suddenly, things from the past caught up with me in the most delightful way. I was missing the stimulation of my career when Garth McDonald, a student at EBHS in 1973, re-entered my world like a lifeline

> *It's Garth McDonald ... one of your choir sopranos from 1973–1976, also band member. I had an epiphany the other night, Mary. Who would I want the most to attend our 40th High School Reunion as the guest of honour, other than the most inspirational and dedicated woman our school, our state and arguably Australia, could ever ask for?*
>
> *Your passion for your music direction and talent nurturing has received the highest accolade. Until two nights ago, I was totally ignorant of your amazing career, post EBHS. I can only feel ultimately honoured to have been guided, nurtured, yelled at ... by the diva of Australian musical arts.*
>
> *Attending our reunion will be: Michael Hogan, front man of the rock band who now acknowledges you as his musical direction in life as a blues singer and blues harp player. Plus, many more who you've made such an impact on their musical lives. We need YOU to join us Mary as our ultimate guest of honour.*
>
> *The reunion was in November and I must say it felt marvellous stepping back to the days when I was a teacher and life was clean and simple. I felt appreciated and valued at that dinner and it also covered the month I would usually be involved with the SS.*

Garth's enthusiasm gave me the confidence and courage to finally begin this book. He reminded me about my passion and my crusade to "spread the word." I was absolutely committed to my belief that it was important for people to sing. Because I loved the sound of boys singing my concentration was on boys' choirs. Garth helped me revisit the real Mary Lopez – the Feneley girl from the country town. Very much pre-SS.

I received a letter from Stuart Davis (another of my EBHS boys) that same year. Stuart is now a highly renowned director of choral music for several organisations including the Education Department's PAU. I still can picture his fine performances in musicals at EBHS not long after I arrived as a music teacher at Epping in the 70s.

25 September 2018

Hi, Mary,

I've just been on the phone to Garth, who's organising the reunion. I'm really disappointed that I can't make it – I have a weekend gig I can't avoid.

It would have been brilliant to catch up, but I reckon we should try anyway, another time.

I understand you've recently retired. In the meantime, I continue to work in the choir area and often credit you as my original inspiration and mentor.

I do quite a bit of work with the PAU, and Louise Barkl (former PAU manager) sings in one of my choirs now.

For the last three years I've been doing a PAU project for boys, and it's one of the most emotional gigs I do – I hope I can inspire at least some of them in the way you did for so many of us.

All the best wishes,
Stuart Davis

On the beach in Culburra, I met Bernie and Roz Carberry who have become good friends. Bernie was an administrator with the School Boys Rugby in 1983 and remembers me coaching the team to sing the National Anthem. He still is now, in 2025, passionately involved with School Boys' Rugby.

It's funny how a chance meeting with someone will spark memories. I ran into another one of the stars to come out of that school, Brett Papworth, who was in the rugby choir and went on to represent Australia as a Wallaby.

Lesson learned
- Karma

22
Australia All Over

2019 was a year when I was free of any working commitments and my family relatively free from any dramas.

Rob's dream was to drive all round Australia. We set off on our big, around-Australia 4WD trip in April. We drove across the Nullarbor to Kalgoorlie and Broome. We were minding an AirBnB for friends in Broome, Annette and Colin Gregory, so we were able to invite Kate, Ivan and Eva over to share the stunning life and scenery around Broome. Six of our aqua friends joined us later, and we introduced them to some good 4WD roads to Fitzroy Crossing and the stunning Cape Leveque, Kimberley. We then drove back to Sydney through Mount Isa, Toowoomba and the Gold Coast. Rob fulfilled his dream to drive around Australia covering some 22,222km, and we loved every minute of it.

In June, I flew back from Broome for the TDP graduation. How delighted I was to see young Arlo Sim graduating. His father, Duncan Sim, was one of my very special and hardworking choir and band members over six years at EBHS. Duncan then sang in the ex-students' singers, Eklipse. Duncan and Kath's son, Arlo continued to achieve success reaching the grand final of *The Voice* in 2021. He graduated from the jazz course at Sydney Conservatorium.

The last six months of 2019 was an incredibly rewarding time for me as I'd reconnected with many of my EBHS ex-students who were involved with me either as their music teacher or choir director. It was especially lovely to meet up again with John Simpson, David Hoffman, Duncan Sim and Scott Dunne. I had so much to do with those boys. When they were students. They became almost like family members over the six years of their EBHS education. Manuel was very fond of them and so were Andy and Kate. The boys were babysitters and frequent visitors to our house in Lane Cove.

In October, I walked the other half of the Camino by myself, setting off from St Jean Pied de Port and finishing in Leon. I took about 28 days to walk almost 400km and have all that time to reflect. There's nothing like being forced into your own company to help you see clearly. Rob and I met in Bangkok for a couple of weeks, in a new country for Rob. It was a contrast to my Camino, but we still enjoyed ourselves.

Where have all the years gone? One minute I'm eight-year-old Mary playing Mary in Paterson Primary School's nativity play, then I'm 22 years old, sitting in the old family farmhouse at Allynbrook, near Gresford in the NSW Hunter Valley, with Mum telling me "you'll never get a big head will you, Mare?" Fast forward to 2018 and 2019 and I'm walking the Camino in Spain and driving all over Australia. The Camino truly helped me move into my own life.

However, I continued to suffer loss in my life, losing my dearest friend Mem Gilchrist, who'd cared for Andy when he was a little boy. She was a wonderful friend with a keenly developed sense of social justice. In particular, the lessons she taught me about the shocking living conditions of Indigenous Australians have helped shape my teaching through the SS.

The year ended beautifully with Andy and Kate and their families having Christmas together in Kingscliff. We got to know each other much better and learnt about the lives we were now living. I feel as if the six weeks from December 2019 through to January 2020 summarised so much of my life, almost like a time capsule, taking in my family and career. It all began with that family Christmas.

Then tragedy struck the McCormack family and all of us, in January. Dear Juliet, daughter of my sister Dot and Robert McCormack, died from kidney failure. Because our children had grown up together, the impact the death had on Andy and Kate was severe. It was a terrible time for Juliet's immediate family and we could see them suffering and could do nothing about it. As soon as we heard about Jules' death, Andy immediately drove from Kingscliff to Dot's house in Surfers Paradise. He then organised a flight for me to be by her side the next day. Finally he bought flights for us both to head back to Sydney. Andy took control and I am so grateful he did this to ease the burden on Dot.

Kate was asked to present the homily for Jules at the funeral. She set about preparing the content by talking to family and friends to make sure she covered all corners of her life. I was surprised at the detail she went into to secure the facts and amazed and impressed by the wonderful words and presentation at the funeral.

I am aware my two fabulous kids have grown up into the most amazing human beings. I'm so proud to be their mother.

Lessons learned
- Listen to others and your inner self
- Don't be afraid to reset your plans

Country music

Encouraged by my music-loving friends, Debbie Hockings and Peter Lorking, Rob and I decided to join them for the Tamworth Country Music Festival at the end of January. By chance I ran into Ian Dundon whom I hadn't seen for fifty years. Ian and I were both teachers at EBHS and Ian was as passionate about teaching as I was. When I told him of my plans to go to the country music festival, he invited me to stay at his home in Tamworth. That was a real coup as accommodation is so hard to get at festival time.

Debbie, Trevor Ashley and Peter

Ian had been an invaluable support for me in creating the first SS. He and a team of five EBHS teachers stage managed the first SS at the Sydney Entertainment Centre. Before that we co-founded the highly innovative and successful Rugby Choir at EBHS. Not only did our meeting re-ignite those memories of EBHS, but I learned he was then managing a famous Tamworth venue, the Longyard Hotel. Many of our TDP graduates have performed on stage there. I had the pleasure of refocusing on those mighty years from my teaching career at EBHS to 50 years on.

I got to see superstar TDP graduate Brad Cox perform live, along with his band members, from TDP days Jackson Beasley, James Edge and Hunter (Tom Beasley), now managed by Kurt Bailey, also a TDP graduate. At the Golden Guitar Awards I ran into many TDP graduates and was proud of the co-hosting role of another alumni, Melanie Dyer. One of the early TDP alumni, Felicity Urquhart received six Golden Guitar awards that night and has continued to win further accolades since then.

What an extraordinarily talented country music family, which grew from the TDP, performed that year at the Country Music Festival. All of them from country and regional NSW areas :

- Felicity Urquhart
- Travis Collins
- Brad Cox with Jackson Beasley and Hunter
- Drew McAllister
- Darren Coggan
- Sam McClymont
- Charlene Bailey
- Max Jackson
- Melanie Dyer
- Christie Lamb.

TDP graduates missing from Tamworth, as they were in Nashville, were Morgan Evans, Anthony Snape and Jedd Hughes.

So many TDP graduates were headlining at the festival. I missed some of those I was looking forward to seeing because Rob and I arrived three days later than we'd intended due to my darling niece's funeral. Tears come as I think back to the terrible sadness of Juliet's illness and death.

Throughout my career I've always been reluctant to seek out TDP graduates for fear that it would seem as if I am expecting some acknowledgment. To tell the truth I was never sure how they really felt about me. I guess also I don't like to push into their lives. But after the warm and enthusiastic greetings I received from so many of the young artists at the festival, I do now feel that they do really appreciate the opportunities I helped give young people from the country.

Lessons learned
- Power of loyalty and mateship
- Regardless of commitments – family comes first

Melanie Dyer – The blossom flowers

I am a country artist and songwriter from Mount Russell in the New England region of NSW.

I met Mary in 2006 at my very first audition for the NSW Schools Spectacular. I was just 12 years old and had grown up watching Schools Spec on TV and dreaming of one day performing on that stage.

Mary was on the judging panel and after I nervously sang a Delta Goodrem cover, she asked me if I had ever tried writing my own songs, encouraging me to try out for a development programme called the Talent Development Project.

After that audition in Sydney, I went back to the farm and sat at the kitchen table and wrote my first original song called **Life On The Land***.*

The song went on to become the theme song for the Woolworths National Drought Appeal where it featured on the television ad and was played in stores right across Australia to support farmers doing it tough.

It was that very first song that opened up my mind to a whole other world and I soon discovered my love of songwriting.

I have since written and released multiple #1 country songs, an ARIA #3 country album, two APRA-nominated country songs, won the APRA Professional Development Award for Songwriting and have been nominated for three Golden Guitar Awards.

I can't say I would never have written a song, but it was certainly Mary who first pushed me to give it a go.

> Mary's ability to see raw talent and nurture it is why she has enjoyed such a long and successful career in the music industry.
>
> The skills and insight I gained while being a student of the TDP from 2006–2010 prepared me for the reality of the music industry and taught me how to navigate a career as an artist and songwriter.
>
> I am so grateful to have received the Mary Lopez Scholarship in 2022 which is another of the many ways Mary continues to support the future of our music industry.
>
> Thank you Mary, for the environment you created for a kid like me from the bush to work hard and dream big.

Culburra, Covid and a book

After my Tamworth visit, I decided to be serious about writing my memoir. During my stay in Tamworth, Joan Douglas, a friend and woman of vast experience in the music industry, arranged for a journalist to interview me because of the strong association I had with so many country performers. The journalist was Anna Rose, also an author of biographies. She gave me the best advice for my memoir project: "Start with a timeline."

I remember calling into Tamworth on a 4WD drive car rally, way back around 2002, for a performance arranged by Joan for her young charges, the Baileys, which began my association with her. A remarkable woman, Joan, with the help of husband Bevan and consultants within the music industry, created Tamworth's very first "listening room." The Bill Chambers Room, at The Pub which they owned at 99 Gunnedah Road, was built to acoustic specifications to enable the ultimate in listening pleasure. The Pub Management was a large part of Joan's life for many years with her taking on guidance of the careers of several young musicians. The shining star from The Pub Management stable was TDP graduate Felicity Urquhart, whose career has gone from strength to strength over the past 30 years.

When the pandemic hit in March 2020, I set myself up in the street bedroom at Culburra during the first lockdown. Luckily, I had kept work diaries from 1992 throughout my career in the events industry. Alongside the diaries I had filed the printed programs for every SS and TDP graduation. Also I had reports, letters and programs from my student days and early teaching years. I have been able to remember my life events from the prompting of these communications. On Anna's advice, I had finished recording the timeline by the end of the first lockdown and I was under way.

I had my second stent inserted on 6 March just before the first lockdown. At my follow-up appointment I had a chance to talk to my cousin, Professor Michael Feneley, who was then head of cardiology at St Vincent's Hospital. His rooms were adjacent to my surgeon, David Roy. How grim and disturbing was Michael's view of the pandemic and the period ahead. He described the dire situation in hospitals in Italy: "You speak to a doctor on the phone in Italy, but don't expect that he will still be alive when next you phone." How terrible and frightening were those two years.

The unprecedented shutdown of the world due to this insidious virus, did have some beneficial aspects if you consider the time it gave us all for reflection. There wasn't much else to do during lockdown except to look within and, in my case, to look way back into the past to create this book. I also used my time isolated in Culburra during lockdown to exercise with my friends also in Culburra, Heather Meadth and Jenny Heesh. Jenny Heesh and I shared the love of our Camino experiences. She has walked it about eight times and volunteers in the pilgrims' free hostels.

During the lockdown periods, I'd been corresponding with my American music and entertainment industry friends, Michael Kerker and Scott Stoner. Michael emailed me that we have: "hands across the water, thanks to you." He is so happy that many of the Broadway scholarship winners have kept in touch with him. All the recipients have been highly successful in their musical theatre or chosen genres and have taken advantage of every opportunity to advance themselves. I would say, of course, the vote of thanks belongs to Michael for opening this window to the world for our graduates.

After a lengthy phone conversation I had with Scott in 2020, I wrote this in my diary:

> *Scott and I agreed that success is always about networking and passion. I see those two qualities along with hard work as being the most important factors determining success (having a unique talent is a given).*

We also talked about the SS and how he saw it, particularly now when we are all isolated and social distancing. The sense of community and belonging that the SS created had gone.

With social distancing came the decision to cancel the SS for 2020. There wouldn't be any trip to Sydney for those thousands of pupils, their teachers and families and no thrill of performing in magnificent venues. I thought, maybe now people will reflect on how big the idea was. How blank was the canvas? This is how it was pre-1984, before the creation of the SS.

The SS team did manage to bravely create an online version of SS during those Covid years

I am particularly proud that the causes about which I was so passionate are still being addressed in SS lessons:

- Australian themes and music
- the inclusion of country performers,
- marginalised groups like disabled and Indigenous performers
- concepts of inclusiveness, tolerance, respect,
- proactive efforts to encourage boys to sing and dance.

Teachers I met during the Covid years helped me realise how important the SS was in their lives.

Sitting on the terrace at our Culburra beach house one afternoon in February 2020, we noticed a group of young women renting the house next door. Rob went to have a chat to our new neighbours (as we usually do) and found that they were all teachers. So, Rob immediately inquired if they'd heard of the SS – and yes, they had. Three of the group had had personal contact with it – either as performers or teachers. Whenever I come across SS teachers it's so rewarding and makes me feel proud. During my career I became somewhat isolated from the teachers and all I ever had was feedback from those in the administration side of the Department. What a relief it was to hear how important and enjoyable the experience of SS was directly from the teachers. They absolutely got it! Twenty to thirty thousand of them!

As I had already begun working on this book, I showed them the programs for the first few SSs where they saw their schools' names and items. I also showed them my pride and joy, watercolours paintings by SS designer the late Laurel Barranikow. These eight small paintings represent the spirits of Australia, which inspired what I consider to be my best SS, "To Be Australian", in 1999. Remember, I had come up with the concept for that SS when I was staying alone at Culburra for a few days.

Belinda Bourne, one of the teachers renting the house next door, taught at Marayong school when my brother, Ian Feneley, was principal there. She admired and respected my brother (Widge) and he also spoke very highly of her.

I love the way, since I started writing this book, that reminders in the form of people who were important in various periods or situations in my past, drop back in to prompt memories.

In March, I was introduced to Sandy and Paul, nearby Culburra neighbours. It turns out Sandy was a teacher, and her daughter was mad about dancing. Her daughter had danced in quite a few SS productions and absolutely loved the experience it gave her. Sandy was thrilled to accompany her every year. A couple of weeks later her daughter came to Culburra and was wildly enthusiastic about her experience. She said it defined her. It was so special for me, standing in the street, to have these passionate conversations. That's what the SS truly meant to me.

On Anzac Day 2020 I wrote:

> *Spending ANZAC Day in lockdown really brought back the 25 years of commitment to teaching the young performers and audiences about the sacrifices our fellow Australians made overseas.*

Driven by a sense of duty for the safety of their families and friends, these men and women gave their lives completely, or in part, in a selfless attitude of sacrifice. The one factor that never ceased to move me was the age of those very young men who enlisted. They were no older than the senior performers in SS. I was so keen to honour those people because I had been educated in the true way by participating in the ANZAC marches as a child. I remember how those very proud men who would then lead us to the cenotaph for the music and remembrance. They created a permanent picture in my heart and mind. Growing up in hotels, of course I thought it was natural then to see them all re-gather for two-up out in the back garden after the march. The shouts of the game – and the mateship – were just what I expected at this time of the year.

I had great support from my creative team of Andrew Bee, Helen Pain and Peter Cook as the years progressed, with all three coming up with different ways to present the theme of the Australian spirit. PAU director of drama Paul Viles dramatized several Anzac segments, which have become legendary. I placed these segments strategically in the program so they'd have the longest-lasting impact for the audience, choir and performers.

I'm so heartened by how Australia has now embraced our ANZACs and I'm glad the detractors didn't put me off all those years ago when they accused me of "glorifying war." I was too passionate about my crusade to honour and thank the servicemen and women to be deterred.

Rob and I proudly stood on our Culburra driveway at dawn with our candles, playing a recording by our dear friend, Dr Frank Cheok of *The Last Post* on his harmonica which he'd recorded the previous year at Villiers-Bretonneux. As usual I was choked up and spent most of the day catching up on the phone with talk about our 2020 ANZAC Day.

Having always wondered whether modern day Australians would sacrifice themselves in the same spirit as our servicemen and women of war, I can see Aussies are still imbued with those same traits and understand the qualities of sacrifice for our mates. This new form of sacrifice could be trucks laden with feed for drought-stricken farmers driven by volunteers; fire hoses held by unpaid heroes in a bid to save lives and houses; doctors, nurses and health workers prepared to face, literally head-on, the coronavirus, risking their own life and limb; and mates all over the country continuing to work in services that brought them into contact with this deadly virus and many more.

During Covid, I was so proud of our politicians for not squabbling over petty, point-scoring rubbish. And how responsible were all our fabulous fellow Australians, complying with the request to stay at home to protect each other?

We were allowed out of lockdown in the middle of the year for a few months. Andy was turning 50 and he had a party in Kingscliff to celebrate. He had kept us all amused with his hilarious lockdown posts on Facebook, so it was his turn to be the recipient of some fun. It was so good to be entertained by Trevor Ashley, a TDP graduate from 1997 and now an internationally acclaimed cabaret and drag artist, musical theatre performer and producer.

My lovely brother Shane passed away in October after spending months of the year isolated during Covid. His wife and children, and my brother Ian, visited when they were allowed. I had visited him as often as I could over the many years he was in the nursing home. My brother, Widge was an almost daily visitor recounting memories and telling stories about their lives together. What a loving and loyal brother he was. I used to take Shane fresh fruit each time I visited which he really enjoyed as a relief from the nursing home food. Sadly, Anthony Feneley, his son from Melbourne, spent many of those final days trying to communicate from outside of the building because of Covid restrictions, as was the case for so many during those pandemic years.

Lesson learned
- Never forget the sacrifice

Thirty years of TDP

I spent four months during the second Covid year, recording and writing the 30-year history of the TDP. It was a most rewarding and worthwhile period. I contacted many graduates, all of whom were suffering from the effects of lockdown. Their livelihood had been snatched away and the entertainment industry ceased to exist. The struggles were especially tough for those with children. They're amazingly resilient, these stoic artists and were positive about their future. I'm full of admiration for them all.

The 30 year Booklet was edited by Meredith Burton, a long-time working colleague involved in the SS, TDP and events. She was perfect for the job because she was able to fill in the gaps because of her long experience with both the SS and TDP and she created a fine professional document. Now we have an accurate record I'm able to use as a reference for the TDP development in my memoir! It was an intense period and as usual, I kept my anxiety well hidden.

Meredith Burton with Trevor in costume

We contacted about 30 graduates for written quotes and birthday wishes. It was reassuring to hear those positive messages, many of which I've included in this memoir. We also had many of the TDP graduate headliners record video messages for the show, including Human Nature and Paulini. Disappointingly, these messages were not included in the Graduation production.

My four months of research and writing appeared in the centre of the printed TDP Graduation program for 2021. I had hoped and expected that there would be a separate booklet which would be available to TDP alumni and all those wonderful consultants who had helped build this incredibly successful training program.

About 10 days after the graduation concert, I was rushed to hospital with a suspected heart attack. It turned at to be Takutsubo cardiomyopathy – Broken Heart syndrome. This is a heart condition which is mostly caused by a sudden, high-stress situation. When the doctor asked about what had been going on recently in my life, it was then I realised the extreme stress and frustration I'd felt when finishing my association with the TDP and the profound feeling of loss.

Apart from that incident, we had a quiet end to the pandemic years and headed for Rob's 80th birthday celebration on 19 October – the last day of lockdown. We had a wonderful few days but were confused by the number of guests we could have for his birthday gatherings with Covid restrictions still in place. We finished up with two parties, one inside venue with Covid restrictions for 20 people and the other, two days later, unrestricted. It's hard to believe we were so compliant.

At the end of the year, Rob and I drove down memory lane, retracing my youth from Paterson through Merriwa, Lithgow, Sofala, Gulgong and Bathurst. We visited my family's graves and saw war memorials naming my father as well as three aunts and uncles from the same family who had enlisted. It was a sobering experience and gave me more information for my memoir. I really have enjoyed so much of country Australia.

Uncle Cecil, Aunty Dot and Uncle Paul: sister and brothers in First Word War. Cecil was killed in France aged 27 years. Paul was with him. The Feneley side of my family. Lest we forget.

Free again in 2022

Australia was recovering after two years of the pandemic, social distancing and lockdowns and I was looking for the next exciting adventure – the book! I had really appreciated slowing down and spending time with Kate, Eva and Ivan in the parks where we were allowed to meet. It was the same with my aqua aerobics friends when we gathered in the open air whilst keeping the required distance. Slowly we all led our lives during these two years. We were so fortunate to live in Australia where we were somewhat protected from great numbers succumbing to Covid.

Hurrah! When we were finally able to move about more freely, Rob and I recaptured our love of the Australian countryside with a trip along the Great Ocean Road to Kangaroo Island and then on to Adelaide. It was a joy to be out and about. Two very significant episodes for me were the morning we spent in Penola, SA, the town where Sister Mary McKillop started the order of the Brown St Joseph's. Remember, I had staged the Life of Mary McKillop in the Sydney Domain in 1995. I loved the whole experience of working with Sister Leonie Farquhar (then head of the order) and Sister Claire Koch, the driving force behind it all. They were good people. Those McKillop nuns are amazing in so many ways. It was a privilege to produce their beatification extravaganza.

In June, I injured my knee and finished up with a torn meniscus and compound fracture. This completely upended my life. My beloved walking was no longer possible, and I was frustratingly restricted to water aerobics and just being mobile. Now, in 2025, I'm still determined to fix it. Like so many other challenges in my life I'm determined that I will win this battle. If I could teach my daughter to walk, then I can teach myself. Yes!

We had three family 50th birthday celebrations this year. In June for Kate, August for Christine and November for Ivan. It was hard to believe that these lovely young people had reached the age of what used to be considered middle age. I was so glad that they were happily settled into their marriages and were loving their children as they had all been loved. The parties were all unique in very different styles suiting their individual personalities.

23
The book

By this point, I'd been in touch with Anna Rose and was full tilt into writing my memoir. We met in Tamworth at Joan and Bevan Douglas's home and had a few very productive days going through the SS programs and what I had written so far.

I must acknowledge the huge efforts of the late Bruce Harris and Richard Spiewak for creating the remarkable printed programs for every production of the SS. Bruce's skills from his career as marketing director for Lintas led him to create professional and descriptive records which tell a true story of this time in the performing arts in public schools and the entertainment industry. Richard Spiewak, now SS Executive Producer, took over the writing and compiling of these program records when Bruce retired in 2000. Richard has driven these pictorial masterpieces to another level and when I congratulated him, he humbly said: "I am but a custodian who should leave SS in a stronger place for the next one." Thank you, Bruce and Richard.

Richard Spiewak and SS finale

My long-time friend and colleague from early SSs and Christmas Pageants, Annie Whealy, conducts a tour to the Adelaide Arts Festival each year and this time Rob and I joined the group. It was a new and inspiring experience. The writers' festival, which some of you will know, runs concurrently, and it was stimulating and motivating. I've never been disciplined when it comes to administration and homework but I found the writers' discussions and insights made me want to write.

The next huge turning point came when Andy decided it was time Rob and I got moving again after the years of the pandemic, so he booked us a trip to the island resort of Likuliku in Fiji. The peace and tranquillity of the resort worked wonders for us, so much so that we booked again for the following year.

I was sad to hear about the death of the legendary Brian Walsh, who gave me so much work and broadened my huge cast and stage horizons with sporting events in the 1990s. He then became a great supporter and mentor for my son, Andy, as he took over the reins of MLP after Manuel died in April 1996. Brian was loving and kind to us when Manuel died and helped us with the funeral. Brian's own partner had died just a short time before way back there in 1996.

In May, we had dinner at the Limelight Thai restaurant with friends, Judy and Chris Luget and were seated next to a table of six. The attractive and vibrant young woman at the end of the next table smiled at me and said: "You remind me very much of someone." When I asked who that might be, she replied: "Mary Lopez." What a laugh we had going over the days when Bronwyn Moreton was a pupil at sister school to EBHS, Cheltenham Girls' HS (CGHS), in the 1980s. She was great friends with the core members of my chamber and senior boys' choirs. They certainly were magical years full of passion and optimism – no hidden agenda, no accusations, and no pulling down tall poppies. We talked about *The Royal Hunt of the Sun* play in which she appeared with other CGHS students who were included in the cast as well as the Gilbert and Sullivan productions with North Sydney Girls' HS.

Since 1985 I've been listening to *Australia All Over* with Macca on Sunday mornings on ABC radio. I can't think how I found him, but I really relate to Macca and his common man approach. He's a kindred spirit who is somewhat like me in his respect for everyday man/woman and loves the unique Aussie spirit. He interviews such wonderful characters on his program, in his own quirky fashion.

An amazing event was staged at Telstra Headquarters in July 2023 to celebrate 40 years of the SS. Dr Sylvia Corish, Executive Director, Student Support and Specialist Programs, and Richard Spiewak, Executive Producer SS, assembled an entertaining and informative program of speeches, film and performances to acknowledge the contribution of the SS pioneering team and sponsors. It was heart-warming and sincere and I truly appreciated their acknowledgment of my creation of the SS. I'm forever thankful for what was to follow.

Sylvie, Murat and Me at the 2023 launch

This new feeling of satisfaction has helped me move forward and cleared the way for me to finish my memoir. I'm so thankful to Sylvia, a self-described "SS tragic having attended a performance nearly every year since its inception", and Richard, and the Secretary, NSW Department of Education, Murat Dizdar. Murat and Sylvia replied to my letter of thanks, saying: "We consider you to be a giant of the public education system and SS. I am so looking forward to our 40th SS and having you with us to celebrate. You should be so very proud – we are of you." That meant the absolute world to me.

I met two livewires who were executives from the major sponsor of SS, Telstra, Arthur Pengrath and Martin Freeman. They were very interested to hear about the origins of the SS. They invited me to be a guest in the Telstra corporate box at the upcoming 40th SS.

Me with Martin Freeman and Arthur Pengrath from Telstra at the SS 2025 launch

Just before we left for Japan on our first adventure since the Covid years, I was invited to a party to celebrate one of my former Epping BHS student's 60th birthday. The gathering for John Simpson was full of music and laughter. John was an enthusiastic member of my choirs at EBHS. He has continued his creative pathway and has enjoyed a successful career as an actor, writer, film maker and producer. I was so excited to meet up with two other men, dedicated choir members, from EBHS days: Michael Spencer, now Head of Music at Frenscham Ladies' College at Mittagong, and Derick Andrews who announced that he was about to retire from his career as an engineer. We missed a generation in time, but I loved hearing the stories about their successful lives and careers and grown-up children. It was hard to believe we were ever separated as teacher/student. Those carefree EBHS years were the happiest of my career.

Lessons learned
- Always say thank you

After Japan

On the flight home from Japan, after a busy and stressful trip, I suffered a stroke - a TIA. After 12 hours of travel from Kyoto to Tokyo which involved a taxi from our hotel to the tour bus, a three-hour wait at Kyoto Airport, the short flight to Tokyo, another five-hour wait at Tokyo, we were finally in the air. It was exhausting.

Anyway, the first thing I noticed was when I went to say good night to Rob, after dinner, who was already asleep was that I couldn't shape my words. I assumed it was because I was wrecked after such a horrific day and promptly went to sleep. When we disembarked I was walking fine and was not confused as we made our way through customs, collected our bags and caught a taxi home. I jokingly said to Rob, I was so tired I felt like I'd had a stroke. We arrived home, did a little unpack and didn't speak much. However, when I spoke to my daughter on the phone my speech was worse. She encouraged me to make an appointment to see a doctor and luckily, I was able to have an appointment that afternoon because he sent me straight to the emergency department at Royal North Shore Hospital.

I had a series of tests and was sent home that night with the advice to have an MRI to determine whether in fact I'd had a stroke. The following Monday I had an MRI and was back to emergency and admitted to the stroke ward for two days. I was assessed by a physio, speech therapist and occupational therapist and given a program I could immediately work with. On discharge I was advised to present to the stroke clinic for rehab. Greenwich Hospital provided the rehab one month later. It was just as well I had followed the advice on rehab from the hospital and was well under way with the recovery.

Every day my body recovered. I am in awe of the brain's ability to find ways to recover my losses. With every improvement I admire my daughter's strength and determination to deal with the severe motor misfunctioning she endures daily. She is my inspiration. I taught Kate to overcome the challenges she had to deal with and now I must use those same skills to teach myself.

People have been so kind. I don't want to forget that. I am overcome by the concern shown by my family, many friends and former workmates. SS executive producer Richard Spiewak and Education Department leader Murat Dizdar sent me lovely floral arrangements and messages. The constant phone calls, visits, and food and coffee drop-offs from my aqua aerobic mates, the Aqua Belles, were invaluable to me in my recovery. Joc Ibels, Wynne Richardson, Barb Hutchinson, Mary Craven and Emanuela Carniato, in particular, were a godsend to me during this time. The other Aqua Belles, Alison Plant, Claire Mallinson, Jean Wheelahan, Diana Savalas, Bev Withers, Marianne Rajkobic, Christine Cook, Wendy Wade and Marilyn

O'Neill were very concerned for me and did everything they could to help me regain who I was. They even had the grace to stay away and stop phoning when I expressed to them the difficulties I had in talking. That's what true friends are.

Rob was by my side making all matters as easy for me as he could. He was very busy with meal preparation and driving me everywhere. At the same time, he also underwent eye surgery and that was very invasive and time consuming.

Lessons learned
- Don't overdo life
- Teacher learn your own lessons

The 40th Anniversary SS

5 year old me with Shanghai "the bulls eye has been hit" – from Paterson to Qudos Bank Arena, Homebush

In November 2023, I was finally able to say my dreams had come true. Rob and I attended the 40th Anniversary SS, held at Qudos Bank Arena in Sydney. I was well enough recovering from my stroke. What a milestone. Forty years of magic. This event was true validation of the creative role and dreams I had all those years ago in 1984.

A most gratifying moment for me was when John Foreman, whom I've known since he was 14, thanked me publicly from the stage for my leadership of the SS. John typifies what I hoped my influence on young performers would be. He is immensely successful, a thoroughly nice man and is "giving back" to support others.

I loved the 40th SS "Fabulous." I was so proud of Executive Producer Richard Spiewak, Creative Director Sonja Sjolander, Musical Director and Conductor Steve Williams, Choral Director Ian Jefferson, Choral Conductor Elizabeth Scott, Sponsorship Coordinator Sandra Henderson and Specfest Producer Peter Hayward, with whom I worked for so many years. All of them were ex public school teachers.

Of course, huge thanks to the massive production team of dance and drama directors, musicians and technicians required to bring the production to life. (A count from program credits is nearly 600). Among the tech experts still on the job were lighting designer Trudi Dalgleish, follow spot caller Chris Snape and audio director, Andrew Crawford and broadcast audio director John Simpson.

Most important of all, thanks and congratulations go to the 1,000-plus marvellous public education teachers, who are the heart and soul of the show.

The SS continues to teach the lessons for which it has become a benchmark – Australian culture and history, inclusiveness, talented soloists, many of whom are now household names, spectacle, creates dazzling costumes and puppets, and is built on a massive cast.

These themes have been performed by nearly 200,000 children over the last 40+ years, supported and encouraged by their loving and proud sacrificing parents. Never underplay the indispensable role that supporting parents play in the family of SS.

The SS has always celebrated our Indigenous culture, and I know my late dear friend Bonita Mabo would be proud of how her words have been carried on: "the Spectacular teaches Indigenous people not to hide their talents but to let the world see what they can do." The Indigenous segment in SS 40, began with an original student composition by Ivy Lennox with didgeridoo played by 12-year-old Lennox Monaghan. Bangarra choreographed the item and created a meaningful and stunning segment called "Culture is a Feeling." It was presented by 250 Indigenous students from across the state and featured a company of 30 dancers which was formed in 2010.

What a long way we've come from when we first presented about six Aboriginal dancers from Darlington Public School back in 1985. The SS paved the way for Indigenous inclusion and certainly "showed the world what they could do."

I wrote the following which was included in the printed program for SS No 40:

> *The Spectacular almost didn't make it past 1988. Doug Swan was no longer at the helm of the department and the new Director-General could not see its value. Fortunately, the community relations unit leader pushed back and the 1989 show happened. We nearly didn't make it past the toddler age of five.*
>
> *Doug Swan contacted me when I retired from Schools Spectacular as director after 25 years. I met Doug for lunch after the 2008 Spectacular. He wanted to set the record straight as he'd been reading reports about what everyone else was claiming were the origins of the Spectacular.*
>
> *It came about through the support of the vision right to the top of the department. There were people with great and bold ideas from both sides of the education and corporate fence. The leap of faith was made right up to the top of the education ladder. It was a team and the start of a new family.*
>
> *Reaching the fabulous age of 40 was never something any of us at the beginning ever thought would happen. The magnitude of the occasion cannot be underestimated. This show is all about dedication to education, goodwill by everyone.*
>
> *The show was born in 1984. It stumbled and got back up as a toddler, charged through the teenage years and settled into its 20s. It took on the challenge of inclusion and made us look at who we were. It strode into the 30s and continued to mature and grow. And now it's 40 and looking to the future. A fine young adult that has become a credit to the family of education.*
>
> *And what about the production team that helped it start and grow? From that very small nucleus in the beginning to the extended family it has become over time, this is a community that looks after one another and is full of goodwill and compassion for all. It is a family that not only has relatives all over the state and country, but*

> all over the world. Teachers, parents, supporters, technical staff are all very much a part of this family.
>
> For me, I see myself as the grandmother of the show, full of pride and so, so proud of the product that it has become. I look forward to seeing it reach its 50s.

Earlier in the same year, Rob and I attended the 20th anniversary of "Creative Generation" in Brisbane. "C Gen" is an annual gala schools spectacular held in Brisbane for State Schools students across Queensland. The dynamic, talented and passionate Liz Williamson proposed and created this production after she resigned from the NSW Performing Arts Unit and moved with her husband to Queensland. She had been the coordinator of SS in the 1990s to 2000 and had worked very closely with Andrew Bee and me for many years. She has produced the "C Gen" since its inception. Liz was smart and creative in bringing onto her Brisbane team some of the fabulous experts from NSW Education with whom she had worked with during her SS years, especially Andrew Bee. He has been alongside Liz as Associate Director and Technical Producer ever since.

I caught up with them all after the show and I feel so very proud of them, not just for the wonderful show, but for the successful, interesting and significant careers they now have. Together with Liz and Andrew, Michelle Mitchell, Chris Snape, Kirstin Dickerson and Peter McVie had been part of the original NSW SS family and were doing it all again, creating magic, in another Stare of Australia! It was no surprise to me to learn that the highly creative and dynamic Kirstin Dickerson had taken over as Director of Starstruck in Newcastle.

What I have discovered as I have been writing about my life is that I have lived the equivalent of five lives rolled into one – family, teacher, SS and TDP, events and travels – no wonder I was always so busy!

I can see how my life was changed in an amazing way because of the SS. The corporate and government world encouraged my innovative way of showcasing young performers and staging spectacular events. They embraced my style of production from 1988–2000 when I established my own events company. Sydney also seemed to enjoy my storytelling with huge cast spectaculars like the 11 Darling Harbour

Christmas Pageants, the Mary McKillop Pageant and Jubilee 2000. I also produced and directed many gala concerts and government ceremonies that combined classical and contemporary artists, sporting event entertainment that combined huge cast spectacles with musicians and stunts – all alongside the SS.

The SS dominated my life for 30+ years. It is a triumph showcasing excellence in public education. For the 20 years since I retired as its director, it has been led by two powerhouses – the dedicated, creative and highly skilled Executive Producer, Richard Spiewak and Creative Director, Sonja Sjolander. Now joined by their Director in the Department of Education, Sylvia Corish, the SS has added to its "performing and arts festival" in the forecourt additional layers for even more student participation.

Rob came into my life in 2001, at the end of my commercial events career, and saw to it that my every need was catered for as I returned to my education roots. My passion for developing young talent and giving everyone a fair go was complete. Now I'm enjoying, in fact relishing, seeing my grandchildren going to school, attending performances, playing sports, having music and art lessons, and even playing video games. I fit in where I can but, never having had a grandparent, I'm not always sure what to do. I learned early though not to interfere, that the parents do know what's best for their children.

Kate had a crack at practising law as a solicitor but found it was not to her liking, so she spent several years working in Andy's company part-time and being a loving wife, devoted mother and amazing home maker. Recently she took up a position in a not-for-profit organisation raising money for Jesuit missionaries, which she loves.

Andy continues to develop his motor events company and is busy being a great boss, constantly travelling for work, investing in real estate and being a dedicated and loving husband and passionate father. I was delighted to attend the 2023 Premier's Senior Citizens' Concert at ICC, produced by the two Andrews through Out There Productions. To see Darren Coggan, Lorenzo Rositano, Paulini and Julie Lee Goodwin, graduates from the TDP, performing so brilliantly was a delicious experience.

Darren Coggan, Julie Lee Goodwin, Me, Paulini, Andy (son), Andrew Bee

And Telstra has come on board as major Sponsor for another 10 years. The SS will live on!

24
March 22, 2024 – A grand age

L to R - Eva, Kate, Ivan, Wu, Mani, me, Andy, Izzy, Rob

Mary's 80th party speech

Thank you all for sharing my life. All the family and friends who have shared a wonderful journey and contributed so much to various periods of my life, patiently waiting while I was so busy.

To Andy and Kate and Rob for putting on this amazing party and for all the arrangements that go with it. The travellers – Andy, Wu, Mani, Izzy, so grateful … Eva for design of invitations and place cards and for sending out invites; Mani and Izzy for taking the time out of school to come from Kingscliff. Proud of them. Andy for running the show. Kate – pushing me for photos, people and places.

Kate and Andy – for their love and loyalty and for their patience. Everything that I could ask for in a son and daughter. I am so proud of them for their kindness, integrity, intelligence and for Andy's wicked sense of humour and Kate's bravery and good humour.

Rob for patiently and encouragingly allowing me to finish my exciting career and then to write my memoir. *Andrew Bee* for being my right-hand man and loyal friend for nearly 30 years.

Wonderful musicians – Rosie, Joshua and Paul Meader – Lorenzo and Maree.

" Happy birthday to me" ♪ ♪ ♪

Born into the most amazing family of 4 brothers and 4 sisters. I felt loved and safe. We had the most beautiful mother who made us all feel special and valued.

Because I've spent 5 years writing my memoir I can see my 80 years divided into childhood, married life and the children, teaching and choirs, Schools Spectacular and Talent Development Project, my 12 year career in great big events and government ceremonies, sporting displays and 11 Christmas Pageants in Darling Harbour, life with Rob, the marriages of Kate and Andy and intro Ivan and Wu and grandchildren to complete my life.

You will know where you fit in – laughs along the way – not taking life too seriously – priorities out of hand – career days – always celebrating. My friends have filled you in about those periods.

The stroke. How Kate and Andy and Rob brought me back to life and my aqua friends bullied me into action.

Anna Rose editing my memoir.

Thank you all her tonight, for the LOVE and LAUGHS

People who shared my life and career, much more than colleagues, they became friends.

With the late Janelle Kidman and Joc Ibels

Mary's 80th – By Anna Rose

What a fabulous night it was celebrating the 80th birthday of Mary Lopez!

The historic Royal Sydney Yacht Squadron Club in Kirribilli was the perfect venue to mark this very memorable occasion, with about 100 or more of her closest friends and family members present.

There were friends, neighbours and relatives from Merriwa, Paterson, Sydney, Kingscliff, Nowra, the Central Coast, Culburra and Melbourne, and I flew up from Geelong.

Of course, we were greeted by music upon arrival, and the obligatory glass of bubbles. How could there not be music and bubbles at this remarkable woman's celebration?

80th birthday messages from TDP graduates

Paulini

Hey, Mary. I just wanted to wish you a happy birthday. You know what? I actually want to thank you for everything you've done for me since I was 16 when I first met you. I want to say thank you and you've been such an inspiration to me. I hope you have the happiest birthday. [Singing] Celebrate and have a margarita! Happy birthday. Bye!

John Foreman

Happy birthday, dear Mary. I'm so sorry I can't be with you tonight. Of course the reason I can't be with you tonight is because I'm working and the reason I'm working, if I really think about it, is because of all the opportunities you gave me all those years ago through the Schools Spectacular and the world of opportunity that you opened for me as you have done for thousands and thousands of people. You are such an inspirational person – you've changed the lives of thousands of Australians. You're a great friend. I'm so grateful to have had the chance to have gotten to know you, especially over the last couple of years with the Talent Development Project. So, thank you for everything you do and happy birthday. Lots of love.

Shannon Brown

Mary! It's Shannon Brown. How are you? I'm stuck here in Indonesia luckily doing some school workshops on music and it's fantastic. A little birdie told me you're turning the big 8-0. Is that correct? I told you what, what a fantastic innings. Thank you for all your support and guidance, especially as a youngster at Schools Spectacular and the Talent Development Project. I've made some wonderful friends and some wonderful memories. So I thank you so much for all your guidance and tutelage because I wouldn't be here without you. So, happy birthday, have a wonderful day and let's catch up when I get back. See ya!

Nicholas Gentile

Hey, Mary. Happy birthday. Thank you for being such a champion of my work and touching the lives of so many others. Here's to the positive impact you continue to have on so many people's lives. Happy birthday.

Anthony Snape

Mary! It's Anthony Snape here. Wishing you a very, very happy birthday. I remember the times back in the TDP when I was petrified to come out on stage because Mary Lopez was in the audience and you were making sure that you were holding us to the highest possible standard you possibly could. You did so much for so many kids especially kids from the country like me. So thank you so much. I hope you have a really wonderful birthday. [Kiss]. Love you. Bye.

Sam Fischer

Hey, Mary. It's Sam Fischer. Happy birthday, sending you so much love. Thank you for always being there to support us. We love you so much. I hope you have an amazing day. [Kiss]

Robert McDougall

Hi, Mary. I just wanted to send a quick message on this special day to say happy birthday and to say thank you for all of the wonderful things you've done for me and for so many other people. You can't swing a cat in the music theatre industry now without running into somebody that's gone through TDP. It was an amazing experience for me and it genuinely changed my life and that's mainly because of you. So happy birthday. Have a very special day. And thank you for everything you've done and continue to do for everybody.

Shaun Rennie

Hi, Mary. It's Shaun Rennie here. I'm coming to you from the beautiful Civic Theatre in Newcastle where I'm bringing my production of Rent. And I can safely say I wouldn't be here without you.

Thank you so much for your belief in me and the very beginning of my time in the arts and your continued support over the years. You were one of my earliest champions and I am so, so grateful. I can honestly, honestly say that I wouldn't be doing what I love today – working in theatre – if it wasn't for you. So congratulations on this milestone. You're an amazing woman. And so many of us have so much to thank you for. I hope you have an amazing, amazing birthday. [Kiss].

Glenn Cunningham

[Singing] Happy Birthday To You a capella (with seven images of himself on the screen) – Happy birthday, Mary. We've known each other for 33 years. Good Lord. I hope you have a fantastic day. I love you lots and I will see you soon. We will get that lunch in. Happy 80th.

Trevor Ashley

Mary Lopez! Happy. My God! So thrilled for you. I hope you're having a brilliant night. You have done so much for me throughout my career and really gave me my start and my introduction to the business. And for that I will forever be grateful. I'm sending you love from my flat here on London's glittering West End, where I'm opening my new show, Priscilla, The Party, can you believe it? here in London and I just wanted to wish you the happiest birthday and thank you so much for everything you've done for me which I know that all of us TDP kids will feel forever. So much love. Happy birthday. [Kiss]

Grant Pearce

Dearest Mary. Where would I be without you? You were not only my teacher but my mentor. You taught me style, wine and food tasting, and in general, gave me everything I needed to take my life forward. Thank you, thank you, thank you, and sending and wishing you best wishes for a wonderful happy birthday. Bye.

Darren Coggan

G'day Mary. This is Darren Coggan. Just wanting to wish you all the love and happiness in the world for your 80th birthday celebration. Thank you so much for your friendship, for your guidance, your support, over so many years. I'll be forever grateful for you making that trek down to Wagga Wagga, my beloved hometown, there back in 1991 and selecting me to be part of the very first Talent Development Project. It was a moment that changed my life and since then has afforded me an incredible career in the performing arts so I'll be forever grateful. Have a wonderful birthday, Mary. We love you; we cherish you and I look forward to many, many more years of a beautiful friendship. [Kiss]

Byron Watson

Happy birthday from London. Mary, 30 years ago you changed the life of a fat little 6'3" boy from Campbelltown and I'll forever be grateful. I wish I was there to celebrate with you but sending you all my love. Happy birthday.

Emma Pask

Hi, Mary. Well, people are saying it's your 80th birthday but I just can't believe them. There's no way that you could possibly be 80 years old. If it is the case and I'm wrong, I'm wishing you a happy birthday surrounded by your loved ones. Wishing you all the best for your special day. Lots of love [kiss] from me. Happy birthday.

Anja Nissen

Happy birthday, Mary. Congratulations on 80 years of being an inspiration to so many. Thank you for all your support and guidance over the years. You are truly remarkable and have had such a lasting impact on my life. I'm sending you all my love, here from Copenhagen in Denmark. Happy birthday.

Lucy Maunder

[Singing] Happy Birthday To You. Hello! It's Lucy here coming to you from Her Majesty's Theatre in Melbourne. Just finished our media call ahead of our opening night of Chicago on Tuesday, where I'm playing Roxie which is a true bucket-list moment for me. I just wanted to send you the hugest, most wonderful wishes for a beautiful birthday and just hope you know how special you are and how grateful we all are to have had you in our lives. As such an inspiration and such a mentor. I hope to see you when I'm there with the show in June. Sending you so so, so, so much love. [Blows a kiss]

Andrew and Michael Tierney (Human Nature)

Mary – it's Andrew and Mike here. Happy birthday. We just want to send a note to you live from Las Vegas. We love you and thank so much for everything you've done for us over the years. Have a great time celebrating with the family. Have a wonderful night and we wish we could be there celebrating with you. We're sending you lots of love. We'll see you soon. Have a great night. Bye.

Felicity Urquhart
[Singing and playing guitar] You are my sunshine, my only sunshine. You make me happy when skies are grey. You'll never know dear how much I love you ... Well, I'm here to tell you I love you, Mary Lopez. Happy birthday. I can't believe you're celebrating 80 years on the planet. I think we first met when I was about 13 and I'll never forget that day you came to Tamworth. You came to the high school and ever since then you've been opening doors for me and filling my heart with opportunities and ideas, I guess. I thank you for that. You believed in me way back then and we've known each other all these years. so enjoy your birthday, celebrate hard and I'll see you soon. [Singing] Please don't take my sunshine away. Love you, Mary. [Kiss]

It's certainly been a busy life. It's a life I have savoured and enjoyed remembering. I had no role model for my career outside of teaching. There was no other female to advise me about events and how to manage my life. That's why I felt so often that I was freewheeling. In fact, Andy and I used to joke with each other at the end of each major event we produced, about how we'd fooled the people in the audience. We had this term that we'd perpetrated a fraud of some sort, as the audience thought we knew what we were doing. Every event was, in fact, a new experience and a big risk for us. And we always managed to pull it off!

Since the big birthday I've sold the Kirribilli apartment and moved back into Walker St. This time I'm in the North Sydney end in a very cool apartment. The complex has a 25 metre heated indoor pool and a gymnasium which will hopefully help keep Rob and I in good health through our old age. I also intend to spend more time in Andy's territory of Kingscliff, where we've purchased another apartment.

We've moved on from our life in Culburra but will never forget the gift of the glorious location and the many friends Rob and I gathered over twenty five years. We never ceased to be in awe of the natural beauty that surrounds us with water everywhere. We have been blessed to have had many warm and friendly neighbours, like Ronelle and Marc Faulks, who fed and entertained us, and also to have our Sydney friends, Judith and Chris Luget and Karen and Andrew Ferry, who built chic holiday houses just down the road. It was exciting to welcome ex-working colleagues and friends to settle in Culburra. Les and Margaret Goch (Song Zu days) built a house which, true to their impeccable sense of style, is like walking into a work of art. Richard Spiewak (Executive Producer SS) and his partner Andrew, own a newly built house on beautiful Lake Wollumboola, Culburra. Rob's going to miss his great fishing mate Les Zezeran and his animal rescuer wife, Pat.

We were fortunate to leave the sale of our house in the hands of our friend Craig Hadflield who in fact had sold it to us twenty years previously. I marvel at the fact that some chance meetings blossom into real friendship. Craig and his wile Geraldine, longtime residents in the Shoalhaven, welcomed us into their lives. We have enjoyed seeing their children grow up having inherited their parents' enormous energy and hard work ethic. This lead to very successful careers for both Lucy and Jake. Geraldine and Craig are a dynamic partnership with Craig now the owner of several highly successful Ray White agencies in the Shoalhaven.

The ever "rolling stone" Mary, is still rolling and enjoying this life that allows me to spend time with many loving family members, old friends and new friends. With the move to Kingscliff, apart from being close to Andy, Christine, Mani and Izzy we formed new friendships with our great neighbours in the small apartment block and the streets close by. Rob and Robyn Hirst have set the benchmark for living a healthy, active and positive retirement. The big bonus in this move north, has also been that dear friends and colleagues from the past are already living nearby. John Tannhauser, a friend for 50 years, has lived in the area for much of his life. His partner Joan Keating and I have an intuitive appreciation of each other since we met some 10 years ago. Peter Lorking and Debbie Hockings and TDP Kim Lemke (now Stevens) with her husband Joff have all settled into the area over the past few years.

I treasure these old and new friendships I have built throughout my life. They are a gift and I certainly don't take them for granted. It's important to keep reaching out and reinforcing those relationships you value. I place great store on those friends who always acknowledge a communication from me. A phone message or an email is always answered. They are the people who are my friends.

I would like to thank my son Andy, my daughter Kate, and my late husband Manuel, for the enormous sacrifices they made for me to have the time required to lead the SS and TDP teams. They had too many people in their lives because of my commitments, but they accepted that world with the utmost generosity and tolerance. The other career I had outside education when I was producing professional major productions and events from 1989–2001 was exciting and rewarding and completely unexpected.

My partner since 2001, Rob Bail has continued his commitment to me and I am ever grateful for the love, encouragement and support I have received from him. He has pushed me gently to write this history knowing that it was important for me to both tell the true story of my career and finally have peace with my very busy and stressful life. I have been constantly amazed at Rob's ability to stand in the background from the time we first met to gently support my career with my rather high profile with no envy or jealousy. I'm sure most women would agree that's a rare man who can do that.

At this stage of my life, I feel such love for my children that it is almost painful. Every night I feel this emotion so deeply and am writing of it because I want to explore it more. I don't want to forget the intensity of this love during the daylight hours.

Writing this memoir has given me immense joy and some sadness. I have relived the world of Mary Feneley and Mary Lopez and it has been both pleasurable and exhausting. I've been up and down with travels around the world and family tragedies and illnesses. But, most importantly it has given me satisfaction and contentment about my life. It has enabled me to focus on the benefits that my career helped bring to thousands of Australians. I can see clearly how my family stood by me through my long and action-packed life.

I loved the army of dedicated teachers in public education who gave their students the opportunity to shine in SS. And shine they did! And still they shine. Hundreds of thousands of children have been enriched with memories of that moment or moments, when they were stars. I'm so thankful to the stunning teams of professionals who so skilfully gave the performers brilliant staging and technical support to present and showcase them. I also thank from the bottom of my heart my own school teachers, who gave me a well-rounded education and a love of music and drama.

I can't let the recent passing in 2024 of two incredible creatives go by without mention. Vale Laurel Barranikow and Ross Milne, who were amongst the pioneers of SS, and remained faithful contributors throughout their lifetimes.

Importantly, I acknowledge the incredible army of TDP and SS parents. These champions sacrificed more than they could ever sum up. They gave love and encouragement, money, transport and time by the bucketload to their talented offspring.

My career was only possible because of the love and training of my mother and sisters who were always available to mind my children; my brothers who were role models of integrity and encouragement; and the financial security from my late husband, Manuel.

I thank with great love the following three rocks in my life. My son Andy, and daughter Kate who sacrificed so much of my mothering time. I always had the encouragement of my partner Rob, who patiently waited for me to discover why I did what I did. Thank you Rob. And thanks for calmy packing up houses and arranging removalists 10 times during our years together (so far).

At this ripe old age I can happily say I lived a spectacular life and I'm glad I did what I did.

Thank you dear reader.

25
Successful TDP Graduates 2024

<u>80th birthday videos lovely greetings compiled by Andy</u>
Pauini 2000
John Foreman 1992
Shannon Brown 2001
Anthony Snape 1997
Sam Fisher 2015
Rob McDougall 2009
Shaun Rennie 1999
Glen Cunningham 1993
Nick Gentile 2009
Trevor Ashley 1997
Grant Pearce EBHS 1983
Darren Coggan 1992
Byron Watson 1997
Emma Pask 1995
Anja Nissen 2012
Lucy Maunder 2004
Andrew and Michael Tierney 1992
Felicity Urquhart 1993

<u>Other TDP Graduates still headlining or with international careers</u>
Drew McAllister 1992
Human Nature 1992
Vanessa Corish 1992
Davis Harris 1994
Nathan Foley 1997
Jedd Hughes 1999

Diana Rouvas 2000
Tonino Speciali 2001
Travis Collins 2002
Angus and Julia Stone 2002
The McClymonts 2002, 2004
Morgan Evans 2004
Brendan Irving 2004
Roshani 2005
Lorenzo Rositano 2005
Katrina Burgoyne 2005
Brendon Boney 2005
Julie Lee Goodwin 2006
Miriam Waks 2006
Robert McDougall 2007
Jess Pollard 2007
Jessica Hitchcock 2008
Michael Lombardi (Vaiasini) 2008
Max Jackson (Micaylie) 2009
David Le'aupepe 2009
Ricki Bloomfield 2009
Alex Gibson-Giorgio 2009
Melanie Dyer 2010
Christie Lamb 2010
Declan Egan 2011
Nathan Lamont 2011
Ashleigh Rubenach 2011
Steven Madsen 2011
Jack Vidgeon 2011
Jacon Neale (late) 2012
Cameron Little 2012
Brad Cox 2012
Imogen Clark 2012
Harry Ward 2013
Clint Crighton 2003
Benny Nelson 2013
Goori Knox 2013
Josh Meader 2015

Rose Shannon-Duhigg 2016
Jeremy Boulton 2017
Rosie Meader 2019

There are many others not mentioned, who have successful careers in choruses, theatre, chorus line dancers, bands, PA Administrative positions and production industries

Producers – great successes – who were not TDP graduates but were part of the SS family
Greg Bowman
Liz Williamson
Michael Cassell

Acknowledgements

In this book I have attempted to acknowledge and say thank you to all my colleagues and friends who supported me in my career with all its variations. They are named throughout the book and I thank them again. I apologise if I have left anyone out.

Thank you to the dedicated Josephite and Dominican Nuns who educated me and gave me the broad musical skills that underpinned my career.

I would like to acknowledge the people who brought this memoir to life.

Firstly I want to acknowledge my partner of 24 years, Rob. Without your encouragement and support this marathon exercise would never have happened. All the meals you cooked and all those cups of tea you delivered kept me working. Since we've been together you have helped me in my career and have been there for all the ups and downs. From me waking you up when I wanted to make notes at midnight and the early hours, to you standing by my side at events, your quiet support in the background was essential. You let me fly!

I also want to acknowledge Andy and Kate for their honest stories included in my memoir and for their patience while I was absent.

Thank you to Anna Rose for the first edit. You helped me start and set me on the path. You prompted me to think about my life and to remember so many of the country artists who came through the TDP and SS.

Thank you to Sarah Plant, my final editor. You cleaned it all up and encouraged me to complete the text. You understood what I wanted to do and helped me pull all the pieces together. You gave me confidence to tell my story for other women and for all the young people out there with dreams.

Thank you to Meredith Burton for working with me on the history of the first 30 years of the TDP. That document was my bible, an invaluable resource that jogged my memory and gave me reference when I needed direction.

Thank you to Craig Hadfield. You inspired me to write and publish, and introduced me to the team at Publicious, who got the book to press.

Thank you to my niece, Louise Feneley for going through all those boxes of photos and helping me to select those most useful in telling the story of our family. Also thanks to my nieces, Merise Feneley and Bronwyn Bailey, for the family stories and for filling the gaps.

Thank you in particular to those who contributed their own words to fill out the narrative: my brother Widge, Andrew Bee, Sandra Copeman, John Simpson, John Foreman, Chris Ryan, Felicity Urquhart, Darren Coggan, Roshani Priddis, Nathan Foley, Max Jackson, Nathan Lamont, Christie Lamb, Melanie Dyer, Ashleigh Rubenach and Lucy Maunder.

Thank you to Maree Montgomery. You introduced me to Culburra and we have shared so much of each others lives. You understand me more than most and you understand my what my career meant to me and to all those I was able to help. You also pushed me in the right direction when you encouraged me to write my memoir because you believed I had something important to say.

Thank you to the TDP Graduates who sent me their letters and messages. Knowing how much the TDP and the SS impacted your lives and mine makes it all worthwhile.

Thank you to Joan Douglas for the accommodation and the introduction to Anna Rose. Your invaluable contribution to the country music scene will not be forgotten.

To Imogen Clark for her diligent early research about the TDP songwriters. Your loyalty to TDP and your longstanding knowledge of the program were important.

Thank you to Jenny Heesh, Robyn Hirst, Debbie Hocking and Kim Stevens for reading early drafts and providing helpful comments. Thank you also to the late Bruce Harris and the current SS Executive Producer, Richard Spiewak for their wonderful program notes for each SS since 1984. These comprehensive and beautiful programs inspired me to write and opened up my memories.

Thank you finally to Murat Dizdar, Secretary, NSW Department of Education, and Dr Sylvia Corish, Executive Director, Student Support and Specialist Programs for making me feel loved, and valued for my work in Public Education. The 40th Anniversary of the SS allowed me to happily reflect on my continuing role as part of the family created by the SS and the TDP. It also gave me closure on my wonderful career as I was finally able to just watch and experience the magic that is the SS.

www.ingramcontent.com/pod-product-compliance
Lightning Source LLC
Chambersburg PA
CBHW041730300426
44115CB00021B/2963